C000094519

COUNTER-*Experiences*

COUNTER-

READING

UNIVERSITY OF NOTRE DAME PRESS

Experiences

JEAN-LUC MARION

edited by

KEVIN HART

NOTRE DAME, INDIANA

Copyright © 2007 by University of Notre Dame
Notre Dame, Indiana 46556
www.undpress.nd.edu
All Rights Reserved

Manufactured in the United States of America

Library of Congress Cataloging-in-Publication Data

Counter-experiences : reading Jean-Luc Marion / edited by Kevin Hart.
p.   cm.
Includes bibliographical references and index.
ISBN-13: 978-0-268-03078-0 (pbk. : alk. paper)
ISBN-10: 0-268-03078-2 (pbk. : alk. paper)
1. Marion, Jean-Luc, 1946–   I. Hart, Kevin, 1954–
B2430.M284C68   2007
194—dc22

                    2006039813

∞ *The paper in this book meets the guidelines for permanence and durability of the Committee on Production Guidelines for Book Longevity of the Council on Library Resources.*

for SARAH *and* CLAIRE

Contents

Acknowledgments

A number of the essays in this collection were first given as papers in a conference, "In Excess: Jean-Luc Marion and the Horizon of Modern Theology," held at the University of Notre Dame, May 7–9, 2004. My thanks to Gerald McKenny who helped me organize the conference. Thanks are due to several offices of the University of Notre Dame—the Henkels Lectures Series, the Dean of Arts and Letters, the Dean of the Graduate School, and the Departments of English, Philosophy, and Theology—for their encouragement and assistance with the conference. I am especially grateful to Jean-Luc Marion for his kind help in supplying material that made the preparation of the bibliographies possible. Tommy Davis, Scott Moringiello, and Becky Davis all helped at various stages of the preparation of the essays collected here. Robyn Horner generously allowed Scott Moringiello to use her bibliographies of Marion's writings in forming his own. Robyn Horner, Jeffrey L. Kosky, and Stephen E. Lewis graciously agreed to translate essays by Emmanuel Falque, Jean-Luc Marion, and Claude Romano, respectively. David Bemelmans provided expert copy-editing, and Julie Henigan helped with proofreading and the preparation of the index. My thanks to all for their help and for the grace with which it was given.

Introduction

KEVIN HART

Jean-Luc Marion's thought is a profound response to two major philosophical events: the beginning of phenomenology and the end of metaphysics. From the vantage point he has gradually achieved over the years, the two events appear as one and the same. Yet their unity is elusive: in order to discern it, one must follow Marion's vigorous and subtle rethinking of the history of modern philosophy and the nature of phenomenology. Having done that, one can begin to make out many things that metaphysics has occluded, especially the nature of selfhood and our relations with God. Also, the newfound unity of the two philosophical developments is productive; it allows Marion to revise and extend the radical way of thinking embedded in the philosophy of disclosure first pursued by Edmund Husserl and Martin Heidegger. With Marion's help not only can we continue to reveal the aberrations of metaphysics but we can also refigure the human subject—as the one who is "called [*l'interloqué*]" or, as he likes better, the "gifted" one [*l'adonné*]—and secure a phenomenological understanding of revelation. Marion does not venture down all the paths his thought makes possible; he finally elects to stay on a track that remains philosophical. Yet he beckons theologians to walk along it, beside it, or even across it in their own ways. Doubtless others will follow in his path or pursue those that he has indicated, for thoughtful scholars of literature and the fine arts will find themselves challenged by his work.[1]

1

In order to identify the beginning of phenomenology with the end of metaphysics Marion has traced the two events from various perspectives in the history of philosophy and under several topics in phenomenology. A wide range of writings has been generated as a consequence, and with time it becomes increasingly evident that they have a relatively sharp focus. Just before we find that satisfying resolution, though, there is a moment when these texts appear in three groups, each somewhat fuzzy partly because they overlap more than a little and partly because of the number of ancillary works that surround them: edited collections, essays in volumes that others have edited, and journal articles. First there is Marion the historian of modern philosophy, member of "L'Équipe Descartes" and one of the major Descartes scholars of our day, the author of scrupulous and venturesome studies of the thinker who marks the advent of philosophical modernity: *Sur l'ontologie grise de Descartes* (1975; rev. ed. 1981); *Index des "Regulae ad directionem ingenii" de René Descartes,* co-edited with Jean-Robert Armogathe (1976); *Sur la théologie blanche de Descartes* (1981; rev. ed. 1991); *Sur le prisme métaphysique de Descartes* (1986); and the two volumes of *Questions cartésiennes* (1991, 1996).[2] It is a body of work that amply testifies to a long and rich career in the history of philosophy.

There is also Marion the theologian who, following his philosophical breakthrough, modulates his endeavors in this area into a phenomenology of revelation. In his early publications Marion appears as a Catholic theologian fired by questions regarding Revelation, Trinity, Eucharist, and Incarnation (the topics of papers in *Résurrection* in the late 1960s), and this strain continues at least until "Hors-Texte" (1982).[3] From its inception in the early 1970s, *Communio* has been an important signpost to his Catholicism, although the names and publications of Henri de Lubac, Hans Urs von Balthasar, and Joseph Ratzinger are at times more precise indications. Even if his religious questions in the 1960s through to the early 1980s are philosophically textured, his way of answering them is distinctly theological, or, as he prefers (since only God can speak of God), *theo*-logical. This is the author of *L'Idol et la distance* (1977); *Dieu sans l'être* (1982, rev. ed. 1991); *Prolégomènes à la charité* (1986, rev. ed. 1991); and, in part, *La Croisée du visible* (1996). Yet with the texts that constitute the third dimension of his work, his resetting of phenomenology, Marion finds that he can stay with philosophical questions all the way until he reaches satisfactory answers. Direct recourse to theology is no longer needed. This is Marion the thinker for whom a revived phenomenology *is* philosophy today, the man deeply concerned to understand, maintain, and if need be rework the central insights of Husserl and Heidegger. He is the author of *Réduction et donation* (1989), a treatise in which a task in the history of philosophy leads to the philosophizing in *Étant donné* (1997; rev. ed. 1998) and *De Surcoît* (2001). When we read these studies we draw near to the center of Marion's *oeuvre* and are close to his most notable contributions to philosophy.

No sooner has one perceived these three groupings and started to look for the deeper unity that holds them together than one's eye is caught by something that seems only now to have come into view, *Le Phénomène érotique* (2003). Under the force of this insight, we are led to reread the whole body of Marion's work, starting with "Amour de Dieu, amour des hommes" (1970), and continuing through to *Being Given* and beyond, as a rethinking of human subjectivity in terms of the possibility of loving and being loved.[4] One of the most provocative contributions that Marion makes to philosophy is his response to the fifth of Husserl's *Cartesian Meditations,* that *point d'appui* in the study of intersubjectivity. Where other philosophers have sought to augment or reform Husserl at this point by way of *mit-da-sein,* being-for-the-other, empathy, friendship or community, Marion argues that phenomenology must supplement itself by a deeper thinking of charity, *agapē,* and do so without relying on religious dogma.[5] We see Marion in sharpest focus when we perceive that he can be grasped in his totality as a philosopher of love.[6]

"The beginning of phenomenology": that is, as I have said, one of the two fundamental events that provide the impetus for Marion's thought. Interpretations of that phrase differ, however, and each requires our attention. First of all, Marion would not be himself—the thinker whose books we read and discuss—had there been no beginning of *phenomenology.* Without the breakthrough of Edmund Husserl's *Logical Investigations* (1900–1) and its reversion "to the 'things themselves' [*'Sachen selbst' zurückgehen*]" there would have been no "Jean-Luc Marion," no philosopher of givenness, of the saturated phenomenon, or of the erotic reduction.[7] For Marion is a thinker of disclosure first and foremost, and he compels our attention because he has made that style of philosophy distinctively his own, as Martin Heidegger, Maurice Merleau-Ponty, Emmanuel Lévinas, Paul Ricœur, Jacques Derrida, and Michel Henry all did before him.

Marion is also a critical thinker of the *beginning* of phenomenology, one who wants firmly to secure its starting point so that we may be fully open to experience and acknowledge what he has come to call "counter-experience." Husserl brought metaphysics to its term, in both senses of the word, Marion argues. Beginning in the *Logical Investigations,* he outlined how *Gegebenheit* [*donation,* givenness] could give itself without any conditions whatsoever, and had he been able to follow that program without deviation he would have overcome metaphysics.[8] For givenness is not presence [*Anwesenheit*]. Giving without conditions is the basis of Husserl's insistence, developed more fully in *Ideas I* (1913), on philosophizing without presuppositions, that is, contenting oneself with accurately describing how things present themselves without their having to meet any conditions that we might have laid down for their reception. As late as the *Cartesian Meditations* (1929), Husserl pointed to phenomenology as a "purely intuitive, concrete, and also apodictic mode of demonstration [that] excludes all 'metaphysical adventure,' all speculative excess."[9] For all that, he proclaimed "the living present" and "transcendental life," notions that have alerted some of his readers to a hidden metaphysics. And much as he desired sheer presentation [*Gegenwärtigung*], not derived re-presentation [*Vergegenwärtigung*], he prized *Gegebenheit,* givenness, as objectivity [*Gegenständlichkeit*], and thereby gave birth to metaphysics in one of its most subtle and intractable forms.[10] The missed opportunity to free thought from a hardened structure of presentness haunted Derrida in his earliest writings, and it also provokes Marion who, as we shall see, comes to a different understanding of Husserl's metaphysics than the author of *Edmund Husserl's "Origin of Geometry": An Introduction* (1962) and *Speech and Phenomena* (1967).

Husserl's commitment to direct awareness of phenomena in terms of objectivity is not the only possibility entertained in his breakthrough volume, the *Logical Investigations,* however. He also indicates a way in which concepts and relations present themselves prior to any deduction of the categories described by Aristotle (with entities in mind) or by Kant (with phenomena in mind). This presentation occurs in a precognitive moment: we encounter concepts and relations in appearances before we seek to know them in a formal manner. As Heidegger and Max Scheler were among the first to see, this notion of "categorial intuition [*kategoriale Anschauung*]," as it is called, expands "experience" beyond the limits to which it had been confined by the British empiricists. Husserl himself would wait until his later works to identify intuition and experience, insisting that "experience is not an opening through which a world, existing prior to all experience, shines into a room of consciousness" but is "the performance in which for me, the experiencer, experienced being 'is there', and is there as what it is, with the whole content and the mode of being that experience itself, by the performance going on in its intentionality, attributes to it."[11] For the first generation who followed Husserl, experience would be taken to cover both sensuous particulars and abstract relations such as negation and conjunction, plurality and totality. Categorial intuition also includes, as Heidegger stresses, the "is" that accompanies sensuous intuitions, and thereby allows us to see being as being-given. Like Heidegger, Marion fastens on categorial intuition, and, if anything, holds onto it longer, until it reveals the priority of givenness with respect to both objectivity and being. In order to see this clearly, we must return to the Husserl of the *Investigations* as well as to the Heidegger for whom "givenness" was the "magic word" of phenomenology.[12] We must go back to the young philosopher whose reading of Husserl formed the ground on which on which *Being and Time* (1927) would be so influential.

In his summer course of 1925, "History of the Concept of Time," Heidegger observes that in the sixth of the *Logical Investigations* the founder of phenomenology establishes that there are different sorts of intuitions that relate to real and ideal objects.[13] As Husserl puts it, "there must at least be an act which renders identical services to the categorial elements of meaning that merely sensuous perception renders to the material elements" (*LI*, II, 785). We can perceive concepts and relations before we formally posit them. "The object with these categorial forms is not merely referred to," Husserl says, "but it is set before our very eyes in just these forms" (II, 785). On hearing talk of "intuition" and "categorial forms" we encounter the vocabulary of phenomenology, which especially in English can distract one from the points at issue because it squares neither with the meanings the words have in ordinary language nor with those they have in standard philosophical usage. Who, untutored, would think that "constitution [*Konstitution*]" in Husserl's *Logical Investigations* means the letting-be-present of an object rather than the construction of it by consciousness? We need to elucidate the technical language of phenomenology as soon as it appears.

Let us start with "intuition." It is not a psychological insight that escapes reason, as one might think. Not at all: the German word is *die Anschauung*, not *die Eingebung;* and for Husserl *Anschauung* denotes that something is directly in my sphere of awareness, this laptop on which I am writing, for example, and not the house on Lake Michigan where I will spend my summer holiday. When I think about that house while working at home in South Bend I have an "empty intuition," as Husserl puts it, but when I finally go up to the lake in August and start to settle into the house and look around the garden my intuition will be filled. "Intention" is another word we must approach with care. In ordinary English it denotes a purpose to do something, while in phenomenology it means being directed to something, whether in the world or in my mind. I intend my holiday house when I have a mental image of it, if I stand before it on the street, or if I remember it years after it has been pulled down. And this brings us to the third of these strange words, and certainly a very important one for the Marion of *Reduction and Givenness.*

"Categorial" does not refer to a category in any of the usual senses philosophers ascribe to that word but to concepts and relations that are prior to the ten classes of predications—substance, quantity, quality, relation, place, time, attitude, circumstance, action, and affection—that Aristotle specifies in the *Categories* as the *summa genera* of our conceptual world. We might dub the "pure forms" that Husserl identified "syntactical categories," for what is at issue is that complexes are always disclosed to us with their syntax in place, as it were. If we do so, however, we should not take the further step and assume that Husserl distinguishes clearly between syntax and semantics, as Rudolf Carnap was later to do when developing his theory of categories.[14] The point Husserl wishes to make is that when I look, for example, at my pet I do not see a furry *and* a tabby *and* a four-legged creature. I see a *cat,* not a collection of different bits and pieces; and if anyone asks what sort of pet I have, I say, "A tabby cat." Or I see that there is something a bit odd about my cat today, look more attentively, and say to myself, "My cat is limping." In both cases I am dealing with synthetic categorial acts in which an object—my cat—cannot be intended without including the elements "tabby" or "limping." Were I talking about animals in a general way, as in a seminar on animal rights, I might begin by mentioning a cat or a bear but would soon abstract myself from any particular animal. Then I would be dealing with ideative categorial acts. Regardless of whether I perceive that my cat is limping or assert "Animals are intrinsically valuable," I am living in categories behind underlying those defined by Aristotle and Kant.

So Husserl maintains that the categorial is given in intuition. When the right circumstances are in place, not only are sensory particulars given but also the relation between them (of part and whole, say) "is truly given with the truly given contents" (*LI,* II, 812). We have, as Heidegger puts it late in life, "two visions: sensuous vision and categorial vision."[15] With this amplification of intuition Husserl makes a decisive advance beyond Kant and distinguishes himself from neo-Kantianism as it runs from Otto Liebmann to Heinrich Rickert. He develops the notion of intuition beyond sense experience, and expands what counts as perception by allowing the categorial to be given concretely in particular acts of perception. It is more direct than the account offered in the *Critique of Pure Reason* where Kant tackles the issue by way of the schematism of judgment (A 80 / B 106) or the table of judgments (A 138 / B 177). Later, in the second edition of the *Logical Investigations* (1913), which was revised in the light of *Ideas I,* Husserl tells us that the sixth investigation is "the most important . . . from a phenomenological point of view" and that, in order to be true to its insights, he has had to revise and enrich it significantly (I, 50). The insight took a long time to be accepted. As late as the *Formal and Transcendental Logic* (1929) he will observe of categorial experience that "even today it still has to fight for its legitimacy" (45). He would have had in mind Moritz Schlick's fierce and sometimes wrongheaded objections to intuitive knowledge in 1910, 1913, and beyond.[16] As Heidegger came to see, categorial perception is not narrowly established but pivots on an analogy with sense perception. Husserl hardly disguises the analogical status of the new mode of perception: "*As the sensible object stands to sense-perception so the state of affairs stands to the 'becoming aware' in which it is* (more or less adequately) *given*—we should like to say simply: so the state of affairs stands to the *perception* of it" (*LI,* II, 783).[17] At any rate, there is no mention by Heidegger of categorial intuition in *Being and Time,* the *Beiträge,* or any of the major works. It is discussed only in early lecture courses and recalled in a late seminar.

For the young Heidegger it was the idea of categorial intuition, along with intentionality and the original sense of the *a priori,* that represented the appeal and the promise of phenomenology. As early as 1916 in his habilitation thesis, *Die Kategorien- und Bedeutungslehre des Duns Scotus,* he used the distinction between sensuous and categorical intuition to help free himself from neo-Kantianism.[18] And in his very last seminar, conducted at Zähringen in 1973, he returns to the sixth investigation, as the following notes from that seminar reveal:

> I see this book before me. But where is the substance in this book? I do not see it in the same way that I see the book. And yet this book is a substance that I must "see" in some fashion, otherwise I could not see

anything at all. We encounter here the Husserlian idea of "surplus" [*Überschuss*]. Heidegger explains: the "is," through which I observe the presence of the inkwell as object or substance, is a "surplus" in relation to the sensuous affections. But in a certain respect the "is" is given *in the same manner* as the sensuous affections: the "is" is not added to the sense data; it is "seen"—even if it is *seen* differently from what is sensibly visible. In order to be "seen" in this way, it *must* be *given*.[19]

Being is not an abstraction but is given in categorial intuition. This insight fascinated Émile Lask in his *Logik der Philosophie* (1911), where the young disciple of Rickert looks past the neo-Kantianism in which he has been educated to argue that empirical categories must rely on prior categories if they are to give rise to knowledge. All cognition requires categorial intuition, he thinks. Heidegger had read Lask before writing his habilitation dissertation, and he was guided by his reading on how best to put to use the sixth investigation. Along with Franz Brentano's *Von der mannigfachen Bedeutung des Seienden nach Aristotles* (1862), "Investigation VI," as mediated by Lask, was one of the signal texts in Heidegger's early philosophical development. No categorial intuition, no Heidegger? With the benefit of hindsight it would seem so. "Through this achievement," the thinker of Todtnauberg says while looking back on his life's work, "I finally had the ground" (ibid., 67).

Husserl's accomplishment in "Investigation VI," at least for the young Heidegger, is more than the widening of the notion of experience; it is nothing less than the liberation of Being from theoretical judgment. But for all his achievement, the master recoils before what he uncovers, Heidegger thinks. Beginning with *The Idea of Phenomenology* (lectures given in 1907) and continuing up to the criticisms of *Ideas I* leveled by Paul Natorp in 1917–18, Husserl converts phenomenology more and more surely into a transcendental philosophy and, as Heidegger sees it, becomes unable and unwilling to pass from disclosing objects to disclosing Being.[20] Preoccupied by the transcendental ego and the problems in the theory of knowledge that it spawns, Husserl goes on to write *The Paris Lectures* and the *Cartesian Meditations* and to develop "transcendental idealism"; Heidegger produces *Being and Time*, a treatise that outlines a fundamental ontology.[21] The one insists on beginning strictly with transcendental consciousness; the other with Dasein, which finds itself always and already thrown into the world and hence irreducible to the Cartesian ego or even the Husserlian transcendental "I." (Far from resembling the *cogito* or any version of the post-Cartesian subject, Dasein is, as Jean-Yves Lacoste mem-orably puts it, "nothing but doors and windows.")²² The one thinker remains within the philosophy of subjectivity, even in his account of intersubjectivity; the other is able to raise the question of the meaning of Being and then, in his later writings, the question of the truth of Being, where "truth," understood as *alētheia,* has come a long way from the fulfillment of intentions. To be sure, there are changes in Husserl's procedure evident in the *Crisis* (1954), including a step back from Cartesianism, but they are too late to influence Heidegger or even attract his close attention.²³

The participants at the Zahringen seminar were not left in any doubt about the limitations of the master's method. For Husserl, they were told, "it goes without saying that 'being' means 'being-object'" (67) and that "[h]e does not unfold the question: 'what does being mean?'" (67). Bypassing that question is not simply one shortcoming among others, as Heidegger sees things. Avoiding the *Seinsfrage* distances Husserl from the animating thought of the Greeks, from Parmenides to Aristotle, who, he insists, had no word for "what stands against [*Gegenstand*]—'object'" (70).²⁴ It was a sign that Husserl had no sense of the "deep meaning of history as Tradition (as that which delivers us), in the sense where Plato is here, Aristotle is here, and they speak to us, they are pres-ent [*gegenwärtig*] to us and must be present to us" (16). It was a sense that Heidegger assiduously cultivated, and at times overcultivated.

From Heidegger's perspective, Husserl was unable to pose the question of the meaning of Being precisely because of his preoccupation with the *epochē* and phenomenological reduction. The two expressions, frequently revised as Husserl sought increasing rigor, need to be glossed.²⁵ *Epochē* names the abstention from "the natural attitude [*die natürliche Einstellung*]," the default reliance on the assumptions that the world exists independently of our con-sciousness and that consciousness is just one more item in the world as factu-ally given. That the world is really and truly there is not to be systematically doubted, as Descartes encouraged us to do; rather, our tendency to use the world to make rough and ready sense of our experience is bracketed so that we may concentrate on the experience as actually lived.²⁶ More technically, the *epochē* suspends all "transcendence," a word that in phenomenology denotes all that is outside lived experience, *Erlebnis,* and its correlates; it includes natu-ral objects and remembered things, as well as God. When we perform the *epochē* we put out of play divine agency, the laws of physics, and experimental psychology as ways of accounting for our experience.

Of course, we can properly understand naturalistic objectivism only from the clear view afforded by carrying out the *epochē*.[27] It is a situation that makes phenomenologists talk of "conversion" almost in a religious sense of the word. In doing so they are encouraged by Husserl who observed "the total phenomenological attitude and the *epochē* belonging to it are destined in essence to effect, at first, a complete personal transformation, comparable in the beginning to a religious conversion."[28] No wonder then that Paul Ricœur, echoing Matt. 10:39, says, "By this act I apparently *lose* the world while truly *gaining* it."[29] Eugen Fink had imagined the reduction as a process of *theosis* that "unhumanizes" the one who performs it and makes him or her like one of the gods, a "player of the world [*Weltspieler*]."[30] More modestly, one might follow the Husserl of the Amsterdam Lectures (1928) and speak of the reduction in Kantian terms as a "*Copernican 180⁰ Turn*."[31] Once the *epochē* has been undertaken, one can proceed to the phenomenological reduction, the leading back of thought to the actual constitution of experience.[32] There are several ways it can be achieved (in the *Crisis* alone Husserl lists five, while the *Formal and Transcendental Logic* offers another) and the task must be perpetually renewed. It would be a mistake to think that the transcendental field is "there," like a distant shore; it is created in the act of reduction. Generally, one might say that with the conversion of the gaze from the natural to the phenomenological attitude, one discovers the world in all its pristine wonder.[33] One finds all the disregarded horizons of one's intentionality and can unfold the full meaning of the objects with which one is in contact. To be a subject, for Husserl, is not to be a self-contained and self-grounding *cogito* but to be always and already in touch with the world.

When phenomenologists use the word "subject," they do not usually name the natural dimension of an individual (the Kevin Hart who was born in London and who walks to work each day) but the transcendental dimension of that same person (the Kevin Hart who is aware of being an "I" and who grasps the principles of being born, place, walking, and work). They are also concerned with the difficult issue of how the two dimensions of the subject interact: Husserl's discussions of the problem in *Cartesian Meditations* §§15–16 and the *Crisis* §§53–54 are essential touchstones, as is Fink's *Sixth Cartesian Meditation*.[34] Yet the transcendental subject encounters experience wholly in itself, Husserl argues, without reference to anything or anyone else. The *epochē* and phenomenological reduction do not disclose the immanence of my psyche. They do not delimit part of the world; they go behind it to disclose the transcendental structures of my being-in-the-world. They reveal what is properly called "absolute" transcendental subjectivity. I encounter phenomena in my experience itself, not derived from the world about me or from psychological data or from abstract speculation. They are there "absolutely" in the etymological sense of the word; they have absolved themselves from all conditions or, as Husserl would want to say, they are without presuppositions.[35]

To repeat, the *epochē* and the reduction lead one back to the immanent life of transcendental consciousness. It is a procedure that, beginning with his Göttingen lectures of 1907, Husserl insisted was essential to phenomenology. But it was not a move that his Göttingen students could always follow, especially when they saw their teacher abandoning the realism of the *Investigations*. Hedwig Conrad-Martius rejected the reduction, regarding it as an impediment to discovering phenomena. Roman Ingarden retained it, believing it necessary for epistemology, but always distanced himself from all tendencies to idealism in Husserl's use of the reduction. Heidegger could not embark for the passage to transcendental consciousness. To do so would put ontology out of play, he thought, since, as Husserl insists in *Ideas III*, "all ontologies become subject to reduction."[36] And what Heidegger wanted, above all, was to show that "*[o]nly as phenomenology, is ontology possible*,"[37] by which he meant that one might seek the Being of beings only by way of phenomenology as reinterpreted in *Being and Time* §7. At all events, when Husserl sought to reduce ontology he was very far from making an unconsidered claim. In 1927, the very year of *Being and Time*, Husserl wrote that "a phenomenology properly carried through is the truly universal ontology."[38] The emphasis falls on "properly" and "truly," since an ontology that has been subject to the reduction would be set against "the only illusory all-embracing ontology in positivity" (32). Several years later, when Husserl sought to develop his thousands of pages of notes in shorthand, the *Forschungsmanuskripte*, into a systematic account of his thought, the second book was to be titled "Ontology and Phenomenology." Unfortunately, it remained a project and so we lack a comprehensive account of the issue.[39]

Precritical ontology had been the subject of withering criticism for several generations of neo-Kantians before Husserl wrote a word on ontology. When he did so he spoke of "formal ontology," the pure categories of objects, which by the time of *Formal and Transcendental Logic* (1929) he twinned with "formal apophantics," the pure categories of meaning. Ontology first entered phenomenology as a branch of logic, which of course Husserl had already recast as an *a priori* science of ideal truths rather than the art of reasoning, which it had been since Aristotle.[40] He had already distinguished formal and regional ontologies in *Ideas I*, §§8–9, underlining the need for a formal ontology to specify the fundamental determinations of whatever can be an object of consciousness. And in *Ideas III*, §§13–17, we see him pursuing an ontological path, even as he criticizes the one-sidedness of ontologies for positing objects rather than examining how they are concretely constituted in lived experience. The very use of the plural, "ontolog*ies*," separates Husserl from the neo-Kantian critics of ontology as well as from those they criticize. We need regional ontologies in order to examine the structures of phenomena as different as mathematical relations, remembering a friend's smile, and touching the rough bark of a tree. What falls before the reduction is "transcendent being" and what remains is "intended being." There may not be any *metaphysica specialis* for Husserl but there will certainly be regions of being.

Be that as it may, Heidegger would retain the reduction only notionally, in terms of the insight gained from the first version of "Investigation VI," and only in his first maturity as a thinker. It was one of the decisive differences between the two founding fathers of phenomenology, as Heidegger made clear to his students at Marburg in the summer of 1927. "*For Husserl,*" he said, "phenomenological reduction . . . is the method of leading phenomenological vision from the natural attitude of the human being whose life is involved in the world of things and persons back to the transcendental life of consciousness."[41] Its positive character, he had memorably observed several years earlier, is the development of "the possibility that every merely possible being comes into view."[42] In 1927 he would put things differently, stressing the risk that the conversion of the gaze never escapes epistemological issues and that Being is always cognized. Not everyone would agree with him, whether because Husserl's orientation to epistemology seemed overstated or because his primary motivation was the structure of life, not knowledge.[43] At any rate, for Heidegger in 1927 the task was to transform phenomenology into "the science of the Being of entities," which would place it in relation with the beginning of philosophy, with the Greeks.[44] And so he distinguishes himself from Husserl: "*For us* phenomenological reduction means leading phenomenological vision back from the apprehension of a being, whatever may be the character of that apprehension, to the understanding of the being of this being (projecting upon the way it is unconcealed)" (*Basic Problems*, 21).

In Marion's terms, Husserl performs the "first reduction," the leading back to the phenomenon as object, and Heidegger engages in the "second reduction," the passage from beings to Being. If phenomenology is to come fully into its own, he thinks, one must go further and perform a "third reduction," a leading back to the originary giving intuition [*originär gebende Anschauung*]— that is, the *self*-givenness [*Selbstgegebenheit*]—of phenomena. Only then will one secure experience as *Evidenz,* evidence or, better, self-evidence: the direct awareness of phenomena as they manifest themselves.[45] Now followers of Husserl before Marion have certainly accented the primacy of givenness— Rudolf Boehm, for example.[46] Others have radicalized the reduction: Fink's meontological reduction (from the Greek *to mē on,* nonbeing), for instance, that takes one back before being. But no one has sought to rethink the reduction in order to yield givenness. Such a reduction is more than a radical strategem in the world of phenomenology; it risks making a total break with the discipline as it has been understood, and inaugurating a new style of thinking, one with a claim to be as upsetting to normative discourse in phenomenology as deconstruction was a generation or two ago. (Perhaps the secret title of *Réduction et donation,* the one that Marion sometimes whispers to himself, would be *De la donatologie.*) Where Derrida disturbed his contemporaries by insisting that interpretation has always and already started, Marion worries his readers, now long conditioned to the primacy of hermeneutics with respect to phenomenology, by implying that hermeneutics, while certainly endless in principle, is subsequent to the self-giving of phenomena.[47] Where Derrida remains in relation with Kant to the extent that grammatology is a critical enterprise, bearing on limits (and especially with their hidden relations with centers), Marion is more surely in relation with Husserl, more occupied with syntheses of fullness and their possible disappointment.

Is there a phenomenology without the horizon of the constituting "I"? Not for Lévinas, not for Derrida, and not for anyone for whom Husserl provides the template for how phenomenology is done. If the history of phenomenology is, as Ricœur says, the history of Husserl's views and the heresies that stem from them, then Marion contributes the most shocking chapter of infidelity to that history by removing the horizon and decreeing multiple horizons.[48] For him, though, it is a chapter that tries to understand and act on Husserl's deepest commitments better than he dealt with them himself. Is the horizon a condition of the reception of phenomena? For Marion it has served as such in phenomenology and is therefore an impediment to full disclosure. At the "Religion and Postmodernism" conference held at Villanova University in September 1997, Marion recalled in a conversation with Derrida, "I said to Lévinas some years ago that in fact the last step for a real phenomenology would be to give up the concept of horizon. Lévinas answered me immediately: 'Without horizon there is no phenomenology.' And I boldly assume he was wrong."[49]

Was he wrong? There is reason to doubt it. One can distinguish between what falls within a horizon, and thereby constitutes the sum total of all possible experience, and the horizon itself—the horizon of horizons, as Husserl would say—which is nothing other than the world in which experience can occur and which is apprehended, if at all, only in a vague and nonthematic manner.[50] The meontic reduction takes us behind the world, and a need for it to be performed has some textual support from Husserl. Marion's reduction, it might seem, leads us not only behind the world but also erases the very idea of "world." I think this would be a hasty reading, based on too quick a response to Marion's anecdote about Lévinas. The horizon remains for Marion, although it no longer restricts the appearing of phenomena in advance. Instead, the phenomenon that is saturated with intuition blurs the horizon, or calls several horizons into play to deal with it, or both events occur together.[51] And here the role of hermeneutics once again comes into view. When a phenomenon with a surplus of intuition runs against the horizon it cannot be constituted as just the one object or even as an object, and it sets in motion a potentially infinite process of interpretation.

Marion's revision of Husserl goes by way of Heidegger, for—at least in *Reduction and Givenness*—he sees his opportunity for originality in Dasein's attunement to boredom. When bored, Dasein finds that the call of Being is suspended, and this recognition opens the possibility of hearing another call, an indeterminate one that has been coming all the while but neglected because one has been attuned to the call of Being. Boredom prompts a reduction—not to objects or Being but to the pure form of the call. Three issues surface here: the reduction, the role of boredom, and the insistence on purity. Each must be addressed, if only briefly, before we continue. Heidegger insists that anxiety [*Angst*], which reveals the world as uncanny, can dislodge one from the world and provoke philosophical reflection on Being. For Marion, this is Heidegger's version of the reduction, an ontological reduction by way of *Befindlichkeit*, and, learning from *Being and Time* §40 and the 1929–30 lecture course, he develops a related version by way of boredom.

Neither reduction would win a nod of approval from Husserl who seeks method and not moods, and to be sure Marion's reduction, as distinct from his account of Husserl's, is one of the most puzzling things in his work. But let us put the issue to the side. No phenomenologist after Husserl is orthodox when it comes to the reduction. "The most important lesson which the reduction teaches us is the impossibility of a complete reduction."[52] Thus Merleau-Ponty: faithful in letter and unfaithful in spirit. Marion would disagree with him, for he seeks a complete reduction but not along transcendental lines. When I suffer from boredom [*Langeweile*], he says, it is unlike an anxiety attack. No gap between the world and myself is felt. I do not encounter being or non-being, as I might in states of astonishment or joy. Only in such a listless state, Marion suggests, can I hear the call, since in boredom time loses its sense and its direction and exposes me to what precedes Being. Here, then, is a rare moment when Marion converges with Maurice Blanchot, yet where Blanchot hears the unsettling whisper of Being ceaselessly passing into nonbeing, the approach of the stagnant void that he calls the "Outside," Marion discerns the fullness of donation.[53] Blanchot and Marion meet, but only with their backs to one another.

What then of purity? It is not an unfamiliar word for readers of Husserl. A section of the Amsterdam Lectures (1928), for instance, is devoted to the meaning of purity [*Reinheit*].[54] There, Husserl is at pains to show that phenomenological purity means the absence of prejudgments and that there has been no contamination from psychophysics. No doubt because of Marion's theological interests, his secular critics have been quick to find a confessional basis for the purity of the call. Derrida, for one, believes it is to be aligned with the call of God the Father, and sees here an instance of Marion's deep desire ultimately to identify givenness as divine gift, a move that Derrida declares illegitimate.[55] Marion would reply that my response to the call is always structured by a delay so that I cannot be sure if I properly name what calls. Such a situation would be intolerable for a Christian who wishes to speak of the Father. The purity in question, Marion insists, is philosophical, not theological, and it arises from his conception of phenomena and evidence.

Things are a little different in *Being Given*. There is no talk of boredom here. Rather, the self-givenness of phenomena addresses me with a counter-intentionality, the shock of exteriority, which Marion names "the call." The claim reminds us of Husserl's remark to Dorian Cairns in 1931 that in his Göttingen days "he used to describe '*originäre*' *Gegebenheit* ["originary" givenness] as the object calling out, *'Ich bin da!'* ['Here I am!'].[56] I attest to the call only in responding to it, yet no attestation can exhaust it.[57] The effect of hearing this call is the exposure of a primordial stage of the subject before Dasein, before any form of the "I"; it dispossesses the claim of any transcendental consciousness to absolute primacy, undercuts any assurance I might have that I coincide perfectly with myself. I receive the phenomenon before I can understand it. This "I" is what Marion first dubs *l'interloqué*, the one who is called, and then *l'adonné*, the one for whom the given is projected as on a screen and who, in and through that very event, receives himself or herself.[58]

Only by proceeding to the third reduction can one address and overcome the metaphysics that, in different ways and to varying extents, still clings to the thought of Husserl and Heidegger.[59] That said, this need is not simply imposed on phenomenology as an innovation by a parvenu but is essentially marked in the *Logical Investigations*. In "Investigation V," the study of intentional experience, Husserl distinguishes several modes of givenness—principally signification, imagination, and perception—and shows that only perceptual givenness directly presents an object. Of special interest to Husserl is that it does not matter if an intentional object exists inside or outside the mind, for what concerns him is the direct awareness of an object: the Roman god Jupiter can become present to us in the stories we read about him in the *Metamorphoses*, even though we do not believe that he exists or even think that Ovid ever believed that he did.

Rather than continue to paraphrase "Investigation V," I will quote the relevant part of it. Note Husserl's elaboration of his general theory of objects, a set of problems inherited from Bernard Bolzano's influential *Wissenshaftslehre* (1837). It is material that, largely because the *Investigations* was not translated until 1970, is better known to Anglo-American philosophers by way of Alexius Meinong's "Über Gegenstandstheorie" (1904) to which Bertrand Russell drew attention in three articles in *Mind* in 1904.[60] For Meinong, even nonexistent and impossible objects—a golden mountain and a round square, for example— have characteristics even if they have no being. The law of noncontradiction takes hold only with real objects; it does not forbid imaginary objects such as round squares. Husserl agrees: "It makes no essential difference to an object presented and given to consciousness whether it exists, or is fictitious, or is perhaps completely absurd [*Für das Bewußtsein ist das Gegebene ein wesentlich Gleiches, ob der vorgestellte Gegenstand existiert oder ob er fingiert und vielleicht gar widersinnig ist*]" (*LI*, II, 559). Husserl is not driven, as Meinong is, to expand a theory of objects so that it includes "homeless objects" but wants rather to asterisk the point that givenness is originary, not existence. Or, as Marion has it, "Already in 1900–01 givenness preceded ('eventual') intuition as much as it did signification."[61] He could have pointed to *The Idea of Phenomenology* (lectures from 1907) where we are told that phenomenology investigates "the sphere of the absolutely given" and that "the idea of *phenomenological reduction* . . . means not the exclusion of the genuinely transcendent . . . but the exclusion of the transcendent as something to be accepted as existent, i.e., everything that is not evident givenness in its true sense, that is not absolutely given to pure 'seeing.'"[62] And he could have indicated the *Dingvorlesung* that followed those lectures, where Husserl noted that "absolute" means "absolute givenness; to be given in the flesh and with the consciousness of indubitable actuality."[63] But he does not; his aim is to find givenness at the very start of phenomenology, in the broadening of the concept of intuition in the *Investigations*.

Marion tells us in clear and strong terms, "Intuition results from givenness without exception"(*Reduction and Givenness*, 15). And then, in a quite remarkable passage, Husserl and Heidgger are interpreted freshly to reveal a deep layer of disclosure:

> Categorial intuition can be admitted only in response to a categorial givenness, and therefore in being thought first as giving. The categorial acts, "in regard to their character as giving [*gebende*] acts . . . are intuitions, they *give* objectivity [*sie* geben *Gegenständlichkeit*]"; and therefore the categorial act "brings the being in this new objectivity to givenness [*zur Gegebenheit*]," precisely because that objectivity is defined by self-givenness, as "self-giving [*sich gebende*]" objectivity. Categorial intuition is never—and this is already true in 1925—directly related to being (still less to Being) as some "intuition of Being"; it always mediates its relation to being through givenness, which originarily determines them both. (37)

And so the third reduction is implicit in the *Logical Investigations,* before even the first formulation of the reduction. Marion merely brings it to light and so remains faithful to the father of phenomenology. This mixture of piety and chutzpah characterizes all Marion's primary research in the philosophy of disclosure, from *Reduction and Givenness* to *In Excess*.

If we ask Marion where Husserl actually inaugurates phenomenology, we will be directed to several places in the master's works, to the *Logical*

Investigations, the *Erste Philosophie,* and *Ideas I.*[64] Of these the "principle of principles" has preeminent status by virtue of its clarity and its title. "No conceivable theory can make us err with respect to the *principle of all principles: that every originary presentive intuition is a legitimizing source of cognition, that everything originarily* (so to speak, in its 'personal' actuality) *offered* to us *in 'intuition' is to be accepted simply as what it is presented as being,* but also *only within the limits in which it is presented there.*"[65] Marion will underline "is presented," and refer us to *The Idea of Phenomenology* where it is admitted that "[t]he word 'phenomenon' is ambiguous in virtue of the essential correlation between *appearance and that which appears*" (11).[66] The phenomenon does not represent anything more primary than itself, is not the emissary of a noumenon that, ghostly and noble, waits afar off, withholding something else that could be given were we only able to receive it.

It is instructive to see how Heidegger responds to the formulation of the master principle. He does so in a late piece, "The End of Philosophy and the Task of Thinking" (1964):

> "The principle of all principles" contains the thesis of the precedence of method. This principle decides what matter alone can suffice for the method. "The principle of principles" requires reduction to absolute subjectivity as the matter of philosophy. The transcendental reduction to absolute subjectivity gives and secures the possibility of grounding the objectivity of all objects (the Being of this being) in its valid structure and consistency, that is, in its constitution, in and through subjectivity. . . .
> If one wanted to ask: Where does "the principle of all principles" get its unshakable right, the answer would have to be: from transcendental subjectivity which is already presupposed as the matter of philosophy.[67]

For Heidegger, the very way in which phenomenology is instituted entrenches Husserl in the metaphysics of subjectivity. In his turn, Marion notes that the principle of principles detaches phenomenology from any reliance on a metaphysical ground: no *a priori* categories or sufficient reasons are required for a phenomenon to appear, not even, as we have seen, a horizon. And he declares Heidegger guilty of the same tendency for which he convicts Husserl, since he "upholds subjectivity in Dasein no less than the privilege of the question of Being."[68]

Despite its authority, the principle of principles stands in need of significant adjustment. Husserl unduly restricts what counts as intuition by limiting it to intentionality, on the one hand, and to the object's transcendence, on the other. It is as though, for the Husserl of *Ideas I* at least, phenomenality must be borrowed from intentionality. Hence Marion's question: Is it not possible for a phenomenon simply to show itself without conforming to the constituting "I" and its horizons? "Husserl hesitates here," he says in *Being Given*. "[O]n the one hand, he seems to claim to liberate appearing (and not only intuition) from every *a priori* principle; on the other hand, he seems to limit appearing to it" (13). A major difficulty with the principle of principles, as Husserl formulates it, is that it is asserted before the reduction has taken place. Strictly speaking, the master principle is not the opening of phenomenology but is a pre-phenomenological, and therefore dogmatic, rule. If phenomena really give themselves, as Husserl wants to say, what need is there for a principle to determine whether or in what degree they do so? To pass beyond these two concerns, Marion argues that the more thoroughly the reduction is deployed, even to the point of self-reduction, the more givenness is made available. It leads to a reformulation of the founding precept of phenomenology: "So much reduction, so much givenness [*Autant de réduction, autant de donation*]."[69]

This new axiom, which Marion calls the "*last* principle" because it follows the phenomenon rather than precedes it, nonetheless echoes other attempts to launch phenomenology.[70] The preformulation of the principle is very far from the philosophy of disclosure, however; it can be found in a treatise that is little read these days, *Hauptpunkte der Metaphysik* (1808), written by Kant's successor at Königsberg, Johann Friedrich Herbart, who is best known today for his philosophy of education. His formulation reads, "So much appearance, so much indicating of being [*wie viel Schein, so viel Hindeutung aufs Seyn*]."[71] Read in context, there can be no doubt that the principle is metaphysical: it hinges on a dualism of appearance and being that is rejected by phenomenology. Husserl slightly misquotes Herbart in his *Erste Philosophie* (1923–24), II, §33, although his adaptation of the formula is heard only years later, in the fifth of the *Cartesian Meditations* (1929): "So much illusion, so much being [*Soviel Schein, soviel (durch ihn nur verdecktes, verfälschtes) Sein*]."[72] Before that magisterial pronouncement was ever penned, Heidegger had noted in his winter semester seminar of 1925, "[S]o much seeming, so much being [*soviel Schein—soviel Sein*]," and then again, in *Being and Time* (1927), "so much semblance, so much 'Being' [*Wieviel Schein jedoch, soviel 'Sein'*]."[73] Marion's inflection of this formula seeks to be more faithful to phenomenology than even Husserl: it insists on the primacy of the reduction, it aims for as complete a reduction as possible, it prizes givenness above both object and being, and it imposes no conditions whatsoever on the self-giving of what shows itself.[74]

With the fresh understanding of phenomenology encapsulated in the new slogan "So much reduction, so much givenness" Marion could make his own breakthrough, his realization that fulfilling intuition does not define all phenomenality. He started shortly after *Reduction and Givenness* (1989) in "The Saturated Phenomenon" (1992) and then elaborated his understanding more surely in *Being Given* (1997) and *In Excess* (2001).[75] For readers familiar with modern French philosophy, the adjective "saturated" will likely bring to mind Gabriel Marcel's notion of "saturated experience" expressed in his Gifford Lectures for 1949–50, later published as *The Mystery of Being*, so it is important to distinguish between Marcel and Marion on this point. Marcel posits two metaphors to help us think about experience, "pure" and "saturated," and suggests that we should think of transcendence not as an overcoming of experience but as an aspiration for pure or at least purer experience. The metaphor of saturation, brought into play in order to show, against the empiricists, that experience is not a homogenous mass, has two poles. There are experiences that are "saturated with prejudices" and others that are saturated with "pure ardor" or "pure receptivity."[76] Now the adjective "pure," as used here, does not make for a clean distinction between pure and saturated experiences, and as it happens Marcel does not think that they are entirely opposed. The apparent contradiction between them disappears "at the spiritual level" (1:55). When I engage in secondary reflection—personal engagement with the deeper, existential questions that life leads me to ask myself—I find that my experience of myself and of others is both purer than it might be otherwise and saturated with feelings, judgments, and values such as faith, hope, and love.

Marcel's idea of saturated experience gives us a placing shot near the more exact and exacting notion of the saturated phenomenon as elaborated by Marion. Following that thought in detail would lead to examining the influence of Lévinas on Marion, especially the former's reflections on the non-adequation of the other person with respect to my intentionality.[77] But I leave the history of influence to others. In *Reduction and Givenness*, Marion discloses two realizations: everything that shows itself must first give itself, and givenness is not always phenomenalized. That is, there are phenomena that give themselves but do not appear in the horizon of either "object" or "being." Philosophers since Kant have been aware of this category, as Marion well knows, but their curiosity has been largely confined to phenomena that are poor in intuition, most notably the formulas of pure mathematics, because they offer something very desirable to modern philosophy, namely certainty. Husserl argued in the *Investigations* that logical truths are given by categorial intuition, but of course they are never rich in intuition. Of more interest in the philosophy of disclosure are common phenomena such as those described and manipulated in chemistry and physics laboratories. Here intention and intuition converge exactly. We may recall Husserl's description in *Ideas II* of "returning rays, coming from the Objects [*Objekte*] back towards the center in manifold changing phenomenological characters."[78] Despite the allure of this canonic image in the philosophy of disclosure, Marion fastens onto those phenomena that cannot be regarded as objects, phenomena that are rich in intuition, that are characterized by intuition giving itself in excess of what can be foreseen or indicated in a concept.

To explore saturated phenomena Marion must question intentional phenomenology. Now the very term "nonintentional" sends a tremor through the world of *Ideas I* and *II*. The structure of intentionality—transcendence in immanence—was seen there to liberate philosophy from the subject–object relation that had bedeviled it for centuries. So important was this structure that it could ground both formal and regional ontologies. Yet doubts over this transcendental grounding have long bothered phenomenologists, requiring an adjustment to the status of intentionality as received from Husserl. "What we understand by call," Marion says in *Being Given*, "comes out of the reversal of intentionality, which is perhaps an essential characteristic of intentionality itself" (266). Only by freeing phenomenology from its reliance on consciousness's intentional rapport with the world can one acknowledge a givenness that is not phenomenalized. Such is the motivation behind what Dominique Janicaud sees as Marion's "maximalist conception of phenomenology."[79] Lévinas's reflections on passivity provide some guidance here. An intentional consciousness, he argues, "is also *indirectly*, and supplementarily, as it were, consciousness of itself: consciousness of the active self that represents the world and objects to itself, as well as consciousness of mental activity. But it would be an indirect consciousness: immediate, but without an intentional aim."[80] To develop this position in the direction of pure immanence would result in a phenomenology of life—the affirmation of self-experience—not the more familiar phenomenology of the world. Michel Henry has already taken this path in his *L'Essence de la manifestation* (1963), which Lévinas taught one year at the Sorbonne. Insisting on the immemorial trace of the Other even in nonintentional life, Lévinas refigures the nonintentional as a reversal of my intentionality. This reversal is Lévinas's "iconic moment," so to speak, the subjection of me by the command of the other person who speaks to me from the heights.[81] It might be said that Marion, while working with Henry's notion of auto-affection in his account of the flesh, also generalizes what is essential to Lévinas's ethics to the whole study of saturated phenomena.

In one of his rare lapidary remarks in the *Critique of Pure Reason* (1781; 2d ed. 1787), Kant observes: "Thoughts without content are empty, intuitions without concepts are blind" (*CPR*, A 51 / B 75).[82] Does Marion transgress this dictum and go in search of intuitions without concepts? Not at all: his point is that intuition must be given before it can be thought, and some phenomena have intuitions that overwhelm signification, intentionality, aim, and so forth. We remember what Heidegger in Zähringen said about "surplus [*Überschuss*] in relation to the sensuous affections."[83] Chiming with that remark, the phenomena that captivate Marion are to be known as "saturated." In his Paris lectures Husserl contended that phenomenology must do without paradoxes, since concepts "must be the genuine foundation-concepts of all knowledge."[84] No univocal sense can be given to Marion's saturated phenomena, however, which is why he sometimes refers to them as "paradoxes." They overflow with meanings that resist being unified or even organized. Each inverts one of the Kantian categories, and none can be accommodated by the sense of experience posited by the critical philosophy.

In the first *Critique* Kant identifies the categories that constrain how we can regard phenomena and hence what we can experience. They fall into four groups: quantity, quality, relation, and modality (A 80 / B 106). Kant takes as normative those phenomena that fall within my intentional horizon. I can aim at them (they have the quantity of unity, for example); I can bear them (they have the quality of limitation, say); they appear within a horizon (they are in a relation of inherence and subsistence, for instance); and I can gaze upon them (they have the modality of possibility, necessity, or existence). Marion is fascinated by those phenomena that, because they are saturated with intuition, exceed the Kantian categories and the notion of experience that they support. I cannot aim at them, or they dazzle me, or they impose themselves on me as absolute, or they rebuke my gaze, or they do all those things at one and the same time. They take me by surprise, giving me an experience of finitude that is not always welcome.

Consider the first sort of saturated phenomenon, that which exceeds the category of quantity and therefore cannot be aimed at. To illustrate it, Marion chooses the perfectly ordinary example of a hall in Paris—the Salle des Actes in the Institut Catholique, where he happens to be giving a lecture—and analyzes the event from the perspectives of the past, the present, and the future.[85] For him to walk into the hall is to encounter a place that, redolent of a past that has little or nothing to do with him personally, could not have been foreseen as the occasion of this lecture. In the present, the hall is the vehicle for a singular event that, in the rapport between lecturer and audience, as well as in innumerable details, is unrepeatable and unable to have been seen beforehand except in the most approximate of ways. And in time to come no one, not even the best informed biographer of Marion, will be able to capture the unique event of the lecture in all the minute inflections of the speaker's voice, tone, and gestures, the audience's guarded and unguarded responses, not to mention the consequences of the lecture in terms of audience members' reflecting on it, judging it, and maybe folding its arguments into their own philosophical reflections. In theory the event could give rise to endless interpretation. It is clear from Marion's example that there is nothing esoteric about saturated phenomena. They impose on us every day of the week.

And consider the third category of saturated phenomenon, in which all analogies fail because the phenomenon is absolute with respect to relation. Marion's example is the flesh, in the sense of *Leib* rather than *Körper*, which he develops brilliantly in *The Erotic Phenomenon* (2007). I can aim my consciousness at the other's body and have my intentions fulfilled. My flesh is different phenomenologically from the other's body; it is before the world in which the other's body, along with everything else, appears to me. I infer *Leib* on the basis of *Körper*, as Husserl thought in the fifth of the *Cartesian Meditations*. My flesh cannot be accounted for in terms of signification and intuition, for intuitions of my flesh precede my intentionality with respect to it. The phenomenon of flesh can give itself to me in a rush of pleasure, for example. It may be because I have just taken in the scent of some early blossoms, or because I am reminded of sitting near a tree in blossom with a girl I loved years ago, or because a line of poetry comes to mind ("And saw the blossoms, snow-bred pink and white") and I am moved once again by the expression "snow-bred."[86] I may be able to isolate the cause, but I will never be able to fit it to an intentional rapport that precedes it. Part of my pleasure is in being taken by surprise. I might smile, or I might not. Either way, no one who passes me will be able to know the intensity of my pleasure. As Marion says, "Flesh is referred to itself as it auto-affects itself . . . it eludes all relation."[87] It is an insight that reveals Marion to have been in dialogue with Ludwig Wittgenstein as well as Merleau-Ponty and, above all, Henry.[88]

The second and fourth saturated phenomena are the best known to Marion's readers, for they have been considered in the analyses of the idol and the icon in *The Idol and Distance* and *God without Being*. Be it a statue, a painting, or a novel, the idol dazzles me when I look at it. I am captivated by what I see. Indeed, the idol reduces visibility to the seen, and fills my gaze to its capacity. I think of Joseph Conrad: "My task which I am trying to achieve is, by the power of the written word, to make you hear, to make you feel—it is, before all, to make you *see*."[89] The novelist is a phenomenologist. As Husserl says, in a certain sense we cannot get beyond seeing, for "*[o]nly in seeing can I bring out what is truly present in a seeing; I must make a seeing explication of the proper essence of seeing.*"[90] Yet in performing his task the novelist risks turning his art into an idol. Unlike Husserl, Marion is equivocal about the act of seeing, especially so in his earlier writings. It is my gaze that makes an idol, not the other way around. "The idol thus acts as a mirror, not as a portrait: a mirror that reflects the gaze's image, or more exactly the image of its aim and of the scope of that aim."[91] As Marion insists, long before he formulates the saturated phenomenon, the idol "saturates" the gaze "with visibility" (12); it calls forth many concepts, no set of which can exhaust it, whether it is a poem like Gerard Manley Hopkins's "The Wreck of the Deutschland," a novel such as Marcel Proust's *A la recherche du temps perdu,* or a painting such as Mark Rothko's "Number 7." With the uncovering of that paradoxical phenomenon, though, Marion's understanding of the idol shifts and deepens. The idol allows what is unseen [*invu*] increasingly to become visible, perhaps over the course of many viewings, and generates an interpretation that is in principle endless. "The painter sees and so gives to be seen what without him would remain forever banished from the visible."[92] The unseen is one thing, the invisible is another; for the idol forbids any and all invisibility to be given. We look at an idol and think that we can judge it, but just the opposite is the case: we are judged by what we admire, we are shown the limits of the phenomenality that we can bear. "Name your idol, and you will know who you are," Marion tells us, and it is all the more pointed when we realize that for him, a professor of philosophy, concepts can be idols.[93]

Things are quite different with the icon. In Marion's early work, it was figured in a context that was heavily freighted with theological themes. *The Idol and Distance* sums up and extends much of his early writing, and it is worth quoting a distinction at the outset: "To the idol, by counterpoint, answers the icon. Whose face does the icon offer? 'Icon of the invisible God' (Colossians 1:15), says Saint Paul of Christ."[94] Part of what is meant here by "counterpoint" is that whereas the idol keeps the divine close, within my gaze, the icon insists on the infinite distance between the divine and me. In this first stage of Marion's intellectual maturity, he tends to treat the idol and the icon as distinct categories. Only later, in *God without Being,* does he begin to grasp them as different modes of disclosure—"a manner of being for beings"—and the fact that this new way of speaking is heard in the opening paragraph of that work suggests Marion's deepening commitment to phenomenology.[95]

That said, *God without Being* remains as theological as it is phenomenological, something sure to generate heated discussion in both groups and once again invite the question how the two discourses can be related. It is a question that has continued to preoccupy Marion, though in another register, one informed by *Being Given,* right through to *Le Visible et le révélé* (2005). Other questions are raised in *God without Being* touching on Marion's ecclesial style as a Catholic; there is, for example, his claim that the bishop is "the theologian par excellence" (152). The statement has often been taken to bespeak Marion's preference for clerical rather than lay theologians, or to insinuate his rejection of female theologians, or to suggest that he believes that all theologians should be under the pastoral authority of the bishop, narrowly conceived, with no freedom to speculate. Of course, Marion wrote "Of the Eucharistic Site of Theology," the chapter of *God without Being* in which the remark occurs, years before *Ex corde ecclesiæ* (1990), and his point addresses the Eucharist as the essential precondition of theology, and not ecclesial surveillance. Only a priest can consecrate the bread and the wine, and theology requires a Eucharistic site: talk of God, whether preaching or teaching, is rooted in the celebration of the liturgy. Not all theologians need be priests, but there can be no theology without them. By virtue of his office, the bishop enjoys the fullness of the priesthood and of course is the one who consecrates men to it. He is the theologian *par excellence* not because, as an empirical individual, he is always gifted in that way but because his office grounds the very possibility of doing theology.

We will appreciate the weight of "theological"—or, better, "*theo*logical"— only when we recall that the bishop derives his authority from Christ and should not act, or be taken to act, as a representative of the pope. Marion's insistence on the primacy of the bishop in matters theological is not only a ground, however, it is also an example. Implicitly he asks us to remember the great bishops who were also major theologians: the three Cappadocians St. Basil of Caesarea, St. Gregory of Nazianzus, and St. Gregory of Nyssa, for example, along with St. Ambrose and St. Augustine, St. Irenaeus, and St. Ignatius of Antioch, and many others. Marion regrets that the offices of bishop and theologian have been increasingly separated since patristic times. Almost never these days do we hear theology being created in homilies as a response by a bishop to an issue in his diocese. Yet Marion's point is broader than what a bishop does or does not do. The theologian interprets the Word, he says, "but on condition that the community itself be interpreted by the Word and assimilated to the place where *theo*logical interpretation can be exercised, thanks to the liturgical service of the theologian par excellence, the bishop" (152). There is no question here that lay theologians are valuable to the church. Were this not so, "Of the Eucharistic Site of Theology" would be a performative contradiction. What is essential is that Christian theologians remain on the Eucharistic site. To go elsewhere would be to fade from being a Christian theologian.

A border between phenomenology and theology runs through *God without Being;* it can be gleaned at the start of "Hors-Texte" and traced near the surface throughout the rest of the book. "If man, by his gaze, renders the idol possible, in reverent contemplation of the icon, on the contrary, the gaze of the invisible, in person, aims at man" (19). To be sure, Marion writes of the face here, yet even when there is no particular image named one is disposed to think of the face of the resurrected Christ or Immaculate Mary or one of the saints. What crosses our vision is the *imago dei,* and it is far more than we can bear. In *Being Given* and *In Excess,* then, the face is presented in terms that are familiar to readers of Lévinas. Still, Heidegger also comes to mind, not the younger philosopher who spoke of boredom, and who unknowingly led Marion to listen for the call of givenness, but the thinker who spoke very late in life of "a phenomenology of the inapparent."[96]

Lévinas's account of the face is invoked by Marion not in order to follow it to the letter but so that it might be adjusted:

The face, saturated phenomenon according to modality, accomplishes the phenomenological operation of the call more, perhaps, than any other phenomenon (saturated or not): it happens (event), without cause of reason (incident / accident), when it decides so (arrival), and imposes the point of view from which to see it (anamorphosis) as a *fait accompli.* That is why what imposes its call must be defined not only as the other person of ethics (Lévinas), but more radically as the icon.[97]

One thing that draws Marion to Lévinas is the latter's insistence that the other person is neither an object nor being. Resistant to being constituted as a phenomenon for me, the other person remains "otherwise than being." What is the givenness proper to the other person that I receive? For Lévinas, it is responsibility for him or her that comes through speech, specifically from the injunction "Thou shalt not kill." I find that my desire to persist in being, my *conatus essendi,* has always and already been interrupted by the trace of the infinite that signifies the other person. A claim is registered in me, one that I cannot satisfy either *de facto* or *de jure* and that therefore denies me the option of retiring from the field of ethical action with a good conscience.

For his part, Marion insists that the face is not merely unseen, which would allow it in principle to be rendered as a phenomenon and hence assigned a concept and a meaning, but is strictly invisible. Lévinas exempts the face from the epistemological meaning that comes from its status as a representation while granting it an ethical meaning to be found in my responsibility for the other person. Marion is unwilling to halt the analysis of the face at this point for two reasons: he finds a flaw in Lévinas's account of the face, and his understanding of the invisibility of the face suggests that we must situate it at the level of the icon. The face, for Lévinas, is that which allows us to escape the blank and heartless rule of the *il y a,* the neutral murmur of Being beneath beings. Does Lévinas thereby escape the philosophy of the Neuter as he claims in *Totality and Infinity?*[98] As early as 1983 Marion says that he does not—or not entirely. He may free himself from Parmenides but he does not affirm the individual person. His case is straightforward: "The injunction of obligation toward the other (*autrui*) leads, in reality, to the neutralization of the other as such. The other is neutralized as other, for another can always be substituted who can offer the face of the other (*d'autrui*) that the universal moral law requires."[99] In 2000 the argument is amplified, for the other person not only appears as "no-one [*personne*]" but also "suppresses and masks individuality," which leads

Marion to a startling claim by way of an allusion to Hannah Arendt's *Eichmann in Jerusalem* (1963), "the banality of evil finds its place in the anonymity of the face itself."[100]

In short, Lévinas fails to push his analysis to the appropriate level. There are three stages required of a thorough account of the face—the elevation of beings over Being; the transfer of intentionality from me to the other person; and the individualization of the other person, the condition that he or she can be loved—and Lévinas halts at the second. However, Marion insists, we must pass from ethics to love because the face of the other person expresses "an infinity of meanings at each moment" that cannot be "reduced to the concept or said adequately."[101] Only the person in love is impatient with the thought that the time with the other must be finite, and longs for an infinite relation with him or her.

Let us turn now to that other major event that has provoked Marion's thought—the end of metaphysics—and in particular let us think first of how it coheres with the beginning of phenomenology, and then ponder how a non-metaphysical phenomenology can help us think theologically.

In the preface to the English edition of *God without Being*, Marion tells us that modernity stands for "the completed and therefore terminal figure of metaphysics" (xx). Heidegger's voice can be heard in the background, and it is his diagnosis in *Identity and Difference* (1957)—that metaphysics is constituted as onto-theo-logy—that Marion adopts and confirms in his own way. "The essential constitution of metaphysics," Heidegger says, "is based on the unity of beings as such in the universal and that which is highest," that is, *ontōs* and the *theîon*.[102] He finds metaphysics in this sense (and in all manner of variations) in philosophy from Plato to Nietzsche. Husserl succumbs to it when he becomes committed to transcendental idealism, and Heidegger is the first to mark it, to signal that it is to be overcome, and then to admit that it must be left to peter out. Derrida agrees broadly with Heidegger but offers another scansion of the thought: the closure, not the end, of metaphysics has become legible.[103] His earliest work convicts Husserl of what he will dub "the meta-physics of presence," which is not one species of metaphysics among others but the thing itself that can be found before Plato, in Heidegger's beloved Parmenides, as well as in a current that runs through Heidegger himself, in his affirmation of *Ereignis* as the unique name of Being.[104] The metaphysics of presence is not confined to philosophy. Not at all: it shapes literary criticism and theology, economics and history, because all these disciplines, along with others, ultimately rely on a thinking of Being as being present in time and knowledge as being present to consciousness. But our focus is phenomenology and metaphysics, so let us stay with them.

Phenomenology begins, as we know, with the *Logical Investigations,* but what this means for us has been rendered opaque by the different interpretations of the text devised by Heidegger and Derrida. For Heidegger, the first version of "Investigation VI," the discovery of categorial intuition, opens the way for the question of the meaning of Being to be unfolded and therefore shows how to reach the far side of metaphysics. Husserl himself did not take this path, but continually revised "Investigation VI" while honing his favorite penknives, the *epochē* and the transcendental reduction.[105] There can be no doubt, however, that he prepared the way for the *Destruktion* of the history of ontology in *Being and Time.* For Derrida, metaphysics is completed rather than overcome in the *Investigations.* No sooner has the prolegomena to pure logic concluded and the "essential distinction" drawn between *Ausdruck* and *Anzeichen,* expression and indication, than one finds the metaphysics of presence structuring Husserl's thought. So where Heidegger sees the *Investigations* pointing away from metaphysics, Derrida sees another, highly seductive, version of it to be addressed. "We have experienced," Derrida says after carefully reviewing Husserl's work, "the systematic interdependence of the concepts of sense, ideality, objectivity, truth, intuition, perception, and expression. Their common matrix is being as *presence:* the absolute proximity of self-identity, the being-in-front of the object available for repetition, the maintenance of the temporal present, whose ideal form is the self-presence of transcendental life, whose ideal identity allows *idealiter* of infinite repetition."[106] The resources for passing beyond this metaphysics of presence are to be found, Derrida thinks, in questioning *Ausdruck* from the perspective of *Anzeichen.* Seen properly, "indication neither degrades nor diverts expression; it dictates it" (97).

Faced with these two powerful interpretations of the *Investigations,* and hence with different understandings of the relation of phenomenology and metaphysics, Marion declines to choose between them. He develops another case in two stages. First, he points out that there is more agreement between the first and the sixth investigations than the opposing interpretations might lead one to believe. It is Husserl's emphasis on the broadening of intuition that joins the first and the last investigations, a situation that becomes clear when one takes into account the "zig-zag" procedure that is adopted in the work as a whole.[107] Second, Heidegger and Derrida miss what is essential in the *Investigations:* "The phenomenological breakthrough consists neither in the broadening of intuition, nor in the autonomy of signification, but solely in the unconditional primacy of the givenness of the phenomenon."[108] It is this insight that, for Marion, allows us to identify the beginning of phenomenology with the end of metaphysics.

His boldest statement of this claim is made in an essay of 1993–94: "Phenomenology goes beyond metaphysics insofar as it renounces the transcendental project, to allow an ultimately radical empiricism to unfold—ultimately radical, because it no longer limits itself to sensible intuition, but admits all intuition that is primarily donative."[109] (The language reminds us of Husserl's early debts to David Hume and William James.) Appropriate shading was added several years later to make it plain that phenomenology does not mark the end of metaphysics in any simple or straightforward way, as is the wish of empiricists. Husserl remains Kantian in his emphasis on transcendental conditions determining phenomenality, and in his reliance on the "I" and its absolute horizon; for his part, Heidegger never quite escapes from the metaphysics of the subject and fails to grant primacy to intuition because he listens exclusively to the call of Being. "It should, therefore, be admitted," Marion says, "that phenomenology does not actually overcome metaphysics so much as it opens the official possibility of leaving it to itself. The border between metaphysics and phenomenology runs within phenomenology—as its highest possibility, and I stick with the phenomenological discipline only in search of the way that it opens and, sometimes, closes."[110]

It might be added that "metaphysics" must be understood in the precise sense that Marion ascribes to it and that the departure from it has been prepared for by Descartes's thought of the infinite, Nietzsche's critique of Platonism, and Heidegger's delimitation of the onto-theo-logical constitution of metaphysics, all of which lack what Marion seeks to provide: a more rigorous understanding of phenomenology as donatology and a nondogmatic account of love, *agapē,* that would help to ease our talk of the subject away from metaphysics (and thereby away from an expression like "the subject"). Now "metaphysics," Marion says, is defined very late in Western history, in St. Thomas Aquinas's commentary on Aristotle's *De generatione et corruptione,* and then, with particular significance for modern philosophy, at the start of Francisco Suárez's *Disputationes Metaphysicæ* (1597). Certainly the meaning of *meta ta physika,* itself a Hellenistic formula rather than an Aristotelian one, changed considerably in the Middle Ages and beyond. No longer did it denote what follows the study of nature but what is above nature in the sense of transcending it. Of course, one might still point to Aristotle's *Metaphysics* 1026ᵃ, 30–31, the discussion of "being as being," in the hope of securing a definite sense of "metaphysics," yet the Philosopher never unites "first philosophy" and the thinking of "being as being" under the one title. It is St. Thomas, in his *Commentary on the Metaphysics of Aristotle*, who speaks of metaphysics as the consideration of "being and the attributes which naturally accompany being" [*Metaphysica, in quantum considerat ens et ea quae consequuutur ipsum*].[111] And he is followed by Suárez for whom metaphysics is "the study of being as being or insofar as it abstracts being from matter [*quæ ens, in quantum ens, seu in quantum a materia abstrahit secundum esse*]," by which he means "being" taken as a noun and not as a participle.[112]

Metaphysics can be regarded as a system of thought (as with the Scholastics) and as a speculative venture. As Marion sees it, Scholastic metaphysics was conceived in terms of a distinction between being in general and essence (or essences); and it was not until Heidegger, in his remarks on the onto-theological constitution of metaphysics, that its speculative nature was finally seized. Strictly speaking, metaphysics runs through Western history from Suárez to Kant. Descartes is a special case: even though he seeks to jettison ontology in his metaphysics, leaving a "grey ontology," he ends up redoubling the onto-theo-logical character of his text.[113] The account of the *cogitatio* leads to a thinking of God as *ens summe perfectum* and the ego as a *cogitatio sui*, while the determination of *causa* implies God as *causa sui* and the ego as *ens causatum* (*Descartes' Metaphysical Prism*, 272; 277). Descartes recognized the limits of his onto-theo-logy, and thereby exposed it to destitution by sheer contrast with a higher order of reality. Once again *agapē* is invoked, and never more seriously: "Pascal does not refute Descartes' redoubled onto-theo-logy; he simply sees it. But he *sees* it from the point of view of a more powerful order, charity, which, simply by considering metaphysics as an inferior order, judges it and leaves it destitute" (351). So for Pascal (and Marion) metaphysics "appears as such—vain in the gaze of charity"; it is still intact but has "lost primacy" (351) and even a certain luster because it cannot save us. "To represent or to love—one must choose."[114] Perhaps Descartes did indeed reach this dilemma. As Marion reads Pascal, it is as though the author of the *Pensées* uncovers a categorial perception of a theological kind, one that allows us to see not just the sun and stars but also the "love that moves the sun and the other stars."[115]

Putting the special case of Descartes to one side, we can see that the end of metaphysics can be discerned positively in Hegel's *Encyclopedia* and negatively in Nietzsche's proclamation of the death of God. Long before either philosopher signed off on the topic, however, the rationalist Christian Wolff formalized metaphysics by distinguishing *metaphysica generalis* (the science of being: ontology) and *metaphysica specialis* (the science of essence: natural theology, psychology, and cosmology) and thus generated the familiar and somewhat tiresome disputes that make up the "metaphysics of the schools." It would be a mistake, Marion gradually came to see, to find this metaphysics in St. Thomas Aquinas. There are three reasons. First, God does not enter metaphysics either as subject or as object, and certainly never as an entity. Second, although entities and their being, *ens commune,* are grounded in God there can be no question that God is himself grounded in being: His *actus essendi* escapes any such determination. And third, God does not ground himself: He is *ipsum esse subsistens,* not *causa sui.*[116] In general, Marion differs from Derrida in assigning a more limited historical scope to metaphysics in the West, and strongly disagrees with his tendency to regard all philosophy as metaphysical. Why? Because phenomenology (now understood as donatology) indicates a way beyond metaphysics because it specifies the originary givenness of phenomena without any conditions being set for their reception, whether they be of height or depth (*theîon*) or generality (*ontōs*). To Husserl's call "Back to the things themselves!" Marion adds, "It is forbidden to forbid!"[117]

If we take this directive seriously, we have no right to deny phenomenality to anything that lays claim to it. As we have seen, Heidegger welcomed phenomenology as opening "the possibility that every merely possible being comes into view."[118] For Marion, of course, "possible being" must be adjusted so that we attend to what gives itself, yet the emphasis on the possible remains intact. Anyone schooled in Aristotle will be perplexed that Marion seeks a way out of metaphysics by way of the possible. For "possibility" is one of the key words in book delta of the *Metaphysics,* the word list that was to supply the basic vocabulary of intelligibility for the Western world. This criticism is misplaced, however, since Marion is far closer to Plato here than to Aristotle, even if his Plato has been interpreted and adapted by the Husserl of *Ideas I* and beyond. Possibility in classical phenomenology is "eidetic existence," which, we are told, is "absolutely necessary possibility," a notion that needs to be teased out before we can grasp what Husserl (and Marion) have in mind.[119] To begin with, we can say that phenomenological possibility is not the same as formal-logical possibility, which guarantees freedom from contradiction. Instead, it names what is given in the *eidōs*, the pure essence that, when seen, is intuition. The obvious reference here is *Ideas I*, §3, the account of *Wesenserschauung* or "eidetic seeing," but for the matter in hand Husserl is never clearer than in the much later work *Experience and Judgment* (1948) when he attends to general essences. "The essence proves to be that without which an object of a particular kind cannot be thought, i.e., without which the object cannot be intuitively imagined as such," he writes. "This general essence is the *eidos*, the *idea* in the Platonic sense, but apprehended in its purity and free from all metaphysical interpretations, therefore taken exactly as it is given to us immediately and intuitively in the vision of the idea which arises in this way."[120]

This intuition of the *eidōs* comes by way of free imaginative variation, the discovery of the principle or essence of the phenomenon by suspending its transcendent status and considering it immanently by way of examples and counter-examples. By ruminating on "revenge," examining it from this angle and that, recalling scenes from Thomas Kyd's *The Spanish Tragedy* or Shakespeare's *Hamlet* as well as unpleasant memories from my childhood, I begin to understand its cruel governing logic. It does not matter if I have had concrete experience of revenge or if I have been mercifully free of the desire for it. "For a pure *eidos*, the factual actuality of the particular cases by means of which we progress in the variation is completely irrelevant," Husserl adds (351). Eidetic generality cannot be limited to phenomena that can be objectified—I can discern the *eidōs* of a Klein bottle, for example—but, by the same token, anything that is admitted to be an actuality has an *eidōs:* the chilled bottle of Passing Clouds chardonnay sitting on my dining room table, for instance. We put out of play all positing of being when seeking a pure *eidōs:* this is the dimension of possibility at issue. At the same time, as Husserl makes clear, "What can be varied . . . bears in itself a necessary structure, an *eidos*, and therewith *necessary laws* which determine what must necessarily belong to an object in order that it can be an object of this kind" (352).

A proper understanding of what "possibility" means for Marion is needed if we are to appreciate his account of the relations between phenomenology and theology. Those relations are approached neither by way of Husserl's personalist religion nor Fink's cosmological religion but by way of revelation.[121] For him, revelation is a possibility in the sense that I have tried to make clear.

More particularly, it is an *a priori* possibility. No reference to the Kant of the first *Critique* is intended here, and certainly neither is any sense of the *a priori* as a condition of possibility that supplies a firm ground for experience. Yet Fichte's *Attempt at a Critique of All Revelation* (2d ed., 1793) is surely in the background of Marion's thinking regarding the possibility of revelation.[122] Specifically, however, *a priori* is used in Husserl's sense of the word. As he says in *Formal and Transcendental Logic*, the *eidōs* is "the only concept belonging to the multisignificant expression *a priori*, that I recognize philosophically."[123] And yet, as we have seen, Husserl acts with reserve toward the possible, restricting what is possible to the horizon and the "I," leading Marion in *Being Given* to state "not only the possibility that surpasses actuality, but the possibility that surpasses the very conditions of possibility, the possibility of unconditioned possibility—in other words, the possibility of the impossible, the saturated phenomenon" (218).

One impossible possibility is revelation, Karl Barth would say; and Marion agrees with him here as well as in his general insistence that theology should learn "to stand on is own feet in relation to philosophy" and to recognize "the point of departure for its method in revelation."[124] In Marion's terms, revelation is a saturation of saturation yet remains an eidetic possibility with an inner structure to be respected and a phenomenality that must be acknowledged even by those without faith in Judaism or Christianity, the positive religions that mostly concern him. Indeed, the death of God—the God of metaphysics—has liberated the Christian God who cannot be confined to the thought of Being. Not that Christianity needed the death of God in order to grasp the divine aseity. That was already fully apparent in Denys the Areopagite. But the death of God that took place with the birth of phenomenology has liberated the Christian God anew, this time as a possibility that does not reduce God. The resurrected Christ, who is for Marion the saturated phenomenon *par excellence,* impinges on us in excess of quantity, quality, relation, and modality.[125] To take just two of the four groups, Marion adjusts the distinction that animates *The Idol and Distance* and *God without Being,* so that Christ is both idol and icon. In the transfiguration he appears as an idol that we cannot bear: "And his raiment became shining, exceeding white as snow; so as no fuller on earth can white them" (Mark 9:2), while St. Paul figures Christ as an icon, "the image [*eikōn*] of the invisible God" (Col. 1:15).

Marion is not the only contemporary French philosopher inspired by Husserl, Heidegger, and all who develop this sort of case. Another is Michel

Henry whose final works propose a rethinking of New Testament Christianity as exhibiting a wholly original structure of phenomenology. Of course, the meaning of "phenomenology" in his writings has been reversed so that the word designates the study not of phenomena but rather of the phenomenality of phenomena.[126] What we find is New Testament Christianity grasped as the essence of immanent manifestation and interpreted by way of Meister Eckhart and Fichte.[127] "In its absolute self-engendering, Life is the Father of whom Christ is the Son," says Henry, and adds later, "*Life self-engenders itself as me.* If, along with Meister Eckhart—and with Christianity—we call Life God, we might say: 'God engenders himself as me.'"[128] The Gnostic flavor of such remarks is evident, but doubtless of more concern to theologians who might take up Henry's radical Christianity than to philosophers concerned with the proper way of doing phenomenology.[129]

Faced with remarks such as Henry's, Janicaud speaks with some exasperation of a "theological turn," an illegal move in the game of phenomenology.[130] For phenomenology is concerned only with immanence, and all transcendence, including God, falls with the reduction. And there are others, Christian theologians mostly, who find the same move worrying because Marion, a devout Catholic, will not (as philosopher) affirm the positivity of the Judeo-Christian revelation and is content to talk of it as a possibility. It is as though for them he is one with the narrator of W. H. Auden's oratorio "For the Time Being" (1941–42) when he reflects rather thinly on Christmas:

> Once again
> As in previous years we have seen the actual Vision and failed
> To do more than entertain it as an agreeable
> Possibility . . . .[131]

Yet Marion is not proposing revelation as a possibility because a possibility can always be realized (by an act of faith, in this case). He deals with revelation as possibility because that is all that phenomenology can do, and indeed must do, if the phenomenality of revelation is to be respected.

Possibility is the way Derrida assimilates the Marion of *Being Given* to a complex response to positive religion that he finds to be variously made by Kant and Hegel, Kierkegaard and Lévinas, Patočka and Marion, maybe even Heidegger. It is a tradition "that consists of proposing a nondogmatic doublet of dogma, a philosophical and metaphysical doublet, in any case a thinking that 'repeats' the possibility of religion without religion."[132] Marion does not dispute that he belongs in this company, although he objects to the identification of philosophy and metaphysics.[133] He believes that phenomenology, as he practices it, is a non-metaphysical form of philosophy, something that Derrida would never admit. Marion might have noted also that, if he belongs to this group, he does so in a quite different way than Kant and Lévinas and, for that matter, Derrida. For these philosophers have different takes on religion but converge on it by way of ethics. Kant establishes that moral action is pleasing to God while works of grace, miracles, mysteries, and means of grace are all parerga to religion considered within the limits of bare reason. Lévinas tries to elucidate how God comes to mind in a phenomenologically concrete way that "cuts across all phenomenality." In helping my neighbor, I move in the trace of God. Or, in the fine words of Rabbi Israel Salanter, which Lévinas likes to quote, "[T]he material needs of my neighbor are my spiritual needs."[134] And Derrida, following Kant and Lévinas but with another end in view, seeks to determine a faith without dogma that is cashed out in responsibility for the other person.[135] If Marion subscribes to "religion without religion," he does so only in the sense that phenomenology constrains him to describe revelation, the saturation of saturation, as a possibility, not as a historical reality. There is no reduction of religion to ethics in his thought.

All this is made quite clear when Marion defends himself against Janicaud and others in the opening pages of *Being Given*. He counters the charge of having made a "theological turn" with two arguments. The first, briefly, is that there is no right by which one can exclude *a priori* revelation from the field of phenomenality. He then develops his second argument:

> *Here,* I am not broaching revelation in its theological pretension to the truth, something faith alone can dare to do. I am outlining it as a possibility—in fact the ultimate possibility, the paradox of paradoxes— of phenomenality, such that it is carried out in a possible saturated phenomenon. The hypothesis that there was historically no such revelation would change nothing in the phenomenological task of offering an account of the fact, itself incontestable, that it has been thinkable, discussible, and even describable. This description therefore does not make an exception to the principle of the reduction to immanence. Here it is perhaps a case of something like the phenomena that Husserl thought could be described only by imaginative variations—imaginary or not,

they appear, and their mere possibility merits analysis and *Sinngebung*. As for the relation that phenomenology, or rather a phenomenology still to be constructed, could maintain with the fact of Revelation, it is not fundamentally different from the relation that philosophy as such maintains with it. (5)

That Christ has been *seen* means that Christ has been *given*, Marion contends. Revelation can be explored formally but not wholly on the terms that philosophy lays down.

Such an exploration would not exhaust the *fides quæ creditur*, however, and maybe it would hardly begin to draw from it. It is one thing to be dazzled by Christ, quite another to enter into life with him and to reflect fully, from all sides, upon that life in faith. That would involve prayerful and rigorous meditation on Christ and the Trinity, on Christ and Our Lady, on Christ and the Kingdom, on Christ and ethics, and so forth. Such is a crucial distinction between phenomenology and theology, and one that Marion fully respects. There is no question, then, of answering a philosophical question with a theological answer, as happens in "Hors-Texte." The task is to find a nondogmatic way of securing for phenomenology what is affirmed in theology. *The Erotic Phenomenon* shows us the way in which Marion will try to determine "love without being." Such is the import of the final formulation of the erotic reduction, "You have loved me first" (331), in which reciprocity in love is firmly rejected as a starting point. I can think *agapē* only if I rigorously exclude all contract and exchange. It scarcely will be expected that Marion will stop here. There is surely more to be done by way of describing from within phenomenology the endlessly strange and compelling idea we learn from Scripture: "God is love" (1 John 4:8). In this statement an infinite number of horizons are called into play.

Like others before him, Marion offers himself as a philosopher of experience. For Kant, experience takes place in space and time through synthetic *a priori* concepts; for Hegel, it is a dialectical process whereby that which is immediate externalizes itself, returns to itself estranged, and thus enters consciousness.[136] Husserl figures experience as "the relevant acts of perceiving, judging etc., with their variable sense-material, their interpretative content, their assertive characters etc.," and concludes that "what the ego or consciousness experiences, are its experience."[137] In his turn, Henry construes experience as pure auto-affection, while for Derrida it is "traversal, voyage, ordeal, both *mediatized* (culture, reading, interpretation, work, generalities, rules and concepts) and *singular*."[138] Certainly Marion discusses lived experience, especially that of the other person.[139] More importantly, though, he attends closely to what cuts across all experience and cannot be folded back into it. "Counter-experience," as he calls it, is discussed in *Being Given* §22, the sketch of the saturated phenomenon, and is elaborated in the essay he has contributed to this collection.

The saturated phenomenon "contradicts the conditions for the poor or common phenomenality of objects" (*Being Given,* 215). It does not appear as an object and so cannot be experienced. Nor does it give itself simply as non-experience. Rather, it "offers the experience of what irreducibly contradicts the conditions for the experience of objects" (215). So Marion is not close, at least not here, to the Lacoste for whom "man's encounter with God gives itself to be thought . . . as nonexperience and nonevent."[140] While he believes with Lacoste that the person attending the liturgy stands *coram Deo* and therefore under the gaze of God, he does not agree that the exposition is "nonexperience" in quite the same way. Lacoste conducts his argument with Schleiermacher's theology of experience, specifically with the claim that religion concerns an "earlier moment" in our consciousness than the present, a time when sense and object "mingle and unite," a moment "which you always experience yet never experience [*den Ihr jedesmal erlebt, aber auch nicht erlebt*]."[141] Marion would agree, but his argument is directed more against Kant's philosophy of experience.

Oddly enough, it is Blanchot rather than Lacoste who is the closer to Marion here, specifically the author of *The Writing of the Disaster* (1980). There we are told of an experience of the disaster, the approach of the Outside, "that is not a lived event, and that does not engage the present of presence." It is "already nonexperience" but with one important qualification: "negation does not deprive it of the peril of that which comes to pass already past." We must talk, then, of an "excess of experience [*excès d'elle-même*]" in which "no experience occurs."[142] Doubtless in placing me under its dark gaze the Outside imposes itself as a saturated phenomenon—unforeseeable, unbearable, absolute and irregardable—a ghastly parody of revelation, one that involves "transdescendance" rather than "transascendance."[143] Yet this would be only one instance of counter-experience, and one that has not thus far motivated

Marion to discuss it. What captivates him is the situation when *l'adonné*'s intentional gaze is rebuked by the intuitions to which it is exposed, not necessarily because he or she is bedazzled but because of being disappointed by unfulfilled or displaced expectations. Husserl certainly took account of disappointment as an event that runs counter to the synthesis of fulfillment, but Marion responds to something else: the sheer resistance of the phenomenon to objectification.[144]

I have titled this collection of essays *Counter-Experiences* partly to highlight Marion's essay "The Banality of Saturation," which extends the account of counter-experience developed in *Being Given,* and partly to emphasize the peculiar resistances that Marion's later writings give his admirers and critics. The essays are themselves set in motion by counter-experiences, chiefly to *Being Given, In Excess,* and *The Erotic Phenomenon,* and not always in Marion's sense of the word. To be sure, there are moments when contributors run counter to Marion because they oppose him on one topic or another. More often than not, people make an angle with his work. All are genuine encounters with a philosopher whose work asks us to rethink much that offers itself to us under the word "phenomenology." Some of the essays given here are revised versions of papers delivered at a conference I organized with Gerald McKenny at the University of Notre Dame (May 9–11, 2004). Others were commissioned to show facets of Marion's thought that did not come to light at that conference. Throughout, I have wanted to host a conversation that would place Marion's work, especially the publications after his breakthrough, in the horizon of modern theology.

The collection begins with three essays that place Marion in context. David Tracy situates his colleague and friend in terms of the old debate between philosophy and theology, seeking to correct two prevalent misunderstandings about Marion's thought: that it is a covert theology posing as a philosophy or a new way in which philosophy can control theology. Tracy offers a clear account of Marion's intellectual development, and brings him into dialogue with his own keen interest in a hermeneutics of retrieval, critique, and suspicion. Could it be that Marion, who has contributed so richly to the phenomenology of the face, might also develop a phenomenology of the voice, and explore the relations between the two? Such is Tracy's hope.

Although Marion first attracted the attention of North American scholars by his work on Descartes, he started to become well known in the United States only because of his differences with Derrida. A pivotal moment was his discussion on the gift at Villanova University in September 1997. John D. Caputo, already beginning to be publicly identified with Derrida, was one of Marion's hosts at the time, and in his essay he compares the new phenomenology with deconstruction. Both perform a religious turn, he thinks, Derrida being animated by desire and Marion by givenness. The debate between Derrida and Marion is structured as much by evasion as by engagement. For Marion to have appeared on stage with Derrida, especially under the sign of "religion," is to have given him a high profile. At the same time, though, it skewed his reception for several years in the English-speaking world. His interest is more in givenness as a general revision of phenomenology, and the gift is to be understood by way of reduction to givenness.[145] Deconstruction for Marion is not opposed to the new phenomenology; it marks a deferring of givenness, an insight that might in time lead to a rereading of Derrida, especially his analyses of Husserl.[146]

Evasion is the keynote of Cyril O'Regan's subtle contribution, and once again Derrida makes an appearance. Why does Marion, who draws so fully from Descartes and Kant, Husserl and Heidegger, avoid a confrontation with Hegel? There is an early piece in *Résurrection* but certainly no sustained dialogue, and this is strange if only because in the 1960s Hegel was an authority among European theologians, Catholic as well as Protestant. In the former group Claude Bruaire and Pierre-Jean Labarrière, Dominique Dubarle and André Léonard, all come to mind, and we must remember that the young Marion was close to Bruaire in the first days of *Communio*. One would not expect a philosopher who, in his mature thought, finds a group of phenomena in which intuition cannot be mastered by concepts to find an ally in Hegel. Yet, as O'Regan shows, Hegel is hidden in the folds of Marion's writings, behind other philosophical and theological figures, Hans Urs von Balthasar not being the least of them.

In the second section of the book, the focus is on God and revelation. Thomas Carlson, Marion's first translator and a lucid expositor of his thought, opens the discussion by suggesting, tongue in cheek, that Marion is a liberation theologian, since he has freed God from the human sciences and from metaphysics. Carlson begins by examining Marion on revelation and the call, paying special attention to different forms of blindness that *l'adonné* might have when faced with saturated phenomena. How could one distinguish the blindness that comes with an excess of intuition from that which results from a lack of intuition? His analysis converges on the final pages of *Being Given,* a section of the treatise devoted to *l'adonné,* and touches on the difficult topic of the humiliation of *l'adonné* by the given. Emmanuel Falque, speaking as theologian, also sees Marion as a liberator of theology. In his adventurous essay he considers the relation of philosophy and theology in Marion, arguing that, despite his protests, Marion allows an interaction between the two disciplines even while respecting their methodological independence. It is not that Marion adopts Descartes's motto *Larvatus prodeo* [I advance masked], but rather, in his consideration of revelation as a possibility, he subscribes to another version of the motto, *Lavartus pro Deo* [masked before God].

American theologian Kathryn Tanner applauds Marion for his strong emphasis on thinking God without conditions, whether these are of Being or the transcendental subject. Warm discussions about the rights and wrongs of a "theological turn" in phenomenology do not disconcert her. Her worry instead is whether phenomenology, however stringently revised, can ever be adequate to the figure of revelation in Christianity. On the one hand, Marion seeks to describe the givenness of revelation without horizons of prejudgment; while, on the other hand, he assumes that revelation will give itself in the four sorts of saturation, thereby giving rise to a saturation to the second degree. Marion will respect revelation as the possibility of the impossible but it is a mode of impossibility that is phenomenologically approved. Whether or not he admits it, "givenness" is a historically determined category, covertly leagued with modernity, and its limited historical range subtly restricts what revelation can be and do. To invert the Kantian categories is not necessarily to have escaped them and opened oneself unreservedly to the self-giving of God that is revelation. Love, Marion's ultimate concern, must be thought outside or beyond the parameters even of sheer self-givenness if it is to be answerable to the love of God in Christ. On hearing Tanner's counter-argument at the conference, Marion responded by saying that counter-experience traces the difference between philosophy and theology. "Counter-experience," he said, "is not only a way to say that, even within the phenomenology of givenness, there is some opposition between my condition for reception and what is appearing to me. Also, it marks a difference between God and me. When you are dealing with God, God is God and you are not God. We cannot anticipate a condition for the manifestation of God."

This brings us to the third section of the book, three considerations of love that take *The Erotic Phenomenon* as a common reference. Robyn Horner, whose two volumes on Marion have greatly clarified his thought for English-speaking readers, begins with the problem of intersubjectivity in the *Cartesian Meditations* and traces Marion's deepening understanding of love as a form of knowing. He reaches the point he has been seeking in the final formulation of the erotic reduction, she thinks, when a metaphysical account of subjectivity (and intersubjectivity) is overcome. At that stage, a phenomenology of love touches a revealed theology of love. Questions remain, needless to say, including one that reverberates throughout this collection: "How would we know that it is God who gives Godself in love?" A quite different approach is adopted by John Milbank who, for over a decade, has been Marion's most demanding conversational partner from within theology. Skeptical about a phenomenological account of love, Marion defends the metaphysical concept so as to retain knowledge and being as co-implicative of love. The erotic reduction, which points to love as a free gift, is bleakly Pascalian for Milbank. If the order of charity is above the orders of body and mind, it becomes all too likely that this world of bodies and minds will be consigned to an inevitable lovelessness. Only an Augustinian model of love as reciprocal, not unilateral, can possibly be of use to us in this world. As he explains in *The Erotic Phenomenon* §15, Marion would disagree with Milbank not over whether love must be reciprocated but over whether we can begin to understand love on the basis of reciprocation. To be sure, we can aim for vows and community; but if we begin with them we risk not talking about love so much as contract and exchange.

Claude Romano, Marion's colleague at the Sorbonne, converges on the problem of the reduction in *The Erotic Phenomenon*. He is quick to note that Marion departs sharply from the transcendental reduction as practiced by Husserl. As we have seen, Marion follows Heidegger in using a mood (in the sense of *Befindlichkeit*) to bring about the reduction. This can only be a partial reduction, Romano observes, and the very fact that Marion writes his study of the erotic in the first person shows that there is nothing universal at stake here. In fact Marion is caught in a paradox. On the one hand, the "I" is the sole condition of possibility for the reduction ("The lover thus makes possible the beloved because he enters into the erotic reduction" (138)), while, on the other hand, the reduction dismisses any and all conditions of possibility. In order to perform the erotic reduction, it would seem, Marion must jettison the account of phenomenology as donatology that he has developed from *Reduction and Givenness* to *In Excess*. Can Marion escape this situation? After Romano gave his paper at the conference, Marion intimated in discussion that the experience of love is indeed universal, so that even though when I fall in love I whisper to myself, "This is utterly unique!" I am not isolated from the rest of humanity. The reduction at issue is not Husserl's, to be sure, but it is a reduction nonetheless, a leading back to see how experience is constituted.

The fourth group of essays attends to the ethical and political worlds that are projected by Marion's writings. Gerald McKenny begins by noticing the tension between ethics and love in Marion. It is an anti-Kantian disposition that runs in a quite different direction from the "ethical turn" we associate with Lévinas and Derrida. Where those two philosophers regard justice as the ultimate horizon of humankind, Marion unabashedly points us instead to love. Does love replace ethics for Marion? Does he evade ethics as such? Or does he preserve part of the ethical in the knowledge that is offered by *agapē?* These are the questions that McKenny draws to our attention, as the opening of a dialogue on Marion and ethics that is certain to develop. Marion himself points us in one direction when he says, in response to McKenny, that he sees his work extending Lévinas's concepts beyond the field of ethics.

Thomas Carlson jokes a little with Marion when he calls him a liberation theologian. However, Michael Kessler is entirely serious when he begins his reflections by pondering the relations between Marion's phenomenology and political theology. A political theology would have the task, as Marion sees it, of rendering visible what cannot be objectified. Accordingly, Kessler asks if there are unconditioned and irreducible phenomena that are politically relevant, and, if so, how can they bear on an objective, rational politics. As a test case—and surely not just any test case—he chooses to examine John Locke's idea of equality. We are led, he thinks, to the task of establishing politics on the basis of the "excessive origin" of the ethical encounter with the other person, and then making sense of equality in those terms. The danger, as McKenny realizes as well, is that we achieve equality only at the cost of neutral interchangeability. If Marion reveals a new way of reading Locke, he also leaves us with a question: How can love hold together responsibility for the unique individual and the daily grind of power politics?

The final contribution is of course Marion's own. He begins by considering a range of objections to saturated phenomena and, having disposed of them, proceeds to expand the notion. Saturated phenomena, he tells us, are actually banal, by which he means that most phenomena that appear deficient in intuition can also be seen as rich in intuition, overflowing the concept or concepts brought into play to interpret them. Our prejudgments are challenged, as Hans-Georg Gadamer would say, or in Marion's terms ordinary things are not so ordinary: they too solicit multiple horizons. It is a lesson that the poets have taught us time and again. We think first of Pablo Neruda's odes on tomatoes, his socks, a lemon and salt, or Francis Ponge's prose poems on rain, blackberries, an oyster and a gymnast, or Charles Simic's lyrics about a butcher shop, a fork, a spoon, and his shoes.[147] And then perhaps we think of Baudelaire's "Le Balcon" or Eugenio Montale's "Arsenio" or long tracts of Rilke's *Neue Gedichte*. These poets bear out what Marion proposes, for they show that ordinary things are not simply objects but have a phenomenality that exceeds the narrow aperture through which we usually see them. We cannot "experience" saturated phenomena, Marion argues, since the conditions of possibility for experience relate only to objects. As soon as a phenomenon exceeds objectivity, it escapes experience as we usually figure it and unfolds in a quite contrary manner, contradicting any and all transcendental conditions. Sometimes we are dazzled, at other times we are disappointed, and at yet other times we simply meet resistance. Such an event leads us to redefine truth as counter-truth, not the opposite of truth but what counteracts me, leading me to love what gives itself to me.

Notes

1. One could begin by pondering the remarks on art and literature in "The Event or the Happening Phenomenon," *In Excess: Studies of Saturated Phenomena*, trans. Robyn Horner and Vincent Berraud (New York: Fordham University Press, 2002), 52–53. Or, in the spirit of Jean-François Lyotard's *The Postmodern Explained to Children*, ed. Julian Pefanis and Morgan Thomas (Sydney: Power Publications, 1992), one could start with "Tintin le terrible," in the book co-authored with Alain Bonfand, *Tintin le Terrible ou l'alphabet des richesses* (Paris: Hachette, 1996), 7–28.

2. "L'Équipe Descartes" is a scholarly group based at the Centre National de la Recherche Scientifique (CNRS) and dedicated to the study of Descartes. It was founded in 1973 by Pierre Costabel. A third volume of *Questions cartésiennes* is forthcoming.

3. See Jean-Luc Marion, "Remarques sur le concept de Révélation chez R. Bultmann," *Résurrection* 27 (1968), 29–42; "La Saisie trinitaire selon l'Esprit de saint Augustin," *Résurrection* 28 (1968), 66–94; "Ce mystère qui juge celui que le juge," *Résurrection* 32 (1969), 54–78; and "La Splendeur de la contemplation eucharistique," *Résurrection* 31 (1969), 84–88. On "Hors-Texte" and theology, see Jean-Luc Marion, *Being Given: Toward a Phenomenology of Givenness*, trans. Jeffrey L. Kosky (Stanford: Stanford University Press, 2002), x.

4. See Jean-Luc Marion, "Amour de Dieu, amour des hommes," *Résurrection* 34 (1970), 89–96. In the same year Marion observes in a discussion with Alain de Benoist, "L'amour est bien le lieu de la communication. Et en un sens, c'est le domaine de la preuve qui est incommunicable." In *Avec ou sans Dieu?* (Paris: Beauchesne, 1970), 42. Also see "Forward to the American Translation," *Prolegomena to Charity,* trans. Stephen E. Lewis (New York: Fordham University Press, 2002), xi. The importance of love, in a nonromantic understanding of the word, is at the heart of Marion's disagreement with Emmanuel Lévinas. See Lévinas, *Autrement que savoir* (Paris: Éditions Osiris, 1986), 74–75; "From the Other to the Individual," trans. Robyn Horner, *Transcendence: Philosophy, Literature, and Theology Approach the Beyond,* ed. Regina Schwartz (London: Routledge, 2004), §7.

5. See Jean-Luc Marion, "What Love Knows," in *Prolegomena to Charity,* 164. Also see the concluding paragraph of *Being Given,* 324. For other attempts implicitly to augment or displace the problem of the fifth meditation, see Martin Heidegger, *Being and Time,* trans. John Macquarrie and Edward Robinson (Oxford: Basil Blackwell, 1973), §26; Emmanuel Lévinas, *Entre Nous: Thinking-of-the-Other,* trans. Michael B. Smith and Barbara Harshav (New York: Columbia University Press, 1998); Edith Stein, *On the Problem of Empathy,* trans. Waltraut Stein (Washington, D.C.: ICS Publications, 1989); Jacques Derrida, *Politics of Friendship,* trans. George Collins (London: Routledge, 1997); Maurice Blanchot, *The Unavowable Community,* trans. Pierre Joris (Barrytown, N.Y.: Station Hill Press, 1988); Jean-Luc Nancy, *The Inoperable Community,* ed. Peter Connor, trans. Peter Conner et al. (Minneapolis: University of Minnesota Press, 1991).

6. Marion encourages us to do this in *Le Phénomène érotique: Six méditations* (Paris: Grasset, 2003), 22–23.

7. Edmund Husserl, *Logical Investigations,* 2 vols., trans. J. N. Findlay (London: Routledge and Kegan Paul, 1970), 1:252.

8. That *donation* (as distinct from *donné,* say) properly translates *Gegebenheit* is disputed by Joseph S. O'Leary, *Religious Pluralism and Christian Truth,* rev. ed. (Edinburgh: Edinburgh University Press, 1996), 191. Also see Dominique Janicaud, *Phenomenology "Wide Open": After the French Debate,* trans. Charles N. Cabral (New York: Fordham University Press, 2005), 35. Derrida expresses reservations about Marion's use of *Gegenbenheit* as implying a gift in "On the Gift: A Discussion between Jacques Derrida and Jean-Luc Marion," in *God, the Gift, and Postmodernism,* ed. John D. Caputo and Michael J. Scanlon (Bloomington: Indiana University Press, 1999), 58–59.

9. Edmund Husserl, *Cartesian Meditations: An Introduction to Phenomenology,* trans. Dorion Cairns (The Hague: Martinus Nijhoff, 1977), §60, 139.

10. See, e.g., Jean-Luc Marion, "Introduction: Phenomenology as Such," *Reduction and Givenness: Investigations of Husserl, Heidegger, and Phenomenology,* trans. Thomas A. Carlson (Evanston: Northwestern University Press, 1998), 2. Also see Jacques Derrida, *Speech and Phenomena: And Other Essays on Husserl's Theory of Signs,* trans. and intro. David B. Allison, pref. Newton Garver (Evanston: Northwestern University Press, 1973), 6.

11. Edmund Husserl, *Formal and Transcendental Logic,* trans. Dorian Cairns (The Hague: Martinus Nijhoff, 1978), 232–33. Also see the papers in *Experience and Judgment:*

Investigations in a Genealogy of Logic, rev. and ed. Ludwig Landgrebe, trans. James S. Churchill and Karl Ameriks (Evanston: Northwestern University Press, 1973), §6.

12. Martin Heidegger, *Grundprobleme der Phänomenologie,* ed. H.-H. Gander (Frankfurt: Klostermann, 1992), *Gesamtausgabe* 58, 5.

13. See Martin Heidegger, *History of the Concept of Time: Prolegomena,* trans. Theodore Kisiel (Bloomington: Indiana University Press, 1985), §6.

14. See Rudolf Carnap, *The Logical Syntax of Language,* trans. Amethe Smeaton (New York: Littlefield, Adams, 1959).

15. Martin Heidegger, *Four Seminars,* trans. Andrew Mitchell and François Raffoul (Bloomington: Indiana University Press, 2003), 66.

16. See Moritz Schlick, "The Nature of Truth in Metaphysics" and "Is There Intuitive Knowledge?" *Philosophical Papers,* 2 vols., ed. Henk L. Mulder and Barbara F. B. Van de Velde-Schlick, trans. Peter Heath (Dordreck: D. Ridel, 1979), 1:1909–22, 41–103, 141–52. For a discussion of the issue, see Paul Livingston, "Husserl and Schlick on the Logical Form of Experience," *Synthese* 132 (2002): 239–72.

17. Heidegger comments on the analogy of sensuous and categorial intuition in *Four Seminars,* 66.

18. See Theodore Kisiel, *The Genesis of Heidegger's "Being and Time"* (Berkeley: University of California Press, 1993), 32–35. Heidegger's thesis was on the speculative grammar of Thomas of Erfurt, which, at the time, was believed to have been written by Scotus.

19. Heidegger, *Four Seminars,* 66.

20. See Paul Natorp, "Husserls *Ideen zu einer reinen Phänomenologie,*" *Logos* 7 (1917–18), 224–46; and Heidegger, "Summary of a Seminar," *On Time and Being,* trans. Joan Stambaugh (New York: Harper and Row, 1972), 44. Husserl had began his transcendental turn some years before *Ideas I* in *The Idea of Phenomenology* (lectures originally given in 1907), trans. W. P. Alston and George Nakhnikian (The Hague: Martinus Nijhoff, 1964). Heidegger tackled Natorp in his first lecture course, the *Kriegsnotsemester* of 1919. See his "The Idea of Philosophy and the Problem of Worldview," in *Towards the Definition of Philosophy,* trans. Ted Sadler (London: Continuum, 2000), §19(c). For a well-conducted defense of Husserl against the neo-Kantians, one that does not chime with Heidegger's interpretation of Natorp's influence and that is fully endorsed by Husserl, see Eugen Fink, "The Phenomenological Philosophy of Edmund Husserl and Contemporary Criticism," in *The Phenomenology of Husserl: Selected Critical Readings,* 2d ed., ed. and intro. R. O. Elveton (Seattle: Noesis Press, 2000), 70–139.

21. Husserl talks of his project as "transcendental idealism" in *The Paris Lectures,* trans. and intro. Peter Koestenbaum (Boston: Kluwer Academic Publishers, 1998), 33.

22. Jean-Yves Lacoste, *Experience and the Absolute: Disputed Questions on the Humanity of Man,* trans. Mark Raftery-Skehan (New York: Fordham University Press, 2004), 11.

23. Consider Husserl's late remark, "[S]ubjectivity is what it is—an ego functioning constitutively—only within intersubjectivity." *The Crisis of European Sciences and Transcendental Phenomenology: An Introduction to Phenomenological Philosophy,* trans. David Carr (Evanston: Northwestern University Press, 1970), §50, 172.

24. Heidegger makes the criticism as early as his lecture course for the winter semester of 1923–24. See *Introduction to Phenomenological Research,* trans. Daniel O. Dahlstrom (Bloomington: Indiana University Press, 2005), 10.

25. Husserl started to talk of the reduction in 1907 when he wrote *The Idea of Phenomenology,* a work that was published only posthumously. *Ideas I* presented the reduction to his contemporaries. In 1924 Husserl would criticize his first account of the reduction. See *Erste Philosophie,* II, 432f. For various senses of the *epochē,* see the index to the *Crisis.*

26. See Edmund Husserl, *Ideas Pertaining to a Pure Phenomenology and to a Phenomenological Philosophy. First Book: General Introduction to a Pure Phenomenology,* trans. F. Kersten (Boston: Kluwer Academic Publishers, 1983), §32.

27. See Husserl, "Philosophy and the Crisis of European Man," *Phenomenology and the Crisis of Philosophy,* trans. and intro. Quentin Lauer (New York: Harper and Row, 1965), 191.

28. Husserl, *Crisis,* 137. Janicaud quotes a letter from Husserl to Edith Stein: "The life of man is nothing other than a road to God. I tried to achieve this goal without the help of either the method of proofs of theology; in other words, I wanted to reach God without God." *Phenomenology "Wide Open,"* 23.

29. Paul Ricœur, "Introduction to *Ideas* of E. Husserl," in *A Key to Husserl's "Ideas I,"* trans. and pref. Bond Harris and Jacqueline Bouchard Spurlock, ed., trans. rev. and intro. Pol Vandervelde (Milwaukee: Marquette University Press, 1996), 43.

30. Eugen Fink, quoted by Ronald Bruzina in his *Edmund Husserl and Eugen Fink: Beginnings and Ends in Phenomenology, 1928–1938* (New Haven: Yale University Press, 2004), 139, 354. Also see Eugen Fink, *Sixth Cartesian Meditation: The Idea of a Transcendental Theory of Method,* trans. Ronald Bruzina (Bloomington: Indiana University Press, 1995), 120.

31. Edmund Husserl, "The Amsterdam Lectures," in *Psychological and Transcendental Phenomenology and the Confrontation with Heidegger (1927–1931),* ed. and trans. Thomas Sheehan and Richard E. Palmer, vol. 6 *Edmund Husserl Collected Works* (Boston: Kluwer, 1997), 235.

32. The phenomenological reduction is to be distinguished from the eidetic reduction in which the fact of a situation [*Tatsache*] is grasped in its essence [*eidōs*]. The eidetic reduction is presupposed by the phenomenological reduction. It should also be noted that Husserl sometimes uses the one word, *epochē,* to designate both abstention and reduction. See his marginal note in Copy D of *Ideen I,* recorded in *Ideas I,* §18.

33. See Eugen Fink, *Die phänomenologische Philosophie Edmund Husserls in der gegenwärtigen Kritik* (Berlin-Charlottenberg: Panverlagsgesellschaft, 1934), 331f.

34. See Fink, *Sixth Cartesian Meditation,* §11, passim.

35. See Husserl, *Formal and Transcendental Logic,* §103.

36. Edmund Husserl, *Ideas III: Phenomenology and the Foundation of the Sciences,* trans. Ted E. Klein and William E. Pohl (The Hague: Martinus Nijhoff, 1980), 65.

37. Heidegger, *Being and Time,* 60.

38. Edmund Husserl, "The Encyclopedia Britannica Article," Draft D, trans. Richard E. Palmer, in *Psychological and Transcendental Phenomenology and the*

Confrontation with Heidegger (1927–1931), 175. The emphasis on ontology as a way of overcoming naturalism is developed early on by Lévinas in his *The Theory of Intuition in Husserl's Phenomenology*, trans. André Orianne (Evanston: Northwestern University Press, 1973). The French original appeared in 1930.

39. See Bruzina, *Edmund Husserl and Eugen Fink*, 422.

40. Husserl's "Prolegomena to Pure Logic" forms the first volume of the *Logical Investigations*. See Marion's account of the ontology present in concept, if not in name, in the *Logical Investigations* in "Being and Region," *Reduction and Givenness*, 146.

41. Martin Heidegger, *The Basic Problems of Phenomenology*, rev. ed., trans., intro., and lexicon Albert Hofstadter (Bloomington: Indiana University Press, 1988), 21.

42. Heidegger, *Introduction to Phenomenological Research*, 200.

43. The former reservation is proposed by Rudolf Benet, Iso Kern, and Eduard Marbach, *An Introduction to Husserlian Phenomenology* (Evanston: Northwestern University Press, 1993), chap. 6, §2. The latter reservation is developed by Fink. See Bruzina, *Edmund Husserl and Eugen Fink*, 333.

44. Heidegger, *Being and Time*, 61. Later, with his "turn," Heidegger would jettison the very idea of philosophy as a rigorous science. Also see Heidegger's remarks on phenomenology and Greek thinking in "My Way to Phenomenology," in *On Time and Being*, 79.

45. See Husserl, *Ideas I*, §141.

46. See, e.g., Rudolf Boehm, "Husserl's Concept of the Absolute," in *Phenomenology of Husserl*, §5.

47. See Marion's remarks on hermeneutics in "The Hermeneutics of Revelation," in Richard Kearney, *Debates in Continental Philosophy: Conversations with Contemporary Thinkers*, 2d ed. (New York: Fordham University Press, 2004), 16–17.

48. See Paul Ricœur, *Husserl: An Analysis of His Phenomenology*, trans. Edward G. Ballard and Lester E. Embree (Evanston: Northwestern University Press, 1967), 4.

49. Derrida replied to Marion, "I am also for the suspension of the horizon, but, for that very reason, by saying so, I am not a phenomenologist anymore," "On the Gift," 66.

50. See Donn Welton's interesting discussion of the world as horizon and as totality in his *The Other Husserl: The Horizons of Transcendental Phenomenology* (Bloomington: Indiana University Press, 2000), chap. 13.

51. See Marion, *Being Given*, 209–12.

52. Maurice Merleau-Ponty, *Phenomenology of Perception*, trans. Colin Smith (London: Routledge, 1962), xiv.

53. See, e.g., Maurice Blanchot, "The Great Refusal," *The Infinite Conversation*, trans. Susan Hanson (Minneapolis: University of Minnesota Press, 1993), 43–48, and *Awaiting Oblivion*, trans. John Gregg (Lincoln: University of Nebraska Press, 1997). I discuss the Outside in my *The Dark Gaze: Maurice Blanchot and the Sacred* (Chicago: University of Chicago Press, 2004), 144–45, passim.

54. See Husserl, "The Amsterdam Lectures," §4, in *Psychological and Transcendental Phenomenology*, 218–20.

55. See Derrida's remarks in *Given Time 1: Counterfeit Money,* trans. Peggy Kamuf (Chicago: University of Chicago Press, 1992), 50–52, n. 10. Also see Derrida's remarks in "On the Gift," 66, and Marion's observation, "The triple reduction of the gift and its reconduction to givenness exclude on principle the possibility that even the least bit of transcendence could subsist—especially transcendence in a theological (or supposedly theological) sense," *Being Given,* 115.

56. Dorian Cairns, *Conversations with Husserl and Fink,* ed. by Husserl Archives in Louvain, foreword Richard M. Zaner (The Hague: Martinus Nijhoff, 1976), 40.

57. See Marion, *Being Given,* §28. Also see, on the call, Jean-Louis Chrétien, *The Call and the Response,* trans. Anne A. Davenport (New York: Fordham University Press, 2004), esp. chap. 1.

58. See Marion, "The Nothing and the Claim," §6, in *Reduction and Givenness,* 192–98. The notion of *l'interloqué* was first explored in 1988 in "L'Interloqué," *Who Comes after the Subject?* ed. Eduardo Cadava, Peter Connor, and Jean-Luc Nancy (London: Routledge, 1991), 236–45. A vivid account of *l'adonné* is given in *In Excess,* 50.

59. See Marion, *Reduction and Givenness,* 204, and *Being Given,* 4.

60. For the troubled relations between Husserl and Meinong over who formulated the general theory of objects, see Herbert Spiegelberg, *The Phenomenological Movement: A Historical Introduction,* 3d ed., with collaboration of Karl Schuhmann (The Hague: Martinus Nijhoff, 1982), 89–92. And for Marion's amusing reflections on "the givenness of non-exisiting objects," see "This is not Funny! From the Quest for the Historical Bibfeldt to Bibfeldt with/without Being," *Criterion* 43, no. 3 (2004): 22.

61. Marion, "The Breakthrough and the Broadening," in *Reduction and Givenness,* 33, and "Phenomenology of Givenness and First Philosophy," in *In Excess,* 16.

62. Husserl, *The Idea of Phenomenology,* 11, 7. Marion cites *The Idea of Phenomenology* in *Being Given,* 14.

63. Edmund Husserl, *Thing and Space: Lectures of 1907,* trans. Richard Rojcewicz (Boston: Kluwer, 1997), 291. Also see p. 15.

64. See Marion, "The Breakthrough and the Broadening," §1, in *Reduction and Givenness,* and *Being Given,* 8–9.

65. Husserl, *Ideas I,* § 24.

66. See Marion, *Being Given,* 69.

67. Martin Heidegger, "The End of Philosophy and the Task of Thinking," in *On Time and Being,* trans. Joan Stambaugh (New York: Harper and Row, 1972), 63.

68. Marion, *Being Given,* 4.

69. Marion, "Conclusion: The Figures of Givenness," in *Reduction and Givenness,* 203.

70. Marion, "Phenomenology of Givenness and First Philosophy," in *In Excess,* 25.

71. J. F. Herbart, *Hauptpunkte der Metaphysik* in *Sämmliche Werke,* 19 vols., ed. Carl Kehrbach et al. (Aalan: Scientia, 1964), 2:187.

72. Husserl, *Cartesian Meditations,* §46. Husserl quotes Herbart as writing "*Soviel Schein, soviel Hindeutung auf Sein*" (47). See Marion, *Being Given,* 329, n. 4.

73. Heidegger, *History of the Concept of Time*, §14 (b); *Being and Time*, §7, 36 (German) and 60 (English).

74. Michel Henry underlines the importance of the new principle for phenomenology in "Quatre principes de la phénomènologie," in *Phénoménologie de la vie*, 4 vols., *De la phénoménologie* (Paris: Presses Universitaires de France, 2003), 1:77–104.

75. See Jean-Luc Marion, "The Saturated Phenomenon," trans. Thomas A. Carlson, in *Phenomenology and the "Theological Turn": The French Debate*, ed. Dominique Janicaud et al. (New York: Fordham University Press, 2000), 176–216.

76. Gabriel Marcel, *The Mystery of Being*, 2 vols. (London: Harvell Press, 1950), 1:55–56. Husserl talks of "saturated consciousness of givenness" in *Thing and Space*, 95. The German original was published only in 1973.

77. See, e.g., Emmanuel Lévinas, *Totality and Infinity: An Essay on Exteriority*, trans. Alphonso Lingis (The Hague: Martinus Nijhoff, 1979), 27.

78. Edmund Husserl, *Ideas Pertaining to a Pure Phenomenology and to a Phenomenological Philosophy*, II: *Studies in the Phenomenology of Constitution*, trans. Richard Rojcewicz and André Schuwer (Boston: Kluwer Academic Publishers, 1989), §25.

79. Janicaud, *Phenomenology "Wide Open,"* 6.

80. Lévinas, "Nonintentional Consciousness," in *Entre Nous*, 127.

81. See Emmanuel Lévinas, *Otherwise than Being or Beyond Essence*, trans. Alphonso Lingis (The Hague: Martinus Nijhoff, 1981), 47. Also see Henry, "Phénoménologie non intentionnelle: une tâche de la phénoménologie," in *De la phénoménologie*, 105–22.

82. Immanuel Kant, *Critique of Pure Reason*, trans. Norman Kemp Smith (London: Macmillan, 1933), A 51 / B 75.

83. Heidegger, *Four Seminars*, 66.

84. Husserl, *The Paris Lectures*, 37.

85. See Marion, "The Event or the Happening Phenomenon," in *In Excess*, 31–34. A slightly earlier version, titled "The Event, the Phenomenon, and the Revealed," and translated by Beata Starwaska, appears in *Transcendence in Philosophy and Religion*, ed. James E. Faulconer (Bloomington: Indiana University Press, 2003), 87–105.

86. Wallace Stevens, "Good Man, Bad Woman," in *Opus Posthumous: Poems, Plays, Prose*, ed. and intro. Samuel French Morse (New York: Vintage Books, 1957), 33.

87. Marion, "Flesh or the Givenness of the Self," in *In Excess*, 100.

88. See the discussion of pain in Ludwig Wittgenstein, *Philosophical Investigations*, trans. G. E. M. Anscombe (Oxford: Blackwell, 1972), §246; the analysis of the flesh in Maurice Merleau-Ponty, *The Visible and the Invisible*, ed. Claude Lefort, trans. Alphonso Lingis (Evanston: Northwestern University Press, 1968); Henry's *Phénoménologie matérielle* (Paris: Presses Universitaires de France, 1990).

89. Joseph Conrad, preface to *The Nigger of the Narcissus*, ed. Cedric Watts (London: Penguin, 1990), xlix.

90. Husserl, *Formal and Transcendental Logic*, 159.

91. Jean-Luc Marion, *God without Being: Hors-Texte*, trans. Thomas A. Carlson (Chicago: Chicago University Press, 1991), 12.

92. Jean-Luc Marion, *The Crossing of the Visible*, trans. James K. A. Smith (Stanford: Stanford University Press, 2004), 25. Marion's work in this area resonates with Henry's. See the latter's *Voir l'invisible: Sur Kandinsky* (Paris: Bourin-Julliard, 1988).

93. Marion, "The Idol or the Radiance of the Painting," in *In Excess*, 61.

94. Jean-Luc Marion, *The Idol and Distance: Five Studies*, trans. Thomas A. Carlson (New York: Fordham University Press, 2001), 8.

95. Marion, *God without Being*, 7.

96. Heidegger, *Four Seminars*, 80.

97. Marion, "The Icon or the Endless Hermeneutic," in *In Excess*, 118.

98. See Lévinas, *Totality and Infinity*, conclusion 7.

99. Marion, "The Intentionality of Love," in *Prolegomena to Charity*, 93.

100. See Marion, "From the Other to the Individual," in *Transcendence*, 50.

101. Marion, "The Icon or the Endless Hermeneutic," in *In Excess*, 122.

102. Martin Heidegger, "The Onto-Theo-Logical Constitution of Metaphysics," in *Identity and Difference*, trans. Joan Stambaugh (Chicago: University of Chicago Press, 2002), 61. Marion notes, "In effect, from the beginning, our studies have been organized by reference to onto-theo-logy." *On Descartes' Metaphysical Prism: The Constitution and the Limits of Onto-Theo-Logy in Cartesian Thought*, trans. Jeffrey L. Kosky (Chicago: University of Chicago Press, 1999), 5.

103. Jacques Derrida, *Of Grammatology*, trans. Gayatri Chakravorty Spivak (Baltimore: Johns Hopkins University Press, 1976), 4.

104. Derrida admits that "one can find several passages in which Heidegger is self-critical and renounces his nostalgia: his practice of canceling and erasing the term in his later texts is an example of such a critique." "Deconstruction and the Other," in Kearney, *Debates in Continental Philosophy*, 142.

105. Husserl once told Lévinas that as a boy he was given a penknife, which he kept trying to sharpen until, in the end, it had no blade at all. The same might be said of the *epochē* and the reduction. See Karl Schuhmann, *Husserl-Chronik: Denk- und Lebensweg Edmund Husserls*, Husserliana Dokumente Bd 1 (The Hague: Martinus Nijhoff, 1977), 2.

106. Derrida, *Speech and Phenomena*, 99. Derrida's reading of Husserl needs to be augmented by a knowledge of Husserl's manuscripts, especially those of the 1920s, that have been published in the *Husserliana* series since the writing of his dissertation, *Le problème de la genèse dans la philosophie de Husserl* (1953–54; published 1990), and the appearance of *La voix et le phénomène* (1967). The publication of the Bernau manuscripts on time-constituting consciousness is likely to require further modifications of Derrida's position on Husserl.

107. Husserl, *Logical Investigations*, 1:261; and see Marion, "The Breakthrough and the Broadening," in *Reduction and Givenness*, 10.

108. Marion, "The Breakthrough and the Broadening," in *Reduction and Givenness*, 32.

109. Jean-Luc Marion, "Metaphysics and Phenomenology: A Summary for Theologians," in *The Postmodern God: A Theological Reader*, ed. Graham Ward (Oxford: Basil Blackwell, 1997), 286.

110. Marion, *Being Given*, 4.

111. St. Thomas Aquinas, *Commentary on the Metaphysics of Aristotle*, 2 vols., trans. John P. Rowan (Chicago: Henry Regnery, 1961), 1:2. Marion multiplies references to Aquinas on metaphysics in *Descartes's Metaphysical Prism*, 54 n. 59. One might also cite *Exposito super librum Boethii De Trinitate*, q. 5, a. 1, *ad* 6.

112. Francisco Suárez, *Disputationes Metaphysicæ*, 2 vols. (Hildesheim: Georg Olms Verlagsbuchhandlung, 1965), 1:3, 1. Marion develops a full account of the history of "metaphysics" in *On Descartes' Metaphysical Prism*, chap. 1.

113. See Marion, *On Descartes' Metaphysical Prism*, §10. Also see "What Is the Metaphysics within the Method? The Metaphysical Situation of the *Discourse on the Method*," in *Cartesian Questions: Method and Metaphysics*, trans. Jeffrey L. Kosky (Chicago: University of Chicago Press, 1999). Also, as Marion points out, Descartes reverses "the Suárezian couple *prima philosophia* / *metaphysica*" so that "the first becomes universal and not theological, the second becomes particular and theological." *On Descartes' Metaphysical Prism*, 42.

114. Marion, "Does the *Ego* Alter the Other? The Solitude of the *Cogito* and the Absence of the *Alter Ego*," in *Cartesian Questions*, 138.

115. Dante, *The Divine Comedy* 3: *Paradise*, trans. Dorothy L. Sayers and Barbara Reynolds (Harmondsworth: Penguin, 1962), 347.

116. See Marion's comments in the preface to the English edition of *God without Being* and, especially, in "Thomas Aquinas and Onto-theo-logy," in *Mystics: Presence and Aporia*, ed. Michael Kessler and Christian Sheppard (Chicago: Chicago University Press, 2003), 38–74, esp. 65. The original French of the latter piece has been added to the new French edition of *Dieu sans l'être* (2002).

117. Marion, "Metaphysics and Phenomenology," in *Postmodern God*, 289.

118. Heidegger, *Introduction to Phenomenological Research*, 200.

119. Husserl, *Ideas I*, §135.

120. Husserl, *Experience and Judgment*, 341.

121. See Bruzina, *Edmund Husserl and Eugen Fink*, 447.

122. See J. G. Fichte, *Attempt at a Critique of All Revelation*, trans. and intro. Garrett Green (Cambridge: Cambridge University Press, 1978), 92.

123. Husserl, *Formal and Transcendental Logic*, 248 n. 1.

124. See Karl Barth, *Epistle to the Romans*, trans. Edwyn C. Hoskyns (London: Oxford University Press, 1933), 79, passim. Also see his *Protestant Theology in the Nineteenth Century: Its Background and History*, n. trans. (Valley Forge: Judson Press, 1973), 307.

125. See Marion, *Being Given*, 236–41.

126. See Michel Henry, *Incarnation: Une philosophie de la chair* (Paris: Seuil, 2000), part 1.

127. The Fichte of interest to Henry here is the author of *The Way towards the Blessed Life; or, The Doctrine of Religion*, lectures delivered at Berlin in 1806. See Fichte, *Popular Works*, with a memoir by William Smith, 2 vols. (London: Trübner, 1873), 1:382–564.

128. Michel Henry, *I Am the Truth: Toward a Philosophy of Christianity*, trans. Susan Emanuel (Stanford: Stanford University Press, 2003), 74, 104.

129. On this issue, see Jad Hatem, *Le Sauveur et les viscères de l'être: Sur le gnosticisme et Michel Henry* (Paris: L'Harmattan, 2004).

130. See Janicaud's contribution to *Phenomenology and the "Theological Turn* and his *Phenomenology "Wide Open."* Also see Jocelyn Benoist, "Le tournant théologique," in *L'Idée de phénoménologie* (Paris: Beauchesne, 2001). For Henry's radical phenomenology at the heart of Christ's preaching, see his *I Am the Truth, Incarnation* and *Paroles du Christ* (Paris: Seuil, 2002).

131. W. H. Auden, "For the Time Being: A Christmas Oratorio," in *Collected Poems*, ed. Edward Mendelson (New York: Random House, 1976), 307.

132. Derrida, *The Gift of Death*, trans. David Wills (Chicago: University of Chicago Press, 1995), 49.

133. See Marion, "Metaphysics and Phenomenology," in *Postmodern God*, 296 n. 27.

134. See Emmanuel Lévinas, "Judaism and Revolution," in *Nine Talmudic Readings*, trans. and intro. Annette Aronowicz (Bloomington: Indiana University Press, 1990), 99.

135. See Kant, *Religion within the Limits of Reason Alone*, trans. Theodore M. Greene and Hoyt H. Hudson (New York: Harper and Row, 1960); Lévinas, *Of God Who Comes to Mind*, trans. Bettina Bergo (Stanford: Stanford University Press, 1998), xi; Derrida, "Faith and Knowledge: The Two Sources of 'Religion' at the Limits of Reason Alone," in *Religion*, ed. Derrida and Gianni Vattimo (Cambridge: Polity Press, 1998), 1–78.

136. See Kant, *Critique of Pure Reason*, B 161; G. W. F. Hegel, *The Phenomenology of Mind*, trans. J. B. Baillie (New York: Harper and Row, 1967), 96.

137. Husserl, *Logical Investigations*, 2:540.

138. Michel Henry, *The Essence of Manifestation*, trans. Girard Etzkorn (The Hague: Martinus Nijhoff, 1973), §IV; Derrida, "A 'Madness' Must Watch over Thinking," *Points . . .: Interviews, 1974–1994*, ed. Elisabeth Weber, trans. Peggy Kamuf et al. (Stanford: Stanford University Press, 1995), 362.

139. See Marion, "The Intentionality of Love," in *Prolegomena to Charity*, esp. 73–75, 88–90.

140. Lacoste, *Experience and the Absolute*, 55.

141. Friedrich Schleiermacher, *On Religion: Speeches to its Cultured Despisers*, trans. John Oman, intro. Rudolf Otto (New York: Harper and Row, 1958), 43. I quote from the second edition.

142. Maurice Blanchot, *The Writing of the Disaster*, trans. Ann Smock (Lincoln: University of Nebraska Press, 1986), 50–51.

143. I take the distinction from Jean Wahl. See his *Existence humaine et Transcendance* (Neuchâtel: Éditions de la Baconnière, 1944), 37.

144. Edmund Husserl, *Analyses Concerning Passive and Active Syntheses: Lectures on Transcendental Logic*, trans. Anthony J. Steinbock, *Edmund Husserl Collected Works*, vol. 9 (Boston: Kluwer, 2001), §5.

145. On this topic see Jean-Luc Marion, "The Reason of the Gift," in *Givenness and God: Questions of Jean-Luc Marion*, ed. Ian Leask and Eoin Cassidy (New York: Fordham University Press, 2005), 112–16.

146. Jacques Taminiaux notes that the reduction for Heidegger has three stages: method, construction, and deconstruction [*Destruktion*]. If so, it would be interesting to read Marion on the reduction in search of the deconstructive dimension of his work. See Taminiaux, *The Metamorphoses of Phenomenological Reduction* (Milwaukee: Marquette University Press, 2004), 34–35.

147. See Pablo Neruda, *Selected Odes of Pablo Neruda,* trans. and intro. Margaret Sayers Peden (Berkeley: University of California Press, 1990); Francis Ponge, *The Voice of Things,* trans. and intro. Beth Archer (New York: McGraw-Hill, 1974); Charles Simic, *Selected Poems: 1963–1983* (New York: George Braziller, 1985).

I

MARION IN CONTEXT

1

Jean-Luc Marion

Phenomenology, Hermeneutics, Theology

DAVID TRACY

There are many ways to approach the thought of Jean-Luc Marion. Some have focused on such inner-phenomenological debates as those with Derrida on gift, Ricœur on two notions of givenness, and Lévinas on the philosophical relationship of justice and love. These debates are highly significant ones in which I, too, like the other contributors to this volume, have a judgment. But none of these inner-phenomenological debates (save later in this essay, where I reflect on the dispute surrounding the relationship of phenomenology and hermeneutics) claim my attention here. Rather, I consider Marion's work as it contributes to the age-old issue of the relationship of philosophy (here, phenomenology) and theology. I do so principally because I believe that Marion's work, if I read him correctly, is enormously fruitful for theology. I also take this focus because I believe his work has, at times, been seriously misread in two opposite ways: either as a philosophy that is a covert theology or as a proposal to control theology by philosophy. Since I do not find either reading persuasive, I feel obliged to give my own reading—influenced no doubt by my own positions in both philosophy and theology—on Professor Marion's work. I, too, will inevitably raise some questions, but they remain, as far as I can see, more in the nature of further questions than internal criticisms. But of that, you—and Professor Marion—must judge.

To complete this task I shall first give my own assessment of the major developments in Professor Marion's impressive intellectual journey and then suggest what questions need further addressing to clarify and advance Marion's enterprise as it affects the relationship of philosophy and theology. In view of Kevin Hart's outline of the chronological stages in Marion's thought, therefore, I shall be silent on several issues in order to concentrate on the philosophy–theology relationship—at times implicit, at other times explicit, in his thought.

Marion's First Stage: The Rereading of Descartes

Marion's first stage of thought was principally a reading of Descartes. In his magisterial interpretation of Descartes, Marion (influenced initially, I believe, by Lévinas's reading of the category of the Infinite in Descartes's *Third Meditation*) spelled out the Infinite in terms of all the relevant texts of Descartes. Only then could a reader understand the significance of that insistence on the Infinite. In brief, the more familiar reading of Descartes by Heidegger was a turn to the subject that instituted a modern onto-theological claim to ground all reality in subjectism rather than the premodern substance. Marion, far more than Heidegger or even Lévinas, spelled out the fuller complexity of Descartes's texts and his influence. In historical context, Descartes's position on God and causality [*causa sui*] was deeply influenced by Suárez's fatal attempt to unite the Scotist *ens commune* and the Thomist analogy. Gilson had already shown this partly and Bernard Lonergan consistently argued for the disastrous intellectual influence of Suárez both in the interpretation of Thomist analogy and in the misinterpretation of causality by modern thought.

However, it is Marion who articulated the full-fledged intellectual debacle that followed in Descartes's wake in the understanding of God in both philosophy and the Cartesian theology that Michael Buckley had persuasively delineated in seventeenth-century French thought: in sum, the historical moment when theology lost its roots in religious life—liturgy, spirituality, prayer, faith—and became, in effect, a second-rate Cartesian philosophy. Neo-Scholasticism was regnant in Catholic theology for almost all theologians before the *resourcement* movement of de Lubac, Congar, Chenu, von Balthasar, Rahner, and Lonergan. Meanwhile, the neo-Scholastics continued their control of Catholic thought under the ironic rubric of responding to Descartes in Cartesian terms and not, as they claimed, on Thomist principles.

In modern philosophy before Marion's groundbreaking work on Descartes, there was a virtual ignoring of Descartes's *Third Meditation* and its recognition that the category of the Infinite is ontologically prior to the category "finite" and thus breaks all our finite categories and disallows the univocity and "common being" that Descartes elsewhere—with his egology and his understanding of causality and God as *causa sui*—employed in the *Meditations*. This move, I suggest, was fatal for not only Catholic theology. Its history of effects has proved equally disturbing for secular philosophical thought and much Protestant theology. Here, unlike the Catholic case, the influence of Spinoza is crucial. Spinoza's impersonal understanding of God is fully dependent on Descartes's notion of causality and therefore a Suárezian "common being" and "univocal language." Moreover, Vincent Carraud has demonstrated the Suárezian formulation of the principle of "sufficient reason" and its enormous influence in modern philosophy. The "atheism controversy" of Jacobi and Fichte, and above all the Kantian formulation of God as a noumenal limit-concept that can be thought but not known, determined much secular and Protestant thinking about God in the modern period.

Lévinas, brilliantly but almost impressionistically, rediscovered the importance of the infinite in Descartes. And Marion demonstrated the complexity of Descartes's thought by a careful, textual analysis of his several namings of God and the contrast in Descartes between the Infinite (in principle not compatible with Suárezian univocity and causality) and *causa sui*—in principle fully compatible with Suárez and the major thinkers (Spinoza, Leibniz, Wolf, and Kant) who followed in Descartes's wake. This study by Marion is far more persuasive than the grand narratives of all Western thought since Plato worked out by Heidegger and by Derrida. For Marion's narrative is the more modest narrative of modern Western thought. Marion, Carraud, Henry, Chrétien, and other "new phenomenologists" delineate with Heidegger the need for a non-metaphysical, more exactly non-onto-theological position for both philosophy and theology. Unlike Heidegger and with Lévinas, they shift phenomenological attention from the self to the other, and, with Marion, in particular, to the saturated phenomenon allied to a new, non-Heideggerian understanding of givenness related to reduction (which the later Heidegger largely ignores). But this is to push the Marion development further along than his actual trajectory took.

Marion's Second Stage: A Phenomenology of Theological Language

It is interesting, certainly for the theologian, that Marion's next move was not to provide the strictly phenomenological (i.e., philosophical) series of reductions needed to defend his phenomenological description of givenness nor his original notion of the fourfold saturated phenomenon. That would come later. In the second stage of his thought, Marion was concerned to recover the Dionysian tradition in Christian theology. A probable influence here was Hans Urs von Balthasar's defense of the Dionysian tradition and the insistence on the liturgical-eucharistic setting of Dionysius' reflections on God, whereby neither cataphatic nor apophatic moves are definitive to understanding Dionysius' insistence in *Mystical Theology* on the Incomprehensible God revealed beyond predication in mystical-liturgical prayer. To show this, Marion wrote phenomenologies on the distinction of "icon" and "idol," and above all his influential *God without Being*. The latter work should be read not as a theology but as a phenomenology of theological language in the Dionysian tradition. Aside from a too narrow reading of Thomas Aquinas on God as *Esse* (a reading he later largely corrected) and a (to me) bizarre claim that the bishop is the authentic theologian, Marion insightfully argued that the Dionysian tradition—once so influential in both Eastern and Western theology prior to Thomas (von Balthasar claims that Dionysius is second in influence only to Augustine in Western theology)—did suffer a setback by Aquinas's choice of *Esse* as the principal cataphatic name for God over the Dionysian "the Good."

Even those of us who believe that Aquinas was far more subtle in this matter (especially in his commentary on Dionysius) than Marion has allowed can still agree, with Marion, that the loss of the cataphatic name "the Good" as the principal name for God did bear some unfortunate consequences—consequences that became fatal even for the presumably Thomist neo-Scholastics after Suárez's linking of the Thomist analogical *Esse* to the Scotist *esse commune*.

As we shall see later, the recovery of the Dionysian strictly theological tradition also allows for a Lévinasian recovery of Plato's "Good beyond Being," which, like Descartes's Infinite, provides a new way to think of God philosophically and theologically freed of the modern "isms": theism, atheism, agnosticism, pantheism, and panentheism—all dependent on modern metaphysical causality and onto-theology.

I have suggested elsewhere that an equally important shift away from the Dionysian tradition in Western Christian theology occurred when Luther, once an admirer of Dionysius, turned violently against him to rethink *Deus Absconditus* not as the "Incomprehensible God" of the Dionysian tradition but as the doubly "Hidden God" of the Reformation tradition. The latter Lutheran and Calvinist positions (reformulated for modernity in Catholic Augustinian but non-Jansenist terms in Pascal's *Pensées*) can be read in two ways: first, as a violent and unfortunate rejection of the Dionysian tradition in almost all Protestant theology—a major misfortune occasioned if not caused by Luther's rejection of that tradition; second, as a healthy corrective of the Dionysian tradition by insisting on the major lack in that tradition (and in Marion's retrieval of it, thus far), namely, a theology of the Cross attentive, as in Luther and Pascal, to Paul's Christ Crucified (not only John's Glory manifested in the givenness of the Lifting-Up of Christ on the Cross).

Again, as in Pascal, this attention to the theological phenomenon of the Cross of Christ also allows more phenomenological attention than Marion has thus far given to Pascalean *misère*—that is, in its full Pascalean sense of *misère* as sin, *misère* as suffering, and *misère* as ineluctable fate. These too are saturated phenomena that deserve, nay demand, attention to any attempt to do justice to the icon of Christ, the one incarnate, crucified, resurrected, and to come again. Could not the recovery of the Dionysian *Dieu sans l'être* also become the occasion for the God without Being, manifested—given in the Cross? Without that retrieval we do not have the full Jesus Christ. Without that we do not have an adequate response to Lévinas's poignant question: Can any philosophy that does not address innocent suffering provide adequacy today? With the full Christological symbols—Incarnation, Cross, Resurrection, Second Coming—contemporary theology might be able to render a fuller and more saturated icon of Jesus Christ beyond not only Being but beyond even Dionysius. That icon would look to the excessive giving, generosity, love—even *kenosis*—of the Dionysian God while realizing with Pascal that the excessive kenotic love of God in Christ must be understood not only by incarnation but by the cross; not only by resurrection, but by the profound not-yet event of the Second Coming.

But these questions, to be sure, are more strictly theological than philosophical-phenomenological. They seem appropriate, however, as comments on the second stage of Marion's work. Hence, in that stage we find a phenomenology of idol and icon and "God without Being" that may be described not as theology but as a phenomenology of theological language and iconic image. There are further questions that do not call into question the persuasive analyses of "God without Being" and the icon but ask for their completion in order to be faithful, beyond Dionysius, to the fuller Christian understanding of Jesus Christ in Incarnation-Cross-Resurrection-Second Coming.

Marion's Third Stage: The New Phenomenology of the Saturated Phenomenon

In Marion's third and present stage of thinking he has left behind (only momentarily one hopes) his phenomenology of theological language and has returned to phenomenology proper. Influenced partly by the debate with Derrida on the possibility of gift, but more by the exigencies of his own thought on phenomenological reduction and givenness, Marion has worked out in his major philosophical work, *Étant donné,* what his work on Descartes implied and his work on the icon and the Dionysian theology needed: a strictly phenomenological defense of givenness related to a critique of both Husserl's notions of intentionality and constitution and Heidegger's formulation of the *es gibt.* Marion has paid less attention, curiously enough, to the Lévinas–Blanchot discussion of the relationship of *es gibt* to *il y a.* Perhaps Marion's relative silence on the latter discussion is partly occasioned by his most original phenomenological breakthrough on the formulation of the "saturated phenomenon"—saturated in all four senses.

Surely the work *Being Given* and the allied text *In Excess,* as well as his exceptional study of the visible in painting and his recent, brilliant and daring study *The Erotic Phenomenon,* constitute Marion's major, strictly philosophical contributions to the "new" phenomenology. The phenomenology of *Being Given,* moreover, establishes the category phenomenologically of both revealability and revelation as the saturated phenomenon *par excellence.*

Quite consistently from a theological viewpoint, and quite persuasively, Marion never presumes that philosophy can establish the fact, the possibility, of an actual revelation, especially the Christian Revelation that his earlier work on icon and Dionysius the Areopagite makes clear that he holds to. Here, surely, his philosophical and theological hesitation is exactly right. The phenomenological defense of "revealability" shows the condition of possibility of the "Impossible" revelation. But only the actual divine revelation itself—the saturated phenomenon *par excellence*—could ever establish it. The actual revelation of God by God is in Christian Trinitarian terms, the revelation of the Father through the Son in the Spirit. The latter, in Christian terms, is clearly a matter of faith—itself a gift/grace by God. Marion is clear that no philosophy could in principle establish that. Even Hegel did not really claim to, since his absolute *Begriff* was possible only because of the absolute Christian *Vorstellung* or revelation. The time wasted by many theologians in the modern period on metaphysical "proofs" for the reality of God is a sad tale with few breakthroughs before the Catholic *resourcement* theologians recovered premodern resources for thought: von Balthasar, Lonergan, Rahner, and the neo-Reformation theologians, especially Karl Barth. There were also, however, other theological and philosophical breakthroughs: Pascal, Kierkegaard, and, most impressively, Franz Rosenzweig.

Phenemonology and Hermeneutics for Theology

More can be said about the relevance of the new phenomenology to theology. As an enterprise that is an endless hermeneutics of revelation, Christian theology is fully dependent on an actual revelation, the pure gift of faith in the revelation to become *fides quaerens intellectum*. As a necessary hermeneutic, theology as faith seeking understanding is also dependent not only on a hermeneutics of retrieval of the primordial revelation but through faith-transformed intelligence (the latter, in sum, not only as the human image as microcosmos but also as *imago dei*). In hermeneutical theology a hermeneutics of critique is at times also necessary. Sometimes critique, not pure retrieval, is the best way to read the witnesses (the Scriptures, creeds, doctrines, symbols, liturgies, prayers, etc.) appropriately (e.g., in not reading Genesis as science). Moreover, when necessary, theology also needs a hermeneutics of suspicion (e.g., on the patriarchal character of the biblical witnesses). This hermeneutical character of theology in its full sense—retrieval, critique, suspicion—is not caused by modern needs (even if they occasion it—e.g., Darwinian science in the first case, secular feminist movements in the second), but by the prophetic character of the revelation itself.

To argue adequately my own position here on hermeneutics of retrieval, critique, and suspicion (which is not Marion's), I realize, would take another essay. For the moment, it is perhaps enough to state that theology should indeed abandon all modern onto-theological attempts and content itself in its philosophical side—first, with a phenomenology without metaphysics both as a first way to describe the givenness of the actual revelation of God as witnessed to us in the texts we name Scripture and the liturgy in all its fullness. The fact that Christian revelation is the event and person of Jesus Christ and that contemporary Christians believe *in* Jesus Christ *with* the apostles shows as well the inevitably hermeneutical character of understanding—beyond the original phenomenology of the actual revelation as the saturated phenomenon *par excellence.*

However, any hermeneutical theology divorced from the givenness of revelation and the transforming *gift* of faith will soon stumble—even on hermeneutical grounds alone, which after all are dependent on a receptivity to the gift of revelation for any hermeneutical conversation. For this move, the kind of phenomenology proposed by Marion in *Being Given* and *In Excess* is invaluable—even, perhaps especially, for hermeneutical theologies. Indeed, Marion himself suggests that phenomenality of actual saturated phenomena (other, face, flesh, gift, eros, etc.) issue forth into what he nicely names "an endless hermeneutic." So it is even more so in theology (e.g., for Christology, Incarnation, Cross, Resurrection, Second Coming).

If this be so, then I suggest that the next step for Marion is not to return to a phenomenology of strictly theological language (Dionysius, St. Thomas, Augustine, Luther, et al.), but first spend more phenomenological time on the original revelation itself, as witnessed in the Scriptures, insofar as Scripture both informs and transforms all later theologies. Hence, my final proposal: once scriptural revelation is more fully described, a phenomenology of the voice will become at least as necessary as any phenomenology of the visible— face or icon. No one can see the face of God and live, as Exodus insists. But the voice of God—for Moses, even for Job in the whirlwind, is always there. And in the New Testament, the fact that the Word becomes flesh also means that, in Jesus the Christ, the voice becomes face. A phenomenology and hermeneutics— of voice and face in the God-man, Jesus the Christ—remains the principal task of any fully Christian theology. Both the new phenomenology and the hermeneutics of the ancients and the moderns have become indispensable philosophical tools for the modern theologian—as indispensable as Platonism was for the patristic period.

A phenomenology of the face connected to a phenomenology of the voice; iconic manifestation and prophetic proclamation; incarnation and cross; Dionysius and Pascal. Can we hope that Jean-Luc Marion, after contributing so much on one of these constant polarities, can be encouraged to turn his attention more fully to the second of these polarities as well?

The Hyperbolization
of Phenomenology

Two Possibilities for Religion in Recent
Continental Philosophy

JOHN D. CAPUTO

What is phenomenology? Of what is phenomenology capable? Is God, who exceeds all our powers and possibilities, one of phenomenology's possibilities? Is phenomenology capable of including the transcendence of God in the field of phenomenological immanence, of encompassing one who is by definition incomprehensible and unencompassable? Or is that impossible? Alternately, is God, for whom all things are possible, capable of making himself manifest, capable of pitching his tent in the field of phenomenological immanence, or are we prepared to deny God that power in advance? Would the entrance of God into phenomenology be the ultimate transgression, exploding its claim to rigor and violating its philosophical integrity? Or does phenomenology itself, however paradoxically, require transgression in order to be true to itself?

My hypothesis in this essay is that phenomenology has recently become religious and it has become so by a series of transgressions I identify as movements of "hyperbolization." By this I mean that the religious element enters phenomenology in the form of a transgression or a passage to the limits [*passage aux frontières*] precisely in order to open phenomenology to God, who exceeds its limits. Such a claim leads us inevitably back to Husserl, who first staked out the rigorous limits and scientific possibility of phenomenology, which this process of becoming religious directly threatens, even as it leads forward to the transgressions, which are ways of radicalizing phenomenology and driving it to excess. The idea behind the excess is to pry phenomenology open, even if in opposing directions—to push it beyond itself, but always in such a way as to force it to be true to itself; for left to itself, to its traditional form, phenomenology cannot be what it wants to be. To radicalize it in the name of God in order to be true to God—that is the surprising thing. The excess and the madness are divine, and the violence against phenomenology religious.

I have in mind two transgressions of phenomenology. The first is represented by the work of Derrida, which I describe here as a "hyperbolization of desire," while the second is represented by the work of what might be called generically the "new phenomenology" in France, spearheaded by Jean-Luc Marion but including Jean-Louis Chrétien, Francois Courtine, Michel Henry, and Jean-Yves Lacoste, which constitutes a "hyperbolization of givenness." Both Marion and Derrida think that it is impossible to avoid Husserl even as it is impossible to avoid exceeding Husserl, to avoid going where Husserl dared not go. Far from simply shutting down phenomenology, both regard this impossible excess as positive and constitutive of a more radical phenomenology or post-phenomenology of the impossible. What I am calling Derrida's "hyperbolic desire" I trace back to what Husserl called "intention" carried to infinity, passing to its limits, pushed beyond its limits to an impossible desire beyond any possible fulfillment. In Marion and the new phenomenologists, we see an almost perfectly opposite movement, where the process of what Husserl called "fulfillment" or "givenness" is carried to infinity, pushed beyond its limits, to an impossible givenness beyond any possible intention. Here the excess of fulfillment, or the frustration of fulfillment by excess, reveals the defect of intention, which is its tendency to short circuit givenness in advance. Two hyperboles, two transgressions, two ways that God has recently found a voice in continental philosophy: in the one by means of a desire beyond desire for a phenomenon without phenomenality, an appearance constituted by its nonappearance; and in the other by means of a saturating event, a phenomenon beyond phenomenality, which is constituted by a hyperbole of givenness.

Deconstruction, thus, on my telling, is not irreligious. On the contrary, its hyperbolic desire issues in a poor and naked religion, a certain religion without religion, making a confession without confessional or doctrinal content of the name of God. In the new phenomenology, on the other hand, we encounter a robustly religious and theological religion that makes no apologies about introducing phenomenology to phenomena of an unmistakably confessional, doctrinal or dogmatic-theological kind. Deconstruction circum-fesses its blindness and poverty, while the new phenomenology moves in the vicinity of a concrete confessional faith, a determinate and sacramental Christian faith.

Thus, if deconstruction has taken a "religious" turn, this is a religion without theology, representing, let us say, a religious but "a-theological" turn, so long as atheology is not confused with atheism and irreligion, while the new phenomenology has taken a decidedly "theological turn," an expression coined by Dominique Janicaud as a criticism of the new phenomenology. Janicaud attacks the second but not the first hyperbolization, the transgression of Husserl's stated methodological constraints to be found in the new phenomenology. Janicaud charged that Lévinas, Marion, and the new phenomenologists violate the strictures of phenomenological method by trying to bootleg the transcendence of God into the immanence of phenomenology. For Janicaud, phenomenology first strayed from the narrow path of phenomenological method in Lévinas, who overwhelmed Husserl not with Being (Heidegger) but with the Good and the transcendence of God.[1] What Lévinas produced is not a "negative phenomenology" but a baldly metaphysical phenomenology that describes the grey on grey of a *tout autre,* a notion that violates the neutrality of phenomenology toward all matters theological and metaphysical.[2] If in *God without Being*[3] Marion was unapologetically theological, Janicaud concedes that Marion has become more circumspect in his later writings. Thus in *Reduction and Givenness*[4] Marion puts on the airs of having methodological rigor by miming the very idea of a "phenomenological reduction." For Janicaud, Marion describes a pseudo-reduction that culminates in the trick move of the "pure call," where he finally tries to make phenomenology what it cannot be, and to do so under the guise of a rigorous method, for the purely "interlocuted" is too thin and meager a thing to have phenomenological substance.[5] With his confession of confusion and surprise in the experience of the pure call, Marion bids farewell to both common sense and phenomenology. The dice of phenomenology are loaded further by Jean-Louis Chrétien,[6] whose search for a body fully manifest and without secret—like a dancer, whose body reveals not only its visibility but its invisible soul—culminates in the confession that the body cannot fully reveal itself here on earth but only in eternity as the resurrected body. That represents a phenomenology that, however edifying, is clearly only for Christians, for no one else can find phenomenology there.[7] It constitutes a phenomenology that is no more phenomenological than Marion's mystifying musings on the "call." These later developments of phenomenology confirm that Husserl did not bracket the transcendence of "God" arbitrarily. In sum, Janicaud concludes, phenomenology and theology are two different things: phenomenology, which has to do with seeing, must recognize its limits within experience and confess that faith, as Luther said, consists in giving oneself over to things we do not see.[8]

Janicaud's critique, which is directed at the transgressions of the new phenomenology, not at Derrida, helps us to focus the issues, which have to do with the nature and extent of the transgressions in which the recent turn to religion is implicated. Are these hyperbolizations necessary, unavoidable, inevitable extensions of phenomenology? Or do they represent a kind of perversion of philosophical inquiry by the perpetual menace of hidden (or not so hidden) theological presuppositions?

Derrida's Hyperbolic Desire for God

If it seems scandalous to link Derrida's name with the name of God, there are also many who will be scandalized by linking him with Husserl and phenomenology. Derrida's early work on Husserl was mistaken as simply a criticism of Husserl's phenomenology, an attempt to debunk phenomenology as something hidebound to the "metaphysics of presence." As usual, nothing is simple in deconstruction and if Derrida was indeed effecting a critical delimitation of Husserl, his intentions were entirely affirmative and productive of something that can pass beyond Husserl only if it first passes through Husserl. Derrida criticized Husserl for concealing what he revealed. That is, Husserl's valorization of presence occludes what Derrida calls an "irreducible non-presence as having a constituting value," which, Derrida maintained, Husserl himself had discovered.[9] So Derrida meant to criticize the metaphysical side of Husserl just in order to emancipate Husserl's more critical, radical, and transcendental side, and Derrida's restlessness with phenomenological presence turned out, in the end, to go hand in hand with a deeply religious aspiration for an excess beyond presence. This delimitation centered on four points in which Husserl could be seen to be resisting his own discoveries, repressing or suppressing what he himself had released.

(1) Having shown that "experience" was the naively lived effect of prior and anonymous transcendental syntheses, Husserl remain attached, nonetheless, to an ideal of pure and primordial experience that provides the founding substratum for all conscious life. When Derrida said that there never was such a

thing as "perception"[10] and when he voiced his suspicion about "experience," he gave voice to a widespread recognition of a residual naivete in Husserl, an innocence about the structures—linguistic, social, and so on—that lay more deeply imbedded within experience and are constituted as effects of a still more anonymous transcendental, or quasi-transcendental, "field" or operation called *différance*. Perception and experience, Derrida was maintaining, are mediated all the way down, or they are not possible at all.

(2) Although Husserl had unearthed the radical principle of constitution, which means that every unity is the effect of a prior synthesis,[11] and hence that every presence was the effect of a certain re-presenting, reproduction, or repetition, he nonetheless treated ideal unities of meaning as having an independent priority and validity, a *Geltung*, of their own and on their own. So when Derrida said that repetition produces what it repeats,[12] including ideal objects, where the scope of repetition was widest of all, he was only holding Husserl's hand to the fire of his own discoveries, of just the sort Husserl made in the "Origin of Geometry" when he showed the constitutive role played by language in the production of geometric ideality.[13]

(3) Husserl introduced a fruitful distinction between intention and fulfillment, but he did so in such a way as to subordinate intention to fulfillment, so that fulfillment is the aim and telos of every intention. But this was again to repress what Husserl had discovered, Derrida maintained, which is the capacity of signifiers (intentions) to function in the absence of the signified (fulfillment), for it is the very idea of a signifier that it can get along by itself when what it signifies is not on hand. His "most audacious" reduction, Derrida said, lies in "putting out of play, as 'non-essential components' of expression, the acts of intuitive cognition which fulfill meaning."[14] When it comes to signs, the whole idea of an intention is to function in the absence of fulfillment, and this Derrida applied to intentions generally. Husserl had liberated signifiers from the rule of intuition, unfettered them from the regime of givenness, and given them a new freedom in which they were able to leap ahead where the leaden feet of intuition and fulfillment could not follow, to produce new effects of which fulfillment and intuition could only dream.

(4) Finally, and here he simply repeated Husserl with a slight difference, Derrida, in the wake of Lévinas, seized on Husserl's description of the analogical apperception of the other ego in the *Fifth Cartesian Meditation*, the constitution of the *tout autre* that Lévinas mistakenly rejected because he had confused "constitution" with creation and did not see that here "constitution"

simply means the "confession" that the other is the shore that I cannot reach. The other for Husserl is not one of my possibilities, as Lévinas charged, but one of my impossibilities, not a part of my powers but the heart of my power-lessness. What interested Derrida here was once again that Husserl had put his finger on the constitutive value of nonpresence, and had identified in a para-digmatic way an appearance that was constituted by its nonappearance. For here was an appearance—the other person—who was precisely and in prin-ciple constituted by its refusal of appearance. Were the mental life, the "secret" life of the other, on display—were it phenomenalizable, even in principle and as an ideal or "Idea" in the Kantian sense—then the very appearance of the other would disappear and its very phenomenality would evaporate under the glare of the sun of knowledge, like the moon and the stars at high noon.[15]

The deeply affirmative point of Derrida's critical delimitation of Husserl was lost on all but the most careful readers. For Derrida's public persona was swallowed up by the tempest over the "free play of signifiers" and the notori-ous saying that "there is nothing outside the text," which grabbed all the head-lines. But that point became unmistakable in Derrida's later writings when he saw fit to characterize deconstruction by resurrecting the word "experience," not of pedestrian presence, but an experience of "the impossible," of an un-foreseeable and unimaginable event called the "coming" or "in-coming of the other" [*l'invention de l'autre*]. What became clear in the later writings, as I argued in 1997, is that deconstruction is structured like a religion, albeit a reli-gion without religion.[16] The errant play of signifiers is not the last word on deconstruction, or the last move deconstruction has to make, as Mark C. Taylor seemed to think in *Erring*,[17] but only its first word or preliminary move, a preamble to its leap of faith. Like Kant, Derrida found it necessary to detain the heady rush of knowledge in order to make room for the risky movements of faith, to defer the day of knowledge in order to make room for the anxious (k)night of faith. That is what structures the "desire" of deconstruction and allows the name of God to gain entrance into phenomenology.

What emerged from Derrida's delimitation of Husserl—not to mention of Heidegger, Lévinas, and Nietzsche, of Plato and Christian neo-Platonism, and of quite a few others—was a certain quasi-phenomenology of the "messianic," a more austere and minimalist post-phenomenology, turning on the structure of the "to come." Derrida was arguing that phenomenology cannot be what it wants to be, a philosophy of fulfilling intuition and givenness, because any such fulfilling presence turns out to be a function of a constitutive nonpresence.

But that is not a result that Derrida viewed with nostalgia or regret; it is not a criticism or a negative result at all. By insinuating the constitutive value of the cut of nonpresence into what phenomenology called "perception," "presence," and "experience," Derrida meant to cut open phenomenology, and philosophy itself, to the future, to reinscribe phenomenology in a framework of messianic expectation and hope in what is always and structurally to come.

We can read Derrida to be saying that phenomenology can only be true to itself by *confessing* the cut of this desire, by confessing or "circum-fessing,"[18] that it desires what cannot be present, and hence that phenomenology cannot be what it wants to be. This confession opens its horizons by cutting or circumcising them, by turning phenomenology, or "thought"—in a sense that is at least as Kantian as it is Heideggerian—toward the unthinkable to come. Deconstruction has to do not with the given or fulfillment but with the cut of what is never given yet is ever to come. In deconstruction, the Messiah is never actually present, never actually comes, and, according to one of the old rabbinic traditions, is never going to show up just because the Messiah represents the very structure of hope and expectation.[19] Deconstruction is structurally advenient or invenient—in the liturgical calendar of its religion it is always advent: always turned toward what is coming, not confined to what is present, with the result that nothing that presents itself in the present can ever measure up to our hope and expectation. The deconstruction of the metaphysics of presence, therefore, belongs not to some sort of skeptical or relativist project of "anything goes," but to an ancient Jewish critique of idols. If in deconstruction one philosophizes with a hammer, it is with the hammer that Moses took to Aaron's golden calf, where the intent is not simply destructive but aimed at inscribing a zone of absolute respect around the *tout autre*. If Derrida underlined the primacy of intentions over givenness, and the capacity of intentions to function in the absence of fulfillment, he did so not out of a nihilist love of emptiness but precisely in the name of messianic expectation, which is structurally turned toward what is to come. The religious turn taken in deconstruction pivots on this messianic turn, which is turned toward what is always and ever to come, which should never be confused with what is present now or in the future. It has to do not with something that will be present at some distant point in the future, but with the very structure of expectation and hope. The messianic structure of the to come, of the democracy or the justice to come, for example, has a prophetic character, not in the sense that it somehow forecasts what will be (as a meteoroligist might do), but in the sense that it announces a justice to come that denounces the injustice in what at present calls itself just or democratic. Like Socrates, it does not know what justice is, but only that nothing present can lay claim to it. Thus the effect of the call to come is not to *predict* anything coming but to *intensify* our desire.

That is why I would say that the religious turn taken in deconstruction represents a kind of Jewish Augustinianism, a post-phenomenology of quasi-Augustinian desire, which is the source of my discontent with the way the atheological turn is worked out in Mark C. Taylor's *Erring*. Taylor catches the cut of errancy and atheology in Derrida but he misses the messianic desire, the religion without theology, the Jewish-Augustinian man of prayers and tears who kisses his tallith before bed every night. He focuses instead on Derrida's critique of the idols of presence that I take to be purely propaedeutic to what is affirmed in deconstruction. Deconstruction is not the hermeneutics of the death of God, as Taylor claims, or at least it is not simply that, but rather the hermeneutics of the desire for God. Taylor is an avant-garde thinker who championed deconstruction as atheology but lost interest in this more religious Derrida. He thinks that we should all be analyzing Times Square right now and forget deconstruction. But this reading of Derrida cuts off in advance a more genuinely religious but nontheological turn Derrida was taking just as *Erring* was published more than twenty years ago. My *Prayers and Tears* was intended in part to displace this death of God reading of Derrida and replace it with a more religious reading, albeit a religion without religion, based on a much more careful reading of what has been published since the appearance of *Erring*. Taylor would, I suspect, not deny but rather regret the religious turn I have been discussing because he would see this return as a regression. The difference between us is that if Taylor thinks that God is dead, I think that God is the name of what we desire, which is how it functions in Derrida.[20]

On the model I defend, deconstruction is structured as a desire beyond desire, as a desire for God, a *cor inquietum*, a restless heart that desires we do not know quite what, where the name of God is the name of our desire even as it is the best name we have for what we do not know. Contrary to the Heideggerian dogma that the name of God puts questioning to sleep, for Derrida it makes everything questionable, makes everything tremble, for we cannot say what we love when we love our God. *Quid ergo amo cum deum (meum) amo?* (*Conf.* X, 6–7). Whenever we love anything we love our God, but what do we love when we love our God? If indeed we say that God is love, does that mean that love is the best name we have for God, which is what the Scriptures mean, or that God is the best name we have for love, which is what a more secularizing theology might say? Or if we say that God is justice, does that mean that justice is the best name we have for God, which is what the prophets say, or that God is the best name we have for justice, which is what a more secularizing theology might say? In deconstruction there is no resolution of this undecidability. Where would it get the authority to bring that endless fluctuation and translatability to halt? Who would authorize it to make such a pronouncement? Where would one be standing when that resolution was pronounced? In what place or time, speaking in which natural language? The task of deconstruction is not to bring that undecidability to a halt but to maintain it and keep it alive because that is the very condition of a decision, of faith, in which what Climacus called the "poor existing individual" decides in the midst of undecidability. The opposite of undecidability is not a decision, but programmability, which obviates decision by reducing decision to the conclusion of a set of premises.

The religious turn in deconstruction is to make everything turn on desire, and to make desire turn on faith, on what Derrida calls the "passion of non-knowing," which is a movement of a desire for I know not what. True, there is much to be said for a desire that knows what it desires and for a faith that knows what it believes. We should not underestimate the inestimable roles such faith and such desire play in life. But such faith and desire belong to the realm of what Derrida calls the "future present," the foreseeable and plannable future, which once it rolls around brings us joy by bringing us what we were waiting for and could foresee. But if that is all that life brings, if our life is entirely circumscribed by the foreseeable and plannable, then for Derrida life has by and large been without "event," without a radical surprise—that is to say, life has by and large passed us by. The more radical quest, the more radical desire, the more radical faith is for Derrida the more radically open-ended one in which we do not know what we desire. Not knowing what we desire is constitutive of desire in its deepest sense. If I set out in search of something that I know, I am not lost. But if I cannot say what I desire then I am truly en route. I do not know what I desire even when I say that what I desire is justice, democracy, or the gift, for these are but the least bad names at my present disposal for what I desire, the least bad words that have been handed down to me from a past that was never present, from a polyphonic and polyvocal complex that I call by the vast and oversimplifying shorthand name of "tradition." Something stirs in these words, something is astir, something is *promised* in them that is not delivered by them, like intentions that intend more than they give us to see. Our best words are empty intentions, promises that have not and cannot be kept, words that we cherish because of the promises they make but do not quite keep. They are what they are if and only if they are what Husserl calls "inadequate" to themselves, not themselves, not yet, never really, but restless with becoming what they can never be.[21] There is a longing in these words— evoked by what Heidegger would call "the force of the most elemental words in which Dasein expresses itself"[22]—that stretches out beyond their fulfill-ment in the present and even beyond their intention, since I cannot even be sure that what I desire when I affirm the "democracy to come" will even bear the name of democracy. When some future historian writes the history of what I desire when I speak of a "democracy to come," it will turn out that what we called democracy today was the name of some antecedent state that is linked by a series of historical transformations to successor states for which we today have neither the name nor the concept.

The religious turn taken in deconstruction is the name of the covenant between desire and the promise of what is to come. But who is making that promise? What is her or his or its name? And what is being promised? If I could say that, if I could answer that, it would compromise the promise: it would represent a lack of fidelity to the faith, of loyalty to the desire, of dedication to the quest. It would be already to know or see in advance what is to come, to maintain one's bearings. There is thus in deconstruction a purer faith, a more perfect prayer. But it is purer not because it is more sublime or uncontaminated but because it is more penurious, more at a loss, more distressed, wounded, cut, and circumcised and less consoled by what Kierkegaard called the "com-forts of the universal," the consolation of the "millions" who congratulate themselves on their common confessional faiths. Derrida's "ankhoral" faith or desire arises in the desert of *khōra*, where the name of God is the name of what I desire, where the desire for God is the desire for I do not know quite what.[23]

Hyperbolic Phenomenology

If Derrida's radicalizing reappropriation of Husserl moves in a messianic direc-tion, which maximizes desire and expectation, Marion and the new phenom-enologists move Husserl in an equally radical but almost perfectly opposite direction, evolving a phenomenology of an impossible of an almost perfectly contrary kind. Derrida had complained that Husserl's distinction between the empty intending of an object and its fulfilling intuition or givenness turned on an implicit valorizing of fulfillment as the telos of intention, and that needed to be overturned in order to release Husserl's discovery of the virtually unlimited capacity of intention to operate in the absence of fulfillment. But Marion makes the opposite complaint, that Husserl's distinction between the empty intention of an object and its fulfilling intuition or givenness turned on an implicit valorizing of intention that is allowed to set the standards for givenness, and that needs to be overturned in order to release Husserl's discovery of the virtually unlimited power of givenness from its subordination to intention.[24] For Husserl, intention sets the parameters of fulfillment, its standard or high water mark, such that the rush of givenness can rise in principle and at the most to the level of the intention. We intend the whole object but not wholly, *totum non totaliter,* so that the complete fulfillment of the intention is regarded as an Idea in the Kantian sense. Givenness is always the givenness of what is previously intended and there will always be something about what is intended that is not given, a certain excess in the intention that givenness can never reach. But for Marion this ideal limit represents a law for only one class, and that a restricted class, of poor pedestrian phenomena, purely formal or scientific phenomena or the sort of medium-sized and quotidian things of everyday experience. If allowed a universal scope or application, Husserl's account would compromise the full power of his own principle of givenness as he stated it in the principle of all principles (*Ideas I,* §24), which is to take what is given just insofar as it is given and in just the way that it is given, and to do so without prescribing any limits for it in advance. Hence Marion explores the provocative and ingenious post-Husserlian possibility of a hyperbolic givenness that exceeds intention, that overflows the high water mark of intention, or as Marion says, that "saturates" the intention with a flood of givenness.[25] I think that we can also see that what is—dare I say ultimately?— at stake for Marion is a theological issue, nothing less than a noncorrelational *theo*logy such as one finds in Barth and von Balthasar, where God is allowed to be God on God's own terms, without submitting God to prior conditions of possibility, where *theo*logy is confessed to be *God*'s word about God, not our word (theo*logy*). Thus these two possibilities for religion in recent phenomenology also represent two possibilities for theology.

That makes for two alternate and even contrary phenomenologies—or two post- or quasi-phenomenologies—of the impossible. In deconstruction, the experience of the impossible means that we have maximized intention and unfettered it from fulfillment, allowing intention an infinite reach beyond the possible to the unforeseeable *tout autre*. Deconstruction turns on an intention that can never be fulfilled, on a gift that never can be given, where presence, intuition, and givenness are constantly being deferred and detained, where intention is permanently haunted by an ungiveable givenness. That does not frustrate desire but is constitutive of desire's very structure. The very idea of this intention is that it intends what will never be given, *can* never be given, its givenness being impossible, *the* impossible, which we always intend and never meet, which we always desire but never have.[26] For Marion, on the other hand, Husserl is pushed in the direction of a hyperbolic givenness. Here the impossible is the givenness that saturates intention,[27] where what is intended is never adequate to what is given, where the horizon of intentional expectation is not fulfilled, not from defect but from excess, because it is shattered or breached. Fulfillment is frustrated not because intention is cut off from intuition but because intention is flooded with a givenness that it cannot contain or intend. Here, *the* impossible is the unimaginable, unforeseeable, inconceivable, uncontainable, givenness with which we are actually visited, where the best that the understanding can report of its experience is to produce in a stammer the halting concept of that than which no greater can be conceived.[28] Hence instead of the desert and the blindness of faith, Marion speaks of the brilliance of transfiguration, the blindness of bedazzling glory; and instead of messianic desire he describes the gift of messianic advent, the flesh of the Messiah, the Christ, the Anointed One, whose coming among us is described in the Scriptures.

Marion describes a two-fold process of saturation, where saturation is said to be a process of maximization, of raising the level of givenness to a "maximum" or "apex."[29] In contrast to the "poor" or commonplace phenomena described in conventional Husserlian phenomenology, where the measure of givenness is taken by intention or signification and givenness never measures up to the intention, the saturated phenomenon of the first order reverses the process and floods intention with a givenness that the intention cannot accommodate. Marion describes four types or classes of such phenomena—events, flesh, the idol, and the icon—a categorization that he has come up with by way of a rather imaginative stretch of the four classes of categories of the understanding in Kant's first *Critique*. On Marion's view, the subject is inundated in four ways by a flood of givenness that the intentional act cannot contain: (1) when it is caught up in the midst of an uncontainable and incomprehensible historical event (e.g., September 11), one that is so latent with sense that there is no privileged perspective from which it can be seen or put in perspective; (2) in the movements of pleasure or the suffering of the flesh (a recent work is titled *The Erotic Phenomenon*),[30] where, as in the extremes of pain or of pleasure, our conceptual powers are inundated; (3) in the work of art whose color, sound, or form overwhelms the subject like an idol; and (4) in the invisible face of the visible other, which reverses the intentional gaze.[31]

But beyond these saturated phenomena of the first order, Marion posits—in a certain sense he hypothesizes—a higher order of saturation in which a phenomenon gives itself by revealing itself, which is the saturated phenomenon of "revelation." This is said to be saturation raised to the second degree, where the saturation is re-saturated. The phenomenon of revelation, or second order saturation, is defined by the confluence or concentration of all four kinds of first order saturation (quantity, quality, relation, and modality; event, idol, flesh, and icon) in one single phenomenon, thereby constituting a fifth form of saturation, a saturation of saturation, a parodox of paradoxes, the possibility of the impossible.[32] In an important footnote that seems like it belongs in the text, this is described as "revelation" with a small "r," as a mere phenomenological possibility: were there to be a revelation, it would be of just this sort [*quid sit*]. But it is not the province of phenomenology to say whether there is an actual fact of "Revelation," an historically actual Revelation [*an sit*], where this time the word is capitalized.[33] Phenomenology has to do with essence; theology with existence. For example, if God reveals or has revealed himself—let us say, in history or in mystical experience—it would be by means of a saturated phenomenon of the second order. But this is a matter for theology alone to determine and strictly in the terms of theology. That, however, does not mean for just any theology, but rather for rigorously non-correlational theologies, like that of Karl Barth and Hans Urs von Balthasar, which are better at finding the fact of Revelation, but not for correlational theologies like Rahner and Bultmann, which compromise the revelatory in Revelation by prescribing antecedent conditions for the hearing of the Word.

As an example of such a pure possibility, Marion chooses the phenomenon of Christ revealed in the New Testament. It is worth noting that, in principle, other phenomena could have been chosen—the life of the Buddha, say, or perhaps literary phenomena—because the requirement is purely formal—namely, that in a saturated phenomenon of the second order all four features are combined in one.[34] The Christ is, according to quantity, the surprising "event" or astonishing advent of the one who is to come; according to quality, he overwhelms what the phenomenological gaze can bear—"his clothes became resplendent, excessively white" (Mark 9:3). In terms of relation, the Christ is an "absolute" phenomenon, because his flesh annuls every mundane horizon of containment and expectation; and finally, in terms of modality, the Christ is an irregardable icon, the counter-gaze that inverts my gaze, who regards me and constitutes me as witness and disciple, while I am unable to constitute him.

All this is said within the framework of a phenomenological hypothesis or sketch, an uncapitalized *r*evelation as a pure phenomenological possibility. Phenomenological intuition—like historical or scholarly research—does not have the resources or the authority to determine whether there are any transfigured bodies or bodies risen from the dead, the phenomena described in the New Testament, as matters of historical *fact,* in *actuality.* Phenomenology is restricted to "the reduced immanence of givenness" and cannot "judge its actual manifestation or ontic status."[35] Thus Revelation has to do with being, actuality, ontic status—a surprising intrusion of the language of *being* into the saturated phenonomen *par excellence,* where one is supposedly sovereignly free from the conditions of being. In the most classically Husserlian terms, phenomenology brackets existence in order to intuit essence.

The shift to existence, to actual Revelation, is made by shifting from a phenomenological to a theological attitude, from the field of immanent givenness to that of faith. But this precaution, which prevents the transformation of phenomenology into theology, is not without another danger: not the theologization of phenomenology (of which Janicaud warns), but the phenomenologizing of theology.[36] In the end, one is struck by the effect of this analysis not so much on phenomenology but on theology, which, having been loosened from its moorings in speculative metaphysics or dogmatic onto-theology, is then transformed from a speculative to a phenomenological discipline. Uncapitalized revelation is the province of a properly philosophical phenomenology, which, unable to experience the actuality of the risen Christ, which is off limits to it, yet can at least delineate its essential possibility. Were there to be a Resurrection or a Transfiguration, Marion is saying, it would have to be of the following sort: certain transfiguring and hyperbolic events would occur that would intensify the structures of quantity, quality, relation, and modality, and concentrate them into a single phenomenon, raising them up to a second level of just this sort. First order phenomenology then leads to the possibility of second order saturated phenomenon on strictly phenomenological grounds. One is thereby led by the hand of phenomenology to the threshold of theology, which can be crossed only by faith and would represent, if confirmed in actuality, an existential and theological "crowning" of phenomenology by actualizing an essential possibility of which phenomenology itself is not capable. Theology would be what phenomenology wants to be but cannot attain. Without confusing itself with theology, and modestly confessing its own limits, phenomenological revelation points to the possibility of a theological Revelation. Without confusing itself with a purely natural phenomenology, a Revealed theology would take over the controls of phenomenology and describe phenomena of maximum paradoxicality and hyper-phenomenality. One might think of Marion as having written, in effect, a kind of phenomenological counterpart to Maritain's classic *Les dégrées du savoir,* which charted an analogous course from (Thomistic) metaphysics to mysticism to the beatific vision. But with Marion the first philosophy is phenomenology, not metaphysics, and the concern is not with the degrees of knowledge but with the degrees of givenness—*les dégrées de la donation.*

On Marion's telling, Revealed theology has to do not with an essential but with an existential order, with phenomena of an ontically actual Revelation, for example, the hyper-experiences the apostles have of the transfigured body of Jesus or the post-Easter appearances of the risen Jesus. To be dazzled by the brilliance of van Gogh is already an excess, but to be dazzled by the brilliance of the transfigured Jesus is to bedazzle that bedazzlement all over again, to exceed that excess, representing a kind of saturation of saturation. One thus "exceeds the very concept of maximum" to a "givenness without reserve."[37] This would mean, for example, that beyond the saturation undergone in contemplating a great painting, vision is further saturated and pushed beyond itself to the point of a breakdown of vision, to what we might call a kind of "hyper-blindness," a hyperbolic blindness from excess not defect, becoming a sight that cannot see because it is blinded by a dazzling light that exceeds its limits. There is no object given to a subject to see or intuit, no being given to Dasein to be comprehended within the horizon of Being, but rather an excess of givenness that pushes us past intuition, past the subject, and past Dasein. Indeed, so true is this that the very idea of such a phenomenon would be undone if it were *not* bedazzling, for its very idea is to be that than which nothing more manifest can be given.

In the language of traditional philosophy, one is reminded of the allegory of the cave, where one moves, to pursue an analogy, from the common law phenomena of sensible things to the saturating phenomena of the pure forms, to the excess of the good, beyond being, which cannot be beheld directly but only in its effects, where there is a kind of hyperbolic blindness in the hyper-vision of the *hyperousios*, in which the eminence of the forms is concentrated. But the more pertinent comparison is to the language of traditional theology, where the transition from the pure phenomenological possibility of revelation to the actuality of Revelation seems to correspond to the natural and super-natural orders. Uncapitalized revelation is accessible in principle to all without the aid of grace and functions as a kind of preamble to faith, while Revelation is accessible only in and through the gift of supernatural faith, which is a spe-cial grace given by God. As grace crowns and perfects nature, grace perfects phenomenology; the wounded vision of phenomenology is perfected by the aid of supernatural faith.

What, then, are we to make of Janicaud's objections? They are largely un-justified once one takes into account Marion's precautions about revelation as a possibility and Revelation as an actuality. When indeed Marion does tread on ground that phenomenology as such and of itself dare not approach—the transfigured body of Christ, resurrected bodies, and so on—he does so with methodological consciousness of the limits of unaided phenomenological experience, knowing full well that phenomenology and theology belong to two different orders, which meets Janicaud's objections. Nor as a phenomeno-logical matter is there anything improper about the confession of confusion and bedazzlement that Marion makes in his phenomenology of the saturated phenomenon. There are comparable phenomena of confusion in phenome-nology's history—the account of the nothingness of *Angst* in *Being and Time,* or of nausea in Sartre, or of the *il y a* in Lévinas, or even, for that matter, of the destructability (the de-constitutability) of the natural world in *Ideas I.* The commitment of phenomenology to the clear description of phenomena does not guarantee that all the phenomena to be described are clear. One can clearly articulate how something is unclear, in which case the unclarity would be essential to the act.

I do not think that it is phenomenology but rather theology that is at stake here. As I have said, and as Marion himself says in that important footnote mentioned above, the noncorrelational theologies of Barth and von Balthasar are closer to *theo*logical Revelation than those of Bultmann and Rahner, where a correlational theo*logy* submits Revelation to anterior conditions. I do not find what Janicaud finds, that phenomenology has been hijacked by theology, but almost the contrary: that theology has been invaded by phenomenology and that it is theology that suffers a distortion. Now Marion recognizes that the phenomenological turn of theology, rather than Janicaud's fear about the theological turn of phenomenology, is the truer "danger" in all this.[38] The danger is that theology would be taken over by a certain sort of phenomenology, one that has itself been overrun by a principle of givenness that has gone out of control. I say this for the following reason.

Marion thinks that one must either admit the paradox of the saturated phenomenon or one cuts off the possibility of Revelation in advance on the basis of preconceived philosophical conditions or prejudices—for example, naturalistic and reductionistic ideas about what is possible—regarding the limits of phenomenality. What would be more astonishing, Marion asks, that God would have the right to inscribe himself within phenomenality or that we should stubbornly refuse God this right?[39] Capitalized Revelation means that God can enter the world unconditionally and on his own terms. So one is either for the saturated phenomenon or against God's Revelation. (One detects a certain imposition of conditions here in the manner of correlational theology: were there to be a Revelation, it would have to be of just this sort; the condition is that it be unconditionally given.) But there is a third possibility, that one might be just as enthusiastic about Revelation as Marion but have a rather different idea of it than he does, namely, a correlationist idea rather than an ultra-conservative literalism about the text of the New Testament. So the real either/or is to be cast as a choice not between the saturated phenomenon and God, but between two ways of doing theology: either for Barth/von Balthasar or for Bultmann/Rahner—or someone like Schillebeeckx.

One does not have far to look to see what sort of scriptural hermeneutics lies behind Marion's position, which appears committed to a kind of historical literalism about the events of the New Testament. Events that many, dare I say most, New Testament scholars like Schillebeeckx (a decidedly correlationalist theologian) regard as "later theological reflections" or expressions of faith by a later community of faith—namely, that God was with Jesus in a preeminent way—are treated by Marion as having *onto-phenomenological* status, as if they were literal, actual, and ontical occurrences that true believers would have witnessed. Suddenly the language of *sans l'être* becomes quite ontic and existential. In the classical manner of negative theology, these phenomena beyond or without being thus acquire a kind of *hyper-entitative* or *hyper-ousiological* status. Thus the hyperbolization of givenness is implicated in a hyperbolization of being, in an historically actual or ontical Revelation of certain existential hyper-events. This is rather like, indeed it is exactly like, giving angels ontical or hyper-ontical—and therefore an onto-phenomenological—status, instead of treating them as literary vehicles. Rather than treating angels as elements of a narrative, one treats them as entities or hyper-entities, forcing theology to come up with some sort of hyper-phenomenology of angelic visitations that would account for the possibility of close encounters of a phenomenological kind, experiences of hyper-beings of dazzling phenomenality sent to us on divine missions. In an ultra-traditional manner, Marion regards narratives written by non-eye witnesses many years after the death of Jesus in order to give expression to their faith as if they described historical actualities, hyper-entities, that were experienced as hyper-events by the faithful.[40]

Let us consider more closely what sort of phenomena they would be. In the Transfiguration narrative, the apostles experienced the unbleachable "white-ness" of the clothes worn by the transfigured body of Christ (Mark 9:3). This is not the normally visible white of the order of commonplace phenomena like a white sheet, but a white of surpassing intensity. Nor could this white have been recorded by a high tech video camera whose lenses could tolerate higher intensities than can the human eye, had one been available at the time, because a mechanical instrument cannot be outfitted with theological faith. No more than the heavenly voice that says "This is my beloved son" (Luke 9:34–35) could have been detected by a super-sensitive microphone. Such devices would experience only static, however high tech they may be. If the whiteness of the garment worn by the transfigured Christ is neither the white of commonplace phenomena nor of measurable scientific objects, neither is it the exquisite use by a master painter of what seems to be a white not of this world to portray the risen Christ's Resurrection,[41] which is a saturated phenomenon of the first order. It is rather a white that dazzles and confuses the senses in a still higher order, where all four features of saturated phenomena of the first order are concentrated in one phenomenon, a white of such extreme and "unbearable" intensity that the eye is blinded by the excess and brilliance of light,[42] so that one sees without sight. Intuition and fulfillment break down, breached by saturation. These are phenomena beyond phenomena, hyperbolic phenome-nological events that leave phenomenology bedazzled and brought to a halt, having reached the *ne plus ultra* of its own order of natural revelation.

At this point, phenomenology passes the baton to faith: only faith can go farther; only the eyes of faith can interpret. Here, then, Marion introduces a theological hermeneutic action, let us say, a theologico-hermeneutical "as" by virtue of which an otherwise confusing phenomenon is taken as an event of Revelation. But it is at just this point, I think, that Marion's account is overtaken by a kind of theological magical realism (a *theo*logical magical realism). By this I mean a method that treats sacred narratives and narrative vehicles as intensified and bedazzling hyper-realities that have acquired existential onto-phenomenological status. This theological magical realism intensifies narratival elements into super-events, with the result that commonplace realities like garments and voices are transformed into a bedazzling hyper-realities. The result is a kind mythological onto-phenomenology of transfigured bodies, risen bodies, dazzling garments, and the like phenomena taken from the extraordinary narratives of the New Testament. I am reminded of Kierkegaard's warning that there would be nothing in the smile of the knight of faith, no "bit of heterogeneous optical telegraphy" that would betray the infinite, no "crack through which the infinite would peek."[43] It would be paganism to think that the divinity of Jesus would have been detectible, as if there were something in the bearing of Jesus, or the look in his eye, that suggests the divinity. The Revelation is revelation *that* Jesus is the anointed one, not a revelation *of* the divinity, which no one can see and still live. The divinity is a matter of faith. By faith, we are given to believe *that* Jesus is divine, to intend Jesus as divine, but the divinity is not itself *given*. Even if you were standing right beside Jesus you would not see the divinity unless you believed it; and if you believed it, that is because you would not see it. You would believe it even though, indeed, in spite of the fact that you did not see it, which is what faith means. Events like the early Christian experience of the resurrection belong to a phenomenology not of the saturated phenomena but to that of invisible credibilia, to the sphere of what eye has not seen nor ear heard.

Let us pursue this point by distinguishing, in Kierkegaardian fashion, the experience of the first generation, the first followers of "the Way," and the experience of later generations. The first generation must have had an experience of the risen Jesus, which can alone explain what got "the Way" underway. If so, this experience admits and demands a phenomenology. But this would surely be a phenomenology of the Spirit, not in the Hegelian sense, but in the sense of being filled with the Holy Spirit, which means of being filled with faith in one who is in some sense still appearing although he has disappeared, who in some sense still lives on in spite of his dying, who is present somehow in spite of his absence. Such filling is not the fulfillment of givenness but the fullness of the living faith/intention. As the disciples reassembled after the crucifixion they began to experience the Spirit in their midst, wherever two or three were gathered together in his name, and a community of faith grew, nourished by the faith that God somehow lived in Jesus even as Jesus now somehow lives with God, which they expressed in the form of the sacred narratives. The narratives would then express what the community later came to believe about who Jesus was before his death; they would express what the first followers came to believe, how they came to interpret his life and death in retrospect, after his life and death among them had transpired. Presumably anyone who met Jesus in the flesh would have been touched by his presence in a special way; but that is a saturated phenomenon of a purely natural order, namely, of human charisma, at most an iconic experience, but not of divinity. The elevation of that purely human experience to an experience of Revelation would not transpire *on the level of saturating givenness but rather on the level of faith,* of a messianic affirmation of Jesus who was born, had died, and who would come again, an affirmation made in the interim time, in a sphere where givenness gives out, for this is revealed, not by "flesh and blood" but by the Father in heaven (Matt. 16:17).

The subsequent generations do not experience Jesus in the flesh, but they experience the memory of Jesus preserved in these narratives and in the *ecclēsia* gathered around them. The narratives of the extraordinary events do indeed have a saturating element—as *narratives.* These are profound and moving narratives in world literature for anyone who can read, which is a saturated phenomenon of a literary order, which exhausts their intuitive content. But if in a special or higher way they touch the lives of those who belong to the community of believers, those for whom these are the founding narratives, they do so *just because and only because of the community's faith, not because of their phenomenal content.* The sacred stories are actualized or fulfilled when they are repeated for the faithful in a life transforming way in the context of faithful preaching and reading. But that existential actualization is not to be confused with the hyperbolic givenness of the narratival elements in higher order saturated phenomena.

The narrative of the transfigured body of Christ can transfigure the lives of the believers who accept it, or who at least accept its point, on faith. New Testament scholars like Schillebeeckx treat the story of the transfigured body of Christ as a later narratival expression of a faith in the preeminent and transfiguring way God was with Jesus during his lifetime. The great religious narratives, Christian and non-Christian, are what Gadamer would call "classics" of the world religions and as such they represent saturated phenomenon of world literature, that is, stories for which we have no adequate concept. There are many such classics in many different traditions. But to be raised beyond that to the level of an actual religious Revelation requires *faith* in what the narrative is getting at, which is something beyond their intuitive or saturating content, which would be the same for believers and nonbelievers. In faith, the sacred narrative is read or heard and made one's own in a special way that transcends what is given. Faith supplies a particular hermeneutic take, an interpretive slant, an *Auffassung*, that allows the believer to intend something that is precisely *not* given, not properly or strictly *given*, but taken on faith. But the hermeneutic reading does not remove the veil of faith in the point of the narrative, which is an intention without givenness.

The first generation stood shoulder to shoulder with Jesus but they accepted him only through faith; the later generation has preserved his memory in the gospels and the church, but they too accepted him only through faith. As Climacus says, both are on equal ground. Neither has the advantage. Both face the same decision; both must effect the same absolute relation, which turns on faith.[44] Now there is a phenomenology here, even a hyberbolic phenomenology, but it is a phenomenology of *faith*, which is an excess in the order of *intention* beyond fulfillment, of how to take or mean something that is only given in part, and not one of saturating *givenness*, which is the same for believers and nonbelievers, otherwise it is not a phenomenological datum. Doubting Thomas is taken to task precisely for taking his stand with givenness and not being content with unfulfilled intentions. There is, to be sure, a phenomenological *surplus* in faith, but the surplus is to affirm more than one is given to see, to affirm what one is not given to see, which is what makes faith blessed. Jesus opposes the *oligopistoi*—those of "little faith"—not to those who see much but to those whose *faith* is great. The excess and the greatness belong to the gift of faith, which is a matter of believing, which is a matter of intending *without* givenness.

To a certain extent Marion concedes this point, just when he introduces the hermeneutic of faith in order to make room for treating saturated phenomena of the second order as matters of Revelation. But at that point his analysis finds itself resubmitted to the most classical Husserlian constraints in which givenness falls short of intention and swings him over to the side of the hyperbolization of intention. Put in Husserlian terms, the gift of faith is a gift that belongs not to the order of givenness but to the order of intention, for the believers are given to believe what they are not given to see, what they cannot see, which is not given but believed. Not every gift has to do with givenness; for faith is a gift in the order of intention, meaning, or signification. The hermeneutic slant provided by faith supplies what Husserl would call an *Auffassung* [taking up (as)], an interpretive reading or a grasping of something given as such and such, one that is not fully or adequately confirmed but only "in part [*ek merous*]" (I Cor. 13:9) or, as Husserl would say, inadequately given. What is given as a saturated phenomenon is bedazzling and not intended clearly; what is intended through the hermeneutic act of faith is the divinity, which is not given or confirmed but believed. Something is given, I know not what, that is intended *as* a presence of the risen Jesus in the community; it could also be intended *as* an hallucination if one does not have faith or has a different faith. In terms of givenness, faith is an unfulfilled or only partially fulfilled intention, which is why the faith-intention will be given up later on when it is completely filled and passes over into knowledge. As Paul says to the Corinthians, what is seen by faith is seen only "in part," through a veil and darkly; "but when the complete [*to telion*] comes, the partial will come to an end" (I Cor. 13:9–13). Then faith will be no more. Faith is not a saturated givenness but an intending that ventures out beyond the given to take the given as something that it is not fully given as.

Marion has successfully described saturated phenomena on the natural order, but he has failed to establish that the phenomena of Revelation are marked by an excess of givenness beyond intention instead of intention beyond givenness. Revelation turns on the interpretive act of faith, of an intensification of the interpretive intention, not on an intensified or redoubled saturation of givenness. The movement to Revelation is effected by means of an interpretive intention, which outstrips what is strictly given. If it belongs anywhere, what Marion calls the "event of Revelation" as a saturated phenomenon belongs to a theology of glory, "when the complete comes," which is what medieval theologians meant by the "beatific vision." But here and now, *in hoc statu vitae*, there is faith, not glory; and faith means being ready, stretching out intentionally toward a completion that is not yet given, that has not yet come. In my view, the hyperbolic phenomenology of the saturated phenomenon *par excellence* is a brilliant but failed experiment or, at least, let us say, it is a hasty or precipitous one. It is perhaps a suitable way to explain how things will be *then*, when faith is no more, not *now*, when things are given only in part, through a glass and darkly. It is an hypothesis better fit for explaining the possibility not of historical Revelation but of post-historical, supra-historical life in eternity. But in the meantime, on the way from here to eternity, we are compelled to make a more circumspect use of phenomenology *in theology*. The excess in faith is not that of phenomena saturated or doubly saturated with plenitudinous givenness, but of venturing out beyond the limits of givenness into deeper and uncharted seas, out upon the sixty thousand fathoms as Kierkegaard used to say. Blessed are those who believe what they do not see, who hope against hope when all seems hopeless, and who love those who do not seem lovable, which from a Husserlian point of view means blessed are those can sustain their intentional acts of faith and hope and love, which are only fulfilled in part while waiting for them to be filled completely, which is akin to what Derrida calls "desire beyond desire."

Conclusions, Confessions

If at the crucial point, in the transition to the order of Revelation, the phenomenology of saturated phenomena has recourse to faith, and if faith belongs to the order of intention not of givenness, what then finally is the difference between the hyperbole of desire and the hyperbole of givenness? What is the difference between Derrida's hyperbolic faith, his more desert-like and pure messianic circumfessional faith, and Marion's more robustly biblical confession of faith, if both confessions in the end turn on faith and faith is an intention that is short on fulfillment? I have not differentiated these two hyperbolizations of phenomenology as religious and antireligious, but as two forms of religion, two ways for phenomenology to become religious, two different possibilities for religion latent in phenomenology. In Derrida's case we have to do with a more indeterminate and a destinerrant faith, a quest more open-ended and lost, a more desert-like "ankhoral" desire, while in Marion faith is nourished in the lush growth of determinate tradition, more anchored than ankhoral. This is the difference between the faith and desire of what in Derrida's own vocabulary is called an "indeterminate messianicity" and the faith and desire of a concrete messianism.

We might even risk saying that it comes down to the difference between a *theological* and an *atheological* religion, which are to be construed as two different possibilities for religion in phenomenology today, the one with and the other without attachment to a determinate theological tradition. The hyper-bolization of phenomenology undertaken in Marion's affirmation of the impossible is nourished by an identifiable, historical theology, highly sacramental and incarnational and very noncorrelational. But Derrida's is a religion without religion, that is, a religious desire without a theology, a religious desire whose terms cannot be fixed within the framework of a determinate and historical theological tradition, a radical quest and questioning for something, it does not know quite what. Marion's confession is deeply confessional, rooted in a Catholic-Christian profession of faith, in a community and a liturgy, in sacred texts and a *traditio*. Derrida's is deeply circum-fessional, cut off from determinate professions of faith, wary of community, somewhat more lost, so that Derrida does not quite know what he professes when he circum-fesses his faith. Derrida's words are more cut and wounded, which does not count against his religion, for that, according to Jean-Louis Chrétien, is the very definition of a prayer, and prayer is the very stuff of religion.[45]

Derrida says of himself that "I quite rightly pass for an atheist."[46] When asked why he does not just say he *is* an atheist, he responds that he does not *know* whether he is one, whether he is *one,* for there are several voices within him and they do not give one another any rest. That, I think, is also a fitting formula for the believer. Did not Johannes Climacus decline to say that he *is* a Christian on the ground that he could at most lay claim to *becoming* one? To quite rightly pass for this or that, while acknowledging the incessant *sic et non* that goes on within us all—what is that if not the very heart of faith, the very heart of the Augustinian *cor inquietum* that, in several different forms, is echoing down the corridors of continental philosophy today?

Notes

The first version of this paper was delivered at a December 2002 symposium of the American Philosophical Association at the invitation of Professor Merold Westphal, and it has profited greatly from the criticisms Merold has made of it—on the sound phenomenological principle he follows that no good deed should go unpunished. See Merold Westphal, "Transfiguration as Saturated Phenomenon," *Journal of Philosophy and Scripture* 1, no. 1 (Fall 2003). Available at www.philosophyandscripture.org.

1. Dominique Janicaud, "The Theological Turn of French Phenomenology," in *Phenomenology and the "Theological Turn": The French Debate,* ed. Jean-François Courtine, trans. Bernard G. Prusak (New York: Fordham University Press, 2000), 39. This is an extremely useful volume for our purposes as it contains papers by Marion,

Jean-Louis Chrétien, Michel Henry, and Paul Ricoeur, all of which address Janicaud's critique, directly or indirectly.

2. Ibid., 46.

3. Jean-Luc Marion, *God without Being*, trans. Thomas A. Carlson (Chicago: University of Chicago Press, 1991).

4. Jean-Luc Marion, *Reduction and Givenness: Investigations of Husserl, Heidegger, and Phenomenology*, trans. Thomas A. Carlson (Evanston: Northwestern University Press, 1998).

5. Janicaud, "Theological Turn of French Phenomenology," 62.

6. See Jean-Louis Chrétien, "The Wounded Word," in *Phenomenology and the "Theological Turn,"* 147–75; *The Unforgettable and the Unhoped For*, trans. Jeffrey Bloechl (New York: Fordham University Press, 2002); *Hand to Hand*, trans. Stephen Lewis (New York: Fordham University Press, 2003); *The Call and the Response*, trans. Anne Davenport (New York: Fordham University Press, 2004).

7. Janicaud, "Theological Turn of French Phenomenology," 101–3.

8. Ibid., 66–68.

9. Jacques Derrida, *Speech and Phenomena and Other Essays on Husserl's Theory of Signs*, trans. David Allison. (Evanston: Northwestern University Press, 1973), 6.

10. Ibid., 103.

11. Edmund Husserl, *Cartesian Mediations: An Introduction to Phenomenology*, trans. Dorian Cairns (Dordrecht: Kluwer Academic Publishers, 1995), 40–41.

12. Derrida, *Speech and Phenomena*, 52.

13. Edmund Husserl, "The Origin of Geometry," in *The Crisis of European Sciences and Transcendental: An Introduction to Phenomenological Philosophy*, trans. David Carr (Evanston: Northwestern University Press, 1970).

14. Derrida, *Speech and Phenomena*, 90.

15. See Jacques Derrida, "Violence and Metaphysics," in *Writing and Difference*, trans. Alan Bass (Chicago: University of Chicago Press, 1978). Derrida sided with Husserl against Lévinas on this point but he criticized both for their "humanism," that is, for not seeing that *tout autre est tout autre*, that every other enjoys such singularity and transcendence, which is a phenomenon that Duns Scotus had called *haecceitas*.

16. See John D. Caputo, *The Prayers and Tears of Jacques Derrida: Religion without Religion* (Bloomington: Indiana University Press, 1997), for a more detailed and patient unpacking of a certain religious—if atheological—turn in deconstruction.

17. Mark C. Taylor, *Erring: A Postmodern A/Theology* (Chicago: University of Chicago Press, 1984).

18. I will make use throughout of Derrida's quasi-Jewish adaptation of Augustine's "confessions" as a circumcisional "circum-fession." See Jacques Derrida, "Circumfession: Fifty-nine Periods and Periphrases," in Geoffrey Bennington and Jacques Derrida, *Jacques Derrida* (Chicago: University of Chicago Press, 1993). See also Caputo, *Prayers and Tears*, 281ff.

19. For a fuller account of the messianic, see *Deconstruction in a Nutshell: A Conversation with Jacques Derrida*, ed. with a commentary by John D. Caputo (New York: Fordham University Press, 1997), chap. 6.

20. See Caputo, *Prayers and Tears,* 14; and see my review of *Erring* in *Man and World* 21 (1988): 107–14.

21. See Jacques Derrida, *Voyous* (Paris: Galilée, 2003), 62–63.

22. Martin Heidegger, *Being and Time,* trans. John Macquarrie and Edward Robinson (New York: Harper and Row, 1962), 262.

23. For a fuller account of Derrida's experience of faith and desire, see my treatment of his "prayer" in "Shedding Tears beyond Being: Derrida's Experience of Prayer," in *Augustine and Postmodernism: Confessions and Circumfession,* eds. John D. Caputo and Michael Scanlon (Bloomington: Indiana University Press, 2005), 95–114.

24. That is the argument of *Reduction and Givenness.*

25. See Marion, "The Saturated Phenomenon," in *Phenomenology and the "Theological Turn,"* 176–216.

26. One proceeds along a shattered horizon of expectation and foreseeability, where the horizon of the future-present, of the "possible" has been breached. Here one reaches the limits of *voir, avoir, savoir, s'avoir*—let us say, of seeing, securing, savvy, and self-possession—in a movement that confesses its cut, that circum-fesses its "blindness" and need for faith, *il faut croire.*

27. See Marion, "The Saturated Phenomenon," in *Phenomenology and the "Theological Turn,"* 176–216.

28. In Derrida, we have no concept that allows us to have a foreconception of what is to come; in Marion, we have no concept for what is given, which is that than which no greater can be given or conceived.

29. Jean-Luc Marion, *Being Given: Toward a Phenomenology of Givenness,* trans. Jeffrey L. Kosky (Stanford: Stanford University Press, 2002), 28–29, 196–97, 225–26.

30. Jean-Luc Marion, *Le phénomène érotique* (Paris: Grasset, 2003); *The Erotic Phenomenon,* trans. Stephen E. Lewis (Chicago: University of Chicago Press, 2007).

31. See Marion, *Being Given,* §§19–24; *In Excess: Studies of Saturated Phenomena,* trans. Robyn Horner and Vincent Berraud (New York: Fordham University Press, 2002). Marion devotes a chapter to each type of saturated phenomenon: chapter 2 describes the event; chapter 3 describes the idol and the painting; chapter 4 describes the flesh; and chapter 5, the icon.

32. Marion, *Being Given,* 235–36.

33. Ibid., 367 n. 90.

34. Every case of theological Revelation would be a phenomenological revelation, but not every phenomenological revelation would be a theological Revelation.

35. Marion, *Being Given,* 236.

36. Ibid., 243.

37. Ibid., 241.

38. Ibid., 243.

39. Ibid., 242–44.

40. I am not a New Testament scholar, but in these matters I follow the account of Edward Schillebeeckx, *Jesus: An Experiment in Christology,* trans. Hubert Hoskins (New York: Crossroad, 1985), 516–72. That is not just more modernist Enlightenment, more secularist reductionism, which would be an unhappy fate to visit upon me—I

who have made a profitable living out of selling postmodernist ideas. To tell a long story briefly, there are three possibilities here. The first (premodern, before the period of historical criticism) is to simply believe that these are historical accounts. The second (modernist, the stance of the *Aufklärer* and the result of historical critical research) is to simply jettison them as the inventions of superstitious believers. The third is the middle (postcritical, postmodern) position taken by Schillebeeckx. That involves taking seriously the work of modern historical research—and not to do so is I think simply intellectual suicide. It is one thing to have one's horizons shattered, another to simply allow one's mind to be shattered. As Thomas Aquinas said, you get nowhere demeaning the world, or the human minds, that God has created. Otherwise, one has to treat the two Genesis creation myths as a (single) physical hypothesis about the origin of the physical world, to imagine that there really was an Adam and Eve, Jonah's whale, and so on. It gets us nowhere to say if you do not think these are literal events, you are just another *Aufklärer*, as there surely is something between literalism and reductionism. This third option does not, in *aufklärisch* style, reduce the New Testament narratives to fiction or superstition, but treats them as narratives linked to some historical core = x, employing inherited Jewish tropes and Jewish models that express and give shape to a growing faith about Jesus, a faith that one would say, in faith, is prompted by the Holy Spirit. When Jesus asks, "Who do men say that I am?" it is the community of faith asking itself that question and clarifying its faith to itself. This is not an ultra-conservative evangelical but a liberal-Catholic, a liberal-Christian way to think about one's faith, with emphasis on *thinking* about one's faith. See my *More Radical Hermeneutics* (Bloomington: Indiana University Press, 2001), chap. 9.

41. Marion, *In Excess*, 65 n. 14.

42. Marion, *Being Given*, 238.

43. *Kierkegaard's Writings*, vol. 6, *Fear and Trembling* and *Repetition*, ed. and trans. Howard Hong and Edna Hong (Princeton: Princeton University Press, 1983), 39.

44. See *Kierkegaard's Writings*, vol. 7, *Philosophical Fragments, or A Fragment of Philosophy* and *Johannes Climacus, or De Omnibus dubitandum est*, ed. and trans. Howard Hong and Edna Hong (Princeton: Princeton University Press, 1985), chaps. 4 and 6.

45. Jean-Louis Chrétien, "The Wounded Word," in *Phenomenology and the "Theological Turn,"* 147.

46. Derrida, "Circumfession," in *Jacques Derrida*, 155.

Jean-Luc Marion

Crossing Hegel

CYRIL O'REGAN

It is not surprising that surprises happen in a discourse that, throughout all its variations in genre and improvisations in theme, is after all a discourse of surprise. But when one stops looking at the texts of Jean-Luc Marion, one notices something, or at least thinks one does. Or rather one notices a nothing, an absence rather than a something. One does not come across Hegel; one does not see Marion crossing in front of, through, or over Hegel, as he so obviously does with Husserl and Heidegger. Why the nonappearance, the failure to show; why the disappearance? With the example of Derrida and Nancy before us,[1] and, arguably, also Lévinas and Deleuze,[2] and Bataille and Blanchot,[3] we have come to expect Hegel to appear, to occupy attention to the same degree as the other two H's. But this would-be third H, what we might have thought to be the (de)generative H, appears to be silent. Although the system never stops speaking, we don't hear a "gug" out of it (an Irish expression calling on/ at the onomatopoeic resources of the English language). Less than white noise, then, the reader is inclined to think here, as with much else, Marion is again just the opposite of Derrida who pronounces somewhat legislatively in *Positions:* "We will never have finished with Hegel."[4] If Marion were to be goaded into translating the disappearance into a thought he might say with equal brio: "We will never have begun with Hegel." Disappeared and invisible, Hegel is dead in Marion's texts, while Marion is dead to him. Perhaps Marion's texts represent a kind of funeral for Hegel, or better, a memorial service, since we cannot find a casket or catafalque. Certainly, no writ of *habeus corpus* is served; a body would give too much presence.

Why has Hegel disappeared; why is his voice—which Hegel's 'postmodern critics and advocates alike realize is precisely not a voice—never sounded? Why does the eagle not land as he does in Derrida,[5] with such troubling consequences for all discourses, even those that would escape metaphysics? As Heidegger has reminded us, "why [*Warum*]" is the biggest word there is and also the most dangerous. It always anticipates a big, usually, portentous answer that puts the principle of sufficient reason in action. Perhaps no important-sounding answer is necessary. Perhaps the answer is so ready at hand that the question never gets going, that it is refused from the outset. So what would this answer be that would do in the question and articulate itself as a journalistic report, a loosely held together set of remarks concerning Marion's ambitions and what he takes, and feels justified in taking, for granted. Given Marion's commitment to phenomenology as *philosophia prima*, it is possible to say with a significant degree of plausibility that Marion finds Husserl and Heidegger much more productive for his own thinking than Hegel, whose phenomenology not only represents a stage toward its overcoming in the logic and the system as a whole, but arguably is overcome from the beginning, anticipating as it does a more self-reflexive scientific elaboration. Marion does not seem to need independently to establish that metaphysics represents a derailment of the primary impulse of philosophy as *thaumazein,* nor struggle toward a genealogy in which, if Descartes represents an egological exacerbation, Hegel represents its elevation and closure in a fully comprehensive and self-reflective network of categories.[6]

Marion can plausibly be read to presuppose Heidegger's general narrative in which Hegelian *Geist* is the realization of the bad dream of metaphysics in its showing of complete self-presence. And Marion rather easily allows himself to be read as presupposing the specifically French coda of Lévinas and Derrida, and maybe Deleuze, in which the imperialism and violence of *Geist* has been exposed, and what remains is thinking otherwise than metaphysics, whether ethically as in the case of Lévinas, grammatologically or semiotically as in the case of Derrida,[7] and plurally in the case of Deleuze.[8] It is thus with a clean conscience that Marion can proceed to an archeological refurbishing of phenomenology that supplies the proper condition for the fulfillment of its vocation for transcendence. Marion then has decided on a project, and its integrity presupposes determination that in turn involves a negation (a peculiarly Heglian note). After all, why do again what has already been done? Hegel has been done, well done, done in, and done to death in French philosophical thought, and not simply in philosophy, with its different arcs from Kojève and Hyppolite, but in theology also. If Marion is more than a little aware of his French precursors who, after Heidegger, both recommend and limit Hegel, he also can take for granted the work of Catholic commentators and critics of Hegel who are focally interested in the effects of Hegelian thought on Christianity. That is, Marion can presuppose the resistance to Hegel provided in different ways by Claude Bruaire and André Léonard, by Xavier Tillette and Albert Chapelle, and also Fessard and Emilio Brito.[9] Presupposing all of this then releases Marion from the obligation of jousting with Hegel's discourse. It may have taken many to bind the strongman—to recall the Markan adage (3:27)—to out the plots and stratagems of Hegel's discourse, which as Jean Hyppolite showed so exemplarily,[10] takes up all speech and silence, all moves and failure to move. It may take many to provide sufficient prophylactics against the speculative suction and the whoosh of the idea. Yet, it is done, and one can go on in gratitude productively to forget.

Such a reading of Marion's texts undoes my question that seemed to hint at something profound in accounting for the disappearance of Hegel, his uncelebrated death in Marion's texts. Likely there is a lesson here: we could prove our true seriousness by being requisitely superficial. And that would not simply be postmodern license. With a nod and a wink we could provide it with the venerable pedigree of one of the more famous aphorisms of Goethe: "In appearances is the depth." Such an interpretation always remains possible. Perhaps, however, it becomes a little less likely when we turn once again to the disappearance of Hegel and more carefully examine its mode. For what is the mode of disappearance? Is Hegel just not there? Do we notice that he is not there because a place seems to be reserved for his discourse that is not filled? Or does the disappearance of Hegel itself appear as the complement of the disappearance of appearance? If the latter case defines the death of Hegel— as it provides the formal definition of death in the *Encyclopedia*[11]—arguably the former would define Hegel as specter. And now our question is whether Hegel does not in fact appear precisely in the mode of disappearance in Marion's texts. Does this appearance of disappearance, just as with the disappearance of appearance, not require tracking? But asking this question is not without consequence: it seems to put out of action the "psychological-sociological" reading that would suggest that Marion is assured of the discursive extra-territoriality of Hegel, his lack of genealogical potency, and his inability to invade discourse and turn it haywire with the linearity of meaning and shadowlessness of truth. When and where has this appearance entered Marion's discourse? What are its conditions? Especially what are its plenary conditions? I begin with the first complex question, and say that essentially the appearance of the disappearance of Hegel happens at the beginning. It has always begun; and can never be completed. Hegel spooks all of Marion's texts, some more than others, never quite giving them rest, provoking them despite Marion's best efforts to ignore or not reflexively take account of the strange goings-on, the way Hegel slinks in to have his say, or turn a picture inside out, or just makes a general noise rendering concentration difficult. Moreover, the signs are not good that the interference will remain limited, as if something like a treaty has been signed and cosigned. The trajectory could be war, as it has been in the case of Derrida.

I want to say that the death and specter of Hegel can be read off texts from all three sectors of Marion's intellectual metropolis: from Marion's historical-genealogical work on Descartes, who represents not only the crossroad of the metaphysical tradition, premodern and modern, but also its accomplishment and its excess; from Marion's excavation of the nature and limits of phenomenology as this requires pealing off Heidegger's occlusion of the phenomenon even as it demands moving beyond the limitations set not only by Husserl's Cartesianism, but by the nature and limits of intentionality itself, thereby releasing Husserl for a future capable of transcending Heidegger's ontological recasting; and finally, and in my view exemplarily, from Marion's more "theologically aspirated" work, that is, those texts that both dare to enlist and interpret discourses that speak to a phenomenon that appears precisely as incognito, and which disturbs and exceeds the sphere of immanence. In this essay, I focus on the second and third sectors of Marion's work, and fold discussion of the presence of Hegel in Marion's historical-genealogical work into my discussion of these. I privilege neither the theologically aspirated band of discourse nor the later more nearly pure phenomenological band, since while Hegel does not appear as Husserl and Heidegger do—thus in some sense he disappears—yet this disappearance appears across both sectors of work, troubling it, wrinkling its smooth folds. Traces of Hegel found in both sectors of Marion's textual production indicate an encounter not fully brought to explicitness. One cannot help wondering whether there is not operative at some implicit level in Marion's texts just the kind of crossing in front and the crossing through and over that are features of Marion's treatment of Husserl and Heidegger. One cannot help speculating also how long the explicit encounter can be avoided.

Hegel and the Emergence from Invisibility in Marion's Theologically Aspirated Works

In speaking of "theologically aspirated" works I mean to mark that portion of Marion's work in which the discourses of the Christian tradition are read to mark an impossible opening beyond the regime of the self and the regime of metaphysics. Moreover, I mean to mark it without prejudice. That is, the somewhat ripe locution is intended to avoid outright "theological" specification. Janicaud and others have made such a designation pejorative: it indicates the confounding of the phenomenological and theological enterprises, which compromises the former as rigorous science and as first philosophy.[12] For present purposes Marion's "theologically aspirated" work is defined by the trilogy of *The Idol and Distance, God without Being*, and *In Excess*. My operative hypothesis is that these texts cannot adequately be understood without reference to the third, what we have been calling the "missing," H.

In *The Idol and Distance* Hegel appears only to be resisted.[13] The resistance to Hegel is most noticeable in chapter 4 on Pseudo-Dionysius (139–95; F 183–250), but implicitly present in chapter 3 on Hölderlin (81–138; F 115–79), even if the constitutive object of resistance in this text, as in the later *God without Being*,[14] is Heidegger's post-metaphysical thought, and derivatively postmodern construals that can be assigned to the Nietzschian fold. However secondary, resistance to Hegel there is. It is prosecuted essentially on three fronts that overlap and imbricate: (1) the possibility for a discourse of the divine; (2) the proper understanding of difference as truly radical and embracing; (3) the Trinity understood as the ultimate horizon for the appearance of Christ who defines the icon. I begin with the first area of the rendering visible of, and the resistance to, a Hegel who tends toward invisibility. Guided by a concern for the possibility of a discourse of the divine, Marion sings the praises of the sixth-century Syrian monk, Pseudo-Dionysius. In arguing that in texts such as the *Divine Names* and *Mystical Theology* Denys points to an affirmation beyond negation that is precisely not a super or a synthetic predication, Marion makes it clear that the prohibition is not generic but rather bears on Hegelian *Aufhebung*. "It is not," he writes, "a question of speaking of the Supreme Being in a predication of which it would be the object. *Nor is it a question of letting the Supreme Being, as absolute subject, state a predication about itself and by itself"* (139–40; F 184) (emphasis added).[15]

Here as elsewhere throughout this text Marion thinks of Hegel as summed up by the speculative proposition. This stance on Hegel, arguably, was made plausible by Hyppolite's *Logic and Existence.*[16] Further it is authorized by Derrida and Nancy,[17] even as, or especially as, they feel that Heidegger's overcoming of Hegel in general, and his overcoming of Hegel's overcoming of the traditional logic of the statement in particular, remains insufficient, and that Hegel's alternative to the standard view of predication requires a separate and deeper overcoming. While Marion's resistance to Hegel on this and other fronts remain in the shadow of his overcoming of Heidegger's ontological difference (141; F 185), it is not simply an implicate of this overcoming. At the very least, this resistance to Hegel has a semi-independent status. Resistance on the front of language takes the specific form of going beyond the polar opposition of speech and silence (143, 150; F 187, 195) that sets the ground conditions for the fundamental Hegelian wager for speech that represents totally transparent enunciation—thus annunciation—of the divine. The Hegelian wager does nothing less than remove the gap between speech *about* the divine and divine speech about itself. Needless to say, Hegel's break with Aristotelian-based predication does nothing to humble the metaphysical ambition of discourse; indeed it absolutizes it. Anticipating a distinction between idol and conceptual idol that is more adequately articulated in *God without Being,* one can say that as the acme of onto-theology—identifying God not only with Being but with a particular being (albeit the highest being)—Hegel's discourse represents the supreme form of "conceptual idolatry." It is a discourse that reflectively justifies idolatry, as it articulates Spirit as the archeoteleological foundation for all appearance.

Still, even if Hegel's discourse could be regarded as a development of prior metaphysical discourse, there are nonetheless at least marks of difference. Certainly, Hegelian discourse undoes the priority of the speech of the empirical subject, even as it invests discourse in the charisma of the actual accomplishment of more than finite speech. In its labors Hegelian speech lives the fruits of the promise of its own blessedness. Marion then seems to agree with others before him in the post-Heideggerian line that the glamour of Hegel requires its own apotropaics. Just as importantly, however, one might recur to the line of *Communio* French commentary. Here the references to Bruaire

(n. 147), the author of the important *Logique et la religion chrétienne dans la philosophie de Hegel* (1964) and an explorer of the metaphysical dimensions of the gift or *ontodology*, is symptomatic.[18] In light of Hegel's being rendered visible as a thinker who requires a discrete and specific overcoming by way of supplement to the overcoming of the metaphysical tradition that he realizes, one can make a case that the doxological matrix of praise and prayer (for present purposes I ignore differences that critics of Marion such as Derrida attempt to exploit)[19] that displaces predication also implies the overcoming of Hegel's simulacrum: the self-referential worship [*Gottesdienst*] in and by thought that brings to completion thought's idolatrous self-celebration in the Stoics (e.g., Epictetus) and in Spinoza.[20]

The second front along which Hegel is brought to visibility and resisted concerns the interpretation of difference. *Distance* points to a difference distinct from ontological difference. But once again Marion is dissatisfied with inference: to go beyond the ontological difference is *ipso facto* to go beyond any and all metaphysical notions of difference, modern or classical. While Heidegger may restrain, he is unable to put to rest Hegelian difference [*Differenz*] or alienation. To use Nancy's expression—but to change his meaning—Hegelian difference remains "restless."[21] Whatever the ratio of rest and restlessness in Hegel's own texts, it cannot be put to rest in ontological difference. The key passage, which in its language transparently evokes Heideggerian commentary on Hegel, is the following:

> This means that the distance does not separate us from the Ab-solute so much as it prepares for us, with all its anteriority, our identity. It denotes, therefore, the positive movement of the Ab-solute which, through it being set at a distance, ecstatically disappropriates itself from Itself in order that man might receive himself ecstatically in difference. In receiving himself from distance, man comprehends not only that distance comprehends him, but that it makes him possible. (153)[22]

Two observations are in order. First, in the above passage the language of the "Absolute" suggests the presence of a conversation with Hegel. Indeed, Hegel's language is used in order to bring out the difference between "distance" and Hegelian difference all the more clearly. The hyphenation in the English translation of "Ab-solute" draws attention to how it would have to be thought if it were to be refigured as distance: the Ab-solute is the event of establishing a difference that cannot be economically contained. At base, Marion is looking at Heidegger looking at Hegel,[23] and naming differently than Heidegger the true nature of absolution. It is distance that gives participation in the "unparticipable" (Maximus).[24] Distance is precisely not the difference that defers participation only to grant it through the mediation of difference in which difference is dialectically overcome. This dialectical schematics is what reinscribes onto-theology in discourse in and to the second degree. Marion agrees formally with Eckhart and Silesius as they are read by Heidegger and, of course, with Heidegger who reads them, that there is no "why" [Warum] for distance and participation. Only a "because" [Weil] can be supplied. Yet materially "distance" crosses over Being, and, most importantly, crosses over the crossing out of Being. In finding the need not to take for granted the closure of the Hegelian system, in not taking it as a dogma, Marion synthesizes two French lines of reflection on Hegelian difference: the Derrida–Nancy line, on the one hand, and the line that can be seen most clearly in a Communio Catholic such as Bruaire, who retains Hegel's language of the absolute in the hope of chastening it, transforming it from an archeteleological discourse into a discourse of origin.[25]

This brings me to my second observation. The above passage represents a denial of Hegel's interpretation of a totally contrastive Jenseits as the paradigmatic form of Christian transcendence. To intrude an Anglo locution, "distance" implies a "'noncontrastive" mode of transcendence.[26] Marion argues that Dionysian aitia supports this kind of distance, as does Maximus's view of participation. With the virtue of hindsight—and some dimming of the lure of Heidegger's monolithic genealogy in which the discourses of creation are reducible in the long run to discourses of efficient causality—neither Thomas nor Augustine need be omitted from Marion's rather elite and Greek-speaking group.[27] Perhaps with sufficient disentanglement from Heidegger, one can risk saying that Latin is not univocally a language of fall, and French hopelessly the language of mere aperçu.

The third front along which Hegel appears, or fails to disappear, is more-explicitly christological and trinitarian. The lesson supplied by Pseudo-Dionysius is nothing less than that the discourse of "distance" is from the very beginning both christologically and trinitarianly inflected. It is the filial relation, which defines Christ, that thereby defines both the space of relation for all of us and its doxological or adorative quality. Christ then establishes the parenthesis within which existence and history happens. But if instead of distance there is dialectically overcomeable alienation, then filiation is put in question. Christ becomes archetype rather than image and his sonship a symbolic counter able to be filled out by world of nature and human spirit. More, Christ becomes not simply contingently replaceable, but necessarily so, if one gives in to the seduction of a Hegelian-style pneumatology in which appropriation constitutes the reality of its provocation.

In a telling footnote in the context of a profound discussion on the Trinity and kenosis (174 n. 54), Marion makes a reference to the concluding paragraphs of the *Encyclopedia of the Philosophical Sciences* (§§564–71), the *locus classicus* of Hegel's syllogistic redescription of the Christian narrative of God's acts. Convinced by Bruaire's 1964 book on Hegel and religion of the pivotal nature of these passages for the interpretation of Hegel,[28] but interpretively more in line with the later Bruaire and other members of *Communio* such as Léonard and Tillette,[29] Marion judges that there is nothing innocent about Hegelian conceptual redescription of the Christian narrative. Such redescription justifies the above substitutions and displacements. Moreover, conceptual makeover (take-over) removes all gratuity and makes distance itself relative in the dialectical absolvance that defines Spirit, which cannot be identified with the Holy Spirit, whose reality is constituted in its complex relations to Son and Father. Here one could say that Hegel's thought is not simply resisted, but in the strict sense measured against the cross that it seems to affirm only to deny. To cross Hegel's *Aufhebung* is to uncover the double-cross of Hegelian narration and the concept, and in effect to double-cross the double-cross by demanding that christologically and trinitarianly inflected discourse bear the unbearable weight of the cross that it so promiscuously announces. To cross Hegel's discourse then is to double-cross, but also recross it and establish the distance that provides the measure of the play between the triune God and human beings whose wildness is neither erring (Heidegger, after him Derrida) nor anticipatory fulfillment (Hegel).

But resistance to Hegel and the various modes of crossing, double-crossing and recrossing are not confined simply to chapter 4. Reading backward from the chapter on Pseudo-Dionysius, the chapter on Hölderlin (chap. 3) can be read as having an anti-Hegelian subtext. Manifestly this chapter offers a reading of Hölderlin's great hymns with the intention of rescuing them from Heidegger's erasure of the gestures of distance that transcend the ontological difference, of compensating for Heidegger's effacement of their kenotic-christological aspect (107, 109–13; also 121–23; F 142, 145–48, 157–59), and of correcting for

Heidegger's singular misunderstanding of the Johannine regulation of Hölderlinian apocalypse, as this is exemplified throughout Hölderlin's major poems,
but perhaps most self-consciously in "Patmos" (105–7, 115; F 141–43, 150–510).[30]
If Marion is assisted in his reading by prior French reflection on Hölderlin,[31]
and if the powerful compression demonstrated in the chapter owes something to the original adaptations of Hölderlin in Char and Bonnefoy (possibly Blanchot),[32] arguably the broad outlines of his position are provided by
Pzywara and possibly Balthasar.[33] Given this determination, it would be easy
to miss Hegel were he to appear. But could an appearance be canceled beforehand? Would it be plausible that discussion of Hölderlin could really avoid
altogether Hegel, Hölderlin's friend and companion, his other, who does not
sing "In lovely blue [In leiblicher Bläue]," who does not submit to the madness
of praise and prayer,[34] but instead in the greatest of all acts of aggrandizement
refines himself out of existence to allow the great autolic poem of the system
to appear? Is it not reasonable to entertain the suspicion that metonymy
alone will determine that at the very least Hegel is folded into this chapter, that
resisting and crossing Heidegger will not exclude resisting and crossing Hegel?
And when one turns to the text and looks more bifocally, the hypothesis seems
to be confirmed. In addition to the theme of distance, perhaps even specifying
it, there are at least three leitmotifs that involve using the cross to diagnose,
resist, and heal a Hegelian emptying of the figure of Christ and the displacement of authority [exousia] onto a nontranscendent Spirit.

The first of these is the Eucharist as the means of establishing not only the
proper relation of human beings to the one who is sent, but also the proper
relation to the one whom he names. The eucharistic site of measure is, as
Marion teases out with extraordinary lucidity, a feature of any number of
Hölderlin's poems (119, 125; F 154, 160) and, of course, above all "Bread and
Wine" (131–33; F 166–69). Even if, as Marion suggests, eucharistic site is less
an interpretation than a principle of interpretation, it can be misinterpreted,
indeed subjected to or substituted for by, another principle of interpretation.
This happens when Real Presence is understood to be without remainder a
function of human appropriation. Raising the prospect of this deformation,
pits Hölderlin against Hegel, who thinks that Real Presence is established in
and by the community and not of our expropriation in and by Christ (116–17;
F 151–53). One can also read Hölderlinian opposition to Hegel on the Eucharist
to be a synedoche of more general resistance to the comprehensive pneuma-
tological displacement that Hegel licenses through a focus on John 16:7. Indeed,

the implication is that Hegel is guilty not only of the fallacy of misplaced concreteness, but also of *eisēgēsis*. By contrast Hölderlin's thought on the Eucharist is holistic, and thus catholic, perhaps even Roman Catholic, and his reading of John faithful and untendentious.

The second leitmotif of importance in unfolding the christological discrimen that regulates discourse of the divine concerns the elaboration of kenosis (connected intrinsically in passage on 110; F 146). In his elaboration Hölderlin genuinely follows Phillippians 2:5–11 in its theological intent as well as pathos (110–13; F 146–48). Speaking of "The Celebration of Peace [*Friendenfeier*]" Marion writes:

> The Hölderlinian meditation here fixes, then, one of the most decisive christological texts of the Christian tradition. There is nothing acciden-tal about this, nor, to be sure, any arbitrariness to the reading, but the inescapable necessity of a convergence, in considering the same paradox. Or if one wants, on condition of understanding the paradox as certain vision of glory and its oblique arrival (*paradoxos*)? (112–13; F 148)[35]

But paradox is just what Hegel will not allow. With Marion it is Hölderlin not Kierkegaard who teaches this lesson, who is, perhaps, better able to teach the lesson, because his language is more nearly slanted at the right angle to repeat the intent of the great hymn. The love affair with kenosis notwithstanding—both inside and outside the divine—Hegel does not repeat the hymn. In his discourse kenosis is limned in such a way as to abolish filial distance, inter-preted in such a way to generalize the tremendous coincidence that Chalcedon as well as Luther attribute uniquely to Jesus Christ.

Third, and finally, there is the leitmotif of apocalypse in which a contrast between the Hölderlinian and Hegelian modes is insinuated. The Hölderlinian mode is valorized: it is nonspecular and nonparousiac. The implied contrast is with the apocalypse form of Hegel. Stated thus, Marion neither transcends Heidegger's reading of Hegel nor Heidegger's own apocalyptic inclinations, which, it could be said, he both reads from or into Hölderlin. Indeed, were he to stop here, Marion could be understood to approve rather than reprove Blanchot's apocalyptic degree zero and Derrida's *apocalypse sans apocalypse*.[36] But if Marion's apocalypse predilection, as figured by Hölderlin, is necessarily interruptive, it is not aniconic. As Marion reads "Patmos," apocalypse is pos-sible only in and through the icon. For his purposes what matters is that the icon be icon and not idol, not a function of desire or the exhaustion of seeing. And the exegetical lesson here is not that Revelation is an impossible text, the economic text *par excellence,* as Blanchot, Derrida, and Caputo would have it.[37] Rather, as a text regulated by the Gospel of John and the hymn of Phillippians, it is a work of the apophatic sublime, which amounts to saying that it is a work of sublime apophasis.[38]

The interpretations of Pseudo-Dionysius and Hölderlin in *The Idol and Distance* suggest that phenomenological description, on the one side, and biblical text and theological commentary, on the other, read each other and do so in essentially a hermeneutic framework. While this mirroring has engendered criticism it is clear that phenomenological description is not made hostage to theology, nor that a systematic program of correlation is going on, or could go on. This doubleness of discourse implies—although it does not state—a resistance to Hegelian discourse with respect to the "science of the experience of consciousness" and, obviously, to Hegel's view of science itself.[39] But it also implies resistance to Hegel's couplings of experience and Christianity, and science and Christianity. Both Pseudo-Dionysius and Hölderlin show that Hegel is guilty of misdescribing experience, and misconstruing the relation between Christianity and absolute discourse. No discourse can catch up to experience; just as no discourse can name that which provokes it. What provokes is what eludes. Thus the need for noncategorial speech—a discourse of hyperbole and allusion.

I turn now to the theologically aspirated text that Marion's critics as well as his followers take to be his most magisterial, that is, *God without Being.* This text also pulls Hegel from the general drift of his invisibility, and even if it is not evident that Hegel has been made urgently visible, and thereby visibly urgent, clearly Hegelian discourse represents the consummate expression of conceptual idolatry in which thought finds in what most dazzles it nothing more nor less than the satisfaction of its constitutive desire. Relative to the earlier *The Idol and Distance,* the text displays a comparable measure of resistance to Hegelian encroachment on Revelation and a comparable effort to compensate for the crossing out of Christ and the cross that identifies him. Unsurprisingly, there is a significant degree of continuity with *The Idol and Distance* regarding the specific aspects of Hegelian discourse that are resisted as well as the manner of that resistance. The first and third foci of resistance discernible in

The Idol and Distance are once again to the fore, that is, Hegel's view of language, especially as this is focused in the speculative proposition or sentence (chap. 7) (189–92; F 266–70), and Hegel's christological and—by implication at least—his trinitarian reflection. Less obvious is the distinction between distance and Hegelian difference, although a good case can be made that the distinction lies in the folds between the resistance to Hegel's language and the resistance to Hegel's conceptual articulation of the Christian narrative that (a)voids christological inflection ironically as it engages in a reflection on Real Presence (chaps. 5–6, esp. 168–69; F 238–39; also 151; F 212–13).

In line with many commentators and critics on Hegel,[40] Marion finds that the clearest and most developed articulation of Hegel's position on Real Presence is in *Lectures on the Philosophy of Religion,* wherein Hegel subjects Real Presence to pneumatic and eschatological torque. The manner of resistance is also relatively continuous to that exhibited in *The Idol and Distance.* Resisting the imperialism of Hegel's discourse, and subjecting his discourse to the rigors of Revelation (in Christ), tends to occur in the spaces between a positive articulation of a God who is beyond Being, and a resistance to Heidegger's trap: formally allowing the prospect for such a God, while materially containing such a God within the ontological difference.[41] Marion desires a recrossing or a different crossing of Being than Heidegger's that at the same time avoids idolatry (chap. 3). Allowing for this, however, it is fair to say that chapters 5 and 6 concerning the eucharistic site of theology and the Eucharist as gift respectively involve a more explicit engagement with Hegel than with anything found in *The Idol and Distance.* In addition, it could be argued that *God without Being* also brings out more clearly the relation between the more formal and material elements of crossing Hegel.

I begin with the more nearly formal element of the speculative proposition whose importance to Marion's thought has already been recognized by Thomas Carlson and laid out with considerable subtlety in that most discreet of texts, *Indiscretion.*[42] What seems to engage Marion is the promise in the speculative proposition not only to open a way beyond metaphysics, but to open a way beyond metaphysics that is specifically Christian. Marion acknowledges in the final chapter (189–92; F 266–70) that Hegel's view of the speculative proposition—indicated awkwardly by a meta-proposition: "God is Being" or "God is Spirit"[43]—is superior to classical subject–predicate discourse in its dynamic articulation of an irreal grammatical subject in and through the attributions that define and actualize it as a real subject.[44] Marion would agree with the critical assessment of Hyppolite and Nancy that the speculative proposition is less intrinsically nominalistic,[45] more appreciative of the disclosive element of reality, than Aristotelian-style predication.[46] On the most favorable reading—the upper end of the French spectrum of French reading—then, Hegel's view of the speculative proposition has not been delivered a knockout blow by Heidegger's critique of Aristotelian logic and grammar, thus its continued status as contender with Heidegger's view of language and poststructuralist alternatives.

Unwilling to support the view that precisely as still standing the speculative proposition is adequate to truth, in chapter 7 Marion makes some fairly standard objections to this view.[47] Specifically, Marion argues that Hegel's view is overdetermined with respect to semantic context, erases the speaker, and ignores the possibility of first-person language being ecstatic or confessional. Most importantly, however, Hegel's view of the speculative proposition represents the betrayal of the promise to chart a way beyond metaphysics that is specifically Christian. In the end, the speculative proposition inscribes Christian discourse in metaphysics. For Marion, the contrary to the speculative proposition is neither the Aristotelian view of predication, Kant's theory of judgment, nor Derridian semiosis: it is rather liturgical discourse, in particular, Christian liturgical discourse. Here Christ is the reality that lies beyond predicative discourse and makes it possible. It is Christ also who bridges the gap between the I and locution. Marion's comments in chapter 7 essentially represent a gloss on the christological view of language articulated in chapter 5, "the eucharistic site of theology," where Christ is taken to be center and principle of theology. The details of the articulation of the eucharistic site bring out with greater clarity the full extent of what is at stake. To deny, as both Marion and Hegel do, the Reformation principle that Scripture is self-interpreting forces a decision as to what constitutes the principle of interpretation, Christ *or* speculative logic. Marion's opts for Christ as the fundamental interpretive principle.

Implicit resistance to Hegel can be read back from chapter 7, where Marion expostulates on the Trinity as the horizon of the christological or Word event. Chapter 7 features the contrast between the logic of dialectics and the logic of charity, the option for the logic of charity, and the indication that this logic cannot be anything other than trinitarian. Marion makes it clear here, as he does in *The Idol and Distance*, that trinitarian discourse is essentially the discourse of filiation, the experience and symbolization of the relation-distance between Father and Son that is anterior and posterior to thought. It can neither be substituted for by a dogma—dogma finds itself therein—nor can it be sublated by a self-constituting series of categories that intercallate subjectivity. It follows that what represents the other of this agapaic trinitarianism is the speculative trinitarianism of Hegel that articulates the speculative proposition,[48] and is folded into the logic of the syllogism that attests to the overcoming of gratuity. That the contrast is laid out in the final chapter suggests that overcoming Heidegger's overcoming of metaphysics will involve a new overcoming of Hegel, only the outlines of which are provided, but which represents in any event something of a titanomachia. For Heidegger's overcoming of Hegel does not appear to be definitive, does not seem to be able to prevent the recurring of Hegel as a Christian simulacrum beyond the ruins of fideism and natural theology.

This is a concern that Marion shares with a French Catholic commentator on Hegel such as Léonard. It is also, however—although for quite different reasons—a concern that Marion shares with Derrida, particularly the Derrida of *Glas*. Sharing a concern, however, is not sharing a position or adopting the same set of hermeneutic postures. In *Glas* Derrida reads Johannine Christianity, as focused in the Eucharist (esp. 167–70),[49] and Hegelian discourse, as a discourse that hides the effects, the waste products,[50] of discourse, to be implicated and mutually enhancing. Hegel does nothing more nor less than "translate John into German" (75).[51] Indeed, without expressly calling on Hegel scholarship, but with typical ingenuity, Derrida reads Hegelian discourse to interpret and elevate Christianity,[52] which finds a considerable part of its identity—perhaps even all of it—in the Gospel of John. At the same time, for Derrida, Hegelian discourse dissimulates its own presuppositions. In particular, Hegelian philosophy disguises its dependence on the symbolic power of Christian discourse as it recodes its symbols and makes them pertinent to modernity that repeats and veils exclusions of otherness, that goes under the different names of matter (e.g., 70), Jew (e.g., 73), woman-mother (e.g., 1, 3, 4, 115, 117), and sister (150ff).[53] The aim of Derrida's tactical discourse is to make the bell toll for Hegelian discourse as it effectively tolls for all those voices it makes inaudible.[54] With Lévinas's 'critique of Hegelian theodicy still not out of mind, and with Lévinas's 'demand for justice very much to the fore,[55] Derrida's seriously playful and playfully serious text implicates Christianity in the discursive machine that justifies and perpetuates death.[56] Here Hegelian discourse is a Christian simulacrum in the sense that a discourse is too much infected by Johanninely Christianity rather than too little.

While Marion does not explicitly engage Derrida's text, and certainly his text cannot be read as *contra* to Derrida's *pro,* it is not a little interesting that, for Marion, Hegelian thought is a Christian simulacrum precisely because it betrays Johannine Christianity—which is capable of phenomenological redemption—even as it recalls it. The relation between Johannine Christianity and Hegelian discourse is then thoroughly critical. The Eucharist does not validate the future present (170–72; F 238–40). Rather it refigures and energizes time, thereby overriding—among other things—periodization between premodern, modern, and postmodern. Nor does the Eucharist imply the obliteration of matter that forms the base of signification. In the Eucharist, the material base finds its transcendence (162; F 226). Similarly, the introduction of the glory of the cross into the economy of Hegelian discourse destroys the specifically Christian view of glory that insists that glory and cross always be thought together, and that the glory of the cross is constitutively excess, that which cannot be thought, that which cannot be adequately rendered. And lastly, the vision of Johannine Christianity is radically different from the Heglian. Johannine aesthetics or Johannine apocalypse can never be pleromatic in the strict sense;[57] it is, as Hölderlin saw clearly—and perhaps also the poets René Char and Yves Bonnefoy who follow him[58]—always but a glimpse, a vision moreover that does not exclude the prophetic.

That Marion is subject in particular to the theological influence of Balthasar is clearly indicated in both chapters 5 and 7. Not only do we see in both Marion and Balthasar that John provides the broad map of divine glory beyond aesthetic domestication, but also that John offers a fully fledged dramatic articulation of paschal mystery that finds its fundamental grammatical form in the union of divine and human will (John 6:38). Of course, the option for John is not simply a matter of exegetical preference, but also a preference for a particular scoping within the theological tradition, particularly that found in Maximus the Confessor. Extrapolating from *The Idol and Distance,* in which Maximus both interprets Pseudo-Dionysius and completes Hölderlin,[59] it is evident that Balthasar's and Marion's fundamental orientation involves a quite different take on Christology in general and John in particular than that found in Hegel, whose interpretive pivot is provided by the linkage of John 1:14 to the reflections on the glory of the cross. In repeating Balthasar on these crucial christological issues, Marion likewise is involved in a repetition of Balthasar's anti-Hegel trinitarian program, centered on Christology, and resting on a fundamentally different reading of the priorities in John than that offered by Hegel,[60] and expressing a fundamentally different posture in reading, one that is oriented toward the presentation of mystery rather than the rigors of explanation.

As I have already indicated, it is Marion's articulation of Real Presence that represents the most conspicuous feature of his resistance to the Hegelian project (chaps. 5–6). When Marion objects in these chapters to the underscoring in contemporary reflection on the Eucharist of the constitutive character of the community context and reference, the basis of the argument is not simply the theological superiority of a Catholic view of transubstantiation over the alternative Reformation views, whether Lutheran or Calvinist. While it is safe to infer that Marion does in fact prefer the Catholic view, perhaps the important ingredient in his argument for a strong view of Real Presence is his genealogy of the Hegelian code of the community view. As Marion points out, *Lectures on the Philosophy of Religion* finalizes the Reformation critique of transubstantiation by determining that the shift of priority from object to subject is underwritten by the shift of emphasis from Christ onto the Spirit that attests to him (162–63, 166–69; F 226–27, 234). If the Hegelian view is philosophically toxic in that its productionist bias reinscribes metaphysics, it is also theologically toxic in that once again it invests itself in the Johannine facade, specifically that of John 16:7, (151; F 212–13), only to undermine Johannine substance. Of particular concern to Marion is the Hegelian figure of recollection [*Erinnerung*] that represents the particular way in which Hegel articulates presence, and at the same time more generally his articulation of time.

In arguing that the modern anti-transubstantiation position—as this is either explicitly expressed or simply assumed—falls foul to Heidegger's objections that it reinscribes the "ordinary view of time" (170, 181; F 239, 257)[61] and thus the priority of the present as the present of attention, Hegel is inextricably implicated. He is so essentially for two reasons. First, as we have seen, it is Hegel who provides the legitimation of the contemporary view that, while it has a philosophical and theological basis, is often more atmosphere and sensibility than argument. Indeed, as has been pointed out by the eminent Hegel scholar Walter Jaeschke,[62] it is Hegel who links the theological critique of transubstantiation with the genealogical and more nearly philosophical argument of the possibility and actuality of the elevation of the subject in and perhaps as modernity.[63] Thus, fatefully the enucleation of the *cogito* and the career of transubstantiation are mapped onto each other. Second, in *God without Being* Marion is fully aware of Heidegger's diagnosis of the deformation of the "ordinary view of time," which has Hegel's articulation of time as one of its supreme instances. The ecstatic temporality of the Eucharist is what destroys past and future as dependent on recollection and anticipation, the having been and to be that form a closed circuit: in the Eucharist the "past" is the immemorial, the immemorial one who inscribes the individual and community into the dynamic of christological kenosis; the future is not simply the not-yet, but the unanticipatable future (outside), or the absolute future that confirms an opened self in participation [*epektasis*] (173–76; F 245–47).[64] Perhaps, even more obviously here in Marion's critique of Hegelian time than with the speculative proposition, Balthasar provides a precedent for Marion's discussion, even if he does not provide the finesse. As is well known, in volume 5 of *Theo-Drama* Balthasar argues against Hegel and Moltmann that Christ is constitutive of time past and to come.[65] Read together with *Glory of the Lord* (vol. 1), in which Balthasar reflects specifically on the Eucharist, Balthasar adumbrates at least a view of eucharistic disturbance and deregulation of discourse and temporality that undermines in advance a conceptual takeover of the hostile sort enacted in Hegel.

I come now to the third and last of our theologically aspirated texts in which Hegel's discourse falls short of full disappearance and where it appears only to be resisted. *Prolegemona to Charity* belongs broadly to the horizon of *The Idol and Distance* and *God without Being*.[66] The essays, which guided in general by the phenomenon of love represent loosely associated raids on the inarticulate or the invisible, are phenomenological in their basic orientation, although once again phenomenology is asked to transcend itself beyond the limits set for it by Husserl and Heidegger. The range of analysis and exposition of phenomena in the text is broad. If in his first essay on evil (1–30; F 13–42) Marion comes closer than anywhere else in his work to the kind of hermeneutic phenomenology practiced by Ricœur in texts such as *The Symbolism of Evil* and *Fallible Man*, between the bookends of the *Symposium* and the New Testament Marion deploys a host of literary figures to illuminate the obscurities of human desire. Baudelaire, Dante, Balzac, Proust, Stendhal, Bernanos, and many others are called on throughout the essays. The influence of Lévinas both with respect to phenomenological style and theme is enormous. Yet, at the very least Marion tempers—one might say "tampers with"—the absolute contrast between *eros* and *agapē*,[67] with the latter, however, getting the last word and thus serving as an exclamation point and regulative principle. In an important sense, however, the final essay in the English translation—"What Loves Knows"—is more decrescendo than crescendo; it is a kind of anticlimactic afterword that offers a kind of x-ray of the structural contrast between an ignorance that attempts to cross the ambition of absolute knowledge only to be crossed by it and an unknowing knowing that marks the beyondness and excess of love, whose humility humiliates knowledge.[68]

The climax of *Prolegomena to Charity* is undoubtedly reached in the theologically aspirated "The Gift of Presence," which is chapter 6 in the English text (124–52; F 147–78), although it is the final chapter in the French edition. This essay essentially repeats the reflections in the *hors-texte* of *God without Being*, in its recurring to Real Presence, and in its unveiling of the insistence of Christ who makes it possible. It seems that here, however, Marion has moved already a little beyond his earlier text in that Real Presence is taken to effect a distention or anamorphosis of the phenomenological space that indicates the possibility of a tear in the tissue of immanence. This distention and possible tear intercallates or calls into being the doxological subject.

It is just at this critical point—(*krisis* in its Greek sense)—that Hegel appears. For it is Hegel, not Heidegger and not even Husserl, who has pledged absolute fealty to the unbroken phenomenological field and the autonomy of the subject that serves as its foundation. If Hegel is right, then Christ cannot serve as breach and a fundamental dislocation of the autonomous subject. Christ will always have been accountable, if only retrospectively. He will always have been a semantic unit that requires appropriation to be effected. The singularity of Christ is simply the effect of grammar, our inability to own up to the incredible constructive power granted by Spirit in its mode of "recollection." If the correspondence between this critique of Hegel and Kierkegaard's critique of Hegel prosecuted in the *Philosophical Fragments* cries out for further exploration, more in plain sight is Marion's resistance to a particular hermeneutic of John, which isolates and privileges 16:7 to the neglect of the christological curtailment of the rest of chapter 16 (139; F 165), and the rampant eucharistic symbolism throughout the text all of which is indissolubly bounded up with Christ's singularity or particularity (140–42; F 166–68). As we have seen already in *The Idol and Distance* and *God without Being*, resisting the hegemony of John 16:7, in which Christ speaks of "going away [*apeltho*]" in order that the Paraclete "comes [*elthē*]," indelibly marks a text as resisting Hegelian transumption. Christ cannot be pneumatologically displaced-replaced (142–43; F 168–69): he cannot be metaphorized, end up elsewhere and as something else. The unrepeatable life and death and death and life of Christ crosses and undoes the autonomous subject in both its individual and more than individual modes, shaves away the subject to reveal its elemental pathos and adorative center.

For the purposes both of phenomenological license and theological warrant, it is not John 1 that is regulative as it was for much of patristic theology, but rather John 6:38.[69] Marion knows well that he is not blazing a trail here. In *God without Being*, Marion shows that he is aware that Maximus made this text the lynchpin of a dramatic Christology that sets the basic terms of his trinitarian thought. Marion is also aware of the pivotal role John 6:38 plays in Balthasar's aesthetics and dramatics, where the claims of Maximus's exemplary elaboration are pressed. But most importantly, he understands that Balthasar's repetition is directed against Hegel's epical construal of the figure of Christ wherein the dramatic tension between human and divine will is overcome in a dialectic dominated by recollection. The other crucial aspect of the Hegelian view that derails the very prospect of transcendence of immanence concerns the way in which in Hegel's reflection on Christian representation the narrative elements of Resurrection (142; F 168) and Ascension (145; F 171) are elided into the community of appropriation. While this has long been a significant theological criticism of Hegel, one certainly that has had some currency in the *Communio* group, especially in Léonard and Brito,[70] the specific form it gets in this text is that the elision of these events effaces an identity that is derived in significant part from actions-passions of Christ, where this identity is the guarantee that the circle of immanence will not close. The issue here is the appearance of what transcends appearance, the name that gives the Name that is nameless. It is this Name who gives the unique name to a subject restlessly seeking to construct, who precisely as renamed is unnamed and named for the first time, and who as named is now able for the first time to praise and to pray, to acknowledge the receipt of the gift of the name, and empowered ecstatically to pledge itself to the repercussions and ricochets of the gift.

Hegel and the Emergence from Invisibility in the Phenomenological Texts

We move now to another trilogy, or at least another textual threesome. It only makes sense that the disappearance of Hegel is broader and deeper in that part of Marion's *oeuvre* that attempts in a fully focused way to bring phenomenology as *first philosophy* beyond the purely contingent limitations set by Husserl and Heidegger. Now while the details of Marion's return to the original promise of phenomenology, that is, its commitment to transcendence, are in the end individual, this is not an entirely new French story. French thought since World War II—on both its literary byways and its philosophical highways—has been engaged in a concerted effort to secure the access to experience at its most ample, and to find means of expositing phenomena beyond the Cartesian straightjacket of Husserl, but also through and beyond Heidegger's double regression, to Dasein in the first instance, and *Sein* in the second, both of which function to legitimate the horizon of possibility as an ineluctable. From the vantage point of Marion's own project it is the most recent phase in such refurbishing, defined by the work of Lévinas and Henry, that provides the proximate, but also the most appropriate, context for his own development. For while Marion tends to pay back all debts by (re)exploring the form and boundaries of phenomena and offering fuller and richer description, nonetheless it is true that he more nearly starts from than moves toward that dimension of the self traumatized by the other, a self always already undone by a substitution that counts as a revelation and by the ecstasy of flesh that eludes the reduction to the body and the doubling of representation. Given the overall shape of the rehabilitation of phenomenology, it is not surprising that the silence of the third H is exacerbated. At the same time, the identity of Marion's proximate precursors forbids us saying outright that Hegel is fully dead, his name removed from the register of possible and actual existents. Both of these thinkers are serious resisters of Hegel, and their presence in Marion's texts include the ghost of Hegel they would exorcise.

At first blush the expectation of a deeper and broader disappearance seems to be borne out by *Reduction and Givenness, Being Given,* and *In Excess.*[71] As one would expect the eclipse of Hegel is starkest in a text that returns to the origins of phenomenology with a view to a revision that chastens, indeed, upsets its egological frame. In *Reduction and Givenness* Husserl is interrogated with respect to his exclusion of the possibility of a third reduction beyond the eidetic and phenomenological reduction, that is, the reduction to givenness, which involves an excess of intuition over intention. The radicality of Heidegger's *apophansis,* the disclosure of the phenomenon of which he speaks so eloquently at the beginning of *Sein und Zeit* §7 is questioned. Questioned also is Heidegger's claim to have transcended Husserl. Indeed, developing a line of thought, which is perhaps inchoate in Lévinas and Henry, it is the work of Husserl rather than Heidegger that remains more faithful to phenomenology's promise of transcendence, even if this promise is betrayed by the developing egological axiomatics.

Ignoring a complex and rich discussion in which Marion outlines the redemption of phenomenology's promise both denied and made possible by Husserl, I confine myself to making the point that in elaborating phenomenology in the mode of the future present, while remaining true to phenomenology's commitment to detailed and precise description of things as they appear, Marion seems to cut off the very possibility of the appearance of Hegel. Very little in Hegel, indeed, very little even in the *Phenomenology,* could be classed as "pure phenomenology."[72] Hegel, however, refuses to disappear entirely. Marion's discussion of Husserl's attempt in *Logical Investigations* to be faithful to a "this" and an "I" that are not taken up in a discourse that sublates particularity and idiosyncracy (27; F 45) obviously recalls the early chapters of Hegel's *Phenomenology,* which evince precisely this vocation.[73] Hegel also appears when in chapter 3 Marion gives general approval to Heidegger's influential genealogical point about Hegel's fulfilling a specifically modern egological trajectory in which knowledge and being are identified, thereby rendering transcendence impossible (84, 93, 223n; F 78, 98).[74]

Undoubtedly, by far the most important of these intrusions of Hegel in Marion's discourse is betrayed in the text's resistance to a conclusion in Hegel to which Descartes—in one of his basic drifts—provides the premises. Hegel articulates the egological frame theologically in a way that is at best inchoate in Descartes, largely because of his balancing emphasis on the infinite that disarticulates the ego and its horizon.[75] More specifically, in Hegel the ontological argument is a means by which the self elevates itself to, and defines itself as, Spirit.[76] Conversely, Hegel articulates the ontological argument not as concluding in existence beyond language and concept, but in an actuality [*Wirklichkeit*] that is self-differentiated absolute subjectivity whose milieu is that of the concept. Thus understood, Hegel's discourse serves as something of a flaming cherub regarding any prospect for transcendence; it serves precisely as the prohibition of excess. If only eventually it turns out that coming through on the unrealized promise of phenomenology involves more than correcting for the inadequacies of Husserl and Heidegger. It also involves rescinding the exile of Hegel and arguing with him. In particular it implies an unflattering comparison with Descartes, whose ontological argument represents a point of rupture with the foundationalist rapture centered on the *ego cogito* that finds its completion, because reflexive justification, in Hegelian *Geist*.

The pattern of disappearance and appearance of Hegel is similar in *Being Given* as that text continues to explore the possibilities of phenomenology, or rather explore what makes phenomenology possible and provides it with real meaning. It is evident that this text has no time for Hegel's discourse that, in its most adequate form, has no time for the time of discourse (55; F 81). This criticism is not an unfamiliar one. It finds a precedent in Ricœur,[77] and even more generatively in Heidegger at the end of *Being and Time* (§82) where, in addition to a general critique of Hegel's view of time as repeating the metaphysical transcription of the "ordinary view of time," Heidegger exposes the Hegelian commitment to the abolition of time precisely as the "being-there [Dasein]" of the nontemporal concept (*Phenomenology,* §§802–8). The truly important appearance of Hegel occurs in the crucial paragraph §24 (236–42; F 325–42) in which Marion brings to a head his discussion of the fundamental modes of the saturated phenomenon—that is, the modes of event, flesh, idol, and icon—by considering revelation as the synthesis of the prior four. In the context of saturated phenomena, which are formally defined as modes of givenness in which intention is exceeded by intuition, as in the context of the text as a whole, "revelation" is still more nearly a phenomenological than a properly theological counter, despite the correlation with Christ.

I have more to say about the correlation later, but for the moment it suffices to say that the base contrast is that of "saturated phenomenon" versus "unsaturated or nonsaturated phenomenon" (the second term is left unspecified). This contrast, however, both supports and hides another—namely, the "intraphilosophical" contrast between revelation and manifestation.[78] By contrast with manifestation, in its properly phenomenological deployment "revelation" signals a fundamental alteration in the laws of appearance that dictate the nature and scope of adequacy and inadequacy regarding the apprehension of phenomena. Phenomenologically rather than theologically deployed, "revelation" denotes a given for which no conditions—transcendental or otherwise—can be supplied. Or stated otherwise, "revelation" provides its own conditions of appearance. Given the synthetic nature of revelation—as "saturation of saturation" (235; F 326–27)—the general resistance to manifestation is, of course, the synthesis of specific resistances.

Understood thus, one begins to see folded in Marion's general resistance to Hegelian manifestation [*Erscheinung*] prior resistances on more local, that is, more modal levels. The assertion of the "event" as the punctiliar that cannot be semantically reduced in a archeoteleological temporal field has a checkered history in modern French thought. Moreover, the assertion has something about it of the parabolic. In the different forms given to it by Lyotard, Deleuze, and Bourdieu, Hegel's exclusion is often the neuralgic point and thus the point of debate. While the excavation in French thought of "flesh" as a primary phenomenon can be pursued without explicit reference to Hegel, as is evidenced in the work of Merleau Ponty, it does not always proceed without such reference. This is so especially in the exemplary exploration of Michel Henry,[79] whose exploration of the dynamics of the of "auto-affection" of self unavailable to semantic and conceptual redescription takes place against the backdrop of a confrontation with Hegel's excision. Obviously, with respect to the mode of the icon, Marion repeats his own resistance to Hegel in earlier works such as *Idol and Distance* and *God without Being,* while also recalling the resistance to Hegel shown and said in Lévinas's articulation of the face of the other, who deposes the ego to uncover a receptivity prior to activity and passivity.

Obviously, given the importance of this text in Marion's later work, much more can and should be said about each aspect of the "saturated phenomenon." Calling for particular attention are Marion's close linking of Christ with icon. Is Christ the supreme instance of iconicity who other individuals follow at a distance, or in whom they participate? What phenomenological features are adduced or adducable that allow Marion to move beyond Lévinas on this front? Again, if Christ is phenomenologically given as icon, can any other figures in any other religion function iconically? Can religions function iconically without reference to a person—for instance, the law in Judaism, the Koran in Islam, the eightfold path in Theravada Buddhism? The evident rehabilitation of the idol also provokes a host of questions. Does art and art alone satisfy idol in the positive sense? Is this form of art already religious? And what does this say about religions of immanence that typically would be the subject of monotheistic critique? Not all of these questions are focally pertinent to our present concerns, but almost all of them bear on it ultimately, since more than any other modern philosopher Hegel is exercised by the disclosive possibilities of art, the question of the historical and systematic relation between art and religion, and the relative adequacy of the disclosive potential of the different religions.

Of course, none of these questions can be answered, indeed, they properly cannot even be asked, unless Marion secures—and keeps secure—the distinction between "revelation" as it functions within phenomenology, and "Revelation" within the language game of theology. Were one reducible to the other, either the enterprise of phenomenology is compromised or that of theology, or probably both. The lexical marking off of "revelation" from "Revelation" in §24 is intended to prevent the confounding of a phenomenological and a theological use. On the surface Marion's position is just the opposite of Hegel's, who has no compunction about reducing the theological rendition to that of philosophy construed in terms of manifestation. In fact, at one point Marion seems to echo Kierkegaard's critique of Hegel in *Concluding Unscientific Postscript* by suggesting that Revelation brings with it its own conditions and thus is free to upset the demands of phenomenality. "It could be that the fact of Revelation provokes and evokes figures and strategies of manifestation that are much more powerful and subtle than what phenomenology, even pushed as far as the phenomenon of revelation (paradox of paradoxes) could ever let us divine" (245; F 339–40). This stance is, of course, as much Barthian as Kierkegaardian. However, beyond the question of its lineage, and even beyond the question of Marion's intention to prevent "revelation" from functioning hegemonically, there is the question of coherence. Given his agenda of (re)defining the phenomenological field in and by "revelation," Marion is entitled to the courtesy of allowing to pass the occasional hyperbole of how revelation itself can be regarded as setting the conditions of whatever appears (118, 235; F 174, 325–26). Still, it does seem on occasions that the worry about the imperialism of "revelation," and by implication the imperalism of phenomenological method, comes as something of an afterthought. Focused on making claims that are as universal in scope as those found in Husserl and Heidegger, Marion has not thought through fully the consequences for Christianity of the claim for the universal rule of revelation, as the phenomenality of phenomenality, and has insufficiently protected Christianity from reduction.

In Excess, which completes the trilogy, arguably represents an amplification of §24 of *Being Given*. "The icon and the Endless Hermeneutic" is a kind of summary essay that covers much the same ground (104–27; 125–53), while opening up the revisionary phenomenological potential of Kant and Descartes, perhaps especially the latter, whose thought on the infinite functions as regulative. Not surprisingly, Lévinas, who is singularly responsible for emphasizing this aspect of Descartes's thought, and thus as gesturing to the possibility of Descartes's being considered not as the rivet of the metaphysical tradition, but as an opening to its undoing, is a major presence in this text. At the same time,

it is not simply an accident of composition, something after the biblical manner of leaving the good wine to last, that these essays on the various forms
or modes of the saturated phenomenon culminate in an essay on negative
theology. In "In the Name: How to Avoid Speaking of It" (128–62; F 155–95),
negative theology is now presented as the discourse of "revelation," thus the
discourse of the saturated phenomenon (158–62; F 190–95). It is this resituating of negative theology as a phenomenological discourse rather than a
hermeneutical discourse—which has as its object the biblical text and through
this text, Christ—that bears the burden of Marion's answer to Derrida's critique in "Sauf le Nom" of Marion's earlier articulation of negative theology
in *The Idol and Distance*.[80]

Marion does not yield much if anything to Derrida respecting hyper-
ousiology and doxology. Despite Derrida's preference for the hypo-ousiologial
khōra, his complaint that doxology intercallates a subject of address (144;
F 173), Marion continues to assert these not only as plausible, but also as truly
necessary post-metaphysical ciphers, indeed, ciphers that are more adequate
than Derrida's suggested alternatives. Defending his earlier account of negative theology necessarily involves a recall of negative theology's resistance to
Hegelian thought's commitment to consuming nonknowledge, to digesting
nonsense, and to enlisting apophasis in the economy of predicative discourse
that inevitably betrays it. On the level of implication, then, Marion cannot
but continue the struggle with Hegel. Hegel's is the first and last word against
excess, the first and last word against revelation. Hegel's discourse represents
their death. Correspondingly negative theology represents the death of Hegel's
discourse, specifically of its semantic triumphalism and its self-satisfaction
in and as the pleroma of self-consciousness. Negative theology then both represents and performs the death of its death by meaning and concept, and thus
represents and performs the opening to life.

As the resituating of negative theology helps bolster the possibility of distention, anamorphosis, and tear in and of the tissue of immanence, it can
also be thought of as redefining the field of the battle with Hegel. The battle,
it is now thought, is best fought on the play of appearance on the screen of
consciousness rather than on the plane of theology, where the concern is the
responsibility of thought to Revelation. Marion would undoubtedly agree with
Balthasar, Tillette, and others that Hegel is completely deficient from a theological point of view. But this would be to take the step outside the realm of
phenomenology that Marion does not in fact take. Proceeding without theo-

logical presuppositions, Marion is convinced that revelation is the appearance of the tear in the field of appearance, the outside of its inside. Lévinas sets the basic terms of this use of revelation, which if positive in its primordiality recalls—at the very least peripherally—the non-other that would deny all otherness and difference.[81]

In defending a purely phenomenological view of revelation here and in *Being Given,* Marion offers a response to criticisms that his phenomenology is impure since it depends on unwarranted theological suppositions. Correlatively Marion's distinction between "revelation" as that which distends and tears the phenomenological field, and "Revelation" as an interruptive event taken by the Christian community to relativize and found the historical, constitutes something like an after-the-fact justification of the distinction between spheres of discourse in the theologically aspirated work. That is, read backward from the point of view of *In Excess* and *Being Given,* Marion can easily suggest that there exists no fundamental confusion between phenomenology and the discourse of theology in the theologically aspirated trilogy. Here it is not simply a matter of paying attention to what is "inside" and what is "outside" the text, but also a matter of distinguishing between the icon as a phenomenological possibility and its actual instantiation, or more broadly between revelation as a possibility and its actuality in Christ as this reality is ecstatically celebrated and enacted in the Christian community.

Borders: Sheer and Sheared Vision

Enough has been exhibited about the appearance of the disappearance of Hegelian discourse, the specter that both complements and completes the disappearance of appearance, the death of Hegelian discourse in Marion's texts. Not even in his obvious marginalization of Hegel in his second, non-theologically aspirated trilogy does Marion manage to inter Hegel. Marion's text certainly do not effect a *requiescat in pace.* At the phenomenological limit, at the boundary of the possible and impossible, which is the troubled place of relation between philosophy and theology, Hegel pervasively, if not always exigently, haunts Marion's texts. Here Hegel has privileges denied Husserl and Heidegger. Unlike the latter two, Hegel is constitutively a thinker of borders. While in Husserl phenomenology's proscription of the theological officially only excludes religion in the dogmatic mode, as *Reduction and Givenness* and

Being Given in particular make clear, Marion thinks that Husserl's actual articulation of phenomenology as "presuppositionless science" masks a presupposition by seeming to insist on the impossibility of a tear within immanence. Thus, the prospect of a nondogmatic religiousness and not simply the actuality of its dogmatic doublet is excluded. The final word of the historical Husserl—who is, of course, lower than his possibility—concerns, then, the nonrelation of the discourses of philosophy and religion, and certainly the nonrelation of philosophy and theology.

Marion recognizes well the greater complexity of Heidegger's discourse that reproves the discourse of the Christian tradition while continually calling selected aspects of it to mind. But throughout both the theologically aspirated trilogy and the phenomenological trilogy a coherent and critical picture of Heidegger emerges that issues in a serious questioning of the intrinsic hospitality of Heideggerian thought to Christianity. Not only does Marion take seriously Heidegger's distinction between the ontological and the ontic, as elaborated in *Being and Time,* he also pays attention to numerous statements made subsequently by Heidegger respecting the differences in method. More importantly, he thinks that Heidegger's consistent and insistent affirmation of the regulative function of the ontological difference gives one reason to worry that Heidegger's so-called 'methodological atheism' is not so indifferent to the claims of religion, or at least not so indifferent to Christianity.[82] Ontological difference functions not only to critique deficient construals of difference in the Western tradition, but also to set stringent limits to the possibility of appearance. Notwithstanding Heidegger's rhetoric of transcendence and the religiousness of his discourse,[83] however, Marion judges that in the final analysis Heidegger's discourse is a discourse in which the impossible does not appear. This judgment is central to Marion's theologically aspirated trilogy. Heidegger's discourse not only stops short of the religious, but effectively imprisons or misprisons it within its own coordinates of possibility. Thus, the need to cross and double-cross Heidegger's discourse, while taking advantage of it, and especially in the guiding protocols of *God without Being* to cross-over the crossing-out of Being. It is no less central in the second trilogy, which attempts to redeem the promise of phenomenology as first philosophy by making regulative the third reduction, the reduction to givenness. In the language of the later trilogy, Heidegger's discourse is not in any unequivocal sense the discourse of the saturated phenomenon.[84] Certainly, Marion is of the opinion that in none of its phases does Heidegger's discourse become a discourse of revelation. As we noted earlier in our treatment of *Being Given,* revelation represents the limits of what is possible in phenomenology, because it represents the appearance of that which transcends to the point of subversion the very conditions of appearance. In any event, in the case of Heidegger, as with Husserl— although for much more complicated reasons than simply guaranteeing a first philosophy—there is once again an exclusion, and the assertion of the impossibility of relation between the discourses of post-metaphysical philosophy and Christianity in either its nondogmatic or dogmatic registers.

As I have said already, relative to Husserl and Heidegger, Hegel is constitutively a thinker of borders, of all kinds of discursive borders, for example, the borders that separate and unite art, politics, history, philosophy, and thus constitute their space or interspace, their "between." Hegel is superbly the thinker of the border(s) between, or the nexus between, the discourses of religion and philosophy, and paradigmatically between Christianity and philosophy. Crucially, for Hegel the border is open, not sealed: considerable traffic flows back and forth between Christian representation [*Vorstellung*] and concept [*Begriff*] without their becoming mixed and confused. Christian representation in general, and especially the Christian narrative,[85] which pivots on the Incarnation and Cross, engender reflection while soliciting conceptual purification and justification. Hegelian thought supplies both. The obvious question is whether anything like parity between Christianity and Hegelian philosophy is preserved, and more specifically whether Christian symbols and forms of life are blessed or cursed in their translation. The question is also unavoidable, given that the concept deposes religious presuppositions in the very act of acknowledging them.

In works such as *Concluding Unscientific Postscript* and *Philosophical Fragments* Kierkegaard experiences the border between faith and reason to be violated in Hegelian mediation [*Vermittlung*]. With its operation of *Aufhebung,* philosophy proves irradicably invasive. Similarly, Franz Anton Staudenmaier,[86] Hegel's most vitriolic nineteenth-century Catholic critic, believed that Hegelian system was totally monistic not only substantively, but also methodologically: in the Hegelian system philosophy is elevated into a master discourse that subsumes all other discourses as relatively adequate adumbrations. In twentieth-century theology Barth and Balthasar offer a similar diagnosis: Hegelian philosophy abolishes the very terms that constitute the between. More interested in articulating the between than Barth, indeed, making its elaboration a constitutive element of his theological vocation, Balthasar comments on the fact and the consequences of the Hegelian discursive nexus in which the discourses of Christianity and philosophy are confounded and mixed. No more than Hegel remained faithful to Chalcedon on the level of substance, does he remain faithful to Chalcedon as a principle of relation between discourses that validates their inseparability while maintaining them as unconfused.

If Marion is not unfamiliar with this history, the proximate context of his somewhat noiseless contestation with Hegel's view of the border is provided by Ricœur and Lévinas, on the one hand, and twentieth-century Catholic commentators on Hegel, on the other. In his well-known essay on the topic of the relation between representation and concept,[87] Ricoeur argues that representation can never be made a function of concept. Against Hegel's image of circle, which presides over the sublation of Christian representation or symbol, thus compromising their integrity, Ricoeur suggests the image of ellipse. Similarly, in his articulation of alterity, Lévinas insists on the collateral nature of religious and philosophical discourses. However much the discourses of philosophy and religion mirror each other, religious presuppositions ought not to be imported into phenomenology, just as philosophy cannot arrogate to itself the right to police religious discourse.[88] In addition, the Catholic philosopher and commentator on Hegel, Claude Bruaire, insists on the noninvasive nature of philosophy while equally insisting that philosophy not be an "embarrassed theology." At the same time, Bruaire does not think that the "border" between discourses constitutes a "no-mans-land" with discourses hermetically sealed from each other. The border is a relation of mutual exposure and solicitation. One can and should place Marion at the intersection of this double tradition of decision about relation.

The generative image of relation offered by Fessard—one of the first Catholic commentators on Hegel in France—seems apropos for Marion's position:[89] truth is a mountain. From one side the activity of philosophy tunnels; from the other side the irrupting absolute reaches toward experience; their jointure is secret. As with all images, this one obscures and well as discloses. But it does disclose. (i) The activity of philosophy is a necessary but not sufficient condition for truth. It requires the supplement of unforeseen irruption. (ii) Barred is a panoptic seeing that would espy and articulate the point of intersection of philosophical eros and Revelation. No such seeing would remain properly finite. Or put in Marion's terms: there is no discourse that can synthesize the possibility and actuality of gift, revelation, and Revelation. With Fessard, with Bruaire, but now also with Marion, all finite seeing is monocular. We can look from the point of view of tunneling *or* impact, philosophical eros *or* Revelation, or the discourses and practices to which it gives rise and which interpret it, but not both simultaneously. From Marion's point of view, binocular vision illustrates the truth of Hölderlin's enigmatic utterance: "Oedipus has one eye too many." Sheer vision is sheared vision, vision cut in half, vision with a halo of blindness. It is almost impossible to stop the reverberations of the figures of seeing: on the borders sheer vision is necessarily cyclopean.

Marion's subscription to Fessard's image serves as a block against the imperialism of Hegelian philosophy in which Revelation is made a function of philosophical eros and impact a function of tunneling. The separation of discourses that Hegel would confound, however, has the effect of proscribing any *method* of correspondence, since this would imply a binocular view that could supply rules of correspondence. While the proscription applies to all views of correspondence justified in terms of a theory or meta-theory, it has particular implications for the Ricœurian model, which, however heroically it struggles to maintain the autonomy of philosophical discourse and theology as the discourse of revelation, nonetheless specifies the rules of correspondence, which in the end are provided by a general hermeneutic to the regional hermeneutic of revelation. Importantly, however, a proscription of a method of correspondence is not the same as a proscription of correspondence. Logically speaking, correspondence could continue to be asserted: but now it would be a matter of perception, thus aesthetics; now a matter of persuasion, thus rhetoric.[90]

One way of typifying the movement in Marion's thought from the first to the second trilogy is his becoming more (a)stringent in his interpretation of the unmediatability of the discourse of philosophy—which may reach to revelation—and the discourse of Revelation as such. That a philosophical discourse might plausibly be claimed to be contaminated by religious or theological presupposition becomes a searing objection. While he vigorously defends his earlier theologically aspirated texts from such a charge—he had after all clearly distinguished what was within the bounds of phenomenology and what was "outside"—in his second trilogy Marion takes no chances. Cutting his philosophical cloth to measure, Marion articulates a phenomenology without possible or actual appeal to Revelation. This separation is, as we have seen, especially ostensible in *Being Given,* where its reiteration plays the apologetic role of attesting that disciplinary boundaries have been observed. Of course, "revelation" is a possible—indeed legitimate—philosophical counter, even as

Marion thinks he has shown that the phenomenological project can be completed only by marking the distention or anamorphosis of the field of immanence.

It would be unfair to suggest that Marion is involved in a reaction formation to the accusations of Janicaud and Derrida of theological foundationalism, on the one hand, and methodological impurity,[91] on the other. One can see the decision, and its correlative asceticism, operative in the very earliest works. The asceticism has something of the tone of Descartes and the substance of Kant. Philosophical discourse and the discourse of Revelation should meticulously be filtered from contaminants supplied by the other. Marion focuses on the philosophical side, leaving it to others, to the magisterium, Barth, or Balthasar in some moods, to filter out philosophical contaminants from the discourse of Revelation. The main question that arises is whether the insistence on the immaculate state of discourses, required among other things to resist Hegelian *Aufhebung*, offers too much prophylaxis, proves in the end too ascetic, too anchorite like? Maybe not, for is not the phenomenological milieu extraordinarily rich and ample, covering all sorts of phenomena even to the very boundaries of the phenomenological field itself in which distention and tear is possible? Moreover, the New Testament, and John's Gospel in particular, are capable of being phenomenologically reduced and relieved.

The news is not bad for philosophy—or at least not all bad—although the richer its domain, the more the flora and fauna of appearance proliferate, the more philosophy allows the rendering visible of the invisible, the more suspicion of theological infiltration. But the suspicion need not be a justified one, and from Marion's point of view is devoid of real warrant: through phenomenology philosophy has restored itself (active) or has been restored (passive) to its original sense of wonder [*thaumazein*], perhaps even to its more original Platonic sense of event [*exaphnēs*]. But is this necessarily good news for Revelation? What content is left to theological discourse? Is Christian discourse put out of work in a way that goes deeper than its bracketing? Are the discourses and performances of Christianity purely factical, their authority different in kind from the persuasive authority of philosophy? Moved by the need to separate and distinguish, and in particular to avoid the hegemony of philosophy, as instanced so clearly in Hegel's articulation of the relation between philosophy and religion, does Marion not risk reducing Christianity to the pure "positivity" that proved both provocation and justification for Hegelian *Aufhebung*?

Given Marion's attestation of the value of Rahner's thought, the question of whether Marion is involved in a repetition becomes unavoidable. Allowing for the irony of Marion's obvious affinities with the thought of Barth and Balthasar, a *prima facie* case for repetition is ready at hand. Both Rahner and Marion would engage in a concerted expansion of a philosophy that moves beyond the objectivity or objectness that has served as the fundamental horizon of philosophy, and especially modern philosophy. As is well known in a classic text such as *Spirit in the World*,[92] Rahner articulates this opening beyond objectivity, which is nothing less than the opening to transcendence, by means of a metaphysics of experience that doubly inflects Thomas with Kant and Heidegger. The opening disclosed in and by philosophy, an opening usually veiled, and graspable only by attention to what is given prethematically, is not predicated on faith. By contrast, operating in the field beyond metaphysics, Marion denies himself recourse to Thomas or any premodern metaphysical surrogate thereof, and retreats behind Heidegger to Husserl, burrowing into the "unsaid" to bring to fruition the transcendent potency of *philosophia prima*.

Still, even if we agree that something like a repetition were afoot, we would have to add that the repetition is nonidentical for two reasons. First, Marion does not follow Rahner all the way down the apologetic path and proceed to demonstrate that Christianity, which is both called into being by and self-consciously bases itself on Revelation as this finds its definitive focus in Christ, offers the unsurpassable dogmatic figuration or refiguration of universal human experience.[93] Second, Marion radicalizes the Rahnerian project by in a sense bringing Scripture itself "inside" phenomenology. Although this is more apparent in Marion's theologically aspirated trilogy, traces of this introjection can be found in the later elaborations of phenomenology as first philosophy. The effect is a disinvesting of one kind of authority and an investing with another. More specifically, the move from one side of the border to another invests—or at least seems to invest—Scripture with a different kind of authority than it would enjoy outside the philosophical (phenomenological) domain. The appearance of introjection raises the question whether outside the precincts of philosophy the authority of Scripture is legitimate and generative, that is an authority that funds other authorities that could be recognized on other non-phenomenological grounds (e.g., magisterium, creeds, theological tradition).

The question is unavoidable, even when Marion tells us in *Being Given* (§24) that there is an authority beyond the phenomenological field. We are told that this authority is Revelation, which is centered on the figure of Christ. But in that text we also find the echo of the position Marion appears to have held in his earlier theologically aspirated writings: that Christ is the Word translated into words, thus transposed into Scripture, to be articulated symphonically by the theological tradition that cannot be other than trinitarian. This symphonic articulation is anything but specular: it is embodied in practices and the making of Christian subjects, which, as Balthasar has emphasized in his reading of Bernanos and Péguy as well as his great trilogy, is the making of saints.[94] But the precincts of Scripture still remains ambiguous: at once an expression of phenomenological intuition that exceeds intention, and a discourse that translates Revelation and plays a role in a different regime of authority.

What I would like to suggest is that this nonidentical repetition of Rahner is a function of the effect of Hegel in Marion's discourse, Hegel's function as a specter. Up until now, I have spoken of the "specter" or "ghost" of Hegel as an object of sight, perhaps simply by being out of sight: he is a reality in Marion's texts, hidden in the folds, hiding behind other figures, for example, Descartes, Husserl, Heidegger, and Lévinas. The task of this essay has been to help us see this figure where possible, for even though Hegel does not seem to appear in Marion's texts, he has not disappeared entirely. One might come to see that Hegel is not buried, come to judge that Hegel is not even dead, come to say that with different urgencies Marion's texts engage and do battle with him—crossing, recrossing, and double-crossing his thought. But this is to fail to announce the ability of a spectral discourse to disturb, worry, and frighten a discourse, even a discourse constituted as a discourse of resistance. Kierkegaard saw this acutely: Hegel's discourse is the most ghastly discourse in that it has the greatest potency to disturb discourse, indeed, nothing short of absolute potency. It has or is this potency because it is a discourse of miming, mincing, and entanglement. As Foucault suggests, a discourse succeeds in resisting Hegelian discourse only by extraordinary vigilance, for the discourse is "insidious": anti-Hegelianism is "possibly one his tricks directed against us, at the end of which he stands, motionless, waiting for us."[95]

At any moment Hegelian discourse can enter, attach itself as a virus to the most innocent of themes, and make a discourse say something other than it intends, especially if it wishes to show—not say—transcendence. The slightest breach and Hegel's discourse makes a host discourse mad. Moreover, the virus is truly demonic: it wants to say one thing, ultimately to say it in one way, with a voice that would be entirely posthumous were it a voice at all. Char captures the dilemma posed by Hegel when in his poem "Le Masque funèbre" he speaks of famine that makes of itself its own meal.

> There was a man, once, who being no longer hungry, no longer ever hungry, what with all the legacies he had devoured, food he had guzzled, neighbors he had impoverished, found his table bare, his bed deserted, his wife pregnant, and the soil bad in the field of his heart.
>
> Having no tomb and wanting to be alive, having nothing to give and even less to receive, with objects shunning him, animals lying to him, he stole famine and made of it a dish that became his mirror and own rout.[96]

Thus the question: has Marion been sufficiently vigilant regarding the spectral properties of Hegelian discourse, its ability to madden a resisting discourse?

Earlier in the essay I sided decisively with Marion against Derrida's dogmatic collapsing of the eucharistic discourse of John's Gospel and Hegel's discourse of the spiritual community [*Gemeinde*], which in modernity constitutes Real Presence, indeed produces itself as nothing less than that parousia of the absolute with itself. Moreover, there is not only something precious, but there may be something naive, most certainly risky, in Derrida's recurring to the scatological discourse of Genet to give a heave to Hegel's eschatologically primed discourse. It is not clear that the Sadean line of discourse that Genet represents is itself not in need of discursive redress, since if it opposes Hegelian discourse in some respects, it repeats it in others, as it generates its own apodictic of experience. One suspects that in the end, however, Derrida knows all this and that for him all critique remains tactical: the critical discourse is also subject to critique, and this third discourse in turn *ad infinitum*. Thus, the anarchism of the text. Still, weaknesses or not, *Glas* remains paradigmatic. First, it reveals, as Kierkegaard's texts do, the enemy with whom no peace treaty is possible. Second, whatever its excesses in argumentation, *Glas* shows graphically that all discourses are contaminated. This is especially true of a discourse such as Hegel's that announces its transcendence of all discursive presuppositions. Earlier in "White Mythology" Derrida had tackled the issue more formally than he does in *Glas* when he made the case that Hegelian conceptuality was defined by a heliocentrism that it could not account for and that it unsuccessfully attempts to erase as a presupposition.[97] *Glas*, however, does more than repeat this point even as it concretizes it. More in line with Kierkegaard it suggests that Hegel's discourse can haunt any discourse, especially resisting discourses that would cross Hegel. As with Kierkegaard, resistance calls for indirection and well as direction, and suppleness in tactics. Although the quotient of vigilance visibly drops from Marion's first trilogy to the second, it is not evident that the vigilance was ever sufficiently hyperbolic, and the tactics ever sufficiently varied and supple. The legerdemain in the texts of Marion is that of a memory of a vaguely unpleasant guest who has come and gone, that of *Glas* the anticipation of a shapeless something always to come, but always having arrived, always having violated discourse.

When Marion pronounces on the purity of philosophical discourse, and when he announces in his second trilogy that philosophical discourse is capable of rendering "revelation," has he not been maddened by Hegelian discourse? The fact that Marion is adamant about the distinction between "revelation" and "Revelation" could turn out to be a difference without a difference, if "Revelation" is pure positivity, for Hegel also realized that this aspect of Christian discourse would have to be excluded from the *Aufhebung*, discarded as so much waste. If the *Phenomenology, Lectures on the Philosophy of Religion*, and the *Encyclopedia of Philosophical Sciences* only bring to fruition a move already made by Kant in *Religion within the Bounds of Reason Alone*, they bring it to an entirely new level. For Hegel's discourse attempts a more ample translation of the symbols, narrative, and performances of Christianity. In particular, it not only says, but shows, that philosophy provides the truly adequate interpretation of Scripture. It not only says, but shows, that the Incarnation and Cross, which Kant was unable to translate into *Verstand*, are exploitable on the level of *Vernunft*. Hegelian discourse discloses that the liturgical practices of the church are at once metaphors of the transformation of the social domain, and instigations to memory in which the self of community enters into the inner sanctum of worship of the divine that is really worship of the self, albeit the self writ large, as the social matrix of interaction and recognition. In the end the details matter less than the comprehensiveness of the enacted program of translation. And it is the mimicking of this comprehensiveness that brings Marion closer to Hegel than to Kant, whose texts he calls on as fundamental opportunities for thought.[98]

Here we notice something extraordinary, or, at very least, something interesting. As Derrida begins to thematize more and more in his later work the relation between philosophical and religious discourse, he begins more and more to repeat Kant. "Religion," as a discourse that admits of justification, is ethically reducible, except of course for the messianic or apocalyptic excess that is a tone rather than a content, although a tone suggesting a motif and motive that are not themselves items of a discursive system. Derrida, it seems, successfully resists Hegel only to reinscribe Kant. By contrast, Marion's discourse consistently crosses and recrosses Hegel, while continually evoking and invoking Kant. But perhaps there is never the sense, even in the first trilogy, that Hegel's discourse is the cross that every discourse must bear, and that like Grendel's victims, one will have been emptied before vigilance was possible. Thus, at no point does Marion's discourse give rise to the hyperbole of vigilance, or rise to the level of hyperbolic vigilance. This is not to say, however, that Marion has definitely fallen victim to Hegel. He knows better than to mimic Hegelian discourse that represents the apotheosis of both philosophy and Christianity. If Hegel is a Protestant Aquinas, then so much the worst for both Protestantism and Aquinas. But resisting the mixing of the discourses of philosophy and religion has the effect of expanding the domain of philosophy's competence, even if the *mise en scène* is the provision of a nondogmatic double of theology. Whatever the motive, the result seems to take on the form that Brito suggests many modern forms of philosophical theology take in modernity, including that of Rahner:[99] they tend to repeat in essential ways the articulation of Christianity displayed within the horizon of the *Phenomenology*, which purports to be "the science of the appearance of consciousness." This is precisely a disarticulation that primes Christian symbols, and particularly Christian christological and trinitarian symbols, for translation into a medium that recollects them as their sanitized abstract.

Marion strikes the note of "revelation" hard in the later trilogy, contrasts it with Revelation, about which from the point of view of phenomenology nothing can be said. There is an abyss, for which the most appropriate figure is Pascal, even if one cannot but think of Wittgenstein. And with Hegel in mind, it is difficult to forget Jacobi and Kierkegaard and their demand of a *salto mortale*. Marion's silence with respect to "Revelation" is not helpful. Perhaps, Revelation is not reductively positivity? Perhaps it does more than simply confirm that possibility—again Rahner—becomes actuality? It is possible that Revelation supplies its own content, just as it is possible that it provides its own authority? We need more clarification on what this content and authority would be. We need Marion to speak theologically and more often. We need Marion to break his silence on the negotiations between these contents and authorities. Even if meta-rules are, as I have indicated, ruled out beforehand, we could do with a sense as to what yields to what and when. We need all of this because now the issue is whether and how borders get crossed.

Borders, nexuses, betweens—this is where Hegelian discourse is to be found; indeed, this is what Hegelian discourse founds. One is forced to encounter, to relent or speak otherwise. If Marion has ducked *agōn* with Hegel by arguing with and from Descartes, Husserl, and Heidegger, it would seem that it was only a postponement of the *agōn* with Hegel who polices all betweens. Hegel is the future cross that Marion must bear, the one whom reflectively he will have to cross, double-cross, cross over and through. Hegel is the future cross whose difficulty greatly exceeds that of the other two H's. The difficulty is in part a function of a promise neither the two other H's make, namely, not simply to save the appearances in general, but of Christianity in particular. This discourse of such saving is, of course, a lie, but more the discourse of the lie, since it is the discourse intoxicated by its own power of naming. But this discourse is also the lie of the simulacrum that makes the eye cross over and not see the real cross. This discourse is the final and greatest test to a specifically Christian parsing of the relation between wisdom and the Cross. For it lies in wait as a complacent and talkative answer to the more cyclopean seeing that befits both the finite subject and the Christian ecstatic.

Hegel's discourse in an important sense constitutes for Marion an apocalypse, specifically the apocalypse of temptation. The siren of this discourse and its *Aufhebung* of Revelation in a revelation that is manifestation will continue to seduce, and will continue to demand that one get clear on whether and where the ecstatic self crosses from revelation to Revelation or where Revelation and revelation come together and separate. The encounter is as inevitable as its resolution is in doubt. But the future of temptation only alters its mode; it does not invent or discover it. If my analysis of Marion's work is correct, the temptation of Hegel and/or the Hegelian temptation belongs to the category of the "always already." The temptation of Hegel is immemorial. The early Christian writers, of whom Marion speaks so approvingly, knew the immemoriality of temptation: temptation had already happened out of sight and mind; one had already been propositioned and acceded to it. The insidious insideness of its outsidedness constitutes the force of temptation. Hegel's discourse is a temptation that Marion occasionally sees and does battle with throughout his two trilogies. There is every reason to suppose that the future of discourse will suffer and unfold a fuller—even a full—encounter, and that his discourse will be called on to name and defeat the hydra of Hegel's discourse+, confirmed as much in the attempt to wound as in surrender.

But Hegel's discourse is also a temptation that Marion is not always aware of, such that it affects his discourse quite out of sight. Moreover, there really is no beginning to the temptation of Hegel and its effect, just as there is no end. The temptation of Hegel has always happened. This is why it is unnecessary to pin the blame on the second trilogy. It has happened in the theologically aspirated trilogy. As the future in the mode of the past, it will have happened even when Marion mindfully has taken care to resist Hegelianism with the desert ecstasy of negative theology.

What is called for in Marion's work is an apotropaics the equal of the lucidity of Monsieur Teste and the mystical theologians. One's wall has already been breached; discourse has to go back before the beginning when another other entered. In the excavation, one is asked to unbury the question "Who are you?" and rediscover the force of the command "Depart from me," and to sign the cross as pointing to oneself and one's speech as a site of resistance. Yet to do all this knowing that it is postponement—that one's discourse is in delay, that its movement is a waiting for an encounter for which it might not be ready—and that there is the apocalyptic razor's edge: what is awaited waits also, and it has been waiting a long time, immemorially in fact, and there are rumors that the speech of the few who returned from the encounter was never the same.

Notes

1. See Jean-Luc Nancy, *La remarque spéculatif: Un bon mot de Hegel* (Paris: Éditions Galilée, 1973); also *Hegel: L'inquiétude du négatif* (Paris: Hachette Littérature, 1997). These texts have been recently translated into English. See *The Speculative Remark: One of Hegel's Bon Mots,* trans. Céline Surprenant (Stanford: Stanford University Press, 2001); *Hegel and the Restlessness of the Negative,* trans. John Smith and Steven Miller (Minneapolis: University of Minnesota Press, 2002). While these texts are basically of a piece with respect to their general attitude toward Hegel's philosophy as representing ambiguously a totalizing discourse and a ceaseless movement toward adequation that is never realized, there are a number of differences between them. First, there is the difference in the level of performance. *The Speculative Remark* is a much more ample and rich text. Second, *The Speculative Remark* is much more conditional and hypothetical about Hegel's transcendence of metaphysics. Third, *The Speculative Remark* appears to show significant traces of Derrida, whereas in the

latter work Derrida is not as exigent a presence. The classic text of Derrida on Hegel is, of course, *Glas* (Paris: Éditions Galilée, 1974). See the English edition, *Glas,* trans. John P. Leavey Jr. and Richard Rand (Lincoln: University of Nebraska Press, 1986). Other important texts of Derrida on Hegel include the essays "From Restricted to General Economy: A Hegelianism without Reserve," in *Writing and Difference,* trans. Alan Bass (Chicago: University of Chicago Press, 1978), 251–77; "Différance" and "White Mythology: Metaphor in the Text of Philosophy," in *Margins of Philosophy,* trans. Alan Bass (Chicago: University of Chicago Press, 1987), 1–27, 207–71. See esp. 13–14, 19–20, and 258–71.

2. For Lévinas, see esp. *Totality and Infinity,* trans. Alphonso Lingis (Pittsburg: Duquesne University Press, 1969). For Deleuze, see esp. *Difference and Repetition,* trans. Paul Patton (New York: Columbia University Press, 1994). For pages in which Deleuze engages in a rebuttal of Hegelian difference as merely conceptual difference, see esp. 26–27, 42–45, 49–50.

3. Bataille's engagement with Hegel is significant. As Derrida recognized, Bataille's theory of religion is through and through an attempt to overcome Hegel, who sets all desire, all sacrifice, and all gift within an economy. As Bataille opposes Hegel's view of giving in which all giving yields a return, indeed a profit, he also opposes Hegel's absolute knowledge. He enters a plea on behalf of nonknowledge, and also an appeal on behalf of negative theology that sets out in a much more antinomian direction than Lévinas, and following him, Marion. This is especially evident in *L'Experience intérieure* (Paris: Gallimard, 1954), originally written in 1943 as the first part of *La somme athéologique.* See *Inner Experience,* trans. with intro. Leslie Anne Boldt (Albany: State University of New York Press, 1988), 52–60, 80–81, 101–3. While Blanchot's engagement is a little less intense, it can be found especially in *L'entretien infini* (Paris: Gallimard, 1969), in which Blanchot challenges Hegel's commitment to the encyclopedia as the figure of absolute knowledge (1–3, 94, 621–22). See also *L'écriture du désastre* (Paris: Gallimard, 1980), in which as a specification of the challenge to Hegelian circularity, Blanchot speaks metaphorically of the undoing of the astral system. This is the meaning of "dis-aster," where "aster" is Latin for "star."

4. See *Positions,* trans. Alan Bass (Chicago: University of Chicago Press, 1981). The quotation is an abbreviation. The full statement reads as follows: "We have never finished with a reading or rereading of Hegel, and, in a certain way, I do nothing other than attempt to explain myself on this point" (77). One should be wary of taking advantage of such a grand statement. Derrida is almost always subtle, but he is not above hyperbole.

5. I am referring here to Derrida's play on the relation between "Hegel" and "aigle," the French word for "eagle," throughout *Glas.* The fact that the relation is not a semantic one is a matter of indifference to Derrida. Semantic relations or chains may not be as important as they are often taken to be, just as superficial relations of sound open up relations and/or differences that are worth exploring. Accidents, in short, represent surprising opportunities for illuminating texts in terms of their repressions and their potentials.

6. Marion accepts then Heidegger's genealogy of modernity in which one can draw a clear line between Descartes and Hegel only in a highly modified form. On Marion's account it is true to say that Hegel represents the terminus of an egological scheme that is first exhibited in Descartes's work. But, Marion contends, egology is a fundamental thrust in Descartes rather than being totally constitutive. The counter-thrust to the egology in Descartes is the dimension of the infinite. Marion's position bears a family resemblance to the position that Ricœur articulates in his work on Husserl, as he associates and dissociates Descartes and Husserl: Descartes's work is fundamentally bipolar and is constituted by the tension between the demands of the *ego cogito* and the demands of transcendence that appear in the *ens perfectissimum*.

7. I realize that while the domains of "grammatology" and "semiology" overlap in Derrida, they may not be identical. Obviously, in the context of Derrida's early work these concepts are coextensive to the degree to which they both indicate a critique of the phonocentrism and logocentrism of the Western tradition. But Derrida is anxious that his project not be exclusively defined in this way, and that the task of the philosopher be more understood as performative than transcendental: that is, the task of the philosopher consists in following different lines of sense and meaning in texts, what is absent or marginalized as well as what is focal.

8. Deleuze's resistance to Hegel is ingredient in his turn away from the two dominant trends in French philosophy, phenomenology and dialectic, and their attempted integration. In this respect he is in line with Jean Wahl, who tried to establish an Anglo dispensation in French philosophy. As it turned out, this dispensation consisted of a synthesis of American pragmatism and Russell's philosophy of external relations, which itself is self-consciously posited as an alternative to a theory of internal relations that had Hegel as its ultimate ancestor. (Russell against the idealist Bradley.) It is clear that in *Difference and Repetition,* for example, Hegel's view is very much to the fore as the foil to the elaboration of a metaphysical pluralism. In particular Deleuze refuses the alternative laid down by Hegel in the first chapter in the *Phenomenology* that our philosophical choice is between temporal and spatial particulars totally devoid of content, and perceptual and conceptual schemes that displace and replace particularity. Deleuze supports a universe of particulars and singularities that have a determinate content resistant to Hegel's semantic chains. See *Difference and Repetition,* esp. 10 and 56.

9. Bruaire's most sustained treatment of Hegel is to be found in *Logique et la religion chrétienne dans la philosophie de Hegel* (Paris: Seuil, 1964). Other texts by Bruaire, which bear on a retrieval of Hegel that has a significant note of resistance, include *L'Affirmation de Dieu: Essai sur la logique de l'existence* (Paris: Seuil, 1964). This text represents the constructive complement of the more exegetical Hegel text. Two other texts by Bruaire are worth noting. The first is *Schelling ou la quête du secret de l'être* (Paris: Seghers, 1970), in which Bruaire tries to find a metaphysical alternative to Hegel that stresses more emphatically freedom and gratuity of a transcendent source of beings. He finds this, as other Catholic French thinkers such as Tillette also have, in the nonidealist later Schelling. Of special interest is *L'être et l'esprit* (Paris:

PUF, 1983). In this text Bruaire articulates a metaphysics of gift in conversation with Christian theology, and especially with trinitarian theology. Continuing to believe that Hegelian texts such as *Lectures on the Philosophy of Religion* provides a template for the conversation between metaphysics and trinitarian theology, he uses Hegel's language of religious and philosophical syllogism while essentially undermining its fundamental commitment to the erasure of mystery and gift. André Léonard is another major French Catholic contributor to the study of Hegel who, precisely because he recognizes Hegel's importance, is anxious to take issue with him. Léonard's most extensive study of Hegel is *Commentaire littéral de la logique de Hegel* (Paris: Vrin, 1974). The more critical side of Léonard's work, however, is exhibited in *La foi chez Hegel* (Paris: Desclée, 1970), and more narrowly, but with great concentration, in "Le primat du négative et l'interpretation de la religion. Un example: la reprise hégélienne du dogme christologique de Chalcédoine," in *Hegels Logik der Philosophie*, ed. Dieter Henrich and Rolf-Peter Horstmann (Stuttgart: Klett-Cotta, 1984), 160–71. Albert Chapelle has written, arguably, the most extensive analysis of Hegel's philosophy of religion in any language. See his *Hegel et la religion*, 3 vols. (Paris: Éditions universitaires, 1964–67). While throughout this text, Chapelle exercises the hermeneutic of generosity and shows himself anxious to underscore how Hegel can be a philosophical resource for thinking the relation between philosophy and theology, he shows his appreciation for those who think otherwise or who believe that Christian philosophers and theologians cannot go all the way with Hegel. See his "L'itineraire philosophique de Claude Bruaire: De Hegel à la métaphysique," in *Revue philosophique* 1 (1990): 5–10; also "Présence de Hegel en France: G. Fessard et Cl. Bruaire," in ibid., 13–26. For Xavier Tillette, see *L'absolu et la philosophie* (Paris: PUF, 1987); and *Schelling: une philosophie en devenir* (Paris: Vrin, 1992). Tillette reads the "later" Schelling as offering a metaphysical correction of Hegel that leads to the possibility of a less hostile and more reciprocal relation between theology and philosophy. For Emilio Brito, see *Hegel et la tâche actuelle de la christologie* (Paris: Letheilleux, 1979), and *La christologie de Hegel: Verbum Crucis* (Paris: Beauchesne, 1983). Like Bruaire and Tillette, Brito too explores the possibility of Schelling's representing an alternative to Hegel and one that is more genuinely open to the Christian tradition in its philosophical and theological deliberations and its assessment of the relation between them. As in the others, the "giftedness" of creation, which is grounded in a dynamic absolute of love, is to the fore. See *La création selon Schelling* (Leuven: Leuven University Press and Peters, 1987). Fessard's influence on the commentary on Hegel was communicated largely through articles he wrote in the late 1940s and 1950s rather than in a book on Hegel that had the stature of the productions of a Kojève or a Hyppolite.

10. The key text here is not Hyppolite's *Genèse et structure de la "Phenomenologie de l'esprit" de Hegel* (Paris: Aubier, 1946), but rather his *Logique et existence: Essai sur la logique de Hegel* (Paris: PUF, 1953). For the English translation, see *Logic and Existence*, trans. Leonard Lawler and Amit Sen (New York: State University of New York Press, 1997).

11. For death as the disappearance of the phenomenon, see esp. *Encyclopedia*, part 3, §381. Other relevant passages on death [*Tod*] as the leaving behind of a particular

include *Encyclopedia*, part 3, §367 Zusatz; and §349. These passages from the third part of the *Encyclopedia*, *The Philosophy of Mind*, pick up and put an exclamation point to earlier reflections on death in the *Philosophy of Nature*, part 2 of the *Encyclopedia*, esp. §251; and the *Logic*, part 1, §§221–22. In §381, in particular, Hegel is conscious of the relation between the general formula for death and the disappearance of the Dasein of Jesus of Nazareth as a condition for the realization of authentic individuality [*Einzenheit*]. Thus, at one and the same time, the death of the divine man [*Tod des göttlichenn Menschen*] Jesus is an example of the phenomenon of death as the disappearance of the phenomenon and regulates the interpretation of death, whose proper domain is that of spirit rather than nature. §381 is connected then with Hegel's more elaborate christological reflections on the death of Christ in Hegel's treatment of "consummate religion" in *Lectures on the Philosophy of Religion*. In the passages in the *Encyclopedia*, Hegel wavers between stronger and weaker versions of what is achieved by death. On the one hand, Hegel seems to adopt the view that death or negativity in and of itself represents the realization of individuality and spirit. There is no gap, therefore, between death and the arrival of deep life as its sublation (See also §19 in the *Phenomenology*.) But in §381, with the death of Jesus in mind—this will be the standard position in *Lectures on the Philosophy of Religion*—Hegel suggests a gap (unspecified as to whether it is logical or temporal) between death and the arrival of individuality and/or spirit in the strict sense. Death fails to bring forth genuine universality [*Allgemeinheit*] or genuinely universal individuality [*allgemeinen Einzelnheit*]. When in addition Hegel suggests that death represents the overcoming of the "being-at-home of life [*Gewohnheit des Lebens*]," then one could say that this "not yet arrived" or "non-arrival" of spirit opens up the space of the specter, the dead that is not fully death and yet not alive. One owes to Althusser the sense that the death of Hegel's thought is not a genuine death, but that his thought continues to have a "half-life" after his death in history and in the discourses of history. Importantly, Althusser defends this position based on an analysis of Hegel's texts themselves. Although the title of the collection of Althusser's essays on Hegel, *The Spectre of Hegel* (London: Verso, 1998), may be undetermined and may represent an echo of Derrida's *Specters of Marx*, in a real sense Althusser's introduction to his essay "The Content in Hegel" not only sets the stage for a spectral analysis of Hegel, but also sets some of the basic terms for Derrida's reflection. (Obviously, not all, given Derrida's allergy to "presence.") In view of Althusser's fascination with psychoanalysis, one cannot rule out the possibility that he is thinking of something like Freud's the "return of the repressed."

    12. See Dominque Janicaud, *Le tournant théologique de la phénoménologie française* (Paris: Éditions de l'Éclat, 1991). For a convenient English translation, see *Phenomenology and the "Theological Turn": The French Debate* (New York: Fordham University Press, 2000), 16–103. I recognize that Janicaud has in mind also Marion's more purely phenomenological works, which he takes to be animated by theology.

    13. Jean-Luc Marion, *L'idole et la distance: cinq études* (Paris: Grasset, 1979). For the English translation, see *The Idol and the Distance: Five Studies*, trans. with intro. Thomas A. Carlson (New York: Fordham University Press, 2001). Throughout I will

first give the page numbers of the English translation and then the page numbers of the original French text. The citation from the French text will be preceded by the letter "F." Only in exceptional cases will I modify the translation.

14. Jean-Luc Marion, *Dieu sans l'être* (Paris: PUF, 1982). For the English translation, see *God without Being*, trans. Thomas A. Carlson with a foreword by David Tracy (Chicago: University of Chicago Press, 1991).

15. The French on p. 184 reads: "Il ne s'agit pas de dire l'Étant suprême, dans une prédication dont il serait l'objet. Ni de le laisser énoncer, comme sujet absolu, une prédication de lui-même par lui-même."

16. See esp. *Logic and Existence*, 129–44, where Hyppolite analyzes Hegel's reflection in the preface to the *Phenomenology* (esp. §§23, 60–65) on the speculative sentence or proposition. Hyppolite understands the speculative sentence to sum up the constitutive Hegelian drive to banish the ineffable, that is, anything that would be exterior to the movement of discourse that is coextensive with the movement of reality. But equally interesting for the purposes of exposing the background assumptions of Marion is Hegel's distinction between the empirical and the speculative sentence. Hyppolite understands Hegel's speculative sentence to represent nothing less than an alternative to Aristotle's understanding of the relation between predicates and subject of attribution. In the speculative sentence there are no subjects subsisting outside of discourse to which attribution of predicates would be adequate. Nor does one need to mark off the speaker from what is spoken. The speaker role gets abolished. See esp. *Logic and Existence*, 142–44.

17. The French commentator-critic of Hegel for whom Hyppolite's work is most formative is, arguably, Jean-Luc Nancy. This is true because of, rather than despite, the fact that Nancy is enormously influenced by early essays of Derrida such as "Différance" and "The Pit and the Pyramid: Introduction to Hegel's Semiology." Both of these essays can be found in *Margins of Philosophy*, 1–27, 69–108. It is interesting that the second of these essays was presented as a paper at the Séminaire de Jean Hyppolite at the Collège de France in 1968 and first appeared in a volume on Hegel titled *Hegel et la pensée moderne* (Paris: PUF, 1971). Nancy's most important text is *La remarque speculative* (1973). Hyppolite provides the basic frame as well as much of the content of Nancy's discussion. Nancy moves to his reflection of the speculative sentence in chapter 4 through a discussion of the Hegelian operation of *Aufhebung* whose essential function is to remove the prospect of chance or surprise (the equivalent to Hyppolite's "ineffable"). And in that chapter (esp. 78–86), Nancy repeats Hyppolite's diagnosis of the monumental nature of Hegel's shift in understanding of the process of predication, and underscores how it has to be dealt with in its own right and not simply as a function of a critique of Aristotle's view of predication.

18. Bruaire's 1983 text *L'être et l'esprit* can be regarded as both the finest expression of his metaphysics of the gift and the summary of the basic drift of the work that preceded it.

19. See, e.g., Derrida's essay "Sauf le nom (Post-Scriptum)," trans. John P. Leavey Jr., in *On the Name*, ed. Thomas Dutoit, trans. David Wood, John P. Leavey Jr., and Ian McLeod (Stanford: Stanford University Press, 1995), 33–85.

20. As is well known, Hegel thinks of both Epictetus and Spinoza as providing templates for his view that philosophy does no less divine service than rites and practices of worship. Indeed, for Hegel's two precursors philosophy is the best kind of worship, since it avoids manipulation and idolatry. As Hegel makes the connection he first cites Epictetus in *Glauben und Wissen* (1801). That the idea does not simply belong to his youthful writings is made clear by his reference throughout the work of his mature period to Epictetus in the *Encyclopedia of Philosophical Sciences*, §§62–63, and throughout *Lectures on the Philosophy of Religion,* especially in his programmatic treatment of the concept [*Begriff*] of religion. In the 1821 manuscript and also in the 1827 Lectures he speaks of knowledge as a form of worship. See *Lectures on the Philosophy of Religion,* vol. 1, ed. Peter Hodgson, trans. R. F. Brown, P. C. Hodgson, and J. M. Steward with assistance of J. P. Fitzer and H. S. Harris (Berkeley: University of California Press, 1984), 84, 153. The influence of Spinoza on this point is also enormous, and this despite Spinoza's almost absolute cleavage between the domains of religion (imagination) and philosophy (thought) licensed in the *Tractatus Theologico-Politicus.* If the Spinoza who links thought and worship is a construction deployed by Herder and Schleiermacher and a considerable number of the romantics as well as Hegel, it was not without support in the texts of Spinoza. Its basis is provided by Spinoza's treatment of the "intellectual love of God [*amor intellectualis ad deum*]," which is a central theme of book 5 of the *Ethics.*

21. See *The Speculative Remark,* 84, for an explicit connection between Hegelian dialectic and "unrest [*Unruhe*]." Of course, "unrest" is the theme of Nancy's small text, *L'inquiétude du négatif.*

22. I have slightly modified the French translation. The passage at 199 of *L'idole et distance* reads: "Ce qui veut dire que la distance ne nous sépare pas tant de l'Ab-solu, qu'elle ne nous ménage, de toute son antériorité, notre identité. Elle dénote donc le mouvment positif de l'Absolu qui, par la mise en distance, se désapproprie extatiquement de Lui-même pour que l'homme se recoive lui-même extatiquement en différence. En se recevent de la distance, l'homme comprend non seulement qu'elle le comprend, mais qu'elle le rend possible." My change in translation is slight but important. Carlson translates "se déappropie extatiquement de Lui-même" as "is disappropriated from itself." The passive construction, however, not only fails to render the reflexive form of the verb but significantly changes the meaning. For the passive form suggests that the Absolute suffers something rather than imposes something on itself gratuitously.

23. In particular Marion is looking at Heidegger's text *Hegels Begriff der Erfahrung* in which Heidegger, focusing on the preface to the *Phenomenology,* speaks of *Geist* as the operation in and through which the parousia of the Absolute with itself and thus the constitution of a self-reflective totality is the goal of negation and difference. Difference is thus always restricted by the constitution and articulation of an immanent network from which transcendence is excluded. Also important is *Hegels Phänomenologie des Geistes,* in *Gesamtausgabe,* vol. 30 (Frankfurt: Klostermann, 1980). This commentary brings together Heidegger's lectures on Hegel in the winter semester of 1930–31.

24. In *L'idol et la distance* Maximus stands for himself, as an authentic interpreter of Pseudo-Dionysius, and for the whole Christian neo-Platonic tradition in which the emphasis on radical transcendence of the triune God (the triune God interpreting the *hyperousias thearchia*) goes hand in hand with a corresponding emphasis on the radical nature of participation. With respect to the details, but also with respect to the basic interpretive posture, Marion seems to be broadly following Balthasar, who quite early on in his career read Maximus to be exemplary for the Christian neo-Platonic tradition. The major difference between Balthasar's earlier view and that elaborated in the chapter on Pseudo-Dionysius in *Herrlichkeit* 2 is that Maximus is now understood not so much to correct Pseudo-Dionysius as ramify his thought. For a treatment of the hermeneutics of the relation between Pseudo-Dionysius and Maximus in Balthasar, see my essay "Von Balthasar and Thick Retrieval: Post-Chalcedonian Symphonic Theology," *Gregorianum* 77, no. 2 (1996): 27–60.

25. Throughout his entire *oeuvre*, from his Hegel book of 1964 to his *L'Être et l'esprit* (1983) defining his competence and purpose as philosophical, Bruaire uses the language of the "Absolute." For him, it was simply a matter of principle that the unconditioned that conditions could not be determined beforehand as the Christian God. On the point of vocabulary then, Hegel was right, and he had to be rebutted by using this language. For Bruaire, Schelling provided part of the answer. He believed that while Christian Revelation gives much for thought to think, even within the limits of philosophy alone the unconditioned could be construed as fecund and replete origin rather than Hegel's self-constituting whole.

26. I allude here to Kathryn Tanner's *God and Creation in Christian Theology: Tyranny or Empowerment* (Oxford: Basil Blackwell, 1988), where the "noncontrastive" relation between God and the world guarantees both God's transcendence of and immanence in the world. This way of construing transcendence is just as important in Tanner's *The Politics of God: Christian Theology and Social Justice* (Minneapolis: Fortress, 1992).

27. All the evidence is that such is the case. See Marion's retraction of his inclusion of Aquinas in the fall of metaphysics as onto-theology. One can take it that Marion's recent interest in Augustine has as one of its motives the urge to release Augustine from Heidegger's dismissal that came before *Sein und Zeit* and that to a significant extent sets the background condition for Derrida in *Of Grammatology*. Marion's own attempts to draw distinctions between Augustine and Descartes in his work on Descartes illustrates the negative capability of Marion's thought to exempt Augustine from the onto-theological deformation constitutive of metaphysics. At the very least he wants to suggest that the self does not serve as the ineluctable foundation and that the dynamics of the love of God and the self undergo serious transformation in Descartes, who is justified in thinking of himself as an original. See, e.g., *On Descartes' Metaphysical Prism: The Constitution and the Limits of Onto-Theo-logy in Cartesian Thought*, trans. Jeffrey Kosky (Chicago: University of Chicago Press, 1999), 129–32.

28. *L'idole et la distance*, 248. Although Marion does not refer to Bruaire here, it seems safe to infer that Bruaire is in the background. Bruaire is referred to earlier in the Denys chapter when the absoluteness of negation gets questioned. See *The Idol*

and Distance, 147 n. 15. There Marion refers to *L'Affirmation de Dieu: Essai sur la logique de l'existence* (Paris: Seuil, 1964), the companion text of *Logique et religion chrétienne dans la philosophie de Hegel.*

29. While it true that Bruaire takes his critical distance from Hegel from the beginning, this is increasingly true of his work even as Bruaire continues to avail of Hegelian vocabulary. *L'Être et l'esprit* represents his definitive statement.

30. What is most important in Marion's interpretation of Hölderlin is how he interprets various poems like "Patmos" and "Brod und Wein" otherwise than Heidegger. But it is also interesting that he tends to avoid poems such as "Der Ister," "Der Rhein," and "Am Quell der Donau" that serve an important function in Heidegger's mythopoesis of the history of the West, which begins with Greece and ends with Germany, since each of these are rivers that rise in the east and flow westward.

31. At the very beginning of his Hölderlin essay, Marion honors previous French scholarship on the German poet, while indicating his intent to strike out in an individual direction. He includes J. Tardieu, F. Fédier, and P. Jaccottet among others. See *The Idol and Distance,* 81 n. 1.

32. The work of Blanchot, which is extraordinarily attentive to both the poetry and literary musings of first Char and then Bonnefoy, treats Hölderlin quite extensively. In addition to "La parole sacrée de Hölderlin" (1946), which deals directly with a Hölderlin who has achieved more than poetic status through the elucidations of Heidegger, there is also extensive reflection on Hölderlin in "La folie par excellence" (1951) and *L'Espace littéraire* (1958). "La parole sacrée," in line with Heidegger, underscores the difference between Hölderlinian apocalypse and that of Hegel. For an excellent account of Blanchot's reading of appropriation of Hölderlin, see Kevin Hart, *The Dark Gaze* (Chicago: University of Chicago Press, 2004). In the poetry of Char, Hölderlin is only rarely an independent source. Still, Char's reflections on the nature of the task of poetry bear more than a resemblance to the task outlined by Hölderlin. In particular, Char's notion of "Archipel" or "archipelago" (1952–60), understood as the surrender of a totalizing meaning, recall the German poet. Char's well-known poem on Prometheus has an epigraph from Hölderlin. The poetry of Bonnefoy is even more obviously determined by encounter with Hölderlin, although throughout Blanchot's reading is singularly important. The epigraph for Bonnefoy's second volume of poetry, *Hier régnant désert* (1958), is from Hölderlin's "Hyperion." That there is a Hölderlin–Hegel contrast in operation is evinced in the fact that Bonnefoy's first volume, *Du movement et de l'immobilité de Douve* (1953), has its epigraph from the *Phenomenology.* In subsequent volumes, both Hölderlin and his Blanchot incarnation are in evidence. See "Les nuées" in *Dans le leuere de seuil* (1975), which invokes all the typical Hölderlinian elements of fire, water, air, and wind, and also the gods to make a case for nonidentity and scattering. The Blanchot resonances are even more apparent in a *L'épars, l'invisible,* in which naming is held never to be completed.

33. Marion refers to Balthasar twice throughout this chapter. See *The Idol and Distance,* 89 n. 15, where he approves of Balthasar's emphasis on Hölderlin's use of kenosis in his interpretation of the great German poet in *Herrlickkeit,* 3/2. The other reference is at 126–27 n. 54, where Marion suggests after Balthasar a Maximan-

Dionysian lens in and through which to read the christological *Tendenz* of Hölderlin's work. Erich Przywara's *Hölderlin: Eine Studie* (Nuremberg: Glock and Lutz, 1949) is mentioned with great appreciation at 105 n. 35.

34. There are two different kinds of madness. First, the largely literary madness invoked as a human norm when Hölderlin recurs to Greek semi-divine mediators such as Empedocles, Diotima, Heracles, and others and when he figures what he takes to be the nature of the poetic enterprise as one of enthusiasm [*enthusiasmos*] and ecstasy. Second, there is his own insanity that finally crystallizes around 1806 of which "in lovely blue" represents a moment of lucidity. Hegel, of course, will ultimately set himself against both excesses: the former because it points to an impossible "non-knowledge" beyond conceptual knowledge, the later because it suggests that conditions exist so insistent that knowledge cannot proceed to do its work. Stimulated in part at least by the work of Foucault on the construct of madness, there has been some reflection by Hegel scholars such as Dieter Henrich and William Desmond on the relation of the Hegelian system to the exclusion of madness whose provocation is exhibited in Hölderlin. By far the most systematic and complete account is provided by Daniel Berthold-Bond. See his *Hegel's Theory of Madness* (Albany: State University of New York Press, 1995).

35. The French at 148 reads: "La méditation hölderlinienne se fixe donc ici sur un des textes christologiques les plus décisifs de la tradition chrétienne. A cela aucun hazard, ni sans doute aucun arbitraire de lecture, mais comme l'inesquivable nécessité d'une convergence, à considérer le même paradoxe. Si l'on veut, à condition, d'entendre le paradoxe comme une certaine vision de la gloire et sa venue de biais (*paradoxos*)."

36. In the North American academy, Blanchot articulation of the apocalyptic of *vien* (which mimes the *maranatha* of Revelation 22:16) largely functions as a presupposition of his assimilation in and by the work of Derrida, and secondly Caputo's translation and apology. Arguably, *D'une ton apocalyptique adopté naguère en philosophie* (Paris: Galilée, 1983), is Derrida's best statement on the necessity and dangers of apocalyptic. For Caputo's translation of the apocalyptic degree zero of Blanchot and Derrida, see part 2 of *The Prayers and Tears of Jacques Derrida* (Bloomington: Indiana University Press, 1997).

37. For disparaging remarks about the book of Revelation in Derrida, see *Ton*, 78, 80–81, 86; for Caputo, see *The Prayers and Tears*, 70, 74, 80, 90–92, 95, 99.

38. A corollary of this is that in the Johannine corpus in general, and in Revelation in particular, we see how *apokalypsis* and *apophasis* define each other. Marion thinks that Hölderlin represents an authentic interpretation of John and is thus exemplary for the Christian tradition. Of course, Balthasar makes the general case for the intervolvement of *apocalypsis* and *apophasis* in *Herrlichkeit*. If anything he is even more insistent on the point in *Theodramatik*, in which the book of Revelation plays an extraordinarily important role in providing the basic coordinates for theodrama.

39. Heidegger is not the only Hegel interpreter anxious to bring out the relation between the *Phenomenology* and the *Logic* by appeal to the subtitle of the *Phenome-

nology as on the way to science. In different ways both Kojève and Hyppolite introduce this protocol into France.

40. Brito in particular has made this point with considerable force in both *La christologie de Hegel* and *La tâche actuelle de la christologie.*

41. Marion's position has been attacked by Laurence Paul Hemming. See his *Heidegger's Atheism: The Refusal of a Theological Voice* (Notre Dame: University of Notre Dame Press, 2002). See esp. chap. 8, "Jean-Luc Marion and the Contemporary Theological Appropriation of Heidegger," 249–69.

42. Thomas A. Carlson, *Indiscretion: Finitude and the Naming of God* (Chicago: University of Chicago Press, 1999), esp. chap. 3, "The Naming of God in Hegel's Speculative Proposition: The Circle of Language and the Annulment of the Singular," 80–112. Carlson understands well the seminal importance of Hyppolite's *Logique et existence* in making language the central French concern (81 n. 1). Helpfully, he also alludes to the contribution made by Jean Beaufret in his article "Hegel et la proposition spéculative," in *Dialogue avec Heidegger: Philosophie moderne* (Paris: Éditions de Minuit, 1973), 82 n. 2.

43. While Marion does not cite Hegel here, he obviously has in mind §§22, 63 of the *Phenomenology,* which have been the object of considerable commentary in French Hegelianism.

44. I take the liberty of invoking Husserl's locution of "irreal" to designate a noetic movement whose reality status is indeterminate, but that nevertheless is teleologically oriented toward fulfillment and actuality.

45. Hyppolite, *Logic and Existence,* 20–21; Nancy, *The Speculative Remark,* 28, 33, 56.

46. Nancy is particularly apropos here. See *The Speculative Remark,* 78–79. Of course, not only is Aristotle's view of predication surpassed in and by the speculative proposition, so also is Kant's view of judgment (80–81). Nancy here merely underscores what is self-conscious in Hegel's appeal to the speculative proposition.

47. One could imagine Paul Ricœur from one angle, and A. J. Austin and Donald Evans of the *Logic of Self-Involvement* from another, expressing similar objections.

48. One could translate the opposition here between very different kinds of trinitarianism into a contrast between agapaic and erotic trinitarianism. Of course, the condition of the possibility of the contrast is that one carefully define the meaning of "erotic." As used here, after the *Symposium* the erotic is a mixture of *poros* [fullness] and *penia* [lack], thus in a sense lack seeking fulfillment. The speculative proposition represents a figure of what is achieved by the Hegelian system as such. The contrast between trinitarianism that articulates and is articulated by different forms of love is made by William Desmond in *Hegel's God: A Counterfeit Double* (Albany: State University of New York Press, 2003). See esp. chap. 3, "Hegel's Trinity and the Erotic Self-Doubling God," 103–19; see also 137–39. The contrast is also a leitmotif of my *The Heterodox Hegel* (Albany: State University of New York Press, 1994).

49. All references are to the English translation of *Glas.* After the manner of Heidegger, Derrida seems to imply—but, of course, without stating—that Hegel represents the completion of Christianity whose basic figuration is Johannine. Of course,

Derrida here is miming "The Spirit of Christianity and its Fate" (1799), in which Hegel seems to make precisely this claim. The eucharistic orientation of Christianity, focused on Real Presence, which Hegel's philosophy submits to conceptual take-over, is a central feature of Johannine theology. Derrida ingeniously notes that the troping of the Eucharist is but one of the ways in which Hegel sublates Johanninely inflected Christianity. Especially important given Marion's reflection on filial distance is Derrida's concern with the Johannine configuration of the relation between Father and Son. In his view this relation and the bond between them that constitutes the Trinity functions basically as a metaphor whose full economic potential Hegel grasps perhaps better than anyone in the Western philosophical tradition. Throughout Derrida also draws attention to the archeo-teleological deployment of Johannine images that articulate both Real Presence and the Father–Son relation, for example, "life" (83), "death and life" (105, 245), "bread of life" (69), "seed" (27, 105).

50. In the left column of *Glas*, which essentially consists of a sustained reading of Hegel's works, both earlier and later (but without genetic gloss), Derrida continually refers to "remains" (e.g., 1, 43, 55, 71, 115, 148). The more scatological right column that presents Genet's response to the excision is full of references to "shit" and its derivatives. The scatological also makes it into the left column, however, in the shape of "vomit" (161, and "waste" 226–28). Derrida could have—but did not—refer to Hegel's use of the alchemical symbol of *caput mortuum* (*Encyclopedia*, §42), which literally means "death's head" and refers to the remains or residue left in the alchemical retort in the work of engendering the philosopher's stone [*lapis philosophorum*]. Interestingly, the philosopher's stone is often associated with the *Sol*, interpretable as both Sun and Son.

51. Here Hegel is led by the Johannine Prologue and particularly its relation to the Incarnation. See *Glas*, 75ff.

52. For Derrida in *Glas*, Hegelian philosophy is a Christian simulacrum (92, 96, 200–1, 218). Hegelian thought is onto-theological in an exemplary way (33); no ontology is possible without the Gospel (56), which presumably means that Hegelianism sums up the limits of metaphysics. Hegel mines biblical narrative for philosophemes (36, 79). Hegel's philosophy is a philosophy of the Christian Logos (75).

53. Derrida uses the figure of Antigone—the sister who demands burial rights for her rebel brother—as a hinge to undo Hegel. As is well known, Hegel thought that Sophocles' drama *Antigone* offered an exemplary instance of classical Greek drama, and also provided in its conflict between the forces of the state (Creon) and the family (Antigone) a figure of dialectic. On the face of it the latter cannot be right, since the conflict has a tragic peritpetia that precisely is not a resolution. Derrida can and does exploit this and shows how the family-earth is repressed rather than sublated, and how Antigone is unassimilatable into the apparatuses of the state or of discourse.

54. Interestingly, it makes the voices of others inaudible, not by being noise [*Klang*], but by excluding it. By contrast, the dialectical movement of the Hegelian system is musical. See *Glas*, 248–51.

55. While Hegel is not the only philosopher who is the object of critique in *Totalité et infini*, he certainly is regarded as one of the major culprits of the Western tradi-

tion whose thought is marked by the ambition of totality. Lévinas's turn to ethics is already implied in the critique of Hegel, but Lévinas also thinks that the domain of ethos can be phenomenologically exhibited. Derrida, and Marion too, are extraordinarily influenced by Lévinas's here, even as both submit Lévinas to amplification and correction.

56. In availing of this oxymoron I am being fully intentional. While, of course, serious play recalls the Schiller of the *Aesthetic Letters,* I have much more in mind Valéry's famous definition of poetry as "serious play" with which Derrida is undoubtedly familiar.

57. In *Glas,* Derrida implies that Johannine apocalypse is pleromatic and that Hegelian thought represents its speculative mime. Derrida's method is to work backward from Hegel's view of vision to its presumed incidence in John. Derrida naively or tactically takes Hegel at his word that he represents the consummation of Johannine visionary Christianity, thus in a sense a pleroma of a pleroma. A marker of Johannine Christianity is the pleromatic view of Christ (8, 59, 63). As this figure is taken up into the system on the basis of a relation to the Father that will demand a trinitarian fulfillment, it encourages a discourse of plerosis (238–39, 255). Pleroma, which is now interpreted more as an operation than a brute given, plays a fundamental role in the *Aufhebung,* since (a) it is interpreted by other dynamic-organic symbols of John such as "seed," "life and death"; and (b) it prefigures dialectic as *dialegein* (72), that is, the gathering together and recollecting that constitutes the archeo-teleological network of *Geist* (e.g., 24, 27, 106, 225). Most interestingly, plerosis is involved in an interesting relation with kenosis. The two mutually interpret each other. The dynamic operation of perfection—ontological and gnoseological—expresses itself in emptying. And kenosis, which is an emptying and a sacrifice, involves plerosis, the coming to be of the perfect realization of being and knowledge. If the last criticism essentially repeats his earlier essay "A Hegelianism without Reserve," the difference is that Christianity—even before explicit theologization—is implicated in the urge to totalization.

58. Although these poets are not referred to copiously throughout *God without Being* (Bonnefoy is cited once, and Char three times) they tend to provide lenses to read Hölderlin and to read the world after his manner. More work needs to be done on the relation between Marion and these poets, and especially with Char, who is cited at least four times in *The Idol and Distance* (6, 23, 25, 157).

59. An epigraph from Maximus frames the text. Marion makes the Hölderlin–Maximus relation explicit (126–27 n. 54), but signs off on bringing out the connection. Obviously, Marion is much influenced by Balthasar's *Kosmische Liturgie, Maximus der Bekenner* (1942). The influence of Balthasar is also evident in Marion's interpretation of Pseudo-Dionysius, who is provided a very-Balthasarian and thus very-Maximan christological reading. See my article "Von Balthasar and Thick Retrieval: Post-Chalcedonian Symphonic Theology," in *Gregorianum* (Spring 1996): 227–60.

60. Balthasar's reading of the New Testament, which concludes *Herrlichkeit* and which is volume 7 of the English translation *The Glory of the Lord,* serves as the definitive perspective from which to judge philosophical and theological regimes that either exclude John from consideration or misread him. In *Theodramatik* Balthasar is

much more concerned with the latter than the former, and different readings of the Johannine corpus—including Revelation—become truly pertinent. For Balthasar, it is crucial that the iconic dimension of the Johannine corpus renders mystery rather than negates or sublates it.

61. Marion refers to *Sein und Zeit,* §§81–82.

62. See Walter Jaeschke, *Reason in Religion: The Formation of Hegel's Philosophy of Religion,* trans. J. Michael Stewart and Peter Hodgson (Berkeley: University of California Press, 1990), 325–58.

63. As with Jaeschke, Marion tracks Hegelian thought in which the Reformation and specifically Lutheran critique of transubstantiation is a necessary condition for the liberation of the self-constituting and self-referring subjectivity. See Marion's long endnote (15) referring to Hegel to be found on 228–29 in which he makes this connection. See this note in *Dieu sans l'être,* 239–40.

64. In *God without Being,* as in *The Idol and Distance,* Nyssa, together with Maximus, Denys, and Bonaventure, is an important Christian neo-Platonic companion with Marion on his journey toward either phenomenological translation of religious texts and/or the finding of something like a phenomenological correlative. Since its deployment is *hors-texte,* the Nyssan construct of *epektasis* belongs to the second rather than first category. The double-displacement of the concept that is enacted in Marion's text should be noted: (i) While Nyssa thought that *epektasis* applied to the eschatological state—although it could be intimated in the pre-eschatological—Marion locates it in the pre-eschatological domain, albeit one that is qualified by connection with the presence that transforms "ordinary time." (ii) Nyssa's construct has been protected from a secondary form of subjectivity by Marion's emphasizing the liturgical-communal rather than individual context of the emptying of self and the self's fallen time that is the correlative of an infinite love that can never be grasped. The construct of *epektasis,* which as a theologoumenon was found problematic by the Western Church and condemned at the Lateran Council, Marion suggests, arguably has more phenomenological heft than the Western alternative of "vision," and has superior critical aptitude for the critique of metaphysics in general and of the critique of the metaphysics of Hegel in particular. Hegel can safely be regarded as the consummate ocular thinker of the West.

65. See *Theo-Drama: Theological Dramatic Theory,* vol. 5: *The Last Act,* trans. Graham Harrison (San Francisco: Ignatius Press, 1998). For Hegel, see 224–29. For Moltmann, see 168–75, 225–27.

66. *Prolegomena to Charity,* trans. Stephen Lewis (New York: Fordham University Press, 2002). This translates *Prolégomènes à la charité* (Paris: La Différence, 1986).

67. The "tampering with" the structural contrast between *eros* and *agapē* finds its most sustained expression in Marion's important recent work *Le phénomène érotique* (Paris: Grasset, 2003), which is translated *The Erotic Phenomenon,* trans. Stephen Lewis (Chicago: University of Chicago Press, 2007).

68. It should be noted that this essay represents an addition and is not to be found in the French text, which has six rather than seven essays and ends with the important "Le don d'une présence," the penultimate essay in the English edition.

69. In the context of *Prolegomena to Charity,* this assertion is controversial. The reason is that John 6:38 is not only not quoted in the important "The Gift of Presence," but is not quoted anywhere in the text. I would argue, however, that even as absent it is regulative in "The Gift of Presence," and that the work it normally does is done by other passages in John in addition to the reflection on mission in Luke.

70. See Léonard's essay, "Le primat du négative." This is an important emphasis in Brito's *La christologie de Hegel.*

71. Jean-Luc Marion, *Reduction and Givenness: Investigations of Husserl, Heidegger, and Phenomenology,* trans. Thomas A. Carlson (Evanston: Northwestern University Press, 1998); *Being Given: Towards a Phenomenology of Givenness,* trans. Jeffrey L. Kosky (Stanford: Stanford University Press, 2002); *In Excess: Studies of Saturated Phenomena,* trans. Robyn Horner and Vincent Berraud (New York: Fordham University Press, 2002). These translate respectively *Réduction et donation: Recherches sur Husserl, Heidegger et la phénomenologie* (Paris: PUF, 1989); *Étant donné: Essai d'une phénoménologie de la donation* (Paris: PUF, 1997); *De surcroît* (Paris: PUF, 2001).

72. This, of course, was also Husserl's opinion, who thinks of Hegel's thought as being incurably speculative.

73. Here Husserl and Hegel are opposed, since in Hegel "this" and "I" (as empirical) are overcome by language and concept. French Hegel interpretation has recognized the importance of Hegel's move since Hyppolite's *Logique et existence.* Without making it explicitly a choice between Husserl and Hegel, in *Difference and Repetition* Deleuze is engaged in working out a non-phenomenological antidote to Hegel's position.

74. See Jean-Luc Marion, *On Descartes's Metaphysical Prism: The Constitution and Limits of Onto-Theo-logy in Cartesian Thought,* trans. Jeffrey L. Kosky (Chicago: University of Chicago Press, 1999). See esp. 119–21; see also 143–44, 206, where Marion underscores the unnuanced nature of Heidegger's genealogy. This text represents a translation of *Sur le prisme métaphysique de Descartes: Constitution et limites de l'onto-théo-logie dans la pensée cartésienne* (Paris: PUF, 1986). See 126–28; see also 153–54, 217–18.

75. Marion here has as his proximate precursor Lévinas, who in *Totality and Infinity* makes this emphasis the basis of his rescue of Descartes from the history of metaphysics that achieves one of its high points in Hegel (the other is the later Heidegger of *es gibt*). One could argue Ricœur's well-known articulation of the Cartesian circle, which stipulates the irreducible bipolarity of Descartes's thought, also represents something of a precedent.

76. In Hegel, the ontological argument also goes by the "speculative proposition," the "syllogisms of the concept," and the "absolute idea."

77. See esp. chap. 9 of *Time and Narrative,* vol. 3, trans. Kathleen Blarney and David Pellauer (Chicago: University of Chicago Press, 1988), 193–206, entitled "Should We Renounce Hegel," where Ricœur worries among other things about the abolition of narrative in the concept. See esp. 199, 206. Ricœur's critique of Hegel in this text is very much in line with the view expressed in his "The Status of *Vorstellung* in Hegel's Philosophy of Religion," in *Meaning, Truth, and God,* ed. Leroy S. Rouner (Notre Dame: Notre Dame University Press, 1982), 70–88.

78. By "intra-philosophical contrast" I wish to mark that the contrast is not generated theologically by a commitment to Revelation as an actual event in which immanence is categorically breached.

79. See Michel Henry, *The Essence of Manifestation,* trans. Girard Etzkorn (The Hague: Martinus Nijhoff, 1973).

80. This is not to deny, however, that in this text Marion does in fact recur to Scripture and to works of theology by his favorites, Gregory of Nyssa and Pseudo-Dionysius, even as he insists that the latter are in the service of the former. Indeed, when Marion talks at length about the non-predicative function of Christian speech and especially about the liturgical context of theology, he does not seem to have gone beyond his earlier texts and is open to the accusation that he has confounded the domains of theology and phenomenology, which is the thrust of Dominque Janicaud's critique in *Le tournant théologique.* The discussion of the "saturated phenomenon" at the end suggests that the language of Scripture and theology reflect or refract at different levels of immediacy what is phenomenologically given.

81. Of course, Lévinas also represents a complicated case in which the enterprise of the expansion of phenomenology goes hand in hand with what appear to be religious commitments. In Lévinas these join forces against Hegelian thought, which is inadequately phenomenological and degeneratively religious in that his philosophy eclipses transcendence. In his notions of "the glory of the infinite" and "inspiration," articulated in *Otherwise than Being,* Levinas obviously anticipates Marion's use of "revelation" as a purely phenomenological counter to undo the plane of immanence. Thus despite appeal to biblical prophets and biblical categories, Lévinas understands his work to move within the horizon of philosophy, not religion. See *Otherwise than Being or Beyond Essence,* trans. Alphonso Lingis (The Hague: Martinus Nijhoff, 1981), 140–52. When Lévinas avails of the concept of "revelation," as he does in an essay "Revelation in the Jewish tradition," he seems to have in mind "Revelation" as this word is capitalized by Marion in *Being Given.* For this essay, see *Beyond the Verse: Talmudic Readings and Lectures,* trans. Gary D. Mole (Bloomington: Indiana University Press, 1992), 129–50. Given the connections between "glory" and the categories of "goodness" and the "infinite," which were both used to chastise Hegelian totalization in *Totality and Infinity,* it is obvious in the final two chapters (chaps. 5 and 6) of *Otherwise than Being* that concepts, which are cognate with "revelation," are intended among other things to humble Hegelian thought by insisting that the other exceeds sense. An obvious base for the attack against Hegel is the Jewish philosopher Franz Rosenzweig, who in *Stern der Erlösung* constructs what he believes is a purely philosophical notion of "revelation" to humble what he takes to be its simulacrum in Hegel, that is, manifestation. Marion, Lévinas, and Rosenzweig here constitute an interesting triangle. It is of no little interest that the Other who is revealed according to *Stern der Erlösung* (part 2) is concealed.

82. A host of critics have wondered whether Heidegger substitutes for Christianity a form of religiousness that admits of very different categorizations. These run the gamut from "pure religiousness" of the type, famously indicated by Rudolph Otto in *Das Heilige,* which is so influential to the pre-*Sein und Zeit* Heidegger; to "paganism,"

which is a consequence of Heidegger's regression to myth (Lévinas, Derrida, Caputo, Vycinas, Zimmerman); to "gnosticism" (Jonas); and to the view that Heidegger represents the meeting of the East and the West, or specifically that his work represents a "revisionist Buddhism" or "revisionist Taoism."

83. As I have indicated already, this point is a controversial one. Marion's reading of Heidegger has been challenged recently by Hemming in *Heidegger's Atheism*, chap. 8. At the same time, although Hemming makes his case in a much more systematic fashion than previous scholars, and provides the outlines of a much more disciplined encounter between philosophy and theology, he is hardly eccentric. For the most part theology's encounter with Heideggerian philosophy has operated under the assumption that, understood properly, Heidegger does not run interference with the more biblical and more mystical aspects of Christianity. Examples of such reading abound in the literature. See, e.g., George Kovacs, *The Question of God in Heidegger's Phenomenology* (Evanston: Northwestern University Press, 1990); John D. Caputo, *The Mystical Element in Heidegger's Thought* (New York: Fordham University Press, 1986).

84. Given the rehabilitation of the "idol" in *Being Given*, it is logically possible that Heidegger's discourse could be assigned a measure of "saturatedness." But only logically possible. It would seem that phenomena that are more nearly first order are in a better position to benefit from Marion's reevaluation and not philosophical discourses whose idolatry is from the beginning reflective and second order.

85. As many of Hegel's more important texts make clear, for example, *Encyclopedia* §§564–71, *Phenomenology* §7, and Hegel's entire treatment of Christianity as "consummate religion [*die vollendete Religion*]" in *Lectures on the Philosophy of Religion*.

86. A considerable portion of Staudenmaier's significant output is directed against Hegel. Staudenmaier's most sustained critique (also analysis) of Hegel is *Darstellung und Kritik des Hegelschen Systems. Aus dem Standpunkte der christlichen Philosophie* (Mainz: Kupferberg, 1844; reprint ed., Frankfurt: Minerva., 1966).

87. See Ricœur, "The Status of *Vorstellung* in Hegel's Philosophy of Religion," 70–88.

88. Thus, Lévinas's scruple to the point of neuralgia in distinguishing between those aspects of his work that are philosophical from those that are religious or theological. For him—if not necessarily his critics—the religious works are defined in large part by his Talmudic exegesis.

89. This is an image that G. Fessard recurred to in his *Dialectique des exercises spirituels de Saint Ignace de Loyola*, 3 vols. (Paris: Aubier, 1956–84).

90. In addition to the aesthetic possibility that remains open, there is also the theo-logical possibility. That is, it is open to Marion to appeal, as Balthasar does, to the Catholic principle that grace completes but surpasses nature. This is not to say that either of these positions would be adopted by Marion, or that they are without problems. Perception or discernment of correspondence or analogy would still have to deal with the issue of communicability, and the formal Catholic principle itself covers a multitude of perspectives that vary from grace being mere superaddition to grace being dialectically related to a creation that is its supposition.

91. It is a little ironic that the "impurity" of discourse is such a problem for Derrida in his later work, and especially in "Sauf le Nom" and "Le ton apocalyptique." It

is after all central to *Grammatology* and even *Glas* that discourses by the nature of the case are impure. Thus, it is not clear what critical edge is gained on Marion by insisting that his discourse is impure beyond suggesting that Marion is involved in a performative contradiction. Arguably, these later texts of Derrida testify to the increasing importance of Kant, even as Derrida claims to go beyond him. What looks as if it is of particular importance is Kant's stipulation of the distinction between the domains of philosophy and theology.

92. *Geist in Welt* was originally written in 1939 and is the most philosophically dense of all of Rahner's texts. See *Spirit in the World,* trans. William Dych (New York: Herder and Herder, 1968).

93. Of course, this is not to say that Marion does not hold such a view, but simply that Marion does not argue for it. The identification of Christ and the icon in Marion's theologically aspirated texts, and the parsing of revelation by reference to Christ and the scriptural witness to Christ in *Being Given* (§24), provide strong indications that Marion is inclined toward such a view.

94. For Balthasar's reflections on Péguy, see *The Glory of the Lord: A Theological Aesthetics,* vol. 3: *Studies in Theological Styles: Lay Styles,* trans. Andrew Louth, John Saward, Martin Simon, and Rowan Williams; ed. John Riches (San Francisco: Ignatius Press, 1986), 400–517; *Bernanos: An Ecclesial Existence,* trans. Erasmo Leiva-Merikakis (San Francisco: Ignatius Press, 1996).

95. See Michel Foucault, *The Archaeology of Knowledge* (New York: Pantheon, 1972), 235.

96. The French reads: "Il était un homme, une fois, qui n'ayant plus faim, plus jamais faim, tant il avait dévoré d'héritages, englouti d'aliments, appauvri son prochain, trouva sa table vide, son lit désert, sa femme grosse, et la terre mauvaise dans le champ de son coeur.

N'ayant pas de tombeau et se voulant en vie, n'ayant rien à donner et moins à recevoir, les objets le fuyant, les bêtes lui mentant, il vola la famine et s'en fit une assiette qui devint son miroir et sa propre déroute." This poem is from *Les Matinaux* (1947–49). I have used but slightly modified a translation of this prose poem that can be found in *The Poems of René Char,* trans. and annot. Mary Ann Caws and Jonathan Griffin (Princeton: Princeton University Press, 1976), 132–33.

97. See "White Mythology: Metaphor in the Text of Philosophy," in *Margins of Philosophy,* 207–71, esp. 266–71.

98. The incidence of Kant in Marion is high. The First and Second Critiques are especially important. One notices, however, in Marion's later work the increasing importance of the Third Critique.

99. Brito, *La tâche actuelle de la christologie.*

II

GOD AND *L'ADONNÉ*

4

Blindness and the Decision to See

On Revelation and Reception in Jean-Luc Marion

THOMAS A. CARLSON

In response to Jean-Luc Marion's work, and in thanks for his writing, teaching, and friendship, I would like first to give him what he may never have received before—the title "liberation theologian." In and through his efforts, both theological and phenomenological, to conceive and to speak of revelation as inconceivable and ineffable because unconditionally self-giving, Marion writes one of the most challenging of liberation theologies—one that seeks primarily, however, not to place the disruptive power of revelation in the service of all too human ends (liberation as we might understand or expect it in its social, political, and economic senses), but much rather to free *God* from the alienation in which he would have been placed by the reign of the human sciences (which would understand revelation in terms of everything but its own unconditional self-showing) and by the metaphysics (especially modern metaphysics) that would undergird the human sciences and culminate in the nihilism of our time.[1] Both in its conception of the human subject (as setting the conditions of possibility for experience and intelligibility, especially in terms of objectivity) and in its conception of God (as prime mover, *causa sui*, sufficient reason, etc.) metaphysics would occlude revelation in its true sense because it would demand that God appear not in his own way but according to the conditions of an objectivized human experience and/or so as to account for and render intelligible, primarily in terms of efficient causality or the logic of sufficient reason, the appearance of all other phenomena. The defining gesture of metaphysics, in its conception of human subject and God alike, is to establish *a priori* grounds or reasons according to which alone anything, including God, might appear and thus to place the reason for appearance somewhere outside, beyond, or behind that appearance itself—thereby yielding only an "alienated phenomenality" and thereby impeding the appearance and reception of any revelation worthy of the name.

It is against the horizon of metaphysics so understood that Marion begins to think revelation in terms that would exceed all horizon; and if this project begins first to unfold within theological texts like *The Idol and Distance, God without Being,* and *Prolegomena to Charity,* his relatively early theological efforts point toward the broader task of giving "pure giving to be thought," as Marion indicates in his preface to the English translation of *God without Being.*[2] If the theological project starts with the scriptural and traditional givens of Christian faith and then opens onto the question of unconditional giving more broadly, the subsequent phenomenological treatment of givenness will make of revelation the norm of self-giving phenomenality,[3] and it will make of a certain faith the necessary condition of such phenomenality. In what follows, I sketch out the operation of such faith in the phenomenology of revelation in order then to ask what its implications might be for Marion's relation both to modern conceptions of freedom in terms of decision and to metaphysical conceptions of will in terms of responsibility and guilt.

Marion has worked brilliantly to reverse philosophy's ideological dismissal of revelation and of its experience as valid and necessary terrain for philosophical questioning, and he has done so primarily through his analysis of the "saturated phenomenon," whose highest form he finds in revelation, and through the reconception of the subjectivity that would be called for in light of the saturated phenomenon.

Indicating a type of phenomenon in which the givenness of intuition would precede and exceed the capacity of any subject to conceive or intend that intuition, the saturated phenomenon overturns the classic understandings of Kant and Husserl, where a concept or intention, an aim or meaning, precedes and then eventually receives either a poor or a relatively adequate fulfilling intuition, and where the possibility is never fully considered that our concepts and intentions, aims and meanings, might prove inadequate to the intuition actually given to us in most experience. Thanks to the excess of its unconditional and irreducible givenness, Marion's saturated phenomenon cannot be constituted as an object nor inscribed within the conditions of any horizon, and for this reason it would require a third phenomenological reduction, beyond Husserl and Heidegger alike, to the pure givenness that defines the phenomenon "in its fullest sense" as that alone which "appears truly as itself, of itself, and starting from itself, since it alone appears without the limits of a horizon, nor the reduction to an *I* and constitutes itself, to the point of giving *itself* as a *self*" (*ED*, 304–5).[4] From this perspective, the most saturated of all saturated phenomena—revelation—would in the paradox of its apparent nonappearance constitute the norm against which all other phenomena might be situated.[5]

If the *self*-giving saturated phenomenon undoes the alienated phenomenality characteristic of metaphysics, then in turn its *self*-manifestation— because setting its *own* conditions for appearing rather than answering to the active, spontaneous subject of modern thought—calls for an alternative conception of the subject in which subjectivity would be characterized "by the submission within itself of its undeniable activity and living spontaneity to the passivity of an absolutely originary receptivity" (*ED*, 425). Marion's conception here of the saturated phenomenon is based in a radical reversal of intentionality, inspired largely by Emmanuel Lévinas, according to which it is not the active, nominative subject of consciousness and language who sets the conditions under which the phenomenon appears, but much rather the unconditional and irreducible givenness of the phenomenon that first gives birth to a radically passive, vocative, and dative "subject"—or no longer a subject but rather what comes (historically) after because (in fact and principle) radically preceding the subject in its modern senses: the one Marion names first the *interloqué* and then the *adonné,* that is, the one who is originarily given to himself or herself in being given over always already to the prior call of givenness.

Now if, as I will elaborate, Marion seeks to overcome the subjection of phenomenality to a metaphysical subjectivity, he seeks also to unsettle the subjection of phenomenality to any metaphysical God—the God, that is, who would constitute the sufficient reason for all appearance and thus, like the modern subject of metaphysics, alienate phenomenality from itself. Despite his thoroughgoing dismissals of the metaphysical God, however, interpreters such as Dominique Janicaud and Jacques Derrida have nonetheless charged that his phenomenology is really a poorly disguised theology or metaphysics— perhaps above all because they suspect that "the call" of givenness giving birth to the *interloqué* or *adonné*, in principle indeterminate and anonymous, is in fact a quite determinate call of the Christian God and Father.[6] Marion's compelling response to this charge is instructive, I think, as much for what it argues about the real work of theology as for what it claims about the scope of phenomenology.

Following in a rich phenomenological tradition of reflection on the "call," while echoing also, to be sure, traditions of Jewish and Christian revelation and liturgy, Marion's third phenomenological reduction is, as I have suggested, both "donative" and "vocative": reduction to the unconditional givenness of the phenomenon is a reduction to the unconditional call or claim exercised by such givenness over a nascent subjectivity. Givenness in fact enters into visibility only through the response made by the *adonné* to the call of givenness; that response, then, is an indispensable pole of phenomenal givenness itself. As Marion indicates, "The call and the responsal [*le répons*] are joined [*s'articulent*] as that which gives itself with that which shows itself, through the go-between of a prism—the *adonné*—that converts the one [i.e., the self-giving call] into the other [i.e., the showing of that call in a response], because it [the *adonné*] receives itself from what gives itself in [the call]" (*ED*, 408). Within this third reduction, then, prior to any constituting ego and prior to any Dasein, there appears the *adonné*, which means the one who, before being (in the subjective mode of consciousness, intention, resoluteness, etc.), is called into a being that is at bottom response, and so already a giving; one who, before becoming a subject in the first person nominative, is originally given over both to givenness and, through givenness, to itself—as already giving once again, for in giving I do not lose but indeed gain myself. Much as with the reversal of intentionality in Lévinas, where it is not I who make possible the appearance of an other whom I would intend but rather the other who first intends me in calling me to responsibility for the other, so here in Marion the priority of the call over my response to it signals that I am always already constituted by an irreducible delay or difference with respect to my own origin: "I am born," Marion writes, "from a call that I have not issued, nor willed, nor even heard. Birth consists solely in this excess of the call and in the delay of my response" (*ED*, 400).[7]

Here, I think, in the inevitable and insurmountable delay of my response to an irreducibly prior and thus excessive call, one might well glimpse the impossibility of identifying the source of that call—an impossibility that would in

principle hold, furthermore, as much (or more) in theology as Marion understands it as in phenomenology:

> The anonymity of the caller (the who or what) . . . does not weaken the
> concept of the call, but confirms it: since I recognize *myself* as sum-
> moned or spoken to [*convoqué ou interloqué*] before any consciousness
> of my subjectivity—which, precisely, would result from that summons
> or interlocution—, any knowledge of the identity of the caller will come
> eventually to be added to the claim after the fact, but it will not precede
> the claim as a presupposition. (*ED*, 412)

In other words, if I were to know or to claim ahead of time that the call is
the call of God—or of Being, the other, or life, as Heidegger, Lévinas, and
Michel Henry might argue, respectively—then I would be subjecting the call
to the precedence of a constituting intention, forcing it to conform to my
expectations, and to do this would be to ignore both the irreducible structure of passivity and delay implied by my birth and thus, on the other side,
the unconditional poverty and anonymity of the call that gives such birth (see
ED, 413).

The argument that Marion's phenomenology of the call *really* understands
that call to be one of the Christian God and Father is an argument that ignores
this insurmountable delay of the *adonné* in its constitutive response. Because
that response necessarily—and forever—lags behind the call that provokes it,
I can as *adonné* name the source of that call only after the fact, and thus always
incompletely and provisionally, never comprehending nor defining the essence
of that which calls. This is true both for each of the four types of saturated
phenomenon that Marion delineates (event, idol, flesh, icon) and for the sum-
mation of those four types within the phenomenon of revelation. Operating
according to the logic of the anonymous call, the phenomenon of revelation
(unforeseeable according to quantity; unbearable according to quality; absolute according to relation; and incapable of being looked at according to
modality) pushes the excess of givenness to an extreme of blinding indeterminacy in which intuitive saturation can appear as intuitive poverty—a poverty
that is essential to the call itself, a kind of weakness that bestows its power to
provoke. That poverty, Marion argues, prohibits any secure naming of the
source of givenness even as it also generates the necessity of an endless attempt

to name over and again that which no name will capture. In the doubly saturated phenomenon of revelation especially,

> the call . . . would not carry any name, because it would assume them all; the anonymity would be reinforced by the very excess of the paradox, which would require an infinite naming; thus no call would offer *less* of a name than that of a phenomenon of revelation. . . . Far, then, from having to fear that such a call leads surreptitiously to naming a transcendent *numen* and to turning—for the worse—to "theology," it is necessary to conclude that, on the contrary, every phenomenon of revelation (as possibility) and especially a Revelation (as actuality) would imply the radical anonymity of that which calls. (*ED*, 410)

Here Marion not only answers the charge that his phenomenology of givenness proves metaphysical for identifying the source of the call as God (givenness as transcendent cause), he goes further to argue that any danger of such identification would, in any case, be least operative in a revealed theology, which his critics wrongly confuse with metaphysical theology.

He develops this line of argument through a remarkable analysis of the Christ, who becomes the figure not of any essential determination of the call or its source but indeed of the call's profound indeterminacy: "The fact that the Christ can receive a plurality of names, of which none speak his essence, is meant to reproduce the property of God himself of admitting all names and of rejecting them all (*polyōnymon kai anōnymon*)—the property of convoking an infinity of horizons of nomination in order to de-nominate the one who saturates not only every horizon, but the incommensurable sum of horizons" (*ED*, 333). Thus, in a line of reasoning that is vintage Marion, phenomenology would be least in danger of identifying the call in theological terms (taken metaphysically) when it treats the givenness of that call in theological terms (taken as revelation)—for revealed theology itself would never be theological in the sense intended by the critics of a "theological turn," since, unlike the theology of metaphysics, revealed theology never actually determines in a concept, and especially that of causality, the source of Revelation's call. Evoking the traditions of mystical theology derived largely from the Pseudo-Dionysius, Marion can argue in equally phenomenological and theological terms that "the paradox of paradoxes does not have to choose between kataphasis and apophasis any more than between the saturation and poverty of intuition—it uses them all to push to its limit the phenomenality of what shows itself only inasmuch as it gives itself" (*ED,* 340). As Dionysian theology insists, mystical theology would signal the inadequacy of affirmative and negative languages alike, for the paradox of revelation gives a "luminous darkness" whose superplenitude, which might appear indeed as lack, cannot be contained or constrained by such an alternative.

The paradox of revelation, whether treated in phenomenology or in theology, would be such that plenitude can appear as lack, or the over-fullness of the phenomenon be received only in blindness—but this, for Marion, is a function of excess and not defect (to evoke the neo-Platonic distinction fundamental to Dionysian theology). The apparent nonappearance of the saturated phenomenon, especially in the paradox of revelation, could be taken as a positive trait of its distinctive visibility: "If the *phenomenon* of revelation could be seen without lack, without indetermination or bedazzlement, would it manifest itself more perfectly as a phenomenon of *revelation,* or on the contrary would it not disqualify itself all the more? Does it not belong essentially to the paradox and its appearance [*apparition*] to contradict the course of appearance in general, to give itself as *para*-dox, and not only as para-*dox?*" (*ED,* 339). In the (immeasurable) measure, then, that the phenomenon of revelation gives itself outside the flow of what we normally expect or count as appearance, its visibility can go unseen—and such unseen givenness Marion names "the abandoned," which is to say the "phenomena of revelation (saturation of saturation), where the excess of the gift can take on the aspect of poverty" (*ED,* 341).

How, though, might we understand here the difference between that which goes unseen because it gives an excess of intuition, a super-plenitude of givenness, and that which goes unseen because it gives no intuition whatsoever? And how, in relation to this distinction, might we understand the role of blindness in the reception of revelation? To elucidate these questions, I'd like to begin by distinguishing two different senses in which blindness might be understood in relation to the saturated phenomenon and hence revelation.

A first form of blindness would be the relatively straightforward function of my finitude, which inevitably prevents me from receiving and converting into visibility through my response to it *all* of the given, which, by contrast to my finitude (according to which I am definitively *not all*), remains, within Marion's basic phenomenological position, without limit or reserve—without exception. According to the logic of the given as abandoned, "it happens sometimes that what gives itself does not manage to show itself" (*ED*, 425), but for Marion this fact does not call into question the principle that what gives itself does finally show itself; rather, it signals only that "the monstration of the given . . . is put into operation within the essential finitude of the *adonné*" (*ED*, 425):

> [A]s its finitude determines the *adonné* essentially, it cannot by definition receive adequately the given such as it gives itself—namely without limit or reserve; and hence the finitude of the phenomenalization put into operation by the *adonné* necessarily does not manage to render visible everything that befalls the *adonné*. The phenomenological principle that what gives itself shows itself remains intact, but it is realized for us only within the limits where the finite *adonné* manages to put it into operation. (*ED*, 425)

Essentially related to this insurmountable finitude of the one whose response alone makes visible that which gives itself and therefore shows itself would be the luminous darkness, the bedazzlement of revelation—a form of blindness resulting from my finitude, according to which I might look at more than I am capable of seeing (at least as a constituted object) and hence experience vision as darkness, super-plenitude as lack. What remains difficult to explain here is my capacity to see, from within the limits of my finitude, and from within the experience of such blindness, the very fact *that* givenness does nonetheless give itself without limit or reserve. Prior to my receiving the given so as to make it visible, how would I see that I do not see? Or how would I distinguish between the blindness of intuitive excess and that of intuitive lack?

Here, I think, it is possible and productive to notice a second form of blindness in Marion, which can be distinguished from the first insofar as the failure to see what nonetheless gives itself and shows itself—including what gives itself so excessively that I could see its light only in darkness—would result not so much from the *finitude* of my capacity to see the excess at which I nonetheless look, but indeed more from that in me which resembles an *infinitude:* namely, from my *will*, where I can prove not simply unable but indeed unwilling to see or receive the given, refusing to be constrained by any obligation or imperative at all—including not only reason or understanding, to which metaphysics would characteristically yoke the will, but also the givenness of what gives itself without limit or reserve, in excess of reason and understanding.

The function of will becomes central to the question of blindness because the gap between givenness and phenomenality is to be understood not only in terms of capability, which is always finite or limited, but also in terms of decision or choice, which might both restrict the capacity I do possess or could exercise and, in the other direction, deny that my capacity even has limits or falls short of the given (and in this sense, as I will suggest, metaphysical blindness to the excess of givenness would be a function of this willful blindness):

> Now, if the *adonné* always phenomenalizes that which gives itself to the *adonné* and always receives itself from that which gives itself, nothing says that the *adonné* should be able or should want [*puisse ou veuille*] to receive *all* that gives itself: one could never exclude some cases where a given would not manage to show itself because the *adonné* would be unable or would simply be unwilling [*ne pourrait ou ne voudrait*] to receive it. (*ED*, 426)

Reception of the unconditionally given, in sum, might be limited not only by the finite capability of the one who receives but also by a constriction or a weakening or a turning of the will, which thus assumes a literally decisive role in staging the given in its visibility.

Indeed, "the decision to respond," Marion writes, "and hence to receive, precedes the possibility of seeing, and hence of conceiving. The more the given is saturated with intuition and rises toward paradox [which means: the closer the given comes to revelation] the more that decision becomes difficult as well as fruitful, because the responsal [*le répons*] proves to be less and less adequate, more and more insufficient and hence to be ceaselessly repeated" (*ED*, 420). In order to see, the *adonné* can and must only decide to see, and that decision cannot be based on what it alone makes possible—the visibility of the given: "the responsal [*le répons*] must only decide, without being able to rely on the visibility of that which does not show itself before the responsal" (*ED*, 421). "Seeing is believing," as the saying goes, which here means not, as one Thomas might think, that belief ensues from the force of evidence seen but rather, indeed, that I must first believe, thanks to a decision made in darkness, in order to see at all.

This decision to see, then, might be understood to fall squarely within the logic of a faith seeking understanding, which means that the possibility of phenomenology itself relies on a necessarily pre-phenomenological movement of faith: "At the birth of the visible (at the conversion of that which gives itself into that which shows itself), there comes into play, in a pre-phenomenological and pre-rational obscurity, the choice or refusal of 'the great reason'—of unconditional givenness" (*ED*, 422). Phenomenology, then, may well be first philosophy, but philosophy is not first, for it cannot get going without faith. If Marion's theological project begins in faith and points finally toward the phenomenological project of giving "pure giving to be thought" (*GWB*, xxv), his phenomenology of givenness proves to depend on this moment of choice or decision whose structure and movement repeat those of the faith whose leap must be without sufficient reason or visible evidence in order to remain faith—as "the evidence of things unseen" (Hebrews 11:1) or as the hope "for what we do not see" (Romans 8:25). Insofar as I would seek reason or evidence in order to see, I rejoin the logic of metaphysics, whose defining trait from this perspective is, precisely, to elide faith and its unfounded decision, granting nothing without foundation or sufficient reason and thus subjecting the absolute freedom of will to the authority of intellect or understanding.

Marion elucidates his phenomenological take on this freedom of will—and he highlights its divergence from metaphysics—by referencing and revaluating the two types of "indifference," finite and infinite, that Descartes evokes within his metaphysical treatment of freedom in the fourth of his *Meditations on First Philosophy*. The decision to see or not to see, the choice or refusal of unconditional givenness, Marion writes,

> recovers and radicalizes what Descartes understood by indifference, but redoubling it. Indeed, Descartes opposed the negative indifference of the finite mind, where the weakness of the understanding leaves the will undecided, to the positive indifference of God, where the initiative of creation precedes every rational state of affairs. Here, the *adonné*, by definition finite and originarily *a posteriori*, finds itself in charge of receiving or of denying the given, that is, the *a priori* of givenness. It is thus inasmuch as it remains negatively indifferent (through a failure to see) that it receives the burden of positive indifference (to make that which gives itself show itself or not). The *adonné*, inasmuch as finite, has nothing less than the charge of opening or closing the entire flux of phenomenality. (*ED*, 422)

In other words, precisely in my finitude as *adonné*, in the measure of the blindness that inevitably conditions such finitude, I become, through a movement of will that can rely on no evidence or reason, the location—or worker—of conversion from the given to the seen. Just as the provocation of the call depends on its poverty, as noted above, so, in a striking sense, my weakness becomes my power, my incapacity my capacity—to the point that I become, through this unconstrained movement of blind will, "the sole given in which the visibility of all the other givens is at stake."[8]

Now, by making my response—itself a function of free decision or unconstrained will—an indispensable pole for the visibility of the phenomenon does Marion not risk imposing on the visibility of the phenomenon, and above all that of revelation, precisely the kind of metaphysical condition from which his entire project seeks to free it? How can we locate a condition of possibility for the appearance of the phenomenon in will and its decision while insisting at the same time that this movement of will escapes the logic of modern metaphysics? Does this need for willful decision deprive the given of its dignity as unconditionally *self*-showing?

In order to avoid the danger of such a metaphysical conception of the will, Marion suggests two lines of response worth noting here—the first more restricted in scope, and perhaps less compelling, the second perhaps more compelling but also more charged in its implications.

The first is framed directly in relation to Descartes and his metaphysical interpretation of will as the source of error in judgment: the exercise of will in Descartes, Marion notes, proves metaphysical because and insofar as Descartes yokes will to the authority of understanding. As Descartes puts it in the fourth *Meditation*, "the source of my mistakes" "must be simply this: the scope of will is wider than that of intellect; but instead of restricting it within the same limits, I extend its use to matters I do not understand."[9] My errors in judgment, then, result neither simply from will and its freedom nor simply from intellect or understanding but from my failure to confine the will's exercise within the scope of understanding; what the metaphysical position seeks to avoid is this "misuse" of freedom beyond reason: "[I]t is surely no imperfection in God," Descartes writes, "that he has given me the freedom to assent or not to assent in those cases where he did not endow my intellect with a clear and distinct perception; but it is undoubtedly an imperfection in me to misuse that freedom and make judgments about matters which I do not fully understand" (AT, VII, 61). The whole thrust of Marion's treatment of revelation shows brilliantly how such a metaphysical restriction on will excludes the possibility of approaching at all the experience actually at stake in revelation (and in so many other cases of saturation, including not only mystical theology but historical events, literature, painting, the psychoanalytic cure, and so on—all instances of intuitive saturation irreducible to the clear and distinct objects of understanding). What Descartes and his modern metaphysics count as error, then, proves to be, for Marion's phenomenology, a necessity and a virtue:[10]

> What metaphysics stigmatizes as error defines, on the contrary, in phenomenological terms, the fundamental exercise of the responsal [répons] such as it converts that which gives itself into that which shows itself. For in order to phenomenalize the given, it is necessary first to admit it ("to will" indeed to see it) and to receive oneself from it as being given over to it, in order thus to see (eventually to comprehend through "understanding") what it shows. The decision to respond, and hence to receive, precedes the possibility of seeing, and hence of conceiving. (ED, 420)

From this perspective, the exercise of the will would not necessarily prove metaphysical, even if that exercise takes on the charge of opening or closing the flux of all phenomenality, for what makes the will metaphysical would be instead the subjection of its exercise to the constraints of understanding.[11] If this seems, however, a relatively narrow terrain within which to define the metaphysical turn of will, insofar as one can imagine other conceptions of will that might prove metaphysical without being yoked in this way to the demands of understanding, a second line of response addresses the question of will in broader and more complex terms.

This second line of response speaks directly to the dynamic of faith that proves indispensable "at the birth of the visible," and in this direction Marion suggests that my decision to see, my wanting or willing to see, which could seem to risk becoming an *a priori* condition of what was purported to be an unconditionally self-giving phenomenon or revelation, is in fact itself a gift: given to me only by givenness itself, such that the first (the unconditionally and unrestrictedly given) can seem to be last (because coming into visibility only through my decision), when in fact what seems to be first (this decision to see) is in fact last (because given by the given that always already precedes me and first calls me to respond): "Nothing of what gives itself can show itself except to the *adonné* and through it. Not through constitution, anticipatory decision, or exposure to the other, but indeed through the will to see [*le vouloir bien voir*] [which is] originally derived from givenness itself" (*ED*, 422).

The logic of a decision that (seemingly first) makes visible the given (seemingly last) while deriving (in fact last) from the givenness of the given itself (in fact first) recalls in more than superficial ways the interplay between conversion and grace in contexts of Christian, especially Augustinian, theology. Just as, phenomenologically speaking, the given appears as visible only to the one whose decision to see derives from the given itself, so, theologically speaking, grace appears only for the one who turns or converts toward that grace, in a conversion that is itself a gift of the grace that appears to the convert only through this very turning. If theologically speaking I am blind to the grace that sustains and saves me until grace itself turns or redirects my will to see it, so phenomenologically speaking I am blind to the given that gives itself to me until I am given—by the given itself—the will that decides to see the given. And just as we might in phenomenology distinguish between a blindness that results from the finitude of my capability and one that results from a misdirection of will, so we could recall the distinction made in theology between my inability, as finite creature, to receive all of God's glory, even in the state of beatitude (as, e.g., with Thomas Aquinas on the illumination of the intellect), and a failure to see God's glory due not to finitude alone but to the sinful turning of my will.[12]

If such Christian thinking on conversion through grace involves a strong notion of alienation, according to whose ambiguity the failure to see grace (both the ground and consequence of my sin) is indeed my failure (not a defect or lack of grace) while my success in seeing grace (and hence also in seeing the sin that blinds me) is a gift of that grace alone, so in Marion's phenomenology there seems to operate an alienation according to whose ambiguity whatever success I achieve, as *adonné*, in seeing givenness is due not to me or my initiative but to that which gives itself beyond my initiative, while my failure to see—my blindness—can be counted as my failure, insofar as that blindness is not a defect of givenness, which can admit no exception, but a function of my will (and here one might wonder whether the will does not in effect count as the exception).

The saturated phenomenon—and its saturation in revelation—is, in this direction, exemplary. When Marion notes that my failure to render the given phenomenal (my blindness) can result both from lack (as, e.g., in the case of death, which gives no intuition to be realized in any present) and from excess (as in the case of revelation, which gives too much intuition to present or to represent), he maintains the possibility of distinguishing blinding revelation (which only appears as poverty but remains over-full) from the darkness of something like death (an actual poverty that gives no intuition): hyper-plenitude and utter barrenness both leave me blind, with nothing to see or conceive, to render present or represent; but I can nonetheless see the difference between them—so long as I have the will. The possibility that the *adonné* would fail to render phenomenal what is in fact an excess of intuitive givenness "is distingushed not only from the preceding possibility (the poverty of intuition) [as with death], because it occupies symmetrically the other end of the spectrum of givenness, but first because it introduces, beyond the impotence of the *adonné* (already constitutive of the witness), its eventual will [*volonté*] not to stage the intuitive excess given to it" (*ED*, 431). The difference between those who stage revelation as phenomenon (even if a phenomenon of the inapparent or the abandoned) and those who do not (not seeing it at all, or confusing it with something other than itself) is a turning of will. Here, then, we see clearly, within Marion's analysis, the distinction between two forms of blindness sketched above—that, inevitable, due simply to my finitude ("the impotence of the *adonné*," "already constitutive of the witness") and that, seemingly avoidable or reversible, which results from my will (my will "not to stage the intuitive excess given to it"). From this perspective, the *adonné* proves, as it were, doubly "guilty": not only always already indebted to a givenness in relation to which its response forever falls short, but then also willfully inadequate, refusing to acknowledge either the given as such (in its excess) or the *adonné*'s own inadequacy to that excess (again, the metaphysical position, or in Augustine the sinful position).

The role assigned to will in converting the given into the phenomenal can seem, then, to introduce into the question of revelation (and of phenomenality more broadly) an understanding of responsiveness and responsibility that entails an essential implication of debt and fault on the part of the one who manages (or not) to make the given visible—and that responsibility, along with the attendant debt or fault, would become even more pressing, more necessary and more overwhelming, as the saturation of phenomenality moves closer to revelation, where the inadequacy of my response, and hence my fault, can only grow in the immeasurable measure of what gives itself.

In this direction, one might note again the deep kinship between Marion and Lévinas, for Marion not only takes up and extends from Lévinas the decisive reversal of intentionality, he also elaborates that reversal in terms of immeasurable responsibility and the insurmountable inadequacy of any response to the given that calls for response. One can at the same time wonder, however, whether Marion does not also differ significantly from Lévinas precisely here, for in Marion reception of the given through response to it is a function of blind decision, made within the freedom of indifference, which implies a measure of activity within the *adonné*'s originary passivity, while by contrast Lévinas insists on "the antecedence of responsibility to freedom" and on a "pre-originary susceptiveness" that would involve a "passivity prior to all receptivity."[13] It could be that Marion's conception of the *adonné*, especially in terms of the will required for reception, involves a greater measure of activity than is found in Lévinas's responsible self, but the responsibility tied to that activity does have, like responsibility in Lévinas, an immeasurable, overwhelming character that stems from the insurmountable delay between the call and my response to it, from the gap, then, between the given and its phenomenalization, which becomes a space and time of inadequacy and fault. If *Being Given* suggests that the choice to see or not see is not a moral choice, and if Marion reworks the Lévinasian reversal of intentionality by extending it beyond its strictly ethical sense to phenomenality more broadly, one might nonetheless read in that choice, and in the conception of will tied to it, a significant trace of traditional Augustinian thinking on sin. Just as Marion closes his treatment of "The Present and the Gift" in *God without Being* by quoting Augustine's assertion, "Not only do we not sin by adoring Him, but we sin by not adoring Him" (Augustine's commentary on Psalm 98:9, in *GWB*, 182), so likewise one might say of the saturated phenomenon: not only are we not guilty in seeing it, but we are guilty in not seeing it.

The struggle at stake here—the choice to be made or not made—is one that shapes, for Marion, the entire history of philosophy in what he takes to be two irreconcilable tendencies: "either to constitute the object [which is] poor in intuition, or to receive the excess of givenness without objectivating it" (*ED*, 421). According to the language and logic with which he frames this alternative, we might understand the decision at stake to be one between arrogance and humility—or one that can be made rightly only when arrogance is beaten down and defeated by humility. In itself, the decision, like any real decision, must remain groundless, and as such it must impose, again like any real decision, some fear and trembling. As Marion puts it, "between these two interpretations of a unique phenomenological situation . . . no reason could decide. For, since it is a matter again and always of receiving the given or not, the responsal must decide alone, without being able to rely on the visibility of what does not show itself before the responsal. The responsal does not know what it wants, because it is necessary first to indeed will it in order to see it, and hence in order to know it. Here opens a space of indecision that one cannot envisage without dread [*effroi*]: the decision for making the given into a phenomenon [*la mise en phénomène du donné*], hence also that for the reason of things, can be made only without vision or reason, since it makes these possible" (*ED*, 422).

From this perspective, the entire history of philosophy, as also that of theology in its split between metaphysical theology and revealed theology, would be divided between those who are blind to the excessive logic of givenness and so persist in the self-reliant, literally arrogant effort of constitution and objectivation, and those who, without any reason or evidence for doing so, manage to acknowledge that the given, even if not yet seen, remains nonetheless given without limit or reserve and so irreducible to constitution or objectivation. This latter position, that of the *adonné*, would depend on a modesty or humility, or even more a humiliation that opens me to the given—which it can do only because it, this humiliation, first comes from or as the given: receptivity to the excess of givenness and hence the abandonment of any self-confidence or self-reliance that would make itself the ground and measure of things (the fundamental arrogance of the subject of modern metaphysics) requires—and grants—the "humiliation of never constituting and of ceaselessly repeating the responsals [*les répons*], in order there to gain the enjoyment of a givenness of paradoxes and there to gain the full status of an *adonné*" (*ED*, 421). The *adonné*'s insurmountable failure to measure up to the given, its "irrevocable weakness [*défaillance*]" (*ED*, 421) is itself seen only to the degree that "the given humiliates the *adonné*" (*ED*, 421). Humiliation, then, which dispossesses me of my arrogance or self-reliance, is itself a necessary gift of the given, the gift required in order for me not only to see the given but also to see what my arrogance prevents me from seeing: that I see the given always inadequately, that my response always falls short.

Humiliation becomes the condition of responsiveness or responsibility insofar as it —much like the operation of grace through the law that humbles me in Paul or Augustine[14]—both free me from the self-assurance or self-reliance in which I actually will to close myself off to the given (by making myself the ground or condition of any appearance at all) and in so freeing me give to me, in my finitude, a "responsibility toward all of the given and prior to any visibility or reason" (*ED*, 422).[15] Such responsibility, note, involves a subtle but important hesitation between passivity and activity in the operation of *reception* that fundamentally defines the *adonné*. As *adonné*, I am characterized indeed by reception, itself the unconditional condition of revelation, and that reception "implies, to be sure, passive receptivity" (*DS*, 57), but it requires also an "active bearing [*contenance*]; for capacity (*capacitas*), in order to grow to the measure of the given and in order to maintain its arrival, must put itself to work—the work of the given to be received, work upon oneself in order to receive" (*DS*, 57). If I am called by the given within my absolute passivity, to decide on that call, or to be decided by it, and so to receive and make it visible, requires, as it were, not only faith but work—a ceaseless work demanded over and again by the given, which stands in need of my decisive response in order to become visible. Through the ongoing work of decision, the *adonné* inhabits, or comprises, according to an "essential phenomenal reciprocity" (*DS*, 60), the space and time of conversion of the given into the seen, which is also necessarily a space and time of fault: "[I]f everything that shows *itself* must in order to do so first give *itself*, it is nevertheless not sufficient that the given give *itself* in order that it show *itself*, since sometimes givenness almost obfuscates manifestation. The function of the *adonné* is precisely to measure *in itself* the gap between the given—which never ceases to impose itself . . . — and phenomenality—which is accomplished only insofar as and to the degree that reception manages to phenomenalize [the given] or, rather, lets it phenomenalize itself" (*DS*, 58).

Now, if this space can be one of my failure or guilt, it can also be one of an elevation or even salvation, for by inhabiting this gap I am charged with opening or closing all phenomenality.[16] As the one who (passively, in all humility) receives, I am also the one who (actively, productively) reveals—and indeed saves or creates, in a movement where creation and salvation would coincide.[17] According to this interplay of passivity and activity, abasement and elevation, in light of this passive reception that is itself active creation or salvation, I myself, as *adonné*, come to function as an image of the Christ—in whose salvific passivity the miracle of creation is actively repeated. To receive the saturated phenomenon of revelation—such as that given in the Christ—I must myself imitate the Christ in a movement where loss or abandon is gain or salvation.

Christ, then, can be read phenomenologically with Marion not only as a name for the saturated phenomenon of revelation but also as a figure of the *adonné* who receives and thus makes visible the saturated phenomenon in and through a self-sacrifice or humiliation that finally saves and elevates. He makes this link within his extraordinary analysis, in *The Crossing of the Visible*, of the painter, whose essential work consists in bringing the unseen from darkness to light: "The painter must lose himself in order to save (and to save himself). Like the Christ, he receives [*acceuille*] and saves only because he gives himself first, without knowing in advance whether he is losing or saving himself" (*CR*, 54). Without any support in the visible, without any *a priori* assurance, working in darkness to bring the unseen to light, the painter in his blindness must take the absolute risk of opening himself to the unseen as the unforeseen *par excellence*, as that which is utterly unforeseeable on the basis of anything already available as visible—in order to resist and thus support the excess of the unseen sufficiently to convert it into visibility, in an act where, again, creation and salvation coincide: the true painter "participates in the simple act of Creation" (*CR*, 54) even as he, or his loving eye, "under the guard of a look that does not yet see anything, but which keeps [*garde*] faith in the visibility to come, leads the unseen to its salvation. It is not in vain that the first Christians claim the title of Orpheus for the Christ, bringing the captives back from Hell. Every painting participates in a resurrection, every painter imitates the Christ, in delivering the unseen to light" (*CR*, 54).

In its unfounded but founding faith, this christological work of the painter is the work, indeed, of a blind man, who is for Marion "painter and seer *par excellence*" because he "sees more than the visible" (*CR*, 52)—which he can do only on the basis of that blind decision made in the freedom or indifference of an absolute innocence:

> The painter works in the obscure chaos that precedes the separation of the waters below from the waters above, the distinction between the unseen and the visible. He works before the creation of the first light. He goes back to the creation of the world, half-witness, half archangelic worker. It is thus that he risks finally losing himself, as if, going back before the separation of the waters, before the separation of light from darkness, he went back also before the distinction between good and evil. For more, no doubt, than any of the other arts, painting has to do directly and essentially with moral choice. (*CR*, 53)

If the painter is an exemplar of that blindness out of which the decision to see must inevitably be made, and if that blindness conditions a decision made in absolute indifference or innocence, prior to any distinction of good and evil, the decision also, at the same time, tears the *adonné* out of its innocence and places it inevitably in a position of failure or guilt—for even the fullest response to the given will always already have failed to respond adequately, in the just measure, to a givenness without measure. From this perspective, all human creation is always already fallen; the decision made in innocence to receive the given as it gives itself, without limit or reserve, becomes, thanks to my always inadequate response, the fault I bear. In this direction, the work of the painter in converting the given into the seen cannot but remind us all, including the painter himself, of our shortcoming—such that every monstration, every showing, becomes the objection or critique of a remonstration:

> The unseen rises again [*remonte*] to the visible: it rises [*monte*] toward the visible. But above all the unseen remonstrates the visible [*en remontre au visible*]: it shows to it and imposes on it what the visible still ignored, it contests the visible's languishing equilibrium through the immigration of a barbaric force. The gates of Hell open ceaselessly, through which the painter brings back to the light of day a new master of the visible, which arises there only in order to remonstrate us and, thus, to show us a monster. *Monstrum,* the showable *par excellence,* the brute unforeseeable, the miracle. *Miraculum,* the admirable *par excellence.* The painter of miracles opens the eyes that had been closed by the visible that was overly foreseen. (*CR,* 56)

If everything is given and the given is without limit or reserve, every moment gives something utterly new—unforeseen and unforeseeable—and thus always still to be seen, and the obligation of the *adonné* in every moment is to decide, without ground, to receive and to see what gives itself by responding to it and so making it phenomenal. In every moment, the *adonné* would be called to affirm the given *as* it gives itself—and to do so fully, without denial or flight, without any of the reserve or suspicion, slander or negation that would seek the reason for that which gives itself and shows itself somewhere outside, beyond, or behind that very self- showing.

We have seen that the *adonné,* in this decisive work of staging the given as phenomenal, is marked by a subtle shifting or hesitation between a radical passivity and receptivity, where the *adonné* would depart significantly from the subject of modern metaphysics, and a related if unexpected activity and productivity, where from out of its radical passivity the *adonné* must decide—and then work creatively—to receive the given by making it seen: an interplay, then, between the abasement or humiliation of one always inadequate to that which is given and the elevation of one who, from within the limits of that very inadequacy, becomes responsible for all phenomenality—to the point of resembling the creator and savior. The two directions of this interplay between passivity and activity, humiliation and elevation, suggest two broad lines of question concerning how we might understand Marion's thinking on given-ness in relation to "the horizon of modern theology." In concluding, then, with a brief formulation of these questions, I aim to open ground for discussions still to come.

Concerning the elevation of the *adonné* to the status of creator and savior, charged with responsibility for all phenomenality on the basis of decision or will: what might such a decisionism or voluntarism—especially as formulated by reference to the indifference of Descartes, "through whom," as Louis Dupré puts it in his masterful study *Passage to Modernity*, "the supremacy of the will entered the mainstream of modern thought"[18]—signify about Marion's rela-tion to distinctively modern, perhaps nominalist, conceptions of freedom in terms of unfounded but founding decision?[19] If Marion clearly and insistently aims to critique and unsettle the modern thought of sovereign subjectivity, does there not remain nonetheless a strange trace of sovereignty in the role that he attributes to decision in the movement from givenness to phenome-nality? And in a related direction, does the understanding of paradox or even miracle as norm stand in any significant continuity with the modern thinking on sovereignty—especially in juridical and political contexts—that likewise, increasingly, turns the exception into the norm in ways whose troubling implications have been explored in the recent work of a thinker like Giorgio Agamben?[20]

To relate this question to our religious—and our military and political—present, and recalling Carl Schmitt's decisionist conception of politics as founded in the distinction between friend and enemy: if the operation of sov-ereign decision might be seen at play in much of the religious violence being carried out today on the part of those who have decided that they are called and given over to a divine truth that summons them to their mission, how might Marion's thinking on decision and revelation help us to elucidate and respond to such violence? What are we to do amidst the clash of irreconcilable decisions, where one unfounded decision seems to confront another in a violence that cannot but prove abyssal? What of the meeting between two *adonnés* in the relation not of love but of hate? And in light of the resonance between our religious violence today and that confronting Descartes in his time, might we appreciate anew his concern to yoke an absolutely unconstrained will to the understanding?[21]

Much turns, of course, on how we understand the obligation of the *adonné* to receive and make visible the given *as* it gives itself. Is every decision to see the given "*as* . . ." therefore also, and always already, an interpretation, and so yielding not the given *itself* but my take on the given, as and in the measure that I manage to receive it? In his emphasis on an infinite hermeneutics, on the unstoppable and inexhaustible play of kataphasis and apophasis, and so on, Marion can seem to tend in this direction. At the same time, however, an equally or even more significant thrust of his project suggests that the given gives itself unconditionally and so before/outside any hermeneutic horizon. To the degree that I would claim to receive the given *itself* as it gives itself (and not simply *as I* manage to receive it—by having a take on it, by interpreting it) do I risk entering a violence that, in the name of the given itself, masks the *as* according to which I decide to receive it?[22] And in a related direction, is the demand that revelation appear unconditionally in the sense that Marion takes the term not itself an interpretive decision or horizon—a horizon of no horizon, which, strangely, ends up placing conditions on the unconditional through the argument that "if an actual revelation must, can, or was able to give itself within phenomenal apparition, it was able, it can, or it will be able only in giving itself according to the type of the paradox *par excellence*—such as we are going to describe it" (*ED*, 327).[23]

A second set of questions, tending now in the direction of the *adonné*'s humiliation or abasement, and looking less to an early modernity associated with nominalist thinking on freedom and more to the late modernity of Nietzsche, concerns also how we take the "as" in the effort to receive the given as it gives itself. As I have suggested, the *adonné* inhabits the gap between the given as it gives itself—but is not yet seen—and the actual phenomenalization of that givenness. Insofar as the given gives itself without limit or reserve, while my response, demanded by the given, always falls short, thanks both to the blindness of limited capacity and to a second, willful blindness, the *adonné* inhabits that gap as a space and time of inadequacy and failure, insurmountable fault or guilt—and the given is thus received unavoidably as humiliation and remonstration. If in his effort to overcome the alienated phenomenality of metaphysics, Marion works in a fairly deep continuity with Nietzsche, who likewise attacks the metaphysical concern to find the real reason or truth of things behind or beyond their appearance, such that the appearance is devalued or degraded, he at the same time seems to maintain—notably through the role attributed to decision and will—the logic of responsibility and guilt that Nietzsche saw at the heart of the metaphysical concept of free will—the last of the Four Great Errors in *Twilight of the Idols*, which he deemed the "foulest of the theologians' artifices" and which drove so much of his attack on Christianity as a "metaphysics of the hangman" that was motivated by the instinct to judge and punish?[24] Is there any tension between the overcoming of metaphysics and the logic of responsibility and fault that defines the situation of the *adonné* as the one who wills (or not) to decide in favor of receptive response? Within the work of the *adonné* to receive the given *as* it gives itself, must the gap between the given and the phenomenal be thought or experienced necessarily as fault or failure (what Marion describes as the greatest crime), a form of guilt tied to the responsibility of will? Does this logic of guilt—this story of crime and punishment—in the work of reception signal a trace of what troubles Nietzsche in the metaphysics (and error) of free will? Does it leave for us still to think the possibility (or impossibility) of receiving that which gives itself beyond obligation and fault, debt and guilt, crime and punishment—the possibility that I might be liberated to receive the given, however I might manage to receive it, without having to suffer humiliation and remonstration, without counting myself always already inadequate to the given and so forever unworthy of it?

Notes

1. A fairly steady position on the human sciences can be noted from the early theological writings through the latest phenomenology. See, e.g., the preface to the English translation of Jean-Luc Marion, *God without Being: Hors-Texte*, trans. Thomas A. Carlson (Chicago: University of Chicago Press, 1991), xix, and *De surcroît: Etudes sur les phénomènes saturés* (Paris: Presses Universitaires de France, 2001), 63.

2. Marion, *God without Being*, xxv. This work is cited parenthetically as *GWB*.

3. Jean-Luc Marion, *Étant donné: Essai d'une phénoménologie de la donation* (Paris: Presses Universitaires de France, 1997), 316. This work is cited parenthetically as *ED*.

4. One should recall the background to this formulation in *Being and Time*'s definition of the phenomenon as "that which shows itself in itself [*das Sich-an-ihm-selbst-zeigende*]," in *Being and Time*, trans. John Macquarrie and Edward Robinson (Oxford: Basil Blackwell, 1962), 54; *Sein und Zeit* (Tübingen: Max Niemeyer Verlag, 1986), 31.

5. See *ED*, 316: "Our whole enterprise tends . . . toward thinking the common-law phenomenon and through it the poor phenomenon starting from the paradigm of the saturated phenomenon, of which they both offer only weakened variants and from which they derive through progressive extenuations. For the saturated phenomenon does not give itself outside of the norm, in exception to the definition of phenomenality; on the contrary, it falls properly to the saturated phenomenon to render the measure of manifestation thinkable starting from givenness and to rediscover it [givenness] in its common-law variation and even in the poor phenomenon. What metaphysics sets apart as an exception (the saturated paradox) phenomenology here takes as its norm—every phenomenon shows itself in the measure (or lack of measure) that it gives itself."

6. Dominique Janicaud, *Le Tournant théologique de la phénoménologie française* (Combas: Editions de l'Eclat, 1991); Jacques Derrida, *Given Time: I. Counterfeit Money*, trans. Peggy Kamuf (Chicago: University of Chicago Press, 1992), 52.

7. One might note here that the child calls and gives birth to the parent at least as much as the reverse. See the beautiful passages in *Étant donné*, whose gendered framing may call for analysis or critique but whose logic should, I believe, hold as much for the mother and maternity as for the father and paternity: "The name that calls the infant is only the response of the father to a nameless call. The anonymity of the call (and of the infant) does not contradict or prohibit paternity but constitutes its terrain, stakes and condition of possibility. The father will therefore be born to his paternity in the measure that he will respond to the anonymous call of the infant with a naming responsal [*répons*]" (*ED*, 415).

8. Jean-Luc Marion, *De surcroît* (Paris: Presses Universitaires de France, 2001), 58. This work is cited parenthetically as *DS*. One might glimpse here the way in which givenness and the *adonné* recast *Being and Time*'s understanding of Being and of Dasein as that being for whom alone Being is an issue. See, e.g., *Being and Time*, §4.

9. *The Philosophical Writings of Descartes*, vol. 2, trans. by John Cottingham, Robert Stoothoff, and Dugald Murdoch (Cambridge: Cambridge University Press, 1984), AT VII, 58. This work is cited parenthetically according to the volume and pagination of the standard edition by Adam and Tannery (AT).

10. Note here that in *Sur le prisme métaphysique de Descartes* (Paris: Presses Universitaires de France, 1986), which is cited parenthetically as *PM*, Marion also suggests that "if the *ego* acquires perfectly a metaphysical status" (*PM*, 215), it may not be wholly exhausted by that status—insofar as the ego can, in the incomprehensible experience of freedom, suspend the metaphysical privilege of presence and representation. On this, see esp. §15, where Marion notes that "inattention to the present and

the fallacious memory of actuality, in suspending the necessity of actual presence, indeed give rise to freedom in its highest form, the freedom of positive indifference" (*PM*, 206). As Marion shows, this freedom of positive indifference, which eludes presence and representation, is linked intimately to the experience of unfounded decision, where the constraints of necessity yield to the openness of possibility: "Freedom is not represented, because representation implies the presence of the object to the *cogitatio* and because all presence tends to persist in its state, and hence to extend its actuality into necessity; thus freedom becomes possible—reaches the possible as its proper domain—only in exceeding present representation. The past found the possible by suspending present evidence through inattentive memory. Here freedom gains its possibility only by opposing to the present evidence of the *cogitatio* the undeniable—and hence unrepresentable—experience of arbitrary choice. Freedom is laid bare in the very measure that it is experienced as the possibility of the impossible. Hence the *aporia* clearly constructed and assumed by Descartes. On the one hand, we understand that the omnipotence of God entails his foreknowledge, and hence necessity . . . . On the other hand, we understand that this necessity contradicts the freedom of which we remain intimately aware . . . . How, then, to reconcile and comprehend these contradictory demands? It is necessary to insist on the Cartesian decision here: Descartes, precisely, decides without attempting a reconciliation that would undoubtedly be—for cognitive representation—impossible; he decides that he can decide (in favor of freedom), even if he cannot comprehend how he can do so; he decides to make a decision that he cannot comprehend, and whose possibility he cannot represent to himself, because he experiences it beyond the *cogitatio* present to actuality . . . . Necessity therefore does not yield to a cognitive representation of possibility in the future; it yields before the incomprehensible experience of freedom, which opens the possibility of an event to come only by exiting the face-to-face of presence with the present, and hence in passing beyond representation. Just as inattentive memory gave rise to the past, and not the inverse, so the decision in favor of freedom opens the possibility to come, and not the inverse" (*PM*, 212–13). See also the discussion of God's power in ibid., §18.

11. Furthermore, Marion elaborates, the will blinds me to the given not so much through an active denial or mistake but rather through a kind of flight or avoidance that leaves the given abandoned and the *adonné* absent: "The willing [*le vouloir*] required here should not be too quickly likened to what metaphysics understands by 'will' [*volonté*], for at least one clear reason: the metaphysical will wills all the more that it relies on an evidence of the understanding (Descartes, Leibniz) or of reason (Kant), even with the intention of resisting it and reversing its primacy (Schopenhauer, Nietzsche), whereas here the willing undertakes only to steal away from the excess of intuition, and therefore from evidence; the willing that the *adonné* opposes to the intuitive excess does not contest it any more than it follows it—it fleas it; the *adonné* avoids the given, becomes the absent *adonné*" (*ED*, 431).

12. See, e.g., *Summa Theologica*, pt. 1, q. 12, art. 7, on "whether those who see the essence of God comprehend him": "But God, whose being is infinite, as was shown above (Q. 7), is infinitely knowable. Now no created intellect can know God infinitely.

For the created intellect knows the divine essence more or less perfectly in proportion as it receives a greater or lesser light of glory. Since therefore the created light of glory received into any created intellect cannot be infinite, it is clearly impossible for any created intellect to know God in an infinite degree. Hence it is impossible that it should comprehend God." In Thomas Aquinas, *The Summa Theologica*, vol. 1, trans. Fathers of the English Domincan Province (New York: Benziger Brothers, 1947).

13. Emmanuel Lévinas, *Otherwise than Being or Beyond Essence*, trans. Alphonso Lingis (Boston: Martinus Nijhof, 1981), 122.

14. See, of course, Romans, where "through the law comes knowledge of sin" (3:20), or Augustine, from the *Confessions*, where "O Lord . . . you teach us by inflicting pain, you smite so that you may heal, and you kill us so that we may not die away from you," through the later anti-Pelagian writings such as *On the Grace of Christ*, where "no one can fulfill the law by the law" and "grace is revealed by the law, so that the law may be fulfilled by grace." *Confessions*, II, 2, trans. R. S. Pine-Coffin (New York: Penguin, 1961), 44; *On the Grace of Christ*, XI, 10, in John E. Rotelle, O.S.A., ed., *Answer to the Pelagians* (Hyde Park, N.Y.: New City Press, 1997), 408.

15. One should also, as Marion noted in responding to the conference presentation of this essay, read the issue of humiliation here against the background of Kant's *Critique of Practical Reason*, where the respectful submission of will to the moral law results from a necessary humiliation that keeps self-conceit in check: "The moral law, which alone is truly, i.e., in every respect, objective, completely excludes the influence of self-love from the highest practical principle and forever checks self-conceit, which decrees the subjective conditions of self-love as laws. If anything checks our self-conceit in our own judgment, it humiliates. Therefore, the moral law inevitably humbles every man when he compares the sensuous propensity of his nature with the law. Now if the idea of something as the determining ground of the will humiliates us in our self-consciousness, it awakens respect for itself so far as it is positive and the ground of determination. The moral law, therefore, is even subjectively a cause for respect." *Critique of Practical Reason*, trans. Lewis White Beck (New York: Macmillan, 1985), 77. See all of pt. 1, chap. 3, "The Incentives of Practical Reason." Just as respect in Kantian moral thought is tied to humiliation, so in Marion's phenomenology of givenness, as exemplified here in the analysis of painting, to lift the eyes in respect would require first lowering them in humility: "Every donation requires that one receive it. Before the least painting, it is therefore necessary to lower one's eyes in order to revere what it gives. Only then can we raise our eyes, with a slow respect, onto what is given by that which gives itself. And then finally attempt to see what gives [*ce que cela donne*]." "Ce que cela donne," in *La croisée du visible* (Paris: Presses Universitaires de France, 1996; 1st ed., Editions de la Différence, 1991), 81; hereafter cited parenthetically as *CR*.

16. The hesitation that one might note here between activity and passivity can be read productively, I think, against the background of Marion's own analyses elsewhere ("What the Ego Is Capable Of," in *Cartesian Questions* [Chicago: University of Chicago Press, 1999]; cited parenthetically as *CQ*) of the inversion that the meaning of *capacitas* can be seen to undergo within the significant shift Marion notes between

the premodern thought of Augustine and Aquinas and a modern thinking that would follow Suárez and Descartes. If in Augustine and Aquinas *capacitas* would involve the receptivity of man toward God, where in and through the expectation (or *epektasis*) of desire *capacitas* can expand infinitely in answer to God's measureless self-giving, such that "capacity is located in a gap, which it constantly crosses and recrosses, between what nature can contain and He who remains to be received" (*CQ,* 88) in the modern context "the paradox of capacity, because it stems from the effective experience of faith, cannot avoid encountering the inevitably triumphant objections of sane reason" (*CQ,* 90) according to which *capacitas* "no longer involves receiving God (*capax Dei*) but rather the exercise of a power (*capax dominii*)" (*CQ,* 91). No longer acknowledging the gap between what is given and what we can by nature manage to receive, modern thought from this perspective ignores exactly what Marion's phenomenology and theology alike aim to think anew. If, however, Marion attempts to rethink the passivity and receptivity that a major trend in modern thought has tended to occlude, one might, as I am suggesting here, still glimpse in Marion's analyses an unresolved tension or hesitation between passive reception and active production— a kind of hesitation that Marion himself notes in those seventeenth-century thinkers, like Pascal, who "wavered between this [Augustinian and Thomistic] passivity and the activity introduced by Descartes" (*CQ,* 95).

17. On such coincidence in Dionysian theology, see Hans Urs von Balthasar: "The concept *sōzein* takes on with Denys an undreamt-of wealth. God is above all *Soter* already as creator, in that he affirms and safeguards the natures in their particularity and the individuals in their individuality and preserves them as such from destruction, the tendency to blend with others and to yield before the superior power of the all, and 'protects each one in the position allotted to it in accordance with its rank and power.'" *Glory of the Lord,* vol. 2 (New York: Crossroad, 1984), 195.

18. Louis Dupré, *Passage to Modernity: An Essay in the Hermeneutics of Nature and Culture* (New Haven: Yale University Press, 1993), 130.

19. The theme of decision in contemporary French thought, and its relation to the heritage of nominalism, deserves more extensive treatment, which might allow one to develop significant proximities between Marion's work, here under discussion, and that of other noted thinkers such as Jacques Derrida and Michel de Certeau. See, e.g., Derrida's "Nombre de Oui," a short but important reading of Certeau that sets up several of the themes elaborated more fully in Derrida's influential essay "Force of Law: 'The Mystical Foundations of Authority.'" The former essay is available in English as "A Number of Yes," trans. Brian Holmes, in *Qui Parle* 2 (1988); the latter is available in Drucilla Cornell, *Deconstruction and the Possibility of Justice* (New York: Routledge, 1992). On nominalism and modern thought, see of course, in addition to Dupré, the important work of Hans Blumenberg, *The Legitimacy of the Modern Age,* trans. Robert Wallace (Cambridge: MIT Press, 1983), and Amos Funkenstein, *Theology and the Scientific Imagination* (Princeton: Princeton University Press, 1986). For a very helpful overview of the main issues surrounding free decision and divine power in nominalist contexts, see William J. Courtenay, *Capacity and Volition: A History of the Distinction of Absolute and Ordained Power* (Bergamo: Pierluigi Lubrina Editore, 1990).

20. See, e.g., Agamben's *Homo Sacer: Sovereign Power and Bare Life* (Stanford: Stanford University Press, 1998), where the very distinction between life and death can be seen to depend on the sovereign decisions yielded by the interplay of medical science and juridical power.

21. Here one thinks of Stephen Toulmin's *Cosmopolis: The Hidden Agenda of Modernity* (Chicago: University of Chicago Press, 1990).

22. In America John Caputo has been a notable voice on the hermeneutic implications of Marion's work. See, e.g., "Holy Hermeneutics versus Devilish Hermeneutics: Textuality and the Word of God," in John D. Caputo, *More Radical Hermeneutics: On not Knowing Who We Are* (Bloomington: Indiana University Press, 2000).

23. See also *ED*, 329 n. 1: "Phenomenology describes possibilities and never considers the phenomenon of revelation except as a possibility of phenomenality, which it formulates as follows: if God manifests himself (or manifested himself), he will make use of a paradox in the second degree; Revelation, if it takes place, will take the phenomenal figure of the phenomenon of revelation, of the paradox of paradoxes, of saturation in the second degree."

24. Friedrich Nietzsche, "The Four Great Errors," in *Twilight of the Idols*, §7, in *The Portable Nietzsche*, trans. Walter Kaufmann (New York: Viking Press, 1982), 499–500.

5

Larvatus pro Deo

Jean-Luc Marion's Phenomenology and Theology

EMMANUEL FALQUE

Translated by Robyn Horner

That Jean-Luc Marion is a philosopher, and even a "great philosopher," no longer needs to be established—and perhaps this is even more true in the United States than in France ("one is never a prophet in one's own country"). I have devoted a lengthy study to his work, published in the journal *Philosophie* under the title "Phénoménologie de l'extraordinaire." The approach I took there, in accordance with the style of the journal, remained purely philosophical and focused on Marion's *Being Given*. By analyzing this work—which in my view is his *magnum opus*—I wanted to show, on the one hand, the novelty of his perspective (the sense of polemics, the way the language works, and the descriptive turn), and, on the other hand, certain limits of the philosophical enterprise (the reversal of the Kantian model without any real "exit" from it, the modeling of phenomenality solely within the framework of the saturated phenomenon, and the forgetting of finitude as such). Here I can do no more than refer to this article and leave it for the reader to judge my expression of profound admiration for the work of Marion, not to mention the friendship with which he has blessed me for such a long time.[1]

Nevertheless, one question remained suspended and had to be revisited, in Marion's opinion as well as my own: namely, the relationship between philosophy and theology. Whence the interrogation that is at the heart of the present essay: should one maintain (and is it necessary to do so) a "theological suspicion" when one is doing philosophy, in such a manner as to disqualify, or

181

virtually disqualify, all that which is within the province of the actuality of the revealed, since one claims only to adhere to the possibility of the phenomeno-logical given? The question is difficult, but nevertheless runs throughout *Being Given*. Must the recourse to eschatology in the parable of the last judgment (Matt. 25), for example, be allowed to be taken over by "the 'gift of self' for the nation (death for one's country, and so on)" because "its *theological origin* could be troubling to the scrupulous" (134 / 93)?[2] Or again, must one truly fear that the saturated phenomenon can be understood "as a vaguely *irrational* (to say it plainly, '*theological*') case of phenomenality" (304 / 218), or that it even "leads surreptitiously to naming a transcendent *numen* and—what is worse— to a theological turn" (410 / 297)? Better, is "some sort of return to 'special metaphysics,' that givenness would perhaps imply, insofar as it is supposed to imply a transcendental, indeed—*horrible dictu*—'theological' giver" (8 / 3) to be feared? In short, isn't defending oneself at this point against the accusa-tion of a (theological) "turn" proof that it has been rightly demonstrated, and that it would be better to assume it rather than turning away from it?

Certainly, the field of interrogation is massive, and would accordingly warrant refinement. It is the particular merit of *Being Given* that it is able to approach the question of the revealed. We find this illustrated in exemplary fashion if we go to paragraph twenty-four, where the "manifestation of Christ" gives itself to be seen as "paradigm of the phenomenon of revelation" (329 / 236). But the question here is not one of objects to be studied, whether not only artistic (the painting of Carravaggio, 391 / 283), historical (the battle of Waterloo, 318 / 228), or literary (the "Madeleine" story of Proust, 238 / 169) or whether also theological. It comes down entirely and solely to the type of rela-tionship sustained by the theologian to his or her object of study. Is it neces-sary to outline with so much clarity the boundary between revelation under-stood as "possible phenomenon" (phenomenology) and Revelation given in its "actuality" (theology)? Marion is emphatic: "*[H]ere* I am not broaching Revelation in its theological pretension to the truth, something faith alone can dare to do" (10 / 5). Later he maintains: "I cannot, however, evoke revealed theology here—first, out of respect for the *distinction of the disciplines* and the fact that I stick *strictly to philosophy* . . ." (163 / 114). In other words, in mark-ing the distinction between phenomenology and theology too scrupulously, would one not risk, on the one hand, forbidding phenomenology its veritable right to phenomenality, and, on the other hand, forbidding theology its mode of being paradigmatic in the saturation of the phenomenon?[3]

The question certainly merits being posed, in that it "pushes to the limit" Marion's thought process, as he himself claims to go beyond Husserl although not ignoring him: "I do not pretend to begin where Husserl stopped, but simply to think what he accomplished perfectly without entirely saying it" (42 / 17). Giving due respect to the quality of Marion's process, the enormous philosophical merit of which I have elsewhere demonstrated (in the journal article cited in note 1), therefore authorizes and demands going beyond it to consider the relationship of Marion's philosophical work to the theological. At stake here is not opposition to the process—we know that the *disputatio* sometimes diverts into a vain discussion—but the proposal and opposition of *another way*, complementary to the preceding one, although more exposed, perhaps because less calculated. It is in honor of the master that his least disciple dares to be compared with him, less in order to overcome him in an immeasurable combat than to break away and discover, thanks to him, one's own limits, as also one's positions: "*Vademecum—vadetecum*," Nietzsche advises his disciple. "Lured by my style and tendency, / you follow and come after me? / *Follow your own self faithfully* / —take time—and thus you follow me."[4]

Larvatus prodeo

The words of the young Descartes are well known, and especially by Marion, who is first and foremost Cartesian in formation: "[C]omedians, called on stage, so as not to let the blush on their faces be seen, put on a mask [*personam induunt*]. Like them, at the moment of making my entry in this theatre of the world, where previously I had only been a spectator, I come forward masked [*larvatus prodeo*, where *prodeo* is a single word]."[5] Is it necessary to come forward masked [*larvatus prodeo*], and must one do so in particular when the philosopher is also a theologian? The question is all the more crucial because Marion combines these disciplines specifically, and perhaps more so than other French philosophers (in particular, Michel Henry), because he has studied and knows the corpus of theology. His double formation therefore ought *rightfully* authorize intersections, or even confrontations between the disciplines. But his work proceeds as if, *in fact*, he was forbidding himself from doing this, or to be more correct, as if he was refusing to do theology when pursuing a work of pure philosophy, and refusing to do philosophy when practicing theology (although this second position is less strongly present than the first). In this way Marion distinguishes the two disciplines as one would distinguish faculties: *The Idol and Distance, God without Being,* and *Prolegomena to Charity* for theology; and the works on Descartes (*L'ontologie grise, La théologie blanche, On Descartes' Metaphysical Prism*), on phenomenology (*Reduction and Givenness*) or starting from phenomenology (*Being Given—Le phénomène érotique* cannot be classified) for philosophy. In a word, this position is classical, and perhaps characterizes French—and thus Cartesian—secularism. "[A]t the moment of making my entry in this theatre of the world . . . I come forward masked [*larvatus prodeo*]," Descartes reminds us, which we can interpret to mean: I pass for a philosopher amongst philosophers, and possibly also amongst theologians, but never for a theologian amongst the philosophers.

The debate certainly goes very widely beyond the case of Marion, and we will also need to go "to the things themselves" with him in order to test the reasonableness of it. There remains, however, the free-French paradox of philosophers not formed in theology who nevertheless do theology without separating the disciplines (cf. *C'est moi la vérité* or *Incarnation* by Michel Henry), and of philosophers passionate about theology who nevertheless repudiate it when they write philosophy (Marion). "Here, as often," *Being Given* emphasizes with regard to Heidegger, "he *hides more than he shows—hiding especially that he hides*" (59 / 38).What is true here of the recovery of givenness [*Gegebenheit*] by the event of appropriation [*Ereignis*] is perhaps truer still of the relationship between philosophy and theology: the one who "believes himself masked [*larvatus prodeo*]" cannot in reality hide that he is only masked in his own eyes, taking the shape of philosophy when nevertheless basically doing theology.

Larvatus pro Deo

The Cartesian position suggests, nevertheless, more than simple dissimulation, and it is the particular merit of Henri Gouhier to have underlined this point and the greatness of Marion to have developed it. "The *fear of God* is the beginning of wisdom" probably pointed—and by way of a preamble—to the *Cogitationes privitae*.[6] The "masked advance [*larvatus prodeo*]" (where *prodeo* is a single word) thus presupposes, and is founded on, a "fear of God [*timor Domini*]." Whence the remark of Léon Brunschvicg in 1927, in the *Revue de métaphysique et de morale*, which this time justifies in full the position of Marion: "Descartes will give *confidence* to his public by *shading* all things, according to the slogan—which was turned against him by the too ingenious formula, but with a little charity, it was not difficult to re-establish the true intention of it—*larvatus pro Deo* [masked before God, with *pro Deo* as two words this time]."[7] To say of Marion that he advances masked, following Descartes, now in the sense of "bedazzlement before the divine glory" is no longer this time to argue in favor of some philosophico-theological comedy (*larvatus prodeo* [I come forward masked]), but to touch the heart of his philosophy itself, and perhaps, too, of the relationship that it maintains with theology: (a) first from the point of view of the Cartesian studies, (b) next from that of theology, and (c) finally from that of phenomenology. This represents a crossing of disciplines that appears with an astonishing unity, without the author ever, nevertheless, claiming this as such, at least in terms of the relation of the philosophical works to the theological ones.

From the point of view of Cartesian studies, *On Descartes' Metaphysical Prism* takes up Descartes's declaration in a letter to Mersenne dated January 28, 1641, which singly sums up the whole of Marion's position: "I have only ever discussed the Infinite in order to submit myself to it."[8] In this way, Descartes's figure of God is first and precisely characterized, which must be understood as a "non-metaphysical statement." Marion stresses that "before God, reverentially, and as a rarity among the metaphysicians, Descartes *stands hidden*—he does not keep secrets, nor does he sneak away, but *hides his face* before that of the infinite—*larvatus pro Deo*" (with *pro Deo* as two words).[9] Second, the themes of the saturation of the infinite before the finite, and of the distance that the infinite imposes, are also and firstly theological, and are insisted on by Marion as such, this time in his 1977 theological work *The Idol and Distance*. "We do not comprehend infinity because it is infinity that comprehends us" (an implicit reference to Descartes). "'The most divine knowledge of God is that which knows through unknowing'" (an explicit reference to Denys the Areopagite).[10] Finally, the saturated phenomenon, most eminently phenomenologically translated in *Being Given*, serves to bring to completion what the study of Cartesianism and Dionysian primacy had already anticipated: "To introduce the concept of the saturated phenomenon into phenomenology, I just described it as unforeseeable in terms of quantity, unbearable in terms of quality, unconditional in terms of relation, and finally irreducible to the I in terms of modality" (303–4 / 218).

The unity of the body of work, over twenty years, is in this sense impressive. Marion draws to a close, in effect, according to different registers—as is often the case with great authors—a single and very great idea: that of the overcoming of the finite by the infinite. What is in this way *in nuce* at the beginning (with Descartes's infinite and the distance of Denys) is recapitulated *in fine* at the end (with Marion's saturated phenomenon). It remains precisely for the beginning to be interrogated, at least in order not to convert anew into the "masked advance [*larvatus prodeo*]" the position of the one who is held "masked before God [*larvatus pro Deo*]." The relationship of Marion to Thomas Aquinas and Anselm of Canterbury becomes in this sense exemplary of a certain attitude.

Natural Theology and the Return of Ontologism

I will not put forward here whatever so *radical* an *orthodoxy* of the thought of Thomas that alone would justify some return to the doctrine of the angelic Doctor against, and sometimes with, the arguments of contemporary philosophy. The packaging of a thought does not suffice to disguise it, and the stakes of the phenomenological reduction are such that they cannot, in a word, correspond to some general objectivism of the given.[11] We will not go back over past debates concerning a God *with* or *without* being. Not that they did not possess in themselves their own justifications, but because they have already been played out, and Marion's noble "*retraction* on this point" suffices to render them, if not out of date, then at least overcome.[12] The question instead depends—as it is conformed, anyway, to my perspective here—on the *type of relationship* maintained between philosophy and theology, and on the possibility for humanity really to remain under the glare of the One who always comes to dazzle us. Is there not, on the one hand, a danger or at least a suspicion about wanting to separate natural philosophy too much from a quasi-Pascalian third order of revealed theology, when Thomas had nevertheless so knowingly united them? And, on the other hand, is the ontologism of thought not such here that one will authorize, without the knowledge of the boundaries of our human thought, a sort of access to the beatific vision forbidden, in a word, in the limits of our earthly life?

Being Given underlines that "any phenomenology of givenness is likely to face a refusal that is based not on a principle but on a suspicion. . . . For with givenness, the natural attitude—and it is in fact a question only of the natural attitude—fears the revival of transcendence in its most resolutely metaphysical, if not to say theological, sense (103 / 71)." In short, the effort to "de-theologize givenness," which paradoxically marks one of the principle aspects of *Being Given,* makes of the "theological suspicion" the spearhead of its properly philosophical development. The main point of the argument, and the claim to be purely philosophical, is found in the response to an objection ("a revival of transcendence?" [103–8 / 71–740]), and according to that response is based on a particular reading of Thomas in view of definitively distributing the genres of thought. Marion emphasizes that "theology, in the sense of revealed theology [*sacra doctrina*], is in no way to be confused with *theologia rationalis,* which belongs to *metaphysica specialis* and arises solely from metaphysics. Rightfully, it should be opposed to it, as the *Revelation of the Wisdom of the Word* is opposed to the *wisdom of the world*" (105 / 72). One will nevertheless wonder: does not Thomas's text, to which this passage from *Being Given* implicitly refers (the allusion is to the *sacra doctrina*), instead say, in the *Summa Theologiae* (Ia.1), that this unique way of pure divine revelation independent of its properly human conditions of access remains strictly impracticable? Accordingly, we read in the *Summa:* "[T]heology that is dependent on sacred doctrine is thus of another genre [*differt secundum genus*] from that which is still a part of philosophy." In this sense natural theology and revealed theology are not "confused," one with the other. But Thomas immediately adds, or rather illustrates, that "nothing thus prevents [*nihil prohibet*] the very objects of which the philosophical sciences treat—according to which they are knowable by the light of natural reason [*lumine naturalis rationis*]— from still being able to be envisaged in another science [*et aliam scientiam*]— according to which they are known by the light of divine revelation [*lumine divinae revelationis*]."[13] In other words, Thomas does not make the separation of the genres or the orders operate here, as Pascal later will, but he introduces, to the contrary, the philosophical at the very heart of the theological—by a *certain* knowledge of the object of faith by the "light of natural reason," however non-indispensable to faith and limited in its claims (the existence of God, q. 2, but not the Trinity or the Incarnation). In short, Thomas does not separate the natural from the supernatural; rather, he inserts the natural at the very heart of the supernatural, only because of "the *weakness* of our minds [*propter defectum intellectus nostri*]" and without "the sciences being *necessary* to the sacred science [*non quod ex necessitate eis indigeat*]."[14] Far from raising the "theological suspicion," Thomas awakens, to the contrary, the "philosophical suspicion" of which his famous detractors accuse him in his renewal and transformation of Aristotle.[15] The problem is the inverse of Marion's, who is concerned more that he does not insert philosophy into theology, and thus poses the question anew, independent of all affiliation with Thomas: is the strict separation of genres, Pascalian more than Thomasian, not at the origin of the impossible meeting of disciplines in the work of Marion himself?[16]

We must also consider here the accusation of an "ontologism of revelation" by Thomas Aquinas against Anselm in the second question of the *Summa,* which has perhaps not ceased to produce certain of its avatars. The essential question today, in phenomenology as in theology, is not uniquely that of the "phenomenon of revelation" or of "God" (with or without being). Instead it concerns the human or the receiving subject in his or her capacity—or lack of capacity—to speak about the phenomenon, or God, whether one starts from the phenomenon itself or from God in the act of self-revelation (the descending ontological way), or starts from the human and the human conditions of existence (*in via*) rendering impossible all direct access to some beyond (*in patria*) (the ascending cosmological way/s). "I say that the proposition, God exists, is *self*-evident [*per se nota est*]," Thomas underlines, "for the predicate is identical to the subject. . . . But as we do not know the essence of God [*quid est*], this proposition is *not evident for us* [*non est nobis per se nota*]; it needs to be demonstrated by things that are more known *by us* [*quoad nos*], though less known in their nature—namely, *by effects* [*scilicet per effectus*]."[17] The detour by these works is certainly the last resort of an impossible direct access to God. But this detour also seeks to speak about our "mere" humanity, when it would remain linked with sin for Thomas.

The decisive test risked by *Cordula,* and well known to theologians in the debate between Hans Urs von Balthasar and Karl Rahner, thus still innervates, although without saying it, the most contemporary debates of phenomenology. Must we necessarily accuse of an "anthropological reduction" a phenomenology that would first take "the human as such," that is to say, in our finitude, for the point of departure of its phenomenality? And must we not, on the contrary, hold at once as impossible and contrary to human freedom all the bedazzlement of the "phenomenon of revelation" that would give itself all at once, almost directly and independently of all the (transcendental) conditions of its reception? The question earlier posed in the framework of theology resounds today more strongly in phenomenological debates.[18] One will also wonder then, with regard to the possible renewal of boundaries: must we still wait, in the manner of Balthasar, to "*win back a philosophy* starting from theology,"[19] or must we not today hope, to the contrary, because philosophy has also become the business of theology, for a *liberation of theology* by philosophy? The treatment of the question of miracles, and further still of the Resurrection, will decide this question, whether in consecrating the *extraordinary* as the norm of divinity, or whether in welcoming the *ordinary* as the average human assumed and transformed by the God-man himself.

To Liberate Theology

In a word, the question of the interpretation of Thomas is not the essential thing. The "theological suspicion" is in reality all the more pressing—for those who practice theology, too—since it fails to free what could (and should) be so: theology itself. *Being Given* emphasizes: "[T]hat there was historically no such theological revelation would change nothing in the phenomenological task" (10 / 4). One will grant, accordingly, that "revelation" is not denied here, but only envisaged as a possibility of the saturated phenomenon, independent of all actuality. "The phenomenon of revelation remains a mere *possibility*. I am going to describe it *without presupposing its actuality,* and yet all the while propose a precise figure for it" (327 / 235).[20] In this sense, section 24 on Christ as "saturated phenomenon," and even "saturation of saturation" (327 / 235) or "paradox of paradoxes" (328 / 236), remains a model of the genre and a courageous lesson. Few are those among philosophers who dare to take the Gospel text as an object to describe, such that one is intentionally confined to the most strict philosophical framework. Two questions nevertheless remain and maintain the ambiguity. First, to link *phenomenology* and *possibility* in this way with *theology* and *actuality,* does one not risk first submitting revelation to the simple role of fulfilment of its transcendental conditions? Second, what will it then be like for theology itself, from its possibility, to be formulated in *the mode of reduction* if it is maintained at the sole level of its actuality, although what founds it cannot be said in the simple historicity of the brute fact—the resurrection itself?

As for the first question just raised, paragraph 24 of *Being Given,* which I have called a courageous lesson and worthy in this sense as such, in the Kantian manner nevertheless seems to indulge in a pure transcendental reduction from revelation: "*If* revelation there must be . . . , *then* it will assume, assumes or assumed the figure of the paradox of paradoxes. . . . In this sense . . . it still remains inscribed within the *transcendental conditions* of possibility" (327–28 / 235).[21] The author nevertheless sees the objection of transcendentalism. Nothing, moreover, is more contrary to his philosophy than to reduce, or better, to submit God in this way to what is not God:

> To be sure, *R*evelation (as actuality) is never confounded with *r*evelation (as possible phenomenon). I will scrupulously respect this conceptual difference by its graphic translation. But phenomenology, which owes it to phenomenality to go this far, does not go beyond and should never pretend to decide the *fact* of Revelation, its historicity, its actuality, or its meaning. It should not do so, not only out of concern for *distinguishing the sciences* and *delimiting their respective regions*, but first of all, because it *does not have the means* to do so. The fact (*if there is one*) of Revelation *exceeds* the scope of all science, *including that of phenomenology.* (Ibid.)[22]

I read this as follows: transcendentally to deduce revelation starting from the possibilities of phenomenology (and no longer from the Kantian categories of the understanding) is not to decide its actuality. Here the main thing is to *remain a philosopher,* without ever encroaching on the theologian. Better, if there were theology, it would go beyond the norms of phenomenology itself, and would prefer the absolute primacy of the Balthasarian revealed to the said Rahnerian transcendental reduction. Marion recognizes that "only a *theology,* and on condition of constructing itself on the basis of this fact alone (Karl Barth or Hans Urs von Balthasar, no doubt more than Rudolf Bultmann or Karl Rahner), could reach it" (ibid.).

In short, and the fact is paramount here, a beyond of phenomenology seems to stand out in profile with the irruption of theology. To recognize in effect that "phenomenology would not have the power to turn to theology" (ibid.) is implicitly to make the admission that "another power" goes beyond it and overflows it through and through, even if one would be forbidden here from making any decision on its place. Marion writes that "one has to be completely ignorant of theology, its procedures, and its problematic, not to imagine this unlikeness (of a phenomenology capable of turning to theology)" (ibid.). The thesis is thus clear, although formulated in implicit fashion: just as phenomenology goes beyond metaphysics, (revealed) theology goes beyond phenomenology in the requisites of its saturation—and in this way opens, to the *theologian philosopher* or the *philosopher theologian* (for I do not believe in the well-founded nature of the pure distinction of the spheres), a path that this time it belongs to him in his own right to occupy. Whence my second question to Marion, or instead, *starting* from him: what would theology become, seeing that it would accept passing over the step of phenomenality to Revelation as such? The treatment of the question of *miracles* and of the *resurrection*, as "limit experiences" of saturation in phenomenology and of divine action in theology, will enable us to see the first delineations of it.[23]

The Miracle in Question

What Marion thus intends to "stitch together" in a quasi-transcendental deduction of revelation starting from the saturated phenomenon is in this way "unstitched" by an overcoming of phenomenology by theology, without, nevertheless, daring *here* to cross swords: "*[R]evealed theology* could, on the other hand, be defined as a thought of the gift without reciprocity. . . . I cannot, however, evoke it here—first, out of respect for the *distinction of disciplines* and the fact that I stick *strictly to philosophy*" (163 / 114).[24] It is, in fact, the right of the philosopher to make his choices and to remain in the strict orthodoxy that his profession of philosopher dictates. Or better, before the crucial alternative of the Kierkegaardian type, *either* a limitation of God to phenomenality *or* an extension of phenomenality to the revealed God (336 / 242), the author explicitly opts for the second term (the extension of phenomenality to the way of revelation)—proof, if there were any, of the new space that he opens in these pages even when he would not inhabit it himself here. "It could be that the *fact of Revelation* provokes and evokes *figures and strategies of manifestation and revelation* that are *much more powerful and more subtle* than what phenomenology, even pushed as far as the phenomenon of revelation (paradox of paradoxes), would ever let us divine" (337 / 243).[25]

Nevertheless, as I have emphasized, Marion is happily, time and again, changed into a theologian, and has shown here or there, always with a radical distinction of the disciplines, what the situation is like with a theology tailored to the measure of the possibility of phenomenology. With two reprises and, then, in an editorial topos properly theological (the journal *Communio*), the author deploys two of his "figures and strategies of manifestation and revelation," more powerful and more subtle than all the clever calculations of phenomenology: the first renewal was before *Being Given* (*Communio* Sept.–

Oct. 1989: "the miracle"); and the second after it (*Communio* Sept.–Oct. 2001: "the sacrament").

The miracle seems in effect to mark Marion's seal of what is actually revelation. The *phenomenology of the extraordinary* (the saturated phenomenon) here rejoins and is allowed to be overcome by *the extraordinary of theology* (the miracle) that notes an actual realization of the "possibility of the impossible." In 1989 Marion emphasized: "[T]he Resurrection, as miracle *par excellence* and in confirming in this way a trait sketched by the other miracles in a smaller measure each time, *saturates* every horizon. By *saturating phenomenon* I understand here one where the manifest given goes beyond not only what a human look can bear without being blinded and dying, but what the world in its essential finitude can receive and contain."[26] Marion's unity of thought here merits emphasizing in order to bring to light how it is sometimes masked but is nevertheless his very strength. In his earlier works, Marion first discovered by way of the theologoumenon of the Resurrection [*Communio* (1989)] the philosophical syntagm of "saturating phenomenon" that he was later to deploy so much in *Being Given.* But the actuality of the miracle, nevertheless, not only of every "sign" of the Gospel but more still the resurrection itself (that I will hesitate, moreover, to name miracle), could not be said theologically under the seal of historicity. Or better, it is the phenomenological type of reduction ("putting between parentheses") of historicity itself or of the factuality of the miracle that demands determining in it the sense—"in order that you may believe" (John 11:15). The author specifies: "[T]he miracle will no longer bear *on a physical event,* but *on my consciousness itself.*" [27] The true miracle, according to Marion, is in this way "a miracle of my consciousness," a lived experience in the conversion of *my* way of looking at things rather than in the things themselves. From phenomenology to revealed theology, the consequence is thus correct: "*[T]he last miracle is that I believe in the miracle par excellence—* the Resurrection where all revelation is accomplished."[28] The miracle is thus not, or more, the "objective fact" of the resurrection as such—the sum total of which in the end is only noticed in the actual absence of the body—but the act by which this resurrection works today *in me* so that I can adhere to it by my consciousness, in this way overflowing all the "good" reasons that I have to "not believe" in the Resurrected One without "having seen" (John 20:29). The true miracle is contained in belief in the miracle, as also, probably, the true saturation is reached in the overflowing of the boundaries within which I believed myself already "saturated."

The thesis of the miracle as *conversion of self in self by another,* as apt phenomenologically as it is pertinent spiritually, comes up, however, against the most ordinary objection from theologians—those most often anchored in a disconcerting objectivism (including Balthasar). The resurrection is not a simple datum of consciousness or a transformation of the subject as such, but a *fact*—valid historically even if only I will live the consequences in me: "[T]his has actually happened"—"this man that you have delivered and suppressed in crucifying him at the hands of the impious, God has raised in delivering him from the pains of death, for it was not possible for death to keep him in its power" (Acts 2:23–24—the *kerygma*). The unresolved question thus remains: how and on what criteria are we to found an actuality of the resurrection if historicity as such has no other principle than its historiality [*Geschichte*], in phenomenology as in theology? Certainly, some have tried—Rahner in exemplary fashion, but in maintaining nevertheless the support of history itself [*Historie*].[29] Marion proposes the only response that suits, or at least the only response consistent with the whole of phenomenology's inability to put in brackets the fact of historicity in its original operation of reduction: "[W]ith this delay continually still to be completed, *l'adonné* opens to its *historicity*" (418 / 303).[30] In other words, and this time translated into theological terms, the resurrection is not first the fact of the God-man in his relationship with the Father in a time and place in history (Jerusalem in approximately the year 33), but principally his givenness *in me* and *for me* today, which, by its reception on the "screen of my consciousness" (351 / 255), phenomenalizes it as such and gives it to appear in its *delay* or its act of "differing." "The receiver, in and through the receptivity of 'feeling,' transforms givenness into manifestation, or more exactly, lets what gives itself through intuition show itself" (364 / 264).[31] Certainly it goes without saying that God has no need for me to exist. But in the framework of the phenomenological reduction where necessary existence is suspended, it only stays appearing in the "for me" of consciousness—if not to be, then at least to be phenomenalized. Far, then, from all the Balthasarian or Rahnerian tradition, which does not renounce a certain objectivity of revelation (probably due to the Hegelian and Thomist tradition in theological matters), a unique theologian—Rudolf Bultmann—is linked here with the thesis put forward by the author, for he too is a phenomenologist by way of being a disciple of Martin Heidegger: "It is thus true that the foundation and the object of faith are identical. They form a single and same thing, for *we cannot speak of what God is in Godself but only of what God does for us and with us.*"[32]

The proximity of the Protestant theologian Bultmann to the Catholic philosopher Marion will astonish those who have never done phenomenology with full knowledge of theology. And the attempted response given by the second (Marion) to the first (Bultmann), in his past definition of the resurrection as "irruption of fact" (*Résurrection*, April 1970), holds the real surprise, maintaining in the framework of theology what phenomenology holds nevertheless as forbidden—the primacy of the fact over the sense. Marion asserts that "it is necessary to pose immediately, with a violent clarity, that the predication of the Resurrection bears, from the start, *on a fact*."[33] The "factuality" of the Resurrection as *fact,* not in the sense derived from *fait accompli* but in the historical sense of "what has *really* happened" no longer seems to hold with regard to the deployment of the subsequent phenomenological vein. Marion, like Bultmann, having become a phenomenological disciple of Heidegger, and beyond Husserl, can nevertheless no longer accord his faith to an objectivity of revelation that, if it is not destroyed by "doubt" (Descartes), is at least suspended in the *epochē* (Husserl). Bultmann, moreover, specifies it: "[F]rom the affirmation, according to which to speak of God is to speak of myself, it does not follow at all that God is *not exterior* to the believer."[34] It remains, nevertheless, that such an exteriority will say nothing to the phenomenologists, if such it is that there is only "transcendence" in phenomenology given most strongly in the "immanence" of consciousness (38–39 / 25).

According to the "sacramental" question, after *Being Given* this time (*Communio,* 2001) it only comes to confirm what was formerly envisaged—but with explicit reference this time to *Being Given.* The objectivism of revelation is now definitively abandoned, and sacramentality becomes a mode of being of counter-intentionality: "[I]t is not a question here (in the case of the sacraments) only of constituting objects starting from a transcendental subjectivity, which masters them by the initiative of an intentionality and certifies them by the assurance of an intuitive fulfilment, but of receiving phenomena that show *themselves starting from the intentionality of God,* such that God reveals Godself in and starting from Godself, contrary to our expectations, anticipations, and plans, according to the deployment of an intuition 'too' strong (Mark 9:3) for our capacity, the very glory of God."[35] The new answer is thus clear and probably founds the whole project of *Being Given:* another intentionality, as absolute as essential to humanity, determines mine in me, and consecrates it as place and act of true sacramentality—"the Spirit, such that

Christ delivers it in delivering himself on the Cross to humanity loved to the point of his desert of love."[36] In short, the subject matter gains its pertinence in being explicit: theology, apparently disconnected from phenomenology in his body of work, nevertheless constitutes for the man as for the work its ultimate sense and reason for being—the Resurrection for the "saturating phenomenon" and sacramentality for "counter-intentionality."

By way of conclusion, we might ask ourselves why there are so many *philosophical* precautions when the point and the scope of all this that Marion has provided remains, in reality, theological. Can one, in a word, have the experience of the saturated phenomenon outside the *actuality* of *Revelation given as such*—that is to say the Resurrection as transformation of self in self by another? To affirm it would be perhaps to settle the question of an impossible experience of bedazzlement or a "seeing otherwise" outside Christianity.[37] To deny it, to the contrary, would come back to losing the way of what characterizes and makes the whole enterprise original: "the intentionality of another in me" (God or the Trinity) starting from which all the phenomena are given to me as not coming from me. In *Being Given* Marion states that "to unravel this thought of the gift as such, it would be necessary to engage in an examination of trinitarian theology, outside the scope of phenomenology as well as of metaphysics" (163 / 114–15), a *philosophical* examination of the Trinity that I wanted to try in my own work on Saint Bonaventure under the direction of Marion.[38] The *theologization of givenness*, against which the author does not cease to put himself on guard—is this not what nevertheless gives him his power, and his true sense? "In the case of the *real presence*," Marion confesses before a June 2000 meeting of bishops assembled at Lourdes for a colloquium on the Eucharist, "[W]e are, exactly, before *this*. We are even before an *exemplary case* of the *saturated phenomenon*."[39]

To all those who accuse Marion of having taken "the theological turn," a charge that he relentlessly defends himself against in the opening pages of *Being Given* (8 n. 4 / 328 n. 8), I respond thus to the contrary, that there is neither shame nor error in assuming and unifying what centuries of recent history have kept radically separate: *the possibility* of the philosophical enterprise and *the actuality* of theological revelation. Michel Henry, moreover, is never deceived, he who in his last works (*C'est moi la vérité*, *Incarnation*, and *Paroles du Christ*), although independent of the tradition itself, is never burdened with such a "theological suspicion" (no more, moreover, than Jean-Louis Chrétien or Jean-Yves Lacoste). In a context where theology and philosophy battle less than they did in the past, the automatic declaration according to which "the theologians . . . undertake or undertake so little to read phenomenologically the events of revelation recorded in the Scriptures, in particular in the New Testament" is no longer adequate, and still less the refuge in a "philosophy that has neither the authority nor the competence to say more, but . . . leaves at least the right to appeal about it to the theologians."[40] Neither the distinction of the disciplines, nor that of the functions, can make thought fertile, and only those who truly possess the formation in both—and Marion by way of being a pioneer—can accomplish its work. In these new times of a possible reciprocal interaction (without confusion or separation of the orders), it comes back in this way to the philosopher to assume his or her "theological task"—or even to the theologian to seek the "philosopher's stone." There is a new future that began yesterday, or at least another mode of thought, that seeks to respond tomorrow to the demands of our today: *non larvatus sed "detecta fronte"* [Ovid] *prodeo*—I come forward not veiled but with an uncovered face.

Notes

1. Emmanuel Falque, "Phénoménologie de l'extraordinaire," *Philosophie* 78 (June 2003): 52–76.

2. I indicate in parenthesis the pages of *Étant donné: Essai d'une phénoménologie de la donation* (Paris: Presses Universitaires de France, 1997), which will serve as the guiding thread for my reflections. [In translation the French reference is given first, followed by a reference to *Being Given: Toward a Phenomenology of Givenness*, trans. Jeffrey L. Kosky (Stanford: Stanford University Press, 2002). While in general I have used Kosky's translation, occasional modifications have been made, as in this case.—Trans.]

3. The distinction between "Revelation" (as actuality) and "revelation" (as possible phenomenon) is one to which it will be necessary for us to return (cf. *Being Given*, 329 n. 1 / 367 n. 90).

4. Friedrich Nietzsche, "Joke, Cunning and Revenge," in *The Gay Science: With a Prelude in Rhymes and an Appendix of Songs,* trans. Walter Kaufman (New York: Vintage, 1974), §7, 43. [Emphasis added in the French by Falque.—Trans.]

5. René Descartes, *Préambules* (*Cogitationes privatae* [1619]), in *Oeuvres philosophiques* (Paris: Classiques Garnier, 1963), t. I (1618–37), 45 [AT, X, 212].

6. Cf. Henri Gouhier, *Les premières pensées de Descartes* (Paris: Vrin, 1979), 66–67. Formula from AT, X, 9, and added to the translation in *Oeuvres Philosophiques*, 45.

7. Léon Brunschvicg, "Mathématique et métaphysique chez Descartes," *Revue de métaphysique et de morale* 34, no. 3 (1927): 323. The article primarily concerns Étienne Gilson's *René Descartes, Discours de la méthode, Texte et commentaire* (Paris: Vrin, 1925).

8. René Descartes, "Lettre à Mersenne, 28 Janvier 1641," AT, III, 293, 24–25. Cited and translated by Jean-Luc Marion, *Sur le prisme métaphysique de Descartes. Constitution et limites de l'onto-théo-logie dans la pensée cartésienne* (Paris: Presses Universitaires de France, 1986), 291.

9. Marion, *Sur le prisme métaphysique*, 292, with reference not only to Brunschvicg but also to Jean-Luc Nancy, *Ego Sum* (Paris: Flammarion, 1979).

10. Jean-Luc Marion, *L'idole et la distance: cinq études* (1977; Paris: Livre de Poche, 1991), 188–89. English trans.: Marion, *The Idol and Distance: Five Studies*, trans. Thomas A. Carlson (New York: Fordham University Press, 2001), 150.

11. On this point see the article of Adrian Pabst, "De la chrétienté à la modernité? Lecture critique des thèses de *Radical orthodoxy* sur la rupture scotiste et ockhamienne et sur le renouveau de la théologie de Saint Thomas d'Aquin," *Revue des sciences philosophiques et théologiques* (RSPT) 86, no. 4 (2002): 561–98, although the critical dimension put forward here is not developed.

12. "Saint Thomas d'Aquin et l'onto-théo-logie," *Revue Thomiste* 95 (1995): 31–66, 65 n. 2: "[I]t is clear that I must, with delight, anyway, today present a *retractatio* on this point."

13. Thomas Aquinas, *Somme théologique*, Ia, q.1, a.1, ad. 2.

14. Ibid., Ia, q.1, a.5, ad. 2.

15. *Correctorium fratris Thomae*, Guillaume de la Marre, 1277.

16. For an interpretation built from and related to this first question of the *Summa Theologiae*, see the very instructive chapter of Jean-François Courtine titled "Philosophie et théologie," in his *Suàrez et le système de la métaphysique* (Paris: Presses Universitaires de France/Épiméthée, 1990), pt. 1, chap. 3, 75–99. Marion's "noble retraction" of the God "without being" attributed unexpectedly to the figure of Thomas Aquinas in *God without Being* could in this way be extended to a new retraction here of a philosophy at least in part "integrated" with, and not "separated" from, *sacra doctrina*, at least with Thomas.

17. Thomas Aquinas, *Somme théologique*, Ia, q.2, a.1, resp.

18. Cf. Hans Urs von Balthasar, *Cordula ou l'épreuve decisive* (Paris: Beauchesne, 1968), esp. 117–20, for the reprise of the animated debate with Karl Rahner: "[M]any have asked me with sadness if it was truly necessary to attack a man so worthy as K. Rahner" (117).

19. Hans Urs von Balthasar, "Regagner une philosophie à partir de la théologie," in *Pour une philosophie chrétienne* (Brussels: Lethielleux, 1983), 182–83.

20. Emphasis added by Falque.—Trans.

21. Emphasis added by Falque.—Trans.

22. Emphasis added by Falque.—Trans.

23. I refer the reader to the two works that illustrate my personal thought on this question (death and resurrection): Emmanuel Falque, *Le passeur de Gethsémani. Angoisse, souffrance et mort. Lecture existentielle et phénoménologique* (Paris: Cerf/La nuit surveilée, 1999), and *Métamorphose de la finitude. Essai philosophique sur la naissance et la resurrection* (Paris: Cerf/La nuit surveilée, 2004).

24. Emphasis added by Falque.—Trans.

25. Emphasis added by Falque.—Trans.

26. Jean-Luc Marion, "À Dieu, rien d'impossible," *Revue Catholique Internationale Communio* 14, no. 5 (1989): 43–58, 56. Note here the important fact that in this article we find for the first time—under the pen of the author—the expression "saturated (or saturating) phenomena." Written some years prior to the famous text on "the saturated phenomenon," which claims to be purely philosophical, in my view the syntagm in this way shows its true source and its most pertinent fecundity. See "Le phénomène saturé," in *Phénoménologie et théologie*, ed. Jean-François Courtine (Paris: Critérion, 1992), 79–128. English trans.: "The Saturated Phenomenon," trans. Thomas A. Carlson, *Philosophy Today* 40, nos. 1–4 (1996): 103–24.

27. Marion, "À Dieu, rien d'impossible," 49.

28. Ibid., 58.

29. Karl Rahner, *Traité fondamental de la foi* (1976; Paris: Centurion, 1983), 258–80, "history (theologically understood)."

30. Emphasis added by Falque. *L'adonné* has been left untranslated because of its wide range of connations. Marion's preference is for "the gifted," but it can also mean "the devoted one," or "the one given over."—Trans.

31. Emphasis added by Falque; English translation modified.—Trans.

32. Rudolf Bultmann, *Jesus, mythologie et demythologisation* (Paris: Seuil, 1968) 234–35.

33. Jean-Luc Marion, "Ce mystère qui juge celui qui le juge," *Résurrection* 32 (1969): 54–78, 55 (emphasis added). Thanks to Marion for having pointed out this refererence.

34. Bultmann, *Jesus, mythologie et demythologisation*, 233.

35. Jean-Luc Marion, "La phénoménalité du sacrement: être et donation," *Communio* (2001): 72.

36. Ibid., 74.

37. Cf. J. Benoist, "Le tournant théologique," in *L'idée de la phénoménologie* (Paris: Beauschesne, 2001), 81, 84, 85: "Dear Jean-Luc Marion, I am an atheist, you are not. . . . There is nothing strongly legitimate in this interpretation, conformed to what you believe *to see,* that is to say to the *believing* in which your *seeing* is deeply rooted, and which orients it. There remains the fact (enigmatic, incomprehensible, we will come back to it) that one can *see otherwise,* that I or others see *otherwise.* . . . For me, for whom atheism has always been obvious . . . , has always been an *existentielle attitude* and not a *theoretical* certitude" (emphasis added).

38. I consider this point in Emmanuel Falque, *Saint Bonaventure et l'entrée de Dieu en théologie* (Paris: Vrin, 2000).

39. Jean-Luc Marion, "Réaliser la presence réelle," *La Maison-Dieu* 225 (2001): 26.

40. Jean-Luc Marion, *De surcroît: Etudes sur les phénomènes saturés* (Paris: Presses Universitaires de France, 2001), 24, 63. English trans.: *In Excess: Studies of Saturated Phenomena,* trans. Robyn Horner and Vincent Berraud (New York: Fordham University Press, 2002), 29, 53.

6

Theology at the Limits of Phenomenology

KATHRYN TANNER

In this essay I speak as a theologian who is not a phenomenologist—for reasons, discussed later, that simply disqualify neither phenomenology nor, I hope, my ability to be an informed critic of it. I share Jean-Luc Marion's theological aim: to think God without conditions, without subjecting God to the *a priori* horizons of either Being or the transcendental subject. I marvel at the brilliance of his efforts to allow the particular subject matters of theological inquiry—for example, the Eucharist or New Testament parables—to establish their own peculiar logic. I applaud his wariness about the way the ordinary and the everyday may straightjacket paths of theological investigation, bending, for example, the trajectories of God's all-giving love in Christ to the commonsense laws of commercial exchange. I am continually refreshed by the way Marion's reminder of the limits of thought is never an excuse for conceptual imprecision: theology has in Marion's hands all the rigor of an alternative logic of love. Theologians should, I agree, be more willing than they have shown themselves so far to take up the challenge, as Marion describes it, "to read phenomenologically the events of revelation . . . instead of always privileging ontic, historic, or semiotic hermeneutics."[1] Whether metaphysics is at an end—and onto-theology with it—the terms of Marion's phenomenology (e.g., "givenness" and the "gifted") provide, I think, enormously suggestive resources for theologians. Besides the ways Marion himself employs them when he speaks as a theologian—primarily on christological, trinitarian, and ecclesiological topics—those terms suggest, for example, a new way of describing the transcendence of God as a dimension of God's immanence to the world, thereby avoiding flat-footed accounts of God as the efficient cause founding and establishing the value of the world from outside it. In short, these new terms hold the promise of a new sort of doctrine of God and Creation.

I suspect, however, a tension between Marion's theological and strictly phenomenological works. Not the usual suspicions here. I do not worry that Marion's phenomenology has been taken captive by a theological aim. That would be an unusual suspicion for a theologian to have in any case. And I think Marion effectively deflects it. The possibility of revelation, as a form of saturated phenomenon, logically arises out of phenomenological attention to givenness according to the usual phenomenological technique of free imaginative variation: if one can consider intuition falling short of consciousness' intentional aim, why not consider the possibility of intuitions exceeding such an aim? Phenomenology is only being true to itself—true to its openness to what gives itself—in asking whether revelation is a possible phenomenon for it, and in considering what would have to be changed about phenomenological analysis in order to allow for that possibility. I am also not worried about whether God is a proper subject matter for phenomenology. I do not think, for example, that the transcendence of God disqualifies God from the pure immanence that phenomenological reduction sustains, since (as I have suggested above) it does not seem to me that the transcendence of God forbids a flexible interpretation of it in terms of immanence—divine transcendence as a dimension of what appears purely to consciousness, in much the way givenness appears in all its excessiveness within the fold of the given and only there.[2] Phenomenological analysis may rule out a metaphysical account of God, in which, for example, God appears as a transcendent efficient cause; but as Marion reminds us there is no reason to equate theology with metaphysics, as if it were some regional subset of metaphysical inquiry into first or self-caused causes. Revealed theology (as Marion calls it) is not the same as rational theology, a mere *metaphysica specialis,* a mere special form of metaphysics.

I worry instead that the theological aim of respecting the unconditionality of God cannot be sustained in light of the way theology and phenomenology are related to one another by Marion. This is the danger that Marion himself acknowledges as the only real one: "If danger there must be, it would reside more in the formal and, in a sense, still transcendental phenomenalization of the question of God than in some sort of theologization of phenomenality. It could be that the fact of Revelation provokes and evokes figures and strategies of manifestation and revelation that are much more powerful and more subtle than what phenomenology, even pushed as far as the phenomenon of revelation (paradox of paradoxes) could ever let us divine."[3] This possibility—this eventuality—that Revelation would exceed the bounds of phenomenological description, however purified, is just what Marion's phenomenology ultimately disallows. If a revelation were to occur (and I agree with Marion that his phenomenology does not prejudge this question) it would have to conform to the dictates of phenomenology concerning the givenness of what appears. Givenness as a universal law of phenomenality permits no exceptions, not even for Revelation, not even for God's coming to us in Christ. "Givenness is never suspended, even if it does not accomplish the phenomenal unfolding in it entirely. Yet again, there can be indefinite degrees of givenness, but no exception from it."[4] More particularly, Revelation, in order to be entertained by phenomenology, has to be fit into the slot marked out for it in advance by Marion's phenomenological description of the degrees and types of givenness; Revelation conforms, and necessarily so, to one of the varieties of the saturated phenomenon—that of the paradox of paradoxes, the saturated phenomenon to the second degree.

> [I]f an actual revelation must, can, or could have been given in phenomenal apparition, it could have, can or will be able to do so only by giving itself according to the type of paradox *par excellence*—such as I will describe it. . . . If revelation there must be (and phenomenology has no authority to decide this), then it will assume, assumes, or assumed the figure of paradox of paradoxes, according to an essential law of phenomenality. In this sense, since revelation remains a variation of saturation, itself a variation of the phenomenality of the phenomenon inasmuch as given, it still remains inscribed within the transcendental conditions of possibility."[5]

The tension I am concerned about—the tension between Marion's phenomenology and his theological aim to respect God's unconditionality—is therefore produced, ironically, by the isomorphism between Marion's theological and phenomenological works, between his treatment of God and his treatment of givenness. The laws of phenomenological appearance may be modified in unexpected ways by God, Revelation, *agapē*. Revelation, God's coming to us in Christ, may necessitate "very particular protocols" from phenomenological analysis;[6] Marion mentions, for example, the need to discuss miracle, election, promise, and certainly the theological virtue of love in the transition from self-giving to self-showing. But the facts of Revelation, while modifying or particularizing them in unexpected ways, cannot in so doing fundamentally violate or trespass the laws of phenomenological appearance. The facts of Revelation are never permitted to fall radically out of sync with the general requirements of phenomenological description. How then can God be beyond all conditions if God's appearance must conform in this way to phenomenological dictates?

Marion has his own ways of responding to this question, which I shall consider in a moment. But we should first be clear about what I am asking of Marion and the character of the challenge being posed. What would it mean for Revelation to exceed the bounds of phenomenological description? What sort of possibility (in Marion's own sense of eventuality) am I asking Marion to admit? Is it a real possibility at all? I am not suggesting that Marion has not sufficiently modified the terms of phenomenological description to allow for the appearance of Revelation. The problem here is not the one that Marion addresses so well, namely, the problem of excluding the phenomenality of Revelation by refusing to reconsider the character, the purity, of the phenomenological reduction—to reconsider, that is, whether phenomenology really allows for the givenness of what appears when it subjects phenomenality to the horizons of Being or transcendental subjectivity or objective intentional aims. I am instead suggesting that, in being open to the phenomenality of revelation, Marion manages to think Revelation too well in phenomenological terms. Revelation thereby becomes what is not at all surprising to phenomenology but just what phenomenology most expects from givenness when givenness is most itself. Marion would thereby do to Revelation what he criticizes a "eucharistic physics" of doing to the eucharistic mystery in *God without Being*. He is so eager to explain the mystery of Revelation in phenomenological terms that he ends up reabsorbing it into a tight conceptual system. "Does one not contradict oneself by seeking, in principle to reinforce credibility, to frame and then to reabsorb the liturgical fact, the mystery of charity [add God's Revelation] in a system (physical, semiotic, etc—[add phenomenological]) at the risk, here again, of attaining only a conceptual idol?"[7]

By making the possibility of revelation something that it has already taken account of as a figure of givenness, phenomenology always preempts, foresees, recuperates for itself what might otherwise surprise it or throw it off balance. Revelation is far from being anything that it is impossible for phenomenology to think—beyond its conceptual capacities, a disturbance to its own sense of adequacy, an evocation of its end. Revelation is instead the very impossible that makes most sense in phenomenological terms—the paradox of paradoxes in a phenomenology geared to paradoxicality. Marion has so well integrated impossible phenomena such as Revelation into phenomenology by reconfiguring its terms of analysis, so well justified the appearance of saturated phenomena such as Revelation thereby,[8] that the coming of Revelation in fact loses its capacity ever to disturb the discipline. Marion refigures the character of phenomenological reduction according to givenness so that phenomenology itself—as a philosophical enterprise—can never be itself disrupted by Revelation, never come to its limit, never meet its match. Phenomenology, just because it has become such an apt instrument for describing a God beyond measure, becomes God's measure.

This consequence is one of the many that rehearse within Marion's own phenomenology the sorts of things he criticized metaphysics and Heidegger for in his theological works. If conditions are not to be placed on God, it is not sufficient, as in Heidegger's case, to think, for once, Being as such, and the ontological difference that metaphysics relegated to oblivion. Even if Heidegger successfully goes beyond metaphysics, this is no guarantee that he does not reinscribe the conditionality of God in a new non-metaphysical mode; this, indeed, is just what Marion argues Heidegger does. And, I would now add, the same would go for Marion's surpassing of Heidegger. Even if God is not considered a ground, or an efficient cause, or the highest being—or Being as such, or associated with the gods within the Fourfold—nothing of Marion's theological aim is served if givenness simply replaces the function of being (metaphysics) and Being as such (Heidegger) as a condition on God. Even if phenomenology escapes metaphysics as Marion hopes (and I see no reason to dispute it), nothing is served if phenomenology takes up the same position in relation to theology that metaphysics and Heideggerian philosophy do, and thereby, like them, sets conditions on God. What Marion argued in Heidegger's case—that his philosophy established a second idolatry despite its attack on metaphysics—would therefore return to haunt Marion's purified phenomenology, beyond

Being and objective intentionality and the transcendental subject: Marion's phenomenology would be haunted by a third idolatry.

Is there after all a significant difference—for all of Marion's rejection of efficient causality, sufficient reason, and the search for metaphysical grounds (all of which I concede)—between saying with metaphysics that God is the highest being and saying with Marion that God appears to us as the highest form or type of saturated phenomena? Is there a real difference—when it comes to the question of sustaining God's unconditionality—between saying that God is the most excellent being, in metaphysics, and that God is "being-given *par excellence,*" "that God "gives himself and allows to be given more than any other being given," for Marion?[9] Doesn't God appear for Marion as one phenomenon among others, albeit the highest, just as God appears as one being among others, the highest being, in a metaphysics forgetful of the onto-logical difference? If divinity is associated with being in metaphysics and with Being as such for Heidegger, who can miss the associations of God with the highest principle of phenomenology for Marion—givenness? God withdraws from what God gives and the trace of this withdrawing is apparent in the given, just as givenness withdraws from the given and is apparent in its with-drawing there (in what Marion terms the "fold"). What is the difference between saying that God is anything at all only insofar as he is subject to Being and say-ing that God can appear to us only insofar as God's appearance conforms to givenness? Marion expends a great deal of effort arguing against his phenome-nologist critics that givenness is not an equivocal term; but isn't the question from a theological point of view whether givenness is univocal? The univocity of givenness[10] means that God gives Himself fundamentally in the same way any phenomenon gives itself, with a simple difference of degree or difference of kind (type). Could the parallel be any stronger with the univocity of being in metaphysics that Marion believes voids God's unconditionality?[11] If the phenomenological laws—that phenomena show themselves in giving them-selves and give themselves to show themselves—establish for Marion the way the world "worlds," isn't God's appearance forced to conform to the ways of the world by his phenomenology in the same way the gods are forced by Heidegger to appear within the world's constitution by the Fourfold? Collaps-ing Revelation into revelation as a universal mode of phenomenality every bit as much as he accuses Heidegger of doing,[12] Marion avers that "the data pro-duced by Revelation— . . . the unique Jewish and Christian Revelation—must be read and be treated as rightfully phenomena, obeying the same operations as those that result from the givens of the world: reduction to the given, eventmentality, reception by *l'adonné*, resistance, saturated phenomena, progressiveness of the transmutation from the self-giving into self-showing, and so on."[13] What indeed, here as in Heidegger's case, happens "to the event that is called God [under erasure] since it claims not to belong to the world (John 18:36)"?[14]

God is subject to the highest term of Marion's phenomenology—givenness—because theology is related to a non-metaphysical philosophy here in the same way theology was related to Heidegger's philosophy—indeed, in the same way theology is related to classical metaphysics—the sort of relationship between theology and philosophy that Marion himself therefore rightly takes strong exception to in his theological works in the effort to be true to God's unconditionality.[15] Conditions are put on God in all these cases because theology has been hijacked by a philosophical aim established independently of it, in such a way that theology can provide a mere ontic or factual corrective to a universal ontological—or in Marion's case, phenomenological—requirement set by philosophy. In all these cases—whether metaphysical or non-metaphysical—philosophy establishes its aims independently of theology and brings God into the picture simply for the sake of furthering those ends. In classical metaphysics God takes up the site that philosophy reserves ahead of time for an ultimate ground, the ultimate reason why there is something rather than nothing, in accordance with its own fundamental aim to seek such grounds and reasons, and in order to fulfill it.

> Onto-theology disengages, of itself, a function and hence a site for every intervention of the divine that would be constituted as metaphysical: the theo-logical pole of metaphysics determines . . . a site for what one later will name "God." Such that "God can come into philosophy only insofar as philosophy of its own accord and by its own nature, requires and determines that and how God enters into it." The advent of something like "God" in philosophy therefore arises less from God himself than from metaphysics. . . . God is determined starting from and to the profit of that which metaphysics is capable, that which it can admit and support.[16]

But the same sort of ultimately idol-making relationship between theology and philosophy affects Heidegger's efforts to surpass the metaphysical search for foundations and the classical metaphysical confusion of Being with beings, according to Marion.[17] Heidegger's philosophy suspends the question of God in a kind of methodological indifference to it, preoccupied as that philosophy is with the more fundamental question of Being as such, which Dasein alone is capable of asking; and it is at this anterior point of the question of Being as such that a new idolatry dawns.[18] The question of God can come into view only as a kind of ontic variation on the invariant question of Being as such; the question of God for philosophy is exhausted in short by its relevance to the invariant ontological question of Being as such, so that God is subjected to an idolatrous precondition.[19] This "indisputable and essential anteriority of the ontological question over the so-called ontic question of God . . . suffices to establish idolatry."[20] The anterior aim of philosophy determines the only God that can appear to it; the only God that appears in philosophy is the one that fills the philosophical gaze, that serves to fulfill a preceding philosophical aim. "Any access to something like 'God,' precisely because of the aim of Being as such, will have to determine him in advance as a being. The precomprehension of 'God' as being is self-evident to the point of exhausting in advance 'God' as a question."[21]

In the case of Marion's phenomenology the preceding, independent philosophical aim would seem to be (in part at least) to exempt phenomenology from the demise of metaphysics in a way that would renew its prospects and rescue its pretensions to be a kind of first philosophy to which all other merely regional philosophies or sciences would have to conform.[22] For a variety of reasons, the only way to ensure this renewal and effectively promote phenomenology's rather grand ambition as first philosophy is for phenomenological reduction, Marion argues, to proceed according to givenness. Givenness as the universal, all-comprehending equivalent of phenomenality justifies (for one) the universal reach of phenomenology and therefore its claim to be the first philosophy rather than a merely regional one: because phenomenology reduces to givenness one can be certain that nothing—indeed, not even nothing—is exempted from phenomenology's proper purview. "Givenness is thus set up, by its certitude and its automatic universality, in principle unconditioned. There could, therefore, be a 'first philosophy' according to phenomenology."[23]

Revelation, the question of God's appearance to us, comes into focus for a phenomenology with these anterior aims for the same reason that any saturated phenomena does for Marion: in order to secure the universal range of givenness. Not even the invisible, the unregardable, the absent, and the unapparent escape givenness. To the contrary, these sorts of cases are often (when not poor phenomena simply lacking in intuition) phenomena characterized by the highest degree of givenness; it is typical of phenomenon at the highest levels of givenness, Marion argues, to be unapparent. One can then quite easily argue that revelation, the highest form of saturated phenomenon, merely serves to reflect givenness back to itself, so as to confirm its universal range and thereby fulfill the prior aim of a purified phenomenology—namely, its aspirations to primacy—to the status of first philosophy. Like any idolatrous mirror, the saturated phenomenon of revelation returns back to givenness the gaze givenness fixes upon it; givenness receives back from revelation what it all along wants to see in it—its own universality, its equivalence with phenomenality. The saturated phenomenon *par excellence* becomes in this way the idol *par excellence* (in the negative sense of "idol" that Marion employs in his theological writings). The saturated phenomena of revelation is the reflective mirror of the question of givenness that precedes any interest in the question of God and that conditions the question of God absolutely, prohibiting all routes of escape.

As I mentioned before, however, Marion has a ready response to these charges.[24] The accusation that phenomenology sets conditions on the appearance of God by submitting it to the phenomenological criterion of givenness is evidently false; and all these parallels I have been drawing between Marion's phenomenology, on the one hand, and classical metaphysics and Heidegger's philosophy, on the other, are specious and superficial—for the same reason: because they ignore what is distinctive about Marion's phenomenological project. That project simply establishes, in the most rigorously consistent way, phenomenological principles and methods of reduction that effectively exclude all *a priori* conditions on phenomenal appearance—God's included. The principles and reductive methods of Marion's phenomenology are doing nothing more than that when they uphold the criterion of givenness as an absolutely comprehensive and inviolable one.

Phenomenology is therefore not a first philosophy in the usual sense of establishing ahead of time the conditions to which all phenomena (and therefore all other subfields of inquiry) must conform—the sort of first philosophy that would always permit a new idolatry to be born. Marion's phenomenology cannot be a first philosophy of that kind since "the originality of its enterprise consists in rendering to the phenomenon an uncontested priority; to let it appear no longer as it must (according to the supposed *a priori* conditions of experience and its objects), but as it gives itself (from itself and as such)."[25]

Marion's renewed phenomenology therefore retains its status as first philosophy only insofar as it is the last philosophy—last in the sense of coming *a posteriori*, after the appearance of phenomena, in order to shore up and respect their priority to give and show themselves without conditions; and last in the sense of doing all this in such an unsurpassably rigorous fashion that it has no successors.

Phenomenology cannot be bending phenomena—say, the possible appearance of divine revelation—to its own anterior aim, so that those phenomena are only ever able to reflect back to it, solipsistically, its own intentions fulfilled. It cannot be doing any of this because the only aim of Marion's phenomenology is to lose itself by way of what Marion terms a paradoxical "counter-method."[26]

> To be sure, like all rigorous science, it decides its own project, its own terrain, and its own method, thus taking the initiative as originally as possible; but counter to all metaphysics, it has no other ambition than to lose this initiative as quickly and as completely as possible, seeing as it claims to connect the apparitions of things in their most initial originarity to the so-to-speak native state of their unconditional manifestation in themselves, therefore starting from themselves. The methodological beginning here establishes the conditions for its own disappearance in the original manifestation of what shows *itself*."[27]

Phenomenology as Marion understands it cannot put conditions on God's appearance because phenomenology's entire philosophical contribution is simply the negative one of ridding phenomena of all conditions hitherto placed on them, of clearing away all the obstacles standing in the way of their manifesting *themselves*. Phenomenology is therefore doing nothing of and for itself, and it would only do what it does successfully by ultimately vacating the field to the unconditional appearance of phenomena themselves, in a final disappearing act.[28]

The criterion of givenness that phenomenology employs is therefore misunderstood if it is viewed as some kind of transcendental condition for the appearance of phenomena: "[T]he principle of givenness does not intervene before the phenomenon in order to fix *a priori* the rules and limits of apparition."[29] To think otherwise is a misunderstanding, not only because it sits uneasily with Marion's project of attacking all transcendental conditions of subjectivity—the transcendental "I"—but because "the principle set up by givenness is precisely that nothing precedes the phenomenon, except its own apparition on its own basis—which amounts to positing that the phenomenon comes forward without any other principle besides itself."[30] In short, "givenness does not submit the given to a transcendent condition, but rather frees it from that condition"; asking after the givenness of phenomena is just a way of asking whether the given phenomenon gives itself starting from itself alone.[31] The criterion of givenness is always employed only after the fact, in order to establish whether what appears is genuinely giving itself in appearing. The criterion serves only to filter out from the appearance everything of which this is not the case so that the appearance might appear absolutely of its own accord, from and by itself.

But are things really so simple? That Marion cannot be setting conditions on the appearance of phenomena—and on God's appearance in particular— follows logically in a kind of *a priori* deductive way from Marion's own understanding of what a purified phenomenology is all about; but do we—without perhaps the same faith in phenomenology's ultimate purity—have reason to believe him? Might not his argument here be subject to confirmation—and therefore possible disconfirmation—in fact, by what in actuality gives itself to be reduced according to givenness? Doesn't Marion's argument here trade indeed on the supposition that no good candidate for phenomenality or Revelation will ever appear that Marion's understanding of givenness must exclude *a priori?* Such an eventuality simply cannot be ruled out in a deductive fashion, because, for example, it exceeds the possibilities that can be generated by phenomenology's own principles of derivation. Marion is confident that nothing of the sort will ever happen, but should we be? Marion tries to enlist our confidence by suggesting that the requirement of givenness is a completely unrestrictive and therefore innocuous one. "About what can we say that it does not appear as given? How could it appear—whatever it is, and in whatever manner it appears—if it did not give itself to any possible degree?"[32] In the case of Revelation too, Marion suggests, this is a completely uncontroversial supposition, to which no theologian of Revelation could possibly have reason to take exception: "[R]evealed theology, by the very fact that it is based on given facts, which are given positively as figures, appearances, and manifestations (indeed, apparitions, miracles, revelations, and so on), takes place in the natural field of phenomenality and is therefore dependent on the competence of phenomenology."[33] Trust then that there is no account of God's coming to us in Christ, within the same negative or mystical theology that Marion believes to escape the pull of onto-theology, which the criterion of givenness would rule out. But what if this trust is misplaced? The burden of proof of course is on me to show, positively, that we do have reason not to follow Marion's seductions here—for either the case of phenomenality in general or Revelation in particular. Marion's purified phenomenology has a limited purview in both cases, I will now try to show.

My argument on the more general question of phenomenality is simply that Marion's treatment of givenness is rather obviously historically circumscribed. When appearances are reduced according to givenness, the result is not a universal form—the pure appearing of phenomena purely given, pure phenomenality that accords with pure givenness—but a particular historical type of phenomenality with a rather limited historical range. Givenness's appearance of universality is only procured, in short, by occluding the historical conditions of its genesis. By overlooking those conditions, Marion is able to pass off as a universal of phenomenality what are in fact rather particular properties of an experience that arises only under exceptional historical conditions.[34] (The fundamentally historical approach I am assuming here explains why I am not a phenomenologist.)

What are these historical conditions that account for the rise of the normative properties Marion attributes to givenness and that therefore limit the reach of Marion's phenomenology? Basically, I suggest those conditions have to do with the growing autonomy of the cultural and economic fields in Western modernity, the growing separation between their respective norms, values, and principles of formation. Marion's treatment of givenness in its opposition to all those aspects of lived experience that it reduces, and, indeed, all the oppositions organizing Marion's phenomenological work—between reduced giving and ordinary gift exchange, between a phenomenological and natural attitude, between openness to what appears and objectifying intentionality— simply reinscribe the opposition between cultural and economic phenomena that is characteristic of the contemporary historical moment in the West. All that to which Marion opposes his phenomenology—objectification, the mastery of the subject, full possession, subsistent presence, efficient causality, and so on—can be summed up under the rubric of "economic exchange." And, conversely, the autonomy of the self of phenomena for Marion (and along with it all the features of givenness that ensure that autonomy)[35] mimics the autonomy of the arts that establishes itself in modernity as the correlate of economy's own formation as an autonomous field. More than mimics: whenever Marion tries to unpack the particular character of givenness he invariably turns, very revealingly, to the figure of painting, following a kind of hyper-Kantian view of art for art's sake.[36]

Painting (his preferred artistic case) escapes the horizons of both being and objects, and therefore reveals what Marion means by givenness very clearly. Givenness, one could say, merely generalizes to all phenomena what Marion believes painting shows, especially when it breaks the hold of representationalist realism, as in impressionism, cubism, and all forms of abstract art. A painting does not depend on its own physical subsistence as a canvas and frame. "The painting . . . subsists only in passing, and the visible in it is not closed up in and as its subsistent but in proportion to the degree to which it is separated from it. The painting therefore does not appear inasmuch as it subsists."[37] The painting does not represent anything—and certainly not anything already existing in the ordinary objective world. "Admiration is concentrated on the resemblance, precisely because it no longer resembles anything";[38] the painter "gives rise to a semblance that resembles nothing already seen before his or her intervention, not in nature, not in other paintings,"[39] and thereby simply dazzles us with a pure semblance that refers us to nothing besides itself. As a result, the painting has no end other than itself, no finality besides itself, and loses indeed all functionality: "[T]he painting appears only as non-used, non-usable, and not even useful, in short, as such," in and for itself.[40] Here is the purity of modern art pushed to excess, purified (as modern art typically strives to be) of all forms of commercialism through its concentration on form rather than content or function, through its appeal to rare inspiration and technical expertise without common measure, and through its refusal of vulgar expectation and reduction, instead, to specifically aesthetic effects.

Repudiating economic exchange, givenness is not freed from it. Like the autonomy of the cultural it reflects, givenness remains bound up with economic exchange in the wider logic of modernity. The autonomy of the aesthetic, for example, depends on specific economic and social circumstances that continue to condition it; without the autonomy of the economic, the autonomy of the aesthetic is impossible. Art was able to liberate itself from the hold of the church and politically powerful patrons—it could serve specifically artistic ends distinct from religious and political pressures—only when a new general market for art opened up with the birth of commercial society.[41] Art is able to liberate itself from the demands that the economic market sets on its "products," in turn, only to the degree the economy purifies itself of anything more than economic concern. Thus Marion's securing of the self of phenomena against all efforts to objectify it is a particular instance of the distinction between persons and things that the market itself requires and sustains. Only when the exchange of material things or goods is no longer dependent on the personal relationships among the parties to it, do those personal relations become free to transpire apart from economic interest—say, out of pure disinterested love. Personal relations were necessarily compromised by considerations of an economic sort—love and giving to others, say, by hopes for a material return on them—when personal relations of giving and loving fealty were the only means to material well being, before the institution of an impersonal market.[42]

Tied up inextricably with the market exchange that is its obverse by the wider logic of modernity, givenness's sights are thereby necessarily limited. What givenness does not allow to be seen are forms of phenomenality that abide by neither one of the autonomous poles of modernity nor their imbrication as enemies. Restricted by this polarity—the play between either givenness or commerce—Marion fails to see possibilities that exceed its scope. Gift exchange is one. Gift exchange is not as easily assimilated to commercial exchange as Marion suggests in book 3 of *Being Given*. Givers are not obviously here the efficient causes of products that are alienated from them and only given in exchange for some sort of future payment. Gift exchange, as many anthropologists tell us, concerns the establishment and maintenance of relationships at a distance, gifts that retain the trace of their givers in them, gifts that always come back unexpectedly and never from the person one gave them to, and so on. Gift exchange is therefore not commercial exchange in that it is quite a bit more like the logic of givenness than Marion admits. But gift exchange is also not exactly the same as the logic of givenness either, for some of the reasons also mentioned in *Being Given* and that become exceptionally clear in Marion's *Prolegomena to Charity*.[43] The reciprocal circle of gift exchange—gifts for gifts, giving only in response to giving, giving that obligates giving, giving that gives only for the sake of a return—is fundamentally unlike the logic of givenness, clearly manifest in charity, that breaks not only the cycle of hate for hate, revenge for revenge, but even the cycle of love for love in its love for enemies. Might there not be other possibilities too (besides gift exchange) not captured—indeed not capturable—by the simple opposition between givenness and commerce that straightjackets Marion's analysis here?

Possibilities more commonly found historically, for example, before the separation of commerce and culture into autonomous fields in the West? Religious possibilities—as I suggest in a moment? The restricted historical circumstances of reduction to givenness simply render it incapable of doing justice to this variety. Reduced according to givenness, their purified form always mimics one narrowly circumscribed possibility of the contemporary moment—the purity of pure love or pure art. The complexity of the historical record—across time periods but just as much within any one of them—suggests indeed a variety of nonequivalent forms of gift giving, which reduction of them all to the same pure givenness necessarily occludes.[44]

Bound up with the commercialism it refuses by the wider logic of modernity, givenness, finally, cannot be fully purified of commercialism. Because it is historically interwoven with the economic exchange it wishes to be autonomous of, Marion's treatment of givenness always threatens to reinstate economy. The logic of exchange infiltrates, for example, his own analysis of givenness through the inclusion of forms of reciprocity that are only very imprecisely distinct from the unreduced forms of gift exchange and commercial transaction that he equates. Despite the fact that givenness gives itself without reserve and with complete abandon, without consideration of return, even to those most unworthy of it—the enemy, the ingrate, and so on—givenness, we are told, especially when it appears in the highest degree in saturated phenomena, can be fully received only in being returned: love fully received only in being returned in love; the call appearing only in that heeding of the call that gives itself in abandon to it, in an appropriate return, a kind of repetition of the call's own abandoning of itself; givenness, if it is to be shown, demanding a receiver willing to align him or herself with givenness's own directives; and the like.

These forms of reciprocity are not clearly distinct from the unreduced forms of exchange Marion opposes to them. First, as I have already suggested, gift exchange is much less like commercial exchange than he gives it credit for. But, more importantly, commercial exchange is much more like his treatment of givenness than Marion would care to admit. The variety of ways that Marion unpacks givenness, including these peculiar forms of reciprocity, seem to fit a market economy quite easily, before any reduction to givenness.[45] Capitalists always risk a nonreturn on their investments; their operations, indeed, are always open to the pure loss of business failure. They must throw out their products onto the market in a kind of abandon to consumer whim, their products, for all the call of advertisement, defenseless before the possible scorn and rejection of the buying public. Especially in late consumer capitalism, production does not strive to meet pre-given consumer tastes, but to best competitors by offering that purely unforeseen eventuality—that unexpectedly novel item—that must work to create its own market, its own demand, through advertisement and word of mouth. Production succeeds only when consumers heed the call of those products, that advertisement, that buzz, losing themselves in them and allowing themselves to be formed by them—as if what they are offered is just what they always wanted.

Finally, givenness remains implicated in economic exchange because the effort to purify givenness, like the effort to purify art, necessarily has its utilities. The ideal of artistic purity cannot avoid becoming both a tool in the struggle for status against more commercial forms of art in the cultural field and a way of naturalizing the differences between economic classes in the wider society. The purely internal end of purifying art or givenness is always predisposed to perform additional, external functions.[46] Thus the effort to purify art from the demands of the general market is always also a way of arguing that this work has greater artistic value than commercial art. Commercial artists are not real artists because they produce representational art of little technical merit that makes no demands of its audience—for example, paintings of Elvis on velvet sold to any passerby in gas station parking lots, or pleasant pictures of pretty things mass produced in Asia for people with no artistic taste to decorate their living rooms with. Only art that is offered as a pure gift without concern for its wide reception among the general buying public, thrown away in an act of unrequited love of art for art's sake—only art that offers itself as a superior reality, irreducible to the vulgar demands of common life or what phenomenology calls the "natural attitude" wins the recompense of recognition as real art, fine art.[47]

Purified art in its refusal of the economic is therefore typically art without much of an audience and therefore art that is always amenable to be used as a mark of distinction by those rare people able to appreciate it. The distance that this art keeps from the economic naturally speaks, indeed, to those classes whose economic position also enables them to keep their distance from economic necessity: a rare taste for a rare class. The few who appreciate fine art are always inclined to use it to naturalize their superior social and economic position. Differences in taste come to legitimize or justify differences in economic class, both within the ranks of the dominant class and between it and the lower class. The elites who owe their position to higher education (e.g., professors) use the purity of their artistic taste against the business class of cultural philistines. Business and educational elites together use their cultured tastes against the poor and the working class: these people are naturally on the lower rungs of society because they are just the sort of people who love velvet Elvis paintings. Such uses for social purposes are possible only by occluding the social conditions for naturally appreciating purified art—for example, a familiarity with it that comes from growing up in a home with it or attending museum exhibitions regularly, a more than minimal level of education, and freedom from an insistent economic need to get by (i.e., freedom from dire poverty or serious economic insecurity). I do not appreciate fine art, then, because I have a particular social background; instead, I both naturally have this social position and merit it at once by virtue of my good taste, my sensitivity to the call of fine art. The occlusion of these social conditions is just, indeed, what purified art demands: pure art offers its gifts to anyone willing to be open to its demanding influence; it creates its own audience through the force of its specifically aesthetic features alone. It therefore becomes inexplicable that only those people with a certain social placement typically respond to difficult art in the way difficult art calls for. Everyone else complains of meaningless squiggles and badly drawn figures, and that even their five-year-olds could do better! In this way pure art—art or art's sake alone—necessarily colludes with its own subversion by an external utility; essential features of its own self-understanding force it to cooperate with its being turned into a tool for the legitimation of domination.

Marion follows pure art's occlusion of the social preconditions for its reception in his treatment of anamorphosis: the idea that givenness requires the self-evacuation of one's prior personal formation, and of all one's preexisting expectations, in favor of the simple decision to open oneself to the phenomenon's own directives, a willingness to take up the position that the phenomenon itself demands, and to follow the lines along which the phenomenon itself directs. Anamorphosis therefore can only enable external utilities rather than prevent them, as Marion thinks. Just like purified art, givenness is offered universally but is in fact rarely perceived, pushed out of the ordinary experience of a world of objects and ready-to-hand tools at human disposal, and completely ignored at its highest reaches of saturated phenomena by the refusal of most people to give themselves over to givenness's own magical powers of conversion. The reception of givenness—its showing of itself in human experience—always comes to the recipient as an unbidden gift but a gift that is always also the consequence of one's own exceptional decision to give oneself over to it. Both a mark of distinction and a pure gift for which one is not responsible, the rare reception of givenness is thereby always available to legitimize social privilege.[48]

Let us turn now to the second question of givenness's restricted purview on Revelation. Is there really nothing that a revealed theology might want to say about God's appearance to us in Christ that Marion's purified phenomenology forbids? Does every account of revelation in Christ, which follows that revelation and not the *a priori* dictates of metaphysics, conform neatly with Marion's account of givenness? Must God always appear according to givenness? I will suggest not by offering a theological view of God's coming to us in Christ that does not follow the lines laid down by givenness, one developed from the same mystical and negative theology strands of the Christian tradition that Marion argues (against Derrida) escape onto-theology.[49] This alternative treatment of God's appearance, I argue, is more in keeping with Marion's theological instincts than his own expressed theological views; it does not succumb to the demands of phenomenology itself as a discipline in ways that promote, as I suggested above, a third idolatry. Not surprisingly, the theological position I advocate is my own, developed in *Jesus, Humanity, and the Trinity,* and garnered, in ways I cannot prove here, from many of the same patristic sources that Marion himself favors as theological resources.[50]

According to this theological alternative, the Greek problematic that revelation in Christ disturbs is not one that equates divinity and humanity so as to permit human comprehension and mastery of the divine (what Marion terms "idolatry"). The Greek problematic incompatible with Christian affirmation is one that refuses direct intimacy between unlikes. The scandal of Christ to the Greeks is therefore the extremely close association, to the point of identification, of God with its opposite: a fully human person, subject to time and change, dying as any mortal would, suffering excruciatingly at his last, an abject failure. For Greek thinking, divinity and a human life of this sort cannot be bound up together this closely without compromising the difference between them.

The distance that, for Marion, establishes difference, and whose traversal unites what must remain at a distance, is just the Greek problematic itself, not a Christian alternative to it that follows the odd logic of God's revelation in Christ. Difference evidently does not require distance if the divine (more specifically, the second person of the Trinity) and the human are one in Christ. Here in Christ, contrary to what Marion says about the icon, the humanity of Christ does not have to appear at a distance from the Word, refer over a distance to its prototype, in order not to be confused with it.[51] In contrast to Marion's typical theological formulations, in Christ it is clear that the divine need not withdraw at a distance—the way givenness always withdraws in what it gives to show itself—so as generously to allow the human to appear; to the contrary, a human being appears here because—only by virtue of the fact that—God is so near. Nor, following Marion's general phenomenological principle that givenness in the highest degree necessarily renders its own manifestations poor, can divinity appear (in what Marion rightly terms an invisible, unapparent fashion) only through the evacuation of Jesus' own humanity, brought to awful culmination on the cross. It is not the case, as Marion avers, that the believer sees the Father in Jesus only if the humanity of Jesus, like the face of an icon, effaces itself, so as to become a transparent window through which one sees the distant Father at a distance.

> The icon does not expect one to see it, but rather gives itself so that one might see or permit oneself to see through it. A dulled, dressed-down image—in short, transpierced—the icon allows another gaze, which it gives to be seen, to suddenly appear through it. . . . The self-renunciation of the image itself—a condition of its transformation into an icon—is thus accomplished in the obedience of the one who sheds his face, renouncing his visibility in order to do the will of God. . . . [I]t is precisely at the moment that he loses his human appearance that Christ becomes the figure of the divine will. . . . His disfigured appearance is thus given as transparency, in order that we might regard there the gaze of God.[52]

Divinity in Jesus is invisible, as Marion says, but this is because, contrary to Marion, all that fills the eye there is a human being miraculously without deficit. Divinity appears unapparently (to follow the beautifully paradoxical phrasing of Marion) in Jesus' human life itself as that life takes on the shape appropriate to that of the Son in relation to Father and Spirit—the mode of the Son transposed into human terms by the incarnation. That shape is not, however, one of self-evacuation at a remove; to the contrary, the divine appears in Jesus as the fullness of Jesus' life and truth, a fullness that not even horrific suffering and untimely death can conquer, a fullness that necessarily spills over for the good of others in the most intimate solidarity with them. It is in these doings that Jesus rehearses in human form the life of the Trinity, a life in which—as every patristic writer I know says—the persons of the Trinity do not empty themselves to fill one another, but spill over into one another out of their fullness, as light or an ever-bubbling fountain would, without self-evacuation or self-loss, so as to mirror one another in what they all have and not in what they have lost to one another, in ways that never produce any sort of gap between them.

This is an unconditional giving following the lines of givenness on Marion's account—unconditional in the sense, first of all, of giving with abandon and without reserve, and second, of giving without regard for a return, even to the unworthy and the ungrateful. This is, however, an account of unconditional giving that can be sustained consistently without succumbing ultimately, as Marion does, to reciprocal forms of either mutually conditioned exchange or mutual hostility among competing actors. This infiltration of economic exchange within Marion's treatment of unconditional giving is just what one would expect if, as I argued above, there is not a sufficient difference between saying, with Marion, that God's appearing to us in Christ is just one type (the highest) among other ways of appearing (according to the degree of givenness), and saying, with the onto-theologians, that God is one kind of being (the highest) among other beings. When God is one kind among others according to the fundamental principles that a philosophy offers for understanding the world (being or phenomenality makes little difference here), God's dealings naturally succumb to the ordinary.

Thus, in order to secure unconditional giving (in both senses), Marion always introduces competitive forms of exchange. For him, giving with abandon, unreservedly, always seems to slide into giving as a form of self-denial or self-emptying, giving at one's own expense, the sort of giving made manifest in dying on a cross. But giving without reserve does not logically require anything like that. To the contrary, as Marion himself recognizes, giving establishes the very self of givenness and therefore cannot work against it. It is in giving unreservedly that God is most properly, fully himself; in so doing, God does not abandon himself but safeguards what is proper to him.[53] Giving at the cost of self-evacuation is instead the demand that the world of everyday phenomena commonly puts on giving (the demand put to Christ by a sinful world in crucifying him); and it is just this demand that a theology of revelation typically refuses. As Dionysius the Areopagite says, God doesn't give himself away in giving all but remains in himself; like the sun (an analogy that no patristic writer repudiates the way Marion does in *The Idol and Distance*),[54] God radiates giving without restriction while maintaining God's own full radiance at the very same time.

Competitive forms of exchange also enter into Marion's account of unconditional giving when he tries to prevent the appearance of reciprocity. Unconditional giving seems to be secured, for Marion, only when it is giving at a complete loss to the giver and without a return.[55] Giving, indeed, is most perfectly itself when the giver is deprived of what it gives[56] and the would-be recipient refuses it: giving perfected in the form of the absolutely abandoned gift. The enemy and the ingrate therefore perfect giving in its perfect unconditionality. When ordinary gift exchange is perfectly reduced according to givenness, those are the forms under which the givee must appear;[57] givenness truly shows its unconditionality only when what it gives is repudiated and scorned. But this is to slide from giving whether or not there is a return to giving that forbids a return. In agreement with Derrida, Marion insists on this forbidding of a return in order to prevent the corruption of a purely generous motive, but it is an unnecessary gambit. As Kant knew full well (and he was not one to compromise on the question of purity of motive!) the mere fact that one might be benefited by one's generosity need not corrupt one's motive of helping others. That lack of corruption is proven by one's willingness to give under every condition (i.e., one's willingness to do so as a categorical imperative), even where such a return is not at issue. Far from securing unconditionality, moreover, forbidding a return overturns unconditional giving by imposing conditions on it: giving is now conditional on the failure of a return.

On the account I am offering, God gives unconditionally but God also does so for the sake of a return; and there is nothing particularly problematic about that. What is problematic is the way Marion has turned the likely eventuality of God's giving to a sinful world—its ingratitude and scorn—into an unsurpassable ideal. God wants the return of our own love and gratitude and devotion to God's own mission of giving to others; that is the soteriological point of God's giving to us. Benefiting others is the end and whether God too might be benefited in some attenuated sense of 'benefit'—our weak chorus of praise drowned in the already fulsome radiance of God's glory—does nothing to corrupt that motive since God gives regardless. The unconditionality of God's giving simply means that God gives before any such return on our part, and that

God continues to give even when that return fails to be made, indeed even if any such return were never to be made, for the sake of enabling it.

For all his efforts to avoid reciprocity in the account of giving and givenness, reciprocity resurfaces quite overtly in Marion's account of the manifestation of givenness: givenness gives itself to show itself but cannot show itself, fully at least, without an appropriate receiver of its manifesting of itself. Givenness gives itself perfectly whether or not it shows itself—indeed gives itself in the highest degree when it does not directly show itself. But if it is to be shown, directly or indirectly, there must be that "to which" givenness shows itself. A "to which" necessarily appears as a seemingly inevitable condition of phenomenality from a phenomenological perspective; there is no appearance without appearance to consciousness. Givenness gives itself but can still only be introduced, for this reason, into the presence of the world by a consciousness that "manages the phenomenological opening where the given must show itself."[58] Despite the fact that givenness gives itself to be shown, that "to which" it shows itself remains the "gate-keeper for the ascent into visibility"; it has "the charge of opening or closing the entire flux of phenomenality."[59] This holds even for the case of saturated phenomena, where givenness is at its height; indeed it holds especially in that case because saturated phenomena require a very special sort of receiver to be made manifest: not the sort of receiver who wants to see only what fits its prior needs, what meets its preconditions, and confirms its expectations or preconceptions, a receiver capable of receiving only an objectified world demystified of all saturation. To be received, to be recognized in their lack of obvious visibility, to be seen in their invisibility, saturated phenomena require receivers who are willing to will themselves over to, unreservedly give themselves over to, the unbearable, the immeasurable, the excessive in absolute degree: receivers who respond in the abandon of whole-hearted devotion and love to what has abandoned itself to them in the same fashion.

In short, unconditional givenness seems to lose its unconditionality upon manifesting itself; this manifesting is conditional on a favorable reception that returns to givenness what it itself gives—love for love, abandonment for abandonment, gift of itself for gift of itself. One receives gifts only in giving them back to the giver in the same way one has been given them. The givenness of what shows itself is only apparent when the receiver perceives that givenness in it and thereby sends it back to givenness in a comparable sort of return giving.[60] The call makes itself heard only in and through the return response—

"You mean me?"—of the one who thereby receives it; the call becomes audible only when it is acknowledged by the one who assumes the role for which it calls, in making a return response.[61] The receiver becomes the gatekeeper of the transition to manifestation only when it exposes itself without protection in the way givenness has already exposed itself without protection to it.[62] And the same sort of necessary return holds for God's manifestation: "God who gives himself as Love only through love, can be reached only so long as one receives him by love, and to receive him by love becomes possible only for he who gives himself to him," surrendering himself to love.[63] Only love can welcome love.[64] "The presence of the Christ, and therefore also that of the Father, discloses itself by a gift; it can therefore be recognized only by a blessing. A presence which gives itself by grace and identifies itself with this gift, can therefore be seen only in being received, and be received only in being blessed."[65]

Because it does not fit our reception of Christ into a phenomenological mold (because, in other words, the paradigm for reception is not appearance to conscious), my account of God's coming in Christ, unlike Marion's, carries over the unconditionality of God's giving to our reception of it. Even if we remain unworthy recipients of it, the divinity of Christ is *ours* (because in Christ that divinity has already been applied to our humanity). The gifts of Christ are fully ours without our having done anything to deserve them, before we have done anything to deserve them, before those gifts themselves turn us into lovers of and witnesses to Christ and givers as he was. They are ours in and through a relationship with Christ that Christ establishes and maintains with us through his doing alone, while we are sinners. Anything that might look like a condition for receiving the gifts of Christ is really something coming after and on the basis of their prior reception.

Marion makes a move like this too, in order to prevent the otherwise strong impression in his account that the receiver places conditions on givenness's showing of itself: the receiver receives itself from what gives itself. Anything that seems to place a condition on givenness's showing of itself—say, the will to open oneself completely to what appears—is itself received, then, from givenness.[66] It is hard to see how this really helps, however, when what calls for the receiver, thereby giving the receiver to itself, is only again manifest in the receiver's heeding of it. The reciprocity Marion tries to avoid in this fashion always reappears at another level down, so to speak.

But the primary way that Marion tries to avoid the impression that the receiver places a condition on the manifestation of givenness is by evacuating the receiver of all activity and control over what is always already happening to it. The receiver is utterly receptive, utterly passive, affected by what gives itself without being able to do anything about it, in a way that exceeds all its abilities to control or anticipate, so that it comes to itself—awakes to itself, one might say—only belatedly, after the fact, in recognizing what, with an irreducible anteriority, is already a *fait accompli*. The receiver receives what gives itself to be shown by it like one receives a car crash: one never sees it coming, one's reactions are always too late to head it off, and one is carried along by the initial force of the impact willy-nilly.[67] The sole initiative of the receiver is therefore to remain ready and open for what will give itself to it according to a time of its own reckoning,[68] and to follow the dictates of what gives itself, to take up the position that giveness itself demands of the receiver in showing itself to it.

Marion, in short, avoids the appearance of a condition here only by making the receiver that givenness needs to show itself next to nothing—not the proud transcendental "I" with its active powers of constituting objects of perception and with its many positive preconditions that force the phenomena of consciousness to conform to it, but a mere negative "precondition," perfectly empty and perfectly powerless, and therefore perfectly pliable to givenness's own inexorable influence. But next to nothing is not simply nothing. And therefore Marion cannot avoid what he himself recognizes as at least a "classic ambiguity of transcendental phenomenology: the givenness of the phenomenon on its own basis to an I can always veer toward a constitution of the phenomena by and on the basis of the I."[69] No matter how reduced the "I" is—reduced indeed by Marion to the "me"—it still plays some undeniable role in givenness's translation into manifestation, a role that givenness simply cannot do without. And therefore all Marion's statements stressing the initiative of givenness in coming upon the receiver are reversible in a way that compromises such a unilateral initiative: givenness may indeed crash upon the screen of consciousness in a way that gives rise to that screen; but what is that crashing, in turn, without the screen?

Marion's refusal of a cooperative relationship between givenness and its receiver in the manifestation of givenness—Marion's refusal of their reciprocal conditioning of one another, in other words—always seems to lead to the proposal of a competitive relationship between them, in keeping with what is ever the way of the world. Givenness must withdraw if it is to show itself; it advances to us in phenomenality only by withdrawing; it shows itself in the phenomena only as a withdrawing. Givenness must retire, in its hiddenness and unnamability, for the receiver to come to itself, come forth as itself; it seems to have to make room thereby for the receiver's own act of conversion. For example, by its absence givenness leaves the decision to be open to it or not to the receiver, a matter of its own responsibility. And then there is the reverse of the same either/or, which we have already been exploring. Givenness shows *itself* only at the expense of the recipient's own initiative. The receiver must be evacuated of any and every desire besides that of whole-heartedly submitting to what givenness dictates; its initiative is simply the refusal to have its own will. Following the law for ordinary worldly phenomena, it is either the autonomy of the phenomena or the autonomy of consciousness. The self of the phenomena must usurp the gravitational center from the self of the receiver.[70] If givenness is self-positing and self-actualizing, what it shows itself to must not be.[71]

But on the account of Christ that I am offering, it is simply not the case that the more God gives the less we are, as the recipients of it. The humanity of Christ is not crushed by God, but raised up into its fullness against the efforts of a sinful world to batter it down. God shows God's giving in the positive building up of the receiver of that giving—in the recipient's own willing and self-propelled activity, a gift of self, indeed, that is not simply submerged into the God it serves and worships. This entrance of the recipient's own acts and operations, moreover, is not the concomitant of God's withdrawal, God's taking up of a position at a distance; we receive ourselves in the fullness of our own activity as God draws near. In Christ, humanity is exalted to its own full glory—Christ has a glorified *humanity*—by virtue of the fact that this human being is one with the second person of the Trinity. Finally, according to the account I am offering, the beauty and glory of the human form need not rival God's, since God is the giver of it. Therefore God's work is not done in the disfiguring of Christ—his beating, his scourging—that, for Marion, allows Christ's humanity to become an icon referring attention entirely away from itself and only to the Father.[72] It is not the case that the human must be as good as nothing to prevent any self-sufficiency, autonomy, or self-affirmation on its part; seen as gifts of God, what humanity has to be proud of only turns humanity all the more to God. Moreover, so long as these gifts are ours only in and through a relationship with God, these gifts need not be sent out in an endless round of circulation, as Marion proposes, in order to avoid the full possession of them that dispossesses the Father.[73] "What's mine is yours and what's yours is mine" holds because what God gives us is only ours in relation to God, because the human and the divine are always with each other (cf. Luke 15:31); the gift endlessly regiven is not, then, required for it to be true. Focusing exclusively, as Marion recommends,[74] on the circulation itself of the gift without any attention to what is being circulated, his position, moreover, becomes indistinguishable from what he rightly criticized in *Prolegomena to Charity*—an endlessly self-repeating cycle of the same—even if it be an endless round of love in response to love, giving in response to giving. What happens here to the love of enemies and the refusal to accuse? If the form of circulation is itself the only thing that matters, one can fill it just as well with hate for hate, act of revenge for act of revenge; hate as well as love can generate the same go-round.

Marion extends the same sort of competitive denial of the receiver even to the full manifestation of givenness in the receiver. When givenness gives itself in the highest degree to the recipient it shows itself in a host of utterly negative phenomena, which remain perfectly final and unsurpassable. The higher the degree or type of givenness in what shows itself, the less the receiver sees, so that this very failure becomes the highest form of showing, according to givenness. The more givenness gives to be shown (in saturated phenomena), the more givenness reveals itself simply in our inability to bear it, our incapacity to grasp or exhaust what we are being given to see. We see the highest forms of saturated phenomena, then, only as all our horizons are trespassed, as our pretensions are humiliated,[75] our certainties stripped from us, as we acknowledge the limitations of our finitude in the always failed effort to name God, as we suffer perturbation and experience our powerlessness to contain what always exceeds our capacities.[76] All of these phenomena are well and good according to the alternative account of God's coming to us in Christ that I am developing; but, on that account, these negative phenomena are all simply a dimension of something positive that itself has an irreducible anteriority in the experience of the graced; all of this happens, as Gregory of Nyssa says, because we are stretched by a fullness received, which always satisfies us at every moment, fills us up, even as it expands our capacities to receive more.

By setting up a competitive relationship between givenness and the receiver who is to show it, between the Father and the Son who is the Father's icon, Marion tends to collapse the latter into the former in a kind of ironic return to immediate identity; all that is left of the latter is made up by the former. Giving myself over completely to what givenness demands, my will simply is that command. Since Christ is nothing of himself but a transparent pointer to the word of the Father, that word can be equated with the otherwise empty Christ; the word of the Father seems to push out the humanity of Christ to appear, for all intents and purposes, alone in his place. By emptying himself of all his own glory, Christ is able to assume the very glory of God;[77] the very glory of God now shines out of his evacuated humanity. Christ does continue to point away from himself across a distance to a distant Father, but this very setting up and traversing of distance again collapses back into simple identity. This emptiness of Christ's humanity is the very emptiness of God; his act of self-renunciation is the very self-renunciation or distancing act that constitutes divinity; this very establishing and traversing of distance reproduces the distance that makes God God.[78] The distance that the Son always maintains to the Father renders perfectly present, then—offers the unmediated appearance of—the very distance of the Father.[79] In a similar collapse into identity for all the distance talk, Christ leaves this world at his Ascension, but in so doing leaves Christians to assume his role perfectly, perfectly evacuating their own wills in a transparent evocation of Christ's.[80] Emptying themselves in abject humility, they nevertheless become themselves little Christs—or better said, they take Christ's glory on themselves just for this reason. By pointing away from themselves across an irreducible distance in praise and prayer to God, Christians, ironically, seem to become indistinguishable from Christ, who did the same, and who is now nowhere (else) to be found. "To recognize Christ, then presupposes that one admit the withdrawal that, between him and us, reveals that other and same withdrawal, in which the Father and the Son recognize one another and are united."[81] All these distances seem to take on a flattened univocity: distances without a difference.

How to conclude? All I really want to say is that to do justice to the peculiar phenomena of revealed theology, to let those phenomena really determine their own terms of discussion (as Marion does so well for the Eucharist in *God without Being*), one must be willing to allow every philosophical perspective to become a merely regional one and admit the possible provisionality of all their methods and conclusions, no matter how thoroughly worked out or apparently basic. There is indeed always the possibility, as Marion says in *God without Being*, of "an irreducible heteronomy, with regard to 'God,' of that which thought (philosophical or poetic?) can do on the one hand, and that which revelation gives."[82] Theology cannot hope to consider God beyond any conditions that philosophy might set for it if phenomenology therefore retains the sort of unquestioned status as a discipline that it has for Marion. Not just the fundamental categories and principles of analysis need to be rethought if phenomenology is to be open to the strange phenomena of Revelation, but the possible limits of the discipline. Phenomenology would thereby give up that self-assurance that so characterizes its search for the indubitable in appearance.[83] It would allow for the possibility of what Marion sometimes hints at in *Being Given:* what revelation gives might simply "transgress the phenomenological field."[84]

At the least, I hope that Marion's full treatment of the rigorous logic of love, promised at the end of *Being Given,* will refuse—especially if it includes the love of God in Christ as one of its highest figures—to follow necessarily and rigidly the lines of givenness. (I assume that *Le Phénomène érotique* is not that work.) And that might mean admitting more. Perhaps the difference between God and the world not only makes the difference between being and non-being a matter of indifference,[85] but also puts to shame phenomenology's preoccupation with the difference between visibility and invisibility, the sort of preoccupation that surrounds the proposal of givenness. To paraphrase Athanasius:[86] "[T]he holy Word of the Father, almighty and all-perfect, uniting with the whole universe and having everywhere unfolded his powers, and illuminating all things—both visible and invisible—holds together and binds to himself both things seen and unseen." What then is the distinction between visibility and invisibility to him? In keeping with such a thought, perhaps it is a mistake—a limited view that phenomenology passes off for the whole—to think that God's coming in Christ is for the primary purpose of destroying idolatry, that the Revelation of God is just for "cleaning the slate of this illusion."[87] Maybe there are greater things to worry about—and greater gifts.

Notes

1. Jean-Luc Marion, *In Excess: Studies of Saturated Phenomena,* trans. Robyn Horner and Vincent Berraud (New York: Fordham University Press, 2002), 29.

2. See Jean-Luc Marion, *Being Given: Toward a Phenomenology of Givenness,* trans. Jeffrey L. Kosky (Stanford: Stanford University Press, 2002), 23–24.

3. Ibid., 243.

4. Marion, *In Excess,* 23.

5. Marion, *Being Given,* 235.

6. Marion, *In Excess,* 53.

7. Jean-Luc Marion, *God without Being: Hors-Texte,* trans. Thomas Carlson (Chicago: University of Chicago Press, 1991), 162.

8. See Marion, *Being Given,* 80, 84, 114, 321–22, where he is arguing against Derrida.

9. Jean-Luc Marion, "Metaphysics and Phenomenology: A Relief for Theology," *Critical Inquiry* 20 (Summer 1991): 588.

10. See Marion, *Being Given,* 118.

11. Marion, *In Excess,* 145; Jean-Luc Marion, *The Idol and Distance: Five Studies,* trans. Thomas Carlson (New York: Fordham University Press, 2001), 7.

12. Marion, *God without Being,* 70.

13. Marion, *In Excess,* 53.

14. Marion, *God without Being,* 71.

15. Ibid., 34–35, 69–71; Marion, *The Idol and Distance,* 208–9.

16. Marion, *God without Being,* 34.

17. Ibid., 41–45; Marion, *The Idol and Distance,* 208–16.

18. Marion, *God without Being,* 43.

19. Marion, *The Idol and Distance,* 208–9.

20. Marion, *God without Being,* 41.

21. Ibid., 43.

22. Marion, *In Excess,* 1–23.

23. Ibid., 23.

24. Marion, *Being Given,* 235–36; *In Excess,* 25–26. See also, more generally, Marion, *Being Given,* 9–10, 18.

25. Marion, *In Excess,* 25.

26. Marion, *Being Given,* 10.

27. Ibid., 9.

28. Ibid., 10.

29. Ibid., 18.

30. Ibid.

31. Marion, *In Excess,* 25.

32. Ibid., 21.

33. Ibid., 28.

34. See Pierre Bourdieu, *The Field of Cultural Production* (New York: Columbia University Press, 1993), 256.

35. Marion, *Being Given,* 213–14.

36. See, e.g., ibid., 39ff, 197ff.

37. Ibid., 41.

38. Marion, *In Excess,* 58.

39. Ibid., 60.

40. Marion, *Being Given,* 43–44.

41. Bourdieu, *The Field of Cultural Production,* 113–14.

42. See Jonathan Parry, "The Gift, the Indian Gift and the 'Indian Gift,'" *Man* 21, no. 3 (September 1986): 467; Allan Silver, "Friendship in Commercial Society: Eighteenth-Century Social Theory and Modern Sociology," *American Journal of Sociology* 95, no. 6 (May 1990): 1474–1504.

43. Jean-Luc Marion, *Prolegomena to Charity*, trans. Stephen Lewis (New York: Fordham University Press, 2002).

44. See Ilana Silber, "Modern Philanthropy: Reassessing the Viability of a Maussian Perspective," in *Marcel Mauss: A Centenary Tribute*, ed. Wendy James and N. J. Allen (New York: Berghahn Books), 146–47.

45. See Jean-Joseph Goux, "General Economics and Postmodern Capitalism," *Yale French Studies* 78 (1990): 206–24.

46. Bourdieu, *The Field of Cultural Production*, 96.

47. Ibid., 101, 114.

48. See ibid., 233–37.

49. Marion, *In Excess*, 148–58.

50. See Kathryn Tanner, *Jesus, Humanity, and the Trinity* (Minneapolis: Fortress Press, 2001).

51. Jean-Luc Marion, *The Crossing of the Visible*, trans. James K. A. Smith (Stanford: Stanford University Press, 2004), 77.

52. Ibid., 61–62.

53. See Marion, *The Idol and Distance*, 241.

54. Ibid., e.g., 117.

55. Marion, *Being Given*, 83, 86.

56. Ibid., 86.

57. Ibid., 89, 91.

58. Ibid., 265.

59. Ibid, 307.

60. Marion, *God without Being*, 104.

61. Marion, *Being Given*, 282–88.

62. Ibid., 307.

63. Marion, *Prolegomena to Charity*, 61.

64. Marion, *The Idol and Distance*, 155.

65. Marion, *Prolegomena to Charity*, 129.

66. Marion, *Being Given*, 307.

67. Ibid., 145–46.

68. Ibid., 138.

69. Ibid., 187.

70. Ibid., 248.

71. Ibid., 111–12, 268–69.

72. Marion, *The Crossing of the Visible*, 61.

73. Marion, *God without Being*, 95–107.

74. Ibid., 99–100.

75. Ibid., 306.

76. Ibid., 216.

77. Marion, *The Crossing of the Visible*, 76.

78. Marion, *The Idol and Distance*, 110.

79. Ibid., 113.

80. Marion, *Prolegomena to Charity*, 136–45.

81. Marion, *The Idol and Distance,* 116.

82. Marion, *God without Being,* 52.

83. Marion, *In Excess,* 18–20.

84. Marion, *Being Given,* 115.

85. Marion, *God without Being,* 88.

86. Athanasius, "Against the Heathen," chap. 42, in *Nicene and Post-Nicene Fathers,* vol. 4, ed. and trans. Philip Schaff and Henry Wace (Grand Rapids, Mich.: Eerdmans, 1957), 26.

87. Marion, *In Excess,* 150.

III

LOVE

7

The Weight of Love

ROBYN HORNER

[W]hat explains the perception of the object—namely its constitution in terms of the lived experiences of my consciousness—is the very thing that forbids love, for love should, by hypothesis, make me transcend my lived experiences and my consciousness in order to reach pure alterity. Whence the infernal paradox, universally suffered by all unfortunate loves as their definitive fatality: when I love, what I experience of the other, in the end, in reality arises from my consciousness alone; what I call love of another bears only on certain lived experiences of my consciousness, inexplicably provoked, in the best of cases, by a chance cause that I call the other, but that the other is not. Love appears as an optical illusion of my consciousness.[1]

One of the most fundamental problems of phenomenology, and of philosophy more generally, is how we are to arrive at knowledge of the personal other precisely as *other*. Jean-Luc Marion argues that we know the other only through loving her or him, and significantly for theologians, this forms the basis of his approach to the divine other: we can know God only by loving God. Yet the "infernal paradox"—what we might call with a more Derridean inflection the *aporia* of love—consists in the fact that love seeks to approach the other as the one who exceeds lived experience [*Erlebnis, vécu*], but with seeming inevitability reduces the other to the content of lived experience in the same intentional movement. For the Edmund Husserl of the *Cartesian Meditations,* it is not yet a question of love: the other is known as an *alter ego,* given to consciousness along with the ego in a type of passive synthesis that Husserl calls "pairing."[2] Like Emmanuel Lévinas, whose criticism of both Husserl and Martin Heidegger relates in part to an apparent thinking of the other person [*autrui*] in terms of the same, Marion maintains that knowledge of the other as other is not that of theoretical consciousness at all.[3]

Lévinas actually suggests that we do not have knowledge of the other as such, writing instead of "an awakening to the other man, which is not knowledge," which he goes on to describe as a "thought that is not an adequation to the other, for whom I can no longer be the measure, and who precisely in his uniqueness is refractory to every measure, but nonetheless a non-in-difference to the other, love breaking the equilibrium of the equanimous soul."[4] For Lévinas, whose thinking of love proceeds differently than Marion's, intentionality is not only theoretical but also "affective, practical, and aesthetic."[5] Love "has a sense"; it signifies without representing.[6] Yet Marion argues that Lévinas "would no longer subscribe completely to the thematization that he gave of love in terms of intentionality."[7] He refers to a debate from 1986, where Lévinas responds to Marion by speaking of love as a relationship with diachrony: "What does this relation signify? I know that it is not an intentionality, but it has a sense."[8] For Marion, love is not a form of intentionality, or at least, not a form of intentionality of a constituting subject, but—strangely— he also describes it as a way of knowing. What he struggles to articulate is how that knowing takes place. Where Lévinas approaches the problem from the perspective of intentionality, Marion will emphasize the other side of the phenomenological equation, arguing for the priority of what gives itself to consciousness so excessively that it saturates intuition. The other gives her or himself, for Marion, as a "saturated phenomenon."

In what follows, we understand better the unfolding of Marion's thinking of love if we place it in the context of his thinking of the overcoming of metaphysics, which has a dual trajectory. On the one hand, metaphysics is overcome by theology; the theological destitution of metaphysics is strongest as a theme in Marion's early works, but is never entirely absent from his writing. On the other hand, from a philosophical perspective, it is phenomenology that may provide a way beyond the metaphysical impasse.[9]

The Knowledge of Love: A Theological Approach

In Marion's theological considerations, love is extolled as a higher order of knowledge, rendering metaphysics meaningless or worthless. Here he reveals an allegiance to Pascal. Metaphysics is an exercise in vanity because the knowledge it delivers cannot bring about salvation.[10] For Pascal, there are three orders, those of the body, the mind, and the heart or will. The order of the body is transgressed by the order of the mind, by thought, or metaphysics. But the order of the mind is also transgressed, this time by the knowledge of love. Marion observes: "[M]etaphysics must from now on recognize the irreducibility of an order that it does not see, but which sees it, grasps it, and judges it, 'the order of charity.'"[11] This order is recognized by loving, that is, by acting according to holiness. But it is also known by the way it interrupts thought. "The third order will thus be revealed indirectly, by the distorting effects that its radiance—the luminosity of charity—will have on the elements of the second order."[12] In both *On Descartes' Metaphysical Prism* and *God without Being*, Marion underwrites the superior knowledge of love with a theological guarantee, but this guarantee rests on its assertion, and he does not always clearly articulate the relationship between love and knowledge.[13] If we sample a number of his texts, we find this relationship constantly at issue.

In 1970, Marion writes: "[T]he revelation that Christ brings, that 'God is love' (1 John 4:18) shows us not only what we can know [*ce que nous pouvons connaître*], but, moreover, how we can know [*comment nous pouvons connaître*]. Love constitutes the content as well as the advancement of faith."[14] The use of *connaître* rather than *savoir*, the verb usually used to refer to conceptual knowledge, suggests that the knowledge of love is based on personal recognition, and this proves to be a consistent feature of Marion's characterization of love. Nevertheless, he indicates that love is not only *how* we know, but also *what* we know—in other words, it has a determined content. In *The Idol and Distance* (1977), Marion argues that love is the content of knowledge of God, but it is a knowledge that is received rather than comprehended:

> The unthinkable, as the distance of Goodness, gives itself—not to be comprehended but to be received. It is therefore not a question of giving up on comprehending (as if it were a question of comprehending,

and not of being comprehended). It is a question of managing to receive that which becomes thinkable, or rather acceptable, only for the one who knows how to receive it. It is not a question of admitting distance despite its unthinkability, but of preciously receiving the unthinkable, as the sign and the seal of the measureless origin of the distance that gives us our measure. If love reveals itself hermetically as distance (which is glossed by *cause* and *goodness*) in order to give itself, only love will be able to welcome it.[15]

Marion invokes the theological trope of "distance" to protect the excessiveness of what is given to thought while allowing it to be thinkable; love is revealed "hermetically," and has to be accepted rather than grasped.[16] In this way it is not unlike the Cartesian idea of the Infinite, excessiveness inserted into the finite, an idea that Lévinas also employs extensively.[17] Knowledge that remains sealed is described in a 1986 article in terms of a "luminous darkness": "Charity allows [us] to know rigorously on the condition, at least, that it is a question of knowing charity itself. The objection that contests the epistemic power of charity does not consider, actually, the exceptional demands that the luminous darkness fixes here on all knowledge [*toute connaissance*] that would wish to be constituted as *theo*logical: to secure knowledge [*un savoir*] without being fixed on an idol, thus to know [*savoir*] without representation of an object."[18] Yet soon after this passage, Marion continues: "[T]he one who loves does not see God as an object, but recognizes God as the dominant logic of his or her own act of love. . . . In short, God is recognized as and in the very act by which God makes me love."[19] We find that love is an item of knowledge [*un savoir*] only in the recognition of or acquaintance with [*la connaissance de*] love in the act of loving. In this instance the "what" and the "how" of love as knowledge are collapsed into one.

While Marion is clear that love does not make an object of God, he notes that love functions as a new way of seeing, and later he observes that as a condition of knowing it allows new phenomena to be seen.[20] Love in some manner functions as a hermeneutic principle, and we cannot underestimate the importance of this point in the context of Marion's theology, particularly when we consider the 1994 essay "What Love Knows."[21] Here Marion writes: "[B]ecause love has also been distinguished from knowledge, we will attempt to think of love itself as a knowledge—and a preeminent knowledge to boot."

In response to what he sees as the failed attempt to account for intersubjectivity in the work of Husserl, and with a view to Kant, Marion maintains that "love opens up knowledge of the other as such."[22] Access to the other person is only possible subsequent to my decision to love him or her. Love is a matter of the will, first of all: "[T]he phenomenality of the other does not precede my (good) will with regard to him, but instead is its result"; "in order for the other to appear to me, I must first love him." Love alone goes beyond object knowledge: "For when it is a question of knowing (and not merely experiencing) the other, the other *I* who, because just such, will never therefore become for me an available and constitutable object—it is necessary to resort to charity. Charity in effect becomes a means of knowledge when our concern is with the other, and no longer with objects."[23] Love is not only a way of seeing, but a will to see in a particular way. Nevertheless, love is not thereby irrational, but allows us "to accede to a knowledge that *surpasses* our ordinary knowledge."[24]

In sum, from a theological perspective, love is knowledge first in the sense that it forms the content of what is known, albeit that this content is known as unknown, since it is "sealed," or given as "distance." In this sense it is superior knowledge, which judges all other knowledge and shows it to be worthless. It is visible by way of the distortions it reveals in that knowledge. Further, it functions to reveal new phenomena and operates as a hermeneutic principle. But love is also knowledge in the second sense that it enables us to know. Love enables us to recognize love, and we only know by choosing to love. The "how" of love here overlaps with the "what" of love, since new phenomena are seen through the will to see and are interpreted in accordance with that choice. Marion's recognition of the role of hermeneutics and of the will is significant, for he has implicitly (and perhaps unintentionally) identified the limitations of a theological understanding of the knowledge of love: we have to interpret the (sealed) content of love as love, and we do this by willing it, in love, to be love. In fact, the knowledge of love—and more specifically of God as love—only comes to us by way of a theological decision, which means that theology is subject to the charge that it only overcomes metaphysics by repeating one of its central moves. While Marion never withdraws from his theological commitments, his thinking of love eventually comes to be supplemented by a phenomenological working out of love as knowledge.

The Knowledge of Love: A Phenomenological Approach

The phenomenological development of Marion's thinking of the other emerges in the context of his work on the icon. While initially this has a theological focus, the icon eventually serves more broadly to incorporate a nontheological consideration of the face, in an extension of Lévinas's use of the face as the means by which the other signifies.[25] The encounter with the other has a basic phenomenological structure throughout Marion's writing. In approaching the other my intentional gaze is drawn to the one place in the other's face where I can see nothing—the pupils of the eyes. I must submit myself to the other, recognizing that here I do not see but am instead seen.[26] The other's intentional gaze crosses my own and is felt as a weight, pressure, or injunction (or call), a counter-intentionality arising in me to which I must respond; in this crossing of gazes I share a common lived experience with the other, which is visible only to us.[27] One of the important questions that Marion seeks to address in his characterization of the encounter with the other is how the other signifies as a particular other, since Lévinas's thinking of the signification of the other—by way of an ethical injunction arising from the face— is open to criticism for its apparent universality. Marion insists on the un-substitutable nature of the other on the twofold basis of my will to respond in love to this particular person, and the submission of the other to me in a gaze, that is, the preparedness of the other to give her or himself to be seen.[28] He also widens the possibilities of the injunctive call: it need not only be ethical but might instead be erotic, existential, or religious, for example.[29] Nevertheless, in this solution we find again the problem that was articulated above: how am I to know the other as particular (and, perhaps, as God rather than another human person) without simply willing or deciding it to be so, especially since the meaning of the call signifies only in the response?[30] We turn to Marion's recent work to consider the most developed form of his argument.[31]

Le phénomène érotique unfolds as a series of meditations in which Marion attempts to bring into view the phenomenon of love—understood as a unity rather than as either eros or agapē—by way of an erotic phenomenological reduction. He formulates this reduction in three progressively deepening ways: "am I loved by another [m'aime-t-on? or m'aime-t-on—d'ailleurs]?"; "can I love first ["puis-je aimer, moi le premier]?"; and "you have loved me first [toi, tu m'as aimé le premier]." The first of these reductions is deemed inadequate, that is, not to bring the erotic phenomenon into view, because it is based on the idea that love must be reciprocal. While the second avoids this pitfall by allowing for a thinking of love as pure loss, it relies on the lover's repeated advances to the other, since the other will never be able to be possessed (in the way an object might be possessed).[32] Further, it delivers neither any assurance of lovableness to the lover nor any certainty that love is genuine, resting solely on a decision to love, expressed in the oath of commitment of the lover. And since it does not rely on the other's self-revelation, it may result in the lover's falling in love only with love, rather than with any specific other. The love intuition that this reduction delivers, in other words, need have no determinate corresponding intention, no specific concept or meaning of the other.[33] Nevertheless, the other might choose to self-reveal in an oath of commitment. In this case, the other provides a meaning for her or himself in the oath, which signifies without the other's being limited by that signification, since it does not fulfil the lover's excessive intuition of the other.[34] What then appears is an erotic phenomenon, produced "without egoic pole" in the crossing of the lover's decision to love (expressed in an oath) and the loved one's imposed signification (the other's oath)—which the lover decides to accept as such.[35] This crossed phenomenon is held in common between the lovers: having a common meaning, it still involves two separate and excessive intuitions.[36] "The lover . . . sees the unique phenomenon, that he or she loves and who loves him or her, by the grace of this oath."[37] The common meaning of the erotic phenomenon depends not simply on the statement of the oath but on its performance, and what is given in the erotic phenomenon is flesh: the flesh of the lover and the flesh of the other. The flesh of the other is accessed not according to the horizon of perception (which is limited to the body) but through naked exposure. Flesh is phenomenalized not through being seen, but through being felt without resistance, through interpenetration.[38] The other person therefore appears as a phenomenon only indirectly, that is, "as the one who phenomenalizes me as my flesh. The difficulty of the phenomenon of the other person does not lie in its distancing, poverty or supposed transcendence; on the contrary, it lies in its absolute immanence: the other person appears to the very extent where he gives me my own flesh, which deploys like a screen on which his [flesh] is projected."[39] The other shows her or himself as a face, but not by means of a quasi-Lévinasian, universal ethical injunction, since here there can be no substitution.[40] "The eroticized face also recapitulates all his or her flesh. . . . I thus see there his or her flesh, insofar as it is felt and is experienced, thus insofar as it is definitively individualized, gifted to itself, in short, insofar as definitively *inaccessible* to mine. I see there the accomplished transcendence of the other person."[41]

According to this characterization, however, the erotic phenomenon can only appear temporarily. Once one of the parties climaxes, the process of eroticization has to be recommenced; the partners become naked bodies again instead of flesh for one another.[42] Since there is no longer any substance of eroticization, there is nothing to see: instead of a saturated phenomenon there remains only a "phenomenon under erasure" about which nothing can be said.[43] Erotic speech—which is non-predicative and, according to Marion, of which there are three types: obscene, infantile, and hyperbolic— no longer applies.[44] Eroticization thus attests to finitude, because each period of eroticization must literally come to an end.[45] Identifying further difficulties, Marion also notes that while eroticization individualizes the other as flesh, it does not always reach the other person *in person*.[46] The possibility of auto-eroticization actually creates a distance between the flesh and the person of the other.[47] And since jealousy and hate can also individualize, individualization—even by means of the face as flesh—does not guarantee truth.[48] How are these difficulties to be overcome? Marion suggests that the answer lies in an eroticization that is not automatic but free, where not only access to flesh but access to the person is gained. This, he claims, can occur without physical contact, through speech: "[M]y word only aims to touch him, to affect him in the most strict sense, so as to make him feel the weight, the insistence, and the non-resistance of my flesh." It is "making love *in person*."[49] In this way, Marion proposes that all loving relationships can be subject to the erotic reduction, not only those that are sexual.[50] "Eroticization" has come to mean giving flesh without physical contact by addressing the person directly.[51]

Although he has thus responded to the problem of reaching the other in person, Marion still has to face the problem of the temporary nature of the erotic phenomenon. According to the erotic reduction, the erotic phenomenon lasts for as long as the oath lasts: fidelity is what allows the phenomenon to be seen. "The erotic phenomenon . . . demands long and profound fidelity. But fidelity requires nothing less than eternity."[52] Fidelity cannot be proved, but only decided upon.[53] The challenge is to establish a means of witnessing to fidelity that does not depend on the limited time of the lovers. Initially Marion tries to do this with another quasi-Lévinasian move by appealing to the child of a loving union.[54] Nevertheless, this strategy fails: "[T]he child definitively ruptures reciprocity by diverting the return of the gift away from the giver, shifting it towards an unknown and as yet non-existent [*non-étant*] recipient (another child, another event still to come). The child thus steals from us, we, the lovers, not only the flesh that our flesh has given to him or her, but especially the return of his or her witness in support of our oath. By definition, the child abandons the lovers to themselves."[55] In a second strategy, Marion suggests that to avoid the constant repetition of the oath, each erotic moment must obtain a sense of final authority. Since only eternity can ensure the permanence of the oath, each moment must take on the character of an eschatological *as if* so that the lovers effectively make eternity rather than waiting for it.[56] Here, God is invoked as the eternal witness: "The lovers accomplish their oath in the *adieu*—in the passage to God [*à Dieu*], who they summon as their final witness, their first witness, the one who never leaves and never lies. Then, for the first time, they say to each other 'adieu': next year in Jerusalem—the next time to God [*à Dieu*]. To think to/about God [*à Dieu*] can only be done, erotically, in this 'adieu.'"[57] Having accomplished fidelity to the oath in a moment that is touched by the eternal, the lovers are finally enabled to discover themselves as lovable because they have been lovers.[58] Marion here arrives at the final formulation of the erotic reduction: "You have loved me first." The capacity to love is actually made possible by finding oneself always and already loved: "[T]o enter into the erotic reduction, there has to have been another lover who has preceded me there and, from there, calls me there in silence."[59] Again, there are Lévinasian antecedents to this position: "[L]ove . . . designates a movement by which the being searches for that to which it was connected even before having taken the initiative to search."[60] Nevertheless, Marion's explication of the universality of the love that enables love perhaps overstates the case. No one, he maintains, can claim "no one loves them or has ever loved them." This hopeful assertion is qualified by the argument that if a person has not been loved in the past then someone may at least love her or him in the future.[61] Ultimately, however, Marion invokes a theological guarantee of love-able-ness. God is the one who loves perfectly, and who always loves before I do: "[God] loves the first and the last. . . . [T]his first lover, forever, has been named God."[62] This has scriptural echoes: we love God because God first loved us (1 John 4:10). The apparently phenomenological study of love has, in fact, been completed by the reassertion of the theological.

From Marion's phenomenological perspective, then, love allows for access to the other person. Finding her or himself already loved (by God, but perhaps also by the other), and therefore lovable, a potential lover is enabled to love another. This love becomes apparent by way of the oath of commitment that the lover makes, as it intersects with an oath made by the other. In the other's oath, he or she appears by imposing an intentional meaning that arises in and is accepted as genuine by the lover, while giving him or herself excessively to intuition as a saturated phenomenon of flesh.[63] The imposed intentional meaning provides a way of identifying the other as a particular other, while not exhausting the saturating intuition, and hence allows for an endless hermeneutics of the other.[64] The fidelity of each party to their respective oaths cannot be proven, but is risked by their entering into the erotic moment with God as—or *as if* God is—an eternal witness. Love is knowledge in the sense that it is an enabling process (one must first be loved in order to love; one must love to know love), and in the sense that it is given as a saturated phenomenon, a phenomenon that is subject to an endless hermeneutics. The phenomenological characterisation of love actually reaches the same conclusions as its theological counterpart, except that it is no longer simply a matter of the dogmatic assertion of superior knowledge.

What Love Gives

There are a number of questions we could address to Marion with regard to his phenomenology of love, but in this context I raise only three, all of which relate to the possibilities of his success in overcoming a metaphysical account of intersubjectivity. First, has Marion avoided "the infernal paradox" and provided a coherent account of the possibility of arriving at knowledge of another person? Marion's most recent thinking of the other depends on a number of factors: the capacity to love; the will to love a particular other; a preparedness to accept as genuine the other's signification in an oath (functioning in much the same way as the call), which is imposed from without but which arises within the lover as a counter-intentionality; and the recognition that to know the other requires an infinite hermeneutics, and hence is a knowledge that is never complete. The most vulnerable points of his argument are those relating to the will to love (it is arbitrary and might be delusional; at the very least, reliance on the will suggests that the other is subject to the constituting "I" of the lover, although Marion always insists on the priority of the other) and the signification of the oath (that it is true depends on the preparedness of the lover to accept it as true, with God as ultimate witness). Both these points demonstrate the way in which phenomenology is inevitably supplemented by a still more basic hermeneutics, and yet the recognition of this necessary supplementation perhaps provides a way forward in thinking the other. To love the other involves the risk of getting it wrong. To allow oneself to be touched by the word of the other, and to address the other in person, requires the risk of faith. The problem of thinking intersubjectivity is therefore not solved as such by Marion, but the conditions for living with the *aporia* are identified.

A second question to be considered is whether Marion's double invocation of God to guarantee his thought of love is a legitimate move in his phenomenology. His use of the *adieu / à Dieu* is not novel: it is also found in the writings of Lévinas and Derrida.[65] While it could be argued that this is an(other) example of Marion's theological completion of phenomenology, it could equally be said that he makes a move like Lévinas, who refers to a God who passes only as a trace in the face of the other, that is, to a God who can never be specified.[66] To the extent that Lévinas is not doing theology, neither is Marion at this point. This is consistent with Marion's treatment of mystical theology in chapter 6 of *In Excess,* where any reference to God is always a mis-reference, a mis-address. More difficult to accommodate phenomenologically is Marion's use of God to initiate the process of loving, which replicates his thought of the gift. His reference to God here appears to depend on an unacknowledged assertion of faith. It seems to me, however, that we can read this in two ways. Perhaps proposing God as the always-prior-lover simply provides a theological solution to the problem of how love gets going, a solution that would be consistent with Marion's earlier writings, and especially with *God without Being.* But this would not account for Marion's later insistence—in *Being Given,* for example—that he now resists the move he made in *God without Being,* the "recourse to theology" as a way of thinking love and the overcoming of metaphysics.[67] Alternatively, Marion's calling upon God could be interpreted within the trajectory of his later works, that is, in light of his recognition that our references to God are basically pragmatic or undecideable. This would require us to read against the letter of the text, although it would be consistent with his use of the *à Dieu*. In other words, in the same way that the *à Dieu* appeals to God with an address that will always be a mis-address, the appeal to God as first lover could also find itself diverted to the other person who, I find in every instance of loving, has in fact always loved me first.

We are brought, then, to a final question, which has to do with the possibility of recognizing God at all as the other whose weight is felt. How would we know that it is God who gives Godself in love? In Marion's thought God is revealed in saturated phenomena: frequently he gives examples of the encounter with God in the person of Jesus—in the face of the icon, in Scripture, and in the Eucharist. This is not the focus of *Le phénomène érotique,* but we can see how Marion might also recharacterize in its light God's gift of self as lover in flesh and in the word, and signification in an oath or promise, accepted as such by the believer. There are evident tensions in Marion's work between an absolute theological hermeneutic of excessive phenomena and a recognition of their necessary undecideability.[68] *Le phénomène érotique* does nothing to resolve those tensions, but to think the oath both in terms of its undecideability and its endless deferral would help to destabilize the metaphysical tendencies of a theological reading. In short, love would guarantee knowledge neither of the divine nor of the human other, but would function only as a quasi-transcendental, a condition of possibility and impossibility for such knowledge.

Notes

1. Jean-Luc Marion, *Prolégomènes à la charité*, 2d ed. (Paris: Éditions de la Différence, 1991), 95; *Prolegomena to Charity*, trans. Stephen Lewis (New York: Fordham University Press, 2002), 75.

2. Edmund Husserl, *Cartesian Meditations: An Introduction to Phenomenology*, trans. Dorion Cairns (The Hague: Martinus Nijhoff, 1960), 112–17.

3. Emmanuel Lévinas, *Totality and Infinity: An Essay on Exteriority*, trans. Alphonso Lingis (The Hague: Martinus Nijhoff, 1979), 67.

4. Emmanuel Lévinas, "Diachrony and Representation," trans. Michael B. Smith and Barbara Harshav, in *Entre Nous: On Thinking-of-the-Other* (New York: Columbia University Press, 1998), 159–77, 168.

5. Emmanuel Lévinas, *The Theory of Intuition in Husserl's Phenomenology*, trans. André Orianne, 2d ed. (Evanston: Northwestern University Press, 1995), 43.

6. Lévinas, *The Theory of Intuition*, 44–45. "The act of love has a sense, but this does not mean that it includes a representation of the object loved together with a purely *subjective* feeling which has no sense and which accompanies the representation. The characteristic of the loved object is precisely to be given in a love intention, an intention which is irreducible to a purely theoretical representation."

7. Marion, *Prolégomènes*, 120 n. 13; *Prolegomena*, 100 n. 15.

8. Emmanuel Lévinas, *Autrement que savoir* (Paris: Osiris, 1988), 75.

9. "I often assume that phenomenology makes an exception to metaphysics. I do not, however, defend this assertion in its entirety, since I emphasize that Husserl upholds Kantian decisions (the conditions for the possibility of phenomenality, the horizon, the constituting function of the I). . . . It should, therefore, be admitted that phenomenology does not actually overcome metaphysics so much as it opens the official possibility of leaving it to itself. The border between metaphysics and phenomenology runs within phenomenology—as its highest possibility, and I stick with the phenomenological discipline only in search of the way that it opens and, sometimes, closes." Jean-Luc Marion, *Étant donné: Essai d'une phénoménologie de la donation* (Paris: Presses Universitaires de France, 1997), 9; *Being Given: Toward a Phenomenology of Givenness*, trans. Jeffrey L. Kosky (Stanford: Stanford University Press, 2002), 4. An expanded presentation of ideas in this essay appears in Robyn Horner, *Jean-Luc Marion: A Theological Introduction* (Aldershot, Hampshire: Ashgate, 2005).

10. Jean-Luc Marion, *Sur le prisme métaphysique de Descartes. Constitution et limites de l'onto-théo-logie dans la pensée cartésienne* (Paris: Presses Universitaires de France, 1986), 310ff; *On Descartes' Metaphysical Prism: The Constitution and the Limits of Onto-theo-logy in Cartesian Thought*, trans. Jeffrey L. Kosky (Chicago: University of Chicago Press, 1999), 293ff.

11. Marion, *Sur le prisme métaphysique*, 358; *On Descartes' Metaphysical Prism*, 335.

12. Marion, *Sur le prisme métaphysique*, 340; *On Descartes' Metaphysical Prism*, 319.

13. See especially chapters 3 and 4 of Jean-Luc Marion, *Dieu sans l'être. Hors-texte*, rev. ed. (Paris: Presses Universitaires de France, 1991); *God without Being*, trans. Thomas A. Carlson (Chicago: University of Chicago Press, 1991).

14. Jean-Luc Marion, "Amour de Dieu, amour des hommes," *Résurrection* 34 (1970): 89–96, 90.

15. Jean-Luc Marion, *L'idole et la distance: Cinq études* (Paris: Grasset, 1977), 194; *The Idol and Distance: Five Studies*, trans. Thomas A. Carlson, Perspectives in Continental Philosophy, ed. John D. Caputo (New York: Fordham University Press, 2001), 155.

16. Here we see the influence on Marion of writers such as Hans Urs von Balthasar, who, with the concept of "diastasis," echoes the idea of "spacing" in Gregory of Nyssa, also a favorite of Marion.

17. See especially chapter 4 of Marion, *Sur le prisme métaphysique de Descartes; On Descartes' Metaphysical Prism*. See also, e.g., Emmanuel Lévinas, "God and Philosophy,"

trans. Bettina Bergo, in *Of God Who Comes to Mind* (Stanford: Stanford University Press, 1998), 55–78.

18. Jean-Luc Marion, "De la 'mort de Dieu' aux noms divins. L'itinéraire théologique de la métaphysique," *Laval Théologique et Philosophique* 41, no. 1 (1985): 25–41, 119. The "luminous darkness" is reminiscent of Gregory of Nyssa: "For leaving behind everything that is observed, not only what sense comprehends but also what the intelligence thinks it sees, it keeps on penetrating deeper until by the intelligence's yearning for understanding it gains access to the invisible and incomprehensible, and there it sees God. This is the true knowledge of what is sought; this is the seeing that consists in not seeing, because that which is sought transcends all knowledge, being separated on all sides by incomprehensibility as by a kind of darkness." *Gregory of Nyssa: The Life of Moses,* ed. A. J. Malherbe and E. Ferguson (New York: Paulist, 1978), §163.

19. Marion, "De la 'mort de Dieu,'" 120.

20. Marion, *Sur le prisme métaphysique,* 333, 336; *On Descartes' Metaphysical Prism,* 313, 316. "[N]ew phenomena appear among the things of this world to an eye that is initiated in charity." "[O]nly those who love see the phenomena of love.... The result is that for many observers, perhaps even most, these phenomena remain invisible, or else are reduced to an arbitrary interpretation, one of several possible interpretations." Jean-Luc Marion, "Christian Philosophy and Charity," *Communio* 17 (1992): 465–73, 469, 470.

21. Published in French as Jean-Luc Marion, "La connaissance de la charité," *Revue Catholique Internationale Communio* 19, no. 6 (1994): 27–42, and appearing as chap. 7 in the English edition of *Prolegomena.*

22. Marion, *Prolegomena,* 160.

23. Ibid., 163, 164.

24. Ibid., 169.

25. See esp. Marion, *Dieu sans l'être; God without Being; Prolégomènes; Prolegomena; La croisée du visible,* rev. ed. (Paris: Éditions de la Différence, 1996); *The Crossing of the Visible,* trans. James K. A. Smith (Stanford: Stanford University Press, 2004); *De surcroît: études sur les phénomènes saturés* (Paris: Presses Universitaires de France, 2001); *In Excess: Studies of Saturated Phenomena,* trans. Robyn Horner and Vincent Berraud (New York: Fordham University Press, 2002); "La connaissance de la charité."

26. On the relationship between the face and flesh, see *De surcroît,* 136ff; *In Excess,* 113ff.

27. See "The Intentionality of Love," in Marion, *Prolegomena; Prolégomènes.*

28. Jean-Luc Marion, "D'Autrui à l'Individu," in *Emmanuel Lévinas: Positivité et transcendence,* ed. Jean-Luc Marion (Paris: Presses Universitaires de France, 1999), 287–308; "From the Other to the Individual," trans. Robyn Horner, in *Transcendence,* ed. Regina Schwartz (New York: Routledge, 2004), 43–59.

29. Marion, *De surcroît,* 142; *In Excess,* 118.

30. Marion, *Étant donné,* 399–400; *Being Given,* 289–90.

31. Jean-Luc Marion, *Le phénomène érotique* (Paris: Grasset, 2003); *The Erotic Phenomenon,* trans. Stephen E. Lewis (Chicago: University of Chicago Press, 2007). English translations of *Le phénomène érotique* found in this essay are those of the author, with page references to the published English translation noted above.

32. Ibid., 133–43; *The Erotic Phenomenon,* 82–89.

33. Ibid., 143–55; *The Erotic Phenomenon,* 89–97.

34. Ibid., 165–66; *The Erotic Phenomenon,* 104.

35. Ibid., 164; *The Erotic Phenomenon,* 103. On the need for acceptance, see ibid., 302; *The Erotic Phenomenon,* 195.

36. Ibid., 166–68; *The Erotic Phenomenon,* 105.

37. Ibid., 168; *The Erotic Phenomenon,* 105.

38. Ibid., 178–90; *The Erotic Phenomenon,* 112–20.

39. Ibid., 192; *The Erotic Phenomenon,* 121.

40. Ibid., 198–99; *The Erotic Phenomenon,* 126. "We must recognize that the privilege of the face . . . no longer depends *here* on a distance, nor on an ethical height. Here the face of the other person, if it wants or can still speak to me, certainly no longer says to me 'Thou shalt not kill!'; not only because the other person is not in any doubt about this point; not only because he or she says to me, in sighs or in words, 'Here I am, come!' (§28); but especially because we [*lui et moi*] have left the universal, even the universal ethic, in order to strive towards particularity—mine and his or hers since it is a question of me and of you and surely not of a universally obligating neighbor. In the situation of mutual eroticization, where each gives to the other the flesh that he or she does not have, each only aims at being individualized in individualizing the other person, thus exactly piercing and transgressing the universal" (198; *The Erotic Phenomenon,* 126).

41. Ibid., 200; *The Erotic Phenomenon,* 127.

42. Ibid., 200–11; *The Erotic Phenomenon,* 127–35.

43. Ibid., 211–16, 224–34; *The Erotic Phenomenon,* 135–38, 143–50.

44. Ibid., 224–34; *The Erotic Phenomenon,* 143–50. Interestingly enough, Marion compares these to the three types of theological discourse: positive, negative, and mystical. The comparison seems forced, except insofar as language is being used nonpredicatively, and except with regard to the mystical and the hyperbolic.

45. Marion, *Le phénomène érotique,* 217–24; *The Erotic Phenomenon,* 138–43.

46. Ibid., 238–42; *The Erotic Phenomenon,* 153–56.

47. Ibid., 242–51; *The Erotic Phenomenon,* 156–62.

48. Ibid., 257–76; *The Erotic Phenomenon,* 166–83.

49. Ibid., 281; *The Erotic Phenomenon,* 182. In this passage Marion uses *ma parole,* which we could translate in the sense of speech or in the sense of a promise made.

50. Ibid., 283; *The Erotic Phenomenon,* 183. This would include relationships between parents and children, between friends, and between humanity and God.

51. Marion argues for an eroticization that can be chaste, that is, he appears to be proposing that all love is on a continuum that includes the sexual as well as the nonsexual. But we have to ask about the kind of address that might occur in such an

eroticization. Marion maintains that it is an address that cannot lie because it does not predicate anything. Is it therefore linked with his earlier description of erotic address—the obscene, the infantile, or the hyperbolic? Presumably, an erotic word that is not destined for genital arousal will not be obscene, while it might possibly be infantile. However, it is more likely to be hyperbolic. Marion does not explicitly make the connection in this context, but such a hyperbolic personal address, of course, bears a striking similarity to the address made to God in mystical theology, a connection Marion has made earlier.

52. Marion, *Le phénomène érotique*, 286; *The Erotic Phenomenon*, 185.

53. Ibid., 293–94; *The Erotic Phenomenon*, 189–90.

54. See Lévinas's comments on fecundity in *Time and the Other*, trans. Richard Cohen (Pittsburgh: Duquesne University Press, 1987).

55. Marion, *Le phénomène érotique*, 316; *The Erotic Phenomenon*, 205. Particular thanks to Shane Mackinlay for his assistance with the translation of this complex passage.

56. Ibid., 321; *The Erotic Phenomenon*, 208.

57. Ibid., 326; *The Erotic Phenomenon*, 212.

58. Ibid., 328; *The Erotic Phenomenon*, 213.

59. Ibid., 331; *The Erotic Phenomenon*, 215.

60. Lévinas, *Totality and Infinity*, 254. This text is quoted in part 7 of Marion, "D'Autrui à L'Individu"; "From the Other to the Individual."

61. Marion, *Le phénomène érotique*, 332; *The Erotic Phenomenon*, 215. In human terms, the assertion is just a little bit too universal. Marion argues that children are conceived by their parents in love, for example, which is not always the case.

62. Ibid., 341; *The Erotic Phenomenon*, 222.

63. It seems to me that while Marion attempts to move from eroticization as a sexual process to one characterized by touching the other with a word, a distinction he maintains by moving from flesh to person, he still considers it a giving of flesh as nonresistance.

64. The endless nature of the hermeneutics is emphasized in chapter 5 of *De Surcroît; In Excess*.

65. Jacques Derrida, *Adieu to Emmanuel Lévinas*, trans. Pascale-Anne Brault and Michael Naas (Stanford: Stanford University Press, 1999). See also, e.g., Emmanuel Lévinas, "Bad Conscience and the Inexorable," in Richard A. Cohen, ed., *Face to Face with Lévinas* (Albany: State University of New York Press, 1986), 35–40.

66. On Marion, theology, and phenomenology, see my discussions in Robyn Horner, "Aporia or Excess: Two Strategies for Thinking r/Revelation," in *Derrida and Religion: Other Testaments*, ed. Kevin Hart and Yvonne Sherwood (London: Routledge, 2004), 325–36; *Jean-Luc Marion; Rethinking God as Gift: Marion, Derrida, and the Limits of Phenomenology*, Perspectives in Continental Philosophy, ed. John D. Caputo (New York: Fordham University Press, 2001). On Lévinas's references to God, see, e.g., his *God, Death, and Time*, trans. Bettina Bergo (Stanford: Stanford University Press, 2000).

67. "Preface to the American Translation," in Marion, *Being Given*: ix–xi, x.

68. See, e.g., Jean-Luc Marion, "Christian Philosophy and Charity," *Communio* 17 (1992): 465–73, 469. See also Jean-Luc Marion, "They Recognized Him; and He Became Invisible to Them," *Modern Theology* 18, no. 2 (2002): 145–52; Shane Mackinlay, "Eyes Wide Shut: A Response to Jean-Luc Marion's Account of the Journey to Emmaus," *Modern Theology* 20, no. 3 (2004): 447–56. On the ambiguity of Marion's thinking of r/Revelation, see Horner, "Aporia or Excess: Two Strategies for Thinking r/Revelation."

8

The Gift and the Mirror

On the Philosophy of Love

JOHN MILBANK

Love, as we commonly speak of it, appears to have three modes or aspects. There is love of the beautiful or of the good as they appear, and this seems to involve some *knowledge* of what is loved. Second, there is the offering, making, or accepting of love and here love seems to concern *gift*—whether donated or received. In its third mode, one speaks of love as prevailing between or among different creatures; here love is spoken of as if it coincided with certain states of *being*.

Jean Luc-Marion would perhaps regard these various locutions as expressing the "natural attitude" with respect to love, and would also perhaps agree that traditional metaphysics—meaning the thought dominant up till the High Middle Ages—sought to "save" the natural attitude by expounding an account of the essence of love that sustains all three aspects. By contrast, Marion retains from the natural attitude only the notion of love as gift, since this, he believes, withstands the most rigorous of all phenomenological reductions that has hitherto been carried through. This reduction achieves, for Marion, for the first time a clarity about love, since at last it knows love on its own and out of its own resources, now no longer entangled with knowledge (in the sense of knowledge of objects or of beings) or being itself.[1] By contrast, love as conceived by us in the everyday that is confirmed by metaphysics contaminates love with knowledge and being and, in the case of metaphysics, dissolves love in known objectivity and mere existence. Neither achieve any clarity about love whatsoever.

In what follows, I wish to question the purely phenomenological project of trying to achieve a clear and distinct concept of love and (and at first by implication) to defend the traditional metaphysical approach to love that left it, often deliberately, in unclarity. In the course of this defense I intermittently compare Marion's phenomenological approach to love as gift with the "ontodology" of Claude Bruaire. I also try to reaffirm the traditional co-implication of love with knowledge and being and to argue that this did not necessarily mean the subordination of the former to the two latter principles. To the contrary, the consequence of Marion's bleakly Pascalian view that the order of love—as charity or eros—lies entirely above and beyond being, power, and knowledge could be that we must hand the physical world, political society, and positive or humane science over to an inevitable lovelessness; for the priority of love in Marion's thought at times scarcely conceals from view its thoroughly ambivalent rarefaction and the consequent inherent limit of its possible reach.

I also wish to suggest that the attempt to think of love alone is the result of a decision, not a phenomenological reduction, which in its apodeictic form I take to be an impossible enterprise. If one asks why Marion has made this decision, it becomes clear that he is reckoning not with the traditional metaphysics of Plato or Proclus or Denys or Maximus or Aquinas, but with the modern metaphysics of Descartes and Heidegger. Descartes (almost) completed the isolation of a loveless and passionless knowledge; Heidegger completed the isolation of an unloving, unlovable, and indeed unknowable being. Marion does not exactly question these philosophies—indeed he seems to think of them as the working through to the end of the ancient metaphysical impulse once unshackled from restraining religious and mystical contexts. The realization of this impulse then becomes, nevertheless, the condition for its supposed overcoming. Once one has a loveless knowledge and being, one can attempt the knowledge of love as beyond being and as more fundamental than all knowing.

But *is* this a post-metaphysical move? Having isolated knowledge from desire and will, an entire sequence of thinkers, from Abelard through Scotus to Descartes, had then to seek another knowledge of will (or of desire or passion) on its own, without reference to theoretical knowledge. Is it after all so clear that Marion's enterprise does not still belong within this long-established supplement to modern metaphysics that confirms metaphysics and does not escape from it? For as in the case of Kant, the further "practical" consideration of the subject in terms of the logic of freedom as such tends to clamp its seal on the isolation of the subject from the objects it represents, which is the main theoretical picture that modern metaphysics has to offer.

Most crucially of all in this context, one can question all residual Heideggerean notions of a fated philosophical destiny. "Metaphysics" has become a hopelessly ambiguous term since it denotes both the Aristotelian-Platonic-Hebraic compound that reigned up till Aquinas and which one might dub "theo-ontology" (since ontological considerations were here subordinate to knowledge of the first principle, and for this reason did not necessarily assume preeminence over henological, gnoseological, or axiological reflections) and the post-Avicennean and Scotist philosophy based rigorously on the priority of ontology over the question of the origin of being, which leads to the reduction of God to an ontic idol as the supreme, infinite instance of a univocal being-in-general. Only the latter can one properly dub "onto-theology." Between the two one could argue there lies no evolution, but only a rupture and a complex collective decision.

The ambivalence in Marion's work is that, at times, he seeks to refuse both theo-ontology and onto-theology. Sometimes, as when he invokes Dionysius or Aquinas, he seems to want to go back behind onto-theology to theo-ontology. But much more consistently—as for example, when he praises Duns Scotus for "completing" metaphysics and at the same time releasing, "beyond metaphysics," the discourse of charity—Marion is a thoroughly modern or postmodern thinker.[2] The true thought of love begins for him, and is only possible as, an initially negative reaction to the eventual secular upshots of onto-theology that have already drained the world and science of any loving warmth. But, as always, the easy and yet inevitable question arises: is a negative reaction—in this case, as Marion puts it, an *adieu* to *le monde*—in fact a sustaining by sublation of what it reacts against? If Marion's supposed phenomenological *vécus* are in fact his own subjective decisions, then are they not still modern metaphysical decisions? In fact I shall eventually argue that they are recognizably *Hegelian* metaphysical decisions.

This, however, only becomes apparent in Marion's recent work *Le Phéno-mène érotique*. In the first section below, I offer an account of its contents interspersed with critical comments and questions, before proceeding to sketch out an alternative approach to the thematic of love.

The Rhapsody of Love

Marion begins the book by suggesting that more fundamental than the forgetting of Being is the forgetting of the "erotic of wisdom" as implied by the term
"philosophy" itself. And one can well agree.[3] Yet here the question immediately
arises as to whether Marion himself in fact perpetuates this forgetting, since
he proposes not to proclaim the love of knowledge alongside the knowledge
of love, but the latter alone (even if love generates for Marion its own form
of knowledge). Indeed the former is briskly discounted in strictly Cartesian
terms: the *jouissance* consequent upon knowledge is not really an enjoyment
of the known object, but an enjoyment of self in the act of knowing. Hence
knowledge is dismissed from the field of love, but it is not lost on the reader
that thereby also, knowledge is sent off on a lonely and comfortless ride, without the consort of *eros*.

In seeking a knowledge of love alone, Marion would appear to face two
possible *aporias*. The first is akin to that with which Socrates confronted the
rhapsode Ion, who claimed to know Homer and only Homer. How, asks
Socrates, can he understand the genre of the *Iliad* with no knowledge of any
literature other than that by Homer?[4] How, moreover, can he understand the
Iliad from the *Iliad* alone, when it speaks of so many things—fighting, rul-
ing, loving, ship-building, cooking—that are not in the first instance located
within literature? Can a rhapsody of Homer, asks Socrates, be a true knowledge of Homer, without divine inspiration? But Socrates' point here is not
pure ridicule—for if the knowledge of only one thing entirely on its own
terms as it displays itself is impossible, then it is not clear that we can ever
quite escape this impossibility. To some degree we must always seek to know
one thing on its own account, even though this one thing can only be adequately known in terms of all its actual and possible relations to everything
else, and the equally infinite ramifications of its own contents.

So if Marion seeks to be the rhapsode of love then one can ask, like
Socrates, can this be true philosophy? But, in his defense, one can also ask how
could there be—at least to some degree—any other approach to love than to
seek to know it lovingly according to the way it displays itself? And if only
divine inspiration can rescue us from the consequent *aporias,* then love itself,
as Marion tends to imply, may demand just this recourse.

Nevertheless, one can still wonder if Marion's rhapsody, like that of Ion, is
too drastic. Perhaps love can *only* be classified by its positive relation to other

genera of being and reflection or else to other semi-transcendental aspects of reality like knowing and *aisthesis*. (For Scholastic thought love, knowledge, and *aisthēsis* are related to, and in spiritual existences coincide with, the full transcendentals good, true, and beautiful; however, noncognizant beings exhibit the latter trio but not the former.) Also, one can note the fact that those involved with love, even in speaking about love, necessarily speak of many things besides love, just as Homer speaks indirectly of poetry by speaking of horses and the sea and so forth. (This is a point recently stressed by Jean-Luc Godard in his film *Éloge d'Amour*.) But Marion tends to speak of love as positively unrelated to anything else and of the discourse of love as speaking of things beside love only with utter irrelevance. One can wonder whether this strategy is a sign of rigor or else dooms itself to eventual evacuation even of the topic of love.

In a modern world where pleasure in knowledge of things is taken to be really self-pleasuring, nothing insofar as it exists actually matters. As Marion says, if (but only if) one supposes, after Heidegger, that the entire being of beings is simply that pure non-ontic being that is identical with nothing and only arrives in time in the delusory guise of this or that, then what follows upon this must be a "So what?" in the face of all reality. As he declares, if such an ontological reduction holds, then all is struck with vanity. Likewise, if in thinking it follows that I am, and this is all that survives the Cartesian *epochē*, then *ennui* may well conclude simply *not* to go on thinking and thereby generating such an airless *esse*. In a world where things *only* are, and I *only* am, what could possibly kindle my interest?

Marion argues that the answer to this question can only be the possibility that I am loved "from elsewhere" or that "someone out there might love me." (Both the literal and idiomatic translations are necessary to grasp the resonance of *m'aime-t-on d'ailleurs*.) Self-love is impossible, because my own existence is empty and (Marion adds, somewhat at random) I am full of faults. But the main point seems to be that, given the success of the Cartesian and the Heideggerean reductions, nothing *deserves* to be loved. As for Luther, so for Marion, love can only be exercised as a free gift or openness to the other as other, not insofar as she in any way inherently deserves such recognition.[5] He frequently stresses that only the exercise of love, and in no sense knowledge of the manifest, renders lovability apparent. Yet in a world struck with vanity, the only residual matter of interest for us is nonetheless that we might perhaps be lovingly recognized. This, however, is nearly impossible for two reasons. First of all, given our reduction by the *cogito* each to the same flat thinking essence beneath all superfluity of biological, cultural, and psychological character, there is nothing *to* recognize—and later in *Le Phénomène érotique* Marion points out the relation of *personne*—person—to *personne:* no one. The second problem of recognition is that, if all are hateful to themselves, then they should be equally unacceptable to others. Such a resulting circumstance of latent mutual hatred is compounded by the fact that the honest person, hating himself, will tend to transfer this hatred to the banally unreflective individual who imagines that he loves himself. This scenario eventually gives rise to a kind of quasi-Hobbesian condition of the hatred of all for all—grounded not, however, as for Hobbes's metaphysics in a primacy of self-love, but in a primacy of self-hatred.

Nevertheless it is enmity that first pierces the veil of boredom. The one who hates me or whom I hate "gets" to me and therefore stands out from the leveled mass as someone for whom I have a negative concern. The enemy therefore figures for Marion as a crucial moment in the process of erotic reduction.

The next moment arises when, having already invoked the possibility of love as acceptance of oneself from elsewhere, and having received negative recognition from my enemy, my attempt to refuse his hatred in the face of my worthiness of it (I am somewhat interpolating here) is resolved by an attempt to reassert possible self-respect by asking "could I love, me first of all [*puis-je aimer, moi le premier*]?" This constitutes for Marion my first "advance" as a lover.[6] He is speaking here of a specifically erotic advance, although (rightly in my view) he does not distinguish this from an *agapēic* advance. But the love involved here exceeds the ethical, even if it is the condition of possibility for the ethical—and here again I think that Marion is profoundly right and surpasses the perspectives of Lévinas (while seeming to side with the Kierkegaard of *Fear and Trembling* rather than the Kierkegaard of *Works of Love*). For to banish (assumed) *ennui,* we require not formal recognition that we fall under the general category of thinking and willing substance and so are the bearer of "rights," but acceptance as a particular individual. Now in the face of the contagion of hatred that prevents this, the issue is whether I myself can achieve this acceptance of another.

Once more though, the operation of recognition in Marion seems to face the insuperable problems of his initial philosophic decisions: beings in the world are only the purveyors of bare meaningless existence, and in space they are counters to be maneuvered about at will, just as they are in time merely punctually to come, or else are present, or yet again have been. Insofar as human beings have spatio-temporally located bodies, then they are exactly like the serial and interchangeable numbers in a telephone book or list of e-mail addresses. To love cannot mean to be drawn by such and such a spatial appearance—which as inter-substitutable is precisely *not*, for Marion, unique and particular. Rather, to love means to be drawn by something invisible, by an other who does not really appear to one, indeed in a more exemplary fashion by a merely absent or possible other. But the question then clearly arises as to how the specific other is isolated at all: it is as if Marion insists that one should love only Homer, but none of the details of Homer, including his name, since they are all in principle transferable from Homer to someone else. Obviously though, the problem then ensues: just how is one to locate Homer, or even *is* Homer at all if one cannot find him?

But for Marion these considerations concerning the knowledge of existence are irrelevant to the logic of love. For love is *without reason,* save this self-abandoning gesture itself. It does not belong in any way to the acceptance offered by love that the lover receives something of the presence of the beloved. For if it did, Marion argues, love would be less than unconditional and therefore less than love. Love must still love even in the face of the absence of the other, since its advance is absolute. It follows that, if love remains even in the face of this reduction, then all that is left behind by such a reduction is not of the essence of love. The counter-question that one could put to Marion here, however, is whether this evidence of remaining love *in extremis* can really carry the weight of locating a kind of *a priori* essence in philosophy (a secure "phenomenon"), or is it rather the *arbitrary* selection of one episode among other characteristic episodes lying within the range of the natural attitude's experience of love. Put very simply: would a woman take it as proof of a man's love if he were faithful to her during a ten-year absence, without even her photograph for consolation, if, nevertheless, when he returned to her he reverted to being the drunken bully she had known before? The enterprise of phenomenological reduction, when deconstructed, seems to suppose that *one* episode of a series or *one* aspect of a natural phenomenon will turn out to be deeper or typical, when perhaps, to the contrary, "love" is complexly spoken of and exemplified just because it is an incurably imprecise analogical concept that indicates no reality other than the mysterious fact that certain diverse experiences and feelings appear, all the same, characteristically to blend together to form a

certain loose unity. Indeed one can go further: if the state of love between creatures itself characteristically blends differences within a kind of mysterious
identity, does not love as such lie close to the cognitive experience of analogical unity?

In contrast to such an approach, Marion is an unremitting *rationalist*. He
specifically renounces the notion that we might primarily learn of love from
history and literature.[7] To the contrary, he says (rather like Descartes in the
face of the humanists) that we would not be able to locate love in history and
literature if we did not first possess a "clear and distinct" concept of it. This
may be contrasted with the "metaphysical" approach of Plato, for whom desire
was involved in our initial obscure apprehension of something that we seek to
know more clearly. His *Dialogues* (supremely the *Meno*) make it clear that this
aporia of searching to know something in some sense already known involves
not just love but also knowledge in the detour of history, biography, myth, and
literature. Knowledge for Plato is always not yet clear, since only as yet desired;
but desiring is also not as yet clear since it could only be fully clarified by the
full presence of the object it desires. For Marion, by contrast, knowledge is
clear without desire, although subject to the *epochē* of tedium (which, inci-
dentally, I doubt can count as an *epochē* in the strict Husserlian sense). But
then it seems as if, of desire itself, taken in rhapsodic isolation, Marion seeks
to have a knowledge *also* without desire.

Things cannot indeed be as simple as this, for he declares that he seeks to
know love only from love, and by love to acquire a special sort of knowledge.
Thus the knower who knows love is not the Cartesian *cogito* nor Heideggerean
Dasein, but the *adonné*, who with priority over these other figures of consciousness knows herself to be there only as also given alongside all of her
objective givenness—who receives herself in fact as primordially acceptance
from elsewhere, even if this be only in the mode of the possibility of such
acceptance. If, however, I am primordially the presence of a welcoming other
who is in me more deeply than I am in myself, and it is only as this myself-
which-is-another that I can acknowledge the phenomenon of love (only by
giving and receiving it), then how can I be the ego who would detachedly look
at love in such a way as to circumscribe it "clearly and distinctly"? My regard
of love is, in fact, not really a regard but, as Marion describes it, a blind urging,
and the regarding ego has here no stable vantage from which to distinguish
himself from the object of his gaze—for as lover, he is already given to and as
himself only by the other.

Hence does not the phenomenological reduction to the *adonné* explode the entire possibility of a pure phenomenology—or of a rhapsodic phenomenology "on its own" and not taken in conjunction with ontology, history, axiomatics, and even theology? Yet if one were to retain the *adonné* outside strict phenomenology, one would then have to regard it more as a speculative decision taken with reasonable, if not *apodeictic*, warrants, to understand the human self as first of all the gift of love.

Just because Marion, in this contradictory fashion, seeks to have a purely phenomenological and therefore rationalist approach to love, he cannot allow that love remains obscure and uncertain precisely to the measure that it seeks to know the other and enter into reciprocity with her. To the contrary, he claims that the will and decision to love is its own clear proof, its own self-acceptance, and its own reward. But to this one could respond, why is this gesture also not subject to a "So what?" In what way is my obstinately stoic commitment of continuing interest, even to myself, if thereby I see nothing and meet with nothing? Can I not become bored with my fidelity, coming to see it only as meaningless obstinacy?

Marion is implicitly aware of this possible objection and the more he faces up to it in the course of the book the more interesting it becomes, yet also the more threatened some of his initial philosophical decisions seem to be. Thus against any Lévinasian or Derridean eulogizing of the purely unilateral, Marion fully insists that the lover who advances goes on *hoping* for a reciprocating response even though he in no way demands it, requires it, or expects it. He also seems to acknowledge that a certain vanity can strike an unshakeable decision to decide to love if in actuality I have failed to love.[8] Is not the possession of a good will as the only indisputable good not somewhat barren and solipsistic? At times Marion seems to admit this and shift from a Kantian to an Hegelian ground. Hence the lover goes on hoping for a response, not only in order to receive acceptance, but also to receive confirmation that his act of love is truly love. In one of the most impressive sections of the book, toward the end, Marion insists that only one's lover can provide assurance that one has been a faithful lover; this is not something one can know for oneself, for faithfulness consists finally in giving to the other that which one does not oneself have—namely, one's most basic identity as *adonné*.[9] As Marion says, faithfulness here resides at the microlevel of consistent small gestures and responses over many years. Yet does not this assertion call into question some of the grand formalism of the will, refusing knowledge and being, that prevails in the rest of the book? If faithfulness must be judged by the other from my acts, words, and gestures, then has it not after all invaded my visible objectivity? Moreover, if only the other can pronounce this judgment, then is not such an appearance in excess of any indisputably reduced phenomenon, since the other's unique spatio-temporal and bodily perspective is of relevance here, besides her act of assessment that exceeds any sheerly ineluctable visibility? And yet this pronouncement of my fidelity by the *autrui* alone for Marion finally gives myself to myself in my own deepest identity as lover. Such an "adonation" would seem to exceed the phenomenological in the direction both of ontological mediation and a hermeneutically, since subjectively invoked, horizon of meaning.

The pronouncement of my fidelity by my lover lies, however, somewhat further down the series of phenomenological moments traced by Marion. Long before this one must pass through the entire drama of *la croisée des chairs* that can be but clumsily rendered into English as "the crossing of fleshes." The drama is inaugurated by the sharing between lovers of the *vow* [*le serment*] that arises at the point where my utter unilateral self-giving in love is crossed by an equivalent abandonment on the part of the other whom I have selected.[10] If there is reciprocity here, it is really the coincidence of two absolute non-reciprocities. Despite his claim that he is speaking of *eros* as well as *agapē*, it is not clear that Marion really allows that lovers are pursuing mutuality for its own sake rather than mutual recognition through mutual sacrificial abandonment (albeit that this is a sacrificial advance or "love without return" in which one gains one's real, irreplaceable self as lover) . That the latter, in ignoring the mediation of spatial encounter and so a shared concrete mutuality for its own sake, can actually result in mutually assured destruction is illustrated by O. Henry's well-known short story *The Gift of the Magi*. Here, for Christmas, a wife sells her hair in order to buy for her husband a coveted watch chain. Meanwhile the husband has sold his watch to buy for his wife a set of combs to bind up her long hair. In receiving the other's sacrifice, both partners now receive a futile because unusable gift that can only make them feel guilty about the other's loss.[11] If love is defined, following Marion, as the meeting of two equal absolute disinterests, rather than as a mutual fulfillment of needs, then this nihilistic upshot must be inevitable. His account of the exchange of vows could open up such a loveless chasm, since the point of crossing composes no "between" or mediating ontological love as a state of analogically blended differences that might be a kind of shared microculture—both the upshot of a shared "affinity" and a public manifestation of this affinity that exhibits a "third," appreciable by others.

To the contrary, "the saturated phenomenon" that arises remains always double—these are really two phenomena for the two different subjects, which coincide with two rich and vague intuitions that reflect the "blinding" of the lover by the other who does not otherwise appear to him. The normal situation of the phenomenological *vécu* is here inverted: one does not have an obscure intention in search of intuitive clarification, but rather an obscure intuition in search of intentional clarification as to the meaningful identity of the other. The latter is given with the vow, which actually provides a shared intentional meaning of *me voici*. It is then, however, conceded by Marion that this vow remains all too formal and abstract if it is to identify the beloved as a particular person responding also to me in particular. Just for this reason one requires the sexual passage through *la croisée des chairs*.

The odd thing here is that the reader is led, at least initially, to ask himself whether this does not attribute too much importance to the physically erotic in the very establishing of our significant identity. Indeed it seems to make true philosophy begin in the shared bedroom rather than on Descartes's lone bed of prevarication. This detour seems only necessary because of a needlessly empty and abstracted understanding of the exchanged vow. The problem would appear to stem from Marion's handing over of all being to existential emptiness and technological manipulation. Why decide, for example, that objects are infinitely interchangeable within a Newtonian absolute space? Why not rather see space in Leibnizian terms as constituted through a web of relations among things that would tend to allow that a place can be irreplaceable in its very spatiality? If that is the case, then I may love not just a person, but also a spatially unique intersection that to a degree may "receive me." Indeed, the very identity of this intersection may be doubled by the love that informs it—as when a crossroads is situated by an ancient bent oak, and then a tavern is later placed there, and so forth. If this spot were to become favored by lovers, then it is not enough to say, with Marion, that it is rendered non-vain by dint of accidental association with their *amours,* since here an objective intersection, loved already for its beauty, becomes part of the very substance of what the lovers share—a common taste. For Marion, such constative discourse does not belong to the true performative and contentless discourse of the erotic voice, but this verdict is surely questionable.[12] If the love also of things is possible, since in their beauty they visibly mediate the invisible—since something about their appearance inspires inexhaustible poetic description tending to apostrophization—then the bodies and voices of lovers may blend with these objects in a mutual augmentation. Things can be adopted as our prostheses, because in a certain way they already address us through themselves by suggesting more than themselves. If things did not speak to us in this way, if they were only the *objects* of representation or manipulation, then how would any speaking, any personal expression, any manifestation of the human will be at all possible, since embodied souls can only think or express themselves by rendering the inert articulate?

Therefore the *éblouissement* of the erotic intuition need not concern only the sublime birth of me as a subject, captivated by the super-categorical imperative of the other in excess of ordinary phenomenalization. It could concern simply a more intense mode of the manifestation of the beautiful in every apparent thing. In which case the "excess" of intuition here still derives from a phenomenally present other and from the outset concerns also and equally an excessive intention or reference to a highly complex conceptual complex. (Intention need not be taken as "mastery" if it is an "inner word" pointing to a reality that in principle it will never grasp in all its aspects.) After all, if it is a Husserlian intellectual intuition we are speaking of here and not only a Kantian sensory intuition (though it is also that), then how can an intuition be in excess of itself as seeing more than can be seen unless, from the beginning, significance is also in excess of itself as grasping more than can be grasped? Since intellectual intuition is a higher mode of understanding than discursivity (a God-like grasp of something "all at once"), it follows that the attempt to "fill out the saturated intuition" conceptually is also the endless attempt to express simply and at once a complex concept that is not merely an internal intention but also belongs to a given and so "external" *eidōs* as such. (It must be external for all phenomenology, at least in some sense, since Husserl refused a "Fichtean" active constitution of a known phenomenon by the knowing subject. But if, following Augustine and Aquinas rather than Husserl, one allows that every intentional thought can only have the character of an inner "sign," then the absence indissociable from sign will tend to support the full realist externality of meaningful *eidōs* as inhering in physical realities themselves.)

If, as for Marion, *only* intuition is in excess of (comprehended) meaning and it is not also the case that (dimly apprehended) meaning is in excess of (comprehended) meaning from the outset, then all that reality supplies is a saturated intuition after the mode of Kantian sensory intuition which is "blind," and then becomes a mere occasion for our subjective supplying of significance. (Although under Marion's scheme, the saturation of the intuition can never heal the "emptiness" of categorial meaning.) But this mode of transcendental idealism on Marion's part ensures that we move endlessly away from intuition toward hidden and latent *a priori* concepts (even if these are never adequate to the incurable blindness of saturation) and indeed toward merely willed positings rather than toward a deeper intuition emanating from the thing itself that carries or points toward a conceptual excess that is thereby also *a posteriori*. There is a "saturated" play between concept and intuition (following Kant) that constitutes the beautiful and keeps us attentive to the sensory and structural visibility of phenomena, whereas to speak of the saturated phenomenon as an initial excess of intuition over concept is to speak of the sublime, and therefore always of a *leaving behind* of the phenomenal in favor of the noumenal.[13]

If one viewed the erotic saturation more in the way just sketched, would one be confined to the bare formalism of the vow? Can it not rather consist in a shared *habitus*, a shared microculture, which through its love and transformation of *things*, including the bodies of the lovers, conceives the exchanged love of the lovers not simply as accidental mutual self-abandonment, but also as a local cultivation of a world conceived as itself springing from and declaring love, since it shows itself to be beautiful and therefore obscurely suggestive of meaning? In this perspective, the love of lovers is not to be taken in rhapsodic isolation, but as part of our entire process of coming to know and coming to be within the world. The speech of the lovers about things other than their love includes precisely the recognition that they, the lovers, are intrinsically lovable at least from certain perspectives, in continuity with the lovability of the world in general and hence the settings they find themselves in.

This perspective would tend to call into question Marion's initial set of presuppositions: if all beings are to some degree beautiful and appear to us in some degree as exhibiting a flourishing in accordance with their own proper ends (which appears to the natural attitude to be the case, and what valid decision can negate this?) then do they not exhibit the Good, and are they not worthy of our attentive love and even of our gifts, insofar as they seem to make manifest unseen powers? For just the same reason, self-love is valid as our self-reception of that portion of the cosmos that we ourselves are and so are closest to—even if, as St. Augustine clearly affirms, we should only love ourselves to the degree that we persist in our *true* selves, as loving God and our neighbors.[14]

In Augustine at least, there is none of that "metaphysical" priority of self-love that Marion denounces, just because the true self loves itself only as the self that loves God and others, which always remains possible because of the inherent goodness and beauty of being as such. (Perhaps Marion is rather attacking a modern, for example Hegelian, priority of self-love; but this would not legitimate the contrary doctrine of initial self-hatred, which seems linked to a notion of the evil of being as such, or at least of some positive evil aspect to being—a thesis that seems again to refuse ancient as well as modern metaphysics.) Here one wants to ask just why Marion takes Heidegger so seriously? No being is present to us except as manifesting an attractive and admirable unity: such unity can only be "voided" if, after Heidegger, Being as such is really the null flux of time, and yet it seems more natural to regard this flux as itself merely ontic. Even if it is not provable, it is more in keeping with "the natural attitude" (and certainly not disprovable), eminently to attribute all the unities of beings to Being as such, which can be regarded as their donating source. Here one would have an *esse* that is as *esse* gift, just as it is, as *esse,* Spirit.

If each apprehended being is not simply a bare object of representation or manipulation, but a kind of *eidōs* or meaningful form, then the lovers, by inserting themselves in the web of such forms with a more adaptive intensity, repeat in some measure the poetic and donating act of Absolute Spirit as such, rendering the forms newly complex, mobile, and regenerating. In that case, the vow of the lovers is as much a kind of established reality as it is also (and undeniably) a formal commitment. They would seem here to be adequately identified without *la croisée des chairs.*

The latter, though, might indeed form the pivot of their poetic and exchanging work, sending it spinning into an ecstatic trance. The irony, however, of Marion's perspective is that his somewhat Manichean demonization of the shaped and apparent is sustained also into the fleshly realm and in such a manner that the invisible and uncontrollable, which constitutes for him in the spiritual realm the most exalted, here becomes sinister and ambiguous and yet unavoidable.[15] For in keeping with the thought of Michel Henry, Marion insists on a strict dualism between the body and the flesh—a Cartesianism no longer of extension versus thought, but of exterior versus interior matter. Hence for Marion, the *croisée des chairs*—even though it is supposed to provide content for a formal framework—is just as invisible a point X as the intersection of promises. True erotic excitation is not for him triggered by any specific sensed surface of the body, any more than the ethical gaze of the *visage* concerns facial expression rather than the black holes of two pupils gazing back at me. It is a case of auto-affection, but nonetheless the most radical and fundamental case, in which I sense the other only insofar as I sense myself sensing, but equally I here sense my most fundamental erotic self only because, in sensing myself sensing the other I can also—and supremely in the sexual act itself—sense myself sensing the other insofar as I sense her sensing me in sensing herself.

In this rather beautiful and exact description, Marion explains how one has here the most radical and defining instance of the *adonné*, where what I am given is myself and therefore, as Claude Bruaire several years ago expressed it, I must as a recipient give myself to myself in a way that ensures that my original relationship to myself is a reflective or auto-affective one.[16]

There is here invoked a very interesting co-implication between the gift, on the one hand, and the *mirror*, on the other. It seems that not only every gift that a man might give a woman is really a mirror in which she might regard herself, but that all gifts are like this—as indeed neo-Platonism already understood. For to be a spirit, to think at all, is to receive one's being and unity and even the being and unity of all that one surveys as the gift that one is oneself. This demands reflexivity—my *prise de conscience* in repeating *as* me the giving of the gift to me. Yet this reflexivity can never be perfect, for one can never, as Plotinus and Proclus put it, recapture in reflection or self-giving the original unity (or one can add beyond neo-Platonism, original being) of the donating source to which as spirit we must assume ourselves to be in debt.

We must assume this debt because spirit as conscious knowledge, or the capacity to give, is in no way derivable from material existence without recourse to a reductive genealogy that would reduce spirit to epiphenomenal illusion. One can agree with Bruaire and Marion: so long as one affirms one's spiritual existence, we discover ourselves as originally given and in debt to a donating source (however diversely the two thinkers may conceive this circumstance). Moreover, one can also agree with both thinkers that the co-implication of mirror and gift has a further consequence. Again, following a Plotinian model, in trying to regard itself in its own mirror spirit is really trying to see also the image of a shadowy donating source that stands behind its back. Since it can never perfectly see this, it can never perfectly see itself either, and this failure of reflection is equally a failure to cancel one's debt or make a perfect return of gratitude to the original donor. But this failure witnesses to the *positivity* of a constitutive spiritual or ontological debt, since the failure ever to be equal to this source or to ourselves ensures that all our spiritual endeavors compose a kind of inadequate compensation for this deficit.

In not fully reaching back to ourselves, we must discursively, or erotically, or poetically create, or else bear witness to, something besides ourselves, and this failure to mirror ourselves in mirroring the donating source paradoxically *recaptures* beyond, but beneath reflection, something of the more original unity of the donating source itself that is already gift, but *not* (since it is simple) already reflection. Our gifts are always already mirrors, but the gift has priority over the mirror, and has the power to shatter even our mirrors into shards.

Hence, as both Marion and Bruaire affirm, by remaining in perpetual debt we reciprocate the original gift, not adequately back to the source, but inadequately by passing the gift in certain measures on to others in space, and more especially by procreative or educatively poetic acts in time down to future generations. The latter indeed will receive our gifts once again as mirrors—of us and of themselves—since they are *adonnés* in relation to us. Here, as Marion implies in his own fashion, the significance of the existence of generations, or of the succession of children through time, is exactly that the problematic of my identity, as of my indebtedness, and so indeed of my salvation, cannot be perfectly resolved by me as an individual alone.[17] I have to leave a legacy of debt, yet in doing so by that gift appropriately called by us in its legal form simply "will" (or "deed"or "testament")—by metaphorically *making my will* in this way—I do further discharge my debt and provide conditions for my descendants further to discharge it on my behalf. And since the debt is infinite, and the donating source does not really *lack* this repayment, the very fact that no repayment reduces the debt or truly reverts to the original giver ensures that the endlessness of our debt possesses no real negativity that would be akin, for example, to the negativity of sin or guilt. For to the contrary, this endlessness of our debt is the transcendental precondition for the possibility that finite spirits may give without end, despite their finitude.

For Marion's version of this complex circumstance of spirit as such in relation to the mirror and the gift, one can see the sexual act, including its relation to procreation, as the point where, as he puts it, the entire phenomenon of love becomes most clearly "intelligible," even though it is not, in fact, its "strongest" instance.

Nevertheless, for Marion, the crucial descent into the flesh that alone defines us, is also a descent into darkness. Here we may salute his realism while questioning his fatalism and even suspecting a certain gnosticism, since *la croisée des chairs* is consistently compared with the hypostatic union of humanity with God in Christ and the darkness seems to concern a relation to being as such, not a fallen contingency.[18] And here also Marion seems once again the victim of his refusal of the possibility that a mere *étant* might be a beautiful *eidōs* itself mediating the ultimate source of love and itself worthy of love in a certain measure. We have seen how the admission of the possibility of a love of *things* might ensure that the makers of the vow could be identified even before and outside the sexual act; but now one faces the problem that the same impossibility for Marion of a love of things (which would allow a non-idolatrous adulation of visible form) ensures that for him true, nonperverse sex always occurs in the ontological darkness, with the lights strictly switched off. Here, as I have said, in the case of the flesh, everything that in Marion's philosophy of the spirit possesses a *positive* valency—namely, invisibility, radical passivity, and derivedness of autonomy—suddenly assumes a negative one. For despite the fact that I am given my erotic flesh by the eroticized flesh of the other, the fact of her invisibility as object of my desire ensures that there remains an autonomous surplus in my auto-affection, just as, in the spiritual realm, the lack of appearance of the *autrui* as phenomenon ensures that, in the last instance, this phenomenon is only present for me by fiat of my will—a point where, as in *Étant donné*, it would seem that a voluntarist decisionism exits phenomenology altogether. Marion is unambiguous: "[S]trictly speaking there is never anything erotic to see . . . . [W]hat is visible here would become at once a ridiculous or obscene object." This matches the fact that the intuition of the advancing lover is "saturated" and "blind" because it "gives itself" "before the other appears as such."[19] In this case erotic love seems to have nothing to do with any specificity of the other that might be publicly apparent—and what other specificity can we be sure of?—and to be entirely a matter of ineffable auto-affection resulting in an entirely mysterious private decision (as if *a*'s predilection for *b* were entirely inscrutable and impossible to judge, despite the entire history of the novel.)

But if spiritual will is positively assessed by Marion—though its formal inadequacy is also acknowledged—our fleshly erotic auto-affection is seen derogatively, just because it supposedly falls outside both the scope of my will and of my response to this specific invisible other. But this seems far too pessimistic. Admirably, Marion argues that the erotic and even the sexually erotic is of itself (in contrast to its perverse substitutes) aligned with fidelity, self-surrender and sacrifice, not with caprice or self-pleasuring, since at bottom it can only enjoy its own pleasure as an enjoying also of the self-pleasuring of the other (which is in turn her self-pleasuring only as the reception of my own). Yet Marion cannot allow that the flesh *also* is tilted toward fidelity; for him the flesh, like the Kantian will, is equally poised between infinite goodness and radical evil—and in a fashion outside our moral control.

This supposed automatism of the flesh is a direct result of its conceptual sundering from the visible body. Unfortunately, Marion follows Michel Henry rather than Maurice Merleau-Ponty in his interpretation of auto-affection and the crossing of touch.[20] If he had followed the latter, then he might have decided to cross phenomenology with semiotics and ontology. (If every appearance must remain a sign, then this, as already argued, encourages a realistic sense of an invisible being manifest in visible phenomena.) For Merleau-Ponty, my touching myself as touching something else is not simply the result of my transcendental constitution as flesh: rather this transcendental constitution is mediated (as for Aristotle in the *De Anima*) by a categorial fold in the surface of being that constitutes the biosphere and in rising degrees of intensity coincides with spiritual self-consciousness. Here the reflexivity of flesh as auto-affection is also the achieved "return upon themselves" of material things as such—as in Aristotle's doctrine of sensation, where the sensed species migrates from the hylomorphic substantial being and bends back upon itself in the being of the sensing creature for which it is inseparably at once "sensation" and "indication." Object sensed and act of sensing are here identical, just as, following this Aristotelian contour, one can think (in a fashion that phenomenology has no rational power to refuse) of the return upon oneself in the act of thinking as equally the holding up of a mirror to beings themselves for the delectation of their unconscious narcissism, which alone nevertheless ensures that our conscious reflection is never merely narcissistic but also (theoretically) receptive and (practically) donating.

If, in this manner, the self-reflection of the flesh is also the folding back upon itself of the body, ensuring that the flesh–body amalgam is constituted as the mediation between matter and spirit, then it would be also the case that the self-reflection of the flesh always goes by the detour of received and given surface sensing of the body, just as for Aquinas the human mind's "return upon itself" goes by the detour of the *conversio ad phantasmata*. It would then further follow that eroticization is never as blind—with an ambiguous blindness for Marion, unlike the good blindness of the spiritual lover—as Marion claims. For it is never entirely obscure to us, but linked to habitual patterns of affinity for certain sensory forms into which we have some degree of conceptual insight and even some capacity to channel in a certain regular direction. Most important of all, eroticization is in fact *most* compulsive when directed toward one individual person who alone has the power to assemble, mingle, and ring changes on a dazzling array of erotic triggers to the maximum synthetic degree. Therefore, beyond Marion, one might claim that, of its own intrinsic bias, when not depleted in terms of its primitive and perverse degrees, eroticization of the flesh favors the vow and fidelity to the vow and to a large degree is responsible for their fostering and furtherance.

For Marion, the automatism of the flesh or *phénomène saturé* reaches its pitch in orgasm. He explicitly declares that "he awaits the crazed" who will claim against him that orgasm is not an entirely impersonal moment where one loses all sense of the *visage* and even the specific identity of the flesh of the other.[21] Here one arrives at the embarrassing moment where the highest stakes of the phenomenological reduction seem to coincide with the all-too-bland investigations of the sex manual. Who will dare to come forth as manifestly crazed for the terms of at least one reduced view? Well one should so dare. In a fallen world, no doubt, all our eroticization is subject to impersonalized automatism. But just because, for theology, fallenness is a mystery, there is no ontological or phenomenological explanation for this. By offering one, in the case of (our undoubted) sexual fallenness, Marion in effect ontologizes sexual sin as premoral lapse in exactly the same gnostic and *not-at-all* Catholic fashion that Heidegger imagines an irresolvable ontological guilt only cancelable by negating our live ontic status when we surrender to the supposed ontological arms of death. It can be noted here (following Marion himself) that ontological debt constitutive of being and spirit has quite a different structure, since its non-cancelability really indicates that this debt is original hyper-abundant gift.

Surely orgasm is sometimes the entry into ecstasy of our sight and touching of the other, just as crossed fleshes can only cross as visible bodies and therefore indeed compose *one* flesh. (Marion negates the literal force of the biblical phase only by the ruse of pretending that it must refer to the produced or possible procreated child.) By the same token, why should there *not* be a shared intuition as well as a shared intended significance? If we are able to use the same complex and sometimes singular words to describe a color experience, then surely the bias should run, after Wittgenstein, toward assuming that we do indeed to some degree share the same experience, since there is *no* experience of color (or of anything else) outside the public and common modes of its imaged and linguistic expressions. These may be inadequate to the experience, but this sense of inadequacy is inseparable from our sense of the nonforeclosed import of images, forms, and signs themselves.

If orgasm is not necessarily impersonal, because it is an experience not altogether disassociated from form and meaning (this would be impossible), then it is not, as Marion implies, in a perhaps somewhat masculine-biased fashion, simply a sign of exhausted eroticization. It is that, but it is equally the sign of consummation and anticipation of eternity, just as Vespers foreshadows sleep and the diurnal *via negativa* of temporary languor of our efforts, yet also anticipates the dawning of the eschatological day that lasts forever. For Marion, by contrast, orgasm is the sign of "radical finitude" and hence is his Kantian counterpart to the saturated phenomenon of the spirit, if one takes the latter as essentially another word for the sublime.

An oscillation between these two poles is linked with Marion's lack of interest in the beautiful as opposed to the sublime and concern less with the semi-decipheral forms and representative *mimēsis* of artistic pictures (and both are present even in an artist like Rothko) than with the way they overwhelm us, look back at us, or anamorphically situate us. (In this way Marion's account of the icon is in fact iconoclastic.) This is inevitable because, for Marion, beauty does not mediate in its visibility the invisible, but rather forecloses a world of idols or of the merely visible and radically finite as reduced to our representing awareness. Ironically, Marion protects the eroticization of the flesh from the seductions of bodily beauty in order to save its sublime impulse toward the infinite. However, without the beautiful mediation of the infinite that may be supplied by form, the fleshly sublime assumes the ambiguity of Kant's *natural* rather than moral sublime, which in Kant may provoke barbaric military heroism as much as heroic virtue.[22] For this reason Marion reads the automatism of the flesh and the periodic lapses of erotic intensity in a transcendental fashion, as marking out an unsurpassable barrier of the finite that dooms our erotic response to the other to an eventual passing away. Yet this reading might be an arbitrary refusal of the possibility that our relative noncontrol of erotic response and its rhythmic lapses and renewals is rather a participation in the infinite donating source of love, which takes the form of a temporality that is, in principle, without end. Marion's decision here would be like the decision to read "evening" as the sign of the phenomenal world's transcendental closure on itself and ultimate passage into night, rather than, as liturgy dictates, the sign of the world's ceaseless preparation for a more adequate and everlasting dawn.

One curious feature of Marion's exposition of the flesh is the way he in certain ways abandons the path of a traditional Catholic metaphysic, yet defends in terms of a strictly modern philosophy most of the strictures of current Catholic sexual teaching—indeed sometimes in an exaggeratedly rigorous form. One might want to oppose to this something like the opposite combination: precisely a more deeply Catholic metaphysical approach could be open to more moral tolerance. This especially applies to an orthodox allowance that physical forms as such can be beautiful, good, and therefore lovable. If such is the case, and if reflective flesh takes the detour of manifest bodily giving and receiving of form, then certain modes of sexual "fetishization" are not, as Marion considers them, a perverse but inevitable visible substitute for the equally inevitable loss of true eroticization by the invisible other, but rather a prosthetic supplement that is always already added to the origins of the erotic impulse, such that indeed flesh as body already is in itself a fetishistic object. (Marion implicitly affirms this circumstance, but reads it negatively.) Such a fetish is at once idol and icon, a combination Marion at times, but all too rarely, permits. And to fetishize is in fact both to acknowledge the continuity of our lovable flesh with the flesh of the touchable world as such, and also to spiritualize this touchable world—since form is always situated at the boundary of mind and matter (or of intelligible and hylomorphic being).

The same goes for a certain mode of sado-masochism. Marion has the rigor to acknowledge that this is unavoidable, since at times we are more entirely focused on the other as physical reality and lose sight of their *visage*. Yet to view this negatively is once more ironically to refuse the possibilities of a more Catholic metaphysic. For the latter, things as well as persons are, in their own degree, properly lovable, and indeed humanity has the privilege of *mediating* between the lowliest material form of existence and the higher intelligible angelic mode of existence and beyond to god-likeness itself. Hence at moments to "reduce" the other to thingness is not wrong within the larger content of an entirely committed love, but rather is a kind of *fuller* recognition of our humanity in its downward-reaching kenotic scope than could be safely allowed in the normal course of affairs. Indeed it can be read positively as a necessary part of *la croisée des chairs*: for just as, normally, my mind seeks to dominate my body and this is a principle of right order, so in the case of sexual love, one hands over one's body to the dominance of the mind of the other, and vice versa. How otherwise could there be a total giving to the other of her rightly ordered identity? Such giving may become so extreme that gestures and embraces with the appearance of violence according to everyday convention in fact betoken the partial recovery of an ontological relation where violence is no longer even conceivable.

For Marion however, fetishism and sado-masochism are signs only of the fading of the erotic—and of course one may agree that there are perverse modes of these phenomena where such is the case and even that, in a fallen world, this perversity is always (inexplicably) to the fore. Yet they are also for Marion inevitable occurrences, since the fading itself is inevitable. Also accompanying this fading is the phenomenon of jealousy, where one wrongly concludes that the desire of the other is due to one, or one resents a feigned desired, and the phenomena of rape, literal or metaphorical, where one seeks to coerce the desire of the other.[23]

Here "rape" for Marion would seem to cover also most instances of "seduction," which coheres with his insistence that, in eroticizing the flesh of the other, I give to her only that which I have not, namely her own flesh—like the Plotinian One, giving by emanation to entities that which it has not, namely Being. In the case of creatures (rather than that of the Christian God who, unlike the Plotinian One, gives only a sharing in what he eminently has), this giving of what one has not most certainly holds, but it is not the only aspect of giving. In the present case, if the invocation of the desire of the other is by the mediation of forms and words, then the infinite opening up by the loving subject (beyond the capacity of things) of a place and a direction that Marion (with deep insight) recognizes as proffered by the advance of the lover is not simply a passive opening but a positive influence that "turns" the impulses of the other somewhat in a new direction, so positively modifying her flesh itself. One always sees oneself, one's desire, and one's body differently in the light of the other's desire: that is just what is so startling about it. But in that case there is no *adonné* without a certain seduction, a certain unasked for forcing of my will and my flesh; and only a shared *judgment* as to the appropriateness of the erotic union—a judgment indeed that may also have to be made from outside the circle of two—ensures that it is not rape or mutual rape in Marion's extended sense.

For Marion, the automatism of the flesh and orgasmic exhaustion means that I as a person—characterized by possession of will under my control—along with the person of the other, cannot really appear in the *croisée des chairs*. Yet just as, originally, an individuated other first appeared as the one hated, so now also, the lover who is no longer a lover but has become the one of whom I am jealous (since she will no longer return my love, or only pretends to do so) now *for the first* time appears to me as a person, because she is more in control, albeit perversely, of her will than the true lover can ever be. In this way, just as hatred is more ontologically fundamental than love, so for Marion the lie is more original than truth, which is not, as for "metaphysics," a *veritas* that is *index sui et falsi*. (In which case the "metaphysics" here refused must include the thought of Plato, Aristotle, Augustine, and Aquinas and not simply that of Descartes and Hegel, etc.) The lie then first of all reveals the person and hatred even attains the reciprocity that eluded love's aspiration.

This dire situation of sterile redemption can, for Marion, nonetheless be salvaged through an eroticization of the flesh that takes place purely through the performative language of love that remains under the control of our will. To this, however, one can object that *either* language is entirely under the control of our will, but then it reduces back to kinship with the formality of the vow (which but imperfectly allowed individualization), *or else,* if it achieves a true intentional individualization, it will deploy metaphors of the body and be driven by impulses of our flesh that are just as manifest in words as in actions. But in that case language is no more under our control or free from periodic exhaustion of inspiration than is our flesh.

Marion then decrees that, since mere language can after all achieve the *croisée des chairs,* it follows that friendship, just as much as the sexual relationship, can achieve the erotic reduction. Here his thought seems ambivalent. On the one hand, love as the negation of enmity and jealousy suggests a kind of Feuerbachian Hegelianism in which the human subject first escapes a void existence in order to seek definition through the other, but must later, and in several moments, negate the otherness of the other as hostile or indifferent to his own identity. In the seemingly paradigmatic instance of sexual union, it would appear that the other is at once the one necessary to my identity and yet is also the one who must be abjected for the sake of my identity. (One is tempted to speak here of Marion's Lacanianism.)

Yet at the same time it might seem as if merely spoken sex or else friendship provides Marion with a path other than the tragically gnostic one of negative dialectics. Nevertheless, he proceeds after all to view love-in-language as still erring toward the formalistic side and hence as not truly guaranteeing the manifestation of the other as unique, and equally as still erring toward the noncontrolledness of the orgasmic since, for example, friendship is also a prey to metaphorical rapine and literal envy. Hence, finally, *Le Phénomène érotique* returns to the centrality of the sexual paradigm for love, since only the child, or at least (and it would seem better) the possible child or the metaphorical child, guarantees the permanence of the lovers vows. Yet the child, as the perfect *adonné*, is only present to its parents in the form of its body that cannot underwrite their invisible flesh. It may seek to honor its parents by naming them, but since it cannot return any of its gift of life to its parents, this honoring in the end takes the form of a departure down the line of time to further and further offspring, so ensuring that the most enduring prize of the lovers' love in the end has nothing to do with the lovers at all.[24]

From the child the lovers must turn finally instead to God, the eternal witness of their once mutual abandonment that intrinsically hopes for eternity. God is alone the stable and infinite lover. Yet, since Marion claims to have uncovered the univocal concept of love in all its necessary moments, God is constituted as love *also* by his advance toward humanity, also by his experience of identification and abjection in the Incarnation and his ascended return from this to the relative formality of spiritual presence among us. In the end it would seem that a Lacanianized Hegelianism of the Left, as it were, is projected back upward as a sexualized Hegelianism of the Right. But in that case, if love applies univocally to God and to us, and if only God redeems us from the problem of love achieved in language that is at once too formal and yet too out of control, then who will redeem Marion's ontic God who is like us in structure, only infinite—in other words, Marion's *onto-theological* God—from what one must presume to be God's *own* predicament of a negation of incarnate negation that must *also* remain at once too formal and unidentified and *too* threatened by contamination by the abjected bride of Israel or the church in her whorish aspect?

The answer can only be *personne*. It would seem that Marion has opened himself to the infinite regress of a third-man problematic just *because* he refuses a genuine Platonism of analogical participation. But in that case Marion offers no phenomenology of love after all, but only another metaphysics of nothingness and absence.

Gift, Matter, and Theurgy

How would one remedy Marion's valiant attempt? In the first place, his phenomenology itself needs to be doubly crossed by a semiotics and an ontology if one is really to be able to speak of loving the other. Phenomenology is certainly an unavoidable gesture since all that is, by token of its excess over nothing, shows itself or *gives* itself. In the end, it seems that existence as such is given, since it is only present insofar as it variously manifests itself in such a fashion that it (at least in principle) affects "something else" in equally multiple ways. If Being itself is in this way a gift, an obscure offering of diverse benefit and meaning, then there are two ways of regarding such a circumstance. Either, for a kind of strict and immanentized Plotinianism, Being itself is nothing (not even Unity—a conclusion already arrived at within neo-Platonism by Damascius) and gives what it has not—namely, the diverse being that resides only in beings; or else Being as such is a giving and is therefore spiritual, which means intellectual and desiring.

In the first case, gifts that in no way derive from the giver are not really gifts at all, but are found, accidental "givens." This means in turn that all the "showings forth" of beings—such as the blue gleaming of a rock's surface for example—do not exhibit an effect that is itself the working out of a cause (like Proclus and Dionysius' *aitia*) but are rather the epiphenomena of the invisible essences of things—for example, their subatomic structures. The latter, like the Plotinian One, "give" what they do not have—namely, the rock and the gleaming—yet since this has no ground in the deeper reality, the hidden essence also "takes back" that which it seems to give. In this way, the showings forth of beings—their phenomena—lapse back into accidental epiphenomenality: the mere way they appear to be for other accidental creatures which, if it is not participating gift, must inevitably sink to the status of given illusion. But it is equally true that sundered from their appearings, beings are handed over to a confused coagulation of "underlying" realities, which themselves may be reduced to epiphenomena in their turn, *ad infinitum*. Without the reality of original being as gift or spirit, the very phenomenality of beings must be denied, such that beings themselves are subject to continuous fractal vanishing.[25]

In this way, nihilism is massively counter-intuitive, while traditional metaphysics and theology works by contrast to save the appearances of the natural attitude. Its sophistication concurs with the unreflexive reception of the world by the yeoman; whereas nihilism seeks to dispossess the yeoman by ensuring that he becomes the urban slave of postponed abstractions.

The traditional metaphysical gesture (Platonic, Aristotelian, Patristic, High Scholastic) therefore saves the constitutive gifts of the world by reading *esse* as originally *donum*. But were *donum* not also *esse*, then gift would be originally and always the gift of that which a preceding X has not and this, as we have seen, would be tantamount to a nihilistic undoing of the gift, as Claude Bruaire concluded.[26] Hence one must conclude that phenomenology alone cannot secure the gift: the phenomenon can only be received as a gift if it is also read as a sign of a reserved being, whose existence we speculatively affirm. To posit this reserve is to posit a source of gift and allow that there may be a giver, without whom the phenomena are not gifts.

If phenomenology is supplemented in this way by ontology, then the appearance of gift is only saved through the metaphysical speculation (which may equally be a spiritual experience, a "phenomenological" reception of the unreachable, beyond phenomenology as strict science) that all being as such is gift. This is the thesis that the world is *created*. Under this thesis one begins to consider the gift not, like Marion, within intersubjective experience, but rather within our speculative experience of all reality. In this section I briefly sketch what such an approach might imply for the philosophy of love. We will see that, in particular, it suggests that love of persons cannot be disentangled from love of things anymore than love itself can be considered apart from being and understanding.

Claude Bruaire argued that, if the Creation is the first receiving of gift such that it is, in itself, through and through gift without remainder, then it must originally subsist as the reflexive reception of itself as gift, which means the giving of a gift to itself, in an inadequate attempt to make the return of gratitude to the ultimate source.[27] As we have already seen, the gift is first received as mirror, even though mirror is preceded by gift. But, as Bruaire further contends, the giving of a gift to oneself involves spirit, and therefore it seems that spirit is *necessarily* the first work of creation; creation is not imaginable without spirit, for if the *logos* is first received entirely as gift by a gift (unlike the Greek instance where logic is first imposed on a purely passive matter) then the order of the world is first of all a conscious reasoning. To deny this, to suppose that there could rather have been a created cosmos without spirit, would be to fail to see that conscious spirit just is the reflexive reception of itself as gift—which must be the fundamental hidden and defining fact of creation. Creation is first of all a mirror as gift, and therefore it is first of all spirit. And this must indeed be why the wisdom literature of the Bible insists that wisdom was the first created of God's works (however one understands this in terms of the role of the angels, a world soul, humanity as microcosmic sustainer of the macrocosm, etc.). If this logic is Proclean, it is all the more creationist.

The material world that lies beneath the spiritual one is, as I have already suggested, in at least one aspect the productive working out of the failure of perfect spiritual reflection (but I mean here that of the angels or the world soul, or ourselves as preexistent souls—never ruled out by Augustine—not of ourselves in this life, as for Fichte). Yet it is more than a kind of guarantee of our separateness from God as the sphere of our freedom, as Bruaire suggests.[28] Unfortunately, he departs from a Proclean (or Dionysian or Maximian) scheme by substituting univocity and dialectics for analogy. Hence for Bruaire God still gives us *matter* that he has not, so constituting us as a kind of negation of his simplicity. Yet Aquinas, for example (in a Proclean line of reasoning), insists that already the angels, never mind God, eminently contain in their purely intellectual substance all that exists in lower domains. In the case of the angels this is a relatively abstract, universal inclusion, but in the case of God, whose perfect intellectuality can bring about the actual from nothing, it is a precise knowledge of material particulars, because God himself is the entire source of their actuality. (Here Aquinas exceeds the Proclean perspective.)[29]

In contrast to Bruaire, one can cleave more closely to Proclus by arguing, as I have already tried to do, that the very failure of mirroring reflection to return the original gift recovers something of the simplicity of the one or of *esse* that precedes reflection. Bruaire has no use for this thematic, since he follows Hegel in attributing reflexivity to God himself. However, Proclus already (if obscurely) envisaged a nonreflexive intelligence coincident with *dosis* [gift] alone (or that eminent possession of *dosis* of which he speaks) as belonging to the divine *henads* or gods who surround the One.[30] Christian theology indeed embraced the perfect thought thinking itself of Aristotle's God, yet it also took full account of the neo-Platonic demand that the first principle be utterly simple and in no way doubled. For Aquinas, God's "return" upon himself is usually reduced to a metaphor of self-subsistent intelligence, or else is seen as referring to God's perception in a simple mode of the return upon himself of creatures, envisaged from all eternity and included in the eternal outgoing of the *Verbum*.[31] Here, as for Dionysius, Maximus, Augustine, and Eriugena, as later for Cusanus, God's thought is a simple internal productive act and a vision only as a kind of absolutely realized *ecstasis* without return—a pure looking without "looking back," a looking that simply *is* the look.

Perhaps this idea of a simple production or *ecstasis* only makes complete sense in Trinitarian terms where the Son as product does *not* mirror the Father, just because the Father entirely *is* the generation of his being imaged (or "mirrored") by the Son. Trinitarian doctrine (at least in its most classic Cappadocian-Augustinian-Thomist lineage) is clearly not built on neo-Platonic doctrines of reflection, just because substantive relation conceives of a kind of hyperbolic reflection never considered by the neo-Platonic writers. Hegel's and Schelling's Trinitarian mediations, by falling back on neo-Platonic notions of reflection, unresolved contradiction, and negative refusal of original indeterminacy, fall behind and beneath these Patristic conceptual gains.

In effect, the latter preserved the neo-Platonic thought of the priority of the gift over the mirror, but by rendering this compatible with an original giver (spiritual, intellectual, and desiring) they rescued the Platonic notion from a destiny of collapse into nihilism, for which a source that gives what it does not have cannot really give (by intention) and may indeed start to be conceived as a monistic gulf before which all notions of emanation are exposed as illusion (as happens with Damascius). For substantive relation just is the thought of a unilateral doubling without reflection, which nonetheless sustains the reserve of the Father as giver over the Son as given-expressed (and so avoids the collapse of the Father–Son relation into a pure impersonal process without gift—as if one could simply see substantive relation as a "drawn line") by insisting that the Father–Son relation can itself proceed outward as a further substantive relation that is the Holy Spirit. If the latter simply *is* the interplay of love between the Father and Son (as Augustine taught), then it ensures that the substantive relation is not accomplished once, but is rather in some unchanging sense perpetual infinite circulation.

As an emphatically unilateral gift—which links the Spirit with that gift of grace that God bestows outward on us—the Holy Spirit nonetheless raises the gift of the Son above mere unilaterality by ensuring that his return to the Father, which is itself entirely given by the Father, is nonetheless also a kind of novelty for the Father that renews the Father in his source—a renewal that all the same constitutes the Father as source in the first place. Another way of putting this is to say that the Spirit's fusion of sign and act as *donum*—since a thing in order to be a gift must be both thing and sign—or the Spirit's pragmatic signifying act as interpreting "third" (in Piercean-Roycean terms) ensures that the Son's perfect expression as *signum* of the Father is nonetheless not a finitely closed expression negating all desire—divine desire that is infinite resource and also infinite and perpetual fulfillment. (My account here has something in common with Bruaire's adaption of Schelling—especially in his view that the Spirit saves the reserve of the Father, in terms of its non-Hegelian expressive positivity, beyond any merely negative reflection in the Son, since otherwise the Son might be held to exhaust and so to "cancel" the Father. However, I diverge from Bruaire's view that thereby all that the Spirit accomplishes is the pure assertion of divine freedom as formally free; to the contrary, it is more that the Spirit saves God as an infinitely determined meaning that yet also has the infinite interpretative openness of the poetic expression.)

Given the Catholic and Trinitarian conception of the ultimate principle as intellectual and *yet* as simple, one can allow a certain adaptation of the Proclean understanding of the material realm. As Jean Trouillard has shown, Proclus partially embraced the priority of the publicly and materially theurgic (or liturgical-magical) over the privately contemplative, just because for him the nonreflexive unity of the material realm in a certain way *recovers* the simplicity of the original One in a way that intellection does not. Moreover, it is body, subject to decay, that most immediately and spontaneously and emphatically "returns" to the ultimate source. Proclus also insisted that, throughout hierarchical descent, the first principle is more *strongly* operative than the lesser principles.[32] Since the latter's power gets weaker and weaker as one descends the hierarchical series, at the bottom of this series, at the nether limit (never really arrived at) of pure matter, *only* the first principle of the One remains causally operative. In this way, the neo-Platonic "series" or hierarchy (but the latter term is Christian, introduced by Dionysius) undergoes a paradoxical kenotic conversion. The "return" of the original gift that constitutes every level of reality happens more powerfully and more automatically beneath the realm of intellectual reflexivity and psychic motion. For this reason, the intellective soul that is perversely too attentive to the material it moves, and not to the unitive principles by which it moves, nevertheless begins its homeopathic cure in this very descent—rather as a man entering a brothel might discover that the only good he could enjoy therein would be something intrinsically demanding liberation from the brothel's confines. Sin is not necessary for redemption, yet the more acute our sin, the more acutely we realize that its only actuality is already the beginning of the work of redemption within us. (This is a great theme of modern Catholic literature that can be traced from Baudelaire through Bloy and Péguy to Bernanos and Graham Greene—perhaps its supreme exponent.) Because the soul in falling loses the vision that would alone prevent its fall, its only remaining recourse is to this homeopathic cure and to the sacramental (relative) innocence of matter that always remains open to the influence of the divine powers, such that through material operations we can reinvoke them. Here it is only our love of matter and our sensory desires that permit divine love once again to operate upon us.

This thematic was much less present in Plotinus, whose doctrine of the partially undescended human soul was allied to a priority of inward retreat and private escape from the world: the beginning of the later "turn to the subject." Nevertheless, even in Plotinus, the *lapsus* of the soul through failed self-mirroring back into productive gift, by which the soul itself gives matter as arising below itself, is not just negatively valued. For in Plotinus the soul also "gives time," and time is the time of discourse (as reflected in the *Enneads* themselves) by which we seek to *perfect* our giving of matter in such a way that we shall both assist and convoke its return to the One, and our poetic giving of matter will ever more nearly approximate to an intellectual self-mirroring.[33] But the gap in this self-mirroring is not to be considered as merely negative, either, since it also represents an echo of the gap between our never foreclosed intellectual reflection and the shadowy Simple One who stands always behind our backs, casting also its dim reflection into the mirror and thereby shattering it. (It remains the case though, that Plotinus, still less than Proclus, could not resolve the *aporia* whereby our advance to true intellectual identity must also resolve that identity into Oneness, even though this is impossible, since Plotinus was not a monist. Hence every true intellectual constructive giving of matter that is also an advance toward a more perfect self-reflection must be equally a deconstruction and a *lapsus* away from the One. Plotinus was in this way incipiently Derridean). In this fashion, as Plotinus sometimes indicates, his own contemplative activity, in its discursive aspect, is itself a mode of theurgy.

On the theurgic view, therefore, whether it regards public ritual or private contemplation, we are redeemed by a further descent into our very lapse—not that we should deliberately choose to fall further, but rather that sin always *is* a dynamic further falling into sin. While for humans to sink to the bestial or the inanimate is evil (because it abases our nature), the very relative good of these levels of reality in their own terms points upward in their inevitable subsistent return upon themselves to their donating source. The beauty of the seashore is never all-contenting—it enraptures us just because it suggests further horizons and obscurely calls forth from us some spiritual response of apostrophic praise.

This reversal of hierarchy is perpetuated by Aquinas when he says that, while God measures truth and our minds are measured by truth, the truth of created material things lies in the middle as both measured (by God) and itself measuring our minds.[34] This places matter *above* finite spirit in the hierarchy, despite the fact that in other places Aquinas insists that all the material creation exists for the sake of finite spirit. Later, Dietrich of Freiburg attempted a resolution of this seeming anomaly in such a way that human self-reflection does not require the detour via sensation, and the occasion of material sensation only provokes a production of knowledge by spirit entirely in its own terms (this foreshadowed German idealism).[35] But there is no anomaly here, if one allows that the human mind stands above the material world in its power to think, desire, and shape, but below the material world insofar as it cannot radically bring even a material thing into being (but only adapt its being or assist the divine bringing about of new being) and is confined to thinking and desiring always within a kind of fictional simulacrum of "conjecture," as the once again authentically Proclean Cusanus later put it. To be able thoughtfully to work places us above the material cosmos, but insofar as the latter is the *divine* work we remain within it and even beneath it. Our conjectural thoughts and vague desires in consequence reach their highest pitch when they attempt to blend poetically with the cosmos in every form of ritual enactment, and especially in the long, slow work of generations that seek to identify themselves and love themselves and their surrounding material reality by molding a "landscape" that realizes and expresses the human dwelling upon the earth and beneath the stars.

Here spirit, by reaching kenotically beneath itself, in fact repairs itself by merging its efforts with the (relatively) uncontaminated ones of matter seeking always its return. In this way human beings perform "rites" that do not command or influence, but nonetheless encourage sympathetically, the descent of the divine with which we thereby become "in tune." Even though our shaping imagination is involved here, and no "god" is present to us without our own mythical fictioning of a god, nevertheless our metaphorical self-expression in terms of material things possessing a simplicity without reflection (like rounded pebbles on the beach) helps to reinvoke the divine intellective power that is itself simple beyond our mode of troubled thought. In Christian terms, though, such is the forgetfulness of the human soul, and such is its pride, even on the seashore, that God himself must land from a boat across the abyssal waters separating Creator from Creation, in order to show us how to worship himself in time by truly loving the cosmos. Christ traces the path of the descent of sin to blood and shattered flesh, and homeopathically cures us by fixing our gaze on the beauty even of the cross and permitting us to taste even slaughtered flesh and shed blood as nourishing bread and wine returning us to spiritual health, since with us and through us they are always, as material elements, embarked on their own uninterrupted return to glory.

Any thought of the priority of the gift and the ultimacy of love requires something like this sketched theurgic metaphysic that has been transfigured by the arrival of love as an event in time—an event that has so cleansed our minds that we can, at least in principle, now see again the ultimacy of the gift that shines out to us through the structures of all being. Without this metaphysic, any merely immanent thought of love is liable to conclude, as with Marion, that it is scarcely attainable and so to threaten a collapse back into nihilism.

The Ontology of Love

Given the foregoing account of the logic of creation as gift and restoration of gift, we can derive an ontology of love that will complete and modify the phenomenology of love. Pure phenomenology seems to exhibit a kind of nominalist bias insofar as it seeks a rhapsodic knowledge of love simply in terms of love. This leads Marion to oppose the convertibility of the transcendentals as "metaphysical"—love as defining the good (in terms of gift) is for him an altogether different (and more basic) phenomenon than Truth, or Beauty, or Being, or Unity. Yet without a continuous overlap with Being, love can never refer to something or someone loved—it is bound to be reduced to a formal structure whose actuality (in terms of an identifiable other who will by reflex provide oneself with an actualized identity) is forever postponed. Yet of course love and Being do not absolutely coincide, for the good or truth or beauty of Being, although "convertible" with it, are also, along with being itself, irreducibly different "transcendental" facets of reality as such. It is in another mode, another register, that we have to speak of Being also as true unified, even if love always obscurely recognizes Being in its "true identity." Besides, love is only transcendental for spirit: Being as such may be lovable, but not all being loves. How can it be that love and Being are always conjoined—since love is of something, and any being whatsoever, as exhibiting some mode of unity, is to some degree lovable—and yet they do not entirely coincide, just as being and the good do not entirely coincide? The answer must be that there is something in ontological finitude that remains always constitutively obscure: we cannot fully describe any being within one transcendental register—say that of truth—and *yet* this register demands of itself that the other registers also be invoked. If it would seem that one must be able to speak of the truth of a being entirely in terms of truth (since the truth of a being ought to encompass everything about a being) and yet truth must refer of itself and ineluctably to other transcendental aspects that are incommensurate with truth—the appearing of a thing as attractively compelling (which alone shows its coherence of truth and so inspires the quest for the truth of this coherence) and so as beautiful, and then also as unified and good (for all truth must be desirable)—then there remains something obscure about truth. Likewise concerning all the other transcendentals and their corresponding spiritual stances of understanding, *aisthēsis, mathēsis,* and love. To remain true to love we must remain true to its unclarity and its continuing manifestation only as the repeated arrival of an obscure event. Christianity after all, especially St. Paul, speaks of the *arrival* of love in time and the showing forth to a fallen world without love that love is indeed the first principle. This is not to be taken as simply the restoration to our sight of a true phenomenology, but rather as the restoration to our sight of the original paradisal process of love that was never even then "clear and distinct" in finite terms, since it exercised itself only as a participation in a love that is infinite.

One should nevertheless note here that Marion's "clear and distinct" is not supposed to preclude the truth that love is a mystery (any more than Descartes's clear and distinct idea of infinity amounts to comprehension). However, if love does not analogically participate in simple and infinite love, then a supposedly "clear" grasp of its formality precludes any further (and endless) *advance* into its mystery, with the consequence that its mystery is reduced to the status of a permanently foreclosed "secret." The projection onto God of an infinite instance of love, univocally comprehended, does not restore love as mystery, but simply infinitizes the secret, which, if penetrable by God, can only concern his will beyond love, since the understanding of love is supposed to be sufficiently secured by its formal definition. (In the same way the "mystery" of the Cartesian infinite lapses into the untrammeled freedom of the divine *voluntas.*)

So in order to sustain the mystery of love, we must remain with the natural attitude, and the contours of ordinary speech, and allow that its reality is tangled up with other apparently "comprehensive" phenomena with which it is not obviously commensurate. This renders love inescapably obscure, such that one cannot "distinctly" define even its mystery. Although the discourse and practice of love should in principle be self-sufficient, since love (like knowledge) is absolute, they are in reality tangled up in the search for knowledge and the vision of the beautiful. We can only read this circumstance as rational and not a delusion if we allow that our finite love remains obscure because it is only an imitative fragment of that infinity that is itself love in exactly the same (for us unknowable) way that it is knowledge, *aisthēsis* and *poesis*. This perspective ensures that infinite love is a boundless mystery whose depths (as St. Paul says) we cannot fathom, and not simply an infinite degree of a phenomenon adequately known to us in finite terms. In the latter case theology would seem only to be involved in a regulative fashion, or else in order to guarantee the reality of our problematic finite love—an attempt that we have seen must fail, since, if our finite love is problematic, an infinite degree of this same univocally understood love will only infinitize its problem.

Where, by contrast, love is but partially understood, since it remains finitely unclear, then nevertheless it can be *somewhat* understood and does not dissolve into the *aporias* that always attend pure formality, just because it is seen as always obscurely linked to the incommensurate register of understanding. Love, since it is love of the known, cannot be fully known only as love; but equally, since knowledge is what is desired by desire, knowledge cannot be fully loved and prized only as knowledge. In finite existence we sense that the transcendentals in reality coincide, but finitude is itself partially constituted by their very division. Finitude declares its secondariness by dividing simplicity into absolutely overlapping aspects and by hinting at an impossible commensurability of seemingly incommensurable registers—of loving, *mathēsis*, *aisthēsis*, and *poesis*.

This points to the second metaphysical modification of a phenomenology of love. Love is analogical, not univocal. One can, however, agree with Marion that friendship is not equivocally diverse from sexual love and *eros* from *agapē*. These are, after all, species of a *genus* of love proper to human*kind* in its own interactions. But perhaps, by contrast, the love of things is only analogous to the higher love of persons and this in turn to the love of God. For one cannot enjoy mutual giving and receiving with things, and yet our experience of caring for things and receiving their benefits tends to a kind of apostrophization that allows one to understand this lower love analogically in terms of the higher love for persons. Inversely, since human (unlike angelic persons) only appear via the medium of thinghood, one has to speak of interhuman love improperly and so analogically in terms of our love for things and bodies, sounds, smells, and images and the expression of our "common sensing," which is language (whose "meaning" springs from the impossible blending of incommensurate sensory sources). It is this inevitably improper and metaphorical speaking of love that Marion tries to avoid. Moreover, the participatory invasion of human love by God, angels, and things ensures that even the variety of human love (irreducible to the species of *agapē, philia, eros,* etc.) assumes an analogical character.

Finally, one is forced to speak even of divine love in terms taken from our love of things as well as persons. Attribution to God and angels of grossly material images must, Dionysius insisted, sometimes theurgically and negatively correct our use of seemingly more appropriate personal images.[36] (In this way he was perhaps more open than Aquinas to the idea that God, by a genuinely analogical use of metaphor, could be eminently "rock" as much as eminently "wisdom" and so forth.) Our speech about divine love is analogical, because in God there is no real division of the transcendentals, even if our *modus cognoscendi* is forced to speak as if there were. Thus to speak of the divine love, as Marion does, in isolation from the divine being and understanding, is to compromise the divine simplicity, if we assume that the God who is indeed "before being" as we experience being, nonetheless also "is" and also infinitely comprehends. How else does one avoid the inappropriate idea of secondary moments in God? Moreover, if God simply is the infinite instance of one aspect of our life in this world—namely love—then God is surely idolized.

However, love has a yet more intimate relation to analogy than the above would suggest. If being is analogical, then, beyond the generic-specific-differential combination of "same in some respects, different in others," being must exhibit more fundamental instances at the transgeneric level where same and different coincide and are impossibly mediated. For Plato, *to know* as such is indeed to know how same and different coincide, and to know ultimate reality without (as in the *Advaida Vedanta*) canceling the ultimate reality of knowledge, is obscurely to know a level where an original monism and an original principle of differentiation are somehow in harmony with other.[37] This is tantamount to declaring that it is the principle of harmony itself that is ultimate. Also, for Plato, this obscurity of our intellectual reach shows that it is always bound up with the *desire* for such a harmonious blending. Yet the latter is in itself the full realization of desire as the demonic *metaxu* or "between," since the blending of the same and the different is the very essence of love. Were friends entirely not alike, says Plato in the *Lysis,* then they would be enemies, but were they entirely alike then they would seem not to require each other as friends.[38] Therefore, friendship requires the coincidence of the like and the unlike.

It follows that, if knowledge seeks ultimately to recognize and adjudicate analogical blending, love is the very source and power of such blending. There can be no univocal concept of love because love is in itself analogy. Where this is apparently denied, as by Marion, one loses the realm of the ontological "between" that fuses the lovers into one flesh. Instead, one has a perfect mirroring of two formally identical acts of love that intersect. But then the lovers need each other only in absolutely not needing each other. It is wholly unclear that there is any real *desire* at work here, since the lover's advance to the other is described rather as absolute commitment and his hope for the other's recognition of himself is framed as the hope for her counter-commitment. In what sense is such commitment desire? Erotic desire must be for the other's presence, for a delightful merging of words and bodies. And in fact, for it to be possible for the lover to advance toward the other, such presence must always already have begun when she permits my unrestricted entry into her eroticized space. The latter is only possible if, *at least to some degree,* I have already admitted her into my space, since otherwise she could not address me or hold my attention at all. Therefore, my relatively unilateral gift of love *presupposes* an already-begun reciprocity. Without at least some sign—albeit perhaps unconscious—that a gift would be welcomed by the recipient, a gift can never even begin to be a gift, as opposed to an unwelcome intrusion. It follows in consequence that reception is coincident with gift, or even precedes it.

For a genuine ontology and phenomenology of the gift, reciprocity is therefore a transcendentally protological condition of possibility for giving, not simply (as for Marion) its eschatological horizon. One may suppose (with Derrida) that this assumed reciprocity must reduce to a balanced trade-off for mutual benefit, thereby canceling the very possibility of giving that it seems to allow. But this is to ignore the further circumstance that this assumed reciprocity is not just transcendental origin and final telos, but also a mutual product—a particular idiolect of *this* unique love, which is already a "third" existing for its own sake as the valued "between" of love and not as any recompense for a preceding expenditure. Marion entirely ignores the Platonic thesis that love is *poros* as well as *penia,* resource as well as lack. He insists that love as lack alone defines us, since we can be robbed of our possessions but not of our need. But I have already argued that desire for the unreserved commitment of the other is scarcely desire for the other as other, and if a lack defines us this is still a lack of a specific thing that we *might* possess. Such a possibility makes no sense without reference to an already at least somewhat present actuality. It is true that a possessed thing might be removed from us, yet *contra* Marion it can still define us, because it may continue to bear our trace—like a book that we have written on in the margins—and so might remain associated with us for many centuries of its passage into other hands. Such a possession is a *product* of our desire to express ourselves as well as to own, and here again Marion refuses to allow that desire is a pregnancy as much as it is frustration. As Plato describes in the *Symposium,* we desire the other because he provides a lacking medium through which we will be able to bring to birth ideas that were so far just struggling to emerge.[39] Therefore the shared and produced *ambience* of love, the *entre-nous* as Marion terms it, is not simply ontological but also cognitive. If love is obscurely mixed with knowledge because there must already be reciprocal knowing if there is to be unconditional gift, then equally knowledge is obscurely mixed with love because friendship and sexual love is an inseparable part of what helps to advance human understanding.

Love, then, can only be known as the obscure love of infinite knowledge; it can only be pursued as the obscure knowledge of infinite love. But in that case it is inherently partial, and can only be culpably deficient when it lacks even that participation of which it is capable. This is the third modification that can be made by ontology to a phenomenological perspective. The latter, in refusing metaphysical speculation (which can, however, also be seen as the phenomenological appearing of the invisible in the visible, apparent only to subjective judgment), tends to disallow that a recognizable subjective reality could be simply the relative absence of what *should* be there were a proper finite speculation (practical as well as theoretical) concerning the infinite properly carried through. Hence it finds it hard to think of evil or falsity simply as deficiencies of true phenomena, rather than as phenomena in their own right. Since hatred is real, runs the argument, it must positively appear to us, else it would be falsely, speculatively, and metaphysically considered.

In Marion's case, this encourages the view that hatred and jealousy are original, basic phenomena that arise inevitably from human existence as such. But this ontologization of hatred is scarcely compatible with Catholic orthodoxy. Furthermore, an *ontology* as well as phenomenology of hatred is implicitly allowed by Marion, where an ontology of love is not conceded by him. This is because, as we have seen, it is the very (supposed) emptiness of being that gives rise to hatred and the very (supposed) inevitable submission of the sexual to the sub-personal and idolatrous that gives rise to jealousy and rapine. But in that case the thesis depends on suppositions that we have already showed to be questionable. We have also already seen how, if love arises only as the phenomenological negation of ontological hatred, it can never quite assume any secure reality. Indeed Marion's admission that confirmation of the vow is always postponed, is tantamount to the further admission that the phenomenon of love actually *seeks* being if it is ever going to be either secure or even identifiable, in which case love can no longer truly "be" before being, as the convolution of this very sentence would suggest. And if love cannot sing its own rhapsody as phenomenon, then it exists only as the gnostic or Manichean gesture of negation in the face of a world of inevitable hatred: a world where being as such is construed as agonistic.

But we have further already seen that this conception is at best highly counter-intuitive. Simply because I and the things that surround me can appear only as, in various ways, unified, they invite my love, and therefore what I hate is nothing positive (since no absolute non-unity could ever appear) but always an absence of a unity that I obscurely sense as lacking.

If, conversely, love is first conceived only as a negative refusal of the actual, then it first arises as a possibility. Yet Marion himself produces instances against his own thesis when he insists, first of all, that even imagined love is always a making love with an imagined actual or once actual lover, and, in the second place, when he finally and rightly insists that no one by virtue of birth can really claim not to have known love.[40] One should radicalize this affirmation by saying that no one can claim by the very "thrownness" of his being not to have known love. Were this not the case, then one would have to ask how it is that love must then be something whose possibility we could envisage out of our own resources alone—and this, *unlike* the notion of self-love, would truly be a solipsistic thesis incompatible with Marion's correct affirmation that love can only be known as the presence of another in me closer to myself than myself to myself. Following Marion's own trajectory, therefore, love must be always already actual in order to be possible, but if this is the case, then it must originally arise within the sphere of Being, of beings, and of visible material beings (in our case). One can note here that Marion's refusal of a privative view of evil again encourages harsher judgments than Catholic ethical theory would truly allow. For if love or hate are either "present or not," one is then led, like Marion, to affirm that the unfaithful lover is not even in any degree faithful or even that infidelity—since it renders the formal gesture of love in its formality an outright lie—ensures that any reconciliation after infidelity becomes more or less impossible. If, by contrast, love is seen more as a continuous habit, then relative interruption of this habit and its resumption seem less inconceivable. (When Marion *also* says, with profundity, that in a real sense we always do remain to a degree faithful to all our advances as lovers, this would seem to suggest that infidelity is only the *privation* of faithfulness.)

One can agree with Marion, as I have just said, that the loved other lies deeper within me than I do to myself. But one should be more cautious than he is concerning this transfer of a theological trope to the intersubjective realm. The transfer can hold if the other in me mediates God in me. That certainly applies for Marion, yet he also affirms the trope in an immanent scenario where God is for the moment bracketed. This seems less satisfactory, for it treats the distance between spirit and spirit as though it were an ontological difference, whereas it is a distance that is but one aspect of an analogical *metaxu,* where differences blend with a certain sureness. For the New Testament, the Christological point of reference for human sexual love is the love of Christ for his Bride, the Church, a love wherein Christ's physical temporal body flows into and mingles with potentially the bodies of all other human beings. Here there is conceived a certain fusion, a certain shared intergenerational (re)production of the body of Christ. But Marion, as we have seen, without biblical warrant conceives of human erotic love on the model of the hypostatic union itself.[41] This means that there is a perfect union but without blending or any change between the intuitions of either lover, just as there is no change in either the divine or human nature within the God-Man. This effectively disallows any real temporal development or mutual influence in human love, and Marion indeed sees the "future" under the erotic reduction simply as an empty waiting for the loved one, rather than as a continuous inventive traversing of all the signs of his coming.[42] It also disallows any true spatial meeting, any eroticization of a shared spatial domain whereby alone, as we have seen, any actual eroticization can arise at all.

Inversely, when Marion considers briefly the Incarnation as such, at the end of *Le Phénomène érotique,* it is precisely the Logos–Bride relation that he has in mind—and this must be included if the entire human scenario of love is to be transferred to the divine instance, since one has (supposedly) secured already the exact univocal concept of love as such. But the implication of the transfer would be that the real relation of Christ to the Bride is unorthodoxly projected back from Christ's humanity onto his divine nature and divine personhood, taken apart from its enhypostasization of the humanity. Hence God would be himself sucked into the tragic erotic drama of ontological reality, in which matter is conceived as being at once a necessary detour and yet also as something finally to be abjected.

Instead of this gnosticism, the perspective of Christianized theurgy suggests rather that God descends to marriage with the Bride so as to realize by kenotic descent his secret affinity with the simplicity of the inanimate—in order to renew the human spirit when it has lost its native animation through prideful self-affirmation and a turning to matter in a desire to dominate it. This can only render matter a wasteland, but God incarnate reactivates the unquenchable healing wells hidden within the wasteland itself.

The metaphysical modification of the phenomenology of love suggests, therefore, that finite love can only be thought of in relation to infinite love and that love belongs to a hierarchical series: to love is to proceed within a process of love that reflexively contemplates and actively gives—a process that begins before us, flows through us, and continues on after us (following the perspective of Dionysius the Areopagite).[43]

Love and Hierarchy

But what might it mean to think of love and gift in terms of hierarchy rather than in terms of equality—or at least only in terms of full equality when it comes to the divine Trinity or "thearchy"? This might seem like an unattractive approach to the concept of love and the notion of gift. But maybe, to the contrary, it permits a final resolution of the *aporias* of gift and love. I have already started to hint how this might be so, but now the thesis must be systematically presented.

The crucial debate about the gift concerns the issue of unilaterality versus reciprocity. Both models, however, seem fundamentally to envisage a situation of equality as pertaining between giver and recipient. One can ask here whether either the realism of this assumption or its implications have ever been fully thought through.

To take the latter first. Kant's ethical theory can be seen as paradigmatic for the unilateral model: ethics is entirely to do with a one-way duty toward the other, and nothing to do with the establishment of mutual affinity. On the other hand, this unilateral duty is to be exercised strictly toward an *equal*, toward an equally free spirit, and therefore toward someone who could in principle reciprocate one's very unilaterality. Therefore, the combination of unilaterality with assumed equality always ensures that the specter of reciprocity will reintrude. We have seen the same thing in the case of Marion's *croisée des chairs*, where the specter is positively embraced. This situation can appear all the more questionable when one reflects that a better paradigm for pure unilaterality would be the hierarchical and impersonal instance where one gives something to an animal or even tends a rose.

The Kantian ethical imperative stands in strict contrast to a contingent interested imperative that could be fulfilled within a market exchange for mutual benefit. Here one has the specifically modern contrast of private, purely "free" ethical gift and public—economic or political—contract. Yet is this contrast so absolute? Is not rather the pure, unilateral gift itself a case of contract—of absolute and completely perfect reciprocal exchange between all and all and for all times in the Kingdom of Ends? My one-way duty is absolute and indifference just *because* I know that it is reversible and due also to me. Lévinas's ethics is an attempt to escape the predicament, but it fails, since the only concreteness of the "face" that he envisages is its negative claim on my compassion, which remains formal and reversible. Marion repeats this formalism in his claim that the *visage* is constituted only by staring pupils—as if the very set and aspect of our face did not convey by habit the modes of our looking at the world and articulating it, along with ourselves within it. Nevertheless, Marion—having ignored the way out of the dilemma just indicated—tries to avoid ethical reversibility by considering regard for the other in its more fundamental erotic rather than ethical form. Yet here also, as we have seen, the reduction of *eros* to total self-commitment ensures its symmetrical correlation with a possible formally mirroring reciprocation. Since Marion never succeeds in rescuing the vow from formalism, his guarding of *eros* against automatism rests in the end entirely upon a *contract*.

Hence the private realm of the free gift in modernity is not one of refuge from the capitalist market—to the contrary, it is its hidden precondition as the ultimately contracted "trust" of all with all. The emptiness of this trust in its regard for abstract freedom is precisely the license that each grants to each to pursue unlimited and pointless commercial production and exchange.

Equal unilaterality therefore reduces to the purest symmetrical reciprocation.

How stands it, by contrast, with equal reciprocation? Here one can take the case of the modern market contract, the aim of which is not one of sharing and mutuality: hence reciprocity is in a certain sense excluded. It is apparently present in the sense of "mutually achieved satisfaction" and a transaction judged to be fair. However, market conditions always secretly coerce the circumstances under which the transaction takes place, such that the participants submit to necessity or ambition (or both), not to any sense of an inherent justice in the exchange as such. Money is given by one party because it has to be given and so according to a one-way inexorable flow in which the payer of the price has no interest in the further destiny of his coinage, nor in that of the person he is buying from. The money passes with *absolute* unilaterality, just because there is only an arbitrary and conventional connection between the coinage and the articles purchased. Likewise, the seller of the article absolutely dispenses with it by a unilateral gesture, since he has no further interest in it, nor in its new owner. Both persons in the transaction wear impersonal masks and make non-intersecting gestures. Inversely, the recipient of the money receives it as a unilateral passage, since this is like money from nowhere, forming no bond with its source, while the recipient of the commodity likewise derives it as coming in a one-way direction toward him, its final destiny, as if from nowhere.

Therefore, if equal unilaterality is deconstructible as reciprocity, equal reciprocity is reciprocally deconstructible as coinciding (or "crossing") unilateralities.

There is in point of fact an interesting circumstance where the modern free (supposedly unilateral) gift and the modern bound (supposedly reciprocal) contract coincide—and that is the crucial instance of the will, testament, or *legacy*.

Here it is notable that gift and contract are only distinguishable in terms of spatial categories. But society is just as fundamentally a continuity in time. And here the contrast breaks down: freedom can only remain outside contract so long as it is exercised in the present and clearly testified to. But the continued free exercise of a *dead* will requires witnesses and a written record if the gift is to pass down through time. Here "gift" becomes a legal category and something that is itself contracted.

But one can also look at this situation the other way round. In this case contract necessarily becomes gift because the contract made by the dead person with the future can never be made between him and others, but must be made in a self-binding fashion with himself—such that the contracted last will and testimony is also the supreme instance of the constitutively personal act by which one gives oneself to oneself. This is possible because the dying person will not live to revise what turns out to be (after death) his "final will and testament." Beyond any possibly revisable act of will lies the will (however regrettable) that one will never live to revise.

Hence—embarrassingly for the bourgeoisie—at death everything private becomes public (personal property) while everything public becomes private (the fate of the public company or corporation). Here contract is entirely unilateral gift of self to self and self to the future, but gift is entirely the contractual binding of future generations—such that every legacy will tend to be curse as much as benefit. In this manner space gives way to time, but time is endlessly entailed to the spatial domain.

The collapse into each other of contract and gift under conditions of spatial equality reveals that both are equally reducible to formal circumstances of transcendental space—which is always both an endless journey without return and a traveling in a circle. However, the coincidence of the two as final testament exhibits a tension and indeterminism affecting gift and contract in relation to time: are we spatially entailed to the past or has a perverse legacy evicted us from spatial security? The introduction of the temporal dimension has in fact upset the equal equation, since now the past is above the present commanding it, even if a well-invested legacy may permit an eventual hierarchical reversal.

I further consider this link between time and hierarchy presently. But for now we might ask how it stands, by contrast, with the reciprocity as found within gift exchange. Here there is no counter-gift due, and yet for the sake of mutuality a counter-gift is in some sense expected. To retain its surplus of gift over contract this gift must be a nonidentical repetition of the first gift, spatially asymmetrical in relation to it and surprising both in its content and timing and *yet* appropriate to the donee. Thus it must show to her a *new* way to go that she will accept. In this sense there is an element of unilaterality within gift exchange, which is confirmed by the fact that giving can never be foreclosed. Though the aim is reciprocal mutuality that constitutes the bonds of love through joint production of a third (that still sustains the distance of the two) and through ever-renewed attention to the specific identity and needs of the other (dimensions that Marion seems to ignore), no counter-gift ever cancels the debt incurred by the original gift, since it always inaugurates a new debt—but a positive debt because it establishes a relationship that allows one to go on being a giver. In this way, mutual human indebtedness participates in our constitutive ontological and spiritual debt to God. Thus for there to be mutual love projected into the future, reciprocity must be ceaselessly interrupted by unilaterality. If modern free gift and liberal formal contract (that immediately cancels any ontological debt, so ridding itself of the irritation of necessary social interaction) collapse into each other, then gift exchange seems rather perpetually to oscillate between the reciprocal and the unilateral.

But this reminds one somewhat of the indeterminacy of the willed legacy that was linked to time. The oscillation in gift exchange arises in part because of the inescapability of the temporal dimension. Yet as in the case of the modern legacy, with time comes hierarchy. The born must be raised; the young must be educated; the present must always first yield to the past if it wishes to reverse the hierarchy and surpass the past in the future. Legacy is ambivalently the opportunity of time or the curse of spatializing entail, because it does not necessarily assume any shared horizon of value. In the case of gift exchange, however, this shared horizon *must* be assumed, because the giver only has an interest in the destiny of his gift and in it returning to him in some (nonidentical) fashion within a shared social universe of meaning that can determine what should count as gifts at all. And if a gift has to be an "appropriate surprise," then it always has a kind of educative dimension within a temporal and temporary hierarchy. The giver (or sometimes the recipient) is *for now* on top and able benignly (or not) to impose himself on the donee. Then she, in turn, can counter-impose. But just because the gift is not a formally unilateral gesture (for the perfectly unilateral and equal gift cannot have a content, as both Marion and Derrida insist, and so cannot be present in being—i.e., exist—as gift at all) but equally is not a perfect reciprocity without debt, gift exchange never really takes place within equal relations but always within hierarchical ones—either in a long series, or in a series of hierarchical oscillations and reversals forming what Jacques Godbout calls a "tangled hierarchy" to complement the "strange loop" of a never fully balanced and so completed reciprocity.[44]

One can see how this is the case even with ordinary conversations, which always exceed, even in modernity, liberal norms. People are not normally granted permission as to when to speak, and still less as to what they may say. Hence every piece of talk is an uncontracted interruption of the other, never truly civil or polite at all. It always offers a gift that opens something up for the other: though she may refuse this, she is always too late to prevent the influence on her will that she has in no sense pre-allowed. The best that freedom and equality can here manage (though this may be the true and the genuinely best equality and freedom) is a mutual play of interferences, a rolling spiral of hierarchical oscillation through time.

In the longest perspective this concerns the relation of one generation to the next. Here, while one can agree with Marion that the child's payment of his debt of love is primarily to his own children, this is not exhaustively the case. There is a sense in which, to the contrary, the parent and the teacher transmit a gift of love with little effort, since they simply convey the treasure-store of the past (genetic and cultural). Children and pupils, however, in their hard struggle to assimilate this, offer back to their guardians the surprising fruit of their inventively loving responses that already starts to reverse the hierarchy—in conveying back (in "theurgic" fashion) to tired reflection simpler and more spontaneous responses that well up from the novice's material energies.

In working with these energies, as in cultivating a garden, we do indeed give what we do not have, since we represent just one strand in the warp of many parallel emanative series. Yet the higher one reaches up the hierarchical chain of being and finally to God, the more one arrives at a giving of what one already has (albeit only in the mode of gift, as the Trinity exemplifies), and even at a giving of a response to this gift. Here finally, reciprocity and unilaterality no longer oscillate but coincide—yet not in the false sense of liberalism, where the two things are equally possible descriptions of one formation, like the drawing of a duck-rabbit, because each in fact *nullifies* the other: free gift is not really gift because it is exact contract; exact contract is not really exact *and just* contract because it is really free gift as the will to power of binding the future.

In the supreme instance of the divine gift, by contrast, the gift is unilateral *because* it is also reciprocal. God gives to be and so he gives also the reception of return of the gift and first of all spirit, as we have seen. It is not that God gives *some part* of the gift of response and the recipient another aspect—as on a Molinist theory of grace. It is rather that at one level God unilaterally does all the work, and yet at another level the responses of spirit and the rest of creation are entirely its own. Here the dualist conditioning/conditioned structure of most (but one should rather say modern) philosophy as identified by Francois Laruelle is already left behind.[45] There is no contrast of a conditioning prime reality—in this case God—and a conditioned reality—in this case Creation—that ensures that the conditioning must really be conceived in terms of the conditioned and therefore can only be idolatrously envisaged. Here instead, the human spirit thinks God and Creation only together, since it thinks of God as emanative giver, not efficient cause, of the Creation, and the Creation as the gift that follows from the fact that God is intrinsically a free-giving love (this allows that the Creation did not have to be, but only because God's being is itself a free affirmation and gift that would betray its own nature if it did not share itself without stint). God is eminently the gift that he gives; the Creation as "effect" is its own cause and reflective explanation, since the effect being gift just is the operation of the "cause" in its intrinsic nature.

Nor does the human spirit seek to represent God to itself by positing a concept of the first principle that it has already presupposed.[46] Rather, the human spirit seeks to enter into the divine gift that provides unilaterally a created response by enacting within itself and its ritual performances in the world the imitative descriptive approximation to the divine source that follows ineluctably upon its "axiomatic" imagining of the divine nature.[47] God is not something we represent, but something we receive, such that to enact the effect is to know, by perpetuating the cause. Likewise, we do not know the world by representing it, but by participating in its constant generation, as gift and return—both by our mystical interior ascent and external ritual descent. The human thinker must be a mystic and a liturgist if he is also to be a philosopher. And ontology can only be delineated through constructive participation in ontogenesis.

Of course one can oppose to theology the counter supreme axiom that reality as such is nothing.[48] But in that case, one's invented and decided-upon worlds (like so many alternative geometries), just because they receive no gift and imitate no reality, will have to collapse into the spectral philosophic space where certain stable "given" (and not gifted) conditions are assumed, presupposed, and conjecturally posited by our descriptions, while everyday reality is regarded as "conditioned" by this imagined foundation. By contrast, the theological supreme axiom liberates us entirely from the indifference and yet mutual confirmation that prevails between condition and conditions. For under its *aegis,* the initial condition is *only* the setting up of the conditioned, since it is itself but the eminent sway of the gift.

In this way gift is "without contrast." God is gift, but creation is the same gift in its return because it is, as Eriugena put it, "created God." Gift is thereby no longer negatively defined, as with Marion, as "not contract," "not reciprocity," "not a thing due," and so forth, but instead it is conceived as transcendentally prior to any thought of necessity, or thing due, or inherent nature. One can think of things as primarily gifts and so as ineluctably return in their deepest presence. Thus one can think of the Creation not as a gift to chaos, but as a production *ex nihilo*. Thus likewise one can think of grace, not as something in addition to the nature of created spirit, but rather as the way spirit must accomplish, like all creatures, its self-constitutive return: since spirit is intellectual, it must make this return intellectually, and therefore in receiving the universal gift of creation it automatically receives also the supplementary gift of deification as the conscious will to return.[49] (Of course this gift must be contingently renewed after the Fall by the event of the arrival of love in time.)

If God alone fully gives without contrast and gives, unilaterally, a reciprocity, nevertheless every finite gift to some extent anticipates and starts to provide, through educative influence of the other, its own counter-gift. Moreover, this is especially true in the case of our loving of children, animals, and even the inanimate. Precisely because gift is a complex hierarchy and ideally a unilateral exchange (in the divine one-way giving of return) love extends also beneath spirit to material creatures whom we help to "raise up" through human apostrophizing *poesis* to a quasi-spiritual level, while their own automatic return is a necessary assistance to our own spiritual return in a fallen world. We love even things, just as they also, and sometimes especially, convey to us the love of God.

As Plato indicates in the *Lysis*, love cannot simply be unilateral—for then one loves ideally enemies and enemies become friends, which is contradictory. But *neither* can love be perfectly mutual, as when one shares what one equally possesses, a love of the good, as on Aristotle's model of friendship. For in that case friends would never assist each other, which seems wrong.[50] The trouble with both modes of love is that they presuppose equality. But if we think of love instead as hierarchical (or rather in terms of oscillating hierarchies), then we can see how love educates the other, opens a path for him, in such a way that a unilateral gift is always the gift also of the possibility of a response. And *this* logic is transhuman and transpersonal: it runs from God through angels to humans to things. In loving even things we give to them also an incitement of their response, which is the speaking of Creation itself. In this way, a metaphysical theology alone thinks love beyond humanism (which is disguised nihilism) as not only human, but also divine and also material. Only such a love can be thought and desired as love at all.

The Haunting of the Phenomenology of Love

In the previous four sections, I have consistently questioned the enterprise of seeking a pure phenomenology of love. This would endeavor to render the logic of love fully apparent for a radically passive subject—a subject receiving love. But the primary problem here is that from the outset such an approach thinks of love, not as an ontological state of affairs pertaining "between" people, but rather in terms of unilateral gift: whether my decision to give or my receiving of the free gift of the other. If, to the contrary, love is inherently interpersonal (or rather, beyond this, inter-ontic) then it is possible that a merely phenomenological approach will never be able to think this interpersonality at all.

That this is a problem in Marion's approach is shown by his oscillation between the priority of the giver and the priority of the recipient. At first it is the latter: in order to banish vanity, one requires recognition from the other —yet this, as we have seen, turns out to be impossible. Then, to the contrary, it is rather the lone ego who must blindly make the advance of the unilateral donation of love. In one sense, Marion's account of this moment has to remain all-sufficient: the one-sided advance is the *entire* ground of love, and the lone lover achieves a self-assurance and self-recognition that appears to lack nothing.[51] The lover here "loves love" itself. But one should question whether this can really be the case. Since, in order to be free of any "interest" nothing of the beloved can here appear to view at all, the lover would appear merely to be in love with the idea of self-abandonment, precisely as that of which he cannot be robbed. Therefore this extreme dispossession of the ego, far from ensuring any priority for alterity, is simply the dialectical realization of egoity itself as pure unshakeable self-possession. (And this is stoicism, not St. Augustine.)

Nevertheless, as we have seen, Marion fully admits that, while the opening to love may be fully gained here (which I would deny), a sense of individual self-identity and of the achievement of love in act is still lacking. For this reason, the initial questions as to whether I can be loved from elsewhere and whether I can love first of all give way to a third synthesizing question—namely, whether the other can manifest herself "from herself" to me by a counter-intention.[52] In the final chapter of *Le Phénomène érotique* this question in turn gives way to an affirmation: "Yes you have loved me first of all," and it is revealed that secretly, all along, the erotic reduction has only been possible in terms of "an advance before my advance" that is at once the love that all, in some sense, receive down the generations and also (somewhat obscurely) the mediation of the love of God.[53] Without this pre-advance, I could never come to love myself, since I am inherently hateful and can only come finally (as the most difficult act of love) to love myself because miraculously—and without reason, without any recognition of anything in me that is objectively good and so lovable—someone has first loved me.

But it is very difficult to understand how this squares with Marion's earlier affirmation of the priority of the unilateral advance or, indeed, how it can be coherent—for it would seem that the counter-advance of the other must be made without his first being loved from elsewhere, and would achieve a self-affirmation or self-love also without being recognized by the other. In the same way it is equally hard to comprehend how, after all, love is always transmitted down the generations, given Marion's initial demonstration that the hatred of all for all is the prior reality—only to be interrupted by the *fiat* of an individual, unilateral advance. If, in fact, one can *neither* first receive love from the other *nor* instigate it oneself, then the prior love from the other must indeed concern the intervention of a *Deus ex machina*. Here it would not be the case that the other mediates to us by participation the love of God— such that God, as prior cause "gives" to the other a capacity to respond in love and in turn to give a love that is fully "his" at the level of secondary causality— on the hierarchical model of "unilateral exchange" that I have already delineated. Instead it would be the case that the other was merely the occasion for a divine intervention that would miraculously override his autonomy.

In this way, Marion's final invocation of God as "infinite subject" who is univocally within the same plane of love as human beings, appears to mark the instability of his phenomenology of love, which fails to locate love either in the pole of the giver or the recipient. He makes a kind of negative obeisance to an ontology of love by insisting that, for mutual identification of personhood and for the actualization of *eros,* there must be a "crossing" of regards and of the flesh. But as this is the invisible intersection of two equally invisible, purely unilateral gestures, no true reciprocity results. We have seen from an invoca- tion of *The Gift of the Magi* that if, truly, one has the *eschaton* of two perfectly symmetrical self-abandoning gestures, then my self-abandonment receives and accepts the self-abandonment of the other and vice versa. What then results is total mutual acceptance only as mutually assured destruction. One can object here that each receives from the other an infinite, indestructible love. But if such love renounces entirely the visibility of the other to oneself as well as one's own visibility for the other, then all one has, after all, is a contractual exchange of a perfect formal idea of love. Such an idea has lost sight of its initial *raison d'être,* which was the actual meeting and narrative merging of specific *characters* expressed through bodily actions and the words of language. This meeting and merging is the diegetic context in which the plot motifs of abandonment and sacrifice alone make sense; whereas to raise self-abandonment into the essence of love is to lose sight of the plot and create a scenario where pure personalism fades into the nihilistic abyss. Love is not by essence self-abandonment, precisely because it concerns also an *attention* to the specificity of the other and the need to provide her with *appropriate* gifts—which means (again *contra* Marion) that the real gift remains always in one dimension a "thing" (albeit not an object) and is not "without content." For this attention to be possible, I must already have negotiated a certain "coexistence" with the other that is more than simply a gesture of commitment.

If, to the contrary, short of the *eschaton,* no perfect crossing of self-abandonments ever ensues, then an *aporia* arises akin to that which notoriously afflicts ethical utilitarianism. When is one lover to be the giver and the other the recipient? In what times and places? This question must arise because, as we have seen, short of the invocation of the *adieu,* there is an inherent instability as to the priority of the advance or the priority of reception—a pure priority of the latter is inconceivable, since this would result in an infinite regress. Therefore, while Marion speaks of a "double passivity" between lovers, it is hard to credit such a reality. It would require a spontaneous simultaneity that would call into question first the necessity of an initial unilateral advance by one lover alone, and second the being loved first of all by a predecessor in time, not a current interlocutor in space. In fact the rigor of Marion's analysis within his own terms indicates that the constant oscillation of "advances" by first one party and then the other means that the counter-advancing that alone secures concretion and recognition is always in arrears, such that reciprocity is always postponed. Indeed he speaks (in very Derridean terms) of a "displaced, differentiated, deferred" reciprocity that is marked by the advent of "the third," which may be an actual child.[54] The arrival is not (as it is for orthodox Catholic teaching) the upshot of a surplus of mutual desire that arises from the very character of desire itself as overflowing generous resource, such that the child is entirely wanted "for itself," but is rather (in relation to the love of the lovers) a kind of compensatory attempt at a guarantee of the lovers vow, which neither sex nor language adequately attains. And we have already seen how even this attempt at confirming reciprocity is ultimately ambivalent.

It follows that Marion realizes that love in the end involves reciprocity, but he is unable to envisage it within the terms of phenomenology. This is perhaps unsurprising, because reciprocity suggests a state of being that pertains *between* two or more persons and therefore seems to require an ontological description of what here occurs that exceeds what is strictly speaking, according to phenomenological reduction, fully apparent to an ego. As I have already argued, Marion's correct appeal to an *adonné* prior to my solipsistic awareness in fact explodes the bounds of this reduction rather than realizing it to the last degree. But since he does not admit this to be the case, the *adonné* cannot evoke an ontological between, but rather conjures up an aporetic shuttle between the priority of recipient and giver: if the other is prior to my ego, yet not according to ontological relation that would allow that we are simultaneously first for each other, then the other can be prior only as an alter ego. Moreover, if he cannot ontologically appear without contaminating his alterity, then, after all, my *ego* must take the lead in auto-affectively affirming his presence. It is hard to see how the coincidental crossing of *adonnés* is not the contracting of self-activating wills as much as it is "double passivity." The latter notion is supposed to exceed the contrast of active and passive, but this could only be the case if my will, in the shape of its actions, were truly *influenced* by the actions of the other, in which case I would have to take account of their manifest forms. "Double passivity" should mean also "joint action" as between actors on the world stage. But on Marion's model it rather suggests the way that actors are passive to the gaze of an audience who cannot intervene in the action, while the audience in turn are passive spectators of a plot that is not really part of their lives. And this "pure looking" can tolerate the spectacle of violence in a way that real interaction cannot.[55] Thus a "double passivity" that excludes mutual bodily and visible interference cannot really differentiate between the disinterest of love and the indifference of cruelty.

So insofar as Marion's discourse on love is haunted by reciprocity, it is also haunted by an ontological "between."[56] In a parallel way it is also haunted by a narrative or history of love. We have seen that Marion denies that history and literature could be primarily instructive as to love's nature. But it is notable that *Le Phénomène érotique* itself seems, confessedly, to take the form of a (riveting) philosophical novel. This is inevitable, if, for the reasons we have just seen, a phenomenological approach to love can arrive only at an unstable oscillation between the poles of self and other. In that case, all one can do is tell the story of this oscillation. But obviously, this cannot simply be one more love story that vaguely illustrates how love may go for some people or other. The phenomenological *vécus* of love must now describe the necessary *moments* of love and in a necessary order (though we have seen that this is unclear on Marion's account). It is for this reason that in this book Husserlian phenomenology seems to slide into a Hegelian phenomenology of spirit. But the latter cannot "reduce" to the transcendental structures of my ego. Rather, its necessarily historical form indicates that it presents the unfolding of absolute spirit, according to an infinite logic that required of Hegel a separate book to describe.

By contrast, Marion's narrative phenomenology of love makes no reference to the actual historical transformations of love. In that sense his enterprise remains sub-Hegelian and not so directly evocative of absolute spirit. Rather, he develops a kind of neo-Kantian approach to the history of love, by claiming to describe how its history must repeatedly go in a series of microhistories— that is to say, the history of each one of us.

In this way, what Marion appears to offer is a kind of Mallarméan "final novel" about love—a novel so accurate and revelatory that all subsequent novels would be mere illustrative novelettes, struck with the vanity of unnecessarily multiplied pedagogy or diversion.

Either he has (perhaps) succeeded or such success is impossible if, as I have argued, love is incurably vague and elusive. In that case, there are an infinite number of ways in which love may go in time and in many different sequences. The history of love is in fact multiply saturated according to its occurrences and plots, and not just according to its appearances and singular events— which can then be categorized in terms of universal metahistorical moments. Philosophy is in consequence confined to an always inadequate reflection on the history of desire that is history as such. But in compensation, it recognizes this history as also the search for wisdom, and so as assisting the task of philosophy itself.

If the phenomenology of love is haunted by ontology and narrative, it is also haunted by semiotics. In a remarkable article on Seneca's *De Beneficiis*, Jean-Joseph Goux has shown how Seneca's treatment of the gift was implicitly related to the Stoic theory of signs.[57] The latter involved perhaps the first account of the triadic structure of semiosis in terms of reference/signifier/ signified. Goux argues that Seneca was able to reflect on the peculiar nature of the gift by seeing that it involved a parallel triadic structure of object/sign/ meaning. This conclusion is supported by the fact that, just as the Stoics and Seneca recognized that there is no human community without signs, so also Seneca declared, anticipating Mauss, that gift is *quae maxime humanum soci-etatem adligat.*[58]

For Seneca, the gift *object,* or commodity, does not exhibit the nature of gift because it is involved merely in the business of trade or *commercium* and is concerned as *feneratio* with interest, loan, and profit. One can suggest here after Jean-Joseph Goux that he is indirectly invoking the lower-rank of the Indo-European triadic hierarchy (knowledge/fame/wealth in one of its manifestations) as discovered by Georges Dumézil. The middle rank of this hierarchy is concerned not with the gain of trade, but with the glory of aristocratic honor. Here one more truly locates the gift in the sense of *munus* (the root of "muni-ficence") because what matters in this instance is not merely the object given—the obvious "referent" of the gift-giving process—but rather gift as sign of generosity. However, such generosity is only partially, or may be not at all, disinterested: it rather belongs to the *agōn* of the display of honor among "big men," as anthropologists would now say, and will usually expect a counter-gift. For Seneca, the *munus* is only a true gift when, as sign, it points to the signi-fied *beneficium,* which is the pure intention to give, for its own sake, that which is of intrinsic and irreducible benefit—which means, for the antique philo-sophical tradition, theoretical knowledge.

Seneca's analysis is somewhat poised between gift exchange and advocacy of the one-way gift. Again like Mauss he spoke of a *commercium dandi, accipendi, reddendi,* but the third component could now, thanks to the triadic distinc-tion, assume the form simply of meaningful gratitude.[59] The true gift was more seen by Seneca as disinterested, and therefore as exceeding established bonds of reciprocal duty: it could go from child to father, slave to free. This accords with his statement, long before Kant, that "the will alone should receive our praise": hence the *beneficium* is finally independent of both sign and object. It is because the *munus* as *sign* inherently points away from itself to benefiting the other that Seneca can state *beneficium sine altero non est.*[60]

Following this indication, Goux argues that because gift is not merely sign, which always indicates beyond itself, but also "the sign of the other" that indicates an action fulfilling this *élan* of the sign, Derrida's deconstruction of the possibility of the gift misses the point. For the *structural* meaning of gift is benefit to the other and therefore the internal consciousness that one is a giver does not cancel gratuity, since this is a mere psychologistic accident. Derrida's perspective here, one might say, is not sufficiently semiotic in character.

This argument, however, is not entirely convincing. For it appears to depend indeed on a "Stoic" claim that *donum* exceeds *signum,* just as thought rises above trade and glory, and meaning above sign and object. Yet Goux himself admits that if the gift needs the other, it is only the gift that gives to us (makes manifest as other) the other. In which case it follows that the other is always indicated by the gift, and that the sign or *munus* dimension of the gift can never really be surpassed in its conveying of gift as *beneficium* to the other for the sake of the other. It follows that Derrida's objection is not just a "psychologistic" one, but that he is saying that, just as there is no pure signified unmediated by the signifier, so also there is no pure benefit unmediated by my reciprocal relation to the benefacted one. It is not merely that I return to myself, congratulate myself as giver, but also that a certain bond of honor and debt has inescapably occurred between me and the one I have sought to benefit. The *beneficium* never finally escapes the *munus,* because its generosity cannot escape the circulation of meanings that always invokes response and so return.

Of course Derrida's *aporia* only holds if one insists that the gift must not involve reciprocity (which I would deny). But in these terms it does hold. This matters because, were Goux entirely right, then his semiotics of the gift would self-collapse in favor of a phenomenology. Gift as sign would be only a secondary instrumental vehicle of gift as inner intention or intuition. But to the contrary, gift is only ever present as sign. It is an expressive gesture and the mark of its sign-character is precisely that it must always be interpreted. An apparent gift may be judged rather as poison. For if we take away timing, content, and circumstance from gift giving, plus the judgment of all these things, gift fades into formal delusion.

Yet if gift is always sign, then certain valuable aspects of Goux's analysis appear in a new light. A gift as sign is more than its reduced appearance, and so it does indeed favor a transport toward an ontologically real other. It helps to reveal her insofar as stumbling on the appropriate gift—especially if it is a success—helps to reveal her character, at the moment where one says to oneself "Yes, that would be suitable." It is not that one simply knew the person already, and then tried to match one's gift to this understanding. At the same time, equally, my gifts alone (including all my words, gestures, etc.) declare my character to the beloved other. And if one refuses Derrida's arbitrary assumption that the necessary mediation of the signified by the signifier renders the former a void, and his assumption that the necessary mediation of unilateral benefit by reciprocal honor renders the former forever postponed, then one can entertain a kind of semiotic realism that is nevertheless a "realism of faith": an ultimate signifier is participated in if never reached; mutual benefit arises because human patterns of asymmetrical reciprocity and non-identical repetition compose a harmony that remotely echoes the infinite divine love.

Part of the excess of *donum* over *signum* concerns the ecstatic reach to the other. However, if the mediation of *signum* can never be left behind, then, equally, another part of its excess concerns the surplus of *res* over *signum*. For if we are always deploying signs and interpreting signs in terms of other signs, then it follows that this necessity of sign for thought also concerns the sign vehicle. In all probability, not even verbal sounds are as arbitrary as Saussure supposed, but in any case verbal signs always invoke more concrete realities that still count as signs because of their metaphorical operation. We think only because we make one thing stand for another, and this at once has a tendency to ignore what a thing is-in-itself and yet still to attend to this and to what it might conjure up, echo, or foreshadow. The sign–gift complex reveals this situation most acutely. Hence exchanged words ("let me tell you about my holiday," etc., or "my new hat") conjure up things and offer ghostly gifts, while gifts, of flowers for example, are resorted to when one needs to say something with more emphatic intensity. The sign always promises a gift, while gifts interpreting signs are themselves more emphatic signs.

In this way, just as the *beneficium* can never really leave behind the *munus*, so also neither can really leave behind the *res*, or the exchanged thing, which need not be merely the object of a trade in self-interest—the *feneratio*—since the "interest" sought by the gift in gift exchange—the obligation always "to give back more"—is a tightening of mutual bonds, not necessarily a gain of power for a benefactor. Were *not* a gift also a thing, it would be no more than a sign, and therefore could not reach and confirm the other in a fashion more radical than words. Here again we see how the elevation of person and action in fact requires the elevation of things: it is the latter's singular history and uniquely acquired character that irreplaceably assists the emergence also of human distinctiveness.

Like Seneca, therefore, a phenomenology that finally underplays the mediating role of signs must tend to evacuate gift of both its relation to an ontological other and its necessary thinghood. One is left with a mere self-affirming security of the will and a collective contractual exchange of mutual assurance of such security. Ironically then, by seeking to discover a present appearance behind the absence of the sign, phenomenology tends to lose concrete reality. And in a doubling of this irony, the gift that is not carried by a thing and does not indicate a worldly other must truly be not a "pure phenomenon" but rather a sign that is *only* a sign, since it merely indicates its own vacuous formality.

But the phenomenology of love is not only haunted by ontology, history, and semiotics. It is also haunted by theology. I have already indicated certain ways in which this is the case for Marion. Above all this emerges in the way he seeks to start with pure immanence, *etsi deus non daretur,* but ends up sounding as if he had rather assumed a certain kind of theology all along. Hence evil and hatred are given a positive identity and it seems as if philosophy can only investigate an entirely *fallen* world, upon which God intervenes purely extrinsically, within the same logic and structure of love that immanence has already disclosed. However, anything other than outrightly Jansenist theology would maintain that the Creation cannot even be sustained in existence (since the Fall cuts us off from God and of itself implies extinction), unless it everywhere receives in some measure the advance benefit of redemption. For this reason philosophy can only investigate a world at once created, fallen, and redeemed: necessarily it gathers something of the original purity of the Creation and something of its destined supernatural end. Theology generously supplies to philosophy a dignity higher than mere autonomy.[61]

Yet because Marion proceeds as if he were investigating a purely fallen world and beyond this (as we have seen) appears even to detect evil structures within being as such, he arrives at a conclusion that seems to make the operation of Christian love problematic. If all are fundamentally foes, and if love only emerges in the rare selection of lovers/friends, then how is love of the neighbor possible? We seem to be close to something like Carl Schmitt's irreducibility of the distinction between friend and foe. One should all the same agree with Marion's thesis of a univocal *genus* of love as regards humankind, so it is not that I am arguing (with Kierkegaard) that love of the friend is other than love of the neighbor. No, it is clear that when Jesus asks in Luke "Who is my neighbor?" whom I should love, the answer is not "the man by the wayside" but rather the Samaritan who helped this man with discreet attention and therefore ineluctably befriended him (Luke 10:29-37).

The point is rather that talk of "unconditional advance" and so forth suggests a rarity of friendship. Yet, to the contrary, one should assume that the smallest gestures of help or communion imply an open-ended commitment. Marion might very well agree to this within his own terms, but the question then arises as to the appropriate distribution of our friendly efforts, the economy of philial time and space. If love is to be possible in general, as the gospels demand, then the question of true friendship cannot evade the political dimension of justice—as Derrida correctly concludes.[62] But the question of justice in friendship necessarily involves issues of the correct placing of bodies, of appropriately shared concerns, and of mutual education in theoretical understanding—all of which Marion seeks to exclude from the true terrain of love.

Finally, Marion appears to fall into the dire theological contradiction of seeking to know love purely by a negative refusal of a fallen world or a tainted being. Yet if the Fall is the refusal of love, then no one, not even the philosopher, can in any way know love without reference (conscious or unconscious) to the event of the full arrival of love in time, which is the Incarnation. Love is first of all manifest in one supreme narrative, subject to endless interpretation. From this narrative alone we learn what love is—whereas for Marion it would seem that it merely supplies an infinite illustration of the univocal concept of love fully known by philosophy.

Moreover, a narrative of love is necessary in order to show us again what love is, just because love is also a matter of justice and can only be revealed or given through an exemplary positioning of human bodies and souls in time and place. Thus in revealing to us the Son of God as love, the gospels also reveal and give to us, through his interactions, the church as the new beginning of the practice of love that alone discloses its reciprocal and distributive nature.

The Theology of Love

From the above we can see that any attempted philosophical discussion of love must pay attention to ontological, historical, semiotic, and theological (or anti-theological) dimensions, as well as to phenomenological ones. The latter cannot themselves be ignored because all that is appears, and we only have access to what is via the apparent. But if the invisible gives itself to the visible as beauty, and not just as sublime invisibility (which dooms visibility to sinister closure), then phenomenology exceeds itself and requires the supplement of the other perspectives.

Within the concerted engagement of all these approaches, love appears as an intrinsic part of our attempt to know a shared ontological reality. The love of knowledge and the knowledge of love involve, perpetually, a never-ending mutual positive debt of all to all and finally all of God, which loops across space and spirals downward through time. Love is perpetually asymmetrical and (reversibly) hierarchical, since it always concerns mutual assistance and education: otherwise we would not need friends and one-way assistance would seek only for enemies. In seeking to assist each other toward the ultimate *beneficium* that is the beatific vision, we cannot have done with the glorious attempt at self-expression in the *munus,* even though we should seek to free this from the will to dominate. Nor can we have done with the destiny of *res* as mediated through trade, even if we should subordinate profit and gain to mutual benefit.

Love therefore, as Proclus and Dionysius surmised, is primarily for humans a participation in a hierarchical series strung through time. Even in the final *henosis,* or the beatific vision (for Dionysius), they both indicate that a sharing in gift stands with or even above the *beneficium* that is contemplation: to receive and to give are, even at this level (or most of all at this level), inseparable and here is one reason why one can argue that Dionysius' bold integration into Christian theology of theurgic neo-Platonism in some ways allowed a *more* evangelical vision to emerge then hitherto.[63] Here mirroring reflection and gift are at last one, when we see ourselves as we are seen and the surpassing of the mirror by the gift is all that remains to be seen, or rather, to be entered into.[64]

Dionysius opened up the idea that the primary orientation of theology is not to private contemplation but to a participation in the liturgy that is at once a collective making and a serial passage as well as an individual *theoria.* The Proclean, serial dimension suggests a certain human primacy to the notion of temporal generation (the angels have their own, other sort of time). Should salvation mean that the individual must conform herself to general, theoretically known norms of love? In that case salvation is, paradoxically, only individual. Or does salvation mean that the individual must seek, in her own time and place, uniquely and irreplaceably to exemplify an unknown love? If that must be her quest, then it can only be the quest of love if it is undertaken along with all others, who are equally in unique situations. In this way one arrives at a symmetrical paradox: the irreducible individuality of the quest to exemplify love beyond general norms (echoing the Kierkegaard of *Fear and Trembling*) ensures that salvation is in fact a collective achievement. But it is such in time as well as in space—since it is an endlessly looping and spiraling mutual enablement in a continuous series.

This gives point to the existence of generations (which theology usually leaves obscure). The positive debt of love can never be repaid in one generation alone—but the future generation gives new significance to earlier efforts, and its own efforts are enabled by what it has learned from those who went before. The salvific work of humanity is something like the realization of a collective work of art through time: accidental but supra-accidental, like a historic landscape (e.g., the landscape of Italy from Etruria to the present, and the landscapes of France and Britain also). Almost the same considerations apply to the repayment of the negative debt of the Fall: this has already been repaid in the theurgic work of the God-Man, but we are now positively in debt to this redemption also, and must actively seek to recuperate it.

This "piety of the generations" is very necessary for today because the realm of generation has been colonized by a Darwinism that sees in it nothing but pointless sex, manipulated by an incomprehensible (including for science) blind self-sustaining of certain genetic formations. So powerful must be this impulse, issuing in sex, that it is today assumed that human culture is little more than the manifestation of a necessitated superfluity of sexual desire by a cautiously over-providing nature. Yet in supreme Freudian "denial" we continue to see this sexual escape from generation as our supreme mode of transcendence.

Religion today also is often tempted to think of its own mode of transcendence, and its own conception of love, in terms of an "escape" from both biological generation and cultural transmission. It seems therefore to augment the "contemplative" (or else a *spatially* political) approach to transcendence over the "liturgical" one. But I have sought to show in this essay just why love is actually unthinkable outside the series of hierarchical transmissions and therefore outside our biological and cultural insertions.

This understanding is perhaps more Johannine than Lukan. Luke exhorts us to "love our neighbor as ourself"—suggesting either that love of self is an initial given, or else that I am within myself already the other—which invites the problem of his prior egoity, and an infinite regression. That indeed a certain either/or as between self and other haunts Luke's exploration of love is suggested by his deep suspicion of reciprocation.[65]

In John of course the opposite is true: there is much about mutual indwelling (John 17:20-26). And this seems to correlate with his rival exhortation to "love as we are loved" (John 15:12). This suggests that we are to give what is initially *not* in our possession and that love is first and foremost a positive debt. So here an allowance of reciprocity also correlates with a hierarchical asymmetry and denial of initial self-presence. This correlation only works if one assumes that the unilateral hierarchical gift itself tends to give (and originally with God entirely gives) the response to this gift. In this context, the Vulgate's translation of *agapē* in the gospels as *dilectio,* but in the Pauline epistles as *caritas,* is perfectly coherent. Mutual delight and unstinting sacrificial care fall together within the hierarchical vision of "unilateral exchange."

But if the goal of hierarchy is education and therefore self-abolition, how will love survive, as it were, the final school prom dance? Here only Trinitarian reflection has the answer (even if Proclus arguably shows some anticipations). It is the doctrine of the Trinity that thinks a thearchic series that remains a series even though its components are equal. Thus Christianity poses an alternative to Seneca's obliteration of hierarchy in favor of the formal mutual recognition of rights and duties that anticipates modern liberalism. As we have seen, this mutual recognition cannot be the exchange of gifts.

For Seneca secretly *accentuated* hierarchy by leaving trade and glory as mere ladders to knowledge, when of course in reality most workers and managers (in every sense) will never attain a social position by which the supposed human essence of pure free motivation could truly be exercised in equality. For true equality one would require rather the elevation of trade and glory, of *feneratio* and *munus.*

But this is just what is thought by the doctrine of the Trinity. Here all the Indo-European triads and their various (possible) echoes are finally leveled. Power, rule, and desire are now on the same plane as are the "remaining, outgoing and return" of neo-Platonism. Likewise, by implication, referent and sign are leveled with meaning. The Father is power and remains and is the ultimate referent as source. The *Logos* is sign and goes outwards and governs. The *Pneuma* or *Donum* is desire and interpreted meaning of the *Logos* who returns to the Paternal source (not in any sense of self-reflection, impossible for God's simplicity, but in the sense, as with the *Logos,* of a necessary and original supplementation).

Because of the "substantive relations" of the Persons of the Trinity (conceived by the Cappadocians and Augustine rather than Dionysius), an asymmetrical mutuality involving a "need" for the other survives here the lapse of hierarchy and is sustained in a kind of divine metahistory. As we ascend the hierarchical scale and assist others to do so down the generations, we climb precisely toward equality and a remote approximation within human interaction to the asymmetry of substantive relations. So the more we ascend, the more we teach to others lessons unique to ourselves that they cannot really assimilate yet are necessary for their redemption (and vice versa).

On this "way of exchange" (as the twentieth-century Anglican lay theologian Charles Williams put it) hierarchy is also gradually canceled, not because we are all accorded (as by liberalism) a fake formal nobility, but rather because the baseness of material things and of self-expressive donating glory are elevated along with aspirations fully to know.

For only the outward-manifesting charitable glory of *munus* points as *signum* to the contemplative *beneficium* of spiritual meaning that is the *Donum* of the *Pneuma.* And the *Pneuma* is only *Donum* because it returns to and renews the mysteriously original (and "material") surplus of "the real" or *res* over the sign that is the *Principium* or God the Father. This *res* as *feneratio* is always entirely loaned out for the sake of interest in a greater return of mutuality that is forever forthcoming only as the immediate increase of the original loan and its positive debt.

Our love may trade in nothing else.

Notes

1. Jean-Luc Marion, *Le phénomène érotique: Six méditations* (Paris: Grasset, 2003); *The Erotic Phenomenon,* trans. Stephen E. Lewis (Chicago: University of Chicago Press, 2007). All translations from *Le phénomène érotique* in this essay are the author's own, with references provided to the published English translation cited above. See esp. 334; *The Erotic Phenomenon,* 217: "To the contrary of that which metaphysics has in the end pretended, love does not lack reason, nor logic, simply it does not admit a reason and a logic other than its own and only becomes legible in terms of its own reason and logic. Love is not uttered: nor made, except in a unique sense, its own."

2. Jean-Luc Marion, "Une époque de Métaphysique," in *Jean Duns Scot ou la revolution subtile,* ed. Christine Goème (Paris: FAC editions, Radio-France, 1982), 87.

3. Marion, *Le phénomène érotique*, 12–97; *The Erotic Phenomenon*, 3–58.

4. Plato, *Ion* 531c and passim.

5. Marion, *Le phénomène érotique*, 94, 127; *The Erotic Phenomenon*, 56, 78. For vanity and hatred, see ibid., 25–109; *The Erotic Phenomenon*, 11–66. Yves-Jean Harder, "Amour," in *Dictionnaire Critique de Théologie*, ed. Jean-Yves Lacoste (Paris: PUF, 1998).

6. Marion, *Le phénomène érotique*, 111–68; *The Erotic Phenomenon*, 67–105.

7. Ibid., 14; *The Erotic Phenomenon*, 4.

8. Ibid., 148, 169ff; *The Erotic Phenomenon*, 92, 106ff.

9. Ibid., 293ff; *The Erotic Phenomenon*, 189ff.

10. Ibid., 161–234; *The Erotic Phenomenon*, 101–50.

11. O. Henry, *The Gift of the Magi*, in *Selected Stories of O. Henry*, ed. Victoria Blake (New York: Barnes and Noble, 2003), 25–31. My reading of the implication of this story may well not be O. Henry's intended one. One can also note here that the wife's sacrifice can be seen either as particularly sinister or particularly cunning. Sinister, since she had deprived her husband of her beauty at Christmas; yet for her this sacrifice is but temporary. She will still one day get to use the combs. Cunning, because she has bought her husband a gift through the mere selling of time: soon her beauty will be restored to him and he will also have the fob for his watch. The husband's sacrifice, however, lacks this cunning that would redeem its mediocre ambiguity. Hence the wife's pleasure in wearing the combs will always be tarnished by the thought of the permanent loss of the cherished watch. In the final analysis, therefore, his action seems the most reprehensible. See also *Le phénomène érotique*, 138–39; *The Erotic Phenomenon*, 85–86, where Marion insists that it is the decision of *one* lover alone that initially opens up the erotic possibility and declares that true love does not ever "care" whether or not it is loved. This seems to conflict with his equal stress on hope for return, but this conflict surely arises from the contradiction of an *entirely* disinterested love hoping to meet a *matching* disinterest.

12. *Le phénomène érotique*, 230; *The Erotic Phenomenon*, 147: "Le langage érotique ne décrit rìen, il met en scene le serment; ou plutôt, comme cette scène ne fait rìen voir, il met en branle l'érotisation"; "Un amour commence quand chacun parle à autrui d'autrui lui-mème et lui seul, et de rìen d'autre; et il finit quand nous éprouvons à nouveau le besoin de parler d'autre chose que d'autrui—bref de faire la conversation." See also ibid.; *The Erotic Phenomenon*, 111: "[t]he erotic reduction abolishes the world and creates an intrigue." But is not the intrigue about and for the world?

13. See Jean-Luc Marion, *Being Given: Toward a Phenomenology of Givenness*, trans. Jeffrey L. Kosky (Stanford: Stanford University Press, 2002), 199–221. See also John Milbank, "The Soul of Reciprocity, Part One," *Modern Theology* 17, no. 3 (July 2001): 335–91, esp. 386 n. 27. Marion takes mathematical knowledge as a paradigm of "penury of intuition." But in, say, geometry, concept and intuition are perfectly in tune: intuition is not here *lacking* but rather *thin*—literally superficial. Marion confuses lacking with a thin but *perfect* intuition. And while Husserl begins with "excess of signification" this does not preclude *advance* to denser and deeper intuition.

14. See John Milbank, "Sacred Triads: Augustine and the Indo-European Soul," *Modern Theology* (October 1997): 451–74.

15. *Le phénomène érotique*, 191–283; *The Erotic Phenomenon*, 120–83.

16. Claude Bruaire, *L'Être et l'Esprit* (Paris: PUF, 1983), 51–64. The background to this *topos* is ultimately Proclean and can be traced through Cusanus, Bérulle, Laberthonnière, and Henri de Lubac. See also John Milbank, *The Suspended Middle: Henri de Lubac and the Debate Concerning the Supernatural* (Grand Rapids: Eerdmans, 2005).

17. *Le phénomène érotique*, 313–18; *The Erotic Phenomenon*, 202–6.

18. Ibid., 211–34; *The Erotic Phenomenon*, 135–150. For the hypostatic union parallel, see ibid. at 200–1; *The Erotic Phenomenon*, 127–28.

19. Ibid., 192, 154–55; *The Erotic Phenomenon*, 121–22, 96–97. And see *Being Given*, 248–320.

20. Marion, *Being Given*, 231–32. And see Milbank, "The Soul of Reciprocity, Part One," 335–93; John Milbank, "The Soul of Reciprocity, Part Two," *Modern Theology* 17, no. 4 (October 2001): 425–509.

21. *Le phénomène érotique*, 244; *The Erotic Phenomenon*, 157; "J'attends les démentis."

22. See Milbank, "The Soul of Reciprocity, Part One," 371–84.

23. *Le phénomène érotique*, 251–71; *The Erotic Phenomenon*, 162–75.

24. For the lie, see ibid., 243–44; *The Erotic Phenomenon*, 156–57; for the child, see ibid., 302–18; *The Erotic Phenomenon*, 195–206.

25. See Wolfgang Smith, *The Wisdom of Ancient Cosmology: Contemporary Science in the Light of Tradition* (Oakton, Va.: Foundation for Traditional Studies, 2003), 37–49.

26. Bruaire, *L'Être et Esprit*, 159–95.

27. Ibid., 51–87.

28. Ibid., 179–95.

29. S.T.I.Q. 57 a 2 resp. See also S-T Bonino, introduction to Thomas D'Aquin, *De La Vérité ou La Science en Dieu*, ed. S-T Bonino (Freiburg: Éditions Universitaries Suisses, 1996), for an excellently detailed discussion of this issue.

30. Proclus, *The Elements of Theology*, ed. E. R. Dodds (Oxford: Oxford Univeristy Press, 2000), props. 120–22.

31. See F-X Putallaz, *Les Sens de la Réflexion chez Thomas d'Aquin* (Paris: Vrin, 1991).

32. Proclus, *The Elements*, prop. 56.

33. Plotinus, *Ennead*, III, 7, 12, 13; VII, 8, 6–7.

34. See, e.g., S.T.I.Q. 14 a 8 ad 3; De Ver. I. 2 ad 4.

35. Dietrich of Freibourg, *Treatise on the Intellect and the Intelligible*, trans. M. L. Führer (Milwaukee: Marquette University Press, 1992). See also Ruedi Imbach, "Le prétendue Primauté de L'Être sur le connaître: Perspectives cavaliers sur Thomas d'Aquin et L'École Dominicaine Allemande," in *Lectionum Varietates: Hommage à Paul Vignaux (1904–1987)* (Paris: Vrin, 1991), 121–32. While one can agree with Imbach that Aquinas is far closer to the German Dominicans' intellectualism than "ontological" readings of Aquinas would suggest, one might debate with him as to whether the "merely theological" foundation of Aquinas's realism is to be considered a weakness, or, likewise, his subordination of humans to things as regards the process of knowing

(in some degree). In a sense one might argue here that while the Germans took the idea of real human knowledge as purely active and human self-reflection as self-sufficient from Proclus (though this was common neo-Platonic currency, ultimately Plotinian, as Gilson claimed) that nevertheless Aquinas's at once more Aristotelian and more creationist view that we remain in our knowing "measured by objects" actually *accentuates* the theurgic dimension of the Proclean legacy. Proclus allowed that at some point the creative influence of intellect and soul over matter runs out—at a nether level only the One is still active—and that just for this reason, the human soul must have, at least initially, recourse to the imagination (and to myth and ritual, argues Trouillard). But Aquinas insisted that being *always* exceeds the reach of created intellect. Implicitly, this points to a yet more indispensable role for imagination, narrative, and ritual. Only in the Renaissance were the theurgic aspects of Proclus seriously reinvoked and further extended.

36. Dionysius the Areopagite, *Celestial Hierarchy*, 140c–145c.

37. See, e.g., Plato, *Sophist*, 258a–e; 259e–260a.

38. Plato, *Lysis*, 214c–215b. And see Catherine Pickstock, "The Problem of Reported Speech: Friendship and Philosophy in Plato's *Lysis* and *Symposium*," *Telos* 123 (Spring 2002): 3–38. The present essay is heavily indebted to this article.

39. Plato, *Symposium*, 206c–210d.

40. *Le phénomène érotique*, 332; *The Erotic Phenomenon*, 215.

41. Ibid., 201–2; *The Erotic Phenomenon*, 128–29.

42. Ibid., 63; *The Erotic Phenomenon*, 37.

43. Dionysius, *The Ecclesiastical Hierarchy*, 376B. And see esp. Ysabel de Andia, *Henosis: L'union à Dieu Chez Denys L'Areopagite* (Leiden: Brill, 1996), in particular, regarding gift, 72–77, 104–9.

44. Jacques T. Godbout and Alan Caillé, *The World of the Gift*, trans. Donald Winkler (Montreal: McGill-Queen's University Press, 1998), 171–223.

45. François Laruelle, *Principes de la non-Philosophie* (Paris: PUF, 1996), esp. "La donation de la non-philosphie," 231–42; Laurelle, "Qu'est ce que la non-Philosophie," in Juan Diego Blanco, *Initiation à la Pensée de François Laurelle* (Paris-Montreal: L'Harmattan, 1997), 13–69, esp. "Radical et unilateral," 47–52.

46. Laruelle, "Qu-est ce que la non-Philosophie?"

47. Laruelle argues that philosophy relies on certain hidden "axioms" (not presuppositions) such that, like non-Euclidean geometry, one can devise a new "non-philosophy" on different axioms—especially ones that deny the conditioning-conditioned duality. But one could point out here that Proclus already consciously axiomatized theology on a Euclidean model and that his axioms concern seamless "series" rather than the forementioned duality (not unrelated to his modification of Euclid in his commentary on the *Elements*). To continue this provocation, could one not further argue that Spinoza's immanentization of Proclus's theological geometry, by abolishing emanation as the unilateral gift of the One itself in favor of substance and modes as fundamental contrasting aspects of the One, *does* in fact lapse into the contrast of conditioning and conditioned such that the two are mutually constitutive?

48. Which is what Laruelle actually does.

49. See Milbank, *The Suspended Middle.*

50. Plato, *Lysis,* 212d–e; Pickstock, "The Problem of Reported Speech."

51. *Le phénomène érotique,* 146; *The Erotic Phenomenon,* 91.

52. Ibid., 161; *The Erotic Phenomenon,* 101.

53. Ibid., 330; *The Erotic Phenomenon,* 214.

54. Ibid., 315; *The Erotic Phenomenon,* 204.

55. See John Milbank, *Being Reconciled* (Oxford: Blackwell, 2003), 26–44.

56. See William Desmond, *Being and the Between* (New York: State University of New York, 1995). I am deeply indebted to Desmond's incomparable reflections.

57. Jean-Joseph Goux, "Seneca against Derrida: Gift and Alterity," in *The Enigma of Gift and Sacrifice,* ed. E. Wyshogrod et al. (New York: Fordham, 2002), 148–61. See also Jacques Derrida, *Given Time,* trans. Peggy Kamuf (Chicago: University of Chicago Press, 1992).

58. Seneca, *De Beneficiis,* I, 4, 2.

59. Ibid.

60. Seneca, *De Beneficiis,* V, 10, 1.

61. See Milbank, *The Suspended Middle.*

62. Jacques Derrida, *Politics of Friendship,* trans. George Collins (London: Verso, 1997).

63. Proclus, *The Elements of Theology,* prop. 10; Dionysius, *The Celestial Hierarchy,* 165D–168B, 212A, 301C–304A.

64. Unlike Gregory of Nyssa, Dionysius does not speak of Moses as "seeing" the invisible God. On a more liturgical model he simply enters into the final inner sanctum where he is "wrapped" in the invisible and "belongs" to it. See Ysabel de Andia, *Henosis,* 319–55; Dionysius, *The Mystical Theology,* 1001A.

65. See Milbank, *Being Reconciled,* 160.

9

Love in Its Concept

Jean-Luc Marion's The Erotic Phenomenon

CLAUDE ROMANO

Translated by Stephen E. Lewis

Jean-Luc Marion's recent book *The Erotic Phenomenon* constitutes the completion of a triptych that began nearly twenty years ago with *The Idol and Distance* and continued with *Prolegomena to Charity*. It is a deeply meditated book that in many ways stands out as the crowning achievement of his entire work. A provisional crowning achievement, of course; but all the same a recapitulatory book: at once clear, refined, stripped of all useless erudition, almost severe in appearance; and disconcerting, complex, indeed, at moments, tortuous, attempting to mold itself to the folds and creases of a phenomenon that is obscure like everything that is evident, and difficult like everything that is simple—a phenomenon that is simplicity itself, known by all, and for that very reason unknown. Love, about which so much has been written, here unfolds with the rigor of a concept, outside of the horizon of metaphysical thought. Indeed, as Marion recalls at the outset, there is an "erotic blindness of metaphysics" that needs first to be surmounted.[1] This is in fact a triple blindness: metaphysics has first of all been ignorant of love's unity, reducing love to a multiplicity of phenomena that are irreducible to one another: *eros* and *agapē*, concupiscient love and benevolent love, sexuality and sentimentality; second, metaphysics has denied love its rationality, preferring to lower it to the level of a phenomenon of passion, and thus a confused and irrational phenomenon; and finally, metaphysics has subordinated the understanding of love to the questions of being and of knowledge.

Marion on the contrary poses three theses, in appearance extremely simple, the consequences of which *The Erotic Phenomenon* opens out methodically: first, that love speaks with one and only one meaning—it is perfectly univocal, whether we are talking about God's love or that of creatures, whether maternal, paternal, or filial love, or the love found in friendship and in carnal love; second, that love sketches "another figure of reason" (15 / 5)—there is an erotic rationality that exceeds (and, according to the author, precedes) metaphysical rationality; and third, we must think a "love without being" (16 / 6) that excepts itself from the horizon of ontology, and which prescribes for phenomenology a new field of research and even a *sui generis* realm of phenomenality.

Such then are the three leading threads running through Jean-Luc Marion's "erotic meditations" (19 / 8), which could be substituted for Descartes's metaphysical *Meditations*. My goal in this essay is to introduce others to this book while formulating the questions that, to my mind, it raises; accordingly, I will follow these three theses through to their ramifications.

The Univocality of Love

It makes sense to begin by taking seriously the book's title. The question here is not "love," that worn-out word that our civilization endlessly invokes, to the point of rendering it almost obscene, the word that metaphysics has employed as a means of "denial," as Marion puts it (12 / 3), in order to rid itself of, rather than to confront, a problem. Instead, and in place of "love," we have "eroticism," a term that, by its semantic tenor, immediately ties love to sexuality, and thus to the flesh. But above all, love is qualified here as a "phenomenon," a word whose neutrality and indetermination is important. To say that love is a phenomenon is to hold implicitly against a tradition that goes from La Rochefoucauld to Proust and from Stendhal to Freud, that love is not an illusion—even if, on occasion, it allows for illusions that are difficult to eradicate. But the word "phenomenon" here has above all the role of excluding customary psychological labels: "feeling," "emotion," "instinct," "desire," "will," "tendency," and so forth. In its indeterminate neutrality, it has almost the same meaning as the word "weight" that St. Augustine, doubtless for analogous reasons, privileged, thus refusing to allow himself to be caught in the trap of these oppositions: "My weight is my love. Wherever I am carried, my love is carry-

ing me [*Pondus meum amor meus; eo feror, quocumque feror*]."[2] Thus Marion
dismisses such questions as whether love is of the order of an emotion or of
an intention. Is it something we undergo or is it voluntary? Does one who
loves seek the good of the other or his own satisfaction? Is love essentially
altruistic or selfish? If love presents itself here in the neutrality of a simple
"phenomenon," it is precisely in order to escape the dichotomies in which the
problem has become mired, to the point of becoming insolvable: the opposition of profane love and holy love, of *eros* and *agapē*, of sexuality and sentimentality, of interested and disinterested love, of benevolent and concupiscent
love,[3] of passionate and intellectual love,[4] of sensual and mystical love, of friendship and passion, of divine and human love. Clearly, for Marion, all of these
oppositions mask the phenomenon, or in any case fracture it to the point of taking away its face. His thesis of the univocality of love, on the contrary, allows
no exception, not even the opposition between human and divine love. In the
command "Come!" from the Book of Revelation,[5] which Marion describes as
"the final word of Revelation and of the mystical theology rooted there" (233 /
149), there still resonates something of the human call, and even of the cry of
human love—in short, "God loves in the same way as we do" (341 / 222).

But in what way, precisely? All of Marion's conceptual work, which is also
terminological work, consists in attempting a description that does not dis-
member the phenomenon, but instead preserves its cohesion and its coherence. For example, he never speaks of "desire," or of "instinct," or of "sexual
drives"—even if the corresponding phenomena are present in his analyses
and even minutely described—alongside which there would come to be added
in a second stage feelings, emotions, or wishes. Love cannot be broken down
into desire, on the one hand, and feelings, on the other. On the contrary, with
sexuality we are already within the dimension of eroticism, which is to say of
love, one and indivisible. Far from desire being a simple "drive" within me,
which turns toward objects and aims blindly at them, the *phenomenon* of
erotic attraction is a global phenomenon that is impossible to break down
into elements or parts (here Marion is particularly sensitive to the teaching of
Heidegger throughout *Sein und Zeit*),[6] a phenomenon in which it is the flesh
of the other that *eroticizes* my flesh: "my eroticization," writes Marion, "comes
to me from the other" (195 / 123). There is not a pre-erotic, stammering stage
of love—the stage of desire—and an accomplished or finished stage—that
of moral engagement, of the promise or the oath. From the very moment that
we are within an attraction, we are also, whether we know it or will it or not,

within the dimension of the oath, and we cannot be within this latter without also being within the former. Thus, one can hold with good reason that everything in love is sexual and that everything in sexuality is erotic—even if the author prefers to avoid the term "sexuality." In reality, the eroticization of our flesh and of that of the other is a phenomenon that wins us over completely, without any remainder: there is an eroticization that begins with the gaze, with the voice, and above all with speech, and which in no way passes through sexuality in the restricted sense. Marion calls this "free eroticization," in contrast to the "automatic" eroticization of desire (§35). This eroticization is the place in which it is at once possible for two flesh [deux chairs] to "cross" and for two beings to relate to one another in person, to offer to one another their true faces.

For the flesh, we must note right away, can in many cases also be the barrier against which the erotic élan breaks itself, barring the other from showing him or herself as such. Often, the flesh "obscures" rather than "accedes to the person" (254 / 164). The flesh, which we want to "possess," hides from us that which it is not possible to possess, for "one only possesses that which cannot love" (257 / 165). Marion describes with care—and not without humor—the diverse modalities of this failed meeting with the other, which stops at automatic eroticization, without ever reaching free eroticization: cruising (245–46 / 158), sweet-talking (246 / 159), infidelity (248–49 / 160), all of which are forms of existential duplicity in which I lie to myself as much as I lie to another, since in refusing the other the chance to show her or himself in person to and for me, I at the same time refuse myself the converse. In other words, these are forms of love that fail by running aground in an endless repetition of automatic eroticization. Opposed to and freeing us from the "bad infinity" of this iterative eroticization is the true infinity of the oath. One may nevertheless wonder whether, at this stage, Marion's analyses are not somewhat distorted by his vocabulary. Does it make sense to oppose at this point the automaticity of desire, wherein the flesh "takes off" or "starts up" (219 / 140), to the freedom of eroticization through the word grounded in the oath, when the very project of the book is, in a sense, to unite them? The notion of "automatism" in particular may appear excessive: the spontaneity of desire is not its automaticity; we do not react to the flesh of another like one of Pavlov's dogs reacting to a conditioned reflex; we allow ourselves to be bewitched, we give in to a tropism, which is different. In opposing "the automatic desire" (219 / 140) of the flesh to the fidelity of the promise, is there not a risk of rendering unthinkable the very *fact* of love, which is to say the surpassing of this alternative *in an act,* which—when it exists, which is rarely—makes the other and her flesh coincide, such that there is no longer any hiatus between loving carnally and simply loving?

But doubtless Marion would respond that, if this possibility exists at the horizon of the erotic phenomenon, then first it is necessary to conquer it, and it is only conquered through the test of the contradiction between the finitude of (automatic) eroticization and the oath that, by its very nature, is willed and hoped to be eternal, which is to say "properly without end" (289 / 187). Here then there is a lived contradiction that makes up the heart of love and that is thus at the center of its manifestation. The oath wills the infinite, and eroticization is finite (223 / 142). In an interview, Marion has affirmed that "in this work I aimed only at describing the logic and the contradiction that we endure when we love."[7] That love is indeed a contradiction in the act, and thus a paradox in the Kierkegaardian sense as well as in the phenomenological sense that Marion intends to confer on this term,[8] results from the fact that it is thought rigorously according to univocality. Indeed, in the cases where thinkers have behaved toward love like the botanist toward his species, seeing only contradictions between *different* loves, Marion, who thinks of love according to univocality, sees *a single center* with multiple contradictions. The contradiction is no longer between several loves, but rather fixed within the heart of love. But this contradiction does not abolish the possibility of love; rather, it grounds it. One might say that love is nothing other than the collection of hopeless efforts that we make in order to hold ourselves to the requirements of love—without ever entirely reaching them.

What are these requirements? In truth, they boil down to a single requirement from which all the others flow: to love first, to arrive ahead of the other in love. That is, to presuppose love in the other, instead of waiting for him to show or to demonstrate it; to dismiss all demands for reciprocity and to move, with regard to the loved one, not within the closed circle of exchange but rather within the *an-economy* of the gift. By making this the unsurpassable requirement of *every* love, whether filial, friendly, or romantic, rather than the limited condition of a limited and particular love—for instance, charitable love as opposed to carnal love, or *agapē* as opposed to *eros*—Marion renders edifying that which was profane, annulling the very distinction. Kierkegaard asked, "But what, then, is love? Love means to presuppose love; to have love means to presuppose love in others; to be loving means to presuppose that others are loving"[9]—thus to arrive before them in love, without even waiting for anything in return. The description of love that Kierkegaard reserved for his edifying discourses is the one that Marion offers for the constant and normative, and thus universal and unsurpassable, phenomenon of love, sacred as well as profane. Anything that does not obey this requirement quite simply is not worthy of being called "love": "Either loving has no meaning at all, or it signifies loving utterly without return" (118 / 72). Marion calls this anticipation of the other's love, which is the only way to enter into love, by the name of "advance." "The more I love at a loss," he writes, "the more I simply love" (117 / 71). Yet in this "loss," in fact, I lose nothing and win everything, beginning with the very possibility of loving. Whence come the different paradoxes that follow: love that risks the most is the most assured; when lovers separate, the one who is most unhappy is the one who no longer loves, not the one who still loves: "[H]e has lost nothing, because he still remains a lover" (140 / 87).

We might ask ourselves at this point whether Marion is proposing a new description or a new designation. Is he analyzing the amorous phenomenon in a new way, or is he simply content to christen it with another name? Does the operation merely consist in giving the name "love" to everything that traditionally has belonged to charity, and refusing this same name to everything that has belonged to *eros*? Such a critique would be deeply unfair: by changing the names, Marion aims very much to reinterpret the phenomena, which is to say, to show concretely the manner in which the requirement of nonreciprocity inheres in every possible form of love. And indeed he accomplishes this aim perfectly. I cannot enter here into the diversity and richness of his analyses—for instance, that of the crossed eroticization of two flesh, the analysis of truth and lies in love, and the particularly luminous analysis of the birth of the third, the child, who is witness to the oath from the very beginning. The requirement of nonreciprocity is not only a common trait, but the only trait common to everything that gives itself as an erotic phenomenon. We understand now why Marion purposely does not choose between a description of love in voluntaristic terms and a description in terms of passivity, or even in terms of permanent disposition. He adopts them one after the other, without opposing them. Thus, as for the description in terms of will and decision: "I can make a primary decision to love without return" (122 / 74; 148 / 92); there is an "incomparable and unstoppable sovereignty of the act of loving" (117 / 71), which is to say that to love is an *act* that I can accomplish. As for the description in terms of passivity: "My flesh eroticizes itself in me without me. Its radical passivity . . . arouses itself like a spontaneousness within me that is not me . . . [and that] takes initiatives and then presents the accomplished facts" (221 / 141). And for the description in terms of *hexis:* "[L]ove grows in loving" (123 / 75). If these descriptions do not contradict one another it is because the unity of the erotic phenomenon is not to be sought in a psychological theory of the faculties, nor in a "grammatical" theory (in Wittgenstein's sense) of action verbs, of verbs referring to a state (of experience), and of dispositional verbs, but rather in the unique and unavoidable phenomenon of the advance. Wherever the lover is in advance of the beloved, love is present, and wherever this advance "melts," love is eclipsed. Thus, for example, friendship just as much as eroticism (in the narrow sense) is characterized by the advance, by the non-reciprocity of gifts, by the unconditional nature of the oath that aspires to the eternal—unless, of course, it degrades into "friendship based on usefulness," as Aristotle would say[10]—but this, Marion would add, no longer merits in any way the name of "friendship."

Thus the thesis of love's univocality can serve as a key to a rereading of metaphysics, a rereading that, within the framework of *The Erotic Phenomenon,* is more sketched and suggested than fully developed. The demand to be loved by another that is expressed by the Pascalian question "Do they love me? *me, myself?*"[11] and that serves as the guiding thread through Marion's first "erotic meditation," is revealed, with regard to the full and rigorous concept of love, as a true *aporia.* Not only does this demand not arise from love, but it emanates from self-hatred and reaches its end in the hatred of others. We must be attentive to the very movement of the text if we are to see that the dismissal of this preliminary question—"Does anyone out there love me?"—can only receive its (retrospective) justification in the third "erotic meditation," that is, in the *positive* presentation of the erotic phenomenon grounded in the advance. Thus, what may seem enigmatic or even arbitrary in the thesis of the "impossibility of self-love" (§9) or, inversely, of the existence of an originary "hatred of self" (§12), disappears, I believe, after a more attentive reading. To the affirmation that self-love is in principle impossible and that self-hatred is "the ultimate affective tonality of the ego" (92 / 55), one is at first tempted to object "How could the possibility of hatred exist where the possibility of love does not exist?" Unless we establish that hatred is not the opposite of love, which Marion does not do, it follows that he who can hate himself must also be able to love himself, and vice versa. In order to "hate his own incompetence" (92 / 55), for instance, mustn't one already have self-love? But these objections, so sensible in appearance, do not hit their mark, for a simple reason (which nevertheless can only appear in the third meditation): the concept of "love" has changed between the first two meditations and those that follow. When Marion denies the possibility of self-love, he does not deny the possibility of selfishness or of self-love in the ordinary sense; rather, he denies the possibility of a love of self in the sense of the full and developed—and solely phenomenological—concept of love, which corresponds to the phenomenon of the advance. Put another way, the possibility of self-love is refused in the name of a concept of love that he who proclaims or who demands such a "love" of himself does not yet possess. There is a distortion here within the "order of reasons" that, as we shall see, results from Marion's use of the method of phenomenological reduction. What is impossible and even absurd is thus simply the possibility of a love of self that is *defined by the phenomenon of the advance,* and thus by the unconditional gift and the absence of reciprocity. Between me and myself, such a love is clearly unthinkable. And, Marion concludes, because I do not love myself with *that love,* I do not love myself *at all,* since love speaks in a univocal manner. But what has been modified as a result: the thing or the vocabulary? For self-love (selfishness) *not defined by these characteristics*— which includes attachment to one's own life, the predilection for what makes it pleasant, and, eventually, self-confidence or self-regard—emerges intact from the critique. We simply do not call it "love" anymore. Let's accept this reform of the language, but not the idea that such an attachment to self would be a "logical contradiction" (89 / 53)! None of Marion's arguments support this point, for at no moment does the reflexivity of a feeling (expressed by the reflexivity of a verb) presuppose that I "precede myself" (77 / 45) or that there is "a gap within myself" (79 / 46)—or indeed a "distance" to traverse!

It is necessary to underscore that the method Marion follows is circular: it is because the univocality of love is presupposed, and thus also its "full" and rigorous concept, grounded in the advance, that there is no love of self *in the restricted sense.* That being so, the circularity of this method can appeal to phenomenology, and to Husserlian phenomenology first and foremost. Indeed, the transcendental reduction must always be presupposed when one describes the natural attitude: this trait does not betray a lack of rigor but simply a particularity of phenomenological analysis. And since Marion himself practices a reduction—the "erotic reduction"—there is no quarter in reproaching him with it. But there remain questions to be asked concerning this reduction itself.

Love's *Logos*

These questions of method lead us to Marion's second thesis: love is a phenomenon that is rational through and through. Love comes under the *logos*, not the passions. Merleau-Ponty used to speak of a "*logos* of the sensible world"; in the same way, it would be necessary to speak of a *logos* of the amorous world, which has nothing to do with formal logic, and concerning which phenomenology must deploy its rigor if it wants to be able to deploy itself with complete rigor. Now, in calling upon both Pascal and Nietzsche, it is necessary to affirm that "the heart has its reasons of which reason knows nothing,"[12] and that these reasons come under a "big reason" that lacks common measure with the "small," hair-splitting reason of the intellect.

Thus, throughout these "Erotic Meditations" we are not, despite misleading appearances, dealing with a logical chain of arguments but rather with the unfolding of a *logos* of the amorous phenomenon (subjective genitive: the amorous phenomenon's *logos*). The amorous phenomenon shows itself here according to its own *logos*, and according to its articulations and inevitable paradoxes. And quite rightly, then, this *logos*, because it is crossed with contradictions, appears (at certain moments, at least) almost to take the form of a dialectical *logos*: "[B]eginning from the crossing of flesh," Marion states, "each erotic phase gives rise immediately to its negative moment, inseparable and inevitable" (338 / 219). For example, the antithesis between automatic desire and the freedom of the oath finds its "synthesis" in the possibility of a free eroticization, grounded in the resources of the spoken word. Or the conflict between the temporal finitude of the flesh that is aroused and the eternity demanded by the oath finds its reconciliation in an eschatological temporality in which each moment is a final moment, a moment that is *sub specie aeterni:* the lover "does not need time to end in order to be finished with time. . . . The lovers do not promise one another eternity, they provoke it and give it to one another starting now" (322 / 209). Each moment in which I love is the final moment, and that is why "the one that I love in the final instant will appear *hic et nunc* as the one that I loved in the final instance" (323 / 210). The journey here is "dialectical" in at least one sense: it is the *logos* of love itself that, as it goes along its way, deploys and suppresses its own contradictions and its own illusions, to end up by identifying itself with the *logos* and the very Word of God, who, while loving "in the same way as we do" (341 / 222), "surpasses us as the best lover" (342 / 222).

But the fact that there is something "dialectical" in Marion's method does not mean that it is not thoroughly phenomenological. On the contrary, *The Erotic Phenomenon* is written in the first person: it is the book of a willingly assumed finitude that, in this regard, is situated at the antipodes of every speculative philosophy. And if description becomes here a development or movement and a journey, that is because the amorous phenomenon does not allow itself to be separated from a story in which I say "I" and in which each person must be able to say the same for him or herself. Referring to *Emile*, Rousseau spoke of a "novel of human nature." Perhaps this is the case too for *The Erotic Phenomenon*, if there is no human nature without love or if man must be defined as "the loving animal" (18 / 7).

For Marion, phenomenology cannot be deployed in a rigorous manner outside of the space opened by reduction. To his mind, reduction is phenomenology's sole method, or at least its preeminent method. "So much reduction, so much givenness," Marion affirmed in *Being Given*. This axiom also underlies *The Erotic Phenomenon*. I must say that it is around this point that my primary difficulties with the book are centered.

What exactly is the status of the "erotic reduction" that the author undertakes to accomplish beginning with the first of his meditations, and which he "radicalizes" in the third meditation? Let us try to follow him step by step on this steep path.

To begin with, we find within the question "Does anyone out there love me?" a reduction that inquires after the erotic phenomenon, or rather, we find a first "way to gain access to the erotic reduction" (112 / 68) that winds up proving unworkable, or at least insufficient. It "remains partial" (113 / 68), Marion tells us, and that is why it must be completed, or rather radicalized. If it is partial, that is because the amorous phenomenon discloses itself there "indirectly, as if negatively" (112 / 68), which is to say because the ego "expects from love only a more or less honest exchange, a negotiated *reciprocity*, an acceptable compromise" (113–14 / 69). "Thus it is necessary to reject reciprocity in love" (115 / 70) and thus "radicalize the erotic reduction in order to reduce even as far as the demand of reciprocity" (116 / 70). It is precisely this that the "erotic reduction (radicalized under the form "[C]an I be the first to love?")" accomplishes (136 / 84). It alone gives me access to the erotic phenomenon in its phenomenological purity and integrity.

A question ("Does anyone love me?") or a decision (to be the first to love) are clearly not in and of themselves reductions: these are acts that are perfectly possible to accomplish within the natural attitude. What then establishes the character of "reduction" in these different reductions considered by the author?

In phenomenology, every reduction, for as much as it concerns a method, puts into play at least three instances: the one who accomplishes the reduction; that which is reduced in such a reduction; and that to which such a reduction is led back, the phenomenon in the reduced (and properly phenomenological) sense. Thus, for Husserl, the one who accomplishes the reduction is the transcendental ego; what is reduced, which is to say bracketed, is the natural thesis of the existence of the world and its correlate, the existence of the ego; that back to which the reduction leads is the transcendental field purified of every thesis of existence, and thus to "phenomena according to phenomenology" such as they are constituted by the pure ego. In the case of Heidegger (who, we should note in passing, takes up as his own the term "reduction" only once in all his work, and within a pedagogical context to boot),[13] the one who accomplishes the reduction is Dasein; what he reduces are beings; and what the reduction leads back to is the being of these beings. To these three characterizations we must also add a fourth: because the reduction is to be the method of access to the phenomenological field as such and in its entirety, it is not only prior to every other method, but *universal by principle,* which is to say practiced without restriction upon the totality of the phenomenal given.

So what about the erotic reduction? To begin with, the one who accomplishes it is the lover and, behind the lover, the gifted thematized in *Being Given.* What, then, does this one who is gifted reduce? The only possible response seems to me to be that the gifted reduces a certain belief that he possesses about what love is—namely, the belief according to which love would demand a certain reciprocity between the lover and the beloved. He therefore suspends *this* belief in particular. To what does this reduction lead? To the phenomenon of love in its full phenomenological consistency and radicality. Two problems appear here: first, what is sought through this reduction is the characterization of *a* phenomenon among many other possible phenomena—the erotic phenomenon. At issue then—at least at first—is a *partial* reduction and not a universal one like that practiced by Husserl; second, what is sought for in the phenomenon of love is that which constitutes it *in its essence.* Now for Husserl, the method allowing access to essences is not phenomenological reduction but rather eidetic reduction. If for me the question is knowing whether reciprocity belongs to the essence of the erotic phenomenon, it is not by freely suspending my belief in a possible reciprocity that I will be able to respond to this question of *essence*. Rather, only once the essence of love has been elucidated will I be able, should the opportunity present itself, to suspend my belief in an eventual reciprocity (or my awaiting such reciprocity). It seems that the passage from the first characterization of love to its second has brought to bear nothing other than an eidetic reduction, which is to say a seizing of *this very particular* phenomenon. But, contrary to these remarks inspired by Husserl, Marion holds that *all* phenomenality finds itself modified by the erotic reduction: the task of the erotic reduction is to give access to a new domain of phenomenality, more originary than that of objects and of beings considered in their being, and thus more originary than the domains brought to light respectively by Husserl and by Heidegger.

How is this affirmation to be understood? I propose the following reading: to accomplish an "erotic reduction," as put forth by Marion, would be *to love*, purely and simply, suspending every requirement of reciprocity. He who has accomplished the erotic reduction loves truly (or is capable of doing so), while he who has not accomplished it remains caught in the logic of exchange, and thus does not even attain to this possibility. Thus two of Marion's affirmations amount to exactly the same thing: "The other is phenomenalized in the exact measure according to which the lover loves him or her" (130 / 80), and "The lover thus renders the beloved possible, because he enters first into the erotic reduction" (138 / 85). This use of the notion of "reduction" is certainly paradoxical: to love is surely not a *method* of phenomenology, not even of the phenomenology of love. It very well can be that, if I love, I see not only the beloved but also the totality of the world differently, and in this way the very world appears "new" to me, because bathed in the light of love. This phenomenon has often been described by poets. Joë Bousquet, for example, writes in his *Lettres à poissons d'or* [*Letters to Goldfish*]: "One day I discovered in you this path toward day; and now the objects that surround me are your presence—a bit more than they are mine."[14] And the narrator of Proust's *Recherche* affirms the following about Albertine: "Albertine had seemed to me to be an obstacle interposed between me and all other things, because she was for me their container, and it was from her alone, as from a vase, that I could receive them."[15]

Nevertheless, if "the event of love" (17 / 6) upsets the world for the one to whom it happens (and it is rather surprising that *The Erotic Phenomenon* never analyzes as such either the event of the amorous encounter or that of amorous rupture or grief, which seem to me to belong entirely to the erotic phenomenon), it only follows that love can spring forth upon the world out of an event (that of *falling in love*) that reconfigures the world and its meaning for the one to whom it happens; it does not follow that such an event, through which the world and others appear in a new light, could constitute in any way a *method* of phenomenology in the sense according to which the reduction, classically understood, is a method.

There is, then, in Jean-Luc Marion's project a tension that I have previously underscored with regard to *Being Given*,[16] which is the following: on the one hand, Marion wants to conserve the reduction, which is to say a method that is transcendental or inspired by transcendental philosophy. Thus he affirms, for example, in *The Erotic Phenomenon* that it is by the intermediary of a reduction that I alone am capable of accomplishing that the beloved appears to me as beloved; thus, that I, myself, by the bias of the reduction, am the unique condition of possibility for the phenomenalization of the erotic phenomenon: "The lover thus renders the beloved possible, because he enters first into the erotic reduction" (138 / 85). But, on the other hand, Marion's entire fundamental project consists in moving beyond a phenomenology of the transcendental style, and thus in thinking of phenomenality as a giving freed of every prior condition of possibility. Put another way, Marion, while using a transcendental method that has been modified according to the needs of his cause, wants to leave the terrain of a transcendental philosophy. In this there is a deliberate paradox on the part of the author of *The Erotic Phenomenon*, because it is necessary to hold at the same time that the lover, through his erotic reduction, makes possible the beloved, and that "the amorous phenomenon is not constituted beginning from the pole of the ego that I am; it rises *of itself* by crossing within itself the lover . . . and the other" (164 / 103 [emphasis added]). This "of itself" refers back to what Marion, in *Being Given*, called the "self" of the phenomenon, which is to say that it refers back to their givenness as such. The post-transcendental reduction that is to be put into place thus leads to passing from the ego classically defined in Cartesian terms to the gifted [*l'adonné*], and consequently, it allows passing beyond the phenomenality of the object (Kant, Husserl) and that of being (Heidegger) toward a new phenomenological field governed by the paradigm of the gift. This project, which was already the project of *Being Given,* remains present in *The Erotic Phenomenon* and in many ways constitutes its heart.

Love without Being

The problem of the beyond of being or of the "otherwise than being," as Lévinas would have put it, is at once very present in *The Erotic Phenomenon* and at the same time little developed. Indeed, this book is not intended as a technical book, and it proceeds—at least on this point—in a fairly allusive manner. If for Marion there is an "erotic reduction," that is because the act of taking love into consideration opens access to a new field of phenomenality, or at least to a new regime of phenomenality.

The first question that occurs to me is how can a phenomenon, however important it may be and whatever definition one might give to it ("feeling," "emotion," "intention," "act," "disposition"), lead us by itself beyond objectivity and beyond being? A first response might be that the erotic phenomenon simply comes under a universal phenomenology of the gift, in relation to which it would be, in some way, a particular case. It would then be the phenomenology of givenness in its entirety—and not "erotic" phenomenology alone—that would be excepted at once from both metaphysical objectivity and from Heideggerian ontological difference. This is doubtless Jean-Luc Marion's thought, but we find numerous passages in *The Erotic Phenomenon* that seem to indicate that love, in and by itself (and not as the given *in general,* with the same status as other "saturated phenomena" such as painting, for example, or the face, or the flesh), is already located beyond (or this side of) being.

Notably, the author affirms: "[T]he presupposition [in metaphysics] is that in order to love or to make oneself loved, one must first be. But the slightest experience of the erotic phenomenon attests to the contrary—I can perfectly well love what is not or is no longer, just as I can make myself loved by what is no longer, by what is not yet, or by something the being of which remains undecided" (16 / 5–6). How can I make myself loved by what no longer is? How can I love or make myself loved by what is not yet?

As much as it is possible to affirm, as Marion did in what certainly remains one of the major books of philosophical theology of the last fifty years, that God is "without being"—since, in keeping with a long tradition rooted in neo-

Platonism that has its purest expression in the apophatic theology of Dionysius the Areopagite, even the attribute of being cannot be predicated of God without having to be denied immediately after by virtue of his very transcendence— just so do I have trouble understanding what it means to say, within the frame of a phenomenology of finitude that treats of love as it is given to be experienced *by us,* that it is not necessary to be in order to love or in order to be loved. Certainly it is not necessary that what we love *be* generally speaking in order for us to be able to love it. We can love a fiction or an idol the being of which remains undecided. We can love a dead person—but in such a case, the person *was.* But we cannot love or make ourselves loved *without being.* Nor can we make ourselves be loved by that which is not. I see no way of escaping these facts, which I admit are rather trivial.

But Marion doubtless wants to say something else: with the affirmation according to which love is beyond being, he wants to say fundamentally that only love *gives a meaning* to being, which otherwise sinks into insignificance and into complete vanity. Marion joins here with Hugh of Saint-Victor who in his *De arrha animae* held that one cannot live or be without loving: "I know that love is your very life [the author is speaking to his soul], and that without love you cannot exist [*vita tua dilectio est, et scio quod sine dilectione esse non potes*]."[17] But is this the same as saying, then, that love opens a field of phenomenality that is beyond being? How is it possible to affirm that, in the erotic reduction, "the entire question of being finds itself hereforward placed in parentheses" (84 / 50), when love is quite rightly seen as giving meaning to the *fact of being,* and thus protecting it from vanity?

Assuredly, there is something hyperbolic in all of these affirmations, as there is in the Lévinasian phenomenology to which Marion in part appeals. The "hyperbole" must be understood here in its etymological sense, notably, in the sense voiced by Glaucon when he exclaims in the sixth book of the *Republic,* upon seeing the idea of the Good, *daimōnias hyperbolēs:* "What a divine transcendence!"[18] Through these hyperboles, Marion's text preserves something of the transcendence of love, which is to say something of the only name that is perfectly and adequately fitting to God, something of the secret that is tied to this phenomenon. At the end of our reading, the secret of love is not so much dissipated as accentuated and deepened.

Does love in the sense spoken of by Marion exist? Yes, it exists insofar as it does not exist, which is to say as a demand we never cease to miss filling, as a possibility that we consistently fall short of and fail. Thus, we must respond to the suspicion formulated by Schopenhauer when he affirmed that love is like the "ghosts of which all speak, but no one has seen,"[19] with the exact response of the character in one of Kafka's stories who has just met a ghost in his room, and encounters a neighbor on the landing outside his door:

> "Going out again already, you rascal?" he asked, pausing with his legs firmly straddled over two steps.
> "What can I do?" I said, "I've just had a ghost in my room."
> "You say that exactly as if you had just found a hair in your soup."
> "You're making a joke of it. But let me tell you, a ghost is a ghost."
> "How true. But what if one doesn't believe in ghosts at all?"
> "Well, do you think I believe in ghosts? But how can my not believing help me?"[20]

Even if love *is* not, when it falls into our lap, when we discover it like a hair in our soup, how can our not believing help us?

Notes

1. Jean-Luc Marion, *Le phénomène érotique: Six méditations* (Paris: Grasset, 2003), 18. English trans.: *The Erotic Phenomenon*, trans. Stephen Lewis (Chicago: University of Chicago Press, 2007), 7. Subsequent references to the French edition of this work are given parenthetically in the text, in each instance followed by the corresponding reference for the English translation.

2. St. Augustine, *Confessiones*, XIII, xi, 10, in *Oeuvres de saint Augustin*, Bibliothèque augustinienne, vol. 14 (Paris: Desclée de Brouwer, 1962), 440. English trans.: *Confessions*, trans. Henry Chadwick (Oxford: Oxford World's Classics, 1998), 278.

3. René Descartes, *Les passions de l'âme*, second part, art. 81, AT, XI, 388; *The Philosophical Writings of Descartes*, trans. John Cottingham, Robert Stoothoff, and Dugald Murdoch (Cambridge: Cambridge University Press, 1983), 1:356.

4. Descartes, letter to Chanut, 1 February 1647, AT, IV, 605; *Philosophical Letters*, ed. and trans., Anthony Kenny (Oxford: Clarendon Press, 1970), 208.

5. Rev. 22:17, 20.

6. Martin Heidegger, *Sein und Zeit*, 16th ed. (Tübingen: Max Niemeyer Verlag, 1986), 53ff.

7. "Entretien avec Jean-Luc Marion," *Etudes*, November 2003, 490.

8. Jean-Luc Marion, *Étant donné: Essai d'une phénoménologie de la donation* (Paris: Presses universitaires de France, 1997), §23, 314ff. English trans.: *Being Given*, trans. Jeffrey Kosky (Stanford: Stanford University Press, 2002), 225ff.

9. Søren Kierkegaard, *Kjerlighedens Gjerninger*, in *Samlede vaerker*, 3d ed. (Copenhagen: Gyldendal, 1963), 12:216. English trans.: *Works of Love*, trans. Howard Hong and Edna Hong (New York: Harper and Row, 1964), 211.

10. Aristotle, *Nicomachean Ethics*, trans. Martin Ostwald (Upper Saddle River, N.J.: Prentice-Hall, 1999), VIII, 3, 218.

11. Pascal, *Pensées*, B 323 / L 688. English trans.: *Pensées*, trans. A. J. Krailsheimer (Harmondsworth: Penguin Books, 1995), 217.

12. Ibid., B 277 / L 423; trans. Krailsheimer, 127.

13. Martin Heidegger, *Die Grundprobleme der Phänomenologie*, in *Gesamtausgabe*, vol. 24 (Frankfurt: Vittorio Klostermann, 1975), 4:29. English trans.: *The Basic Problems of Phenomenology*, trans. Albert Hofstadter (Bloomington: Indiana University Press, 1982), 21: "*For Husserl* the phenomenological reduction ... is the method of leading phenomenological vision from the natural attitude of the human being whose life is involved in the world of things and persons back to the transcendental life of consciousness and its noetic-noematic experiences, in which objects are constituted as correlates of consciousness. *For us* phenomenological reduction means leading phenomenological vision back from the apprehension of a being, whatever may be the character of that apprehension, to the understanding of the being of this being."

14. Joë Bousquet, *Lettres à poissons d'or* (Paris: Gallimard, 1967), 202.

15. Marcel Proust, *A la recherche du temps perdu*, ed. Jean-Yves Tadié (Paris: Gallimard/Bibliothèque de la Pléiade, 1987–89), 4:65. English trans.: *Rememberance of Things Past*, trans. C.K. Scott Moncrieff, Terence Kilmartin, and Andreas Mayor (New York: Vintage Books, 1982), 3:492.

16. Claude Romano, "Remarques sur la méthode phénoménologique dans *Étant donné*," *Annales de philosophie* 21 (2000): 6–14 (esp. 11–12). Marion recognized the pertinence of this objection in *De surcroît: Etudes sur les phénomènes saturés* (Paris: Presses Universitaires de France, 2001), 54. English trans.: *In Excess: Studies of Saturated Phenomena*, trans. Robyn Horner and Vincent Berraud (New York: Fordham University Press, 2002), 45, affirming that "such a difficulty cannot be resolved all at once" (original 55, trans. 46), while nevertheless maintaining his demand for a reduction that is not simply this "performative contradiction": "[T]he phenomenon gives *itself* from itself—the *ego* must get rid of all transcendental pretensions. This is not to say that the reduction is compromised, but inversely, that it is accomplished even in the one who makes it possible, *l'adonné* [the gifted]. *L'adonné* [the gifted] does not compromise the reduction to the given but instead confirms it in transferring the *self* from itself to the phenomenon" (original 57, trans. 48).

17. Hugh of Saint-Victor, *Soliloquium de arrha animae*, 25–26. English trans.: *Soliloquy on the Earnest Money of the Soul*, trans. Kevin Herbert (Milwaukee: Marquette University Press, 1956), 13.

18. Plato, *Republic*, VI, 509 c.

19. Arthur Schopenhauer, *The World as Will and Representation*, vol. 2, trans. E. F. J. Payne (New York: Dover, 1958), 2:531.

20. Franz Kafka, *Unhappiness*, in *The Metamorphosis, In the Penal Colony, and Other Stories*, trans. Willa and Edwin Muir (New York: Schocken Books, 1948, 1995), 43–44.

IV

ETHICS AND POLITICS

10

(Re)placing Ethics

Jean-Luc Marion and the Horizon of Modern Morality

GERALD McKENNY

In an essay on love Jean-Luc Marion speaks of "the *aporia* that, from Descartes to Lévinas, haunts modern philosophy—access to the other, the most faraway neighbor." He then issues a challenge. "It is doubtful that Christians, if they want seriously to contribute to the rationality of the world and manifest what has come to them, have anything better to do than to work in this vein."[1] By "this vein" Marion refers to Pascal's third order, namely "to know following love, and to know what love itself reveals." What he has in mind is a theology of charity, which would take primacy over the theologies of faith and hope that, he thinks, dominated the twentieth century. These remarks exhibit two general characteristics of Marion's theology and philosophy. One is that the privileged route to the other is love rather than justice; the second is that love of the other comes to expression more in knowledge than in deed. The privilege enjoyed by this pairing of love and knowledge in access to the other raises the question of what place, if any, the ethical relation to the other person might have in the program to which Marion calls Christians—and certainly not only Christians. The question is not incidental. As Marion himself frequently points out, to love or to know the other seems to involve the very *aporia* with respect to the other—namely, that while what we seek is love or knowledge of the other as other, love and knowledge seem to offer us only the other as object of my consciousness or intentionality—which the ethical relation to the other is thought to have overcome. In light of this *aporia* of love and knowledge, it is ethics, not love or knowledge, that is the privileged route to the other as such—or so it has seemed to many who work in the tradition that runs from Descartes to Lévinas.

Marion seems to break sharply with the ethical solution to this *aporia*. At a somewhat superficial level there is an apparent evasion of the ethical in Marion's work—evident not only in the fact that he has never written a book on ethics but more significantly in the fact that he seems determined to avoid speaking of ethics even where his inquiries seem to demand it, for example, in some of his references to the love commandments in the Gospels.[2] Yet at a deeper level Marion's positive aim is to restore the primacy of love or charity among the virtues.[3] To accomplish this restoration, love or charity must be rescued from the scorn of objectification it suffers in metaphysical thought about love, from the destructive polarity of thinking that opposes *eros* to *agapē* and passion to knowledge.[4] Marion finds in the privilege granted to ethics as the route of access to the other a continuation of this denigration of love in modern thought.[5] Yet in his restoration of love to the privileged place now granted to ethics Marion does not simply ignore or reject the ethical. Rather, love and ethics appear to involve one another in an endless intrigue in his thought: love seems to be a necessary condition for an ethical relation to the other, while ethics seems able to complete itself only by surpassing itself in love.

These mutual implications are the source of some difficulties in Marion's work. First, love can only assume its status as the privileged mode of access to the other by taking on some ethical characteristics, yet these characteristics are in tension with certain things we expect of love, at least at some level, including genuine mutuality and attachment to another on the grounds of her particular features. Second, if love does bring the ethical to completion, it seems able to do so only at the risk of introducing preference into the relation to the other in a way that is inimical to justice. I consider both these issues below along with a third difficulty, which is that Marion's understanding of love focuses on knowledge of the other in a way that seems to ignore, and perhaps even to denigrate, the ethical deed. Before examining this complex relationship of love and ethics in Marion's thought, however, it is necessary to examine the place of ethics in his phenomenological project more generally. What emerges from this examination is Marion's discomfort with Kantian notions of the autonomy of ethics. This anti-Kantian thrust is critical for understanding why Marion is determined to find in love the privileged route of access to the other.

Phenomenology and the Ethical

The denial of a privileged status to ethics lies at the deepest levels of Marion's philosophical project. It is especially acute when we consider his place in the phenomenological tradition. It has become common among some philosophers and theologians to narrate the development of phenomenology from Husserl to Lévinas as a progressive effort to bring to the fore the ethical relation to the other, an effort finally realized in Lévinas's phenomenology of the face. Phenomenology according to this narrative culminates in the recognition of the primacy of the ethical, of ethics as first philosophy.[6] According to this narrative, Marion's phenomenology would appear to signal a retreat, for he quite explicitly holds that "first philosophy," in the sense of that term he endorses, is the phenomenology of givenness, not ethics.[7] Nor is the honor of counting as first philosophy the only privilege ethics loses in Marion's phenomenology. A central characteristic of the phenomenology of givenness itself is the shift it marks from the subject, whose primacy from Descartes to Heidegger involves numerous *aporias,* to the "gifted [*adonné*]," who (unlike the subject) does not begin with himself but receives himself from the phenomenon. Here Marion draws on Lévinas's notion of the call, which for Lévinas opposes to my intentionality the counter-intentionality of the other. For Lévinas this inversion of intentionality is what characterizes the ethical as such; it establishes my responsibility for and to the other. However, Marion recognizes a more general applicability of this analysis of the call. He argues that Lévinas was mistaken to suppose that the call is enacted only in the relation to the other. Rather, it characterizes every saturated phenomenon as such inasmuch as every saturated phenomenon involves an excess of intuition that subverts my intention.[8] In short, what for Lévinas marks the ethical relation to the other in distinction from the constituting subject for Marion marks every saturated phenomenon.

Thus even the phenomenology of the face is no longer a privileged site for the ethical. Whereas for Lévinas the injunction "Thou shalt not kill" proceeds from the face and establishes the relation to the other as an ethical relation, for Marion the call as such precedes its content, and that content may take any number of forms besides the ethical "Thou shalt not kill." For Lévinas, at least in some of his earlier work, this ethical injunction takes priority because it uniquely identifies the other as other. The other is the one whose negation by me can only be total, that is, murder, in contrast to the partial negation involved in the violence of understanding—in which I grasp things, possess them, in terms of being in general. Yet the other is also precisely the one whom I cannot kill, because to kill would be to grasp the other in terms of being in general, yet what I grasp in this way is precisely *not* the other. The other eludes me in the very moment I would negate him.[9] In killing the other, I kill what belongs to the world of being; I cannot kill the other as other. The injunction, therefore, opens up an ethical dimension distinct from ontology. This is why for Lévinas the very meaning of the face is expressed in the injunction "Thou shalt not kill." By contrast, Marion argues that the injunction that identifies the other as other is prior to any particular form—ethical, religious, existential, existentielle—that it might take. The ethical injunction takes its place along-side these other forms of the injunction, which itself is therefore properly treated in terms of the call.[10] The face imposes itself on me in the call, accomplishing its phenomenality not by making itself visible—that would reduce it to an object of my gaze—but by making itself heard. It is clear that this kind of phenomenality can be accomplished in a variety of modes, not only in the ethical. Not only the other person of ethics but the icon more generally, or more fundamentally, imposes itself on me in the call. That Marion has argued that in the end Lévinas himself eventually doubted that the transcendence of the face occurs exclusively in the ethical relation is beside the point—or rather it confirms the point, which is that throughout his work Marion insists on removing the ethical from its privileged position and treating it as one instance of a more general kind of phenomenality. He thus reverses what some moral theologians and moral philosophers might call the "ethical turn" in phenomenology accomplished by Lévinas.

While the ethical has clearly lost its privileged status in Marion's phenomenology, it does not follow that he is indifferent or inimical to ethics. Indeed, it is possible to argue that, despite an undeniable lack of interest in ethics, Marion nevertheless wants to preserve the ethical against the nihilism of modern thought—a nihilism that he finds lurking in the conviction, from Kant to Lévinas, of the autonomy of the ethical. First, we should note that Marion does not deny the ethical in the Lévinasian sense of responsibility but rather opens up other saturated phenomena besides the face of the other to a kind of analysis that was previously restricted to the ethical. While this certainly involves a de-privileging of the ethical, it by no means entails its exclusion, as Marion makes clear.[11] But of course, it is trivial simply to point out that Marion's phenomenology de-privileges the ethical without excluding it. I therefore turn to two essays in which Marion attempts to preserve ethics from distinct forms of modern nihilism. In an essay titled "The Freedom to be Free," written around the time of *God without Being,* Marion traces the fate of ethics with the modern closure of metaphysics.

Perhaps surprisingly, Marion declares at the outset that ethics "belongs . . . to metaphysics." He quotes Heraclitus: *ēthos anthrōpō daimōn*—in Marion's rendering, ethos is "that which either determines or is lacking from the very humanity of man."[12] Marion poses the unavoidable question: if ethics belongs to metaphysics, what happens to ethics if modernity brings metaphysics to a close? In what follows of his essay, Marion traces what he calls the "undoing [*défaite*]" of ethics, which unfolds as a series of episodes in the history of modern metaphysics. By the undoing of ethics Marion has in mind the loss of moral normativity itself, that is, the refusal of a universal law capable of imposing itself on me as such. Here, as everywhere in Marion's thought, the moral is understood in terms of Kant's notion of the feeling of respect for the moral law, the feeling inspired in me by the moral law itself as the effect of its rationality on my sensibility. Marion traces the modern undoing of the ethical, the way to nihilism, in terms of various refusals of a universal moral law that makes demands on me, passing through the Hegelian reversal by which the moral law that enjoins my conformity to it is transformed into a demand that the world conform to a rational project, and finally to its denouement in Nietzsche, for whom the moral law can only be a symptom of a will that seeks to, and can, will only itself. Here free will itself, as indetermination and indifference, disappears in the necessity of the will to power; metaphysics culminates in the destruction of the metaphysical conditions of morality.

In sum, ethics belongs to metaphysics yet metaphysics is the undoing of ethics. It is futile, then, to try to restore metaphysics to save ethics; one would only risk repeating a history that culminates in nihilism. This genealogy of nihilism is familiar in its broad outlines; what makes Marion's version worth considering in this context is his response to the question of how to rehabilitate ethics after metaphysics. That solution emerges more clearly when we contrast it to the solutions of Heidegger and Lévinas. Heidegger, as is well known, sought to recover an "originary ethics" by understanding the *ēthos* of the Heraclitean fragment quoted by Marion as a concern with dwelling rather than character, and thus finding in it an understanding of ethics older than that of Aristotle—what we might call an "ethos without ethics"—as an alternative to the entire metaphysical tradition whose implication in nihilism runs far longer and far deeper than the trajectory that runs from Kant to Nietzsche.[13] Lévinas broke sharply with this effort, returning ethics to metaphysics in the sense of that term Lévinas drew from the third of Descartes' *Meditations*, formulating the ethical relation to the other in terms of the metaphysical relation of a being to the Infinite rather than in terms of an ontological relation to being in general.[14]

Both of these responses involve a departure from the metaphysics of the will that from Kant to Nietzsche is the condition of the ethical as such. By contrast, Marion situates himself at the precise point where the metaphysics of the will arrives at its nihilistic conclusion, fashioning an argument for morality out of the Nietzschean rubble. He begins by noting that while the will to power can put any allegedly moral act under suspicion of being merely a symptom of itself, it cannot prevent one from going ahead and acting on a moral interpretation of that act even at the risk that this act is merely a symptom of the will to power. An act is moral precisely insofar as one assumes this risk. The will to power can reduce the morality of an act to itself, but one is still free to attempt a moral act after that reduction, to assume the risk that in doing so one is under an illusion. One is free, that is, to take up an attitude of indifference toward the determinants of one's actions; free to go on *as if* one were free.

Thus far the argument resembles William James's "will to believe," but Marion sketches a phenomenology of freedom that goes considerably beyond James. He points out that the *as if* ensures that this freedom admits no prior condition—least of all the will, which as the will to power has already destroyed free will. In the form of the *as if*, freedom is no being, it is no cause, and it is no effect. In other words, freedom here is a phenomenon *par excellence*. With this freedom, says Marion, morality "already establishes by itself an *ethos*," one which opens up the horizon of all that is possible and "opens man himself as the unique instance and stake in possibilization [coming into possibility] in general."[15] *Ēthos* is still the *daimōn* in *anthrōpos*. But after the culmination of metaphysics in nihilism, Marion gives the Heraclitean fragment a phenomenological expression, in which the relation of freedom to man anticipates, in several ways, the relation of the saturated phenomenon to the *adonné*.[16] Here phenomenology rescues the ethical from nihilism by a thinking of the metaphysical location of the ethical beyond metaphysics.[17]

More recently, Marion published an essay titled "The Original Otherness of the Ego," which consisted of a detailed textual study of Descartes in light of an alternative characterization of nihilism. Marion here locates nihilism in the divorce between ontology as the question of being, on the one hand, and ethics as the concern with the infinite, on the other hand.[18] While he does not name Heidegger or Lévinas, the references are unmistakable. Marion finds the origin of this divorce in the transcendental "I" and illustrates in the cases of Kant and Husserl the separation of ethics from ontology that occurs when ontology becomes the science of the phenomenon in its knowability. Marion then poses the question of whether the transcendental "I" responsible for the divorce first emerges as the *ego cogito* of Descartes. The standard view holds that the ego of the *ego cogito, ergo sum* is mediated by thought such that thinking and being are equated. But in the second of his *Meditations* Descartes also uses the formula *ego sum, ego existo.* Marion argues that with this formula the ego guarantees itself of its existence only in a space of interlocution where an indeterminate and anonymous other (later identified as God) speaks to me (dative *mihi*), thus recognizing me as existing and assigning me my being. Remarkably, under this second formula there is no divorce between ontology (as the way of being of the ego who presides over the science of being in general) and ethics (as the experience of the other), since the way of being of the ego is governed originarily by the interlocution of an other. Ontology and ethics originate in precisely the same interlocutionary space. It follows that the divorce between ethics and ontology would originate in Descartes only if the standard formula, *ego cogito, ergo sum,* is privileged.[19]

Marion's analysis of the second *Meditation* enables us to revisit the de-privileging of the ethical in the description of the call and the *interloqué* in *Being Given.* Three questions are worth posing here. First, in denying Lévinas's assumption that the call and the *interloqué* are confined to the other but rather apply to the relation between the saturated phenomenon and the *adonné* more generally, can we understand Marion to be not merely de-privileging the ethical but also "saving" it from nihilism—a nihilism, we may suppose, that for Marion would result from treating the ethical as exceptional, that is, as divorced from all other phenomena? In other words, is the rejection of the exceptionality of the ethical—the claim that the phenomenology of the call as such is indifferent to whether it comes from God, the moral law, or whatever—undertaken at least in part to preserve the ethical from nihilism? This question leads to a second: if interlocution, in which the call addresses me in the dative case, replaces the Lévinasian Other, who places me in the accusative, then what does this mean for ethics? How, if at all, would ethics in the dative case differ from ethics in the accusative? How would Marion's ethic, were he to develop one, differ from Lévinas's? As for the third question, if the *interloqué* takes the dative rather than the accusative case, and if ethics in the dative case differs from ethics in the accusative case, does Marion's phenomenology exclude an ethical relation to the other that would take the form of the accusative? To answer these questions would require extrapolation, which is not without risk. In any case, our investigation to this point makes clear that Marion's de-privileging of ethics does not entail indifference toward ethics, much less hostility. While ethics is far from central in his thought, that thought does indicate an interest in showing how his phenomenology addresses the fundamental ethical problem of late modernity, namely, the problem of nihilism. We may summarize this by saying that Marion re-places ethics in a broader phenomenological context and also replaces it, in its privileged position, with love. While this clearly de-privileges ethics, and while that de-privileging indicates a lesser level of concern for ethics, it seems to be at least partly grounded also in Marion's fundamental conviction that the nature and status of the ethical from Kant to Lévinas is in the end inimical to ethics itself.

Love and Justice

We have seen that for Marion the first virtue is not justice, but rather charity. This already sets him against much of modern moral philosophy. The priority of charity, or love, rests on its status as the privileged mode of access to the other. Yet why does love rather than justice enjoy this privilege? After the analyses of Lévinas it would seem to be indisputable that ethics alone gives us access to the other as such. On what grounds does Marion dispute this claim?

First, love is necessary because knowledge of the other as other requires not only a phenomenology of alterity as such but also that I seek the other as such. For Marion, the phenomenology of alterity enables us to distinguish knowledge of the other as object of consciousness or intention, a knowledge in which the object of knowledge returns my own gaze (the idol), on the one hand, from knowledge of the other as the one who opposes a counter-gaze to my gaze (the icon), on the other hand. But on any particular occasion, what determines which alternative occurs? What determines whether the other will appear as genuinely other or as an object? For Marion, this question was not addressed sufficiently either by Husserl, who simply assumed that I will make the analogical inference to the other as another ego, or by Lévinas, who avoided the well-known problems with Husserl's analogical argument to the other in his description of the phenomenon of the face (to the extent that the face is a phenomenon for Lévinas) but did not explore the conditions under which I accept or reject the other—conditions under which, for Marion, the face attains its phenomenality. Marion seems to accept a certain privilege (though, as we have seen, not exclusivity) of ethics in defining the phenomenality of the other as such, and to this extent his own phenomenology of alterity does not depart radically from that of Lévinas. The difference with Lévinas emerges where Marion points to love as a condition of the appearance of the other as other, insisting that "the phenomenality of the other does not precede my (good) will with regard to him, but instead is its result."[20] Only love determines whether I will deal with the other as an object that returns my gaze or as a counter-gaze. "The other appears only if I gratuitously give him the space in which to appear." Ethics is therefore not sufficient to account for the appearance of the other as other; "its phenomenality depends upon the fact that I indeed will it."[21]

Here we arrive at the theme of the "advance," the notion that love, precisely as love, always arrives first, is always the first to love.[22] In Kierkegaard's understanding, love discovers the neighbor.[23] It therefore appears that for Marion the one who loves is the *adonné* who, precisely by responding to the call issued by the gaze of the other person, enables that gaze to appear. Precisely as a phenomenon, alterity requires the priority of charity over ethics. Once again, however, we should not conclude that the priority of love entails indifference or hostility to ethics. Marion continues to insist that the phenomenality of the face is accomplished, or at least can be accomplished also, and perhaps even first, through the ethical injunction.[24] Ethics in a Lévinasian sense remains at least one way (and perhaps the initial way) by which we understand the phenomenality of the face while love is what receives it as such and thereby enables it to appear.

Yet if love is in this way the condition of the phenomenality of the other, it is still the case that the knowledge love seeks is, precisely, knowledge of the other. For Marion, the phenomenology of love is always in part a matter of describing in what sense I can know the other who cannot be constituted as an object.[25] But Marion consistently recognizes that it is justice that prohibits reducing the other solely to an object. If love is a condition for the appearance of the other as such, that is, as the other and not as an object, then love is a condition for what justice demands—namely, that the other not be reduced to an object. There are points in Marion's texts where this notion that love does what justice requires—enacts the condition under which it is the other and not an object that appears to me—seems to emerge more or less clearly. In addressing the question whether I can envisage what envisages me without turning it into an object, Marion argues that while the face that envisages me expresses itself without signification, and thus evades any conceptualizable meaning, this does not mean that it is unintelligible. Rather, as a saturated phenomenon the face expresses an infinity of meanings. It follows that knowledge of the other must take the form of an "endless hermeneutic" correlative to the infinity of meanings expressed by the face. What is interesting is that Marion presents the envisaging of the other in an ethical context, in terms of the injunction "Thou shalt not kill," that is, "Thou shalt not objectivize the other" by reducing its endless flux of meanings to a determinate meaning or, at the limit, by annulling it as the other who envisages me.[26] The knowledge of the other that love seeks also meets a demand of justice.

At the same time, Marion quite explicitly argues for the superiority of love over justice by showing how it is necessary that justice surpass itself in (and as) love. Marion's most extensive reflections on ethics occur in two essays on Lévinas.[27] In both essays Marion points to *aporias* or paradoxes in the ethics of Kant and Lévinas. In the earlier of the two essays, Marion turns again to the injunction that exposes one to the other as other rather than as object. He points out a limitation of the injunction. In itself, the injunction opens me to any other and thus to every possible other. As such it possesses universality. According to this universality, however, the role played by the particular other opened up by the injunction could be played by anyone. And the respect the injunction imposes on me is not respect for *this* other but for the universal law instead. Paradoxically, by way of the very injunction that demands that I treat the other as end and never as a means only, I end up using the particular other as a means to accomplish the universal. It is precisely at this point, Marion notes, that Lévinas reformulates the injunction in terms of singularity: the other does not place me before the injunction as a universal law; rather the injunction places me directly before the singularity of the other, making me responsible for her precisely in her singularity. However, Marion points out that this singularity still allows for substitution, for any face can compel my responsibility. How, then, can the other opened up by the injunction be not only singular but also unsubstitutable? This can occur only if the injunction extends beyond the universal to the unique, to an other who is the other of all the others—that is, if it extends to love.

Thus Marion unfolds the injunction that opens up the face of the other as such in the passage from (Kantian) obligation to (Lévinasian) responsibility to love, a passage marked by an increasing degree of singularity or unsubstitutability of the other that is required by ethics in its orientation to the other. If we may sum up obligation and responsibility under the heading of justice, we can think of this passage as one in which love completes justice insofar as it alone accomplishes the singularity of the other as her unsubstitutability that is required by justice itself. Justice is unable to accomplish its own requirement and therefore must complete itself in love. At the same time, love clearly surpasses justice in that it alone opens up the particular other.

This same trajectory from justice to love also governs "From the Other to the Individual," although here Marion credits Lévinas, in some late writings and interviews, with having eventually arrived at the view Marion espouses. This essay focuses on Lévinas's early contrast of the ethical with the anonymity of being, arguing that the very anonymity Lévinas objected to in ontology reappears in his ethics. Lévinasian alterity, Marion points out at length, requires an other without individuating features. Here Marion links Lévinas more closely to the Kantian paradox in which morality delivers the other over to the universal law. For Kant, according to Marion, respect as the moral motive bears not on any individual at all but rather on the universal law, which itself requires indifference to the individuating features of those who fall under it. This paradox emerges clearly in a passage where Kant insists that reverence is for the moral law itself rather than for the individual. In other words, morality not only relates the other solely to the anonymous neutrality of the universal law but insists that this is all that the other can expect or require of me.[28] As in the earlier essay, the paradox is that ethics requires a kind of particularity that it cannot deliver, namely, the unsubstitutability of the other in her particularity. As Marion puts it in the later essay, "It remains no less a necessity, even and especially in ethics, . . . to particularize the face, to individuate it."[29] Yet, as Marion points out, only love can individuate the face, that is, accomplish its unsubstitutability. Thus only love can fulfill what ethics itself, in the name of justice, demands.

We have now identified various senses in which love, while clearly in a position of privilege with respect to justice, nevertheless relates positively to justice. The crucial point is this: for Marion it remains a matter of justice whether the other is received as other or is objectivized or delivered over to the neutrality of law. In Kant's terms, justice demands that I treat the other as an "end" and never as a "means" only, though for Marion the fulfillment of this imperative requires that I accept the other person as another person in the first place and that I not (as Kant did in his very formula, which enjoins me to treat as an end not the other person herself but humanity in her as well as in myself) refer her to the universal but receive her in her unsubstitutable particularity. Justice, then, is subordinated to love less because love involves an alternative way of relating to the other than because justice is radically dependent on love.

Of course, for Marion the unsubstitutability love offers goes well beyond justice. Nevertheless, is it not precisely the traces of justice that remain in love that present the greatest problem according to critics of Marion? Central to Marion's effort to deliver love from its modern denigration and restore it to its rightful place is his insistence that love is the privileged route of access to the other. Love, he shows, does not reduce the other to the subjectivity of my consciousness or my intentionality, nor is it mere intellectual representation. In other words, love does not reduce the other to an object; it truly is the other whose phenomenality love accomplishes. Yet this alternative—either other or object—is the alternative on which the ethical is founded. It forbids, as the unjust reduction of the other to the same, not only the grounding of my relation to the beloved in my lived experience of her—in the effect of her particular features on my consciousness or in my election of her on the grounds of her particular features—but also the grounding of my relation to the other in a shared mutuality. Love goes beyond justice not by accomplishing a relation to the other that is "deeper" than the relation to her as unsubstitutable, but by accomplishing a common unsubstitutability in a crossing of the gazes that is known to the lovers alone. The gaze that accomplishes the unsubstitutable in its identity with the injunction enjoins me to accomplish my own unsubstitutability, resulting in what Marion calls "a common, though not symmetrical, unsubstitutability."[30] Thus the injunction that begins with obligation ends in what we might call a "commonality without reciprocity" in which justice seems to be inscribed within the very heart of love.[31] There is, in short, an ethical reservation that seems to govern Marion's entire phenomenology of love.[32] Love is delivered from the thought that holds it to be vulgar by being lifted to the status of justice, which indeed it surpasses but whose trace it still retains.

Just as the trace of justice that remains in love invites the suspicion that love as Marion describes it is not adequate to certain aspects of love, Marion's conviction that love completes justice seems to invite the criticism that justice so completed is not really justice. Having argued for the necessity of the particularity of the other in contrast to the delivery of the other to the anonymity of the universal, Marion appears to foreclose the possibility of a responsibility beyond particularity: "For could I be responsible for the universal? Could my responsibility, even limitless, exercise itself on me, if it was not exercising itself against a particular Other, where alone the universal phenomenalizes itself?"[33] Unlike Lévinas, Marion does not show how the relation to the singular other requires while at the same time limits the universal, which is necessary for justice in its concrete forms. By responding to the other in her uniqueness, love offers what justice ultimately requires and is unable to deliver. But justice also requires that I not respond to the other only in her uniqueness; it also requires placing the unique other amid the multiple others even as it limits and qualifies this delivery of the other to the universality of the moral law. While Lévinas understands the difficulty and gravity of this problem of particularity and universality in justice, Marion seems to ignore it. If so, then love in his thought does not so much complete justice as pass through it.

Love as Knowledge, Love as Deed

We now turn to a final instance of the de-privileging of ethics. In this instance love does appear to involve an indifference to ethics. The problem of the other for Marion is fundamentally a problem of knowledge of the other: how can I know the other as other without reducing her to an object of intention or consciousness? In posing this question Marion returns to the problem Husserl faced in the fifth of his *Cartesian Meditations,* only now it cannot be knowledge of another I or the envisaging of the other in the same way she envisages me, but rather a knowledge that occurs in the crossing of incomparable and asymmetrical gazes. Nevertheless, it is knowledge that Marion privileges in love; here his tendency, noted at the outset, to treat the love commandments of the Gospels in terms of knowledge of the other rather than in terms of ethical deeds is indicative of a more fundamental privilege granted to knowledge over deed in his work. That privilege is also apparent in the treatment of the endless hermeneutic as a problem for knowledge of the other, as if the obligation to respond to the pain, the hunger, the anguish, and the fear of the other did not weigh on me as much as the obligation to interpret the other. "To know following love, and to know what love itself reveals"—if Christians and others are to work in this vein, it is to be hoped that love reveals more of the neighbor than what appeals to my knowledge in abstraction from my deed.

This problem in Marion's thought concerning love is especially apparent in his essay "What Love Knows." Early in this essay Marion points out that the parables of the Last Judgment hinge not on faith or hope but on charity: "Have we helped our neighbor, given even from our surplus, loved the least among us? This is the only criteria [sic], the only crisis, the only test."[34] Yet, later in the same essay, Marion treats the parable of the Good Samaritan as a figure of the acceptance or occultation of the other as other, ignoring the fact that it was the naked, beaten body of the Samaritan that provokes the question of the other.[35] Finally, near the end of the essay he speaks of the reduction of charity to "doing charity" as a betrayal of charity, its submission "to the iron law of '. . . doing'" and thus objectification of the other.[36] The reduction of charity to doing in a crude sense is, of course, its betrayal; the stereotypical mechanical, bureaucratic delivery of "services" does indeed objectify the other. But it is also crude to characterize the deed as such in these terms, as if it took only this form. Yet, the only alternative Marion offers in this essay—and not only in this essay—is love as knowledge of the other that appears to abstract from the deed altogether. Unlike the tensions between love and justice discussed above, the effacement of the deed in favor of knowledge in Marion's phenomenology of love suggests an exclusion of the ethical.

I referred above to the endless hermeneutic in which one who would envisage the face is involved. For Marion, revealed theology has an eschatological solution to this problem, which in philosophy can be resolved only through resort to the notion of the infinite. Theology has recourse to faith in the final manifestation of the face of the other, when its truth will be manifested in the glorification of the infinite Face. Until then, "the face of the other person remains a phenomenon of inaccessible meaning."[37] But what does faith do while it awaits the return of Christ? Many things, of course, but at least one of the parables of the Last Judgment (which, as Marion notes, is where the last judgment, the interpretation in which the meaning of the face is fully expressed, is accomplished) holds that it is precisely in the ethical deed in the present—feeding the hungry, welcoming the stranger, clothing the naked, caring for the sick, visiting the prisoner—that the infinite Face, now inaccessible, will manifest itself. "Lord, when was it that we saw [eidomen] you hungry?" and so on. "Truly I tell you, just as you did it to one of the least of these . . . you did it to me" (Matt. 25:37, 40 [NRSB]). The eschatological disclosure of the now inaccessible meaning is anticipated in the present by the ethical deed, and this is one important sense in which faith without works is dead. For revealed theology, at least, knowledge of the other is inseparable from the deed.

Conclusion

In raising the question of ethics in Marion's work we have admittedly approached that work from its margins. Yet for the most part the demotion of ethics in favor of love as the privileged route of access to the other in Marion's thought does not mean that ethics is ignored or rejected. To the contrary, we have seen that in his phenomenological project generally and in his phenomenology of love in particular Marion aims in part to preserve the ethical. In principle, his claims that love is a condition of the possibility of justice and that love completes justice point in the direction theology and philosophy should move if they are to overcome the split between love and justice that is characteristic of much of modern ethics. I have raised questions about whether, in Marion's particular formulation of this relation of love and justice, love can really be love and justice really be justice, but these are not questions about the relation of love and justice in itself. However, we have seen the indifference to love as deed in Marion's work, which is due to a nearly exclusive emphasis on love as knowledge and which seems to involve a denigration of ethics at the hands of love.

Whether Marion will ever address the ethical phenomenon in the same detail he has devoted to the erotic phenomenon is, of course, unknown. But perhaps more important than the relative degrees of attention he has addressed to love and ethics are his gestures beyond the modern fractures between ontology and ethics and between love and justice, fractures that have had such a debilitating effect on modern theology and philosophy alike.

Notes

1. Jean-Luc Marion, "What Love Knows," in *Prolegomena to Charity*, trans. Stephen Lewis (New York: Fordham University Press, 2002), 169.

2. See esp. Jean-Luc Marion, "The Gift of a Presence" and "What Love Knows," both in *Prolegomena to Charity.* Marion privileges the Johannine formulation of the

love commandment over the synoptic formulations and treats even the latter in terms of knowledge of the other rather than the ethical deed.

3. Marion, "What Love Knows," in *Prolegomena to Charity*, 153.

4. Ibid., 155–60, 68; Jean-Luc Marion, *Le phénomène érotique: six méditations* (Paris: Grasset, 2003), 15.

5. Specifically, he finds this in the early work of Lévinas. See Jean-Luc Marion, "From the Other to the Individual," in *Transcendence: Philosophy, Literature, and Theology: Approach the Beyond*, ed. Regina Schwartz (New York: Routledge, 2004), 52.

6. See, e.g., Edith Wyschogrod, *Emmanuel Lévinas: The Problem of Ethical Metaphysics* (The Hague: Martinus Nijhoff, 1974); Robert Gibbs, *Why Ethics?* (Princeton: Princeton University Press, 2000).

7. Jean-Luc Marion, *In Excess: Studies in the Saturated Phenomenon*, trans. Robyn Horner and Vincent Berrau (New York: Fordham University Press, 2001), 25–26.

8. Jean-Luc Marion, *Being Given: Toward a Phenomenology of Givenness*, trans. Jeffrey L. Kosky (Stanford: Stanford University Press, 2002), 266f.

9. Emmanuel Lévinas, "Is Ontology Fundamental?" in *Entre Nous*, trans. Michael B. Smith and Barbara Harshav (New York: Columbia University Press, 1998), 9–10; and Lévinas, *Totality and Infinity: An Essay on Exteriority*, trans. Alphonso Lingis (Pittsburgh: Dusquesne University Press, 1969), 198–99.

10. Marion, *In Excess*, 118–19.

11. See also the analysis of the responsal that the *adonné* makes to the call in terms of responsibility in *Being Given*, 293–94.

12. Jean-Luc Marion, "The Freedom to Be Free," in *Prolegomena to Charity*, 31.

13. Martin Heidegger, "Letter on 'Humanism,'" in *Pathmarks*, ed. William McNeill (Cambridge: Cambridge University Press, 1998), 268–71.

14. Lévinas, *Totality and Infinity*, 40–52.

15. Marion, "The Freedom to Be Free," 49.

16. See ibid., 48–52.

17. Freedom without being, without cause, and without effect can also be understood as a phenomenological return to Kant's notion of freedom as noumenal.

18. Jean-Luc Marion, "The Original Otherness of the Ego," in *The Ethical* (Oxford: Blackwell, 2003), 33–53.

19. Ibid., 43, 49.

20. Marion, "What Love Knows," in *Prolegomena to Charity*, 163.

21. Ibid., 166.

22. This is explored most fully in Marion, *Le phénomène érotique*, 111–68.

23. Søren Kierkegaard, *Works of Love*, trans. Howard Hong and Edna Hong (Princeton: Princeton University Press, 1995), 44.

24. Marion, *In Excess*, 117.

25. Jean-Luc Marion, "The Intentionality of Love," in *Prolegomena to Charity*, 73–75; Marion, "What Love Knows," in *Prolegomena to Charity*, 164.

26. Marion, *In Excess*, 117–27. Marion finds a profound example of obedience to this injunction in Mark Rothko's "self-mutilation," that is, his refusal to objectify the face by painting it (ibid., 78f). See also Marion, "What Love Knows," in *Prolegomena*

to Charity, 164, where in criticism of Husserl's analogical route to the other, Marion points out various ways we may, and do, ignore or reject the analogy, and thus fail to recognize the other as other.

27. Marion, "The Intentionality of Love," in *Prolegomena to Charity*, 71–101; Marion, "From the Other to the Individual," in *Transcendence*, 43–59.

28. Ibid., 51. Marion quotes Kant's *Metaphysics of Morals*, AK, VI, 468. However, it is not clear that Lévinas follows Kant at this point. For Lévinas, the neutrality of the universal arises in the question of the third or of the multiple others of whom I must also take account in my responsibility to the other. Marion's earlier essay, where he distinguishes Lévinasian responsibility for the singular but still substitutable other from Kantian universality, is more adequate to Lévinas's position.

29. Marion, "From the Other to the Individual," in *Transcendence*, 49.

30. Marion, "The Intentionality of Love," in *Prolegomena to Charity*, 100.

31. This nonreciprocity seems also to be a fundamental characteristic of the erotic phenomenon just to the extent that the phenomenality of the latter is defined by the advance: if love is love by virtue of my loving first, love excludes reciprocity, as Marion explicitly points out on pages 115–16 of *Le phénomène érotique*.

32. This does not mean that Marion's argument for the nonreciprocality of love depends on ethics. In *Le phénomène érotique* this nonreciprocality is grounded in the centrality of love as advance.

33. Marion, "From the Other to the Individual," in *Transcendence*, 154.

34. Marion, "What Love Knows," in *Prolegomena to Charity*, 154–55.

35. Ibid., 166.

36. Ibid., 168.

37. Marion, *In Excess*, 124.

11

Responsibility within Politics

The Origin of Locke's Idea of Equality

MICHAEL KESSLER

To offer a judgment about Jean-Luc Marion's relation to political theology is a daunting task: there seems to be little that is immediately relevant to politics in his large corpus of writings. This has been a source of consternation for those compelled by his boldly creative phenomenology who would like him to develop its possible implications for a theory of justice. Perhaps he learned from Heidegger, his phenomenological predecessor, that merging ontological insight with political prescription leads to naïve, if not disastrous, consequences. Or it may be that he actually believes what he once quipped to me when I asked why he did not develop specifically political ideas: "It is more than I can accomplish to rule myself, let alone to rule the world."

We can leave aside the question whether engaging political theory necessarily first requires self-mastery. Other issues press upon us. Within the trajectory of phenomenology, little precise detail has been given about the relation of responsibility for the "other"—as this term is developed by thinkers such as Lévinas and Marion—and political obligations.[1] Often, the principles offered extend little beyond vague statements of wishful ideals: "[T]he recognition of and respect for difference calls for democratic deliberation in the ever dangerous presence of violence as the act of effacing the otherness of the Other."[2] This formulation, not an uncommon gesture in phenomenological discussions of responsibility, offers no specification about how deliberation should be instituted, maintained, or related to the exercise of power. Nor does this determine how responsibility, phenomenologically understood, might serve as a regulative ideal to control and direct power or be a foundation for *political* ideas of justice. If our best ideas about ethical responsibility are to matter—and I tend to believe that these principles are nowhere more keenly discussed than in phenomenology—they must be able to establish a link between notions of responsibility and practical politics: how can we make our political associations practically yield equality and respect for persons.

Ethical responsibility, as articulated by Lévinas and Marion, claims a realm of human value that is neither limited to personal interactions nor ignorant of collective life. Phenomenological responsibility respects no material boundaries of national border, political party, or ethnic identity. The task is not completed if we simply say that our ethical obligations toward others are satisfied by assigning certain tasks to the democratic state; this is a naïve view of the realities of power politics. The state's presence does not relieve me of these tasks arising from responsibility. The political tasks set before phenomenologists involve clarifying how the appearance of the human phenomenon obliges not only our unending personal pursuit of ethical responsibility, but also makes specific demands on our material political systems.

Liberal democratic political theory bases its legitimacy on an account of equality that demands respect for human dignity. Such modern political theory largely eschews any lingering attempt to ground ideas such as dignity and equality on anything but rational grounds. We must press this point, however, since the attempt to account sufficiently for these ideas on solely rational bases appears unsuccessful. This difficulty does not necessarily indicate a return to theocracy. Rather, if we admit the mere *possibility* that rational accounts of the dignity of the human may be insufficient to account for the dignity of the human, we carve out a twofold task: first, to articulate how rational political processes, laws, and institutions build on these ideas about the human, sustain themselves objectively, yet do not exhaust the human dignity on which they are founded; and second, to define how these ideas of the human can be known or experienced, if at all.

The latter question compels us to ask about the very possibility of political *theology.* To ask fundamental questions about the grounds of political systems and allegiance is to engage questions about the nature of human being. Such anthropologies run the risk of falling into the trap Marion described for the religious phenomenon itself: either "it would be a question of phenomena that are objectively definable but lose their religious specificity," or "it would be a question of phenomena that are specifically religious but cannot be described objectively."[3] Does political theory, if it takes seriously fundamental anthropology, necessarily betray a basic objectivity? If political theology points to (or depends on) a claim about a set of core human characteristics that are excessive of reason, does political theology have anything of value to contribute toward modern political thought? What if rational politics is found to have a set of core claims that cannot be accounted for objectively? Must it be dismissed as pseudo-theological or might we find a way to admit properly basic claims that themselves are not fully objective? Can phenomenology help to illuminate a way out of this predicament, if there is one, such that nonobjective sources of the imperative to responsibility can be admitted, while at the same time acknowledging rigorous standards for political processes that are rationally defensible and public?

If the claims of politics can be objective, which we certainly must hope is the case, then political theology, which (properly and, may we say, most honestly) makes claims about a nonobjective core of the human (e.g. inherent dignity, freedom of the will, basic and inalienable rights), would have as its task to "render visible what nevertheless could not be objectivized" ("Saturated," 103). An account of these human attributes and rights that hopes to experience their fullness would (must) hesitate from reducing these core attributes into objectivity, since their proper richness (saturation) might very well be lost in the translation into purely rational accounts. While political theology would render them visible for the wider discussion of rights and institutions, political theology would simultaneously demand that they not be reduced to a common range object. For any political theology to be relevant to politics, a system of human interactions that demands the bases of claims to be objective and rational, requires that such claims be made visible in a public and universal way. Yet for political theology to treat its object seriously—the human in all of their manifold complexity and sacrality—it must reject any purely objectivizing account of the human phenomenon. The task of political theology is thus *to render visible the "unconditioned and irreducible phenomena" of human life that ground political life.*

In this essay, I explore how one such phenomenon—the idea of equality—was developed by John Locke and used as the basis of his political theory. Try as he might, Locke's exposition leaves the reader unconvinced that equality is a properly rational idea, that is, an idea derived from objective, rational grounds. While Locke attempts to show how equality is a rational idea, in the end he assigns a *divine* origin to the idea of human equality. The human had a noble birth by God and was, as such, a natural phenomenon harboring an inexhaustible surplus of value. Locke's whole political project extends from this idea of equality in a rational manner, yet it fundamentally rests on a fideistic claim about human dignity. This presents a significant problem, for which I shall turn to Marion's phenomenology as an aid to help in understanding how Locke derives his account of political foundations and related it to rational politics.

Some have cursorily recognized this problem and subsequently dismissed this element of Locke as cryptotheological, calling into question the entire political edifice built on his idea of equality.[4] However, these dismissals most often fail to understand what Locke thought was at stake. He was not simply using theological categories as fairy tales to explain away difficult problems. Rather, we shall see that rational concepts appear to have been insufficient to assist him in accounting for the human phenomenon he described. This being the case, we might learn much from Locke, even as we move beyond him. An account of the dignity of the human may require a foundational claim that cannot be rendered wholly visible according to the schematic of objective reason, yet nonetheless does not sacrifice our duty to articulate a rational political system. For it may be the case that the abundant reality of the human phenomenon finds rational categories like equality too poor to adequately contain its nobility.

Locke develops his principal foundation for politics through the idea of equality: humans are equal, rational creatures and this fact requires their equal standing and treatment before legal institutions and a complete reciprocity of rights between each individual. They cannot be legitimately subordinated one to another without due process of law. Locke develops this idea, and its political consequences, in his *Second Treatise on Government* (1690), where he espouses perhaps the most influential theory of modern, liberal political theory. There Locke argues that each individual, including the sovereign, is bound by criteria of transcendental justice known through natural reason, which teaches that every human, being equal and independent, should not harm any other in his or her life, liberty, health, or property. Indeed, equality in the Lockean system is the benchmark against which every political claim is to be judged.

Let us briefly review Locke's major aims in the *Two Treatises on Government*. He sought to marshal his idea of equality against Robert Filmer, who espoused a natural hierarchy of human authority that supported monarchial rule. The *First Treatise* proves, in Locke's mind, that it is "impossible that the Rulers now on Earth, should make any benefit, or derive any the least shadow of Authority from that which is held to be the Fountain of all Power, *Adam's Private Dominion and Paternal Jurisdiction*" (*First Treatise*, I, 1, 267). On this basis, Locke claims that the dominion Adam inherited from God was the birthright of *all* humanity, not singularly Adam's and his appointed successors. This fundamentally undercut any claim to the divine right of monarchial succession from Adam's initial authority.

While the *First Treatise* shows that Adam's dominion in and over the world is shared by all humanity, the *Second Treatise* spells out the nature of the political order befitting such independently free and equal creatures. Locke's goal was to show, against Hobbes, that it is not the case that "all Government in the World is the product only of Force and Violence, and that Men live together by no other Rules but that of Beasts, where the strongest carries it, and so lay a Foundation for perpetual discord and Mischief, Tumult, Sedition and Rebellion" (*Second Treatise*, I, 1, 267–68). Locke instead forcefully asserts that humans are the kinds of creatures that cannot legitimately live by might alone. While Hobbes grounded the need for political society on the selfish, rational calculation that without law and order one's own pursuits could never be stably achieved, Locke describes a more noble vision of the obligations we humans owe to each other. Leaving aside the question whether this is superior to Hobbesist anthropology, Locke's vision took root as the basis of modern democracy, most notably underlying the American constitutional experiment.

Locke's theory is based on a transcendental account of reason and equality. He aimed to "understand Political Power right," (i.e., objectively and properly), and "derive it from its Original," (i.e., a proper account of the way the human actually *is*). Politics would henceforth be based, he thought, not on an anthropology of force, but on a nonnegotiable, authentic duty to respect others because they are equal to ourselves. But from where does this idea of equality arise?

Locke argues that we must uncover the original, natural conditions of the human if we are to rightly understand this obligation and its consequent politics.[5] Any quest for political origins drives us back to the state of human-kind prior to all attempts to autonomously structure the world through politics and culture, the so-called state of nature. This move, toward the *pure phenomenon* of the human, interests us here. Insofar as Locke purports to show us the human as a natural phenomenon, we must illuminate his connection between the natural state of the human phenomenon and the idea of equality that he claims emerges from the experience of that phenomenon.

His description of the pure phenomenon of the human in the state of nature comes in the early part of the *Second Treatise:*

> We must consider what State all Men are naturally in, and that is, a *State of perfect Freedom* to order their Actions, and dispose of their Possessions, and Persons as they think fit, within the bounds of the Law of Nature, without asking leave, or depending upon the Will of any other Man.
>
> A *State* also of *Equality,* wherein all the Power and Jurisdiction is reciprocal, no one having more than another: there being nothing more evident, than that Creatures of the same species and rank promiscu-ously born to all the same advantages of Nature, and the use of the same faculties, should also be equal one amongst another without Subordina-tion or Subjection. (*Second Treatise,* II, 4, 269)

Locke's attempt here is to isolate the human in its *pure* state, unblemished by cultural constructs, presented to our rational investigation. He claims that the human bears a set of ideal characteristics (freedom and equality) that are available to the perception of others: when looking on my fellow human beings, I can see that they have such attributes. Locke seems to think that these human phenomena—the human as equal and free—are so self-evident they barely need more than mere assertion to gain our assent to their reality. Far from holding them to be obvious, however, we must question how it may be possible that such a phenomenon—a human we know to be our equal and are obliged to respect—could appear to us as such.

Marion can aid us in this investigation since he instructively posed a simi-lar question in "The Saturated Phenomenon." There he articulated, with ref-erence to Kant, the necessary conditions under which a phenomenon may possibly appear. In general, for a phenomenon to be possible, it must agree "with the formal conditions of experience, that is, with the conditions of intu-ition and concepts."[6] That is, for something to be possible for humans, the "thing" must submit to the formal conditions of human experience: "The postulate of the possibility of things requires that the concept of things should agree with the formal conditions of an experience in general."[7] A phenomenon can be possible as a thing appearing within the human world insofar as what objectively appears [*Erscheinenden*] correlates to appearance in general [*Erscheinen*], that is, the subjective appearing to the intentional agent who actively seeks out and perceives or receives the appearance ("Saturated," 107–8).

Thus any phenomenon is "possible that grants itself to the finitude of the power of knowing and its requirements" ("Saturated," 104). The "formal conditions" and "requirements" of this appearing are intuition (the "originary data" of the appearing) and concepts (the mental categories of understanding by which the mind is able to understand anything in the manifold of intuition). "Intuition and the concept determine in advance the possibility of appearing for any phenomenon" ("Saturated," 104). As Kant articulated their relation:

> [W]ithout sensibility, no object would be given to us, without understanding no object would be thought. Thoughts without content are empty, intuitions without concepts are blind. It is, therefore, just as necessary to make our concepts sensible (that is, to add the object to them in intuition), as to make our intuitions intelligible (that is, to bring them under concepts). These two powers or capacities cannot exchange their functions. The understanding can intuit nothing, the senses can think nothing.[8]

The concept is "king" in terms of understanding the appearance, since it provides the form by which the appearance is organized. Yet "before an object is seen and in order to be seen, its appearance must be given; even if it does not see what it gives, intuition alone enjoys the privilege of giving" ("Saturated," 109). Thus intuition "ensures the concept's condition of possibility—its possibility itself: 'intuitions in general, through which objects can be given to us, constitute the field or whole object of possible experience.'"[9]

The distinction between intuition and concepts focuses our inquiry into Locke's presentation of the idea of equality. If a lack of intuition does plague certain phenomena, as Marion has described it, might it be the case that Locke's position suffers because our concepts for the idea of equality are stronger than the intuitions that emanate from the phenomenon? Does he assume a rational category of equality whose application to the human being he finds troubled by a deficit of intuition? Or does he encounter the converse problem: do humans appear through a saturation of intuition for which there are insufficient corresponding categories of reason. Was Locke therefore plagued by the persistent metaphysical problem that "in order for the phenomenon to be reduced to an obviously finite 'I' who constitutes it, the phenomenon must be reduced to the status of finite objectivity" ("Saturated," 111). Could it be that in trying to show us that humans are equal to each other, grand and noble creatures that we are, Locke ends up treating us as objects? Is our collective inability to sufficiently ground this idea of equality based on a lack within the concept of equality? We must contend with this basic problem in Locke's analysis and determine whether it is our concept of equality or our intuitions of the human that are deficient.

Armed with this distinction, let us explore in more detail Locke's argument that humans appear as equals to each other by turning to the first stipulation that humans are in a state of freedom. Locke relies on the *lingua franca* of his day to support his claims about the free capacities of the human species. Hobbes and Spinoza provided an idea of the will that isolated the function of self-preservation as the goal of each individual substance. The individual's passions, or endeavor, are the interior inclinations that prompt one to persevere in existence: pain is avoided and pleasure is sought.[10] The passions are internal forces that push the human along to ends of subjective pleasure while avoiding those stimuli that bring displeasure and consequent harm (*Leviathan*, 6). For Hobbes, the will is, strictly speaking, the last appetite or aversion immediately adhering to the action. In this respect, the will is always disposed to act, awaiting the completion of deliberation between competing appetites and aversions, until one is chosen (*Leviathan*, 44). Thus the will is at rest only because it is restrained by some external force that prevents it from acting, whether that external force is another agent, physical constraints, or internal checks on action.

According to Hobbes, the will possesses *infinite* freedom before determining itself to a concrete action; it can choose any direction in which to act, any aversion or appetite to follow. Thus in the state of nature, humans have unconditional freedom: "[B]y Liberty, is understood . . . the absence of externall

Impediments" (*Leviathan*, 91). In its efforts to self-preserve, the will has license to expend its power without constraint toward the goal of furthering its own existence: "[T]he right of nature . . . is the liberty each man hath, to use his own power, as he will himselfe, for the preservation of his Nature; that is to say, of his own Life; and consequently, of doing any thing, which in his own Judgment, and Reason, hee shall conceive to be the aptest means thereunto" (*Leviathan*, 91). The law of nature in this passage refers to the self-preserving tendencies of the human will. In extending their own existence, they act according to the most basic law of nature, to self-preserve: "A Law of Nature, (*Lex Naturalis*,) is a Precept, or generall Rule, found out by Reason, by which a man is forbidden to do, that, which is destructive of his life, or taketh away the means of preserving the same; and to omit, that, by which he thinketh it may be best preserved" (*Leviathan*, 91).

Locke adopts this principle of human freedom but adds another dimension: the individual's use of reason can (and should) constrain the individual's desires and ends for more than individual preservation; every freedom is bound by the law of reason.[11] Because reason is objective in the Lockean world, the state of nature is not a condition of pure license but one in which individuals are constrained by a rational law that obligates them with respect to how they discharge their actions, especially against and around other human beings. The will cannot simply act on its whims or arbitrary desires; desires may abound but actions must conform to principles that correspond to rational laws that transcend the ego. Those laws teach that actions that bear on another individual cannot intentionally bring undue harm to that other: "Reason . . . teaches all Mankind . . . *that being all equal*, and independent, no one ought to harm another in his Life, Health, Liberty, or Possessions" (*Second Treatise*, II, 6, 271, emphasis added). Whereas Hobbesian rationality could lead one to more cleverly and effectively gain one's goals irrespective of the aims of other agents—after all, their respective inequalities of capacities and skill might be manipulated to another's advantage—Lockean rationality requires one to regard the other agent as a constraint on our unbridled freedom. But why are we so obliged to other humans? Locke answers: because we have this idea through a law of nature, given somehow by reason, that all humans are in a state of equality with each other. A *concept* of equality informs our experience of humans as he states it here. Regardless of our desires for power or superiority, perhaps coincidental to our desires to treat others well, the fount of this notion is a concept that the mind *assigns* to the experience. But from where does this concept arise in the mind? Is it derived from reason or given in the interpersonal experience?

We must note the extent to which *everything* depends on equality; without it, Locke's idea of human freedom could not transcend Hobbes's doctrine of a state of license. Without the principle of equality, human freedom would have no obligation to constrain itself when confronted with another human being. For Locke, equality demands respect and responsibility among human agents. Equality grounds an obligation imposed on us whether or not we choose to obey it, regardless of whether we recognize it, irrespective of our desires to act against it.

For his part, Hobbes presents a peculiar version of human equality that illuminates Locke by way of contrast. Each person, striving for their own preservation, has the right to "secure himself by his own strength, and to invade a suspected neighbor, by way of prevention" (*Leviathan,* 26). Free agents, after all, have the capacity to render harm to others; the potential victim therefore has a due right to protect himself, toward the natural end of his own self-preservation. For Hobbes, this creates a condition of interminable strife and perpetual enmity. Thus, the condition of the state of nature is perpetually insecure, due to the conflicts arising between individual agents. For Hobbes, this means first—and here is the substance of his political theory—that one needs the all-powerful sovereign to coerce compliance with laws that aim to achieve security between otherwise free and unbridled agents. Second, and more to our specific point, each agent represents an *equal* threat to every other agent:

> Nature hath made men so equall, in the faculties of body, and mind; as that though there bee found one man sometimes manifestly stronger in body, or of quicker mind then another; yet when all is reckoned together, the difference between man, and man, is not so considerable, as that one man can thereupon claim to himselfe any benefit, to which another may not pretend, as well as he. For as to the strength of body, the weakest has strength enough to kill the strongest, either by secret machination, or by confederacy with others, that are in the same danger with himselfe. (*Leviathan,* 87)

For Hobbes, equality in the state of nature is due to the material fact that each human is equally able to kill every other. Consequently, each human is equally vulnerable to perish at the hands of even the weakest member of the species. For Hobbes, equality amounts to the equivalent capacity of each member of the species to harm every other and the equivalent state of vulnerability of each at the hands of every other (*Leviathan*, 87).

Locke claims much more than this: equality is a transcendentally affirmed obligation such that "all the Power and Jurisdiction is reciprocal, no one having more than another" (*Second Treatise*, II, 4, 269). Thus equality has to do more with an *objective claim* to the equal right to exercise some set of powers, not simply the equivalent material capacity to discharge those powers. Locke first asserts that this objective right is rationally self-evident when he cites the origin of the idea in Richard Hooker's legal theory: "This *equality* of Men by Nature, the Judicious *Hooker* looks upon as so evident in it self, and beyond all question, that he makes it the Foundation of that Obligation to mutual Love amongst Men, on which he Builds the Duties they owe one another, and from whence he derives the great Maxims *of Justice* and *Charity* (*Second Treatise*, II, 5, 270).

However, Locke's gesture toward Hooker doesn't get him what he wants: a strong and express claim that each human is equal and we are, therefore, obliged to act toward each other in certain ways. But why is Hooker's pronouncement insufficient? The answer is that he makes this claim in the midst of his purported discovery of the "natural way, whereby rules have been found out concerning that goodness wherewith the will of man ought to be moved in human actions."[12] Hooker asserts that it is *plain and clear by the natural light* that every human is equal one to another, and with this knowledge comes an imperative to respect every other:

> The like natural inducement hath brought men to know, that it is their duty no less to love others than themselves. For seeing those things which are equal, must needs all have one measure; if I cannot but wish to receive all good, even as much at every man's hand as any man can wish unto his own soul: how should I look to have any part of my desire herein satisfied, unless myself be careful to satisfy the like desire, which is undoubtedly in other men, we all being one, and the same nature? . . . My desire therefore to be loved of my equals in nature as much as possibly may be, imposeth upon me a natural duty of bearing to them-ward fully the like affection. From which relation of equality between ourselves and them that are as ourselves, what several rules and canons

natural reason hath drawn for direction of life, no man is ignorant. (*Laws*, 80)

Hooker bases the equality of the human species on their common striving for affection, a need arising from a capacity. He posits the principle that those things that are equal in capacity are all due the same measure. That is, those entities that bear the same capacities are to be judged according to the same standard and accorded the same rights. We know other humans are our equals *because* we see in them a common desire for affection and a common harm suffered when that desire is not met.

However, there is nothing in the empirical experience of the common desire for esteem that would seem, on the face of it, to necessarily oblige another human being in an objective sense. Why should I be moved to action based on someone else's desires, even if I share those desires for myself? That some person shares a desire similar to mine does not entail that I owe them something substantially more than any other person with whom I share fewer capacities. Nor does the fact that I wish my peers to hold me in esteem necessarily entail that, in hoping to achieve that end, I will either desire to hold them in reciprocal esteem, or even actually need to esteem them. Indeed, my desire for esteem often may result in competing against the others' interests, since esteem may very well involve achieving a superior position over a peer's, at their expense. Ultimately, there is nothing in this version of the idea of equality that necessarily moves us out of the Hobbesian world of egoistic strife. Indeed, Hooker's position is not that different from Hobbes's account of equality on one important point: equality is based on a similarity of capacities. Where for Hobbes, humans are equal in that one is equally vulnerable at the hands of any other (because of common capacities they possess), Hooker claims that humans are equal out of this one capacity: the desire for affection. Neither position gets us to a firm answer for why anyone else should, or must, care and act accordingly.

While Locke initially claims obedience to Hooker's principle of equality, he ends up articulating something different: "Creatures of the same species and rank promiscuously born to all the same advantages of Nature, and the use of the same faculties, should also be equal one amongst another without Subordination or Subjection" (*Second Treatise*, II, 4, 269).[13] For Hooker, as we saw above, the desire that I have to be loved by others forces my recognition that they hope for the same, thereby imposing on me an obligation to respect this striving in the other. In essence, as I do not want to be disappointed in this desire, neither should I disappoint others. We are equal *due to* our awareness of an equivalent desire for recognition in them that we also possess. For Locke, however, the idea of equality, as he discusses it here, is based not on some similar act of striving or some common goal of that striving, but on a principle of taxonomic similarity: those possessing similar faculties are equal and should not suffer intraspecies subordination. The principle Locke espouses is akin to saying that every member of a species is equal since they have equivalent faculties. Since we intuit that creatures of the same species share equivalent capacities, we are supposed to conclude that there is nothing within a species to properly justify a hierarchy or subordination of some members over others. For this assertion to work, however, requires holding an unstated premise: a *qualitative* difference of natural capacities is required objectively to justify any real difference in the quantity of power that is exercised between members of the same species. To be just in exercising dominion requires more than mere quantitative surplus; one must possess more complex and different capacities. I can legitimately subordinate a tiger, who is physically stronger than me, because I possess reason and it does not. Yet I cannot justifiably enslave my weaker, younger brother because as humans we all share the same capacities, even though my strength in their use may, compared with my brother, be greater.[14]

This fails, however, to rise to the level of a proof for the obligation. Locke is trying to show that free capacities involve a "State of Liberty" but not a "State of License" (*Second Treatise*, II, 5, 270). For this, he needs a reason why liberty is constrained. Yet Locke has not provided an obligatory account of equality that arises *in me* through the phenomenal experience of the other. To address this, Locke extends the concept of equality beyond the notion of similarity of capacity and focuses on the specific capacity of freedom of intellect and will:

> And Reason, which is that Law [of nature], teaches all Mankind, who will but consult it, that being all equal, and independent, no one ought to harm another in his Life, Health, Liberty, or Possessions. (*Second Treatise*, II, 6, 271)

> All this [range of varied abilities] consists with the *Equality*, which all Men are in, in respect of Jurisdiction or Dominion one over another,

which was the *Equality* I there spoke of, as proper to the Business in hand, being that *equal Right* that every Man hath, *to his Natural Freedom,* without being subjected to the Will or Authority of any other Man. (*Second Treatise*, VI, 54, 304)

Here, Locke asserts that our status as equals is not based on the whole commonality of our capacities, but on the presence of the specific capacity we have for intellectual, self-directed action, or freedom. Since we are all free to discharge our intentions without interference from others, this freedom displays our equal status and grounds the prohibition on any intraspecies subjection. Our intellectual capacity and freedom to act on those intellectual directives ground a right to be equal among others so equipped. Hobbes, too, held that every agent is explicitly at liberty, but in the absence of the coercive state, he could find no *objective* bases on which to impose limitations on the exercise of that freedom with respect to other agents. Jeremy Waldron honed Locke's argument about commonality of capacity more directly: all creatures with the power of *abstraction* are to be considered equal.[15] Waldron holds that the capacity for abstract thought is the proper basis for human equality *because* Locke insists that abstraction can expose the divine reality via the light of natural reason. Anyone with the capacity for abstraction, who sees this same reflective capacity in another, must concede that this other agent should be accorded the same rights that one claims for oneself, since one's rights are understood to derive from having this reflective capacity.[16] To do otherwise would be a performative contradiction.

We can note an important result of this approach. Locke expresses something more pointed when he describes intuitive accounts of similar capacities: the human phenomenon with equivalent capacities is more than what we intuit because we know *by reason* that a human is a free agent with certain rights. Our experience of others gives rise to an idea about the other human we encounter—this other is an agent whose actions appear to be free, laden with rights we must respect. Yet the origin of this idea of equality is still unclear: do we impose it as a concept on the encounter or does this concept arise from our intuitive experience of the encounter? We have seen Locke assert that humans are equal to each other because they possess similar characteristics and bear equivalent capabilities, and in particular have similar powers of rational freedom. Yet we are left with the same difficulty: the intuitive encounter with the other as Locke describes it does not yet satisfy our demand for *strong* grounds for the obligation to respect others. How does this imperative arise *necessarily* from Locke's description of our interpersonal experience of seeing the reflective capacity in another? Might Locke face the conundrum we posed at the outset: how the concept of equality that grounds the imperative of respect is capable of either filling in for a deficit of intuition or attempting, however inadequately, to describe an encounter with a phenomenon saturated with intuition?

Locke must have recognized the deficiency of this result since he developed another, wholly different approach to ground the idea of equality. Back in the *First Treatise*, Locke specifically linked intellectual capacity with possession of the office of dominion, the divinely sanctioned capacity and authority to rule over inferior creatures (*First Treatise*, IV, 30, 162; IX, 92, 209). Lordship over the inferior creatures, so Locke read from the theological tradition, was explicitly forbidden to extend to intraspecies subordination. Since *every* human received a like share of the same dominion over the inferior animals, no one has authority over another human (*First Treatise*, IV, 29, 161). This claim is at the heart of Locke's rejection in the *First Treatise* of Filmer's position, in which Adam was held to have been given a special dispensation of authority, handed down through monarchial succession. For Locke, instead, the right of dominion over the world is given to every human equally. Humans must then respect each other as bearing this same capacity for dominion.

In the *Second Treatise*, after providing the (insufficient) capacities approach, Locke returns to this theological assertion from the *First Treatise* by assigning the ultimate basis for the prohibition against intrahuman subordination to a reading of the Creation narrative. Locke finds the ultimate ground for the idea of equality, not in a rational principle, but in the *origin* of the capacity: God, the Creator: "For Men being all the Workmanship of one Omnipotent, and infinitely wise Maker; All the Servants of one Sovereign Master, sent into the World by his order and about his business, they are his Property, whose Workmanship they are, made to last during his, not one anothers Pleasure" (*Second Treatise*, II, 6, 271).

After trying to ground the idea of equality on rational and empirical bases, Locke opts to rest it on a theological assertion. The only ground that works for an obligatory idea of equality is this bedrock theological stipulation. Because humans are created in common by the Divine to have dominion, because their obedience in how they discharge their capacity is due alone to God, they can only be the property of God alone. Elsewhere he insisted on this same point:

> Man made not himself nor any other man.
> Man made not the world which he found made at his birth.
> Therefore man at his birth can have no right to anything in the world
>   more than another.[17]

Since humans were created by a common, transcendent source they are limited in their range of dominion and, more to our point, are obligated to hold the other as a co-equal creature. The fact of creation imparts ownership rights to God; only the Divine can hold another as a subject. As fellow creatures of the same Divine Maker, humans share the same image: "God makes him *in his own Image after his own Likeness,* makes him an intellectual Creature, and so capable of *Dominion*" (*First Treatise,* IV, 30, 162). This dominion is a special capacity, according to Locke, because it makes us *like* the creator. In relation to other animals and the physical world, every human can exercise dominion analogous to God's dominion over us. In relation to each other, humans are fellow creatures of the same divine origin and cannot subject another to dominion.

Consequently, the traction of the idea of equality and the imperative to hold no other human in subjection does not ultimately arise from possessing the common capacity for dominion. Rather, its obligatory nature comes through divine promulgation. We hold our fellows as equal because their true nature is only known when we see them *through* our relation to the Divine. Without this theological concept to provide the objective and universal ground for the obligation to respect the equality of each other, Locke's political theory would be nothing more than a grand dream. Nor would Locke have gotten anywhere beyond Hobbes's position.

It is now clear that, for Locke, the concept of equality is imposed from on high. We do not intuit the human as equal through their phenomenal appearance; our empirical observations are insufficient to ground an obligation to treat them as equal and deserving of respect. The equality of all others cannot be derived from natural reason; it is instead built on a theological premise, perhaps the product of scriptural hermeneutics and Revelation, but functionally in the text as a basic stipulation *that just appears.* It seems that the depth of meaning for the idea of equality is one of those "many Things, wherein we have very imperfect Notions, or none at all . . . being beyond the Discovery of *Reason*" and which are, as such, "purely Matters of *Faith*."[18]

We immediately confront a significant issue at this juncture: Locke's rational politics articulates its core claim by recourse to a nonobjective account of human being. Such nonobjectivity appears in a double sense. First, this idea of equality is a nonobjective claim staked at the foundation of a rational system, given without deeper proof. Second, it is a claim to which some will assent because they see in Locke's account resonance with their intuitive experience of other people, while others will disagree, citing a lack of evidence. The claim that we are equal and obliged to act in certain ways toward each other is a deeply contested, intractable issue. How dubious is Locke's method of confronting the most important task of human community—building a political order—by grounding an objective state of affairs on a nonobjective and excessive idea of equality? If Locke's assertion of the dignity of the human is neither grasped in our experience, nor something about which we are rationally certain, what is the status of the political system built upon this claim? Is the objectivity of politics—and, therefore, its very claim to legitimacy—compromised by a foundation that exceeds strict objectivity and cannot be rationally defended all the way down to its deepest core assumptions? For if our answer is affirmative, then the rationalized politics of justice of our day is parasitic upon a notion for which it cannot account by its own devices.

We have established that in Locke, the concept of equality arises from outside the encounter with the other, as a theological concept imposed on the experience. Even while Locke admits that we are unable to completely synthesize this other that we encounter without divine assistance, our rational minds still proceed: in order to preserve and respect each person we encounter, we build objective and fair systems of politics. What do we make of this move by the rationalist Locke? Why, in the midst of articulating a system of purely rational politics, where he rejects many politico-theological arguments for the state as arbitrary and tyrannical justifications of unbridled power, does he turn to a theological ground for the fundamental concept of his system? One answer presents itself—that Locke is attempting to address a deficiency in reason itself, such that it is incapable of fully articulating the experience of the other human. That is, the encounter with others overwhelms one's intuition and exceeds the capacity of reason to supply an adequate concept—"a phenomenon in which intuition would give *more, indeed immeasurably more,* than intention ever would have intended or foreseen?" (112).

Of course, we should not arbitrarily privilege intuition without good cause, and the deficiency of reason in Locke's account is not necessarily sufficient for assuming that ideas of responsibility for the other can thereby adequately emerge from the intuition in the interpersonal encounter. But we know from Marion, and Lévinas before him, that responsibility may have a different origin, from within the human to human encounter itself. If the other human captures my "sight and attention" in the way of phenomenological responsibility, the Lockean political agent likewise "calls me and holds me at a distance by the weight of an invisible look, by its silent appeal" that commands my respect and induces a political duty.[19] Aren't the demands of phenomenological responsibility precisely those arising from the mode of encounter that we have seen Locke claim each human experiences when in proximity to another? The political human is saturated, presented to us with an excess of demands for how we ought to treat each individual, an ethical charge to respect every other in an endless hermeneutics, an encounter that obliges us to refuse arbitrary authority and choose instead to act toward the other as a unique, infinite bearer of the *imago dei*.

Given the analysis above, we could then base our reading of Locke's idea of equality on a newfound understanding of the limitations he faced in accounting for the excessive dignity of the human. We know from Locke that strictly rational and empirical grounds were never an adequate basis on which to view the core essence of the human being. Locke teaches us that strict objectivity in political theory down to its deepest foundations would be a misapplication of a rationality that does not know its limits. I take Locke's move toward the theological ground for equality as recognizing that both empirical and rational accounts are inadequate. We are more troubled by this maneuver than Locke, but the structure of the move is instructive: where rational categories are inadequate to correspond to the experience, we must find other ways to account for the phenomena in order to preserve the dignity of the human encountered. Instead, we could read in Locke, where he asserts a theological basis for the idea of equality, the equally excessive thought of responsibility as taught to us by the phenomenologists.

As Marion describes this failure of concepts and the understanding, to try to perceive the other by strictly rational means would yield insufficient results: "All that I would perceive of the other person as regards significations and intentions will remain always and by definition in the background and in deficit in relation to his or her face, a saturated phenomenon. And, therefore, I will only be able to bear this paradox and do it justice in consecrating myself to its infinite hermeneutic" (*Excess*, 126). Here, the objection that there is no necessary obligation of justice toward the other person is not due to a lack of evidence, but results from a problem of inattention toward their actual being. Stated more precisely, we misappropriate rational categories by applying them to a phenomenon (other human/political agent) for which reason is not properly the privileged operator of the experience. As Marion suggests, "the other person only appears to me starting from the moment when I expose myself to him or her, thus when I am no longer the master or constitute the other and admit that he or she expressed self without signification" (*Excess*, 122). That is, since the injunction of the other person appears as an excessive, saturated phenomenon, it is "self-evident that the face gives itself as a call and shows itself (phenomenalizes itself) only to the degree that the gifted responds to it."[20]

Yet, for Locke, we do encounter the other as the irreducible creature of the transcendent God, a fellow lord and master, an agent of dominion to whom we owe respect and whom we must not subjugate. If the other's status as an equal is only opened to me through the horizon of our own relation to the excessive Divine Creation, then we encounter the other *in the mode of* a saturated phenomena, exceeding the "categories and the principles of the understanding" ("Saturated," 113). The stumbling block for Locke is not that he insufficiently envisions the human as excessively dignified and demanding our responsibility. In fact, his turn to the theological ground for equality shows just how much he wants this category to reign supreme in interpersonal relationships. Rather, by Locke's account, our interpersonal relations are always discharged across the triangular grid of *self—other—divine*; similarly, our political relations are always enacted across the triangular grid of *political self— other citizen/political agent—sovereign*. In this way, the other human being is always a construct of divinely imposed categories, ensuring that we engage the other in a manner befitting their nature as equal agents. The infamous argument Locke takes up in the *Letter Concerning Toleration*, concerning why the political community ought not tolerate the atheist, confirms this view: the atheist, in their rejection of the Divine, necessarily destroys the possibility of assuring others that they can keep promises, since promise-keeping is a function of how we view those to whom we make promises.[21] We can only view others as agents deserving respect and having the capacity of dominion if we affirm their *created* status. In the end, every human, according to Locke, is an *imago dei*, who evades my intentionality and conceptualization. The other is neither reduced in its particularity into an abstract universality, nor does Locke fail to expose to us the other human as an unenvisageable creature to whom we owe an inexhaustible duty of respect.[22]

The more precise problem arises from Locke's grounding this claim about the other exclusively on the theological vision that they are a *creature* of the sovereign and unenvisageable Divine. For Locke, the other human's claim over me, its injunction on my being as one whom I must respect, comes from the transcendent Creator's claim on my life. The particular other is encountered *based on* this prior theological concept of its status as a fellow creature. For Locke, the unenvisageability of the other and the injunction to respect that person finally derives, not from the encounter with the particular other, but from God alone. By preserving the dignity of the human through the only means he could ultimately find in the conceptual language of his day—the theological basis for the idea of equality—Locke inadvertently displaces the irreducible other altogether. Such a displacement subverts the claim of responsibility, as developed by Marion and other phenomenologists, which comes directly from the encounter with the other human, where the intuition of the other overpowers us. We now have phenomenological tools more precisely to understand this encounter and articulate the responsibility that arises. Locke's idea of equality, even as it richly preserves the sanctity of the particular other in light of the Divine reality, elides the possibility of this particular kind of responsibility. We must now hope that Marion's creative vision of responsibility, because it shows us that humans who encounter each other find beings saturated with dignity, can exceed this Lockean shortcoming. The challenge for Marion and his students is now hopefully a bit more clear: how can love, the most demanding horizon for responsible humans, articulate and refine the duties of responsibility *within* the mundane realm of power politics?

Notes

1. For a helpful overview of the approaches and issues, see Bettina Bergo, *Lévinas between Ethics and Politics: For the Beauty That Adorns the Earth* (Dordrecht: Kluwer Academic Publishers, 1999).

2. Hwa Yol Jung, "Taking Responsibility Seriously," in *Phenomenology of the Political,* ed. Kevin Thompson and Lester Embree (Dordrecht: Kluwer Academic Publishers, 2000), 160.

3. Jean-Luc Marion, "The Saturated Phenomenon," trans. Thomas Carlson, *Philosophy Today* (Spring 1996): 103, hereafter cited in text as "Saturated."

4. The problem is basic in Lockean interpretation and centers most fundamentally on whether natural law can be known by reason. For a thorough study, see Leo Strauss, *Natural Right and History* (Chicago: Chicago University Press, 1953), 202ff. Foremost among those who see Locke as having limited application to contemporary political theory is John Dunn. See his *The Political Thought of John Locke* (Cambridge: Cambridge University Press, 1969). Cf. John Dunn, "What Is Living and What Is Dead in John Locke?" in *Interpreting Political Responsibility: Essays 1981–1989* (Cambridge: Polity Press, 1990).

5. Locke proceeded to an understanding of politics by articulating the original anthropological conditions of the capacity and need for political life. This move has been held by some to be suspect, because it is unclear that hypotheses about the state of nature are nothing more than fanciful products of the wishes of the author. Thus Rousseau urged his reader caution: such inquiries into political origins "ought not be taken for historical truths, but only for hypothetical and conditional reasonings; better suited to elucidate the Nature of things than to show their genuine origin." Rousseau, *The Discourses,* ed. Victor Gourevitch (Cambridge: Cambridge University Press, 1997), 132.

6. Marion quoting Immanuel Kant, *Critique of Pure Reason* (New York: St. Martin's Press, 1965), A218 / B265, 239, hereafter cited in text as *CPR*.

7. *CPR*, A220 / B267, 239, quoted by Marion at "Saturated," 104.

8. *CPR*, A51 / B75, 93, quoted by Marion at "Saturated," 109.

9. *CPR*, A95 / B129, 129, quoted by Marion at "Saturated," 110.

10. See Thomas Hobbes, *Leviathan,* ed. Richard Tuck (Cambridge: Cambridge University Press, 1997), esp. chap. VI, hereafter cited as *Leviathan.* Hobbes built on the tradition of this idea of endeavor, which itself rested on the doctrine of the *conatus*— as it was handed down from Spinoza. The *conatus* is the primal component of the human ego, driving toward satisfaction and preservation, and is disposed such that it should start to move if external constraints are removed. See esp. Spinoza, *The Ethics,* trans. Edwin Curley (Princeton: Princeton University Press, 1994), III, 6: "Each thing, as far as it can by its own power, strives to persevere in its being," and III, 7: "The striving by which each thing strives to persevere in its being is nothing but the actual essence of the thing."

11. For further explanation of the "law of nature," see Locke's insistence in the "Essays on the Law of Nature" (1663–64) that there are no "moral propositions inborn in the mind and as it were engraved upon it such that they are as natural and familiar to it as its own faculties." Rather, they are developed through interaction with others (tradition), observation of particulars, and proof by induction. See John Locke, *Political Essays* (Cambridge: Cambridge University Press, 1997), 96–100.

12. Richard Hooker, *Of The Laws of Ecclesiastical Polity*, ed. Arthur Stephen McGrade (Cambridge: Cambridge University Press, 1989), hereafter cited as *Laws*.

13. Jeremy Waldron makes a mildly convincing case that Locke's skepticism about species forces him to turn away from the idea that all humans are part of a common species and that there can be no intraspecies domination. His skepticism thus forces him to consider particular characteristics as the common, and crucial, trait for determining who and what is subject to another. See Waldron, *God, Locke, and Equality: Christian Foundations in Locke's Political Thought* (Cambridge: Cambridge University Press, 2002), 67.

14. Locke does admit that inequity between humans regarding innate abilities is real, yet does not change the injunction to not subordinate those in my same species. This has been nicely explained in detail by Waldron in *God, Locke, and Equality*, esp. chaps. 2–4. In the *Second Treatise*, Locke insists that "[t]hough I have said above, Chap. II, That all Men by Nature are equal, I cannot be supposed to understand all sorts of Equality: Age or Virtue may give men a just Precedency: Excellency of Parts and Merit may place others above the Common Level . . . ." (*Second Treatise*, VI, 54, 304). That is, humans have varying levels of skill and gifts in using their faculties, the range of which may reasonably call into serious question any claim that we are equal due to shared capacities. However, Locke clearly insists that regardless of any variation among humans in their ability to exercise capacities, the fact that they all have the same faculties and capacities makes them in some basic sense equal.

15. Waldron, *God, Locke, and Equality*, 75–80.

16. It does seem to be the case that this is the basis on which Locke insists that the atheist must not be tolerated in civil society. Locke holds that if belief in God is taken away, then the ability to hold promises, covenants, and oaths—the bonds of society itself—is made impossible.

17. See John Locke, "Morality" (1677–78), in *Political Essays* (Cambridge: Cambridge University Press, 1997), 268.

18. John Locke, *An Essay Concerning Human Understanding*, ed. Peter Nidditch (Oxford: Oxford University Press, 1979), IV, 18. 7. This does not mean that reason has nothing to do with these claims of faith, because they are issues for reason to judge about their relation to our lives, even while the initial truth or experience of the claim is not discovered by reason. Locke continually makes reference to Scripture, especially in the *First Treatise*, but often with an eye toward its equivocal content (see *First Treatise*, I, 112) and always with the understanding that Scripture does not merely present itself as some sort of pure intuition but must be interpreted by the natural, rational capacities. For a thorough discussion of Locke's use of scriptural argument, see Waldron, *God, Locke, and Equality*, 16–19, 188–216.

19. Jean-Luc Marion, "The Icon or the Endless Hermeneutic," in *In Excess: Studies of Saturated Phenomena*, trans. Robyn Horner (New York: Fordham University Press, 2002), 119, hereafter cited as *Excess*.

20. Jean-Luc Marion, *Being Given: Toward a Phenomenology of Givenness*, trans. Jeffrey L. Kosky (Stanford: Stanford University Press, 2002), 293.

21. John Locke, *A Letter Concerning Toleration,* ed. James Tully (Indianapolis: Hackett, 1983).

22. If we attempt to build politics from this "excessive origin" of the human ethical encounter, and if in the case of Locke this ethical encounter is built on a doctrine of equality, do we not fall into the trap of creating a political order that reduces humans to neutral interchangeability? That is, does the Lockean "other," understood as my equal, get reduced necessarily to the anonymous third, thereby destroying the particularity of the individual, and the possibility of the injunction to responsibility arising from that particularity? Does political interaction, when based on "the formal universality of the obligation," only occur if the other "opened by the injunction can be played by anyone" and is thereby erased in their particularity (*Prolegomena to Charity,* trans. Stephen E. Lewis and Jeffrey Kosky (New York: Fordham University Press, 2002), 92.

V

COUNTER-EXPERIENCE

12

The Banality of Saturation

JEAN-LUC MARION

Translated by Jeffrey L. Kosky

I sometimes see within a banal theater.
Baudelaire, "L'irréperable"

In several steps and not without some stumbling and a few retractions, I proposed a new concept for phenomenology: the saturated phenomenon. This concept will pose the question for my reflections in this essay.

A Reminder

The innovation I proposed should still be understood cautiously. For formally at least, it does not mark a revolution but merely a development of one of the possibilities that is, by right, already inscribed within the commonly accepted definition of the phenomenon. By "commonly accepted definition" I mean that of Kant and Husserl—the two philosophers, if not the only ones then at least the first in modernity, to have saved the phenomenon by according it the right to appear unreservedly. For them, a phenomenon is a representation that ceases to refer, like a symptom, only to its subject (like an inadequate idea in Spinoza), and instead gives access to a thing placed facing it (possibly an object), because some intuition in general (sensible or not, the question remains open), one actually given, finds itself assumed, framed, and controlled by a concept, playing the role of a category. On these two conditions, the representation is modeled after its objective—concentrated on it and absorbed in it—such that the representation becomes the direct presentation of its objective, its appearance passes through to this object and becomes its apparition. Intuition can then become objectively intentional (like an apparition, no longer a mere appearance) in and through the concept that actively fixes it (according to the spontaneity of the understanding). But reciprocally, the concept becomes objectively intentional (and plays the role of a category) only in and through the intuition that fills it from the outside, by virtue of the passivity that it transmits to it (according to intuition). Without underestimating the no doubt significant differences in how each philosopher states his case, I therefore assume the compatibility, indeed the equivalence, of Kant's and Husserl's definitions of the phenomenon.[1]

There are then two variations of this initial formulation, according as one considers the two relations that the two constitutive elements can maintain. Kant and Husserl traced one variation each. On one hand, truth is accomplished in perfect evidence, when intuition completely fills the concept, thereby validating it without remainder; this is the paradigmatic situation, and for that reason the least frequent. On the other hand, we have the partial validation of a concept by an intuition that does not fulfill it totally, but is enough to certify it or verify it; this is the more ordinary situation (truth in the common sense of verification, validation, confirmation), even though it can seem unsatisfying. My innovation intervenes only in the wake of these two: it consists only in paying attention to a third possible relation between intuition and concept— that in which, inverting the common situation where the concept exceeds intuition and the exceptional situation of an equality between them, intuition would surpass (in multiple senses) the concept. In other words, it concerns the situation in which intuition would not only validate all that to which the concept ensures intelligibility, but would also add a given (sensations, experiences, information, it matters little) that this concept would no longer be able to constitute as an object or render objectively intelligible. Such an excess of intuition beyond the concept would invert the common situation, without however abandoning phenomenality (nor the terms of its definition), since the two elements of the phenomenon are still operative. The ideal norm of evidence (equality between intuition and the concept) is no longer threatened only and as usual by a shortage of intuition, but indeed by its excess. I have already designated and explained this phenomenon by excess as the (intuitively) saturated phenomenon.

I have not only formally identified this new determination of the phenomenon. I have also tried to apply it to the task of offering reasons for phenomena that have hitherto been left in the margins of ordinary phenomenality—indeed excluded by it. Or rather, not to offer reason, since what is at issue is liberating a phenomenon from the requirement of the principle of (sufficient) reason, but to offer it *its own* reason so as to give it a rationality against all the objections, the interdictions, and the conditions that weigh on it in metaphysics (indeed for the most part in the history of phenomenology). What is at stake here is offering legitimacy to nonobjectifiable, even nonbeing phenomena: the event (which exceeds all quantity), the work of art (which exceeds all quality), the flesh (which exceeds all relation), and the face of the Other (which exceeds all modality). Each of these excesses identifies a type of saturated phenomenon, which functions exactly like a paradox. I then suggested the possibility of combining, on one hand, some of these types and, on the other hand, all four together in order to describe other, still more complex saturated phenomena. For example, the face of the Other doubtlessly combines the transgression of all modality with the surpassing of quantity, quality, and relation.[2] Finally, this combining provides access to a radicalized mode of saturation, one that I designated with the name "phenomenon of revelation." And finally, on the basis of this complex of saturations, what might possibly become thinkable is the case of Revelation. But it would no longer fall within phenomenology (which deals only with possibility, not the fact of its phenomenality) to decide about the latter, which it could only admit formally. For that, one would have to call on theology.

Objections

As a general rule, one should neither expect nor hope that an innovation be adopted immediately and unreservedly. For especially if by chance it should be borne out, an assertion cannot lay claim to novelty and to success at the same time. If it meets with no resistance, it is doing nothing more than responding to already established convictions, which is a matter of yielding to the (always) dominant ideology. If instead it incites a reaction, it could be because it is innovative (provided that it is not simply mad). Criticism therefore pays homage despite itself to the innovation that it helps to validate. Even if it does not validate more than it invalidates what it challenges, criticism remains inevitable and indispensable because it alone lays bare, by the resistance it opposes, the truly symptomatic points of what is thus advanced. The criticism can thus open a royal road to what is at stake. This seems to be the case for the objections addressed to the legitimacy of a saturated phenomenon; for they let us identify at least two resistances, therefore two questions. To simplify, I will use two particularly clear formulations of these objections, ones that sum up all the others. The first questions the terms in which the saturated phenomenon is defined, the other its principle. Though aware of the "appalling uselessness of explaining anything whatever to anyone whatever,"[3] I will try, in examining the objections, to answer their assault, but I will above all try to extend their lines of attack so as to once again reach, through them, the heart of the question.

The first objection points to two contradictions, which lead to two impasses. First, the hypothesis of the saturated phenomenon pretends to go "beyond what canonical phenomenology has recognized as the possibility of *experience* itself," all the while pretending at the same time "to be inscribed within an experience."[4] What is more, because "there is no 'pure experience,'"[5] especially not of "full transcendence [and] its pure alterity,"[6] it follows that, "no Revelation, with a capital R, can be given within phenomenality."[7] In short, we do not have any experience of what passes beyond the conditions for the possibility of experience; and yet the so-called saturated phenomenon passes beyond, by its very definition, the limits of experience; therefore we have absolutely no experience of it. And concerning what cannot (and therefore should not) be thought, there isn't even any discussion. But who does not see that this objection presupposes, without critiquing or even admitting, that experience has only one meaning and that this meaning is the one suited to the experience of objects? In short, who does not see that the objection presupposes the univocity of experience and of objectivity? Now the entire question of the saturated phenomenon concerns solely and specifically the possibility that certain phenomena do not manifest themselves in the mode of objects, and yet do still manifest themselves. All the difficulty consists specifically in describing what could manifest itself without our being able to constitute (or synthesize) it as an object (by a concept or an intentionality adequate to its intuition).

From the outset, by its simple formulation, the objection misses the sole and central question, substituting for it a pure and simple fiction—the fiction of a "pure experience," a "full transcendence [and] its pure alterity"—whose absurdity is easy to show. Not only does the description of the saturated phenomenon never use such pompous formulations, it does not even speak willingly of experience (except in the mode of counter-experience). That is, under the guise of modest showiness, the very notion of experience already presupposes too much—nothing less than a subject, whose measure and anteriority define from the start the conditions of experience and therefore of objectification. Consequently, if, in order to do justice to the possibility of the saturated phenomenon, one wants to contest the horizon of the object, one must also contest the conditions for the subject of experience, therefore the univocal notion of experience itself.

To this first invented contradiction a second is added—namely, that even if one can rigorously admit an experience without object, one cannot think "an experience without subject."[8] And this is why, even if it pretends to stick with an "entirely empty, passive, seized upon, affected, powerless and s.o."[9] subject, the saturated phenomenon should maintain intact its role within phenomenality: "[I]ts function (which is to allow the appearing of phenomena) remains unchanged . . . ; the character of subjectivity is maintained throughout and . . . the promised dispossession or dismissal has not taken place." Thus, "[I] reestablish, without admitting it, what [I] claim to have dismissed."[10] This contradiction supposes that the (in principle) criticized subject coincides exactly with the (in fact) maintained subject; in other words, it rests on the univocity of the concept of subject. And yet, how can one feign not knowing that the entire question—and the entire difficulty—consists in seeing if "subject" cannot and should not be understood in many senses or, in other words, if the critique of the transcendental subject does not free another sense of "subject" or more exactly of "who comes after the subject" (to borrow a helpful phrase from Jean-Luc Nancy)?[11] And I can hardly see why such an equivocalness should be dismissed, seeing as phenomenology has already broached it—be it only in passing from Husserl (the transcendental subject) to Heidegger (Dasein), indeed within Heidegger's own thought (from Dasein to what succeeds it), not to mention the questioning of the subject who is master of experience in Jean-Paul Sartre, Maurice Merleau-Ponty, Emmanuel Lévinas, and Michel Henry. And anyway, why should the "subject" or whoever comes after it disappear without remainder if it no longer plays any role within the process of phenomenalization except that of response and "resistance" to what gives itself, then of screen where what gives itself would show itself? Why should the "subject" or whoever comes after it be abolished simply because it has lost the activity of the understanding in favor of a more originary receptivity, the spontaneity of representation (or intentionality) to the benefit of a more radical, and perhaps in another mode more powerful, passivity? In not asking these questions, the first criticism betrays an extraordinarily noncritical sense of who comes after the subject—possibly the gifted.[12]

The second objection remains. It evidences, at least apparently, a ruthless radicality since it contests the very principle of the possibility (and therefore the actuality) of a saturated phenomenon: "There remains the (enigmatic, incomprehensible . . .) fact that one could *see otherwise*—that I or the others, we saw otherwise." See what? Saturated phenomena no doubt, but more simply, by a slippage that is as hasty as obsessive, "God," always and already. In fact, according to this objection, the one counts for all the others since in all cases it is a question of denying purely and simply that there be anything whatsoever to see: first in the saturated phenomenon in general ("one no longer speaks of anything—that is of nothing that can be assigned");[13] next in a phenomenon of revelation in particular ("What will you say to me if I say to you that there where you see God, I see nothing?").[14] What to respond? But the brutality of the argument can be turned against the one who uses it. For the fact of not comprehending and seeing nothing should not always or even most often disqualify what it is a question of comprehending and seeing, but rather the one who understands nothing and sees only a ruse. No more than admitting an insurmountable powerlessness to see or comprehend guarantees that something does indeed give itself to be seen and comprehended do the glorious claims of blindness directly and of themselves constitute a theoretical argument against this possibility of seeing or comprehending. To be sure, it is not enough to claim to see in order to prove that one saw. But the fact or the pretense not to see does not prove that there is nothing to see.[15] It can simply suggest that there is indeed something to see, but that in order to see it, it is necessary to learn to see otherwise because it could be a question of another phenomenality besides that which manifests objects. In phenomenology where it is a matter only of seeing what manifests itself (and describing how it manifests itself), resting on the authority of one's blindness in order to call a halt to research constitutes the weakest argument possible; indeed, it is the admission of defeat, to be used only in the last instance—and then again. In any case, it is not fitting to flaunt it as a strength, a profound mystery, and a great discovery. After all, blindness can also be explained in the sense that, as Aristotle says, "as the eyes of bats are to the light of the day, so is the reason in our soul to the things which are most visible of all nature."[16] Until the contrary is proven, it behooves us to persist in making evident what at first appears to obfuscate itself. "Whether convenient or inconvenient, and even though (because of no matter what prejudices) it may sound monstrous to me, it[17] is *the primal matter of fact to which I must hold fast* [*Ursache die ich standhalten muss*], which I, as a philosopher, must not disregard for a single instant. For children in philosophy [*philosophische Kinder*], this may be the dark corner haunted by the specters of solipsism and, perhaps, of psychologism, of relativism. The true philosopher, instead of running away, will prefer to fill the dark corner with light."[18]

Frequency and Banality

The hypothesis of the saturated phenomenon quite naturally, therefore, incited a discussion that, despite or because of my detailed accounts,[19] is still ongoing. A serious motive must underlie this refusal or, at the least, skepticism. Which one, if not the fear that phenomena are saturated only in the case of "exceptional intuitions"[20] and in a "maximalist" mode?[21] Do saturated phenomena touch us only rarely, in a confused and out of the ordinary ravishing?

To address this objection, we must distinguish between the *frequency* and the *banality* of phenomena. Common or poor phenomena appear frequently, and this is a consequence of their very definition. First, because their constitution as objects requires only an empty or poor intuition, such that the difficulty of comprehending them consists most of the time only in determining the concept or concepts, not in the ordeal of intuition. It follows that their actual production does not mobilize uncommon experiential resources. They therefore appear frequently. Next, if these phenomena with no or poor intuition assume the status of technically produced objects (which is most frequently the case), their mode of production demands no other intuition besides that which gives us their material (a material that itself becomes at once perfectly appropriate to the concept and available in an, on principle, limitless quantity). Hence nothing or very little opposes itself to what their production reproduces according to the needs of consumption, itself without assignable limit. The mode of constitution of available objects [*Vorhandenheit*], namely production, of itself authorizes their reproduction for use [*Zuhandenheit*]. Whence follows a frequency of technical objects and their phenomenality that accumulates day by day. It could even be said that the world is covered with a layer, invasive and most visible, of poor phenomena (namely, the technical objects produced and reproduced without end), which ends up obfuscating what it covers. And what does it cover, if not other phenomena (e.g., the event, the painting, the flesh, or the Other) that I proposed naming "saturated phenomena"? In this specific sense, poor and common phenomenality not only guarantees a higher frequency to technical objects, but it makes this frequency, by virtue of its very definition, inevitable and irrepressible. In this specific sense, saturated phenomena can appear only in less frequent, therefore exceptional, cases.

Banality must be understood in an entirely different way than frequency.[22] In the strict sense, that which becomes banal concerns, by political and legal decision, all and is accessible to all. All, that is to say, the vassals and their vassals [*le ban et l'arrière-ban*]—the men that the lord can mobilize from his own fiefs and then also, in perilous times, from the fiefs of his men for the purpose of waging a war, by derivation the men in the force who are of age and then the others, the elders. Calling on his vassals and their vassals obviously does not happen frequently; at least all those concerned by this banality hope it to be as rare as possible. By extension, one speaks of the banalization of a forge, a mill, a field, and so on, which means that these facilities, properties of the lord, are either used obligatorily (nobody can use another stove, another mill, etc.) or else are used only by those who need them (a field whose pastures are open to those who do not possess their own). But neither one nor the other banality (obligatory or gracious) have anything frequent about them; only the lord can grant them and one turns to them only in cases of need. Banality, which is open to all, does not equal frequent; indeed it sometimes opposes it.

To speak of a banal saturated phenomenon, therefore, does not imply that it becomes current and frequent, nor *a contrario* that it must become exceptional and rare and therefore be confined to the margins of common phenomenality, which supposedly fixes the norm. The banality of the saturated phenomenon suggests that *the majority of phenomena, if not all* can undergo saturation by the excess in them of intuition over the concept or signification. In other terms, the majority of phenomena that appear at first glance as poor in intuition could be described not only as objects, but also as phenomena that intuition saturates and therefore exceeds all univocal concept. Before the majority of phenomena, even the most simple (the majority of objects, produced technically and reproduced industrially), there opens the possibility of double interpretations, which depends only on the demands of my ever changing relation to them. Or rather, when the description demands it, I most often have the possibility of passing from one interpretation to the other, from a poor or common phenomenality to a saturated phenomenality. That is, "those things that are the clearest and the most common are the same things that are most obscure and understanding them is a novelty [*nova est intentio eorum*]."[23] At least that is what I am going to try to show.

It seems reasonable not to yield to an anti-theological obsession, one that would refuse *en masse* the hypothesis of saturated phenomena out of fear of having to admit one particular and exceptional case (God). In short, it seems reasonable not to hide from what is more evident so as to avoid a less evident, though indisputably possible, consequence.[24] I therefore suggest that we provisionally disconnect these two questions so as to avoid a willing phenomenological blindness. Or, and this amounts to the same thing, before deciding about the possibility of saturated phenomena and the legitimacy of their appearing, it is appropriate first to examine if such a thing can be found in fact. In other words, when and why must we make recourse to the hypothesis of the saturated phenomenon? We must each time that we admit that it is impossible to assume an intuition in an adequate concept, as we always do in the case of a poor or common law phenomenon—in other words, each time that we must renounce thinking a phenomenon as an object, if we want to think it as it shows itself.

The Banality of Saturated Phenomena

There is no shortage of experiences that would let us trace the border between these two phenomenalities; we have only to follow the five senses of perception.

Suppose that I perceive, or rather that I undergo, the sensation of three colors arranged one on top of the other—for example, green, orange, and red, it matters little in what figure (circle, horizontal bands, etc.). This intuition, as simple and primary as it is (after all, the color red is, literally, primary), opens onto two radically different types of phenomena. In the first case, a concept lets us synthesize the phenomenon in an objective mode, and the intuition is inscribed adequately in this concept, which contains and comprehends it all. So it goes if I assign these three colors to the flag of a nation or the traffic signal that regulates traffic at an intersection. In this case, the concept (either the country at issue, here something like Ethiopia or Guinea, or the authorization or prohibition to cross) grasps the intuition without remainder, and the intuition literally disappears in it—to the point that it becomes insignificant, pointless, and even dangerous to concentrate one's attention on the exact form of the colored spots, their intensity, or their nuances. For if you do so, you are distracted from the signification that alone is important to practical knowledge and therefore to the use of this phenomenon. That is, when it is a question of phenomena produced as signs, their intuitions and their forms pass without remainder into their significations, and they appear as signs, thus in terms of their concepts, only on condition of disappearing as autonomous intuitions of color. This is why it always remains possible to change arbitrarily the intuited colors (of the flag or the crossing signal) or else blatantly dispense with them, replacing their visual intuition with another type of intuition—for example, by substituting the sounds of a national anthem or an alarm. For in these cases, intuition plays only a very minor role in relation to the concept (signification, intention) precisely because the phenomenon does not rest first on intuition or appear in its light, but is governed and comprehended through and through by the concept. Eventually, the concept can even be substituted for the lacking intuition because more radically it dispenses with it. In this way the phenomenon of an object is manifest.

But there remains another way for these three colors to appear. Suppose they are imposed vertically over one another in three horizontal bands in a rectangular frame, as in Mark Rothko's canvas *Number 212*.[25] Here the phenomenon (this painting) appears with a manifest conceptual shortage or, if you prefer, an evident intuitive excess. There is first of all no concept in the sense of form: first because each of the horizontal bands resembles only approximately a rectangle; second because the very imprecision of their edges (in the sense of an ideal and geometric precision) plays the positive function of making the two contiguous colors vibrate each in relation to the other (all the more so as a vague and indistinct strip of yellow comes between the green and the red, then between the green and the orange); third because the arrangement of the three bands of color resembles nothing at all: it shows nothing other than these very colors and the play among them, without making evident anything else in the world, without producing any object, and without transmitting any information. There is no concept in the sense of a signification, still less of a sign that would refer arbitrarily to a second signification. The painting means nothing that we can comprehend; it is not connected to any signification that would assume it; it is not assumed in anything that would permit coding it, by doing away with the intuition of its formless colors.

A painting is distinguished from other visibles (objects) in that no signification can comprehend it or do away with our encountering its intuition. A painting consists first in its intuition, which discourages all the concepts that one can mobilize for its comprehension, indeed which submerges them. You always have to go to see a painting; the *only* thing you have to do is *see* it, without any other "exceptional" intuition besides that of simply, but truly, seeing it. On condition that one should speak only one meaning, all intuition as such, even the most simple, turns out to be exceptional insofar as it and it alone gives (to see). Before this Rothko painting, no form, no signification, no concept, nothing can dismiss us from our vigil over its intuition and from responding to its mute summons. And this intuition to be seen resembles nothing besides itself, refers only to the visible itself, and refers us to it with it. This saturated phenomenon does not have to be constituted or comprehended as an object; it has only to be confronted, submitted to such as it comes upon me.

This gap between the objective phenomenon and the saturated phenomenon (a phenomenological difference) is something we undergo not only in the case of sight, but also in each of the other senses. Consider hearing: between the simple sound, the sound as signal, the sound as voice, and the sound as song, what differences arise? In each case, the acoustic experience remains of the same order, and yet the intuition is enriched and made more complex from moment to moment. When the hostess who greets you in the train station or airport makes an announcement or answers a question, she produces an acoustic effect that is pleasant enough as such (she was chosen precisely for the tone of her voice, articulate and yet reassuring, seductive and yet informative), comparable to that of a jazz singer in Chicago or an alto in the aria of a Bach cantata. And yet this voice differs from that voice as an object differs from a saturated phenomenon. By what do we notice this difference? By the fact that in order to listen to an announcement at the airport, one must comprehend it—that is to say, reduce it immediately to its signification (or to its meaning), without remaining frozen in the sonic intuition used to communicate it; for if by contrast, I linger over this sonic intuition as such, I would no longer comprehend the information, either because I succumb to the charm of the voice and the woman that I imagine to proffer it or because I do not comprehend the language she is using. In this case, hearing demands comprehending— that is to say, leaping over the sounds and passing directly to the signification.

Hearing becomes (as in most languages) synonymous with comprehending, therefore with *not* hearing. In the case of listening to the voice of an alto, however, in her song or in her aria, I can perfectly well not comprehend the text clearly (it is in English or Italian) or I can know the words by heart without paying the least attention to them because, in both cases, I am not asked to learn a text or gather information, but to enjoy the voice—the pure and simple listening of the sonic intuition that it delivers. I listen to *the* Bergenza, *the* Schwarzkopf, almost without concern for what is sung, but because she sings it. When it is a matter of the sound in such an intuition, no clear and distinct signification can, in the role of concept, subsume it. I could attempt to explain the pleasure I find in listening, to find arguments to blame or praise the song, to discuss the performance with other listeners, therefore mobilize an indefinite number of concepts (those of music criticism, of musicology, of acoustics, etc.), but assuming I am not a philistine, I would never imagine that I could successfully include this sonic intuition within the limits of one or several concepts. Not that it pleases without concept—but rather because it calls for all, and calls for them because it saturates them all. Then, we listen to a saturated phenomenon.[26]

We can trace the gap just as clearly in the case of touch; for it falls to us to touch in two distinct, indeed opposed, manners. In one sense, to touch means to follow a surface in its twists and turns in order to gain information about the form of an object—as in the case when one fumbles about in the darkness in order to know where one is located and where objects are found, or more exactly what objects there are. In this case, we are not seeking intuition (which a flat or rough, hot or cold, convex or concave surface reveals), so much as a signification, comprehended even without anything being seen. I would like to know if I have run up against a wall or a door to open, if I am bumping against the corner of a table or perched against the back of a chair, where the light switch is, and so on. In this darkness, I therefore do not first touch surfaces or materials; rather I recognize objects, which is to say that I touch significations directly. Moreover, as soon as these significations are recognized (the room where I locate myself, the door by which I pass, the chair in which I sit, etc.), I no longer have to touch them by groping with an intuition that touches. Even in the darkness, I can see them directly and spot them in space. To touch means here to see a signification with eyes wide shut. With Braille, touching lets a meaning be read, significations be reached, and objects known with nothing being seen in intuition, therefore without intuition *par excellence.*

On the other hand, when I rest my flesh on another flesh, that which I love because it does not resist me (a gesture that should not be reduced to the convention of the caress), when I touch the one I desire or the one who suffers and dies, I no longer have any signification to transmit to him, no information to communicate to him; often he does not want to, indeed cannot, hear any. I do not caress in order to know nor to make known, as I do when groping about in order to orient myself in space and to identify objects. I caress in order to love, therefore in silence, in order to console and soothe, to excite and enjoy, therefore without objective signification, indeed without identifiable or sayable signification. Thus touch does not manifest an object, but a saturated phenomenon: an intuition that no concept will assume adequately, but that will demand a multiplicity of them.[27]

And we can oppose two modes of phenomenalization in terms of taste. On the one hand, taste can serve only to distinguish two objects—for example, a poison (cocaine) from a food (sugar)—by limiting intuition to the maximum (one does not want to put oneself in danger by exposing oneself to too much) so as merely to anticipate a difference that is ultimately conceptual (two physical bodies, two chemical compositions) and can be expressed exhaustively by numbers and symbols. In this instance, even taste reaches what Descartes would call a "clear and distinct idea": "[I]t is so precise and sharply separated from all other perceptions that it contains within itself only what appears to one who considers it as he should."[28] Thus taste can give the intuition of objects and be exhausted in a concept. On the other hand, taste can be exercised over what escapes all concept. For example, when I taste a wine and especially if I participate in a blind tasting, it is not a matter of reconducting clear and confused intuition as quickly as possible to a supposedly distinct concept. The definition that a chemist can quickly and accurately fix for it offers no response to the vintner's questions: for example, is this wine worthy of its name and which one? To answer this question, one must not pass from intuition to the concept and substitute the latter for the former, but rather prolong the intuition to its maximum and plumb its depths. It is a matter of not making the taste of the wine pass away, but of following it in time (does it have a long finish, does it open out at the end?), in density (does it have body, tannin, bouquet, etc.). It is even necessary to summon sight (its color) and smell (the aroma) so as to reach in the end a precise and exact identification (this grape, this harvest, this plot of land, this year, this producer), yet one that is nevertheless inexplicable in conceptual terms and not transmittable by information.

The support provided by custom or by the oenological guide serve only to make it understood that one has not tasted the wine or, having mistasted it, that one perceived nothing or almost nothing. The vintner knows what he has tasted and can discuss it precisely, though without concept, with an equal. Or else with an endless series of quasi-concepts that take on a meaning only after and only according to the intuition, sole and definitive authority. This intuition indicates its privilege in that it can never be dispensed with. One must always return to it—from one year to the next, from one wine to the other, from one moment of the same wine to another moment; it changes, obliges the description to be resumed, all the metaphors to be rediscovered. What is more, this intuition cannot be shared immediately from one to the other taster; accordingly only one possibility remains to them, which is to speak of it endlessly—whence a paradoxical conviviality: that of the incommunicable and through it.[29] At issue is an idea that is at once clear and confused for whoever does not participate in wine culture, but clear and distinct for those in the know. In short, wine tasted has nothing objective about it, but appears according to a saturation of intuition that incites a plurality of quasi-concepts and approximate significations.[30]

The same goes for smell. When I sense an odor of gas or a solvent, of humidity or fire, I am constrained to approach intuitively what could, if I had the free time and the means, be described by models and parameters (graphs of temperature, pressure, humidity, etc.). I would then immediately transform the intuition into evident significations (danger of flood, of fire, of an explosion, etc.) on which my attention and my activity would at once be concentrated. I would no longer remain with my nose in the air, drinking in the smell for pleasure. In other words, in these cases, smell refers to a concept (or even a group of concepts) that is on principle able to grasp the intuitive totality. It does not merely refer to it, but disappears in it by letting itself be coded in rational equivalents. It is reducible to information concerning the state of things, objective phenomenon. But smell also smells in an entirely different way: when someone with a nose for things—as we call the experts whose sense of smell is so refined that they can combine fragrances into new perfumes—takes a whiff, it is clear that no univocal concept, no signification will ever succeed in designating it or distinguishing it. And yet the perfume thus produced can, if it is a success, provoke an experience recognizable by thousands, to the point that even without taste each can recognize this Chanel and distinguish it from

Guerlain. The names, arbitrarily and naïvely sophistic, that we impose on these perfumes do not identify them like a concept or a definition; to the contrary, only their firm and stable intuitions ensure them an identifiable signification, which never detaches them from the arbitrary. The names signify nothing, for the perfumes do not have a univocal signification any more than a definition. They draw their strength from their intuition—ever to be resumed, impossible to comprehend—that provokes each time new significations, necessary and provisional: "Perfumes there are . . . / Green as the prairies, fresh as a child's caress." The uniqueness of smell stems no doubt from the fact that it receives at the outset and almost always saturated phenomena, which can only in exceptional cases and after the fact be assigned to a concept; for before making themselves sensed "the myrrh, or musk, or amber" provoke significations without assignable object; they have straightaway "the expansiveness of infinite things."[31] As soon as its vapors rise, perfume makes something other than itself appear, a pure unforeseeable: "Languorous Asia, burning Africa, / And a far world, defunct almost, absent, / Within your aromatic forest stay! / As other souls on music drift away, / Mine, o my love! still floats upon your scent."[32] Thus the relation between common law and saturated phenomena is reversed: though the former arise most often and from the outset, the latter offer, by virtue of their very banality, a more originary determination of phenomenality.

Thus considering each of the five senses opens a gap between the phenomenon as object and the phenomenon that "fills the soul beyond its capacity."[33] And in this gap become visible saturated phenomena. Thus the hypothesis of a saturation of the visible by intuition proves to be not only possible but inevitable: first, of course, in order to do justice to "exceptional intuitions" that saturate from the beginning all the thinkable significations of certain phenomena nonobjective from the outset; but next and especially to do justice to the belated saturation of phenomena at first glance banal, but more originally irreducible to an objective constitution. This hypothesis therefore has nothing optional about it, since the range of the "everyday banality"[34] that gives itself to appear calls for it and confirms it. Without admitting the hypothesis of saturated phenomena, either one cannot see certain phenomena that nevertheless appear banally or one has to deny what one nevertheless sees. One impugns it therefore only at one's own risk. And is there a greater crime for a phenomenologist than not seeing or, worse, not accepting what he sees—in short, blindness undergone or willed?[35]

The Conditions of Possibility

The question of fact is thus settled. What remains is to consider the question of right: in making an exception to the conditions of common-law phenomenality, doesn't the saturated phenomenon give up the power to claim legitimately the name "phenomenon"?[36] In wanting to be free from the constraint of every phenomenological *a priori*, do we not find ourselves in the position of the "light dove," which "cleaving the air in her free flight, and feeling its resistance, might imagine that its flight would be still easier in empty space"?[37] Whoever wants to see too much and to do so imagines that he can cross all limits of experience, doesn't he by that very move abolish the conditions of experience and remain sunk in the illusion of seeing more and better, while in fact he no longer sees anything?

Though repeated in many different voices, this objection is not valid. For the hypothesis of saturated phenomena never consisted in annulling or overcoming the conditions for the possibility of experience, but in examining if certain phenomena contradict or exceed those conditions and if they nevertheless still appear—precisely by exceeding or contradicting them. In other words, the experience of saturated phenomena proves, *de facto,* that the question is not confined to a choice between, on the one hand, an objective experience (in conformity with the conditions for the possibility of experience) and, on the other, a nonexperience of objects (contradicting all the conditions for the possibility of experience). A third option remains: the veritable and verifiable experience of a nonobjective phenomenon, one that would truly appear all the while contradicting the conditions for the possibility of objects of experience because it would arise with a nonobjective experience. Or, if one shudders at the formulation of a positively nonobjective experience, one can speak instead of the experience of what, contradicting the conditions of experience, appears in the mode of their saturation in a counter-experience.

This other option can already be detected in Kant's own argument, which is often invoked to deny it. How must we understand conditions for the possibility of experience? Obviously in terms of the famous formulation according to which "the *a priori* conditions of a possible experience in general are at the same time [*zugleich*] conditions of the possibility of *objects* of experience."[38] The first consequence to follow is this: the conditions for the possibility of experience concern only objects and therefore are valid only for phenomena understood as objects; for that matter, one can, in general, invoke *a priori* conditions and, in particular, identify the conditions of experience with those of the objects of experience only by referring to these very objects: namely, to that which alone can admit being thought in advance (in contrast to that which comes upon me without warning and counter to my foresight). But as all phenomena are not reducible to conditioned and foreseeable, produced and reproduced objects, a second consequence follows: contradicting the conditions of possibility (of the objects) of experience means at the same time contradicting the condition of objectness for the phenomena in experience. It is therefore not enough to make the objection that by admitting nonobjective phenomena we risk contradicting the conditions for the possibility of experience in general. For by what right can we speak of experience *in general*, or why should experience admit conditions? In other words, on what condition must experience always submit to conditions? Or if experience in general is identified with certain conditions, of what experience is one speaking and is *this* concept of experience self-evident?

It could be that we can legitimately contradict the so little critiqued use of the concept of experience by highlighting the presuppositions that ground it— the first of which might well be the pre-veiling pre-valence of a "subject" (or whatever one wants to call it) supposed to know and always already present, in advance, in relation to which conditions can be imposed on experience. These conditions are imposed only on condition that we cut experience in general to the measure of what the "subject" can receive. But this condition of all conditions is not self-evident, and here the modest, empirical showiness of the *tabula rasa* hides quite poorly the prideful assumption of a consciousness that, in order to remain empty, nevertheless stays always already in place *a priori*, so as to keep, even in this arrangement, a transcendental posture.[39] This transcendental posture governs experience with a certain legitimacy only because it knows how to know only persisting, certain, and constant objects— in short, present beings [*vorhanden*] whose presence is indisputable. Moreover, when one so quickly and so solemnly calls on experience as the judge and the last bastion of defense against other possibilities that phenomenality holds in reserve, one doubtlessly does so only for this very reason: to assure oneself of the enduring presence of being, which constitutes the sole privilege of objects. It could be that this assumption, far from closing the debate, sets its terms and therefore opens it. I therefore ask: is experience limited to the experience of objects, or does the constitution of objects define only one particular and restricted field of experience, which contradicts the immense banality of the intuitive saturation of phenomenality? Does it go without saying that presence in the present should determine the Being of all beings? Does it even go without saying that all that appears should first be? This empiricism remains thoroughly rooted in the most ponderous metaphysical presuppositions, and it dares even less to question them as it doesn't even suspect them (while Descartes, Kant, and Husserl, to speak only of the greatest, knew perfectly well that the object constitutes only a species, and not even the most usual, of what appears).[40] There is therefore no authority that could legitimate challenging or even disputing the hypothesis of saturated phenomena and the phenomenology of givenness that renders it thinkable. Nothing proves that experience is reducible to the conditions imposed on it by the concern for objectness and objectivity nor that, when I have the experience of what does not appear as an object, I experience nothing or that nothing appears if it does not appear as an object. A third way remains: to experience what contradicts the conditions of objective experience; to experience, at the very least, what this contradiction leaves always accessible and possible for us—the counter-experience itself.

We must therefore set out from this decisive point: the notion of experience is equivocal. It does not always aim at an object nor is it always determined by a transcendental subject; it can also expose an "I" that is nontranscendental (and nonempirical), but given over to [adonné à] a nonconstitutable because saturated phenomenon. In this case, do the conditions for the possibility of experience miraculously disappear? In no way. They remain in place but insofar as they are contradicted and subverted by phenomena that are not limited by them, that do not bow to them, and that are no longer constituted by them as objects. The conditions of experience (of objects) themselves thus become all the more visible and clear as they are more evidently contradicted. For their contradiction does not annul phenomenality as such; it simply testifies that this phenomenality runs up against the finitude of the gifted (of the "subject") who undergoes it without possessing the power to objectify it. Far from leading to the denial of finitude, the ordeal of the saturated phenomenon confirms it and attests it perfectly.[41] One should not conclude from the fact that the saturated phenomenon cannot be said univocally nor defined adequately that it is simply lacking—in short that there are none. For this lack itself is not at all lacking. It instead raises a question that demands a specific response: either the concept is lacking because it simply is not a question of a phenomenon or the concept is lacking because intuition exceeds it. To be sure, the lacking concept is not enough to prove that a saturated phenomenon gives itself, rather than nothing; but this lack is enough to demand that one should investigate its status and, subsequently, that of a possible saturated phenomenon.[42] As a result, it is not a question of deciding on a whim if there is, if there must be, if there can be in general saturated phenomena; it is a question of seeing, when confronted with this phenomenon, if I can describe it as an object (a common law phenomenon whose intuition is contained within the concept) or if I must describe it as a saturated phenomenon (whose intuition exceeds the concept). This affair is not decided abstractly and arbitrarily. In each case, attentiveness, discernment, time, and hermeneutics are necessary. But what else is there in philosophy, and are we still philosophers if we refuse this work?

Counter-experience

A question remains: even if we admit the legitimacy of such a contradiction of the conditions of experience, what can it still describe since it no longer describes objects? If it permits the description of nothing, of what phenomenon are we speaking and what phenomenology are we practicing?

Without going back over analyses conducted elsewhere,[43] I would like to recall briefly the chief characteristic of the experience of the saturated phenomenon: it is always a contrary experience or rather one that always counteracts. In contradicting the conditions for the experience of an object, such an experience does not contradict itself by forbidding the experience of anything at all; rather, it does nothing but counteract experience understood in the transcendental sense as the subsuming of intuition under the concept; it is confined to counteracting the counteracting of intuition by the concept. Thus, far from counteracting all experience, it liberates the possibility of an unconditioned experience of giving intuition. Let it not be objected once again that an experience without conditions would become impossible and untenable, for it would be a self-contradiction. For the issue is precisely to decide if the conditions for the experience of objects are always and at the same time the conditions of all experience in general, or if, by contrast, experience can sometimes (indeed banally) cross the conditions of objectification. In other words, nothing suggests that the possibility of experience should be equivalent to the possibility of experiencing objects or to what a transcendental subject can synthesize, constitute, and maintain in an objective condition. That experience might also contradict the conditions for the possibility of objects means only this: experience does not always or only give access to objects, but also to non-objective phenomena. That experience is not limited to the field of objectivity does not suggest that it is self-contradictory, but only that it contradicts the conditions for the experience of objects by a transcendental subject, therefore that it can sometimes (indeed banally) *contradict its transcendental acceptation.* According to this hypothesis, experience would unfurl as contrary or rather as *counteractive.* The counter-experience does not contradict the possibility of experience, but to the contrary frees it insofar as it counteracts its assignation to an object, therefore to its subjection to the transcendental subject.

Henceforth the finitude of the transcendental subject (and therefore of his intuition) is not transposed or declined automatically in a finitude of univocally objective experience; rather it is suffered and experienced as such in the contradiction that the excess of intuition imposes on it with each saturated phenomenon. It imposes on the transcendental subject that he must confess himself a gifted. Such a counter-experience can be recognized by several specific characteristics.

(1) Contradicted by the excess of intuition, intentionality can no longer aim at a signification (or a concept) that would permit it to constitute an object; it no longer hits any intentional "object," because what it hits no longer has objective status. Intentionality is therefore turned back against itself, no longer indicating the signification of a definite object but the limits of its aim, disqualified precisely by the intuitive excess. I always see, but what I see does not attest something; rather it measures the range of my disappointed vision. I no longer hit any vision, but I undergo the limits of my sight: "on an island charged by air / not with visions but with sight."[44] As it undergoes the trial of itself inasmuch as refused and rebuked by intuition, the intentional aim hits less an object to signify or conceptualize than it is itself hit by the rebound off an ungraspable objective, one that no concept permitted it to foresee or foretell. Hit in return by what it intended, intentionality rediscovers itself displaced, beside itself, "moved"—in short *altered.*

(2) Counter-experience is marked by the saturation of every concept by intuition. This saturation can of course be translated by a positive bedazzlement,[45] but not always or necessarily. Or rather bedazzlement can itself be conjugated in *disappointment:* not a shortfall of all signification, but the fulfillment of another signification besides that intentionally aimed at, a sort of displaced fulfillment, at an unforeseeable distance from the fulfillment that intention awaited and foresaw; not so much a nothing as an unforeseen signification—

seen, not fore-seen—by the foresight of any object. Such a disappointment, provoked by no lack but by a displacement of the overabundant intuition, proposes to fill *another* concept, one not foreseen, indeed an unknown and not yet identified concept; and for what it's worth, this characterizes the scientific attitude, at least in the case of a revolution of scientific paradigms.[46]

(3) Above all, the saturation of the aim by intuition can be signaled by the very perturbation induced by the reception of its excess. In the case of saturated phenomena, I no longer see anything by an excess of light, I no longer hear anything by an excess of sounds, taste or smell anything by an excess of excitations—at least nothing objectifiable, realizable as a thing other than myself and able to be looked at as placed before me. Here it must be emphasized that these excesses never face the danger of being illusory—for example, of imagining there to be excess of intuition while there is "nothing." This is so, first, because the (supposed) illusion of an intuitive excess becomes at once an intuitive excess of the illusion itself, since I undoubtedly undergo this excess (it alters me, perturbs me, disappoints me, etc.) as veritable and verifiable. If I believe I see too much light, even if no excess of "objective" light can be found,[47] I do indeed undergo an excess. Second (and the excess is verified precisely for this reason), the ordeal of excess is actually attested by the resistance, eventually the pain, that it imposes on the one who receives it, and this resistance can no more be disputed than one can doubt undergoing his own pain (for we "feel our pain" without any doubt or separation). This *resistance* suggests a wholly other sense of objectivity: objectivity would no longer mean access to an objective that is targeted, foreseen, and constructed according only to the demands and possibilities of intelligibility, such that "object" ends up designating precisely what does *not resist* the cognitive intention but yields to it without offering any resistance whatsoever, to the point that the object designates the alienation of the thing from itself and its seizure by method. Inversely, counter-experience is an issue of the obstinate resistance of what refuses itself to the transparency of knowledge that leaves out nothing, of what withdraws into its dark origin (the unseen, unheard, unscathed, etc.), as is sometimes the case with the resistance of another gaze to my gaze, which marks the irreducibility of this gaze to my own. For what we call "meeting the gaze of the Other" (maintaining eye contact) is in fact equivalent to deadening the blow, to challenging his power to annihilate, and to returning upon him the weight of an aim.[48]

Thus counter-experience can be defined precisely according to the *notae* alteration, disappointment, and resistance. The experience counteracting, or more precisely the contrariety that the saturated phenomenon imposes on the one who undergoes it *etiam invito*,[49] is imposed not only on the side of the experience of objects, but resists the reproach of subjectivism by its very over-coming of objectivity. That is, the gifted verifies itself infinitely more when face-to-face with a saturated phenomenon than before an object since it experiences itself as such in the counter-experience that resists it. For resistance can go so far as to expose me to a danger, the danger of seeing too much [*l'oeil en trop*], hearing too much, sensing too much, tasting too much, smelling too much. This resistance imposes itself as suffering, and what does one feel better than one's suffering?

The Truth That Counteracts

Such a resistance can and should be experienced in at least two senses. (1) Either as the ordeal of what gives itself in the encounter with finitude, by a definitive excess of intuition over every concept that I could impose on it. In this case, resistance translates the effect of the phenomenon on he who sees it, without however objectifying it. It is a matter of the reverential fear of the finite before what surpasses it, frightening and attracting it at the same time. Respect (for the good use of my free will, for the moral law, for the face of the Other, for holiness, etc.), the sublime, or enjoyment—all of these that are never not accompanied by some suffering or humiliation are described in this way. This resistance recoils by definition before what it glimpses, precisely because it recognizes its excess. (2) Or this same resistance can take the form of the denial of what gives itself to sight, not because we see it poorly (indistinctly or doubtfully), but precisely because we see it (clearly if not distinctly, indubitably) and this vision treats us so poorly. In other words, my resistance does not so much undergo as it represses what doubtlessly affects it precisely because this affection becomes an unbearable suffering. In seeing what I see, I also see the obligatory darkness created by the all too clear excess of light; and this obligatory darkness spills over the one who sees the truth because it imposes on him a dark obligation: that of revising his own self to the (scaleless) scale of the saturating excess of intuition. That is, since the saturated phenomenon cannot be reduced to the measure of objectivity or objectness, it demands of the one it affects that he see it and admit it in its very excess, without the security of a concept. It therefore demands of the affected that he give himself over [*de s'adonner*], let himself be (re-)made, (re-)defined, and, so to speak, (un-)measured by the measure of its own excess. Instead of summing up the given within the limits of my own finitude (of my concept), I undergo the obscure obligation of letting myself conform to (and by) the excess of intuition over every intention that my gaze could oppose to it. This demand can no longer merely provoke a bedazzlement, a disappointment, or a resistance; rather it incites a second-order resistance (resistance to the resistance, evade it) to the point of a recoil, a denial, a refusal. It is possible that the intuitive evidence of the saturated phenomenon might not produce the recognition of its truth, or its disclosure, but to the contrary and quite logically the impossibility of receiving it, therefore the impossibility of rejecting it. The disclosure of the saturated phenomenon might forbid its reception because, by dint of excess and bedazzlement, its evidence seems to accuse as well as clarify, challenge as well as illuminate.

To do justice to this ambivalence, Saint Augustine did not hesitate to offer a radical redefinition of the essence of truth: to its straightforward (Greek) phenomenality, in which the more evidence discloses the thing the more its truth is disclosed, he added and perhaps opposed a counteracting phenomenality in which the more the evidence discloses the thing the more access to it is shut, the more it becomes the object of a refusal, indeed a scandal. Object? Of course, in the sense of the objective around which denial focuses, the objective to be destroyed precisely because it offers no object, but exceeds objectivity and objectness. Here where the truth concerns the unveiling not of a common law phenomenon (one that is objectifiable within the limits of my finitude) but a saturated phenomenon, we have to pass from the *veritas lucens,* the truth that shows and demonstrates [*montre et démontre*] in a straightforward fashion, to a *veritas redarguens,* a truth that shows [*montre*] only inasmuch as it remonstrates [*remontre*] with he who receives it. This remonstrating truth inevitably accuses he who recuses it, as it does he who excuses himself from it. Thus the criteria for reaching the truth are modified; for the evidence of disclosure is substituted the love of excess: "Truth is loved, [but] in such a way that those who love something else would like it if what they love were the truth, and because they do not like to be deceived, they also do not want to be shown that they are deceived. And so they hate the truth for the sake of whatever it is they love instead of the truth. They love the truth insofar as it illuminates [*lucens*], but hate it when it turns its light upon them [*redarguens*]."[50] This text does not concern the demand to love the truth already seen nor even to love the truth in order to see it;[51] rather it concerns loving the truth so as to bear it, to bear, without faltering or condemning oneself, the cruel clarity that its radiance poses and imposes on he who risks gazing at it and the charge it imposes on him, "because glory overwhelms he who sees it, when it does not glorify him [*porque la gloria oprime al que la mira cuando no glorifica*]."[52] Before all moral or religious sense, it is first of all a matter of a strictly phenomenological necessity. The bedazzlement and the disappointment of intentionality by the saturated phenomenon imposes on the aim the necessity of confronting directly—without the mediation of the concept or the screen of the object that it permits constituting—the excess of intuition. This excess that pours itself out without intermediary over my gaze affects it, constrains it, and wounds it. This can, indeed almost inevitably *must*, lead the gaze to refuse what shows itself [*se montre*] only by remonstrating [*en remontrant*] with this gaze and what gives itself without giving way before me. This *veritas redarguens* turns its merciless evidence upon and therefore against he who sees it (or rather can no longer see it). It can therefore be defined as a light counter to my sight, a light that goes up against my [fore-]sight, rendering it confused and me with it. I become confused before this light, in all senses of the term: my sight loses its clarity and grows blurred, I lose my confidence, my good sense, and my security—to such a degree that this truth, that accuses me of untruth, can indeed be called a "counter-truth." But here counter-truth does not at all mean the contrary of truth or the simple lie that I could oppose to it, but *the truth that counteracts he whom it affects*—me. It counteracts me; for it requires of me, if I am to see it without danger, that I love it and lend myself to its radiance by conforming myself to its purity.

The Witness

It now becomes possible to broach a final difficulty, one which bears on he whom a saturated phenomenon affects. The objections often challenge the gifted by privileging the "subject" (quite possibly "without subjectivity") or, inversely, the "subjectivity (sometimes "without subject"); often they consider it a subject less or more transcendental or, inversely, more or less empirical, according as they prefer one or the other title. These approximations indicate the difficulty of, if not the powerlessness to think "who comes after the subject." I limit myself to two basic remarks.

(1) The distinction between "subject" and "subjectivity," a hazy one at that, loses all pertinence as soon as the phenomenon concerned can no longer be constituted as an object. Therefore if there be a saturated phenomenon, it will not affect a "subject" or a "subjectivity" precisely because both the one and the other function only in a metaphysical situation where it is a question of constituting and not of admitting an affection, of constituting objects, phenomena poor in intuition or common law phenomena. That which or he whom a saturated phenomenon affects no longer precedes it, conditions it, constitutes it; therefore he or it cannot claim any "subjectivity" nor any "subject."[53] (2) *A fortiori,* one cannot play on the opposition between a transcendental "subject" and an empirical "me." This is so, first, because the givenness of the phenomenon (which renders it nonobjective, but perhaps determines it also even when it seems objective) makes it always come upon me, by its own unpredictable landing, before, without, or counter to the conditions of possibility that the transcendental instance would impose on it.[54] On principle, a phenomenology of the given frees (or tries to free) the phenomenon from all transcendental subjection. Second, an empirical "me" has no meaning or legitimacy except in opposition to a transcendental *I,* that it balances and whose shadow it extends. If one is lacking, the other disappears. As I observed above, the supposed empiricity of such a "me" remains doubtful so long as the concept of experience that it puts into operation remains essentially burdened by a transcendental pretension: that of receiving the empirical given without also receiving itself in this givenness. Consequently it seems to me to be more wise to renounce hypotheses that are as imprecise as they are metaphysically charged. To the novelty of the hypothesis of the saturated phenomenon must correspond, at least as an attempt, a new determination of what or whom it affects.

I suggest that here we consider anew the figure of the *witness.*[55] So as not to stray from what is essential, let me restate the paradox: the witness sees the phenomenon but he does not know what he sees and will not comprehend what he saw. He sees it indisputably, in perfect clarity, with all requisite intuition, often with an intuitive excess that profoundly and enduringly affected him, possibly wounded him. He knows what he saw and knows it so well that he stands ready to witness it, again and again, often counter to his immediate interests. Witnessing becomes for him a second nature, a job, and a social function, which can end up rendering him tiresome, if not odious to those who have to deal with his "obligation to remember." And for all that, the witness still does not ever succeed in saying, comprehending, or making us comprehend what he saw. Most of the time, he does not even claim to do so; indeed he ends by plunging into silence. Which is nevertheless its own explanation; for what he saw remains withdrawn from the complete comprehension of the event, a comprehension that the concept alone could secure; but precisely the witness does not have available the concept or concepts that would be adequate to the intuition unfurling over him. He develops *his* vision of things, *his* story, *his* details, and *his* information—in short, he tells *his* story, which never achieves the rank of *the* story—history. Most of the time, he is wise enough not to claim to produce a global interpretation and gladly leaves that to the labor of the historians. In short, the witness plays his part in the interval between, on the one hand, the indisputable and incontestable excess of intuition lived and, on the other, the never compensated lack of the concepts that would render this experience an objective experience—in other words, that would make it an object. The witness, who knows what he saw and that he saw it, does not comprehend it by one or more adequate concepts. As a result, he undergoes an affection of the event and remains forever late to it. Never will he (re-)constitute it, which distinguishes him from the engineer, the inventor or the "conceiver" who produces objects because he comprehends them in terms of their concept before turning to any actual intuition, indeed without recourse to it at all. And in *this* sense, it could be said that the "conceiver," in contrast to the witness, accomplishes the "creation of events." This oxymoron becomes thinkable only as the denegation of the saturated phenomenon by the power of technics, which attempts to produce objects even there where the event unrolls.

Described thus, the witness escapes the majority of the criticisms, however contradictory, that are often addressed to what or whom a saturated phenomenon affects. (a) Does it remain sunk in pure passivity, reduced to recording the given and submitting to the monstrous excess of intuition? Obviously not, since the witness does not stop thinking this intuitive excess by having recourse to all the concepts available to him, in a labor that can be called an "infinite hermeneutic." Writing the history of the historians, but also constructing his own identity (or that of others) by the narrative of his individual story imply an ongoing effort that, remaining without an end that concepts could set, requires no less the activity of response—the response by concepts delayed behind the precedence of the intuitions. The gifted has nothing passive about it since by its response (hermeneutic) to the call (intuitive), it, and it alone, allows what gives itself to become, partially but really, what shows itself. (b) Does it by contrast exercise without admitting a spontaneous activity, thus betraying the unexamined persistence of the transcendental attitude? Obviously not, since the witness never exercises the transcendental privilege of fixing in advance conditions for experience, by formatting it within the limits of objectivity and objectness. Its activity always remains that of response, determined and even decided by the advent (unpredictable landing, the event) of intuition. This responsive posture imposes on the witness not only that he receive himself from what he receives, without any advance warning, precaution, or patrimony, but that he remain always in radical dependence on the event that gave him to himself. The figure, so often criticized as excessive and hyperbolic, of the *hostage* here finds its legitimacy: *de facto* and *de jure,* the witness is himself only through an other, more interior to himself than the most intimate within him—more him than he himself, and forever because always already. (c) Would it abandon phenomenological rigor by importing ethical or theological thinking? This reproach itself raises more questions than it resolves. First because it presupposes that ethics or theology escape rationality or are confined to derivative uses of it. Arguing this way, one fails to see that rationality not only holds sway over all domains, but that it often arises or flows forth there where thought did not or no longer expects it. What right do we have to rule out the possibility that the model of rationality might migrate from mathematics and physics to biology or information, but also to the poetic word, the ethical exigency or theological revelation? Next who can fix limits to phenomenology and by what right? One thing is clear: the real phenomenologists, I mean those who actually made visible phenomena heretofore unseen, never stopped crossing these limits, or rather ignoring them, such that after them phenomenology became, each time, infinitely more powerful than it had been before them. It could be that one defends the limits of phenomenology, its orthodoxy, and its past when one has simply given up practicing it. But perhaps involving oneself in phenomenology does not consist in involving oneself in phenomenological doctrines, their history, and their archaeology, but in what the phenomenologists themselves are involved in—the things themselves—that is to say in the phenomena and their description.

As for deciding if saturated phenomena actually give themselves and which ones, how are we to decide for another besides ourselves? And yet it can be supposed that some impose themselves on all—at the first rank of which is found the erotic phenomenon.

List of English Editions Cited

English versions of works previously translated and cited in this essay were taken from the following editions. Note that translations have sometimes been modified to capture the author's reading. When that is the case, it is marked. Works originally in English and cited in the text are also listed below.

Aristotle. *Metaphysics.* In *The Complete Works of Aristotle,* vol. 2. Trans. Jonathan Barnes. Princeton: Princeton University Press, 1984.

Augustine. *Confessiones. Confessions.* Trans. Rex Warner. New York: Signet, 2001.

Balthasar, Han Urs von. *Herrlichkeit,* vol. 3. *The Glory of the Lord.* San Francisco: Ignatius Press, 1986

Baudelaire, Charles. *Les Fleurs du mal. The Flowers of Evil.* Eds. Marthiel and Jackson Mathews. New York: New Directions, 1989.

Descartes, René. *Meditationes* and *Principia. The Philosophical Writings of Descartes.* Trans. John Cottingham, Robert Stoothof, and Dugald Murdoch. Cambridge: Cambridge University Press, 1985.

Faulconer, James, ed. *Transcendence in Philosophy and Religion.* Bloomington: Indiana University Press, 2003.

Husserl, Edmund. *Formal and Transcendental Logic.* Trans. Dorion Cairns. The Hague: Martinus Nijhoff, 1978.

Janicaud, Dominique. *Le tournant théologique de la phénoménologie française.* In Dominique Janicaud et al. *Phenomenology and the "Theological Turn": The French Debate.* Trans. Bernard G. Prusak and Jeffrey L. Kosky. New York: Fordham University Press, 2000.

Kant, Immanuel. *Critique of Pure Reason.* Trans. Norman Kemp Smith. New York: St. Martin's Press, 1965.

Kessler, Michael, and Christian Sheppard, eds. *Mystics: Presence and Aporia.* Chicago: University of Chicago Press, 2003.

Leibniz, G. W. *New Essays Concerning Human Understanding.* Trans. Peter Remnant and Jonathan Bennett. Cambridge: Cambridge University Press, 1981.

Lévinas, Emmanuel. *De Dieu qui vient à l'idée. Of God Who Comes to Mind.* Trans. Bettina Bergo. Stanford: Stanford University Press, 1998.

Mallarmé, Stéphane. *Prose pour des Esseintes.* In *Stéphane Mallarmé: Selected Poems.* Trans. C. F. MacIntyre. Berkeley: University of California Press, 1957.

Marion, Jean-Luc. *Étant donné: Essai d'une phénoménologie de la donation. Being Given: Toward a Phenomenology of Givenness.* Trans. Jeffrey L. Kosky. Stanford: Stanford University Press, 2002.

———. *De Surcroît. In Excess: Studies of Saturated Phenomena.* Trans. Robyn Horner and Vincent Berraud. New York: Fordham University Press, 2002.

———. "Le Phénomène saturé." In *Phénoménologie et théologie.* "The Saturated Phenomenon." In *Phenomenology and the "Theological Turn."*

Pascal, Blaise. *Pensées.* Trans. A. J. Krailsheimer. New York: Penguin Books, 1966.

Notes

1. The reproach—sometimes explicit, often implicit—that I remain within "metaphysics" because I take my point of departure from Kant's typology (and Husserl's) seems to me perfectly unjust and inadmissible for several reason. First methodologically, even if I do start with a "metaphysical" definition of the phenomenon for the purpose of reaching that of the phenomenon as it shows itself from itself and insofar as it gives itself, I am only repeating the Husserlian and Heideggerian movement of starting with a "natural" or "inauthentic" situation so as to pass, by reduction or destruction, to a "reduced" or "authentic" situation. Next historically, in defining the phenomenon for the first time as *Erscheinung* and not as mere *Schein*, Kant indicated a way to overcome all metaphysical senses. Heidegger made no mistake about this as he took the Kantian definition as his point of departure in constructing the "phenomenological" acceptation of the phenomenon in *Sein und Zeit*, §7. Finally conceptually, it should be necessary to define, at least once, what one means precisely, therefore *conceptually*, by the term "metaphysics," a task all the more delicate (as confirmed by Heidegger's successive positions on its use) as the term has perhaps never received a stable or univocal definition. See my study "La science toujours recherché et toujours manguante," in J.-M. Narbonne and L. Langlois, eds., *La Métaphysique. Son histoire, sa critique ses enjeux* (Paris: Vrin, 1999).

2. See *Étant donné: Essai d'une phénoménologie de la donation* (Paris 1998) §24. [English trans. in *Being Given: Toward a Phenomenology of Givenness*, §24]. Here, in distinction from my first approach at the saturated phenomenon ("Le phénomène saturé" in Jean-François Courtine, ed. *Phénoménologie et théologie* (Paris 1992) [English trans., 176–216]), I no longer include Revelation in the list of simple paradoxes or saturated phenomena. Supposing that it can enter phenomenality, Revelation demands at least a combination of the four figures of saturation, ending up at a radicalized paradox. On this point, see *Being Given*, §25 and *De surcroît* (Paris 2001), chap. 6, [English trans., in *In Excess: Studies of Saturated Phenomena*, chap. 6].

3. Baudelaire, "Three Drafts of a Preface" to *The Flowers of Evil*, xxvii.

4. Marlene Zarader, "Phenomenology and Transcendence," in James Faulconer, ed., *Transcendence in Philosophy and Religion* (Bloomington: Indiana University Press, 2003), 110. What is more, this text often assumes what it calls a "canonical" phenomenology, but this formulation is puzzling. Would this be a moment in the history of phenomenological doctrines? But then we would need to know who defines the "canon." Husserl? Which Husserl? And why the one rather than the other? As things stand, none of these questions receives an answer, since not one of them is even posed. Does this concern an abstract and nontemporal model of phenomenology? But what legitimacy can be granted to this? Often the most dogmatic defenders of the (presumed) orthodoxy of phenomenology seem also to ignore, voluntarily or not it matters little, its real history and development.

5. Ibid., p. 113.

6. Ibid., p. 110.

7. Ibid., p.118.

8. Ibid., p. 114. This is an allusion to Rudolf Bernet, *La vie du sujet. Recherches sur l'interpretation de Husserl dans la phénoménologie* (Paris: PUF, 1994), who evokes, in concluding, the question of "an intentional life without subject or object" (297ff). This concession, one that is inevitable in phenomenological terms (not only in reference to the dispute between Bolzano, Twardowski, Meinong, and Husserl about nonexistant objects, but also in regard to the overcoming of *Vorhandenheit* by *Zuhandenheit* in *Sein und Zeit*, §§15–17), already grants a lot, in fact almost everything to the saturated phenomenon's claim to legitimacy, whose chief ambition is precisely to do justice to phenomena that are irreducible to objectification.

9. Ibid., 115. Of course, the gifted was never defined in such a way since it finds itself charged, at the very moment when it receives itself with what gives itself, with the visibility of the very thing that gives itself. Here there is nothing like so simple a choice between "activity" and "passivity," with no other option (these are for that matter only categories borrowed from Aristotle, radically metaphysical and whose phenomenological usefulness can be disputed). The gifted operates according to the call and response and manages the passage of what gives itself to what shows itself: neither the one nor the other correspond to these categories. "Passivity" and "activity" intervene only once the characteristics of the gifted are misconstrued. One can make the same observations concerning Charles Larmore's criticisms of the supposed passivity of the gifted (*Les pratiques du moi* (Paris: PUF, 2004), 221ff.).

10. Ibid., 114. Obviously the problem consists in deciding not if the gifted maintains a "character of subjectivity," but *which one*—transcendental, empirical, or something else? The outrageously simplified alternative loses all pertinence. And for that matter, why reproach it for *keeping* a subjective function when other criticisms (or even the same ones) will give it grief for *losing* this function?

11. Title of the collection, *Who Comes after the Subject?* (New York: Routledge, 1991).

12. Throughout this essay "the gifted" translates the French *l'adonné*—a term that could be rendered more literally as "the one given over" and that is used in French to designate what English would call "the addict." The theme is elaborated at length in book 5 of Marion's *Being Given.*—Trans.

13. Jocelyn Benoist, "L'écart plotôt que l'excédant," *Philosophie* 78 (June 2003): 89. See "there was nothing to overcome" (ibid., 93). One remark: what does it mean to say "nothing that can be assigned [*rien d'assignable*]"? Is this the same as seeing absolutely nothing? No, without a doubt, since it is specified that what is at stake is challenging "some *absolute* form of appearing" in the name of some phenomenon (89). "To assign" therefore means *not to absolutize the phenomenon* (77), to accord (to all phenomena) only a relative phenomenality. But, we ask, relative to what or to whom? Such a presupposition should be argued or at least explained more fully. Once it is admitted, no doubt a saturated phenomenon (not to mention a phenomenon of revelation) cannot be admitted. But doesn't the entire question rest on the legitimacy of this presupposition?

14. Jocelyn Benoist, *L'idée de phénoménologie* (Paris 2001), 102. Let me observe that this question, one far too personal to remain purely philosophical, goes on: "I see

nothing or something else, for example the infinite forest of sensible life or the meta-morphoses of the divine in our daily affair of being loved, rather than the monotheistic idol?" ibid. Or: "[The phenomenon's] intuitive richness and the unbelievable complexity of the forest of the sensible" (Benoist, "L'écart plutôt que l'excédent," 92). This simple addition calls for some remarks. (a) Can one describe the supposed "infinite forest of the sensible" and its "frightening complexity" without having recourse to one or several saturated phenomena? (b) How can one describe what is here named, quite rightly for that matter, "our daily affair of being loved" without, once again, a nonobjectifying phenomenology, therefore a phenomenology of saturated phenomena (as I attempted in *Le phénomène érotique* [Paris 2003])? (c) Finally, with what right and by what procedures can one recognize (once again rightly) "metamorphoses of the divine," indeed oppose them to a presumed "idol," except by presupposing a rationality of this very divinity, therefore the means to think it, for example as paradox of paradoxes (*In Excess*, chap. 6)? But then if one wants not to remain sunk in platitudes and edifying discourses but reach the level of the concept, what philosophy will let one do this? At the very least, one can say it is not a positivism decked out in Husserlian rags that tries the patience, the diligence, and the effort of the one who describes phenomena such as they give themselves.

15. I think here of a remark Husserl made: "He [Wundt] refuses to, because he deduces, as the real *a priori* philosophy, that he can have absolutely nothing like it. Against this *a priori*, there is no cure. One cannot make oneself understood with someone who and does not want to see" ("Preface to Logical Investigations" (1913), *Tijdschrift voor Philosophie* [Louvain 1939]). I owe this reference to Benoist himself (*L'idée de phénoménologie*, 102), whom I thank.

16. Aristotle, *Metaphysics*, I, 993b 9–11 [English trans., 1570 (modified)] (or also *Physics*, I, 2, 185a 1–2), commented on by Thomas Aquinas *In Metaphysicorum Libros*, XX, n. 282. For the angels, another caution is in order: "Sicut igitur maximae amentiae esset idiota, qui ea quae a philosopho proponnutur falsa esse assereret propter hoc, quod ea capere non potest; ita et multo amplius nimiae stultiae esset homo, si ea quae divinitus angelorum ministerio revelantur, falsa esse suspicaretur ex hoc quod ratione investigari non posset" (*Summa contra gentes*, I, 3).

17. Husserl here makes reference to the "I am" as the sole intentional ground of the entire ideal world, even that of the Other. I would gladly substitute here the saturated phenomenon as official model of phenomenality, even (as we will see) for poor or common phenomenality.

18. Edmund Husserl, *Formal and Transcendental Logic*, §95, trans. Darian Cairns (The Hague: Martinus Nijhoff, 1969), 237.

19. Efforts that for the most part remain in vain since the criticisms of the saturated phenomenon, all the while calling for precise and concrete analyses, do not, most of the time, consider the descriptions offered in *In Excess* (and thereafter), but stick to the still abstract scheme in *Being Given*, if not just to the essay of 1992 ("The Saturated Phenomenon").

20. Benoist: "I believe instead that it is necessary, continuing some Husserlian analyses, and like numerous philosophies today, to recognize the fundamental and relatively

uniform *richness of intuition*. What need is there to go out looking for exceptional intuitions?" ("L'écart plutôt que l'excédent," 87). This is to say too much and to say it too quickly: (a) what are these "Husserlian analyses" and these "numerous philoso-phies" (aren't these precisely ones that the author rejects elsewhere?). (b) Why, finally, couldn't this "fundamental richness" of intuition exercise an influence in the defini-tion of the phenomenon itself, perhaps even modify this definition? (c) Does the "relatively *uniform* richness of intuition" designate some specific characteristic for this uniformity or not? If that is the case, doesn't it suggest a model common to all the phenomena endowed with this "rich" intuition and wouldn't it therefore join my attempt to establish a new paradigm of phenomenality?

21. Dominique Janicaud, *La phénoménologie éclatée* (Combas: Éditions de l'éclat, 1998), 69 (though the same author had previously denounced a "watered-down expe-rience" in *Le tournant théologique de la phénoménologie française* (Combas: Éditions de l'éclat, 1998) [English trans., in *Phenomenology and the "Theological Turn,"* 50].

22. See, on this apparently unexpected point, *Being Given*, §23 (and also §§3–4), which already sketched this banality without, it is true, formulating it as such.

23. Saint Augustine: "manifestissima et usitatissima sunt et eadem rursus nimis latent et nova est intentio eorum" (*Confessions*, XI, 22, 28 [English trans., 270–1 (mod-ified)], in regard to time).

24. Without question, the confusion, willed or not, of these two questions weighs heavily on Dominique Janicaud's criticism (*La phénoménologie éclatée*, esp. chap. 3, 63ff, to the point of leaving it too confused to be really useful and worth discussing.

25. Reproduced in Diane Waldman, *Mark Rothko, 1903–1970: A Retrospective* (New York: Abrams, 1978), plate no. 173. See the analysis of other paintings by Rothko (and Klee), as well as other phenomena saturated in terms of quality (idol), in *In Excess*, chap. 3, §§2–4.

26. The detailed and argued application of the concept of the saturated phenom-enon to music itself (and not just to listening) was more than sketched by S. Van Maas, "On Preferring Mozart," *Bijdragen. International Journal in Philosophy and Theology* 65, no. 1 (2004).

27. To the objective sense of touch are attached derived usages: touching in the sense of taking possession (money, military equipment) or else of hitting a distant target (that is to say in fact not touching directly, from flesh to thing). To its sense in terms of the saturated phenomenon, other uses are attached: to touch someone in conversation (wound him, move him, beyond what is said to him or without saying anything specific to him), to touch on something or other while with someone (without saying anything, without the intention of saying anything specific, but doing so nevertheless), to stay out of touch (in fact, to lose all contact with society or a group).

28. *Principles of Philosophy*, I, §45 [English translation, 207–8 (modified)]. Even taste can admit coding in terms of order and measure, insofar as one can assign it causes that, in extension (intelligible and producing intelligibility), determine it as their effect.

29. Signification, in the sense of what can be communicated clearly and distinctly in language, is lacking here; but precisely this shortcoming opens space for public discussion about the least communicable intuition—as if the chasm between common and private language were blurred.

30. "Hence a perception can be clear without being distinct, but not distinct without being clear" (Descartes, *Principles of Philosophy,* I, §46 [English trans., 209]). We could introduce a distinction: certain clear items of knowledge become distinct, though without a unique concept, such that it is indeed clear but not necessarily clear for just anyone. There is an excellent description of the saturation of taste in Phillipe Delerm, *La première gorge de bière* (Paris: Gallimard, 1997) (but why stick with just poor old beer?).

31. Baudelaire, "Correspondances," *Les Fleurs du mal,* IV [English trans., 12 (modified)].

32. Baudelaire, "La chevelure," *Les Fleurs du mal,* XXIV [English trans., 32].

33. Baudelaire, "Le poison," *Les Fleurs du mal,* LII [English trans., 62 (modified)].

34. In the wonderful words of Dominique Janicaud (*La phénoménologie éclatée,* 112). I am contesting nothing, except this: that such a banality impugns the hypothesis of saturated phenomena; to the contrary, it implies them.

35. One thinks of Marcel Aymé's character: "Vouturier knew to recognize the evidence and, in the same moment, to refuse its consequences. . . . He gave up the blessed springs of paradise in favor of remaining faithful to its lieutenant and its ideal of secularity" (*La Vouivre,* chap. 8, Ed. Pléiade, vol. 3, 581.

36. An objection raised quite often though with very different intentions, by among others Janicaud in *La phénoménologie éclatée,* 67; B. Han in "Transcendence and the Hermeneutic Circle" (in *Transcendence and Philosophy of Religion,* ed. James Faulconer), 136ff); and R. Welten in "Saturation and Disappointment. Marion according to Husserl."

37. Immanuel Kant, *Critique of Pure Reason* A5 / B7 [English trans., 47].

38. Ibid., A 111 (my emphasis) [English trans., 138]. See also A 158 / B 197.

39. Leibniz had already seen this: "Does the soul have windows? Is it similar to writing tablets, or like wax? Clearly those who take this view of the soul are treating it as fundamentally corporeal. Someone will confront me with this accepted philosophical maxim, that there is nothing in the soul that does not come from the senses. But an exception must be made of the soul itself. *Nihil est in intellectu quod non fuerit in sensu excipe nisi ipse intellectus*" (*New Essays Concerning Human Understanding,* trans. Peter Remnant and Jonathan Bennett [Cambridge: Cambridge University Press, 1981], II, 1, §2, 110). Even *rasa,* the *tabula* remains a table erased and therefore available for the *self,* for the *ego cogitans* before the experience cogitated—in short, it already posits, in a certain fashion, an *a priori.* If empiricism itself already implies a transcendental posture (consciously or not, it doesn't really matter), we can be free from it only by one path: thinking the ego as the gifted; for the gifted does not precede the given that it receives (as a *tabula rasa* already there awaiting it still does), since it *receives itself* from what it receives (see *Being Given,* §26).

40. Let me refer to the analyses of the infinite (Descartes), of the sublime (Kant), and the originary impression of time (Husserl) as nonobjective phenomena, sketched in *Being Given*, §22.

41. There is no greater misreading than to imagine that I attribute an *intuitus originarius* to the gifted so as to permit him to experience directly, clearly, and distinctly the Divine Absolute (Han, "Transcendence and the Hermeneutic Circle," 137). There is no better illustration of the situation of saturation of the gifted than what Kant identifies with reason as our *intuitus derivatives* because here this finitude is not limited to sensible intuition, but determines the entire experience of phenomenality.

42. For example, in the (arbitrarily) privileged case of God, Jocelyn Benoist objects: "But *is it enough not to be a concept to be God*" (*L'idée de phénoménologie*, 86). Or: "[R]epeating my criticism of your thought, *it is not enough not to be a concept to be God*" (ibid., 96). Let me pass over the fact that respect for the basic rules of mystical (so-called negative) theology would have permitted avoiding this gross syntactical error. But to speak more precisely, several remarks are called for. (a) Of course, God is not a concept, but it happens too often that we want to identify him by a concept (be it only the very concept "God"). (b) Yes, God should not be identified with *a* concept since his incomprehensibility requires all concepts [*via affirmativa*]. (c) Agreed, it is not enough that God exceed each concept (and demand them all), but that nevertheless remains a necessary, though not sufficient, condition; for as soon as we invoke a concept, it is no longer a question of God. (d) God *is* not a concept, for a more radical reason: he does not have *to be*, in contrast with everything that this polemic supposes in continually returning to the opposition between "atheist" and "believer" ("I am an atheist, you are not," ibid., 84), without at any time accepting the need to dispute the grounds or even the meaning of this opposition. For it could be that "believer" is no more opposed to "atheist" than to "theist" or "deist" or what have you, but to "nonbeliever," he who refuses to believe what he already knows well enough, be it only so as to have the power to refuse it.

43. See in particular *Being Given*, §22; *In Excess*, passim.

44. Mallarmé, *Prose pour Des Esseintes* [English trans., 63]. One can also speak of "the eye exceeded by light" (Emmanuel Lévinas, *De Dieu Qui vient à l'idée* [Paris: Vrin, 1982], 57) [English trans., 30].

45. On bedazzlement, see *Being Given*, §21. Benoist notes, as an objection, that "the only bedazzlement I know of is that of our organs' sensibility, sometimes submitted to a stimulation too strong for them" ("L'écart plutôt que l'excédent," 91). But whoever asked for a different definition of bedazzlement? I can only suggest the following: (a) The "organs" submitted to this stimulation "too strong for them" cease to give us an object exactly in the sense that I indicated (I suggest elsewhere that "this bedazzlement counts for intelligible intuition as well as for sensible intuition," *Being Given*, §21). (b) In such a situation, "our organs" extend more broadly than to sensation understood in the most sensualist sense, as I suggested earlier. (c) Theology itself (to return to the case always privileged by our dear reader) always considered the "spiritual senses" as the senses of "our organs," suggesting only that the sensibility of the latter is not limited to sensualism. It is in this sense that one must understand the

sensibility of categorical intuition in Husserl. (See *Reduction and Givenness: Investigations of Husserl, Heidegger and Phenomenology,* trans. Thomas A. Carlson (Evanston: Northwestern University Press, 1998).

46. I owe it to R. Welten ("Saturation and Disappointment. Marion according to Husserl") to have drawn my attention to this essential point.

47. Let me note that this hypothesis is quite contrived, indeed inconceivable. For who, how, and by what right could someone convince me that I do not experience the excess of light that makes me blink, indeed close my eyes? Descartes's argument (and its exegesis by Michel Henry) are fully valid here: "videlicet iam lucem video, strepitum audio, calorem sentio. Falsa haec sunt, dormio enim. At certe videre videor, audire, calescere. Hoc falsum esse non potest; hoc est proprie quod in me sentire appellatur" (*Meditatio* II, AT VII, 29).

48. On this resistance, see *In Excess,* II, §5; IV, §5. If one neglects it, the decisive phenomenological gap between "giving itself" and "manifesting itself" disappears. Then one remains stuck in the misreadings that give rise to the objections concerning the supposed passivity of the gifted or the supposed infinity of manifestation, and so on.

49. Descartes, *Meditationes de prima Philosophia,* AT VII 22, 6 (See also 28, 27; 79, 14).

50. Saint Augustine: "sic amatur veritas, ut, quicumque aliud amant, hoc quod amant velint esse veritatem, et quia falli nollent, nolunt convinci quod falis sint. Itaque propter eam rem oderut veritatem, quam pro veritate amant. Amant eam lucentem, oderunt eam redarguentem" (*Confessiones,* X, 23, ed. James O'Donnell, Oxford, 1992, vol. 1, 133 [English trans., 226–27 (modified)]).

51. In the sense of *gaudium de Deo* or *de veritate* (as in *Confessiones,* X, 29–22, 33; or *De vita beata,* IV, 35) or of Pascal's "Truth is so obscured nowadays and lies so well established that unless we love the truth we shall never recognize it" (*Pensées,* §739 [New York: Penguin Books, 1966]).

52. St. John of the Cross, *Llama de amor viva,* IV, 11. Hans Urs von Balthasar has commented: "The illuminating light is in the first instance predominantly purificatory," such that we can speak of an "experience of the absolute in the non-experience of all content or finite activity" (*Herrlichkeit,* vol. 2. *Fächer der Style* (Einsiedeln: Johannes Verlag, 1962), 527 [English trans., 138]. Kevin Hart offers an excellent commentary on this formula in "The Experience of Non-experience" in *Mystics, Presence and Aporia,* ed. Michael Kessler and Christian Sheppard (Chicago: University of Chicago Press, 2003), 196ff.

53. We should therefore take quite seriously—as is rarely the case, in my experience—the fact that Descartes himself avoids these terms. No doubt, because for him at least, the ego (as well as the *mens* or the *anima,* etc.) never exerts itself toward an object, according to the rules of the method, but sometimes admits an affection.

54. See *Being Given,* I, §1. Be it only for this reason, there is no occasion for theologians to be worried about the surreptitious reestablishment of a transcendental condition of possibility being assigned to Revelation (see, e.g., V. Holtzer, "La foi, ses saviors et sa rationalité. Esquisse des débats fondamentaux en théologie catholique contemporaine," a presentation at the conference "L'intelligence de la foi parmi les

rationalités contemporaines," Institut catholique de Paris, March 5, 2004; K. Tanner, discussion at the conference "*In Excess:* Jean-Luc Marion and the Horizon of Modern Theology," University of Notre Dame, May 9–11, 2004. For that matter, *Being Given* had already evoked this possible objection explicitly and answered it (235–36, 243).

    55. See *Being Given,* IV, §22.

Appendix A

Primary Bibliography of Jean-Luc Marion

An earlier version of this bibliography was published in Robyn Horner's *Jean-Luc Marion: A* Theo-*logical Introduction* (London: Ashgate, 2005) and was compiled on the basis of a number of resources: Marion's own records, including a list put together by Marc Loriaux; an online bibliography compiled by James K. A. Smith; and independent searches completed by Robyn Horner, Mark Manolopoulos, and Glenn Morrison. Where possible, entries in the primary bibliography are cross-referenced, although later translations falling into the same category (for either book chapters or articles) are listed with the originals rather than reentered. The primary bibliography is chronological and the secondary alphabetical by author and then chronological. While every effort has been made to track down primary and secondary works, these bibliographies are, doubtlessly, not exhaustive. Special thanks to Stijn Van den Bossche, Peter Howard, and Luz Imbriano for their proofreading assistance. Scott D. Moringiello made additions to the bibliography for the present volume.

Books in French and Their English Translations
(partial translations not listed)

Marion, Jean-Luc. *Sur l'ontologie grise de Descartes. Science cartésienne et savoir aristotélicien dans les "Regulae."* Paris: Vrin, 1975. Rev. ed. 1981. 3d ed. Paris:

Vrin, 1993. 4th ed., 2000. *Sobre a ontologia cinzenta da Descartes*. Lisbonne: Instituto Piaget, 1997. *Descartes' Grey Ontology: Cartesian Science and Aristotelian Thought in the* Regulae. Trans. S. Donohue. South Bend, Ind.: St. Augustine's Press, 2004.

———. *L'idole et la distance: cinq études*. Paris: Grasset, 1977. 2d ed. 1989. 3d ed. Paris: Livre de Poche, 1991. *L'idolo e la distanza*. Trans. A. dell'Asta. Milan: Jaca Book, 1979. *El ídolo y la distancia*. Trans. M. Pascual and N. Latrille. Salamanque: Ediciones Segime, 1999. *The Idol and Distance: Five Studies*. Trans. Thomas A. Carlson. Perspectives in Continental Philosophy. Ed. John D. Caputo. New York: Fordham University Press, 2001.

———. *Sur la théologie blanche de Descartes. Analogie, création des vérités éternelles et fondement*. Paris : Presses universitaires de France, 1981. Rev. ed. Paris: Presses Universitaires de France, 1991. English translation forthcoming.

———. *Dieu sans l'être. Hors-texte*. Paris: Arthème Fayard, 1982. Rev. ed. Paris: Presses Universitaires de France, 1991. *Dio senza essere*. Trans. A. dell'Asta. Milan: Jaca Book, 1987. *God without Being*. Trans. Thomas A. Carlson. Chicago: University of Chicago Press, 1991. Japanese translation by S. Nagai and M. Nakajima. Tokyo: Hosei University Press, 1995. *Bog bez bycia*. Trans. M. Franiewicz and K. Tarnowski. Carcovie: Znak, 1996. *Dieu sans l'être. Hors-texte*. 2d ed. Paris: Presses Universitaires de France, 2002. Chinese translation forthcoming. Japanese translation forthcoming.

———. *"Ce que cela donne." Jean-François Lacalmontie*. Paris: Éditions de la Différence, 1986. Completely revised in *La croisée du visible*. 1991. Rev. ed. Paris: Éditions de la Différence, 1996.

———. *Prolégomènes à la charité*. 1986. 2d ed. Paris: Éditions de la Différence, 1991. *Prolegomenos a la Caridad*. Trans. C. Diaz. Madrid: Caparros Editores, 1993. *Prolegomena to Charity*. Trans. Stephen Lewis. Perspectives in Continental Philosophy. Ed. John D. Caputo. New York: Fordham University Press, 2002.

———. *Sur le prisme métaphysique de Descartes. Constitution et limites de l'onto-théo-logie dans la pensée cartésienne*. Paris: Presses Universitaires de France, 1986. *Il prismo metafisico di Descartes*. Trans. F. Ciro Papparo and G. Belgioioso. Milan, 1998. *On Descartes' Metaphysical Prism: The Constitution and the Limits of the Onto-theo-logy of Cartesian Thought*. Trans. Jeffrey L. Kosky. Chicago: University of Chicago Press, 1999.

————. *Réduction et donation: recherches sur Husserl, Heidegger et la phénom-énologie.* Paris: Presses Universitaires de France, 1989. Japanese translation. Tokyo: Kora Sha, 1995. *Reduction and Givenness: Investigations of Husserl, Heidegger and Phenomenology.* Trans. Thomas A. Carlson. Evanston, Ill.: Northwestern University Press, 1998.

————. *La croisée du visible.* 1991. Rev. ed. Paris: Éditions de la Différence, 1996. Presses Universitaires de France, 1996. *Crucea vizibilului. Tablou, tele-viziune, iciana—o privire fenomenologica.* Trans. M. Neauytu. Sibiu: Deisis, 2000. *Atvaizdo dovana.* Trans. N. Keryté. Vilnius: Vertimas, 2002. *The Cross-ing of the Visible.* Trans. James K. A. Smith. Stanford: Stanford University Press, 2004. Romanian translation forthcoming.

————. *Questions cartésiennes. Méthode et métaphysique.* Paris: Presses Uni-versitaires de France, 1991. *Cartesian Questions: Method and Metaphysics.* Trans. Jeffrey L. Kosky, John Cottingham, and Stephen Voss. Chicago: Uni-versity of Chicago Press, 1999.

————. *Questions cartésiennes II. Sur l'ego et sur Dieu.* Paris: Presses Univer-sitaires de France, 1996.

————. *Étant donné: Essai d'une phénoménologie de la donation.* Paris: Presses Universitaires de France, 1997. *Being Given: Toward a Phenomenology of Givenness.* Trans. Jeffrey L. Kosky. Stanford: Stanford University Press, 2002. Italian translation by R. Caderone. Turin: S.E.I., 2002.

————. *De surcroît: études sur les phénomènes saturés.* Paris: Presses Uni-versitaires de France, 2001. *In Excess: Studies of Saturated Phenomena.* Trans. Robyn Horner and Vincent Berraud. Perspectives in Continental Philosophy. Ed. John D. Caputo. New York: Fordham University Press, 2002. *In plus. Studii asupra fenomenelor saturata.* Trans. I. Biliuta. Sibiu: Deisis, 2003.

————. *Le phénomène érotique: Six méditations.* Paris: Grasset, 2003. *The Erotic Phenomenon.* Trans. Stephen E. Lewis. Chicago: University of Chicago Press, 2007. Romanian translation forthcoming.

Books Translated into English

Marion, Jean-Luc. *God without Being.* Trans. Thomas A. Carlson. Chicago: University of Chicago Press, 1991.

———. *Reduction and Givenness: Investigations of Husserl, Heidegger and Phenomenology.* Trans. Thomas A. Carlson. Evanston: Northwestern University Press, 1998.

———. *Cartesian Questions: Method and Metaphysics.* Trans. Jeffrey L. Kosky, John Cottingham, and Stephen Voss. Chicago: University of Chicago Press, 1999.

———. *On Descartes' Metaphysical Prism: The Constitution and the Limits of the Onto-theo-logy in Cartesian Thought.* Trans. Jeffrey L. Kosky. Chicago: University of Chicago Press, 1999.

———. *The Idol and Distance: Five Studies.* Trans. Thomas A. Carlson. Perspectives in Continental Philosophy. Ed. John D. Caputo. New York: Fordham University Press, 2001.

———. *Being Given: Toward a Phenomenology of Givenness.* Trans. Jeffrey L. Kosky. Stanford: Stanford University Press, 2002.

———. *In Excess: Studies of Saturated Phenomena.* Trans. Robyn Horner and Vincent Berraud. Perspectives in Continental Philosophy. Ed. John D. Caputo. New York: Fordham University Press, 2002.

———. *Prolegomena to Charity.* Trans. Stephen Lewis. Perspectives in Continental Philosophy. Ed. John D. Caputo. New York: Fordham University Press, 2002.

———. *The Crossing of the Visible.* Trans. James K. A. Smith. Stanford: Stanford University Press, 2004.

———. *Descartes' Grey Ontology. Cartesian Science and Aristotelian Thought in the* Regulae. Trans. S. Donohue. South Bend, Ind.: St. Augustine's Press, 2004.

———. *The Erotic Phenomenon.* Trans. Stephen E. Lewis. Chicago: University of Chicago Press, 2006.

Co-authored Books

Marion, Jean-Luc, and Alain de Benoist. *Avec ou sans Dieu? Carrefour des Jeunes.* Ed. Guy Baret. Paris: Beauchesne, 1970.

Marion, Jean-Luc, and Jacques Lacourt. *La difficulté de croire.* Limoges: Droguet and Ardant, 1980.

Marion, Jean-Luc, and Jacques Lacourt. *Foi à l'épreuve de l'incroyance.* Limoges: Droguet and Ardant, 1990.

Marion, Jean-Luc, and Alain Bonfand. *Hergé: Tintin le Terrible ou l'alphabet des richesses.* Paris: Hachette, 1996.

Edited Books and Translations

Marion, Jean-Luc, ed. *Emmanuel Lévinas: Positivité et transcendence. Suivi de Lévinas et la phénoménologie.* Paris: Presses Universitaires de France, 1999.

Marion, Jean-Luc, and Jean-Robert Armogathe, eds. *Index des "Regulae ad directionem ingenii" de René Descartes.* Rome: Edizioni dell'Ateneo, 1976.

Marion, Jean-Luc and Pierre Costabel trans. and eds., *René Descartes. Regles utiles et claires pour la direction de l'esprit en la recherche de la vérité.* The Hague: Martinus Nijhoff, 1977.

Marion, Jean-Luc, and Jean Deprun, eds. *La passion de la raison. Hommage à Ferdinand Alquié.* Paris: Presses Universitaires de France, 1983.

Marion, Jean-Luc, and Guy Planty-Bonjour, eds. *Phénoménologie et métaphysique.* Paris: Presses Universitaires de France, 1984.

Marion, Jean-Luc, Alain Bonfand, and Gérard Labrot, eds. *Trois essais sur la perspective.* 2d ed. Paris: Éditions de la Différence, 1985.

Marion, Jean-Luc, and Nicolas Grimaldi, eds. *Le discours et sa Méthode.* Paris: Presses Universitaires de France, 1987.

Marion, Jean-Luc, and Jean-Marie Beyssade, eds. *Descartes: objecter et répondre.* Paris: Presses Universitaires de France, 1994.

Marion, Jean-Luc, and Marc B. de Launay, trans. and eds. *Edmund Husserl: Méditations cartésiennes.* Paris: Presses Universitaires de France, 1994.

Marion, Jean-Luc, et al., eds. *René Descartes: Index des Meditationes de prima Philosophia de R. Descartes.* Besançon: Annales littéraires de l'université de Franche-Compté, 1996.

Marion, Jean-Luc, and P. F. Moreau, trans. and eds. *Spinoza. Cogitata Metaphysica.* In *Spinoza. Oeuvres Complètes.* Paris: Presses Universitaires de France, 2000.

Marion, Jean-Luc, and Vincent Carraud. *Montaigne. Scepticisme, métaphysique et théologie.* Paris: Presses Universitaires de France, 2004.

Book Sections

Marion, Jean-Luc. "La rigueur de la louange." *Confession de la foi chrétienne.* Ed. Claude Bruaire. Paris: Fayard, 1977. 261–76. Trans. L. Wenzler. *Gott nennen. Phänomenologische Zugänge.* Ed. Bernhard Casper. Freiburg: Alber Verlag, 1981. Revised in *Dieu sans l'être. Hors-texte.* Paris: Arthème Fayard, 1982.

————. "La double idolâtrie. Remarques sur la différence ontologique et la pensée de Dieu." *Heidegger et la question de Dieu*. Eds. Richard Kearney and Joseph S. O'Leary. Paris: Grasset, 1980. Revised in *Dieu sans l'être. Hors-texte*. Paris: Arthème Fayard, 1982. Castilian translation. "La doble idolatria: Observaciones sobre la diferencia ontologica y el pensamiento de Dios." *Nombres 96*.

————. "L'instauration de la rupture: Gilson à la lecture de Descartes." *Étienne Gilson et nous: la philosophie et son histoire*. Ed. M. Couratier. Paris: Vrin, 1980. 13–34.

————. "Quelques objections à quelques réponses." *Heidegger et la question de Dieu*. Eds. Richard Kearney and Joseph S. O'Leary. Paris: Grasset, 1980. 304–9.

————. "Die Strenge der Liebe." *Gott nennen: Phänomenologische Zugänge*. Ed. Bernhard Casper. Freiburg: Alber Verlag, 1981. 165–87.

————. "Idol und Bild." *Phänomenologie des Idols*. Ed. Bernhard Casper. Freiburg: Alber Verlag, 1981. 107–32.

————. "Une nouvelle morale provisoire: la liberté d'être libre." *La morale, sagesse et salut*. Ed. Claude Bruaire. Paris: Communio Fayard, 1981.

————. "Avertissement." *E. Gilson. La liberté chez Descartes et la théologie*. Paris: Vrin, 1982. i–v.

————. "La vanité d'être et le nom de Dieu." *Analogie et dialectique. Essais de théologie fondamentale*. Eds. P. Gisel and P. Secretan. Geneva: Labor et Fides, 1982. 17–49. Revised in *Dieu sans l'être. Hors-texte*. Paris: Arthème Fayard, 1982. 17–50.

————. "Du pareil au même, ou: comment Heidegger permet de refaire de l'histoire de la philosophie." *Martin Heidegger*. Ed. Michel Haar. Paris: Éditions de l'Herne, 1983. 177–91.

————. "Les trois songes ou l'éveil du philosophe." *La passion de la raison. Hommage à Ferdinand Alquié*. Eds. J. Deprun and Jean-Luc Marion. Paris: Presses Universitaires de France, 1983. *Questions cartésiennes. Méthode et métaphysique*. Paris: Presses Universitaires de France, 1991.

————. "Avant propos." *Phénoménologie et métaphysique*. Eds. Jean-Luc Marion and Guy Planty-Bonjour. Paris: Presses Universitaires de France, 1984. 7–14.

————. "L'étant et le phénomène." *Phénoménologie et Métaphysique*. Eds. Jean-Luc Marion and G. Planty-Bonjour. Paris: Presses Universitaires de France, 1984. 159–209. Revised in *Réduction et donation*. Paris: Presses Universitaires de France, 1989.

———. "L'intentionnalité de l'amour." *Emmanuel Lévinas.* Ed. Jacques Rolland. Lagrasse: Éditions Verdier, 1984. 225–45. "L'intenzionalità dell'amore." *E si sporco le mani Prossimità ed estraneità.* Perugia: Collevanlenza, 1984. Hungarian translation in *Pannonhalmi Szemle,* 1994. Revised in *Prolégomènes à la charité.* Paris: Éditions de la différence, 1986.

———. "Splendeur de la contemplation eucharistique." *La politique de la mystique. Hommage à Mgr Maxime Charles.* Limoges: Critérion, 1984. 17–28.

———. "La croisée du visible et l'invisible." *Trois essais sur la perspective.* Eds. Jean-Luc Marion, A. Bonfand, and G. Labrot. 2d ed. Paris: Éditions de la Différence, 1985. Revised in *La croisée du visible.* 1991. Paris: Presses Universitaires de France, 1996.

———. "Wahrheit in der europäischen Geschichte: Grund oder Gabe?" *Das europäische Erbe und seine christliche Zukunft.* Ed. N. von Lobkowicz. Munich: Hanns Martin Schleyer-Stiftung, 1985.

———. "De la 'mort de Dieu' aux noms divins. L'itinéraire théologique de la métaphysique." *L'être et Dieu.* Ed. D. Bourg. Paris: Cerf, 1986.

———. "The Essential Incoherence of Descartes' Definition of Divinity." Trans. F. Van de Pitte. *Essays on Descartes' Meditations.* Ed. Amélie Oksenberg Rorty. Berkeley: University of California Press, 1986. 297–338.

———. "Aspekte der Religionsphänomenologie: Grund, Horizont und Offenbarung." *Religionsphilosophie heute: Chancen und Bedeutung in Philosophie und Theologie.* Eds. Lois Halder, Klaus Kienzler, and Joseph Möller. Düsseldorf, 1987. 84–102.

———. "La situation métaphysique du *Discours de la Méthode.*" *Le discours et sa Méthode.* Eds. Jean-Luc Marion and Nicolas Grimaldi. Paris: Presses Universitaires de France, 1987. 365–94. "The Metaphysical Situation of the *Discourse on Method.*" Trans. Rosalind Gill and Roger Gannon. *René Descartes: Critical Assessments.* Ed. G. Moyal. London: Routledge, 1991. Revised in *Questions cartésiennes. Méthode et métaphysique.* Paris: Presses Universitaires de France, 1991.

———. "Le prototype de l'image." *Nicée II, 787–1987. Douze siècles d'images religieuses.* Ed. F. Bloesflug and N. Lossky. Paris: Cerf, 1987. 451–70. Revised in *La croisée du visible.* 1991. Rev. ed. Paris: Éditions de la Différence, 1996.

———. "Descartes à l'encontre d'Aristote." *Aristote aujourd'hui.* Ed. M. A. Sinaceur. Paris: Érès, 1988. 326–30.

———. *Emmanuel Lévinas: Autrement que Savoir.* Eds. G. Petitdemande and J. Rolland. Paris: Éditions Osiris, 1988. 74–76.

————."L'interloqué." *Après le sujet qui vient?* Ed. Jean-Luc Nancy. Paris: Aubier, 1989. Who *Comes after the Subject?* Ed. E. Cadava, P. Connor, J.-L. Nancy. London: Routledge, 1991. "Podmiot w Wezwaniu." *Zawierzyc czlowiekowi. Ksiedzu Jozefowi Tischerowi na szescdziesiate urodziny.* Crocovie: Znaxk, 1992. Revised in "Le sujet en dernier appeal." *Revue de Métaphysique et de Morale* 96.1 (1991): 77–96. "L'essere e la rivendicazione." *Heidegger e la metafisica.* Ed. M. Ruggenini. Genova: Marietti, 1991. "El sujeto en última instancia." Trans. R. Rodriguea. *Revista de Filosofía* VI.10 (1993). "The Final Appeal of the Subject." Trans. Simon Critchley. *Deconstructive Subjectivities.* Eds. Simon Critchley and Peter Dews. Albany: State University of New York Press, 1996. 85–104. Reprinted in *The Religious.* Ed. John D. Caputo. Oxford: Blackwell, 2002. 131-44.

————. "Phänomenologie und Offenbarung." Trans. R. Funk. *Religionsphilosophie heute: Chancen und Bedeutung in Philosophie und Theologie.* Eds. Lois Halder, Klaus Kienzler, and Joseph Möller. Düsseldorf: Patmos, 1988. "Filosofia e Rivelazione. Trans. F. Volpi. *Studia Patavina. Revista di Scienze religiose* XXXI.3 (1989). "Le possible et la Révélation." *Eros et Eris. Contributions to a Hermeneutical Phenomenology. Liber amicorum for Adriaan Peperzak.* Ed. P. J. M. van Tongeren et al. The Hague: Kluwer Academic, 1992. 217–32.

————. ". . . plus en pratique qu'en théorie." *Problématique et réception du Discours de la Méthode et des Essais.* Ed. H. Méchoulan. Paris: Vrin, 1988.

————. "Préface." *René Descartes et Martin Schook. La querelle d'Utrecht.* Ed. T. Verbeek. Paris: Les impressiones nouvelles, 1988. 7–17.

————. "Théo-logique." *Encyclopédie philosophique universelle.* Eds. André Jacob and Jean-François Mattei. Vol. I. Paris: Presses Universitaires de France, 1989. 17–25.

————. "L'interprétation criticiste de Descartes et Leibniz: Critique d'une critique." *Ernst Cassirer. De Marbourg à New York: L'itinéraire philosophique.* Ed. Jean Seidengart. Paris: Les éditions du Cerf, 1990. 29–42.

————. "Spinoza et les trois noms de Dieu." *Herméneutique et ontologie: mélanges en hommage à Pierre Aubenque.* Eds. Remi Brague and Jean-François Courtine. Paris: Presses Universitaires de France, 1990. 225–45. "The Coherence of Spinoza's Definitions of God in *Ethics I,* Proposition 11." *God and Nature: Spinoza's Metaphysics.* Ed. Yirmayhu Yovel. Leiden: E. J. Brill, 1991. 61–77.

————. "Cartesian Metaphysics and the Role of the Simple Natures." *The Cambridge Companion to Descartes*. Ed. J. Cottingham. New York: Cambridge University Press, 1992. *Questions cartésiennes. Méthode et métaphysique*. Paris: Presses Universitaires de France, 1991. Metodo e metafisica: la nature simplici. *Cartesiana*. Ed. Giulia Belgioioso. Lecce: Università degli Studi di Lecce, 1992.

————. "Constitution et crise de la métaphysique." *Le XVIIè siecle. Diversité et cohérence*. Ed. J. Truchet. Paris: Berger-Levrault, 1992.

————. "Heidegger and Descartes." *Martin Heidegger: Critical Assessments*. Ed. Christopher Macann. London: Routledge, 1992. 178–207.

————. "Le colloque de Lecce et les perspectives des études cartésiennes." *Cartesiana*. Ed. Giulia Belgioioso. Lecce: Università degli Studi di Lecce, 1992.

————. "Le phénomène saturé." *Phénoménologie et théologie*. Ed. Jean-François Courtine. Paris: Critérion, 1992. 79–128. "The Saturated Phenomenon." Trans. Thomas A. Carlson. *Philosophy Today* 40.1–4 (1996): 103–24. "Fenomenaul saturat." Trans. N. Ionel. *Fenomenolgie si Teologie*. Iasi: Edituri Polirom Trinitas, 1996.

————. "Vorwort." Michel Henry. *Radikale Lebensphänomenologie*. Freiburg: Alber Verlag, 1992. 9–16.

————. "Generosity and Phenomenology: Remarks on Michel Henry's Interpretation of the Cartesian *Cogito*." Trans. Stephen Voss. *Essays on the Philosophy and Science of René Descartes*. Ed. Stephen Voss. New York: Oxford University Press, 1993. 52–74. *Questions cartésiennes. Méthode et métaphysique*. Paris: Presses Universitaires de France, 1991.

————. "L'image et la liberté." *Saint Bernard et la philosophie*. Ed. Remi Brague. Paris: Presses Universitaires de France, 1993. 49–72.

————. "Note sur l'indifférence ontologique." *Emmanuel Lévinas. L'éthique comme philosophie première*. Eds. Jean Greisch and Jacques Rolland. Paris: Cerf, 1993. 47–62. Trans. Jeffrey L. Kosky. *Graduate Faculty Philosophy Journal* (1996).

————. "Métaphysique et phénoménologie: une relève pour la théologie." *L'avenir de la métaphysique*. Toulouse: Bulletin de littérature ecclésiastique, 1993–94. 189–206. "Metaphysics and Phenomenology: A Relief for Theology." Trans. Thomas A. Carlson. *Critical Inquiry* 20.4 (1994): 572–91. "Metaphysics and Phenomenology: A Summary for Theologians." Trans.

A. McGeoch. *The Postmodern God: A Theological Reader.* Ed. Graham Ward. Oxford: Blackwell, 1997. 279–96.

————. "*Aporias* and the Origins of Spinoza's Theory of Adequate Ideas." *Spinoza on Knowledge and the Human Mind.* Ed. Y. Yovel. Leiden: E. J. Brill, 1994. 129–58. "Aporie ed origini della teoria spinoziana dell'idea adeguata." *L'etica e il suo altro.* Ed. Carmelo Vigna. Milan, 1994. "Apories et origines de la théorie spinoziste de l'idée adéquate." *Philosophiques.* Paris: Kimé, 1998.

————. "Entre analogie et principe de raison suffisante: la *causa sui.*" *Descartes. Objecter et répondre.* Eds. Jean-Luc Marion and Jean-Marie Beyssade. Paris: Presses Universitaires de France, 1994. 305–35. *Questions cartésiennes II. Sur l'ego et sur Dieu.* Paris: Presses Universitaires de France, 1996.

————. "Konstanten der kritischen Vernunft." *Vernunftbegriffe in der Moderne.* Eds. H. F. Fulda and R. P. Hortsmann. Stuttgart: Hegel-Vereinigung, 1994. 104–26. Revised in *Questions cartésiennes II. Sur l'ego et sur Dieu.* Paris: Presses Universitaires de France, 1996.

————. "Le statut originairement responsorial des *Meditationes.*" *Descartes. Objecter et répondre.* Eds. Jean-Luc Marion and Jean-Marie Beyssade. Paris: Presses Universitaires de France, 1994. 3–19. "The Place of the *Objections* in the Development of Cartesian Metaphysics." *Descartes and His Contemporaries: Meditations, Objections and Replies.* Eds. Roger Ariew and Marjorie Grene. Chicago: University of Chicago Press, 1995. *Questions cartésiennes II. Sur l'ego et sur Dieu.* Paris: Presses Universitaires de France, 1996.

————. "L'ego cartesiano e le sue interpretazioni fenomenologiche: al di là della representatione." *Descartes metafisico. Interpretationi del Novecento.* Eds. Jean-Robert Armogathe and Giulia Belgioioso. Rome: Istituto della Enciclopedia Italiana, 1994.

————. "Préface." Philippe Cormier. *Généalogie de personne.* Paris: Critérion, 1994.

————. "Tintin le terrible." Jean-Luc Marion and Alain Bonfand, eds. *Hergé: Tintin le Terrible ou l'alphabet des richesses.* Paris: Hachette, 1996.

————. "Nothing and Nothing Else." *The Ancients and the Moderns.* Ed. Reginald Lilly. *Studies in Continental Thought.* Bloomington: Indiana University Press, 1996. 183–95.

————. "The Idea of God." Trans. Thomas A. Carlson and Daniel Garber. *The Cambridge History of Seventeenth-Century Philosophy.* Eds. Daniel Garber and Michael Ayers. Vol. I. Cambridge: Cambridge University Press, 1998.

265–304. Revised in *Questions cartésiennes II. Sur l'ego et sur Dieu.* Paris: Presses Universitaires de France, 1996.

———. "La 'règle générale' de vérité. Meditatio III, AT VII, 34–36." *Lire Descartes Aujourd'hui.* Eds. O. Depré and D. Lories. *Actes du Colloque de Louvain-la-Neuve.* June, 1996. Louvain: Editions Peeters, 1997. *Questions cartésiennes II. Sur l'ego et sur Dieu.* Paris: Presses Universitaires de France, 1996.

———. "Notes sur les modalités de l'ego." *Chemins de Descartes.* Eds. P. Soual and Miklos Vetö. Paris: L'Harmattan, 1997.

———. "La voix sans nom." *Rue Descartes: Emmanuel Lévinas.* Paris: Collège International de Philosophie, 1998. 11–26. "The Voice without Name: Homage to Lévinas." *The Face of the Other and the Trace of God: Essays on the Philosophy of Emmanuel Lévinas.* Ed. Jeffrey Bloechl. New York: Fordham University Press, 2000.

———. "La création des vérités éternelles—le réseau d'une 'question.'" *La biografia intellettuale di René Descartes Attraverso la correspondance.* Eds. Jean-Robert Armogathe, Guilia Belgioioso, and C. Verti. Naples: Vivarium, 1999.

———. "La prise de chair comme donation de soi." *Encyclopédie philosophique universelle.* Ed. Jean-François Mattei. Vol. IV. Paris: Presses Universitaires de France, 1999. "La prise de chair comme donation de soi." *Incarnation. Archivio di Filosofia.* Ed. Marco M. Olivetti. Roma, 1999. Revised in *De surcroît: études sur les phénomènes saturés.* Paris: Presses Universitaires de France, 2001.

———. "Specificità filosofica della storia delle filosofia." *La filosofia e le sue storie.* Lecce: Milella, 1998. "D'une quadruple méthode pour lire les textes de la philosophie: la pertinence d'Henri Gouhier." *Le regard d'Henri Gouhier.* Ed. Denise Leduc-Fayette. Paris: Vrin, 1999. 103–20.

———. "'Christian Philosophy': Hermeneutic or Heuristic?" *The Question of Christian Philosophy Today.* Ed. Francis J. Ambrosio. New York: Fordham University Press, 1999. 247–64.

———. "États des études philosophiques dans la Revue XVIIème siècle: acquis, déficits et prospectives." *XVIIème siècle* 203.2 (1999).

———. "In the Name: How to Avoid Speaking of 'Negative Theology' (including Derrida's Response to Jean-Luc Marion)." *God, the Gift and Postmodernism.* Eds. John D. Caputo and Michael Scanlon. Bloomington: Indiana University Press, 1999. 122–53. Revised in *In Excess: Studies of Saturated Phenomena.* Trans. Robyn Horner and Vincent Berraud. New York: Fordham University Press, 2002.

————. "La science toujours recherché et toujours manquante." *La méta-physique. Son histoire, sa critique, ses enjeux (Acts of the XXVIIth Congress of the Association des sociétés de philosophie de langue française).* Eds. Jean-Marc Narbonne and Luc Langois. Québec-Paris: Vrin/Presses de L'Université Laval, 1999. 13–36. "La scienza sempre cercata e sempre mancante." *Ri-pensar Diritto.* Ed. P. Ventura. Turin: Giappichelli, 2000.

————. "The Original Otherness of the Ego: A Re-reading of Descartes' Meditatio II." *The Ethical.* Ed. Edith Wyschogrod and G. McKenny. Oxford: Blackwell, 1999. *Questions cartésiennes II. Sur l'ego et sur Dieu.* Paris: Presses Universitaires de France, 1996.

————. "D'Autrui à L'Individu." *Emmanuel Lévinas: Positivité et transcendence.* Ed. Jean-Luc Marion. Paris: Presses Universitaires de France, 2000. 287–308. "From the Other to the Individual." Trans. Robyn Horner. *Transcendence.* Ed. Regina Schwartz. London: Routledge, 2004.

————. "Descartes et l'expérience de la finitude." *L'Esprit cartésien.* Eds. Berard Bourgois and J. Havet. Paris: Vrin, 2000.

————. "Préface." *Pétrarque: Le repos religieux.* Ed. and trans. Christophe Carraud. Grenoble: J. Millon, 2000.

————. "La conscience du don." *Le don. Théologie, philosophie, psychologie, sociologie.* Ed. Jean-Noël Dumont. Colloque interdisciplinaire sous la direction de J.-L. Marion. Lyon: Editions de l' Emmanuel, 2001. "L'incoscienza del dono." *Il codice del dono. Verità e gratuità nelle ontologie del novecento.* Ed. Giovanni Ferretti. Atti del IX Colloquio su Filosopfia e Religione. Macerata: Università degli studio di Macerata, 2003. Revised in *Die Normativität des Wirklichen. Robert Spaemann, zum 75. Geburtstag* Ed. T. Buchheim, R. Schönberger, and W. Schweidler. Stuttgart: Klett-Cotta, 2002. 458–82.

————. "Ils le reconnurent et lui-même leur devint invisible." *Demain l'église.* Eds. Jean Duchesne and Jacques Ollier. Paris: Flammarion, 2001. 134-43. "They Recognized Him; and He Became Invisible to Them." *Modern Theology* 18.2 (2002): 145–52.

————. "The Formal Reason for the Infinite." *The Blackwell Companion to Postmodern Theology.* Ed. Graham Ward. *Blackwell Companions to Religion.* Oxford: Blackwell, 2001. "La raison formelle de l'infini." *Christiannisme. Héritages et destins.* Paris: Le livre de poche, 2002.

————. "La fenomenalita del sacramento: essere e donazione." *Il mondo del sacramento. Teologia e filosofia a confronto.* Ed. Nicola Reali. Milano: Paoline, 2001. 134–54. "La phénoménalité du sacrement: être et donation." *Communio* XXVI.5 (2001).

———. "Phänomen und Transzendenz." *Mythisierung Der Transzendenz als Entwurf ihrer Erfahrung: Arbeitsdokumentation eines Symposiums.* Eds. Gerhard Oberhammer and Marcus Schmeicher. Vienna: Verlag der Österreichischen Akademie der Wissenschaften, 2003.

———. "Préface." Emmanuel Housset. *L'Intelligence de la Pitié. Phénoménologie et Communiauté.* Paris: Cerf, 2003.

———. "The End of Metaphysics as a Possibility." *Religion after Metaphysics.* Ed. Mark A. Wrathall. Cambridge: Cambridge University Press, 2003. 166–89.

———. "The Original Otherness of the *Ego:* A Rereading of Descartes' *Meditatio II." The Ethical.* Eds. E. Wyschogrod and G. McKenny. Oxford: Blackwell, 2003.

———. "Objectivité et donation." *Le souci du passage. Mélanges offerts à Jean Greisch.* Eds. Ph. Capelle, G. Hébert, and M.-D. Popelard. Paris: Cerf, 2004.

———. "Qui suis-je pour ne pas dire *ego sum, ego existo?" Montaigne: scepticisme, métaphysique, théologie.* Eds. V. Carraud and J.-L. Marion. Paris, Presses Universitaires de France, 2004.

Marion, Jean-Luc, and Jean-Robert Armogathe. "Contribution à la sémantèse d'*ordre/ordo* chez Descartes." *Ordo Atti del II Colloquio Internationale del Lessico Intellectuale Europeo.* Rome: Edizioni dell'Ateneo, 1980.

Marion, Jean-Luc, and Richard Kearney. "Giving More: Jean-Luc Marion and Richard Kearney in Dialogue." Eds. Ian Leask and Coin Cassidy. *Givenness and God: Questions of Jean-Luc Marion.* New York: Fordham University Press, 2005. 243–56.

Kearney, Richard, Jacques Derrida, and Jean-Luc Marion. "On the Gift: A Discussion between Jacques Derrida and Jean-Luc Marion, Moderated by Richard Kearney." *God, the Gift and Postmodernism.* Eds. John D. Caputo and Michael J. Scanlon. Bloomington: Indiana University Press, 1999. 54–78.

Journal Articles

Marion, Jean-Luc. "Distance et béatitude: sur le mot capacitas chez Saint Augustin." *Résurrection* 29 (1968): 58–80.

———. "La saisie trinitaire selon l'Esprit de saint Augustin." *Résurrection* 28 (1968): 66–94.

———. "Remarques sur le concept de Révélation chez R. Bultmann." *Résurrection* 27 (1968): 29–42.

———. "Ce mystère qui juge celui qui le juge." *Résurrection* 32 (1969): 54–78.

———. "La splendeur de la contemplation eucharistique." *Résurrection* 31 (1969): 84–88.

———. "Penser juste ou trahir le mystère: notes sur l'elaboration patristique du dogme de l'incarnation." *Résurrection* 30 (1969): 68–93.

———. "Amour de Dieu, amour des hommes." *Résurrection* 34 (1970): 89–96.

———. "Distance et louange." *Résurrection* 38 (1971): 89–118.

———. "Généalogie de la 'Mort de Dieu.'" *Résurrection* 36 (1971): 30–53.

———. "Note sur l'athéisme conceptuel." *Résurrection* 38 (1971): 119–20.

———. "Note sur le choix d'un analogon." *Résurrection* 38 (1971): 121–22.

———. "Le fondement de la *cogitatio* selon le *De Intellectus Emendatione:* Essai d'une lecture des §§104–105." *Les Études Philosophiques* (1972): 357–68.

———. "Les deux volontés du Christ selon saint Maxime le Confesseur." *Résurrection* 41 (1972): 48–66.

———. "A propos d'une sémantique de la Méthode." *Revue Internationale de Philosophie* 27.103 (1973): 37–48.

———. "De la divinisation à la domination: étude sur la sémantique de *capax/ capable* chez Descartes." *Revue philosophique de Louvain* (1973). Revised in *Questions cartésiennes. Méthode et métaphysique.* Paris: Presses Universitaires de France, 1991.

———. "Ordre et relation. Sur la situation aristotélicienne de la théorie cartésienne de l'ordre selon les *Regulae V* et *VI.*" *Archives de Philosophie* 37 (1974): 243–74.

———. "Présence et distance: remarques sur l'implication réciproque de la contemplation eucharistique et de la présence réelle." *Résurrection* 43–44 (1974): 31–58.

———. "Bulletin cartésien IV." *Archives Philosophie* 38 (1975): 253–309.

———. "Droit à l confession." *Communio* 1 (1975): 17–27.

———. "Heidegger et la situation métaphysique de Descartes." *Archives de Philosophie* 38.2 (1975): 253–63.

———. "Intimität durch Abstand: Grundgesetz christlichen Betens." *Internationale Katholische Zeitschrift "Communio"* 4 (1975): 218–27.

———. "Le verbe et le texte." *Résurrection* 46 (1975): 63–80.

———. "Après Ecône." *Communio* I.8 (1976): 87–91.

———. "L'ambivalence de la métaphysique cartésienne." *Les Études Philosophiques* 4 (1976): 443–60.

———. "Le présent et le don." *Revue Catholique Internationale Communio* II.6 (1977): 50–70. Reprinted in *L'eucharistie, pain nouveau pour un monde rompu*. Paris: Fayard, 1980. Revised in *Dieu sans l'être. Hors–texte*. Paris: Arthème Fayard, 1982. Rev. ed. Paris: Presses Universitaires de France, 1991.

———. "De connaître à aimer: l'éblouissement." *Revue Catholique Internationale Communio* III (1978): 17–28. "L'évidence et l'éblouissement." *Prolégomènes à la charité*. 2d. Ed. Paris: Éditions de la Différence, 1986.

———. "A interdisciplinaridade como questao para a filosofia." *Presença filosofica* 1 (1978): 15–27. French text in *A Filosofia e as ciencias*. IV. Rio de Janiero: Semana Internacional de Filosofía, 1978.

———. "Clavel philosophe?" *Revue Catholique Internationale Communio* IV (1979): 73–75.

———. "De l'éminente dignité des pauvres baptisés." *Revue Catholique Internationale Communio* IV.2 (1979): 27–44.

———. "Fragments sur l'idole et l'icone." *Revue de Métaphysique et de Morale* 84.4 (1979): 433–45. Trans. L. Wenzler. *Phänomenologie des Idols*. Ed. Berhard Casper. Freiburg: Alber Verlag, 1981. "Ce que montre l'idole." *Rencontres de l'École du Louvre. L'idolatrie*. Paris: Documentation française, 1990. 23–34. Trans. A. Vassiliu. *Viata Româneasca* (1996). Revised in *Dieu sans l'être. Hors–texte*. Paris: Arthème Fayard, 1982. Rev. ed. Paris: Presses Universitaires de France, 1991. "Idollul si icoana."

———. "Le mal en personne." *Revue Catholique Internationale Communio* IV.3 (1979): 28–42. "Das Böse in Person." *Internationale Katholique Zeitschrift Communio* 8 (1979): 243–50. *Prolégomènes à la charité*. 1986. 2d ed. Paris: Éditions de la Différence, 1991.

———. "L'angoisse et l'ennui. Pout interpréter 'Was ist Metaphysik?'" *Archives de Philosophie* 43.1 (1980): 121–46.

———. "Le système ou l'étoile. Étude de l'ouvrage de F. Rosenzweig, *Der Stern der Erlösung*." *Archives de Philosophie* 43.1 (1980).

———. "Les chemins de la recherche sur le jeune Descartes. Notes bibliographiques sur quelques ouvrages récents (1966–1977)." *XVIIe siècle* 1 (1980).

———. "L'être et l'affection. A propos de *La conscience affective* de F. Alquié." *Archives de Philosophie* 43.1 (1980): 433–41.

————. "L'idéologie, ou la violence sans ombre." *Revue Catholique Internationale Communio* V.6 (1980): 82–92.

————. "Paradoxe sur une doctrine." *Revue Catholique Internationale Communio* VI.2 (1981): 2–5."Paradox van een benaming." *Internationale Katholique Zeitschrift Communio* 6 (1981): 81–86.

————. "Descartes et l'onto–théologie." *Bulletin de la Société française de Philosophie* 76.4 (1982): 117–71. *Giornale di Metafisica* (1984). "Die cartesianische Ontotheologie." *Zeitschrift für philosophische Forschung* (1984). *Auslegungen. Descartes*. Ed. T. Keutner. Frankfurt: Peter Lang, 1993. "Descartes and Onto–theo–logy." Trans. B. Bergo. *Post-Secular Philosophy: Between Philosophy and Theology*. Ed. Phillip Blond. London: Routledge and Paul, 1998. Revised in *Sur le prisme métaphysique de Descartes. Constitution et limites de l'onto–théo–logie dans la pensée cartésienne*. Paris: Presses Universitaires de France, 1986. *On Descartes' Metaphysical Prism: The Constitution and the Limits of the Onto–theo–logy of Cartesian Thought*. Trans. Jeffrey L. Kosky. Chicago: University of Chicago Press, 1999.

————. "Le présent de l'homme." *Revue Catholique Internationale Communio* VII.4 (1982): 2–9.

————. "La crise et la Croix." *Revue Catholique Internationale Communio* VIII.3 (1983): 8–22. *Prolégomènes à la charité*. 1986. 2d ed. Paris: Éditions de la Différence, 1991.

————. "Le don glorieux d'une présence." *Revue Catholique Internationale Communio* VIII (1983): 35–51. *Prolégomènes à la charité*. 1986. 2d ed. Paris: Éditions de la Différence, 1991.

————. "Le système ou l'étoile. Étude de l'ouvrage de F. Rosenzweig, *Der Stern der Erlösung* dont une traduction française vient de paraître." *Archives de Philosophie* 46.3 (1983): 429–43.

————. "La percée et l'élargissement. Contribution à l'interprétation des *Recherches Loqiques* de Husserl." *Philosophie* 2 (1984): 67–91, 3 (1984): 67–88. *Réduction et donation*. Paris: Presses Universitaires de France, 1989.

————. "L'âme et la paix. A propos du pacifisme." *Commentaire* 7.26 (1984): 237–42. *Identit'culturale dell'Europa. La vie della pace*. Turin: A.I.C., 1984. "Limpegno del cristiano." *Strumento internazionale per un lavoro teologico Communio* 83–84 (1985). "Per costruire la pace." *Strumento internazionale per un lavoro teologico Communio* 104 (1989). "Das Herz des Friedens. Anmerkungen zum Pazifismus." *Internationale katholische Zeitschrift Communio*

(1985). "El alma de la paz. A propósito del pacifismo." *Revista Católica Internacional Communio* V.7 (1985).

———. "L'autre regard." *Presença filosofica* 10.3–4 (1984): 60–65.

———. "De la création des vérités au principe de raison suffisante. Remarques sur l'anti–cartésianisme de Spinoza, Malebranche et Leibniz." *XVIIè siècle* 147.2 (1985): 143–64. Revised in *Questions cartésiennes II. Sur l'ego et sur Dieu.* Paris: Presses Universitaires de France, 1996.

———. "De la 'mort de Dieu' aux noms divins. L'itinéraire théologique de la métaphysique." *Laval Théologique et Philosophique* 41.1 (1985): 25–41. *L'être et Dieu.* Ed. D. Bourg. Paris: Cerf, 1986.

———. "L'avenir du catholicisme." *Revue Catholique Internationale Communio* X.5–6 (1985): 38–47.

———. "La fin de la fin de la métaphysique." *Laval Théologique et Philosophique* 42.1 (1986): 23–33. "The End of the 'End of Metaphysics.'" *Epoche: A Journal for the History of Philosophy* 2 (1996): 1–22.

———. "L'unique ego et l'altération de l'autre." *Archivio di Filosofia* 54.1–3 (1986): 607–24. Revised in *Questions cartésiennes. Méthode et métaphysique.* Paris: Presses Universitaires de France, 1991.

———. "On Descartes' Constitution of Metaphysics." *Graduate Faculty of Philosophy Journal* 11.1 (1986): 21–33.

———. "Sur les figures de la relation entre rationalité et progrès." *Revue tunisienne des Études Philosophiques* 5 (1986).

———. "Différence ontologique ou question de l'être; une indécidé de *Sein und Zeit*." *Tijdschrift voor Filosofie* 49.4 (1987): 602–45. Revised in *Réduction et donation.* Paris: Presses Universitaires de France, 1989.

———. "La conversion de la volonté selon 'L'action.'" *Revue Philosophique de la France et de l'Étranger* (1987): 33–46. *Maurice Blondel: une dramatique de la modernité.* Ed. D. Folscheid. Paris: Presses Universitaires de France, 1990. 154–65.

———. "L'aveugle à Siloé ou le report de l'image à son original." *Revue Catholique Internationale Communio* XII.6 (1987): 17–34. Revised in *La croisée du visible.* 1991. Rev. ed. Paris: Éditions de la Différence, 1996.

———. "L'ego et le *Dasein*. Heidegger et la 'Destruktion' de Descartes dans *Sein und Zeit*." *Revue de Métaphysique et de Morale* 92.1 (1987): 25–53. *Réduction et donation.* Paris: Presses Universitaires de France, 1989. *Critical Heidegger.* Ed. C. McCann. London: Routledge and Paul, 1996.

———. "L'exactitude de l'ego." *Les Études Philosophiques* (1987): 3–10. *Destins et enjeux du XVIIIe siècle.* Paris: Presses Universitaires de France, 1985. "The Exactitude of the 'Ego.'" Trans. Stephen Voss. *American Catholic Philosophical Quarterly* 67.4 (1993).

———. "'Ego autem substantia.' Überlegungen über den metaphysischen Status des ersten Prinzips bei Descartes." *Philos. Jahrb.* 95 (1988): 54–71.

———. "Générosité et phénoménologie. Remarques sur l'interprétation du *cogito* cartésien par Michel Henry." *Études Philosophiques* 1 (1988). Revised in *Questions cartésiennes. Méthode et métaphysique.* Paris: Presses Universitaires de France, 1991. *Essays on the Philosophy and Science of René Descartes.* Ed. S. Voss. New York: Oxford University Press, 1993. Greek translation by D. Rosakis. Athens, 1997. *Cartesian Questions: Method and Metaphysics.* Trans. Jeffrey L. Kosky, John Cottingham, and Stephen Voss. Chicago: University of Chicago Press, 1999.

———. "L'interloqué." Trans. E. Cadava and A. Tomiche. *Topoi* 7.2 (1988): 175–80. French version in *Confrontation.* Cahier 20. Paris, 1989. *Après le sujet qui vient?* Ed. Jean-Luc Nancy. Paris: Aubier, 1989. "El Interpelado." Trans. J.-L. Vermal. *Taula. Quaderns de pesament.* Palma de Majorque: Universitat de les Illes Balears, 1990. "L'interloqué." *Who Comes after the Subject?* Eds. E. Cadava, P. Connor, and J.-L. Nancy. London, 1991. "Podmiot w Wezwaniu." *Zawierzyc czlowiekowi. Ksiedzu Jozefowi Tischerowi na szescdziesiate urodziny.* Crocovie: Znaxk, 1992. Revised in "Le sujet en dernier appeal." *Revue de Métaphysique et de Morale* 96.1 (1991): 77–96. "L'essere e la rivendicazione." *Heidegger e la metafisica.* Ed. Mario Ruggenini. Genova: Marietti, 1991. "El sujeto en última instancia." Trans. R. Rodriguea. *Revista de Filosofía* VI.10 (1993). "The Final Appeal of the Subject." Trans. Simon Critchley. *Deconstructive Subjectivities.* Eds. Simon Critchley and Peter Dews. 85–104. Albany: State University of New York Press, 1996. Reprinted in *The Religious.* Ed. John D. Caputo. Oxford: Blackwell, 2002. 131–44.

———. "À Dieu, rien d'impossible." *Revue Catholique Internationale Communio* XIV.5 (1989): 43–58.

———. "L'analogie." *Les Études Philosophiques* 3.4 (1989).

———. "L'argument relève–t–il de l'ontologie?" *Archivio di Filosofia* 57 (1990). *L'argomento ontologico. The Ontological Argument. L'argument ontologique. Der ontologische Gottesbeweis.* Rome: Biblioteca dell' "Archivio di Filosofia," 1990. *Questions cartésiennes. Méthode et métaphysique.* Paris: Presses Universitaires de France, 1991. "Is the Ontological Argument Ontological?" *Jour-*

nal of the History of Philosophy 28 (1992). *Cartesian Questions: Method and Metaphysics.* Trans. Jeffrey L. Kosky, John Cottingham, and Stephen Voss. Chicago: University of Chicago Press, 1999. "Is the Ontological Argument Ontological? The Argument According to Anselm and Its Metaphysical Interpretation According to Kant." *Flight of the Gods: Philosophical Perspectives on Negative Theology.* Eds. Ilse N. Bulhof and Laurens ten Kate. New York: Fordham University Press, 2000. 78–99.

―――. "Réponses à quelques questions." *Revue de Métaphysique et de Morale* 96 (1991): 65–76.

―――. "Apologie de l'argument." *Revue Catholique Internationale Communio* XVII.2–3 (1992): 12–33.

―――. "Christian Philosophy and Charity." *Communio* XVII (1992): 465–73.

―――. "Esquisse d'une histoire du nom de Dieu dans la philosophie du XVII siècle." *Nouvelles de la République des Lettres* 2 (1993). Revised in "The Idea of God." Trans. Thomas A. Carlson and Daniel Garber. *The Cambridge History of Seventeenth-Century Philosophy.* Eds. Daniel Garber and Michael Ayers. Vol. I. Cambridge: Cambridge University Press, 1998. 265–304. *Questions cartésiennes II. Sur l'ego et sur Dieu.* Paris: Presses Universitaires de France, 1996.

―――. "Philosophie chrétienne et herméneutique de la charité." *Revue Catholique Internationale Communio* XVIII.2 (1993): 89–96.

―――. "Erkenntnis durch Liebe." *Internationale Katholische Zeitschrift "Communio"* (1994): 387–99.

―――. "Esquisse d'un concept phénoménologique du don." *Archivio di Filosofia* LXII.1–3 (1994): 75–94. *Phénoménologie et herméneutique.* Lausanne: Payot, 1997. "Sketch of a Phenomenological Concept of the Gift." *Postmodern Philosophy and Christian Thought.* Eds. J. Conley and D. Poe. Bloomington: Indiana University Press, 1999.

―――. "La connaissance de la charité." *Revue Catholique Internationale Communio* XIX.6 (1994): 27–42. "What Love Knows." *Prolegomena to Charity.* Trans. Stephen Lewis. New York: Fordham, 2002. 153–69.

―――. "Le concept de métaphysique selon Mersenne." *Les Études Philosophiques* 106.1–2 (1994): 129–43. Revised in *Questions cartésiennes II. Sur l'ego et* tatto della substantia nei Principia I, §51–54." *Descartes: Principia Philosophiae.* Eds. Jean-Robert Armogathe and Guilia Belgioioso. Naples: Vivarium, 1996. *Questions cartésiennes II.* Paris: Presses Universitaires de France, 1996.

————. "L'obscure évidence de la volonté. Pascal au–delà de la *regula generalis* de Descartes." *XVIIè siècle* 185.4 (1994). Revised in *Questions cartésiennes II. Sur l'ego et sur Dieu.* Paris: Presses Universitaires de France, 1996.

————. "Réponses à J.- L. Vieillard-Baron à propos d'une hypothèse sur saint Bernard et l'image de Dieu." *Philosophie* 42 (1994): 62–68.

————. "Saint Thomas d'Aquin et l'onto–théo–logie." *Revue Thomiste* XCV (1995): 31–66. *Dieu sans l'être. Hors–texte.* 2d ed. Paris: Presses Universitaires de France, 2002. "Saint Thomas Aquinas and Onto–theo–logy." Trans. B. Gendreau, R. Rethy, and M. Sweeney. *Mystic: Presence and Aporia.* Eds. M. Kessler and C. Sheppard. Chicago: University of Chicago Press, 2003.

————. "L'altérité de l'ego. Une relecture de Descartes, Meditatio II." *Archivio di Filosofia* VXIV.1–3 (1996): 583–602.

————. "L'autre philosophie première et la question de la donation." *Philosophie* 49 (1996). Revised in *Le statut contemporain de la philosophie première.* Ed. P. Capelle. Paris: Beauchesne, 1996. "La donazione in filosofia." *Annuario filosofica* 12 (1996). German translation in *Festschrift für Bernhard Casper.* Freibourg. "The Other First Philosophy and the Question of Givenness." *Critical Inquiry* 25.4 (1999): 784–800. *De surcroît: études sur les phénomènes saturés.* Paris. P.... .. iversitaires de France, 2001.

————. "Présentation de travaux actuels." *Études Philosophiques* (1996): 1–2.

————. "À propos de Descartes et Suarez." *Revue Internationale de Philosophie* 50.1 (1996): 109–31. Revised in *Questions cartésiennes II. Sur l'ego et sur Dieu.* Paris: Presses Universitaires de France, 1996.

————. "Quelques règles en l'histoire de la philosophie." *Études Philosophiques* 4 (1996): 495–510.

————. "The Saturated Phenomenon." *Philosophy Today* 40.1–4 (1996): 103–24.

————. "Le paradigme cartésien de la métaphysique." *Laval Théologique et Philosophique* 53.3 (1997): 785–91.

————. "A Note Concerning the Ontological Difference." *Graduate Faculty of Philosophy Journal* 20.2 (1998): 25–40.

————. "Justice et transcendance." *Difficile Liberté. Dans la trace d'Emmanuel Levinas.* Paris: Albin Michel, 1998. 53ff.

————. "Au nom. Comment ne pas parler de 'théologie négative.'" *Laval théologique et philosophique* 55.3 (1999): 339–63. "In the Name: How to Avoid Speaking of 'Negative Theology' (including Derrida's Response to Jean-Luc Marion)." *God, the Gift and Postmodernism.* Eds. John D. Caputo and Michael Scanlon. Bloomington: Indiana University Press, 1999. 20–53. Revised in *De surcroît: études sur les phénomènes saturés*. Paris: Presses Universitaires de France, 2001.

———. "État des études philosophiques dans la revue XVIIe siècle: Acquis, déficits et prospective." *XVIIe siècle* 51.203 (1999): 227–33.

———. "Le visage, une herméneutique sans fin." *Conférences* 9 (1999). "The Face: An Endless Hermeneutics." *Harvard Divinity Bulletin* 28.2–3 (1999): 9–10. Revised in *De surcroît: études sur les phénomènes saturés*. Paris: Presses Universitaires de France, 2001.

———. "L'évènement, le phénomène, et le révélé." *Transversalités: Revue de L'Institut Catholique de Paris* 70 (1999): 4–26. Revised in *De surcroît: études sur les phénomènes saturés*. Paris: Presses Universitaires de France, 2001. "The Event, the Phenomenon, and the Revealed. *Transcendence in Philosophy and Religion*. Ed. James E. Faulconer. Bloomington: Indiana University Press, 2003.

———. "Quelques règles en l'histoire de la philosophie." *Études Philosophiques* 109.4 (1999): 495–510.

———. "Le paradoxe de la personne." *Études* (1999). Spanish translation in *Criterio* 2251 (2000).

———. "Ratiunea formalata a infintului." *Echinox* XXXI.1–3 (2000). "The Formal Reason For the Infinite." *The Blackwell Companion to Postmodern Theology*. Ed. Graham Ward. *Blackwell Companions to Religion*. Oxford: Blackwell, 2001.

———. "Remarques sur des questions." *Annales de Philosophie* 21 (2000).

———. "The Blind Man of Siloe." *Image* 29 (2001).

———. "La phénoménalité du sacrement: être et donation." *Communio* XXVI.5 (2001).

———. "Réaliser la présence réelle." *La Maison-Dieu* 225 (2001).

———. "Ce qui ne se dit pas: Remarques sur l'apophase dans le discours amoureux." *Théologie négative*. Ed. M.-M. Ollivetti. *Actes du Colloque «Castelli»* Rome, January 4–7, 2002.

———. "Parlare d'amore." *Il Regno* 901 (2002).

———. "Notes sur le phénomène et son évènement." *Iris. Annales de philosophie. Université Saint-Joseph Beyrouth*. Vol. 23. Beyrouth, 2002. Revised in "Le phénomène et l'évènement." *Quaes* (2003). *L'existenzia/L'existence/Die Existenz/Existence*. Eds. C. Esposito and P. Porro. Bari: Turnhout, 2004.

———. "La raison du don." *Philosophie. Jean-Luc Marion*. Vol. 78. Paris: Minuit, 2003. 3–32. "The Reason of the Gift." Trans. Shane Mackinlay and Nicholas de Warren. *Bijdragen* 65.1 (2004): 5–37. *Givenness and God: Questions of Jean-Luc Marion.* Eds. Eoin Cassidy and Ian Leask. New York: Fordham University Press, 2004. 101–34.

————. "On Love and Phenomenological Reduction." Trans. Anne Davenport. *New Arcadia Review* (2004).

Marion, Jean-Luc, and Michel Henry, et al. "Préalables philosophiques à une lecture de Marx." *Bulletin de la Société française de Philosophie* 77.4 (1983): 117–51.

Marion, Jean-Luc, and Vincent Carraud. "De quelque citations cartésiennes de l'Écriture Sainte." *Archives de Philosophie* 59.1 (1996).

Interviews

"La modernité sans avenir." *Le Débat. Histoire, Politique, Société* (September 1980): 54–60.

"Phénoménologiques." *Magazine Littéraire* (November 1986): 47–48.

"Si tu m'aimes ou si tu me hais." *Art Pressï* (June 1987).

"La fin de la bêtise." *Le Nouvel Observateur* (December 22–28, 1988).

"Pour une philosophie de la charité." *France Catholique* (May 15, 1992).

"De l'histoire de l'être à la donation du possible." *Le Débat. Histoire, Politique, Société* (November–December 1992).

"Ni passion, ni vertu." *La charité. Revue Autrement* (April 1993).

"Si je veux." *Libération* (August 30, 1993).

"Descartes." *Le Point* (1995).

"Descartes—à revoir." *Magazine littéraire* (March 1996): 31–32.

"La fin de la métaphysique?" *Page* (January–February 1996).

"Interview with Jean-Luc Marion." *Leuven Philosophy Newsletter* 6 (1997).

"Après tout, l'être se donne." *Le Nouvel Observateur* (1998).

"La fin de la métaphysique ouvre une nouvelle carrière à la métaphysique." *Le Monde* (September 22, 1998).

"Auf der Suche nach einer neuen Phänomenologie" (Paris, June 17, 1997); "Ruf und Gabe als formale Bestimmung der Sübjektivität" in der Phänomenologie" (Bonn, June 25, 1998). Jean-Luc Marion and Josef Wolmuth. *Ruf und Gabe. Zum Verhältnis von Phänomenologie und Theologie.* Bonn: Borengässer, 2000.

"Le paradoxe de la personne." *Études* (October 1999).

"A quoi pensez-vous?—A penser." *Libération* (January 1, 2000).

Interview with V. Citôt and P. Godo. *Le philosophoire* (Spring–Summer 2000).

"Les vrais sujets sont délaissés." *Le Figaro* (September 27, 2000).

"Réaliser la présence réelle." *La Maison-Dieu,* 1er trimestre 2001.

"Entretien avec D. Janicaud." *Heidegger en France. II. Entretiens.* (Paris, 2001): 210–227.

"Un moment français de la phénoménologie." *Phénoménologies françaises. Revue Descartes* 35 (Paris, 2002).

"Qu'est-ce que l'amour?" *Le Nouvel Observateur* (April 17–23, 2003).

"L'amour et ses raisons." *Valeurs Actuelles* (June 20, 2003).

"Un clair devoir d'universalité." *Le Figaro* (August 19, 2003).

"Le phénomène érotique." *Études* (November 2003).

"The Hermeneutics of Revelation." *Debates in Continental Philosophy: Conversations with Contemporary Thinkers.* Ed. R. Kearney. New York: Fordham University Press, 2004.

God's Advocates: Christian Thinkers in Conversation. Ed. Rupert Short. Grand Rapids, Mich:. Eerdmans, 2005.

Appendix B

Secondary Bibliography of Jean-Luc Marion

Many of these works are substantial studies of Marion, but in line with Marion's own records, entries include texts where he is briefly mentioned.

Rev. of Jean-Luc Marion. *God without Being*. Trans. Thomas A. Carlson. Chicago: University of Chicago Press, 1991. *First Things* (1996): 67–73.

Rev. of Jean-Luc Marion. *Prolegomena to Charity*. Trans. Stephen Lewis. New York: Fordham University Press, 2002. *First Things* 20.3 (2003): 75–79.

Ahn, Taekyun. "The Gift and the Understanding of God: Iconic Theology of J.-L. Marion." Ph.D. diss. Drew University, 2003.

Alferi, T. "'Der unvorgreifbare Appell der Wirklichkeit' : Fundamentaltheologische impulse aus dem Denken Jean-Luc Marion?" (Teil 1, Teil 2). *Orientierung*, 68. 18–19 (Sept.–Oct. 2004).

Alessi, A. *Salesianum* 52.1 (1990): 53–111.

Alliez, Eric. *De l'impossibilité de la phénoménologie. Sur la philosophie française contemporaine.* Paris: Vrin, 1995.

Alweiss, Lillian. "I Am, I Exist." *Givenness and God: Questions of Jean-Luc Marion*. Eds. Ian Leask and Eoin Cassidy. New York: Fordham Unversity Press, 2005. 37–46.

Ambrosio, Francis J. "Concluding Roundtable Discussion (R. Adams, A. Peperzak, M. Adams, J. Ladriere, J. Richardson, L. Dupré, J.-L. Marion)." *The*

Question of Christian Philosophy Today. Ed. Francis J. Ambrosio. New York: Fordham University Press, 1999.

Ansaldi, Jean. "Approche doxologique de la Trinité de Dieu: Dialogue avec Jean-Luc Marion." *Études théologiques et religieuses* 62.1 (1987): 81–95.

Armour, Ellen T. "Beyond Belief? Sexual Difference and Religion after Ontotheology." *The Religious.* Ed. John D. Caputo. Oxford: Blackwell, 2002. 212–26.

Armour, Leslie. "The Idealist Philosophers' God ."*Laval Theologique et Philosophique* 58.3 (2002): 443–55.

Audi, P. "S'adonner à la phénoménologie." *Le Monde,* November 21, 1997.

Ayres, Lewis, and Gareth Jones, eds. *Christian Origins: Theology, Rhetoric and Community.* London: Routledge, 1998.

Badiou, Alain. *Saint Paul: The Foundation of Universalism.* Trans. Paul Brassier. Stanford: Stanford University Press, 2003.

Barber, Michael D. "Theory and Alterity: Dussel's Marx and Marion on Idolatry." *Thinking from the Underside of History: Enrique Dussel's Philosophy of Liberation.* Ed. Linda Martin Alcoff. Lanham, Md.: Rowman and Littlefield, 2000.

Batstone, David, et al., eds. *Liberation Theologies, Postmodernity, and the Americas.* London: Routledge, 1997.

Bauerschmidt, Frederick Christian. "Aesthetics. The Theological Sublime." *Radical Orthodoxy: A New Theology.* Eds. John Milbank, Catherine Pickstock, and Graham Ward. London: Routledge, 1999. 201–19.

Beaufret, Jean. "Heidegger et la théologie." *Heidegger et la question de Dieu.* Eds. Richard Kearney and Joseph S. O'Leary. Paris: Vrin, 1980. 19–35.

Begbie, Jeremy S. *Theology, Music and Time.* Cambridge: Cambridge University Press, 2000.

Belgioioso, Giulia. "L'année Descartes 1996: un bilan historiographique." *Nouvelles de la République des Lettres* (1996).

Bella, S. di. *Le Meditazioni Metafisiche di Cartesio. Introduzione alla lettura.* Rome: NIS, 1997.

Ben–Smit, Peter. "The Bishop and His/Her Eucharistic Community: A Critique of Jean-Luc Marion's Eucharistic Hermeneutic." *Modern Theology* 19.1 (2003): 29–40.

Benoist, Jocelyn. "Répondre de soi." *Philosophie* 34 (1992): 37–44.

———. "Vingt ans de phénoménologie française." *Philosophie Contemporaine en France.* Paris: Ministère des Affaires Étrangères, 1994.

————. "Qu'est ce qui est donné? La pensée et l'évènement." *Archives de Philosophie* 59.4 (1996).

————. "Le tournant théologique." *L'Idée de phénoménologie.* Paris: Beauchesne, 2001.

————. "Les voix du soliloque. Sur quelques interprétations récentes du *cogito.*" *Études Philosophiques* 4 (1997): 541–55.

————. "L'écart plutôt que l'excédent." *Philosophie. Jean-Luc Marion.* Vol. 78. Paris: Minuit, 2003.

Benson, Bruce Ellis. *Graven Ideologies: Nietzsche, Derrida and Marion on Modern Idolatry.* Downers Grove, Ill.: InterVarsity Press, 2002.

————. "Jean-Luc Marion Tests the Limits of Logic: Love Is a Given." *Christian Century* 120.3 (2003): 22–25.

Beyssade, Jean-Marie. "The Idea of God and the Proofs of his Existence." Trans. J. Cottingham. *The Cambridge Companion to Descartes.* Ed. J. Cottingham. Cambridge: Cambridge University Press, 1992. 174–99.

————. "On the Idea of God: Incomprehensibility or Incompatibilities?" Trans. Charles Paul. *Essays on the Philosophy and Science of René Descartes.* Ed. Stephen Voss. New York: Oxford University Press, 1993.

————. "Méditer, objecter, répondre." *Descartes. Objecter et répondre.* Eds. Jean-Luc Marion and Jean-Marie Beyssade. Paris: Presses Universitaires de France, 1994. 21–38.

Bloechl, Jeffrey. "Dialectical Approaches to Retrieving God after Heidegger: Premises and Consequences (Lacoste and Marion)." *Pacifia: Journal of the Melbourne College of Divinity* 13 (2000): 288–98.

————. "The Postmodern Context and Sacramental Presence: Disputed Questions." *The Presence of Transcendence.* Eds. Lieven Boeve and John C. Ries. Leuven: Uitgeverij Peeters, 2001. 3–17.

————. "Translator's Introduction." *Jean-Louis Chrétien. The Unforgettable and the Unhoped For.* New York: Fordham University Press, 2002. vii–xv.

Bloesch, Donald G. *God the Almighty: Power, Wisdom, Holiness, Love.* Downers Grove, Ill.: Intervarsity Press, 1995.

Blond, Philip, ed. *Post-Secular Philosophy: Between Philosophy and Theology.* London: Routledge, 1998.

————. "Perception: From Modern Painting to the Vision in Christ." *Radical Orthodoxy: A New Theology.* Eds. John Milbank, Catherine Pickstock, and Graham Ward. London: Routledge, 1999. 220–42.

Boeve, Lieven. "Method in Postmodern Theology: A Case Study." *The Presence of Transcendence.* Eds. Lieven Boeve and John C. Ries. Leuven: Uitgeverij Peeters, 2001. 19–39.

Boldor, Marius. "O incursiune fenomenologică în lumea vizibilului împreună cu Jean-Luc Marion." *Studia Theologica* 1.4 (2003): 178–95.

Bonfand, Alain. *L'ombre de la nuit. Essai sur la mélancolie et l'angoisse dans les oeuvres de Mario Sironi et de Paul Klee entre 1933 et 1940.* Paris: La Différence, 1993.

———. *L'expérience esthétique à l'épreuve de la phénoménologie. La tristesse du roi.* Paris: Presses Universitaires de France, 1995.

Bottum, J. "Christians and Postmodernists." *First Things* 40 (1994): 28–32.

Bouttes, M. "Analogie et question de l'infini chez Descartes." *Cartesiana.* Eds. M. Bouttes and G. Granel. Mauvezin: TER, 1984. 69–85.

Bracken, Joseph A. "Toward a New Philosophical Theology Based on Intersubjectivity." *Theological Studies* 59.4 (1998): 703–19.

Bradley, Arthur. "God *Sans* Being: Derrida, Marion and 'a Paradoxical Writing of the Word *Without.*'" *Literature and Theology* 14.3 (2000): 299–312.

Brennan, Teresa, and Martin Jay, eds. *Vision in Context: Historical and Contemporary Perspectives on Sight.* London: Routledge, 1996.

Bres, Yvon. "L'avenir du judéo–christianisme (suite et fin)." *Revue Philosophique de la France et de l'Étranger* (2002): 65–83.

Breton, Stanislas. Rev. of Jean-Luc Marion. *L'idole et la distance.* Paris: Grasset, 1977. *Archives de Philosophie* 43 (1980): 152–57.

———. "La querelle des dénominations." *Heidegger et la question de Dieu.* Eds. Richard Kearney and Joseph S. O'Leary. Paris: Vrin, 1980. 248–68.

Brito, Emilio. "La réception de la pensée de Heidegger dans la théologie catholique." *Nouvelle Revue Théologique* 119.3 (1997): 352–74.

Broughton, Janet. *Descartes's Method of Doubt.* Princeton: Princeton University Press, 2003.

Bulhof, Ilse N. "Being Open as a Form of Negative Theology: On Nominalism, Negative Theology, and Derrida's Performative Interpretation of 'Khôra.'" *Flight of the Gods: Philosophical Perspectives on Negative Theology.* Eds. Ilse N. Bulhof and Laurens ten Kate. New York: Fordham University Press, 2000. 194–221.

Bulhof, Ilse N., and Laurens ten Kate, eds. *Flight of the Gods: Philosophical Perspectives on Negative Theology.* New York: Fordham University Press, 2000.

Bultmann, Rudolf, et al. *Philosophie. Phénomenologie et théologie.* Vol. 42. Paris: Minuit, 1994.

Burrell, David B. "Reflections on 'Negative Theology' in the Light of a Recent Venture to Speak of 'God without Being.'" *Postmodernism and Christian Philosophy.* Ed. R. T. Ciapalo. Washington, D.C.: Catholic University of America Press, 1997. 58–67.

Cacciari, M. "Il problema del sacro in Heidegger." *La recezione italiana di Heidegger.* Ed. Marco Olivetti. Padua: Cedam, 1989. 203–17.

Canullo, C. *La fenomenologia rovesciata. Percorsi tentati in J.-L. Marion, M. Henry et J.-L. Chrétien.* Turin: Rosenberg and Sellier, 2004.

Calderone, R. "Eros e filosofia. A partire da *le phénomène érotique* di Jean-Luc Marion," *Fieri. Annali del Dipartimento di Filosofia, Storia e Critica dei Saperi,* Université de Palerme, I, 2004.

Canziani, G. "Ermeneutica cartesiana. In margine ad un recente libro di J.-L. Marion [*Sur la théologie blanche de Descartes,* vol. I, no. 5]." *Rivista di Storia della Filosofia* (1984).

Caputo, John D. "How to Avoid Speaking of God: The Violence of Natural Theology." *Prospects for Natural Theology.* Ed. E. T. Long. Washington, D.C.: Catholic University of America Press, 1992.

———. "God Is Wholly Other—Almost: 'Différance' and the Hyperbolic Alterity of God." *The Otherness of God.* Ed. O. F. Summerell. Charlottesville: University Press of Virginia, 1998. 190–205.

———. "Apostles of the Impossible." *God, the Gift and Postmodernism.* Eds. John D. Caputo and Michael Scanlon. Bloomington: Indiana University Press, 1999. 185–222. "Apôtres de l'impossible: sur Dieu et le don chez Derrida et Marion." *Philosophie. Jean-Luc Marion.* Vol. 78. Paris: Minuit, 2003.

Caputo, John D., Mark Dooley, and Richard Kearney, eds. *Questioning God.* Bloomington: Indiana University Press, 2001.

Caputo, John D., and Michael Scanlon. "Apology for the Impossible: Religion and Postmodernism." *God, the Gift, and Postmodernism.* Eds. John D. Caputo and Michael Scanlon. Bloomington: Indiana University Press, 1999. 1–19.

Caputo, John D., and Michael Scanlon, eds. *God, the Gift, and Postmodernism.* Bloomington: Indiana University Press, 1999.

Carabine, Deirdre. *John Scottus Eriugena.* Great Medieval Thinkers. Oxford: Oxford University Press, 2000.

Carlson, Thomas A. "Finitude and the Naming of God: A Study of Onto-theology and the Apophatic Traditions." Ph.D. diss. University of Chicago, 1995.

———. *Indiscretion: Finitude and the Naming of God. A Study of Onto–theology and the Apophatic Traditions.* Chicago: University of Chicago Press, 1999.

———. "Translator's Introduction." *The Idol and Distance: Five Studies.* New York: Fordham University Press, 2001. xi–xxxi.

Carraud, Vincent. "Descartes appartienne alla storia della metafisica?" *Descartes metafisico. Interpretationi del Novecento.* Eds. Jean-Robert Armogathe and Guilia Belgioioso. Roma: Instituto della Enciclopedia Italiana, 1995.

Cassidy, Eoin. "*Le phénomène érotique:* Augustinian Resonances in Marion's Phenomenology of Love." *Givenness and God: Questions of Jean-Luc Marion.* Eds. Ian Leask and Eoin Cassidy. New York: Fordham Unversity Press, 2005. 201–19.

Cavanaugh, William T. "The City: Beyond Secular Parodies." *Radical Orthodoxy: A New Theology.* Eds. John Milbank, Catherine Pickstock, and Graham Ward. London: Routledge, 1999. 182–200.

Chambers, Iain. *Migrancy, Culture, Identity.* London: Routledge, 1994.

Chrétien, Jean-Louis. *The Call and the Response.* Trans. Anne A. Davenport. New York: Fordham University Press, 2004.

Clark, David A. "Otherwise than God: Schelling, Marion." *Trajectories of Mysticism in Theory and Literature.* New York: St. Martin's Press, 2000. 133–76.

Coda, P. "Dono e abbandono: con Heidegger sulle tracce dell'Essere." *La Trinità e il pensare: figure percorsi prospettive.* Eds. P. Coda and A. Tapken. Rome: Città Nuovo, 1994. 165–70.

Colette, Jacques. "Phénoménologie et métaphysique." *Critique* 548–49 (1993): 56–73.

Cooke, Alexander. "What Saturates? Jean-Luc Marion's Phenomenological Theology." *Philosophy Today* 48.2 (2004): 179–87.

Corbin, Michel. "Négation et transcendance dans l'oeuvre de Denys." *Revue des sciences philosophiques et théologiques* 69.1 (1985): 41–75.

Corvet, M. *Revue Théologique* 1 (1979): 124–32.

Cottingham, John, ed. *The Cambridge Companion to Descartes.* Cambridge: Cambridge University Press, 1992.

———. Rev. of *Cartesian Questions: Method and Metaphysics.* Trans. Jeffrey L. Kosky, John Cottingham, and Stephen Voss. Chicago: University of Chicago Press, 1999. *Mind* 111.442 (2002): 447–49.

Courtine, Jean-François, et al. *Phénoménologie et théologie*. Paris: Critérion, 1992.

Craig, Edward, ed. *Routledge Encyclopedia of Philosophy*. London: Routledge, 1998.

Critchley, Simon, and Robert Bernasconi, eds. *The Cambridge Companion to Lévinas*. Cambridge: Cambridge University Press, 2002.

Crockett, Clayton. *Secular Theology: American Radical Theological Thought*. London: Routledge, 2001.

————. *A Theology of the Sublime*. London: Routledge, 2001.

Crowell, Steven-Galt. "Authentic Thinking and Phenomenological Method." *The New Yearbook for Phenomenology and Phenomenological Philosophy*. Ed. Burt C. Hopkins. Seattle: Noesis–Press, 2002. 23–37.

Crump, Eric H. Rev. of Jean-Luc Marion. *God without Being*. Trans. Thomas A. Carlson. Chicago: University of Chicago Press, 1991. *Modern Theology* 9.3 (1993): 309.

Cunningham, Conor. *Genealogy of Nihilism: Philosophies of Nothing and the Difference of Theology*. Radical Orthodoxy. London: Routledge, 2002.

Davenport, John, et al., eds. *Kierkegaard after MacIntyre: Essays on Freedom, Narrative, and Virtue*. Chicago: Open Court, 2001.

Davis, Stephen T., Daniel Kendall, and Gerald O'Collins, eds. *The Trinity: An Interdisciplinary Symposium on the Trinity*. Oxford: Oxford University Press, 2002.

Decartes, René. *Discourse on Method and Related Writings*. Trans. Desmond M. Clarke. New York: Penguin, 2000.

DeHart, Paul J. *Beyond the Necessary God: Trinitarian Faith and Philosophy in the Thought of Eberhard Jüngel*. Reflection and Theory in the Study of Religion, No. 15. Atlanta, GA: Scholars Press, 2000.

————. "The Ambiguous Infinite: Jüngel, Marion, and the God of Descartes." *Journal of Religion* 82.1 (2002): 75–96.

Delacampagne, Christian. *A History of Philosophy in the Twentieth Century*. Trans. M. B. Debevoise. Reprint ed. Baltimore: Johns Hopkins University Press, 2001.

Depraz, Natalie. "Gibt es eine Gebung des Unendlichen." *Perspektiven der Philosophie*. Ed. R. Berlinger. Amsterdam: Rodopi, 1997.

————. "The Return of Phenomenology in Recent French Moral Philosophy." *Phenomenological Approaches to Moral Philosophy*. Ed. John Drummond. Dordrecht: Kluwer Academic Publishers, 2002.

Derrida, Jacques. *Donner le temps. I. La fausse monnaie.* Paris: Galilée, 1991. *Given Time. I. Counterfeit Money.* Trans. Peggy Kamuf. Chicago: University of Chicago Press, 1992.

Deverell, Gary. *The Bonds of Freedom: Vow, Sacraments, and the Formation of the Christian Self.* Ph.D. diss. Monash University, 1998.

Devillairs, Laurence. "Le phénomène érotique. Entretien avec Jean-Luc Marion." *Études* 10 (2003): 483–94.

Dooley, Mark. "Marion's Ambition of Transcendence." *Givenness and God: Questions of Jean-Luc Marion.* Eds. Ian Leask and Eoin Cassidy. New York: Fordham Unversity Press, 2005. 190–98.

Dostal, Robert J., ed. *The Cambridge Companion to Gadamer.* Cambridge: Cambridge University Press, 2002.

Drabinski, J. E. "Sense and Icon: The Problem of *Sinngebung* in Lévinas and Marion." *Philosophy Today* 42 SPEP Supplement (1998): 47–58.

Duquesne, Marcel. "À propos d'un livre récent: Jean-Luc Marion, *Dieu sans l'être* (à suivre)." *Mélanges de Science Religieuse* XLII.2 (1985): 57–76.

―――. "À propos d'un livre récent: Jean-Luc Marion, *Dieu sans l'être.*" *Mélanges de Science Religieuse* XLII (1985): 127–40.

Elliott, Brian. "Reduced Phenomena and Unreserved Debts in Marion's Reading of Heidegger." *Givenness and God: Questions of Jean-Luc Marion.* Eds. Ian Leask and Eoin Cassidy. New York: Fordham Unversity Press, 2005. 87–100.

English, Adam C. "Structure, Mystery, Power: The Christian Ontology of Maurice Blondel (John Milbank, Henri de Lubac, Karl Rahner, Jean-Luc Marion)." Ph.D. diss. Baylor University, 2003.

Esposito, C. "Ritorno a Suarez. Le *Disputationes Metaphysicae* nella critica contemporanea." *La filosofia nel siglo de Oro. Studi sul tardo rinascimento spagnolo.* Ed. Ada Lammachia. Bari: Levante, 1995.

Ewbank, Michael B. "Of Idols, Icons, and Aquinas's Esse: Reflections on Jean-Luc Marion." *International Philosophical Quarterly* 42.2 (2002): 161–75.

Fabrègues, J. de. "Non à l'idole, oui à l'icône." *France Catholique–Ecclesia* (September 24, 1982): 12–13.

Falque, Emmanuel. *Saint Bonaventure et l'entrée de Dieu en théologie.* Paris: Vrin, 2000.

―――. "Phénoménologie de l'extraordinaire." *Philosophie. Jean-Luc Marion.* Vol. 78. Paris: Minuit, 2003.

―――. "*Larvatus pro Deo.* Phénoménologie et théologie chez J.-L.Marion," *Gregorianum* 86.1 (2005).

Faulconer, James E., ed. *Transcendence in Philosophy and Religion.* Bloomington: Indiana University Press, 2003.

Fédier, F. "Heidegger et Dieu." *Heidegger et la question de Dieu.* Eds. Richard Kearney and Joseph S. O'Lery. Paris: Vrin, 1980. 37–45.

Flanagan, Kieran, and Peter C Jupp. *Postmodernity, Sociology and Religion.* London : Macmillan, 1996.

Fletcher, Paul. "Writing of(f) Victims: hors texte." *New Blackfriars* 78.916 (1997): 267–78.

Floucat, Y. "Chronique de philosophie." *Revue Théologique* (1983).

Ford, David F. *Self and Salvation: Being Transformed.* Cambridge: Cambridge University Press, 1999.

Fountain, J. Stephen. "Postmodernism, A/Theology, and the Possibility of Language as Universal Eucharist." *The Nature of Religious Language.* Ed. Stanley E. Porter. Sheffield: Sheffield Academic Press, 1996. 131–47.

Foutz, S. D. "Postmetaphysic[al?] Theology—A Case Study: Jean-Luc Marion." *Quodlibet: Online Journal of Christian Theology and Philosophy* 1.3 (1999).

Frank, Daniel H., and Oliver Leaman, eds. *History of Jewish Philosophy.* Vol. 2. London: Routledge, 1997.

Gabellieri, E. "De la métaphysique à la phénoménologies: une 'relève'?" *Revue philosophique de Louvain* 94.4 (1996): 625–45.

Gagnon, M. "La phénoménologie à la limite." *Eidos: The Canadian Graduate Journal of Philosophy* 11 (1993): 111–30.

Gamba, F. "Della reduzione alla donazione: Svilluppi della fenomenologia contemporanea." *Filosofia* 49.3 (1998): 315–31.

Garber, Daniel. "Foreword." *Cartesian Questions: Method and Metaphysics.* Chicago: University of Chicago Press, 1999. ix–xiii.

———. *Descartes Embodied: Reading Cartesian Philosophy through Cartesian Science.* Cambridge: Cambridge University Press, 2000.

Garcia Murga, Jose R. "Como decir hoy que Dios es amor." *Miscelanea Comillas* 45 (1987): 289–321.

Gaukroger, Stephen, John Schuster, and John Sutton, eds. *Descartes' Natural Philosophy.* London: Routledge, 2000.

Gicquel, Herve-Marie. "L'intervention de l'inconnu dans la vie personnelle." Ph.D. diss. University of Ottawa, 1996.

Gilbert, Paul. "Substance et présence: Derrida et Marion, critiques de Husserl." *Gregorianum* 75.1 (1994): 95–133.

Godzieba, Anthony J. "Ontotheology to Excess: Imagining God without Being." *Theological Studies* 56 (1995): 3–20.

Goodchild, Philip. *Capitalism and Religion: The Price of Piety.* London: Routledge, 2002.

Greisch, Jean. "Actualité ou inactualité de la théologie naturelle?" *Revue des sciences philosophiques et théologiques* 67.3 (1983): 443–53.

———. "L'herméneutique dans la 'phénoménologie comme telle.'" *Revue de Métaphysique et de Morale* 96.1 (1991): 43–76.

———. "Index sui et non dati: Les paradoxes d'une phénoménologie de la donation." *Transversalités: Revue de L'Institut Catholique de Paris* (1999): 27–54.

———. *Le cogito herméneutique: l'herméneutique philosophique et l'heritage cartésien.* Paris: Vrin, 2000.

Grene, Marjorie Glicksman, Lewis Edward Hahn, and Randall E. Auxier, eds. *The Philosophy of Marjorie Grene.* Chicago: Open Court, 2003.

Grimwood, Steven. "Iconography and Postmodernity." *Literature and Theology* 17.1 (2003): 76–97.

Grondin, Jean. Rev. of Jean-Luc Marion, *Sur le prisme métaphysique de Descartes.* Paris: Presses Universitaires de France, 1986. *Laval Théologique et Philosophique* 43.3 (1987): 409–13.

———. "La phénoménologie sans herméneutique." *L'horizon herméneutique de la pensée contemporaine.* Paris: Vrin, 1993. 81–90.

———. "La tension de la donation ultime et de la pensée herméneutique de l'application chez Jean-Luc Marion." *Dialogue* 38.3 (1999): 547–59.

Gschwandtner, Christina Margrit. "Sparks of Meaning at the Points of Friction: At the Boundary between Philosophy and Theology in the Work of Jean-Luc Marion (René Descartes)." Ph.D. diss. Depaul University, 2003.

Guarino, Thomas. "Postmodernity and Five Fundamental Theological Issues." *Theological Studies* 57.4 (1996): 654–89.

Guitton, Jean. "Le fini de l'homme et l'infini de Dieu." *France Catholique–Ecclesia* (September 24, 1982): 12–13.

Gutting, Gary. *French Philosophy in the Twentieth Century.* Cambridge: Cambridge University Press, 2001.

Hankey, Wayne J. "The Postmodern Retrieval of Neoplatonism in Jean-Luc Marion and John Milbank and the Origins of Western Subjectivity in Augustine and Eriugena." *Hermathena* 165 (1998): 9–70.

————. "Theoria versus Poesis: Neoplatonism and Trinitarian Difference in Aquinas, John Milbank, Jean-Luc Marion and John Zizoulas." *Modern Theology* 15.4 (1999): 387–415.

————. "Between and Beyond Augustine and Descartes: More Than a Source of the Self." *Augustinian–Studies* 32.1 (2001): 65–88.

————. "Why Philosophy Abides for Aquinas." *Heythrop Journal* 42.3 (2001): 329–48.

Hannay, Alastair, and Gordon Daniel Marino, eds. *The Cambridge Companion to Kierkegaard.* Cambridge: Cambridge University Press, 1997.

Hancock, Stuart C. "Postmodernism." *Mars Hill Review* 12 (1998): 9–104.

Hanson, J. A. "Jean-Luc Marion and the Possibility of a Postmodern Theology." *Mars Hill Review* 12 (1998): 93–104.

Happel, Stephen. *Metaphors for God's Time in Science and Religion.* Houndmills, Hampshire: Palgrave Macmillan, 2003.

Hart, Kevin. *Postmodernism. A Beginner's Guide.* London: Oneworld, 2004.

Heinich, Nathalie. *The Glory of van Gogh.* Trans. Paul Leduc Browne. Princeton: Princeton University Press, 1997.

Heller–Roazen, Daniel, Stephen G. Nichols, and Gerald Prince, eds. *Fortune's Faces: The Roma de la Rose and the Poetics of Contingency.* Baltimore: Johns Hopkins University Press, 2003.

Hemming, Laurence. "Reading Heidegger: Is God without Being? Jean-Luc Marion's Reading of Martin Heidegger in *God without Being.*" *New Blackfriars* 76.895 (1995): 343–50.

————. "To Say Nothing of the Existence of God." Ph.D. diss. Cambridge University, 1999.

————. "Nihilism: Heidegger and the Grounds of Redemption." *Radical Orthodoxy: A New Theology.* Eds. John Milbank, Catherine Pickstock, and Graham Ward. London: Routledge, 1999. 91–108.

————. *Postmodernity's Transcending: Devaluing God.* London: SCM Press, 2005.

Hengel, John van den. "God with/out Being." *Method: Journal of Lonergan Studies* 12.2 (1994): 251–79.

Henry, Michel. "Quatres principes de la phénoménologie." *Revue de Métaphysique et de Morale* 96.1 (1991): 3–26.

Hoff, A. E. van. "Sein als Idol? Erwägungen zu Jean-Luc Marion, *Dieu sans l'être.*" *Archivio di Filosofia* 54 (1986).

Höhn, G. "Suche nach Ursprünglichkeit. Die Wiedergeburt der Metaphysik aus dem Erbe der Phänomenologie." *Frankfurter Rundschau* (1994).

Holzer, Vincent. "Phénoménologie radicale et phénomène de révélation." *Transversalités: Revue de L'Institut Catholique de Paris* (1999): 55–68.

Horner, Robyn. "Rethinking God as Gift: Jean-Luc Marion and a Theology of Donation." Ph.D. diss. Monash University, 1998.

———. "The Eucharist and the Postmodern." *Eucharist: Experience and Testimony.* Ed. Tom Knowles. Ringwood, VIC: David Lovell, 2001. 3–24.

———. *Rethinking God as Gift: Marion, Derrida, and the Limits of Phenomenology.* Perspectives in Continental Philosophy. Ed. John D. Caputo. New York: Fordham University Press, 2001.

———. "Problème du mal et péché des origines." *Recherches de Science Religieuse* 90.1 (2002): 63–86.

———. "Translator's Introduction." *Jean-Luc Marion. In Excess: Studies of Saturated Phenomena.* New York: Fordham University Press, 2002. ix–xx.

———. "Aporia or Excess: Two Strategies for Thinking r/Revelation." *Other Testaments: Derrida and Religion.* Eds. Kevin Hart and Yvonne Sherwood. London: Routledge, 2004.

———. "The Betrayal of Transcendence." *Transcendence.* Ed. Regina Schwartz. New York: Routledge, 2004.

———. "The Face as Icon." *Australasian Catholic Record* (2004).

———. *Jean-Luc Marion. A Theo–logical Introduction,* London: Ashgate, 2005.

Houtepen, A. *God, een open vraag. Theologische perspectieven in een cultuur van agnosme.* Zoetermeer: Meinema, 1997.

Hureaux, R. "Au *Dasein* prisonnier, la libération." *Liberté politique,* 27, Paris, November 2004.

Hutter, Reinhard. Rev. of Jean-Luc Marion. *God without Being. Hors–Texte.* Trans. Thomas. A. Carlson. Chicago: University of Chicago Press, 1991. *Pro–Ecclesia* 3 (1994): 239–44.

Iezzoni, E. *Il Dar–si dell' Essere nell' ecstasi del' altro. Antropologia filosofics e ontologia trinitaria nel peniero di Jean-Luc Marion e Klaus Hemmerle.* Chieti: University of Chieti, 1997.

Inglis, John, ed. *Medieval Philosophy and the Classical Tradition in Islam, Judaism and Christianity.* London: Curzon Press, 2001.

Janicaud, Dominique. Rev. of Jean-Luc Marion. *L'idole et la distance.* Paris: Grasset, 1977. *Les Études Philosophiques* 2 (1979): 250–52.

————. Rev. of Jean-Luc Marion. *Dieu sans l'être*. Paris: Fayard, 1982. *Les Études Philosophiques* 4 (1983): 496–98.

————. *Le tournant théologique de la phénoménologie française*. Combas: Éditions de l'Éclat, 1991.

————. *La phénoménologie éclatée*. Combas: Éditions de l'éclat, 1998.

————. "'Veerings' from *The Theological Turn of French Phenomenology*." *The Religious*. Ed. John D. Caputo. Oxford: Blackwell, 2002. 145–58.

Janicaud, Dominique, et al. *Phenomenology and the "Theological Turn": The French Debate*. Perspectives in Continental Philosophy. Ed. John D. Caputo. New York: Fordham University Press, 2001.

Janz, Denis R. "Syllogism or Paradox: Aquinas and Luther on Theological Method." *Theological Studies* 59.1 (1998): 3–21.

Javaux, J. Rev. of Jean-Luc Marion. *L'idole et la distance*. Paris: Grasset, 1977. *Nouvelle Revue Théologique* 100.2 (1978): 297–99.

————. Rev. of Jean-Luc Marion. *Dieu sans l'être*. Paris: Fayard, 1982. *Nouvelle Revue Théologique* 105.5 (1983): 731–32.

Jenson, Robert W. *Systematic Theology: The Triune God*. Oxford: Oxford University Press, 2001.

Jonkers, Peter, and Ruud Welten, eds. *God in Frankrijk. Zes hedendaagse Franse filosofen over God*. Budel: Damon, 2003.

Kal, Victor. "Being Unable to Speak, Seen As a Period: Difference and Distance in Jean-Luc Marion." *Flight of the Gods: Philosophical Perspectives on Negative Theology*. Eds. Ilse N. Bulhof and Laurens ten Kate. New York: Fordham University Press, 2000. 143–64.

Kalinowski, G. "Discours de louange et discours métaphysique: Denys l'aréopagite et Thomas D'Aquin." *Rivista di Filosofia Neo Scolastica* 73 (1981): 399–404.

Kate, Laurens ten. "The Gift of Loss: A Study of the Fugitive God in Bataille's Atheology, with Reference to Jean-Luc Nancy." *Flight of the Gods: Philosophical Perspectives on Negative Theology*. Eds. Ilse N. Bulhof and Laurens ten Kate. New York: Fordham University Press, 2000. 249–91.

Kearney, Richard. *The God Who May Be: A Hermeneutics of Religion*. Bloomington: Indiana University Press, 2001.

————. "Eschatology of the Possible God." *The Religious*. Ed. John D. Caputo. Oxford: Blackwell, 2002. 175–96.

————. *Strangers, Gods, and Monsters*. London: Routledge, 2002.

———. "A Dialogue with Jean Luc Marion." *Philosophy Today* 48.1 2004: 12–26.

———. "Hermeneutics of the Possible God." *Givenness and God: Questions of Jean-Luc Marion.* Eds. Ian Leask and Eoin Cassidy. New York: Fordham Unversity Press, 2005. 220–42.

Kearney, Richard, Jacques Derrida, and Jean-Luc Marion. "On the Gift: A Discussion between Jacques Derrida and Jean-Luc Marion, Moderated by Richard Kearney." *God, the Gift and Postmodernism.* Eds. John D. Caputo and Michael J. Scanlon. Bloomington: Indiana University Press, 1999. 54–78.

Kearney, Richard, and Mark Dooley, eds. *Questioning Ethics: Contemporary Debates in Philosophy.* London: Routledge, 1999.

Kearney, Richard, and Joseph S. O'Leary, eds. *Heidegger et la question de Dieu.* Paris: Grasset, 1980.

Kelly, Anthony. "A Trinitarian Moral Theology." *Studia Moralia* 39 (2001): 245–89.

———. "The 'Horrible Wrappers' of Aquinas' God." *Pacifica: Journal of the Melbourne College of Divinity* 9.2 (1996): 185–203.

Kelly, Anthoy, and Francis J. Moloney. *The Experience of God in the Gospel of John.* New York: Paulist, 2003.

Kerr, Fergus. "Aquinas after Marion." *New Blackfriars* 76.895 (1995): 354–64.

Kinnard, Jacob N. *Imaging Wisdom: Seeing and Knowing in the Art of Indian Buddhism.* London: Curzon Press, 1999.

Klein, Julie Rachel. "Descartes' Occluded Metaphysics." Ph.D. diss. Vanderbilt University, 1996.

Kosky, Jeffrey L. "The Disqualification of Intentionality: The Gift in Derrida, Lévinas, and Michel Henry." *Philosophy Today* 41 SPEP Supplement (1997): 186–97.

Kraftson-Hogue, Mike. "Predication Turning to Praise: Marion and Augustine on God and Hermeneutics (Giver, Gift, Giving)." *Literature and Theology* 14.4 (2000): 399–411.

Kroesen, J. O. *Kwaad en Zin. Over de betekenis van de filosofie van Emmanuel Lévinas voor de theologische vraag van het kwade.* Kampen: Kok. 1991.

Kühn, R. *Französische Reflexions–und Geisterphilosophie.* Frankfurt: Anton Hain, 1993.

———. "Langweile und Anruf. Eine Heidegger–und Husserl–Revision mit dem Problemhintergrund 'absoluter Phänomene' bei Jean-Luc Marion." *Philosophisches Jahrbuch* 102.1 (1995): 144–55.

————. "'Sättinung' als absolutes Phänomen. Zur Kritik der klassische Phänomenalität (Kant, Husserl) bei Jean-Luc Marion." *Mesotes. Zeitschrift für philosophischen Ost–West–Dialog* 3 (1995).

Labarrière, Pierre-Jean. Rev. of Jean-Luc Marion. *Dieu sans l'être.* Paris: Fayard, 1982. *Études: Revue Mensuelle* (1983): 285–88.

Labate, S. *La verità buona. Sens e figure del dono nel pensiero contemporaneo.* Assisi: Cittadella, 2004

Lacocque, André, and Paul Ricoeur. *Penser la Bible.* Paris: Éditions du Seuil, 1998.

Lacoste, Jean-Yves. Rev. of Jean-Luc Marion. *L'idole et la distance.* Paris: Grasset, 1977. *Résurrection* 56 (1977): 78–83.

————. "Penser à Dieu en l'aimant: philosophie et théologie de Jean-Luc Marion." *Archives de Philosophie* 50 (1987): 245–70.

Lafont, Ghislain. "Mystique de la croix et question de 'être. À propos d'un livre récent de Jean-Luc Marion." *Revue Théologique de Louvain* (1979): 259–304.

————. "Écouter Heidegger en théologien." *Revue des sciences philosophiques et théologiques* 67.3 (1983): 371–98.

Laird, Martin. "'Whereof We Speak': Gregory of Nyssa, Jean-Luc Marion and the Current Apophatic Rage." *Heythrop Journal* 42.1 (2001): 1–12.

Lakeland, Paul. "Is the Holy Wholly Other, and is the Wholly Other Really Holy?" *Divine Aporia.* Lewisberg, Penn.: Bucknell University Press, 2000. 57–69.

Lamore, C. Rev. of Jean-Luc Marion. *Sur la théologie blanche de Descartes.* Paris: Presses Universitaires de France, 1981. *Journal of Philosophy* 81.3 (1984): 156–62.

Laramée, Martin. Rev. of Jean-Luc Marion. *De surcroît: études sur les phénomènes saturés.* Paris: Presses Universitaires de France, 2001. *Religiologiques* 26 (2002).

Laruelle, François. "L'Appel et le Phénomène." *Revue de Métaphysique et de Morale* 96.1 (1991): 27–42.

Launay, M. B. de. *Le Figaro,* September 22, 1997.

Laurens, Camille. "Qu'est–ce que l'amour?" *Le Nouvel Observateur,* April 17, 2003.

Leask, Ian. "The Dative Subject (and the 'Principle of Principles')." *Givenness and God: Questions of Jean-Luc Marion.* Eds. Ian Leask and Eoin Cassidy. New York: Fordham Unversity Press, 2005. 182–89.

Leask, Ian and Cassidy, Eoin, eds. *Givenness and God: Questions of Jean-Luc Marion*. New York: Fordham University Press, 2005.

Lee, Richard A. *Science, the Singular, and the Question of Theology*. Houndmills, Hampshire: Palgrave Macmillan, 2002.

Lévinas, Emmanuel. *Entre Nous*. Trans. Michael B. Smith and Barbara Harshav. New York: Columbia University Press, 2000.

Lilly, R. *The Ancients and the Moderns*. Bloomington: Indiana University Press, 1996.

Lindbeck, George A., Dennis L. Okholm, and Timothy R. Phillips, eds. *The Nature of Confession: Evangelicals & Postliberals in Conversation*. Downers Grove, Ill.: Intervarsity Press, 1996.

Llewelyn, John. "Meanings Reserved, Re-served, and Reduced." *Southern Journal of Philosophy* XXXII, Supplement (1994): 27–54.

Lock, Charles. "Against Being: An Introduction to the Thought of Jean-Luc Marion." *Saint Vladimir's Theological Quarterly* 37.4 (1993): 370–80.

Lojacono, E. "Le letture delle *Meditationes* di Jean-Luc Marion." *Descartes metafisico. Interpretationi del Novecento*. Eds. Jean-Robert Armogathe and Giulia Belgioioso. Rome: Instituto della Enciclopedia Italiana, 1994. 129–51.

Long, D. Stephen. *Divine Economy: Theology and the Market*. Radical Orthodoxy. London: Routledge, 2000.

Look, Brandon. Rev. of Jean-Luc Marion. *Cartesian Questions: Method and Metaphysics*. Chicago: University of Chicago Press, 1999. *Review of Metaphysics* 54.1 (2000): 160–61.

Loparic, Z. "A propos du cartésianisme gris de J.-L. Marion." *Manuscripto* 11.2 (1988).

Loughlin, Gerard. "Transubstantiation: Eucharist as Pure Gift." *Christ*. London: SPCK, 1996. 123–41.

———. *Telling God's Story. Bible, Church and Narrative Theology*. Oxford: Oxford University Press, 1997.

Lowe, Walter. "Second Thoughts about Transcendence." *The Religious*. Ed. John D. Caputo. Oxford: Blackwell, 2002. 241–51.

Macann, Christopher. *Four Phenomenological Philosophers: Husserl, Heidegger, Sartre, Merleau-Ponty*. London: Routledge, 1994.

Macann, Christopher, ed. *Critical Heidegger*. London: Routledge, 1996.

MacGregor, Lorie. "The Role of the Ego in Religious Experience." *Aporia* 12.2 (2002).

Mackinlay, Shane. "Eyes Wide Shut: A Response to Jean-Luc Marion's Account of the Journey to Emmaus." *Modern Theology* 20.3 (2004): 447–56.

———. "Phenomenality in the Middle. Marion, Romano, and the Hermeneutics of the Event." *Givenness and God: Questions of Jean-Luc Marion.* Eds. Eoin Cassidy and Ian Leask. New York: Fordham University Press, 2004. 167–81.

———. *Interpreting Excess. The Implicit Hermeneutics of Jean-Luc Marion's Saturated Phenomena,* Ph.D. diss. Hoger Instituut voor Wijsbegeerte, Katholieke Universiteit Leuven, 2004.

Macquarrie, John. Rev. of Jean Luc Marion. *God without Being.* Trans. Thomas A. Carlson. Chicago: University of Chicago Press, 1991. *Journal of Religion* 73.1 (1992): 99–101.

———. "Postmodernism in Philosophy of Religion and Theology." *International Journal for Philosophy of Religion* 50 (2001): 9–27.

Maggiori, Robert. "Le sens de l'amour." March 27, 2003. Internet. *Libération.* Available: http://www.liberation.com/page.php?Article=98845. April 14, 2003.

Magnard, Pierre. *Le Dieu des philosophes.* Collection Philosophie Européenne. Ed. Henri Hude: MAME Éditions universitaires, 1992.

Makarian, Christian. "Aimer pour comprendre: La superbe réflexion philosophique de Jean-Luc Marion sur l'amour." April 14, 2003. Internet. *L'Express Livres.* Available: http://livres.lexpress.fr/critique.asp?idC=6552/idR=12/idG=8. April 14, 2003.

Manolopoulos, Mark. *If Creation is a Gift.* Ph.D. diss. Monash University, 2003.

Manoussakis, John P. "The Phenomenon of God: From Husserl to Marion" *American Catholic Philosophical Quarterly* 78(1) (2004): 53–68.

Marshall, D. J. "J.-L. Marion: Werke zu Descartes." *Philosophische Rundschau* 31.1–2 (1984).

Martineau, Emmanuel. "L'ontologie de l'ordre." *Études Philosophiques* 81.4 (1976): 469–94.

Martis, John. "Postmodernism and God as Giver." *The Way* 36 (1996): 236–43.

———. "Thomistic *Esse*—Idol or Icon? Jean-Luc Marion's God without Being." *Pacifica: Journal of the Melbourne College of Divinity* 9.1 (1996): 55–68.

Marty, F. "L'analogie perdue. La métaphysique sur les chemins de la science de Descartes à Kant." *Archives de Philosophie* 46.3 (1983).

Mason, Richard. *The God of Spinoza: A Philosophical Study.* Cambridge: Cambridge University Press, 1999.

Mastin, Jean-Clet. *Cents mots pour cents philosophes. De Héraclite à Derrida*, Paris: Empêcheurs de penser en rond, 2005

Mattes, Mark Christopher. "Toward Divine Relationality: Eberhard Jungel's New Trinitarian, Postmetaphysical Approach." Ph.D. diss. University of Chicago, 1995.

McCarthy, John C. Rev. of Jean-Luc Marion. *God without Being*. Trans. Thomas A. Carlson. Chicago: University of Chicago Press, 1991. *Review of Metaphysics* 46.3 (1993): 627–29.

———. "Amo Ergo Sum." Rev. of Jean-Luc Marion. *Prolegomena to Charity*. Trans. Stephen Lewis. New York: Fordham University Press, 2002. *Crisis: Politics, Culture, and the Church* (2002).

McKenna, Andrew J. "Derrida, Death, and Forgiveness." *First Things* 71 (1997): 34–37.

Mendez, A. F. "God and Alterity." *New Blackfriars* 80.946 (1999): 552–67.

Menn, Stephen. *Descartes and Augustine*. Cambridge: Cambridge University Press, 2002.

Mensch, James. "Givenness and Alterity." *Issues Confronting the Post-European World*. Eds. Chan-Fai Cheung et al. Prague, 2002. 1–8 of Essays in Celebration of the Founding of the Organization of Phenomenological Organizations.

Milbank, John. "Can a Gift Be Given? Prolegomena to a Future Trinitarian Metaphysic." *Rethinking Metaphysics*. Eds. L. Gregory Jones and Stephen E. Fowl. Oxford: Blackwell, 1995. 119–61.

———. "Only Theology Overcomes Metaphysics." *New Blackfriars* 76.895 (1995): 325–42. *The Word Made Strange*. Oxford: Blackwell, 1997. 36–52.

———. "The Ethics of Self–Sacrifice." *First Things* 91 (1999): 33–38.

———. "The Soul of Reciprocity. Reciprocity Refused Part One." *Modern Theology* 17.3 (2001): 335–91.

———. *Being Reconciled: Ontology and Pardon*. London: Routledge, 2003.

Milbank, John, and Catherine Pickstock. *Truth in Aquinas*. Radical Orthodoxy. London: Routledge, 2001.

Monnoyer, Jean-Maurice. "Individualisme cartésien et sémantique externaliste." *Philosophie analytique et histoire de la philosophie*. Ed. Jean-Michel Vienne. Paris: Vrin, 1997. 167–69.

Mooney, Timothy. "Hubris and Humility: Husserl's Reduction and Givenness." *Givenness and God: Questions of Jean-Luc Marion*. Eds. Ian Leask and Eoin Cassidy. New York: Fordham Unversity Press, 2005. 47–68.

Morrow, Derek J. "The Conceptual Idolatry of Descartes's Gray Ontology: An Epistemology 'Without Being." *Givenness and God: Questions of Jean-Luc Marion.* Eds. Ian Leask and Eoin Cassidy. New York: Fordham Unversity Press, 2005. 11–36.

Moss, David. "Costly Giving: On Jean-Luc Marion's Theology of the Gift." *New Blackfriars* 74 (1993): 393–99.

Nadler, S. Rev. of Jean-Luc Marion. *Cartesian Questions: Method and Metaphysics.* Trans. Jeffrey L. Kosky, John Cottingham, and Stephen Voss. Chicago: University of Chicago Press, 1999. *Journal of the History of Philosophy* (2000).

Neatu, M. "Le relief théologique de la pensée de Jean-Luc Marion." Thèse de license en Philosophie. Cluj–Napoca, Romanie, 2000.

Nemoianu, Virgil. "Literary Play and Religious Referentiality." *Play, Literature, and Religion.* Albany: State University of New York Press, 1992. 1–18.

Neutsch, M. "La révélation est un vrai phénomène." *La crois,* September 1997.

Newman, L. "Descartes on Unknown Faculties and Our Knowledge of the Eternal World." *Philosophical Review* 103.3 (1994): 489–531.

Nicolas, Jean-Hervé. "La suprême logique de l'amour et la théologie." *Revue Thomiste* LXXXIII.4 (1983): 639–59.

O'Donoghe, John. "The Absent Threshold: An Eckhartian Afterword." *Givenness and God: Questions of Jean-Luc Marion.* Eds. Ian Leask and Eoin Cassidy. New York: Fordham Unversity Press, 2005. 258–83.

O'Donoghue, Noel Dermot. "In the Beginning Was the Gift: A Marginal Note on *God without Being.*" *New Blackfriars* 76.895 (1995): 351–53.

O'Leary, Joseph S. *La vérité chrétienne à l'âge du pluralisme religieux.* Paris: Cerf, 1994. *Religious Pluralism and Christian Truth.* Edinburgh: Edinburgh University Press, 1996.

———. "The Gift: A Trojan Horse in the Citadel of Phenomenology?" *Givenness and God: Questions of Jean-Luc Marion.* Eds. Ian Leask and Eoin Cassidy. New York: Fordham Unversity Press, 2005. 135–66.

Ó Murchadha, Felix. "Glory, Idolatry, Kairos: Revelation and the Ontological Difference in Marion." *Givenness and God: Questions of Jean-Luc Marion.* Eds. Ian Leask and Eoin Cassidy. New York: Fordham Unversity Press, 2005. 69–86.

O'Rourke, F. *Pseudo-Dionysius and the Metaphysics of Aquinas.* Leiden: E. J. Brill, 1992.

Oliveros, Chris, and Frank King, eds. *Drawn & Quarterly.* Vol. 4. Montreal: Drawn & Quarterly Publications, 2001.

Olivetti, Marco M. "Ueber J.-L. Marions Beitrag Zur Neueren Religionsphilosophie." *Archivio di Filosofia* LIV.1–3 (1986): 625–36.

————. "L'argomento ontologico." *Archivio di Filosofia* 1–3 (1990).

Olthuis, James H., ed. *Knowing Other–wise: Philosophy at the Threshold of
Spirituality.* New York: Fordham University Press, 1997.

————. *Religion With/Out Religion: The Prayers and Tears of John D. Caputo.*
London: Routledge, 2001.

Onimus, Jean. Rev. of Jean-Luc Marion. *L'idole et la distance.* Paris: Grasset,
1977. *Revue de Métaphysique et de Morale* 2 (1980): 280.

Overton, J. "See(k)ing God through the Icon: A Semiotic Analysis of Marion's
God without Being." *Semiotica* 110 (1996): 87–126.

Pagé, Jean-Guy. "Dieu et l'être." *Laval Théologique et Philosophique* XXXVII.1
(1981): 33–43.

Pedemonte Feu, Bonaventura. "Le sujet convoqué: à partir de la pensée de
Buber, de Rosenzweig, de Lévinas, de Marion et de Ricoeur." Ph.D. diss.
Institut Catholique de Paris, 1995.

Pelluchon, Corine. Rev. of Jean-Luc Marion. *Le phénomène érotique.* Paris:
Grasset, 2003. *Religiologiques* 28 (2003).

Peperzak, Adriaan T. *Ethics As First Philosophy: The Significance of Emmanuel
Lévinas for Philosophy, Literature and Religion.* London: Routledge, 1995.

Perl, E. Rev. of Jean-Luc Marion. *God without Being.* Trans. Thomas A. Carlson. Chicago: University of Chicago Press, 1991. *American Catholic Philosophical Quarterly* 68.4 (1994): 554–57.

Petrosino, S. "D'un livre à l'autre. *Totalité et l'infini–Autrement qu'être.*"
Emmanuel Lévinas: Cahiers de la nuit surveillée. Lagrasse: Verdier, 1984.
199ff.

Pickstock, Catherine. *After Writing: On the Liturgical Consummation of Philosophy.* Oxford: Blackwell, 1998.

Popkin, Richard Henry. *The History of Scepticism: From Savanorola to Bayle.*
Oxford: Oxford Press, 2003.

Power, David N. "Sacramental Theology: Postmodern Approaches." *Theological Studies* 55 (1994): 684–93.

————. "Roman Catholic Theologies of Eucharistic Communion: A Contribution to Ecumenical Conversation." *Theological Studies* 57.4 (1996): 587–610.

————. *Sacraments: The Language of God's Giving.* New York: Crossroad, 1999.

Prouvost, G. "La tension irrésolue." *Revue Thomiste* 98.1 (1998): 95–102.

Purcell, Michael. "'This Is My Body' Which Is 'for you' . . . Ethically speaking . . ." *The Presence of Transcendence.* Eds. Lieven Boeve and John C. Ries. Leuven: Uitgeverij Peeters, 2001. 135–51.

Pyle, Andrew. *Malebranche.* London: Routledge, 2003.

Reali, Nicola. *Fino all'abbandono: l'eucaristia nella fenomenologia di Jean-Luc Marion.* Rome: Città Nuova, 2001.

Reiter, J. Rev. of Jean-Luc Marion, *L'idole et la distance.* Paris, Editions Grasset and Fasquelle, 1977. *Philosophischer Literaturanzeiger* 32.4 (1979). 369–72.

Renaut, Alain. *The Era of the Individual.* Trans. M. B. Debevoise and Franklin Philip. Princeton: Princeton University Press, 1999.

Ricard, Marie-Andrée. "La question de la donation chez Jean-Luc Marion." *Laval Théologique et Philosophique* 57.1 (2001): 83–94.

Ricci, R. "Da Heidegger a Marion: rifless sulla metafisica cartesiana come ontologia." *Discipline filosofiche* 1.1 (1991).

Richardson, William J. *Theological Studies* 54.3 (1993): 576.

Robbins, Jeffrey W. "Overcoming Overcoming: In Praise of Ontotheology." *Explorations in Contemporary Continental Philosophy of Religion.* Ed. Deane-Peter Baker. New York: Rodopi, 2003. 9–21.

Robert, Jean-Dominique. "Autour de *Dieu sans l'être* de Jean-Luc Marion." *Laval Théologique et Philosophique* 39.3 (1983): 341–47.

———. "'Dieu sans l'être': À propos d'un livre récent." *Nouvelle Revue Théologique* 105.3 (1983): 406–10.

Rockmore, Tom. *Heidegger and French Philosophy: Humanism, Antihumanism and Being.* London: Routledge, 1994.

Röd, W. Rev. of *Sur le prisme métaphysique de Descartes. Constitution et limites de l'onto-théo-logie dans la pensée cartésienne.* Paris: Presses Universitaires de France, 1986. *Archiv för Geschichte der Philosophie* 75.2 (1993). 229–32.

Rolland, Jacques. *Parcours de l'autrement: lecture d'Emmanuel Lévinas.* Paris: Presses Universitaires de France, 2000.

Rolland, Jacques, and S. Petrosino. *La vérité nomade. Introduction à Emmanuel Lévinas.* Paris: Cerf, 1984.

Romano, C. "Remarques sur la méthode phénoménologique dans *Étant donné.*" *Annales de Philosophie* 21. Beyrouth: Université Saint-Joseph, 2000.

Rosemann, Philipp W. "Der maskierte Philosoph. Die verborgene Theologie des Cartesianismus." *Frankfurter Allgemeine Zeitung* 2.3 (1992).

———. "Der Melancholiker sieht wie Gott. Aber weil er das Andere ver-weigert, blickt er ins Nichts: Jean-Luc Marion's negative Theologie." *Frankfurter Allgemeine Zeitung* 7.14 (1993).

———. "Penser l'Autre: théologie négative et 'postmodernite.'" *Revue philosophique de Louvain* 91.90 (1993): 296–310.

———. *Understanding Scholastic Thought with Foucault*. Houndmills, Hampshire: Palgrave Macmillan, 1999.

———. "J.-L. Marion's Eucharistic Realism." *The Mystery of Faith. Reflections on the Encyclical* Ecclesia de Eucharistia. Eds. James McEvoy and Maurice Hogan. Dublin: Columba Press, 2005.

Rostagno, Sergio. "La ragione teologica: Rassegna di teologia sistematica." *Protestantesimo* 53.1 (1998): 35–42.

Sanders, T. "The Otherness of God and the Bodies of Others." *Journal of Religion* 76 (1996): 572–87.

Sansonetti, G. "Distanza e differenza. A proposito del libro di Jean-Luc Marion." *Archives de Philosophie* 50.1 (1987).

Schlegel, Jean-Louis. "*Dieu sans l'être*. À propos de J.-L. Marion." *Esprit* (1984): 26–36.

Schmitz, K. L. "The God of Love." *The Thomist* 57.3 (1993): 495–508.

Sebba, G. "Retroversion and the History of Ideas: J.-L. Marion's Translation of the *Regulae* of Descartes." *Studia Cartesiana* 1 (1979).

Secher, Tobias. *Einen anderen Gott denken. Zum Verständnis der Alterität Gottes bei Jean-Luc Marion*. Frankfurt: Knecht, 2002.

Seubert, Xavier John. "A Discussion on the Eucharistic Theology in Jean-Luc Marion's *God without Being*." *The Catholic Theological Society of America— Proceedings of the Fifty–second Annual Convention*. Ed. Judith Dwyer. New York: CTSA, 1997. 111–12.

Shanks, Andrew. *God and Modernity: A New and Better Way to Do Theology*. London/New York: Routledge, 2000.

Shanley, Brian J. "Saint Thomas, Onto–theology, and Marion." *The Thomist* 60.4 (1996): 617–25.

Sichère, B. *Cinquante ans de philosophie française*. Paris: Ministère des Affaires Étrangères, 1998.

Smith, James K. A. "How to Avoid Not Speaking: Attestations." *Knowing Otherwise: Philosophy at the Threshold of Spirituality*. Ed. James H. Olthuis. Perspectives in Continental Philosophy. New York: Fordham University Press, 1997. 217–34.

————. "Respect and Donation: A Critique of Marion's Critique of Husserl." *American Catholic Philosophical Quarterly* 71.4 (1997): 523–38.

————. "How to Avoid Not Speaking: On the Phenomenological Possibility of Theology." Ph.D. diss. Villanova University, 1999.

————. "Liberating Religion from Theology: Marion and Heidegger on the Possibility of a Phenomenology of Religion." *International Journal for Philosophy of Religion* 46.1 (1999): 17–33.

————. "Between Predication and Silence: Augustine on How (Not) to Speak of God." *Heythrop Journal* 41.1 (2000): 66–86.

————. *The Fall of Interpretation: Philosophical Foundations for a Creational Hermeneutic.* Downer Grove, Ill.: Intervarsity Press, 2000.

————. "How (Not) to Tell a Secret: Interiority and the Strategy of 'Confession.'" *American Catholic Philosophical Quarterly* 74.1 (2000): 135–51.

————. *Speech and Theology: Language and the Logic of Incarnation.* Radical Orthodoxy. London: Routledge, 2002.

Sneller, Rico. "Incarnation as a Prerequisite: Marion and Derrida." *Bijdragen* 65.1 (2004): 38–54.

Sommavilla, G. "La nuova teologia di Marion e la sua logica." *Rasegna di teologia* 3 (1979).

Steinbock, A. "Saturated Intentionality." *Resituating Merleau-Ponty.* Atlantic Highlands, N.J.: Humanities Press, 1995.

Stoppa, A. "Verso l'*in–visibile.* Fenomenologia ed ontologia in J.-L. Marion," Ph.D. diss. University of Bologna, 2004.

Stout, Jeffrey. *Democracy and Tradition.* Princeton: Princeton University Press, 2003.

Svenungsson, Jayne. "Guds aterkomst. En studie av gudsbegreppet inom postmodern filosofi." Ph.D. diss. Lund University, 2002.

Sweetman, Brendan. Rev. of Jean-Luc Marion. *God without Being.* Trans. Thomas A. Carlson. Chicago: University of Chicago Press, 1991. *New Oxford Review* (July-August 1993). 25–26.

Tarnowski, K. "God after Metaphysics?" *Kwartalnik Filozof* 24.1 (1996): 31–47.

Taylor, Victor E., and Charles E. Winquist, eds. *Encyclopedia of Postmodernism.* London: Routledge, 2001.

Tilliette, Xavier. Rev. of Jean-Luc Marion. *Étant donné.* Paris: Presses Universitaires de France, 1997. *Archives de Philosophie* 61.4 (1998): 759–63.

Tracy, David. "Foreword." *God Without Being.* Trans. Thomas A. Carlson. Chicago: University of Chicago Press, 1991. ix–xv.

Turner, Denys. *Faith,Reason, and the Existence of God.* Cambridge: Cambridge University Press, 2005.

Valadier, Paul. *Jésus-Christ ou Dionysos: La foi chrétienne en confrontation avec Nietzsche.* Paris: Desclée, 1979.

Van den Bossche, Stijn. "God verschijnt toch in de immanentie. De fenomenologische neerlegging van de theologie in Jean-Luc Marion's *Étant donné.*" *God en het Denken. Over de filosofie van Jean-Luc Marion.* Ed. Ruud Welten. Nijmegen: Annalen van het Thijmgenootschap 88.2, 2000. 128–53.

———. "God Does Appear in Immanence After All: Jean-Luc Marion's Phenomenology as a New First Philosophy for Theology." *Sacramental Presence in a Postmodern Context.* Leuven: Peeters, 2001. 325–46.

———. "Twee verschillende kijkwijzen. Jean-Luc Marion over idool en icoon." *God ondergronds.*

———. *Opstellen voor een theologisch vrijdenker.* Eds. L. Boeve and J. Haers. Averbode: Uitg. Averbode, 2001. 339–56.

———. "Gott ist ganz anders." *Philokles. Zeitschrift für populäre Philosophie* 1 (2001): 35–38.

———. Rev. of Jean-Luc Marion and Josef Wolmuth. *Ruf und Gabe. Zum Verhältnis von Phänomenologie und Theologie.* Bonn: Borengässer, 2000. *Bijdragen* 62.2 (2001): 239–40.

———. "A Possible Present for Theology." *Bijdragen* 65.1 (2004): 55–78.

Van den Bossche, Stijn, and Ruud Welten. "Preface." *Bijdragen* 65.1 (2004): 3–4.

Van Maas, Sander. "On Preferring Mozart." *Bijdragen* 65.1 (2004): 97–110.

Vanhoozer, Kevin J. *First Theology: God, Scriptures and Hermeneutics.* Downers Grove, Ill.: Intervarsity Press, 2002.

Vanhoozer, Kevin J, ed. *The Cambridge Companion to Postmodern Theology.* Cambridge: Cambridge University Press, 2003.

Verneaux, Roger. *Étude critique du livre Dieu sans l'être.* Paris: Téqui, 1986.

Vienne, Jean-Michel. *Philosophie analytique et histoire de la philosophie.* Paris: Vrin, 1997.

Villela-Petit, M. "Heidegger est–il idolâtre?" *Heidegger et la question de Dieu.* Eds. Richard Kearney and Joseph S. O'Leary. Paris: Vrin, 1980. 75–102.

Virgoulay, René. "Dieu ou l'être? Relecture de Heidegger en marge de J.-L. Marion, *Dieu sans l'être.*" *Recherches de Science Religieuse* 72.2 (1984): 163–98.

Vogel, Arthur A. "Catching Up with Jean-Luc Marion." *Anglican Theological Review* 82.4 (2000): 803–11.

Vries, Hent De. *Philosophy & the Turn to Religion*. Baltimore: Johns Hopkins University Press, 1999.

Vries, Hent de. "Theotopographies: Nancy, Hölderlin, Heidegger." *MLN* 109.3 (1994): 445–77.

———. *Religion and Violence: Philosophical Perspectives from Kant to Derrida*. Baltimore: Johns Hopkins University Press, 2002.

Wall, John Schweiker, and W. David Hall, eds. *Paul Ricoeur and Contemporary Moral Thought*. London: Routledge, 2002.

Ward, Graham. "Introducing Jean-Luc Marion." *New Blackfriars* 76.895 (1995): 317–24.

———. "Theology and the Crisis of Representation." *Literature and Theology at Century's End*. Atlanta: Scholar's Press, 1995. 131–58.

———. "Between Postmodernism and Postmodernity: The Theology of Jean-Luc Marion." *Postmodernity, Sociology and Religion*. Eds. Kieran Flanagan and Peter C. Jupp. London: Macmillan, 1996. 190–205.

———. "Introduction." *The Postmodern God*. Ed. Graham Ward. Oxford: Blackwell, 1997. xv–xlvii.

———. "The Theological Project of Jean-Luc Marion." *Post-Secular Philosophy: Between Philosophy and Theology*. Ed. Philip Blond. London: Routledge, 1998. 67–106.

———. *Cities of God*. London: Routledge, 2000.

Ware, K. "Spirituality of the Icon." *The Study of Spirituality*. Eds. C. Jones and G. Wainwright. New York: Oxford University Press, 1986. 195ff.

Webb, S. H. *The Gifting God*. Oxford: Oxford University Press, 1996.

Weinstein, Idit Dobbs. *Maimonides and St. Thomas on the Limits of Reason*. Albany: State University of New York, 1995.

Welten, Ruud. "Het andere ego van Descartes." *Tijdschrift voor Filosofie* 60.3 (1998): 572–79.

———. *Fenomenologie en Beeldverbod bij Emmanuel Lévinas en Jean-Luc Marion*. Damon: Budel, 2001.

———. "Saturation and Disappointment. Marion According to Husserl." *Bijdragen* 65.1 (2004): 79–96.

Welten, Ruud, ed. *God en het Denken. Over de filosofie van Jean-Luc Marion*. Nijmegen: Annalen van het Thijmgenootschap 88.2, 2000.

Westphal, Merold. "Postmodernism and Religious Reflection." *International Journal for Philosophy of Religion* 38 (1995): 127–43.

————. *Overcoming Onto–theology*. Perspectives in Continental Philosophy. Ed. John D. Caputo. New York: Fordham University Press, 2001.

————. "Divine Excess: The God Who Comes After." *The Religious*. Ed. John D. Caputo. Oxford: Blackwell, 2002. 259–76.

————. "Transfiguration as Saturated Phenomenon." *Journal of Philosophy and Scripture* 1.1 (2003): 1–10.

Westphal, Merold, ed. *Postmodern Philosophy and Christian Thought*. Bloomington: Indiana University Press, 1999.

Winkler, K. "Descartes and the Three Names of God." *American Catholic Philosophical Quarterly* 67.4 (1993): 451–65.

Wirzba, Norman. Rev. of Jean-Luc Marion. *God without Being*. Trans. Thomas A. Carlson. Chicago: University of Chicago Press, 1991. *Christian Century* 109.15 (1992): 458.

Wolmuth, Josef. *Ruf und Gabe. Zum Verhältnis von Phänomenologie und Theologie*. Bonn: Borengässer, 2000.

————. "'Geben ist seliger als nehmen' (Apg 20, 35). Vorüberlegungen zur einer Theologie der Gabe." *Einander Zugewandt. Die Rezeption des christlich–jüdischen Dialogs in der Dogmatik*. Eds. E. Dirschel, S. Sandherr, M. Tomé, and B. Wunder, Paderborn: Schöningh, 2005.

Wood, John. *The Virtual Embodied: Presence/Practice/Technology*. London: Routledge, 1998.

Wrathall, Mark A., ed. *Religion after Metaphysics*. Cambridge: Cambridge University Press: 2003

Wright, John P., and Paul Potter, eds. *Psyche and Soma: Physicians and Metaphysicians on the Mind–Body Problem from Antiquity to Enlightenment*. Oxford: Oxford University Press, 2003.

Wyschogrod, Edith. *Emmanuel Lévinas: The Problem of Ethical Metaphysics*. Perspectives in Continental Philosophy. Ed. John D. Caputo. New York: Fordham University Press, 2000.

Wyschogrod, Edith, and John D. Caputo. "Postmodernism and the Desire for God." *Cross Currents* 48.3 (1998).

Yovel, Yirmiyahu. *Spinoza and Other Heretics*. Reprint ed. Vol. 1. Princeton: Princeton University Press, 1992.

Yun, W.-J. "The 'Gift' With/Of No-Return: A Christian (De)Constructive Ethic of Alterity." Ph.D. diss. Southwestern Baptist Theological Seminary, 1999.

Zanardo, S. "La Regola d'oro e la fenomenologia della donazione di Jean-Luc Marion." *La regola d'Oro come etica universale.* Eds. C. Vigna and S. Zanardo. Milan: Vita e pensiero, 2005.

Zhang, Ellen Y. "Icon without Logos; Theology without Ontology." Rev. of Jean-Luc Marion. *God without Being: Hors–Texte.* Chicago: University of Chicago Press, 1991. *Cross Currents* (1993): 273–77.

Ziarek, K. "The Language of Praise: Lévinas and Marion." *Religion and Literature* 22 (1990): 93–107.

Contributors

JOHN D. CAPUTO

is the Thomas J. Watson Professor of Religion and Humanities at Syracuse University and David R. Cook Professor Emeritus of Philosophy at Villanova University, where he taught from 1968 until 2004. His most recent books are *The Weakness of God: A Theology of the Event* (2006) and *Augustine and Postmodernism: Confessions and Circumfession*, co-edited with Michael Scanlon (2005). Recent publications include *On Religion* (2001), *More Radical Hermeneutics: On Not Knowing Who We Are* (2000), *The Prayers and Tears of Jacques Derrida: Religion without Religion* (1997), *Deconstruction in a Nutshell: A Conversation with Jacques Derrida* (1997), and *God, the Gift and Postmodernism* (1999), based on the conference that brought Marion and Derrida together for the first time.

THOMAS A. CARLSON

is associate professor in the Department of Religious Studies at the University of California, Santa Barbara, where he teaches courses in religion and modern philosophy, contemporary theory, and the history of Christian thought. He is the author of *Indiscretion: Finitude and the Naming of God* (1999), an investigation of negative and mystical theologies in light of deconstructive and phenomenological thought, and translator of several works by Jean-Luc Marion, including *God without Being* (1991), *Reduction and Givenness: Investigations of Husserl, Heidegger, and Phenomenology* (1998), and *The Idol and Distance* (2001).

EMMANUEL FALQUE

is professor of philosophy at the Institut Catholique in Paris, where he specializes in medieval philosophy and phenomenology. His most recent publications include *Le passeur de Gethsémani* (1999), *Saint Bonaventure et l'entrée de Dieu en théologie* (2000), and *Métamorphose de la finitude* (2004).

KEVIN HART

is Notre Dame Professor of Philosophy and Literature and Concurrent Professor of Philosophy at the University of Notre Dame. He is the author of *The Trespass of the Sign* (1989; 2000), *A. D. Hope* (1992), *Samuel Johnson and the Culture of Property* (1999), *Postmodernism* (2004), and *The Dark Gaze: Maurice Blanchot and the Sacred* (2004). He co-edited, with Geoffrey Hartman, *The Power of Contestation: Perspectives on Maurice Blanchot* (2004), with Yvonne Sherwood, *Derrida and Religion: Other Testaments* (2004), and with Barbara Wall, *The Experience of God* (2005). Kevin Hart is the author of several volumes of poetry, the most recent being *Flame Tree: Selected Poems* (2002).

ROBYN HORNER

is a lecturer in theology at the Melbourne campus of the Australian Catholic University, and a research associate of Monash University. She is the author of *Rethinking God as Gift: Marion, Derrida and the Limits of Phenomenology* (2001) and *Jean-Luc Marion: A Theo-logical Introduction* (2005), as well as articles on Marion, Lévinas, and Derrida. With Vincent Berraud she translated Marion's *In Excess: Studies of Saturated Phenomena* (2002).

MICHAEL KESSLER

is assistant dean in the College at Georgetown University and a lecturer in the Department of Theology. He teaches and writes about the intersection of religion, law, and ethics. His most recent work appears in *The Encyclopedia of Religion* (2d ed.) and *Religion and Literature;* he co-edited with Christian Sheppard *Mystics: Presence and Aporia* (2003).

JEAN-LUC MARION

is professor of philosophy at the University of Paris IV—Sorbonne and John Nuveen Professor of the Philosophy of Religion and Theology in the Divinity School at the University of Chicago, where he also teaches on the Committee on Social Thought. His books in English include *On Descartes's Metaphysical Prism: The Constitution and Limits of Onto-Theo-Logy in Cartesian Thought* (1999), *Cartesian Questions: Method and Metaphysics* (1999), *Descartes's Grey Ontology: Cartesian Science and Aristotelian Thought in the Regulæ* (2006), *The Idol and Distance: Five Studies* (2001), *God without Being: Hors-Texte* (1991), *Prolegomena to Charity* (2002), *The Crossing of the Visible* (2004), *Reduction and Givenness: Investigations of Husserl, Heidegger, and Phenomenology* (1998), *Being Given: Toward a Phenomenology of Givenness* (2002), *In Excess: Studies of Saturated Phenomena* (2002), and *The Erotic Phenomenon* (2007).

GERALD MCKENNY

is associate professor of Christian ethics and director of the John J. Reilly Center for Science, Technology, and Values at the University of Notre Dame. He is author of *To Relieve the Human Condition: Bioethics, Technology, and the Body* (1997), is co-editor (with Edith Wyschogrod) of *The Ethical* (2003), and has published widely in the fields of theological ethics, moral philosophy, and bioethics.

JOHN MILBANK

is Research Professor of Religion, Politics, and Ethics at the University of Nottingham. He previously taught at the Universities of Lancaster, Cambridge, and Virginia. He is the author of *Theology and Social Theory: Beyond Secular Reason* (2d ed. 2005) among other books and articles. His most recent books are *Being Reconciled: Ontology and Pardon* (2002) and *The Suspended Middle: Henri de Lubac and the Debate Concerning the Supernatural* (2005).

CYRIL O'REGAN

is Huisking Professor of Theology at the University of Notre Dame. He is the author of *The Heterodox Hegel* (1994), *Gnostic Return in Modernity* (2001), and *Gnostic Apocalypse: Jacob Boehme's Haunted Narrative* (2002).

CLAUDE ROMANO

is associate professor of philosophy at the University of Paris IV—Sorbonne. He has published several books on phenomenology, including *L'événement et le monde* (1998), *L'événement et le temps* (1999), *Il y a* (2003), and *Le chant de la vie: phénoménologie de Faulkner* (2005).

KATHRYN TANNER

is professor of theology at the University of Chicago Divinity School. She is the author of *God and Creation in Christian Theology* (1988), *The Politics of God, Theories of Culture: A New Agenda for Theology* (1994), *Jesus, Humanity, and the Trinity*, and *Economy of Grace* (2001).

DAVID TRACY

is Andrew Thomas Greeley and Grace McNichols Greeley Distinguished
Service Professor of Catholic Studies and professor of theology and the phi-
losophy of religion in the Divinity School of the University of Chicago, where
he also teaches in the Committee on Social Thought. His books include *The
Achievement of Bernard Lonergan* (1970), *Blessed Rage for Order: The New
Pluralism in Theology* (1975), *The Analogical Imagination: Christian Theology
and the Cultue of Pluralism* (1981), and *On Naming the Present: Reflections on
God, Hermeneutics, and Church* (1994).

Index